W9-ADH-736

IN THE BEGINNING

Decked out for the hunt, King Assurbanipal of Assyria pursues his quarry, as depicted in a bas-relief from the seventh century B.C.

BRIAN M. FAGAN
University of California, Santa Barbara

IN THE BEGINNING

AN INTRODUCTION TO ARCHAEOLOGY

Fifth Edition

WITHDRAWN

LITTLE, BROWN AND COMPANY
Boston   Toronto

Library of Congress Cataloging in Publication Data

Fagan, Brian M.
  In the beginning.

  Bibliography: p. 558
  Includes index.
  1. Archaeology—Methodology. 2. Archaeology—History.
I. Title.
  CC75.F34 1985   930.1'028   84-7887
  ISBN 0-316-25988-8

Burgess
CC
75
.F34
1985
Copy 1

Copyright © 1985 by The Lindbriar Corporation

All rights reserved. No part of this book may be reproduced in any form or by any electronic or mechanical means including information storage and retrieval systems without permission in writing from the publisher, except by a reviewer who may quote brief passages in a review.

Library of Congress Catalog Card No. 84-7887

ISBN 0-316-25988-8

9 8 7 6 5 4 3

HAL

Published simultaneously in Canada by Little, Brown & Company (Canada) Limited

Printed in the United States of America

Cover photo: Courtesy of Jane Roos Neville.

The author wishes to thank the publishers, authors, photographers, and illustrators for granting permission to use their material. The sources for the text appear below, except for those given with the illustration. The figures without specific credits have been drawn specially for this book.

Frontispiece: Courtesy of the Trustees of the British Museum.

Chapter 1: *Fig. 1.2*, The Bettmann Archive, Inc.; *Fig. 1.3*, Courtesy of the trustees of the British Museum; *Fig. 1.4*, Hester A. Davis, "Is There a Future for the Past?" *Archaeology*, Vol. 24, no. 4, copyright 1971, Archaeological Institute of America; *Fig. 1.5*, The Metropolitan Museum of Art, bequest of Joseph H. Durkee, gift of Darius Mills, and gift of C. Ruxton Love, by Exchange, 1972; *Fig. 1.6*, The Bettmann Archive, Inc.; *Fig. 1.7*, George Holton/Photo Researchers, Inc., *Fig. 1.8*, Courtesy of Colonial Williamsburg; *Fig. 1.9*, Courtesy of Dr. Braidwood and the Oriental Institute, University of Chicago.

Chapter 2: *Fig. 2.1*, From Michael Grant, *Cities of Vesuvius: Pompeii and Herclaneum*, 1971. Reprinted by permission of Macmillan Publishing Co. Inc., New York and Weidenfeld and Nicholson Archives; *Fig. 2.2*, George Gerster/Photo Researchers, Inc.; *Fig. 2.4*, Courtesy of the Royal Anthropological Institute of Great Britain and Ireland. Redrawn from "The Swanscombe Skull: A Survey of Research on a Pleistocene Site" (Occasional paper No. 20, Fig. 26.3); *Fig. 2.5*, The Bettmann Archive, Inc.; *Fig. 2.6*, Robert Lackenbach/Black Star; *Fig. 2.7*, From the collection of the Musée de l'Homme, J. Oster, photographer.

Chapter 4: *Fig. 4.1*, DeVore/Anthro-Photo File.

Chapter 5: *Fig. 5.1*, By courtesy of Electa Editrice, Milano; *Fig. 5.2*, Richard Lee/Anthro-Photo File; *Fig. 5.3*, Courtesy of the Trustees of the British Museum; *Fig. 5.5*, Courtesy of the Society of Antiquaries of London; *Fig. 5.6*, From James Deetz, *Invitation to Archaeology*, illustrated by Eric G. Engstrom. Copyright © 1967 by James Deetz.

(Continued on page 594.)

TO THE READER ❧

Many people think of archaeology as a romantic subject, a glamorous pastime spent with pyramids, mysterious inscriptions, and buried treasure. This stereotype originated in the nineteenth century, when both archaeologists and the ancient civilizations they uncovered became legendary. Today, more than 150 years of archaeological investigations have turned archaeology into a meticulous scientific discipline. But the excitement is still there, in the many diverse and highly detailed reconstructions of life in the past from finds that sometimes seem trivial. Archaeologists have established the direction of the wind during a bison hunt on the Great Plains about 8000 years ago, learned which plants made up the wreaths created for Tutankhamun's funeral, and even examined the garbage produced in modern urban America. In this book I describe how archaeologists make and study such finds to illuminate the human past.

In the Beginning introduces the history and methods of archaeology and its significance today. I discuss archaeological concepts and procedures, and show how archaeologists describe cultures as part of time and space to interpret the prehistoric past. One objective in this book is to provide a comprehensive summary of the field for people who have little or no experience with it. A second objective is to alert you to a major crisis facing archaeology in the 1980s. All archaeological sites are finite records of the past; once destroyed they can never be replaced. But treasure hunting by individuals and an explosive increase in construction of buildings, roads, dams, and the like have destroyed thousands of archaeological sites all over the world. Without access to intact sites, we cannot possibly complete a picture of the human past. The crisis of site destruction is, in its way, as important as the ecological crisis we face. *In the Beginning* is meant to arouse you to the need for living responsibly with your cultural heritage.

Archaeology has been struck by a knowledge explosion and must rely more and more on sophisticated systems models and apply quantitative methods. But this relatively small book and the necessity for providing an overall view of the subject prevent me from considering too many technical nuances of contemporary archaeology. I hope you will pursue the topics that interest you in more advanced and specialized archaeology courses or in the many excellent books and articles listed in the Bibliography and Suggested Readings at the back of the book or in the Guide to Further Reading following each chapter.

The chapters open with previews highlighting the major themes and concepts. Whenever practicable, drawings and photographs illustrate the subjects the text describes in words. I use specialized terminology as little as possible and define every new term when it first appears. In addition, a glossary at the back of the book provides definitions of the words used in the book as well as of some words you may encounter in other reading.

I have written this book from predominantly English-language sources for two main reasons. First, my reading in the vast archaeological literature has been necessarily selective and mostly in English. And, second, for most of you English is your native tongue. Although linguistic abilities and time have thus biased this volume toward the achievements and writings of English-speaking archaeologists, archaeology is indeed a global activity, conducted with great energy and intelligence by every nation and in every corner of the world.

B. M. F.

TO THE INSTRUCTOR ✒

When I started writing the first edition of this book in 1968, I had no idea that I would be revising it for the fifth time fifteen years later. *In the Beginning* has been in print during a period of profound change in archaeology. One has only to glance through the first edition and then through this one to see just how much it has changed in the 1970s and early 1980s. Hundreds of instructors have assigned the first four editions, and thousands of students have used them. A few respected teachers have even told me that they were introduced to archaeology by *In the Beginning*, which indeed reflects the passage of years. They and many others have helped improve the book by writing to me with suggestions, criticisms, even reprints of their own work. Of course, the fifth edition also reflects my own perceptions of contemporary archaeology and of the way in which the discipline is evolving. Archaeology's many traits, interacting variables, and different forms of feedback make it almost as much a cultural system, evolving multilinearly, as the many cultures it studies.

The fifth edition of *In the Beginning* reflects a number of important trends in archaeology in the past five years. These include:

- An explosion of archaeological data from all over the world, resulting from a vastly expanded community of archaeologists everywhere. This growth has led to a mountain of archaeological literature in dozens of languages, making the task of keeping up to date even more challenging.
- A growing emphasis on regional studies, cultural resource management, and nondestructive ways of investigating the past. Remote sensing and computers are increasingly important in archaeology today, for destructive excavation is now seen as a strategy of last resort in many areas.
- Renewed emphasis on multidisciplinary research, especially in the general area of geoarchaeology, placing human activities within an environmental context.
- Vastly increased use of instrumentation and highly scientific approaches to the past. Almost no archaeological research is carried out in this day and age without a battery of equipment and scientific instruments. These sophisticated tools can include remote sensing devices like side-scan radar, lasers, and electron

microscopes. Thus, the cost of archaeological research is rising. Quantitative methods are now common, with computers applied to create huge banks of data on local, regional, state, and even national archaeology.

- Quickened interest in site-formation processes, and "middle-range theory." Interpretation of the archaeological record is now a major theoretical debate.

- Potentially most important, a profound change has occurred in archaeology itself. A decade ago, most archaeologists were academic scholars in universities, colleges, or museums. Today, most American archaeologists are involved with conservation and management, known as cultural resource management. We are now a more "professional discipline," undergoing a revolution that geology, for one, underwent some decades ago. This switch in our ways of thinking about and teaching archaeology is likely to affect us profoundly.

These are but a few of the fascinating trends in contemporary archaeology that form this edition of *In the Beginning*. This is an interesting time in archaeology, for the "new" archaeology of the 1960s and 1970s is no longer new. Then it set out some bold and promising objectives: imposing great scientific rigor, creating a body of archaeological theory, and searching for general laws of cultural behavior. At first the new archaeologists attacked every concept in archaeology. Today, the level of bombast has subsided, to be replaced by better-focused theoretical debate about everything from style and function to ethnographic analogy. But there is frustration, too, and a widespread feeling that the new archaeology has not delivered its promised advances; that some of its high-minded objectives will never be fulfilled. In part, many of those who are disappointed feel that way because they believed that creating a new body of archaeological theory would be much easier than it has proved. It is also because the interpretative problems of much regional and spatial archaeology are obdurate, sophisticated, and difficult, especially when approached with borrowed concepts. Archaeology has spent two decades borrowing concepts like general systems theory and cluster analysis from other disciplines. These ideas have often proved inadequate or inappropriate for archaeological application, except in the most general way. At the moment, we are midway in a long period of transition, with archaeologists divided into a minority engaged in intensive theoretical debate, and the remainder carrying out the same forms of empirical research, albeit in more scientific ways, as were commonplace before processual archaeology came along. Those who believe that this dichotomy will endure are false prophets! What is happening in archaeology has already happened in many matured sciences, and is still taking place in much of biology—the development of distinctive and scientific archaeological method and theory that not only enrich our understanding of the past but add something to the sum of Westerners' better understanding of themselves. We may hope that the short remainder of this century will see archaeology achieve this lofty goal; it depends on the work and cooperation of archaeologists of all theoretical and methodological persuasions. Please encourage your students to think of archaeology as one enterprise, not as dozens of unrelated activities!

I have changed about 40 percent of this edition, much of it by updating methods, theoretical approaches, and case examples. Parts I and II are little changed except for some minor updating. Part I covers the significance, goals, and current crisis in archaeology; Part II the early origins of archaeology and how it developed into the science it is today. Part III covers the basic concepts of archaeology. Here I have retained the format and coverage of earlier editions at the request of reviewers, as a good introduction to Part IV, which deals with the recovery of archaeological data. I have rewritten much of the survey chapter, incorporating renewed interest in survey and remote sensing as a major new archaeological tool. I have also reworked the sections on sampling and now pay more attention to processes of site formation than in earlier editions. Part V has revisions in the metallurgy sections and increased coverage of artifact classification, as well as added material on lithic wear studies and refitting.

The second half of In the Beginning retains its organization from earlier editions, but is substantially updated. New advances in taphonomy and zooarchaeology are incorporated, and the influence of Lewis R. Binford's Bones: Ancient Men and Modern Myths (1981) can be found throughout Parts V and VI. The most extensively changed chapter in the book is 15, completely rewritten to incorporate the latest thinking on analogy, middle-range theory, and approaches to interpretation of the archaeological record. Parts VII and VIII have been updated throughout, and Cultural Resource Management, Chapter 20, now reflects current thinking on CRM research designs.

Modern archaeology is so wide ranging and complex that one could easily write a 1000-page text on the subject. Thus I have had to skate over some topics, such as population carrying capacity, in almost indecent haste. These topics are important, to be sure, but the limitations of space require concentration on basics rather than on the more experimental methodologies. I leave it to each of you to fill in details on topics you think are given inadequate treatment. I urge you, however, to give full coverage to one vital topic: the growing crisis of site destruction. This subject demands full factual and moral coverage in introductory courses, where many students arrive with the notion of finding buried treasure or collecting beautiful artifacts. Many of us have first-hand experience with treasure hunters and with tragically bulldozed sites. Every course in archaeology must place responsibility for preserving the past emphatically on the public. It is for this reason that the book ends with a stark statement of basic archaeological ethics for everyone.

In the Beginning is a comprehensive, introductory look at contemporary archaeology. With the very first edition, I decided not to espouse any one theory of archaeology, but to give each instructor a basis for amplifying the text with his or her own viewpoint and theoretical persuasion. This decision has turned out to be endorsed by many users. A reviewer said a couple of editions ago: "This is the fun with the book." Long may it continue to be so.

Many people have assisted in preparing this fifth edition. Their comments have always been challenging and provocative. I only hope that my efforts to navigate between conflicting viewpoints and priorities meet with their approval. I am especially indebted to the wise advice of Margaret Conkey, State University of New York at Binghamton; Paul R. Fish, Arizona State Museum, The University of Arizona; Donald K. Grayson, Thomas Burke Memorial Washington State Museum, U. of Washington; and William A. Turnbaugh, University of Rhode Island.

My friendships within the College Division of Little, Brown extend back more than fifteen years and through no fewer than six anthropology editors. Brad Gray joins the list of those who have supported and encouraged *In the Beginning*. To him, and the production staff in Boston, my most grateful thanks. My association with Little, Brown has enriched not only this book, but also my life.

B.M.F.

CONTENTS 🌿

PART I

BACKGROUND TO ARCHAEOLOGY

Like earnest mastodons petrified in the forests of their own apparatus the archaeologists come and go, each with his pocket Odyssey and his lack of modern Greek. Diligently working upon the refuse-heaps of some township for a number of years they erect on the basis of a few sherds or a piece of dramatic drainage, a sickly and enfeebled portrait of a way of life. How true it is we cannot say; but if an Eskimo were asked to describe our way of life, deducing all his evidence from a search in a contemporary refuse dump, his picture might lack certain formidable essentials.

LAWRENCE DURRELL
Prospero's Cell

Why study archaeology? What is the importance of this popular and apparently romantic subject? We begin to answer these questions by looking at the place of archaeology in the twentieth-century world, at its important role in our cultural enrichment and in the writing of world history. Unfortunately, the discipline faces a crisis brought about by rapid destruction of important sites by industrial development and treasure hunting. Furthermore, the credibility of archaeologists is undermined by all sorts of pseudo-archaeologies purporting to tell the truth about lost worlds, ancient astronauts, and sunken continents.

The reality of archaeology is much less romantic but just as fascinating. We define archaeology by placing it within its broad context as part of anthropology and history.

CHAPTER 1 🐾

ARCHAEOLOGY INTRODUCED

Preview

- Modern archaeology is the scientific study of past cultures and technologies—whether ancient or recent—by scientific methods and theoretical concepts devised for that purpose.
- Archaeology covers the human past, from the earliest peoples up to modern times.
- Archaeology had its origins in treasure hunting, Renaissance classicism, and grave robbing, but it has evolved into a highly precise discipline. It has become an integral part of twentieth-century life as a component of popular culture and modern intellectual curiosity.
- Archaeology provides the only viable means of discovering the history of many of the world's societies whose documented past began in recent times. As such, it is a vital support for nationalist feeling and for fostering cultural identity.
- Archaeologists have major contributions to make to the resolution of modern land disputes and to modern management of resources.
- The destruction of sites, fostered by greedy collectors and industrial development, is the crisis that archaeology is faced with today. Archaeological sites are a finite resource that can never be replaced. If the present rate of destruction continues, the danger

is real that few undisturbed archaeological sites will remain by the end of this century.

- Archaeologists also face a challenge from people who promote "pseudo-archaeologies" purporting to explain the past, such as extravagant theories that Ancient Egyptians or Phoenicians landed in the New World thousands of years before Columbus.
- Archaeology is part of the science of anthropology, which is the study of humanity in the widest possible sense. Archaeologists use a battery of special methods and techniques to examine human societies of the past.
- There are many types of archaeologists. Prehistoric archaeologists study prehistory, that is, human history before written records; historical archaeologists use archaeology to supplement documentary history; and Classical archaeologists study ancient Greece and Rome.
- Modern archaeology has three basic goals: studying culture history, reconstructing past lifeways, and studying cultural process.
- In contrast to American archaeologists, Old World scholars think of archaeology as extending documentary history into the remote past.

Archaeology has always been thought of as a romantic subject. In fact, however, modern archaeology is a rigorous and demanding scientific discipline. We use the word discipline because archaeology consists of a broad range of scientific methods and techniques for studying the past, used carefully and in a disciplined way. In this chapter we explore archaeology's role in the twentieth-century world and the crisis of destruction that archaeology faces; define archaeology in relation to anthropology and history; and look at the different types of archaeologists.

WHY STUDY ARCHAEOLOGY?

Most people associate archaeologists with buried treasure, the Great Pyramids, and grinning skeletons. They are often depicted as elderly, eccentric scholars in sun helmets digging up inscribed tablets in the shadow of Egyptian temples. They are thought to be typical absentminded professors, so deeply absorbed in the details of ancient life that they care little for the pressures and frustrations of modern life. Archaeology is believed to open doors to a world of romance and excitement, to discoveries like the spectacular tomb of the Egyptian pharaoh Tutankhamun, opened by English archaeologists Howard Carter and Lord Carnarvon in 1922. Even today, many people believe that archaeologists spend their lives solving great mysteries and finding lost civilizations. Any course or lecture on archaeology is filled with people who are indulging their fascination with the past. I hope you are reading this book for the same reason.

Few archaeologists are fortunate enough to discover a royal burial or a forgotten civilization, however. Most of them excavate for a lifetime finding nothing more spectacular than some fine pottery or delicately made stone tools. But archaeology is still a fascinating subject and captures the imagination of scholar and public alike. It was British archaeologist Stuart Piggott who called archaeology "the science of rubbish." And there is much truth in that statement. Archaeologists spend their lives investigating the surviving and abandoned remains of ancient societies. It is not gold or fine objects that interest them, though, but the information that comes from digging up finds and properly recording them. The archaeologist today is as interested in why people live the way they do, as in the objects they made and the buildings they erected.

On the face of it, the study of archaeology, however fascinating, seems a luxury we can ill afford in a world confronted by economic recessions and widespread poverty and famine. But to regard archaeology in such a way would be to treat the entire cultural heritage of humanity as irrelevant and unnecessary to the quality of our lives; in reality, it is integral (White, 1974).

Early Archaeologists. The first people to study archaeology did so because they enjoyed digging into the past (Daniel, 1981), both out of curiosity and for fun. A century and a quarter ago, archaeology was no more than a lighthearted pastime. People would gather from far and wide to witness the unbandaging of an Egyptian mummy or the excavation of an ancient burial mound. "Eight barrows were examined," wrote Englishman Thomas Wright (1852) of an archaeological picnic in 1844. "Most of them contained skeletons, more or less entire, with the remains of weapons in iron, bosses of shields, urns, beads, brooches, armlets, bones, amulets, and occasionally more vessels." The day's festivities ended with a

"sumptuous repast" and a tour through the landowner's "interesting collection of antiquities" (Daniel, 1975) (Figure 1.1).

The first archaeologists to dig in Egypt, as well as those who discovered the Maya and the Assyrians, were no more than amateurs
(Fagan, 1975; 1979; Willey and Sabloff, 1980). Normally ardent trav-

Figure 1.1   A nineteenth-century barrow excavation as depicted in *Gentlemen's
Magazine,* 1840.

elers, they learned how to dig as they went along, their objective being to discover and remove as many spectacular finds as they could in the time they had. Englishman Austen Henry Layard was in his twenties during the mid-1840s, when he dug into the ancient mounds of the Biblical sites of Calah and Nineveh in Iraq. He discovered the lost civilization of the Assyrians and gave up archaeology by the time he was thirty-five. Layard achieved worldwide fame with his bestselling book *Nineveh and Its Remains* (Layard, 1849). The Mayan civilization of Mexico and Guatemala was first described by American travel writer John Lloyd Stephens, who traveled in the forests of the Yucatan with artist Frederick Catherwood in 1839 (Figure 1.2). His *Incidents of Travel* (Stephens, 1841) was an instant bestseller. Both Layard's and Stephens's works were as much volumes of travel and adventure as they were archaeological reports. One has the impression that they had great fun on their travels. "The reader is perhaps curious to know how old cities sell in Central America. Like other articles of trade they are regulated by the quality in the market and the demand," wrote Stephens. "I paid fifty dollars for Copán ... for which Don José Maria thought me only a fool; if I had offered more, he would probably have considered me something worse." Stephens wanted to transport the Copán sculptures to New York, as others had removed antiquities from Egypt and Mesopotamia to the museums of Europe. Fortu-

Figure 1.2   A lithograph by Frederick Catherwood of the Mayan site, Chichén Itzá.

nately for science, he failed (Fagan, 1977), and today's traveler can still enjoy the sculptures in their natural setting.

The foundations of modern archaeology lie not only in the adventuresome spirit, but also in the intellectual curiosity of the early travelers and archaeologists. None was more single-minded than Heinrich Schliemann, a German businessman who made several fortunes before retiring and devoting the remainder of his life to searching for the cities that were described in Homer's poems (Ceram, 1953). His career reads like a dream. He was born into a poor German family and started work as a grocer's assistant at age fifteen. During a period as a merchant's clerk in Amsterdam, Schliemann devoted himself to learning Russian and other languages with fanatical intensity. Within a few years he was a wealthy merchant in St. Petersburg, Russia. In his early forties he gave up business, married a young Greek woman, and set out to find Homer's legendary city of Troy. His feverish search ended at the mound of Hissarlik in northwestern Turkey. Schliemann always worked on a large scale. He recruited 150 men and moved 325,000 cubic yards of soil in his early seasons. His excavation techniques were modeled on those used to dig the Suez Canal in Egypt some years earlier. By 1873, Schliemann had found no fewer than seven cities and a great gold treasure, which he proudly displayed on his wife's neck (Ceram, 1953; Deuel, 1977; Stone, 1975). But his archaeological methods were brutal—he destroyed almost as much as he discovered.

Until the last decades of the nineteenth century, archaeological excavations still resembled treasure hunts—and that they often were. "It is sickening to see the rate at which everything is being destroyed, and the little regard paid to preservation," wrote Egyptologist Flinders Petrie in 1883. One can hardly blame him for his remark. Early excavators in Egypt, such as the notorious Giovanni Belzoni, a strongman turned tomb robber, literally mined the ancient Egyptians for gold. Belzoni would push his way into mummy caves and even sit down on a corpse to rest. "When my weight bore on the body of an Egyptian, it crushed like a bandbox," he recalled (Fagan, 1975). Belzoni often found himself smothered in dust and decayed bones, and he was not above using corpses and coffins for firewood. The losses to science from such activities were incalculable. How often do we read that such and such a find "crumbled to dust," or that exposed to the open air the object "dissolved before our very eyes"?

Most early archaeologists were interested in carrying away precious objects for display in foreign museums and minimally in preserving the great sites they dug for future generations. But their depredations did lead to the popular fascination that archaeology holds for many today.

Archaeology as Entertainment. Scientific archaeology began a century ago, but has become a serious and popular field of investigation only within the past half century. Sixty years ago professional archaeologists were few; today hundreds of museums, archaeological surveys, and universities are staffed with trained graduates in archaeology. Popular interest in the past has sharply increased in recent decades, sparked in part by an explosion of popular literature on archaeology. Colorful, imaginative reconstructions of early human beings camping on the African savannah appear in Time-Life books and on the pages of *National Geographic*. Spectacular archaeological discoveries merit prominent headlines in many newspapers. Archaeology is as much a part of popular culture as football or the automobile. Thousands of people read archaeology books for entertainment, join archaeological societies, and flock to popular lectures on the past.

The jetliner and the package tour have helped make archaeology a medium of popular entertainment as well. Fifty years ago only the wealthy and privileged could take a tour up the Nile, visit the Greek temples, and explore Mayan civilization. Now package tours can take you to Egypt, to the Parthenon, and to Teotihuacán. The jumbo jet and the air-conditioned bus can take you to such remote sites as Petra in Jordan or the Inca cities in Peru. The famous sites of antiquity give the modern traveler a sense of time that dwarfs the day-to-day cares of the twentieth century. The immense pyramids of Gizeh in Egypt, and the prodigious labor that built them; the white columns of the Temple of Poseidon at Sounion, touched with pink by the setting sun; the ruins at Tikal bathed in the full moon's light—as sights alone, these overwhelm the senses. Tutankhamun's golden mask or a giant Olmec head with its snarling grin (Figure 1.3) lifts us to a realm where achievement endures and perceptions seem of a higher order. It is this sense of physical reality carried from the past which holds our human secrets, if only we could read its meaning, which draws people to archaeology—a casual interest for some, but for others a consuming passion.

Archaeology and Cultural Heritage. Every society on earth has some form of the origin myth: folklore that is the official, sanc-

Figure 1.3   A ceremonial Olmec axe head, depicting a god who combines the features of a man and a jaguar. His face is stylized, with flamelike eyelashes and drooping mouth. (One-half actual size.)

tioned account of how it came into being. Our own society is no exception. "And God said, 'Let us make man in our image, after our likeness: and let them have dominion over the fish of the sea, and over the fowl of the air, and over the cattle, and over all the earth, and over every creeping thing that creepeth on the earth.'"—thus reads the first chapter of Genesis, a majestic account of the Creation that was accepted as the authorized version of human origin for centuries.

Origin myths, such as that of Genesis, developed in response to humanity's deep-seated curiosity about its origins. For more than two thousand years, Westerners have speculated about their ancestry and tried to develop theoretical models to explain their origins. Some of these models are purely philosophical; others are based on scientifically collected data. Much of these data come from archaeological surveys and excavations. Archaeology is fascinating because it enables us to test theoretical models of evolving societies: why some people have flourished, others have vanished without trace, and still others have sunk into obscurity.

Our curiosity about the past stems not only from preoccupation with our ultimate origins, but from strong feelings of nostalgia as well. We live in a world of rapid change and diminishing natural resources, in a crowded, overpopulated urban environment. As population increases and ecological problems deepen, we find ourselves nostalgic for simpler, earlier times. The life of prehistoric peoples, determined by the seasons of vegetable foods and the movements of game, is perceived as a time of natural simplicity. Archaeology gives insight into those less complicated societies of the past.

Archaeology also contributes valuable information to our collective cultural heritage. Most American Indian groups came into contact with literate Western civilization only in the past three centuries. Before European contact, Indian history was not written; it consisted mostly of oral traditions handed down from generation to generation. Archaeology and archaeological sites are the only other possible sources for American Indian history. Only as archaeologists probe into their ancestry will the first chapter of American history be written.

One of the most remarkable examples of archaeology's ability to reveal the history of the Indian comes from Ozette, Washington, where Richard Daugherty has excavated the remains of a Makah Indian village that was buried by mud slides about 500 years ago (Kirk, 1974). Conditions for preservation at the site were so exceptional that archaeologists were able to recover complete details of the village's plank houses and their contents, down to stored food and whalebone harpoons. By working closely with the Tribal Council, Daugherty was able not only to interpret the objects found on the site, but also to help the Council raise a large sum of money for a local museum in which to display the finds. In this way, he brought the hitherto forgotten history of the Makah into the consciousness of the Indians themselves and of the public as well (Fagan, 1978a). Though scientific monographs on this site have yet to appear, the public is fully informed on the results of the excavation.

The Ozette example is by no means unique, for more and more archaeologists are working closely with American Indians and other ethnic groups. E. Charles Adams has excavated at the Hopi village of Walpi in the Southwest, and has worked closely with the local people. Pre-civil war lifeways among slave communities in the Southeast are the subject of long-term excavations there, and archaeologists working in Alexandria, Virginia, have studied the history of black neighborhoods using archaeology, historical records, and oral traditions (Cressey, 1980).

Political Uses of Archaeology. Many newly independent nations, eager to foster nationalism, are encouraging archaeological research as the only way to uncover the early roots of the peoples who lived there before colonial times. For years the Tanzanian and Zambian governments in Africa have sponsored excavations, whose results soon appear in university textbooks and schoolbooks. The primary goal of archaeology there, as in many parts of the world, is to write unwritten history, not from archives and dusty documents, but from long-abandoned villages and rubbish heaps. That this type of archaeology is essential is clear from the remarks by President Kenneth Kaunda of Zambia, when presented with a book on Zambian history written by a group of archaeologists and historians. With intense pride he said, "This is our history. Now we can look people from other countries in the face and tell them that we have a history and a national identity to be proud of." It is difficult to convey the feeling that came through in his remarks.

In a far less admirable way, a number of governments have used archaeology for political ends. With it the Nazis produced "evidence" for the evolution of a master race in Europe (Clark, G., 1939). During the late 1960s, the government of Rhodesia in southern Africa claimed that the Zimbabwe ruins, a famous complex of stone buildings, were the work of Phoenician colonists who had settled south of the Zambezi River more than 2,000 years ago. They chose to ignore half a century and more of archaeological research that showed Zimbabwe had been built by indigenous African peoples between A.D. 1000 and 1500. The reason for the claim was easily discerned: A Phoenician date for Zimbabwe would be evidence for white settlement in southern Africa long before the local people arrived (Garlake, 1973). Oddly, the controversy has a new twist now that Zimbabwe is an independent nation. Local politicians accuse white archaeologists of not understanding the true significance of the site, even though they had proved it was built by Africans. Only locally born scholars, they argue, have adequate "cultural background" to interpret the symbolism in the ruins.

Archaeology as a Social Science. Archaeologists bring a unique tool to the social sciences of which they are a part: a perspective that enables them to understand how people have dealt with the world around them from the earliest times. This facility contributes to a much better understanding of our own history, as well as that of the environment, the world climate, and the landscape. The long-abandoned settlements that archaeologists study are repositories of precisely dated geological, biological, and environmental data that can add a vital time depth to studies of the contemporary world. In the dry pueblos of Arizona preservation conditions are so good that wood, fossil pollen grains, and other environmental evidence are found in abundance. It is proving to be possible to study the gradual evolution of southwestern agriculture through many centuries and determine how the local people responded to uneven rainfall and other environmental changes. Information from such researches is invaluable to students of agriculture who are trying to expand crop production in the desert. Archaeological sites are storehouses of information for a host of natural and physical sciences.

Chemists and physicists have made great contributions to the study of the past as well, by developing such approaches as the radiocarbon dating method and sophisticated spectrographic analysis for studying prehistoric trade.

Archaeologists have many practical tasks in today's world that further amplify their role as social scientists. One such task is the settling of territorial claims by excavation. In the eighteenth century an archaeological investigation figured in the settling of a border dispute between the British and the Americans over the site of Samuel de Champlain's settlement at Dochet Island on the St. Croix River, between Maine and Canada. An antiquarian dug to find the site of the fort, but the results were inconclusive. Excavations have occasionally featured in disputes over Indian lands and we can expect that archaeologists will provide expert testimony in many future cases.

Recent federal legislation requires that archaeological impact studies be done on all government-funded development projects to ensure that minimal damage is done to archaeological resources during construction work. This legislation has massively expanded archaeological work throughout North America (see Chapter 21). It is designed to protect the finite data base of archaeological sites that are studied by archaeologists and by scientists from many other disciplines.

Archaeology has also worked directly for contemporary American society, especially in management of resources and waste. University of Arizona archaeologist William Rathje has studied the garbage dumps in Tucson for a long time (Rathje, 1974). He examines patterns in garbage disposed of by Tucson households, analyzes evidence from the dump with the latest archaeological research designs and techniques, and joins to it data gleaned from interviews with householders and other sources. His study has revealed startlingly wasteful habits in Arizona households of many economic and social backgrounds, information that could be used to suggest better strategies for consumer buying and resource management.

Rathje argues that such studies of modern garbage can supply unique knowledge about ourselves, as well as about the past. Because the objects we use shape our lives in many ways, we need to understand how they affect us to learn about the past and anticipate the future (Rathje, 1979).

The archaeologist's task, then, is significant in the twentieth-century world, in which we must understand other cultures if we are to survive. To say that archaeology is a luxury is to deny the cultural achievements of our predecessors, and to deprive many millions of the opportunity to learn about their roots and ancestry. For generations white Americans believed that the Midwest was populated by ancient European civilizations extinct long before the American Indians arrived. This "mound-builder" theory, so named after the great earthworks found in the Midwest, was discredited by archaeological researches in the Ohio Valley and elsewhere late in the nineteenth century (Silverberg, 1968).

As more and more non-Western societies abandon their traditional ways of life to become part of modern technological civilization, archaeologists have to be guardians of the world's dying cultures. People move from their traditional village sites into cities or modern housing, leaving their old settlements to crumble to the ground. Only with the archaeologist's spade, combined with oral tradition and the work of early anthropologists, can we hope to recover many details about the dying culture. Richard Lee and others made remarkable anthropological studies of San hunter-gatherers in the Kalahari desert of Southern Africa, to learn about the living people and their recently abandoned campsites (Yellen,

1977). In this and other field studies, the archaeologist and the anthropologist together hurry to describe a society that is slowly becoming extinct as it reacts to pressure from the outside world.

In short, archaeology also satisfies our intellectual curiosity about the nature of humanity. Perhaps its greatest achievement is to have established the tremendous antiquity of human existence on earth. With their broad perspective on time and circumstance, archaeologists are as much part of our lives as are historians, anthropologists, physicists, and an army of more exotic specialists. It is the only source of cultural history for some.

THE CRISIS IN ARCHAEOLOGY

Unfortunately, archaeologists are an endangered species. The sites that cry out to be investigated are being destroyed so rapidly that a sizable portion of the world's archaeological heritage has already vanished forever. Unlike trees or animals, archaeological sites are a finite resource. Once a bulldozer or treasure hunter moves in, archaeological evidence is wiped out. The archaeologist's archives are buried in the soil, and the only way to preserve them is to leave them alone, intact, until they can be investigated with rigorous scientific care. Both human nature and the world's growing populations' insatiable needs have wrought terrible destruction on the discipline.

Collectors and the Morality of Collecting. Our materialistic society greatly emphasizes wealth and the possession of valuable things. Many people feel an urge to possess the past, to keep a piece of antiquity on the mantel. Projectile points, Acheulian hand axes, Benin bronzes, or Maya pots add an exotic touch to the prosaic American living room. Many archaeological artifacts, such as those Benin bronzes, have high antique and commercial value. They are "Buried Treasure," valued as museum pieces and by the world's major collectors, commanding enormous prices at auction and in salesrooms. Glorious finds of antiquity are displayed without context, often because their archaeological associations are unknown. High commercial prices and the human urge to own have incited unscrupulous treasure hunting and a flourishing illegal trade in antiquities, raping sites for gold and other precious ornaments, as well as pottery, sculpture, and all the other artifacts that today's covetous collectors seek to own and sell.

The destruction of archaeological sites for commercial ends has grown to alarming proportions, but it is nothing new. The dilettantes of eighteenth-century Italy, Giovanni Belzoni in Egypt, and Lord Elgin in Greece were merely the best known of those who satisfied the educated European's lust for antiquities. The thirst for pre-Columbian antiquities goes back as least a century. The only difference is that today the traffic in tomb robbing and illegal antiquities is better organized, more lucrative, and fueled by inflation, greed, and the aggressive policies on acquisition of heavily endowed public and private museums.

This pressure to acquire objects of interest and value has escalated in the twentieth century as more museums compete for fewer and fewer valuable and authentic pieces. In some countries, like Italy and Costa Rica, tomb robbing is a full-time, if technically illegal, profession. The Italian *tombaroli* concentrate on Etruscan tombs (Hamblin, 1970). Their finds command high prices from foreign dealers, and the government does little to control either the looting or the export trade. Entire Inca cemeteries have been dug up for gold ornaments. Thousands of Egyptian tombs have been rifled for papyri and statues. And the problem is not confined to ancient civilizations. North America bristles with pot hunters, who think nothing of ravaging sites for their projectile heads and potsherds. Looting even one projectile head destroys a small part of our nation's limited archaeological resource. The cumulative effects of treasure hunting, pot hunting, and metal detectors is catastrophic.

Why do people collect antiquities? In 1921 Henri Codet, a French medical doctor, wrote a pioneering dissertation on collecting. He concluded that it has four underlying motives: "the need to possess, the need for spontaneous activity, the impulse to self-advancement, and the tendency to classify things" (Meyer, 1977). Another Frenchman said of collecting: "It is not a pastime, but a passion and often so violent that it is inferior to love or ambition only in the pettiness of its aims." People collect everything from beer-bottle caps to phallic symbols, and anything collectible is considered by collectors to be portable and private—and it is their duty to preserve it. It follows that everything has a market value and can be purchased, the market value depending on the demand for the category of artifact or its rarity or aesthetic appeal. The archaeological context of the artifact is unimportant, and information about the people who made it is usually irrelevant: all that matters is the object itself (Figure 1.4).

Figure 1.4 The wrong and the right way to dig. Archaeology is a hobby for both these groups, but the top group is destroying evidence of the past by their digging "techniques" and the bottom group is preserving it. The latter, alas, happens all too rarely.

Protecting antiquities is complex and incredibly difficult, for in the final analysis, it involves appealing to people's moral values and requires almost unenforceable legislation that ultimately would take away a potential source of livelihood, however illegal, from thousands of poverty-striken peasants and more prosperous middlemen who have some political influence. Many countries are now feeling more nationalistic about their past and their own archaeological sites. When collecting began, such countries as Egypt or Turkey had no museums to house the finds of early archaeologists. Now most countries have museums, and many have antiquities services and stringent archaeology laws controlling export of archaeological finds—at least in theory. The trouble is that the laws cost a fortune to administer and enforce, and even such comparatively wealthy countries as Mexico are unable to police even the most famous of sites. But public opinion in Egypt and other countries shows some pride in the national heritage. It is galling to see the prized sculptures and antiquities of one's past adorning museums in London, Copenhagen, and New York. Yet the tide of public opinion cannot stem the collectors' mania or the ruthless policies of major museums. Perhaps the most notorious example of questionable acquisition by a large museum was perpetrated by the Metropolitan Museum of Art in New York when it purchased a Greek painted vase priced at no less than a million dollars in 1972 (Hess, 1974). The Euphronios vase dates to the sixth century B.C. and is one of the finest examples of its type ever found (Figure 1.5). The Met claimed that the vase came from a private collection that had been intact for almost half a century. But others suspected that the vase was found in an illegal excavation of an Etruscan tomb north of Rome and sold by tomb robbers. The controversy continues. Fortunately some universities and museums have adopted more stringent acquisitions policies, although it is too early to say whether they have had any efffect. Changing public attitudes, more cautious policies, and a shortage of fine antiquities may slow the traffic, but the damage has already been done.

Destruction of Archaeological Sites. Pot hunters and treasure hunters have left thousands of archaeological sites looking like rabbit burrows and have so damaged them that archaeological inquiry is impossible. The ravages of industrial activity, strip mining, and agriculture have all taken their catastrophic toll on many sites as well.

In some of the Unites States, damaging sites is an uncontrolled

Figure 1.5 The Euphronios Vase, sixth century B.C., showing dead Sarpedon being carried by Thanatos and Hypnos. (Height, 18 inches; diameter, 21¹¹⁄₁₆ inches.)

epidemic; virtually no undisturbed sites remain. It has been estimated that fewer than 5 percent of the sites in Los Angeles county remain untouched by pot hunters or developers. Charles McGimsey points out in his landmark book, *Public Archaeology* (1972): "This nation's past is contained in the soil. That soil is being disturbed and redistributed at an ever-increasing rate. Those of us alive today will be the last ever to see any significant portion of it in an undisturbed state."

How can we stem this wanton destruction? Don Graybill (1978) estimates that we are rapidly losing the opportunity to study many ancient societies on more than a local basis because the sites have been destroyed. The only way to minimize future damage is to spend vast sums to enforce much stricter antiquities laws, and to carry out large surveys to inventory the finite resource of sites before it is too late. At the same time, a massive shift in public attitudes toward archaeology is needed—one that makes people respect the past as a valued possession. We need to educate people to learn a responsible attitude toward the past—to consider destruction of vital sites an invalid exchange for prestige and wealth. Archaeologists have done little to educate the general public about the crisis facing the irreplaceable archives of the prehistoric and historic past. McGimsey (1972) describes the situation tersely: "No one may act in such a manner that the public right to knowledge of the past is unduly endangered or destroyed."

PSEUDO-ARCHAEOLOGIES

Modern archaeology is highly technical and—let us be honest—sometimes rather dull. In contrast, the flood of "pseudo-archaeologies" that has appeared in recent years positively drip with romance and excitement, with "unexplained" secrets, lost civilizations, and great temples buried in dense rain forests. The Lost Continent of Atlantis, the Ten Lost Tribes of Israel, expeditions in search of Noah's Ark—all provide superb raw material for the armchair adventurer.

Pseudo-archaeologies are not new, and they have always been lucrative businesses. In the mid-nineteenth century, thousands of Americans bought books that described great mound-building civilizations that flourished and did battle in the Midwest. Their descendants supposedly have moved from earth into space. Perhaps the most notorious pseudo-archaeology of recent times was perpetuated in the early 1970s by a popular writer with dubious archaeological credentials named Erich von Däniken. He took advantage of general fascination with space to argue that people from other worlds had lived on earth long before our civilization arose. With his books and films he earned millions of dollars by arguing that "foreign astronauts visited the earth thousands of years ago. The crew of the spaceship soon realized that the earth could support intelligent life" (von Däniken, 1970; 1971). They found primitive humans on earth and fertilized some of the females. Millennia later the spacemen returned and found *Homo sapiens* scattered over the earth. They repeated their breeding experiment and eventually produced a "creature intelligent enough to have the rules of society imparted to it" (von Däniken, 1970). These new beings started art and agriculture and eventually their own civilizations, regarding their progenitors as "benevolent gods who were interested in their welfare." But soon warfare began and people began to destroy many of the sacred places. Centuries later, people started to excavate these ancient temples. The astronauts' influence on prehistoric people, argued von Däniken, was about equivalent to that of Captain Cook and his mariners on the Tahitians—devastating.

The world at large adored von Däniken's incredible hypotheses, but archaeologists were puzzled. His extravagant theories—they are nothing less—are a superb example of misused archaeological data. Most scholars find it impossible to follow von Däniken's reasoning, for his archaeological "evidence" is laced with Biblical allusions, in one of which he claims that Sodom and Gomorrah were destroyed by an atomic bomb! The Ark of the Covenant was an electrified transmitter that enabled Moses to communicate with the astronauts. After this theological *tour de force* we are led through a mishmash of archaeological evidence from all over the world cited as grounds for proving that astronauts did land on earth thousands of years ago. Von Däniken claims that an astronaut complete with helmet was carved at Copán in Guatemala and that the Sun God statue at Tiahuanaco, Bolivia (Figure 1.6), depicts a golden spaceship that came from the stars.

Von Däniken's brand of pseudo-archaeology is unusual only because he has moved into space for his heroes. Like his predecessors, and like many people fascinated by escapism and space fiction, he is intoxicated with the mystery and lure of vanished tribes and lost cities engulfed in swirling mists. (Story, 1976; Wauchope, 1972).

Figure 1.6 The Gate of the Sun God at Tiahuanaco, Bolivia. According to von Däniken, the gate represents "a flying god flanked by forty-eight mysterious figures. Legend tells of a golden spaceship which comes from the stars."

Of course, the pseudo-archaeologists do not all turn to space for their explanations. In order to answer the intense controversy that surrounds the question of early settlements in the Americas, Barry Fell and other authors have alleged that North America was settled by foreigners long before the Vikings and Christopher Columbus arrived. They use as evidence isolated artifacts and alleged inscriptions that are sometimes little more than crude forgeries and are invariably without well-documented archaeological contexts. Many of their theories bear no resemblance whatsoever to archaeological reality (Fell, 1976).

Flamboyant nonarchaeology of the type espoused by von Däniken and Fell will always appeal to those who are impatient with the deliberate pace of science, and to people who believe in "a faint possibility that...." Some of these cult archaeologies—they are nothing more—show all the symptoms of becoming personality cults, even religious movements (Cole, 1980). The theories espoused by the leaders become articles of faith, the object of personal conversion. They are attempts to give meaning to being human, and often are steeped in symbolism and religious activity. Almost invariably the cultists dismiss archaeologists as "elitists" or "scientific fuddy-duddies" because they reject wild theories that are unsupported by scientifically gathered evidence. Until recently, archaeologists made little effort to popularize their findings, leaving a clear field for the bizarre and the eccentric.

The credibility of modern archaeology depends on archaeologist's ability to communicate the results of their scientific research to wide audiences in intelligible and enjoyable forms. They have a formidable task, for as we have seen, popular attitudes toward archaeology tend toward the romantic and the exotic. Today's archaeology is far from exotic, and although it is highly technical, it is still extremely fascinating. I hope this book will give you an understanding of how scientific archaeologists go about their work.

ARCHAEOLOGY, ANTHROPOLOGY, AND HISTORY

Anthropology and Archaeology.   Anthropology is the scientific study of humanity in the widest possible sense. Anthropologists study human beings as biological organisms and as people with a distinctive and unique characteristic—culture. They carry out research on contemporary human societies and on human development from the very earliest times. This enormous field is divided into subdisciplines:

Physical anthropology involves the study of human biological evolution and the variations among different living populations. Physical anthropologists also study the behavior of living nonhuman primates, such as the chimpanzee and the gorilla, research that can suggest explanations for behavior among the earliest human beings.

Cultural anthropology deals with the analysis of human social life, both past and present. It is primarily a study of human culture and how culture adapts to the environment. Within cultural anthropology are a number of specialists:

Ethnographers spend most of their time describing the culture, technology, and economic life of living and extinct societies.
Ethnologists engage in comparative studies of societies, a process that involves attempts to reconstruct general principles of human behavior.
Social anthropologists analyze social organization, the ways in which people organize themeslves.

Many of the archaeologist's objectives are the same as those of the cultural anthropologist, one difference being that archaeologists study ancient societies. Thus one could describe an archaeologist as a special type of anthropologist, one who studies the past. This definition is somewhat inadequate, however, for archaeologists use many theoretical frameworks to link their excavated evidence to actual human behavior, and do far more than merely use evidence different from that of their anthropological colleagues.

Archaeology. Archaeologists both build theories and apply scientific techniques and theoretical concepts in studying the material remains of culture (Clark, 1939; Deetz, 1967; Fagan, 1983). They cover all of human history, from the time of the earliest human beings right up to the present.

To understand what archaeology involves requires some knowledge of the material evidence we examine. As we shall see in Chapter 8, some raw materials survive much longer than others. Stone and clay vessels are nearly indestructible; wood, skin, metals, and bone are much more friable. In most archaeological sites, only the most durable remains of human material culture are preserved for the archaeologist to study. Any picture of life in the prehistoric past derived from archaeological investigations is likely to be very one-sided. As a result, the unfortunate archaeologist is like a detective fitting together a complicated collection of clues to give a general impression and explanation of prehistoric culture and society. Much effort has gone into developing sophisticated methods for studying the prehistoric past. Often, it can be like taking a handful of miscellaneous objects—say two spark plugs, a fragment of a china cup, a needle, a grindstone, and a candleholder—and trying to reconstruct the culture of those who made these diverse objects on the basis of these alone.

Some people think that archaeology is an assortment of techniques, such as accurate recording, precise excavation, and detailed laboratory analysis. This narrow definition, however, deals only with "doing archaeology," the actual work of recovering data from the soil. Modern archaeology is far more than a gathering of techniques, for it involves not only recovering, ordering, and describing things from the past, but also interpreting the evidence from the earth. In fact, it is an *interactive* discipline, striking a balance between practical excavation and description and theoretical interpretation.

Theory in Archaeology.   The word "theory" has many uses among social scientists. In archaeology it is the overall framework within which a scholar operates. Theory is still little developed in archaeology, as in the other social sciences, partly because working with variable human behavior is difficult, and also because of inadequate research methods. Normally, archaeologists work within procedural rules and a classification system that is also used by other scholars with the same basic theoretical leanings. Truly interactive archaeology is a constant dialogue between theory and observation, a more or less uniquely self-critical procedure that is very much based on inferences about the past, in turn built on phenomena found in the contemporary world. Theoretical approaches to archaeology are numerous, among them:

Cultural materialism seeks the causes behind sociocultural diversity in the modern world. Thus technoeconomic and technoenvironmental conditions exert selective pressures on society and its ideologies (Harris, 1968; White, 1960). Cultural materialism is closely associated with the teachings of Engels and Marx. It is especially attractive to archaeologists, because it stresses technology, economy, and environment, data for which survive in the archaeological record. The majority of archaeologists would probably consider themselves cultural materialists (Chapter 4).

Structural approaches treat human cultures as shared symbolic structures that are cumulative creations of the human mind. Structural analyses are designed to discover the basic principles of the human mind, an approach associated in particular with famed French anthropologist Claude Lévi-Strauss. The difficulty with this approach for archaeologists is that the intangibles of the human mind are difficult to verify from the archaeological record (Chapter 19).

Ecological approaches stress the study of ancient societies within their ecosystem (Chapter 16). They are fundamental to contemporary archaeology.

Evolutionary approaches have been popular in archaeology since the nineteenth century. The concepts that form multilinear cultural evolution are inextricable from modern archaeological research (Chapters 4 and 19).

A broad definition of archaeology includes not only the subject matter but also the techniques used to describe and explain it. More than a century and a half of work all over the world has developed a battery of methods and techniques for describing and explaining the past. But these are not enough; they are related to a body of theory that provides both a framework and a means for archaeologists to look beyond the facts and material objects for explanations of events that took place during our long history.

Much archaeological research and theory is strongly influenced by contributions made by other academic disciplines, such as specialists in other fields of anthropology and in biology, chemistry, geography, history, physics, and computer technology. Multidisciplinary research is essential to modern archaeology, but much of it does not handle the archaeological record itself, and is meaningless unless combined with such data.

Archaeology and Prehistory. The term *archaeology* originally embraced the study of ancient history as a whole, but the word was gradually narrowed to its present definition—the study of material remains and human cultures using archaeological theory and techniques (Daniel, 1981).

In 1833, French scholar Paul Tournal (1805–1872) coined the name *période anti-historique* for the period of human history extending back before the time of written documents (Grayson, 1983). In time, this phrase shrank to "prehistory," and now encompasses the enormous span of human cultural evolution that extends back at least three million years. This is the time frame studied by prehistoric archaeologists.

Archaeology and History. The earliest known written records were compiled on the banks of the Tigris and Euphrates rivers where Iraq is now, about 5,000 years ago. There *history*, the study of human experience in written documents, begins.

Archaeology is our primary source of information for 99 percent of human history. Written history describes less than one-tenth of 1 percent of that enormous time span. Although written records extend back 5,000 years in the Near East, the earlier portions of that period are but dimly illuminated by the documents. In other parts of the world, prehistory ended much later. Continuous written history in Britain began with the Roman conquest some 2,000 years ago; decipherable records in the New World commenced with Christopher Columbus, even though the Maya long had a record-keeping system and a form of calendar. Some parts of the world did not come into contact with literate peoples until much more recently. The pastoral Khoi Khoi of the Cape of Good Hope came out of prehistory in 1652 and were first known to the outside world when Portuguese explorer Bartholomew Diaz met them in the late fifteenth century. The tribes of the Central African interior had their first contact with David Livingstone in 1855. Continuous government records of this area did not begin until late in the nineteenth century, and parts of New Guinea and the Amazon basin are still leaving their prehistoric past.

Documentary history contrasts sharply with the view of our past as it is reconstructed from the archaeological record. In the first place, historians work with accurate chronologies (Dymond, 1974). They can date an event with certainty to within a year, and possibly even as closely as a minute or second. Second, their history is that of individuals, groups, governments, and even several nations interacting with each other, reacting to events, and struggling for power. They are able to glimpse the subtle interplay of human intellects, for their principal players have often recorded their impressions or deeds on paper. But the historian's record often has gaps. Details of political events are likely to be far more complete than those of day-to-day existence or the trivia of village life, which often mattered little to contemporary observers, no doubt because they experienced such commonplace things in the same way as we do in driving our cars. Such minor details of past human behavior do absorb students of ancient society, especially archaeologists interested in broad patterns of human change and early cultures, and it is here that the archaeologist may be useful to the historian (Finley, 1971).

DIVERSITY OF ARCHAEOLOGISTS

Because no one could possible be expert in the entire time span of archaeology, most archaeologists specialize, pursuing one of these specialties:

Prehistoric Archaeologists (prehistorians) study prehistoric times, from the day of the earliest human beings right up to the frontiers of documentary history. Their dozens of specialties include paleoanthropologists, who are experts in the living floors and artifacts of the earliest human beings. This specialty requires close cooperation with physical anthropologists interested in human biological evolution, and with geologists studying the complex strata in which the earliest human dwellings are found. Others are experts in stone technology, studying the early peopling of the world and the subsistence strategies used by prehistoric hunter-gatherers. Those who specialize in the origins of agriculture and literate civilization work with ceramics, domesticated grains and animal bones, and a wide range of site types and economic lifeways. Because modern prehistoric archaeology covers the globe, it is divided between New and Old World archaeologists, each focusing on specific regions such as the North American Southwest, Meso-america, or Peru. Even these large areas are too big for specialist researchers to work alone, and so they tackle a specific region, site, or detailed problem within a larger site, region, or area. Our knowledge of world prehistory today was gathered by hundreds of archaeologists working in all parts of the world, on small problems or larger ones, on a regional survey or a ten-year excavation at one settlement. And, of course, some prehistorians are experts on soil analysis, ancient animal bones, computer applications and statistical methods in archaeology, or simply on excavation itself.

Classical archaeologists study the remains of the great Classical civilizations of Greece and Rome (Figure 1.7). Many of them work

Figure 1.7 The Parthenon in Athens. Most Classical archaeologists give much attention to art history and architecture.

closely with historians, amplifying documentary records and filling in details of architectural and art history. Traditionally, Classical archaeologists have given much attention to art objects and buildings, but some are now beginning to study the types of economic and social problems discussed by prehistoric archaeologists in this book (Wheeler, 1954).

Egyptologists and *Assyriologists* are among the many specialist archaeologists who work on specific civilizations or time periods. These specialties require unusual skills. Egyptologists have to acquire fluent knowledge of hieroglyphs to help them study the ancient Egyptians, and Assyriologists, experts on the Assyrians of ancient Iraq, have to be conversant with cuneiform script.

Historical archaeologists study archaeological sites in written records. They examine medieval cities, such as Winchester and York in England; they excavate Colonial American settlements (Figure 1.8), Spanish missions, and nineteenth-century forts in the west; and they study a range of interesting historical artifacts, from bottles to uniform buttons (Fontana, 1968; Noël Hume, 1969, 1982; South, 1977).

Both historical and archaeological data are such that gaps always remain in the reconstruction of the past. Even on sites where historical records are exceptionally complete, though, archaeology can provide invaluable information to amplify them (Schuyler, 1978). Medieval Winchester is known to us from a rich archive of official records, which include title deeds for houses. In the Brooks area of the city, Martin Biddle and his colleagues were able to connect houses found in excavations with their long-dead owners. They excavated the quarter where humble artisans had lived, then carried out a lengthy title search in the city archives. They were then able to identify the owners of individual houses whose foundations were exposed in their trenches (Selkirk, 1970). One of the most vivid discoveries in historical archaeology comes from the fortress of Masada in Israel. The first-century historian Josephus Flavius describes how the Romans besieged a group of Jewish patriots in the fortress in A.D. 73. The defenders chose to commit mass suicide rather than surrender. Excavations in the mid-1960s revealed minute details in the daily lives of the besieged and their heroic deaths. Thus, archaeology and history combined painted a vivid and surprisingly complete picture of the siege.

Figure 1.8   Foundations of the Public Hospital for the Insane at Colonial Williamsburg in Virginia, which were revealed by archaeological excavation in 1972.

Historical archaeology comes into its own in studies of the last 5,000 years, for which abundant documentary records are available. But historical records can also be important in telling us about societies that had limited written records. The Classic Mayan civilization, which flourished in Mesoamerica between about A.D. 200 and 900, had developed a complex writing system. With it the Maya could record religious, political, and astronomical events with elaborate glyphs sculpted on stone and wood, as well as set down in large books. Although still only partially deciphered, these records are beginning to provide an invaluable new perspective on a civilization hitherto known almost entirely from archaeological investigations (Hammond, 1982).

Underwater archaeologists study sites and ancient shipwrecks on the sea floor and lake bottoms, and even under rapids in Canadian streams. Scuba-diving archaeologists now have an array of specialist techniques for recording these underwater sites (Bass, 1966). This field of archaeology is so specialized that we lack the space to cover it here.

Industrial archaeologists study buildings and other structures dating to the Industrial Revolution or later, such as Victorian railway stations, old cotton plantations, windmills, and even slum housing in England (Buchanon, 1972; Hudson, 1982). Anyone entering this field needs at least some training as an architectural historian.

Ethnoarchaeologists study living societies as a way of better understanding and interpreting the past. They examine the dynamics of modern hunter-gatherer, horticultural, and peasant societies, and collect empirical data on the present, which can be used to interpret the archaeological record. Ethnoarchaeologists examine such phenomena as recently abandoned campsites and the hunter-gatherer's ways of acquiring food at different seasons. This type of "middle-range" research is gaining importance in archaeology (Chapter 15).

These are but a few of the specialties in archaeology. The modern science is so complex as to have experts in dozens of aspects of the subject, from mouse bones to soil profiles to techniques in ancient metallurgy. All are unified by their common interest in studying humanity in the past.

GOALS OF ARCHAEOLOGY

Whether they concentrate on the most ancient human societies or those of more recent centuries, most archaeologists agree that their research has four broad goals:

Studying sites and their contents in a context of time and space, to derive descriptions of long sequences of human culture. This descriptive activity reconstructs culture history.

Reconstructing past lifeways.

Studying cultural process (Trigger, 1978).

Understanding the archaeological record, including sites, artifacts, food remains, and so on, which is part of our contemporary world, and is studied as part of it (Binford, 1983).

By no means would every scholar agree that all four of these objectives are equally valid, or indeed that they should coexist. In practice, however, each usually complements the others, especially when archaeologists design their research to answer specific questions, rather than merely digging as a preliminary to describing rows of excavated objects.

Culture History.   The expression *culture history* means, quite simply, description of human cultures as they extend backward thousands of years into the past. An archaeologist working on the culture history of an area describes the prehistoric cultures of that region. Culture history is derived from the study of sites and the artifacts and structures in them in a temporal and spatial context. By investigating groups of prehistoric sites and the many artifacts in them, it is possible to erect local and regional *sequences* of human cultures that extend over centuries, even millennia (see Chapters 12 and 18). Most of the activity is descriptive, accumulating minute chronological and spatial frameworks of archaeological data as a basis for observing how particular cultures evolved and changed through prehistoric times. Culture history is reconstructed by building up local sequences of archaeological sites into regional and even larger frameworks of changing human cultures. It is an essential preliminary to any work on lifeways or cultural process (see Chapter 19).

Many archaeologists who work on culture history feel inhibited by poor preservation of artifacts and sites about making inferences on the more intangible aspects of human prehistory, such as religion and social organization. They argue that archaeologists can legitimately deal only with the material remains of ancient human behavior. Unfortunately, this rather narrow view of culture history has sent many people off in unprofitable directions, into a long and painstaking preoccupation with artifact types and local chronologies that turned much of archaeology into a glorified type of classification.

Past Lifeways. The study of past lifeways—the ways in which people have made their livings in the past—has developed into a major goal since the 1930s. This new purpose for archaeology became evident as people realized that the prehistory of human-kind was played out against a complicated background of changing environments. Every human culture was, they realized, a complex and constantly changing adaptation to specific environmental conditions.

Prehistoric lifeways were first studied in their environmental contexts by Grahame Clark at Star Carr and other sites in Europe (Chapter 4), and with Julian Steward and others in the United States (Clark, 1954; Steward, 1955; Steward and Setzler, 1977). These scholars realized that artifacts and structures without environmental context give a one-sided view of humanity and its adaptations to the environment. They began to concentrate on reconstructing ancient subsistence patterns from animal bones, carbonized seeds, and other food residues recovered in meticulous excavation. They called for assistance by pollen analysts and soil scientists, as well as botanists, so that they could look at archaeological sites in a much wider, multidisciplinary context. The context of such studies was still descriptive archaeology, preoccupied with space and time, but the emphasis was different: the contexts supplied by space and time related to interplay among changing patterns of human settlement, subsistence strategies, and ancient environments.

Robert Braidwood took with him a team of scientists from other disciplines when he started work on the early history of agriculture in the Zagros Mountains of the Near East (Figure 1.9). He recovered evidence of domesticated animals as early as 6000 B.C. and based a new theory for the origins of food production on more precise environmental data than ever before (Braidwood and Howe, 1962). Richard MacNeish worked closely with botanists as he traced the early history of maize in the Tehuacán Valley in Mexico (MacNeish, 1970). Conditions there were so dry that he was able to show how settlements of the Tehuacán people had slowly changed as they relied more heavily on maize cultivation after 5000 B.C. As long ago as 1948, Gordon Willey surveyed in detail the coastal Virú Valley in Peru, where he plotted the distributions of hundreds of prehistoric sites from different chronological periods against the valley's changing environment (Willey, 1953). This was a pioneer attempt at reconstructing prehistoric patterns of settlement, obviously a key part in any attempts to reconstruct prehistoric lifeways.

Such factors as population density and carrying capacity of agri-

Figure 1.9 Robert Braidwood's excavation at the village of Jarmo in the Zagros Mountains of the Near East was among the first team investigations to study early agriculture.

cultural land are clearly required to understand ancient lifeways. The intent in this goal of archaeology is still, however, descriptive, within a theoretical framework that saw human cultures as complicated, ever-changing systems. These systems interacted not only with others but with the natural environment as well.

Cultural Process. A third archaeological goal in the past twenty years not only describes the past but also explains culture change in prehistory. Archaeologists with this goal attempt to explain cultural change, process, and evolution in prehistory, topics that we explore more fully in Chapter 19 (definitions are in the Glossary). The ultimate goal of these prehistoric archaeologists is to explain why human cultures in all parts of the world reached their various stages of cultural evolution. Human tools are seen as part of a system of related phenomena that include both culture and the natural environment. Prehistoric archaeology, they argue, is a science in which research methods must be much more rigorous than hitherto. Archaeologists should design their research work within a framework of testable propositions that may be supported, modified, or rejected when they review all the excavated and analyzed archaeological data.

This approach to archaeology, once called the "new archaeology," is primarily meant to find out the "ways in which human populations (in their own way) do the things other systems do" (Binford and Binford, 1968). The many archaeologists of this persuasion believe that the past is inherently knowable, provided that rigorous research methods and designs are used and that field methods are impeccable. They feel strongly that archaeology is more than a descriptive science and that archaeologists can explain cultural change in the past (Binford, 1983).

This activity is often called "processual archaeology," a label that emphasizes its concentration on cultural process and explanation of the past.

Understanding the Archaeological Record. "The archaeological record is here with us in the present," writes Lewis Binford (1983). He emphasizes how much a part of the contemporary world the artifacts and sites that make up the remains of our past are. Our observations about the past are made today, in the 1980s, for we are describing sites and artifacts as they come from the soil today, centuries, often millennia after they were abandoned. In this way the archaeologist differs from the historian, who reads a document written in, say, 1492, which conveys information written by a contemporary observer, and unchanged since that year. The archaeological record is made up of material things, and arrangements of material objects in the soil. The only way we can *understand* this record is by knowing something about how the finds of which it consists came into being. Binford likens archaeological data to a kind of untranslated language that has to be decoded if we are to make statements about human behavior in the past. "The challenge that archaeology offers, then, is to take contemporary observations of static material things and, quite literally, translate them into statements about the dynamics of past ways of life and about the conditions in the past which brought into being the things that have survived for us to see," writes Binford (1983). Archaeologists have to be deeply aware of phenomena in the contemporary world if they are to make inferences about the past. They cannot study it directly, but must consider it with reference to the present. For this reason, controlled experiments, observations of contemporary hunter-gatherers and horticulturalists, and the formulation that

Binford and others call "Middle Range Theory" are vital to archaeologists (Chapter 15).

Differing Goals: New and Old World Archaeologists. Not only do disagreements about goals divide archaeologists as a whole, but American scholars have a viewpoint different from that of many Old World prehistorians as well. In the United States, archaeologists have long considered their discipline as part of anthropology. European archaeologists, on the other hand, lean toward defining archaeology as part of history. In the Old World, the arts of excavation have been highly developed by a historical tradition that began with A. H. L. Fox Pitt-Rivers and continued with Sir Mortimer Wheeler and many post–World War II archaeologists. Both British and Continental prehistorians have greatly emphasized recovery of data from the ground, tracing settlement patterns and structures, reconstructing economics, and analyzing in detail artifact types and complicated typologies. Many European archaeologists have acquired international reputations for their skill as excavators or museum people. The archaeologist is seen as an artisan with diverse skills, not the least of which is effective reconstruction of the past, both to amplify the written record and to create a historical story, albeit incomplete, for periods when no archives record the deeds of chiefs or the attitudes of individuals.

One reason for the difference in approach may be that European archaeologists think of prehistory as "their own" history, whereas prehistorians in the Americas are conscious that they are studying prehistoric peoples from a background completely different from their own, a non-Western tradition.

But, for all the differences in approaches and goals, every archaeologist, of whatever viewpoint, would agree that we cannot hope to carry out archaeological research without a body of sound theory, good descriptive archaeology, and detailed information from both the contemporary world and prehistoric lifeways. Above all, the present and the phenomena of the world we live in are there to help us achieve better understanding of the major issues in archaeology:

- What were our earliest ancestors like and when did they come into being? How old is "human" behavior, and when did such phenomena as language evolve? What distinguishes our behavior from that of other animals?
- How and when did humanity people the globe?

- What were the conditions and when and how did human beings begin to abandon the hunter-gatherer lifeway and domesticate animals and plants, becoming sedentary farmers?
- What brought about civilization, and what caused complex societies to evolve—the urban societies from which, ultimately, our own industrial civilization grew?
- Last, and a long-neglected question, how did the expansion of Western civilization affect the hunter-gatherer, agricultural, and even urban states of the world that it encountered after Classical times? As more and more of the world's hunter-gatherer and peasant societies are assimilated into the fringes of our industrialized economy, archaeology is becoming the primary way of studying the tragic, closing centuries of prehistory between A.D. 1400 and our own era.

In the Beginning is not meant to describe these major developments in world prehistory. Rather, I summarize the multitude of methods and theoretical approaches that archaeologists have used to better understand our long past.

Guide to Further Reading

These books may be helpful as general reading about archaeology today, but I advise you to consult a specialist before starting in on them:

Binford, Lewis R. *In Pursuit of the Past.* New York: Thames and Hudson, 1983.
  A closely argued essay on archaeology that integrates ethnoarchaeology with the archaeological record. Recommended for more advanced readers.

Ceram, C. W. *Gods, Graves, and Scholars.* New York: Alfred A. Knopf, 1953.
  A classic account of early archaeologists; a wonderful introduction to the heroic days of archaeology.

Deetz, James, *Invitation to Archaeology.* Garden City, N.Y.: Natural History Press, 1967.
  An admirable brief introduction to prehistoric archaeology that gives a brief overview of the subject.

Fagan, Brian M. *Archaeology: A Brief Introduction,* 2nd ed. Boston: Little, Brown, 1983.
  A short version of In the Beginning *that covers more ground than Deetz in about the same length.*

McGimsey, Charles. *Public Archaeology.* New York: Seminar Press, 1972.
  A pungent statement about the crisis in archaeology; should be read by everyone interested in preserving the past.

PART II

A SHORT HISTORY OF ARCHAEOLOGY

SIXTH CENTURY B.C. TO 1980

The Four Stages of Public Opinion

 I (Just after publication)
   The Novelty is absurd and subversive of Religion & Morality. The propounder both fool & knave.
 II (Twenty years later)
   The Novelty is absolute Truth and will yield a full & satisfactory explanation of things in general—The propounder man of sublime genius & perfect virtue.
III (Forty years later)
   The Novelty won't explain things in general after all and therefore is a wretched failure. The propounder a very ordinary person advertised by a clique.
 IV (A century later)
   The Novelty a mixture of truth & error. Explains as much as could reasonably be expected. The propounder worthy of all honour in spite of his share of human frailties, as one who has added to the permanent possessions of science.

THOMAS HUXLEY
Notes, 1873

No one can fully understand modern scientific archaeology without having some notion of its roots. The first archaeologists were little more than philosophers and antiquarians who were searching for curiosities, buried treasure, and intellectual enlightenment. These treasure hunters were the predecessors of the early professionals, scholars who concentrated on site description and believed that human society evolved through simple stages, the final stage being modern civilizations. Since World War II, archaeology has undergone a major transformation, from a basically descriptive discipline into a many-sided activity that is greatly absorbed in trying to understand how human cultures changed and evolved in the past. If there is one major lesson to be learned from the history of archaeology, it is that no development in the field took place in isolation. All innovations in archaeology are the result of steady advances in the quality of scientific research.

CHAPTER 2 ❧

ORIGINS OF ARCHAEOLOGY

SIXTH CENTURY B.C. TO 1870

Preview

- Archaeology has its origins in the intellectual curiosity about the past felt by a number of Classical writers, such as Hesiod, who engaged in much speculation about the stages in early human history.
- With the Renaissance this curiosity about the past, which manifested itself in excavations at Pompeii and elsewhere, was renewed. But speculations about early prehistory were shackled by the dogma of the Christian church.
- With greater knowledge of human biological and cultural diversity late in the eighteenth century, people began to speculate about the relationships between different groups and about the notion of human progress from simple to complex societies.
- Proof that humanity had existed for more than 6,000 years was the discovery in the Somme Valley, France, and elsewhere, of the bones of extinct animals directly associated with tools made by human beings. These discoveries could not be placed in a scientific context, however, until both uniformitarian geology—the new science of paleontology—and the theory of evolution by natural selection were created.
- The notion of human social evolution followed that of biological evolution. Many archaeologists thought of prehistoric cultures as

arranged in stratum-like layers of progress from the simple to the complex. A simple form of unilinear evolution was espoused by such pioneer anthropologists as Sir Edward Tylor and Lewis Morgan, who portrayed humanity as having progressed from simple savagery to complex, literate civilization.

In this chapter we examine the early history of archaeology as it developed out of philosophical speculations by Classical and Renaissance scholars. Much early nineteenth-century archaeology probed for the origins of humankind and evidence that people lived on earth long before 4004 B.C., the date for the Creation determined by Archbishop James Ussher in the seventeenth century. Developments in evolutionary biology, geology, and paleontology strongly influenced nineteenth-century archaeology. Anthropology, the study of humanity, grew out of the social sciences in the 1870s, and immediately formed a close relationship with archaeology. A sign of this bond was the common scholarly belief that all human societies evolved from a state of simple hunting and gathering to civilization in stages, but that not all societies reached the highest pinnacle of achievement—modern civilization. The material in Chapter 2 covers everything up to the time when scholars began to challenge this evolutionary approach.

THE FIRST ARCHAEOLOGISTS

Philosophical Speculations. Archaeology grew into a scientific discipline only in the last two hundred years, and though young and vigorous, its basic principles are still much debated. But philosophical interest in the prehistoric past goes back far earlier than the eighteenth century. The Greeks and Romans reflected about human origins and about human diversity. Homer had written about a glorious, heroic past of kings and warriors, a time when gods mingled freely with people. But how had humanity fared before the time of Homer's *Iliad?* In the eighth century B.C. the philosopher Hesiod wrote that humanity had passed through five great ages of history—the earliest, one of Gold, when people "dwelt in ease"; the last, an Age of War, when people worked terribly hard and experienced great sorrow (Daniel, 1981; Plumb, 1969). Speculations of this type, reflecting the idle curiosity of the day, are widespread in Classical and even early Chinese writings.

The Renaissance. The centuries of the Renaissance saw quickened intellectual curiosity, not only about humanity but about the Classical world as well. People of leisure and wealth began to follow the paths of the Renaissance scholars, traveling widely in Greece and Italy, studying antiquities, and collecting examples of Classical art. The same travelers were not above a little illicit excavation to recover fine statuary from ancient temples and Roman villas. Soon the cabinets of wealthy collectors bulged with fine art objects, and the study of Classical art became a major scholarly preoccupation. When the King of the Two Sicilies commissioned the Cavaliere Alcubierre to excavate the famed Roman City of Herculaneum in 1738, a new era in Classical archaeology began, making it into a discipline dealing mostly with art and architecture, with temples and other large, spectacular monuments (Ceram, 1953) (Figure 2.1). And the Herculaneum excavations revealed incredibly full details of a Roman town destroyed by an eruption of Vesuvius in A.D. 79. The many fine objects dug up by Alcubierre and his successors transported Classical archaeology into spectacular artistic realms holding exciting prospects for wealthy collectors and those scholars who considered themselves expert antiquarians.

Antiquarians and Excavators. Many of the early collectors and scholars were from Britain, France, and Germany. Their less wealthy colleagues stayed at home and instead spent their time speculating about ancient British and European history. Who were the ancient Britons? Were they the sophisticated warriors Julius Caesar had described when he visited Britain in 55 B.C.? Or were they to be compared to the American Indians? When the renowned English artist John White returned from North America with his vivid drawings of the simple Indian tribes in the new colony, intellectual curiosity about the ancient Britons was feverish. Pioneer antiquarian John Aubrey (1626–1697) described them as "two or three degrees less savage than the Americans. The Romans subdued and civilized them" (Daniel, 1975).

There was little enough in the record for people to go on. The prehistoric Europeans left behind few tangible signs of their existence, except for thousands of earthen mounds, some extensive

Figure 2.1   Body of a beggar smothered by volcanic ash outside the Nucerian Gate at Pompeii.

earth fortification works, and a few very conspicuous monuments, the best known of which was Stonehenge in southern England (Figure 2.2). This remarkable group of stone circles was hailed as a celebrated temple. It was here that the ancient Druids, a flamboyant priesthood decribed by Julius Caesar, had performed their pagan rites, just as Aubrey believed (Piggott, 1968). Everyone realized that Europe had been populated by primitive tribes long before the Roman conquest. But how long had they lived there, and what was their history? If the American Indians and South Sea islanders, first revealed to an astonished world in the eighteenth century, were any guide, then the ancient Europeans had enjoyed many life-styles and elaborate customs. There were only two ways to tackle the problem—by excavating ancient burial mounds and settlements and by philosophical speculation about human conditions and origins.

Figure 2.2 Stonehenge, the Bronze Age ceremonial center in southern England that was an early focus of antiquarian interest. This picture was taken before restoration of the stones in 1958.

Tools and burials left by the ancient Europeans had been turning up for centuries, revealed by the plowshare and house-building operations. Stone and bronze axes, strange clay pots, gold ornaments, and skeletons found buried with elaborate ornaments formed a jumble of information about prehistoric times. When local landowners began to excavate burial mounds and other monuments on their properties, the confusion was compounded. Some burials contained bronze and gold ornaments, others only stone implements; still others were mere cremations deposited in large urns. Which burial mounds were the earliest? Who had deposited the skeletons, and how long ago? No one yet had a way of putting in order the thousands of years of prehistory that preceded the Greeks, Romans, and ancient Egyptians of Biblical fame (for extended discussion, see Piggott, 1976).

SCRIPTURES AND FOSSILS

The Biblical Legend.   One reason antiquarians in the seventeenth and eighteenth centuries were confused was that they had no idea how long people had been living on earth. They had no means of dating the past or of classifying the finds that cluttered their cabinets.

At the time, most people believed that Genesis, chapter 1, told the true story of the Creation. The Old Testament stated that God had created the world and its inhabitants in six days. The story of Adam and Eve provided an entirely consistent explanation for the creation of humankind and the world's population. The Bible's early chapters are full of complicated genealogical tables for the early families that populated the earth. Scholars used these to calculate the date of the Flood and of the Creation itself. In the seventeenth century, Archbishop James Ussher used the same genealogies and calculated that the world was created on the night preceding October 23, 4004 B.C. (Grayson, 1983). These calculations and propositions were accepted almost universally. They became a dogmatic canon defended with almost frenzied fanatism early in the nineteenth century. It was a comfortable proposition, allowing approximately 6,000 years for all of human history. All kinds of romantic legends were concocted to fill these 4,000 years, to arrive at some explanation for the chaos of antiquities found by the antiquarians.

What Is Humanity?   While antiquarians were puzzling over prehistoric artifacts and their meaning, political and social philosophers were speculating intensely about the state of human society. The great scientist Sir Isaac Newton argued that the universe ran more like a clock than like a body moved by the hand of God (Slotkin, 1965). This clock notion led writers of the Enlightenment, such as John Locke and Jean-Jacques Rousseau, to philosophize about the rules and laws that could perpetuate a sophisticated civilization. "What is humanity?" they asked. "Does it need a despotic government—or a minimum of social control?"

Many scholars began to feel that such human beings as the South Sea islanders, the American Indians, and the Australian aborigines—people who lived in a "state of nature" with minimal social controls—were inferior, for they were deprived of the benefits of modern civilization. Others, like Rousseau, depicted contemporary savages such as the Tahitians as living in Eden-like innocence in pastoral groves (Fagan, 1984b). People were better off, he said, without civilization's institutions, rules, and repressions.

The philosophers began to rebel openly against the church and its way of interpreting the world and its history, and their grounds for doing so were sound. Captain Cook, who traveled in the South

Seas, and others who traveled in the Americas and Africa, had brought home new information about all manner of primitive societies flourishing at various levels of cultural development; none of them, however, were as advanced as that of eighteenth-century Europe (Figure 2.3). Daringly, in a world where an accusation of heresy could mean death, they began to formulate a theory of human progress that would help explain how Europeans had achieved a life-style so different from that of the South Sea islands, but also to put human prehistory in a new perspective. People like the Marquis de Cordorcet theorized that humanity had progressed through successively higher stages of development up to modern times. But the question of questions remained unanswered: How long had this progress been going on? Could it really have happened within the short time allowed by Biblical chronologies? (Esti-

Figure 2.3   An Australian aborigine with his lightweight toolkit. (A nineteenth-century engraving.)

mates by those who disagreed with Ussher varied between 5,000 and 8,000 years.)

Axes and Animals. As antiquarians dug into burial mounds and philosophers argued about human progress, discoveries were beginning to cast doubt on Biblical chronologies. For centuries, farmers had happened upon ancient bones from large animals in clays and river gravels in the banks of such rivers as the Somme in France and the Douro in Portugal (Rudwick, 1972). They had found hundreds of strange stones as well, whose shapes so differed from those of natural stones that it was difficult to explain them away as anything but human-made axes. Scientists generally scoffed at the idea that these "thunderbolts" or "meteorites" were of human manufacture. But a few people had quietly disagreed, among them the sixteenth-century scholar Michele Mercati, who called the alleged thunderbolts "weapons used by people ignorant of the use of metals" (Mercati, 1717). A century later, an author said that Mercati's "weapons" were made by people who lived before Adam: his works were burned in public.

Then the bones of large tropical animals such as the elephant and hippopotamus began to be found in European river gravels. These bones were mingled with Mercati's axes so that the tropical animals and human tools appeared to have been contemporary. In 1797, English country squire John Frere collected carefully chipped stone axes from a gravel pit near the small village of Hoxne, Suffolk (Figure 2.4). The axes were 3.7 meters (12 feet) below the surface of the ground, at the same level as bones of extinct animals. Frere took the trouble to publish his remarkable finds, describing the axes as weapons of war used by people ignorant of metals. "The situation," he wrote, "in which these weapons were found may tempt us to refer them to a very remote period indeed, even beyond that of the present world." In other words, the tools dated to a time when the world was not yet geologically modern (Grayson, 1983).

John Frere's remarkable discovery caused little excitement at the time. Early in the nineteenth century, most people, even the most eminent scientists, still fervently believed that God created the world in 4004 B.C. Humanity had inhabited the world for 6,000 glorious years, a beautiful world that "teemed with delighted existence" created by the Lord. Although scholars were now familiar enough with stone implements, they were not ready to accept the idea that they came from a world much older than the Garden of Eden. A parallel question, the age of the earth, was still very open.

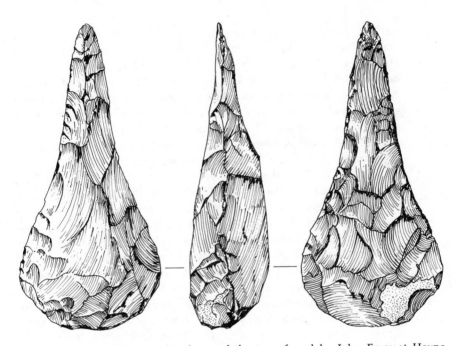

Figure 2.4   A stone hand axe of the type found by John Frere at Hoxne, England, in 1797.

Most people still believed that the world was relatively modern, for the science of geology was yet in the future (Grayson, 1983). That humanity had existed longer than 6,000 years, and that the earth and living organisms had developed over a far larger scale of time than the Ussherian estimate—these were still treated as wild ideas. And until proofs of these notions could be established, no one would be able to explain the discoveries of extinct animals and stone tools at all satisfactorily.

Catastrophism and Uniformitarianism.   The eighteenth century was a period of awakening interest in archaeology and also in geology and the natural sciences. It was then that the science of paleontology was born, devoted to studying fossil animals. A remarkable Frenchman, Georges Cuvier (1769–1832) spent his life working with fossil mammals, distinguishing hundreds of species and developing paleontology into a complex science. He laid out a geological history of the world using dozens of fossil animals as type indicators for different geological layers and epochs. He discovered a period when great dinosaurs had been the dominant creatures on earth. Cuvier sought to explain periods with massive extinctions of animals by saying that there had been widespread flooding on earth before human beings had been created. Some theologians and religion-minded geologists went so far as to argue that God had wiped out successive populations of animals now long extinct with gigantic cataclysms, the last of which was the Biblical Flood.

Cuvier's flooding theory, called catastrophism, gained some acceptance among serious geologists, many of whom were examining deep geological strata exposed during great canal-building excavations during the early stages of the Industrial Revolution. Some scientists delved beyond Cuvier's work and tried to explain the formation of the earth by examining the evidence in the field. James Hutton (1726–1797) was one such expert. In his *Theory of the Earth*, he proposed that the earth was formed by quite natural and gradual processes. He recognized that the geological processes of erosion, accumulation, weathering, and earthquake movement, which were still occurring, were far more likely to be the agents of geological change than were successive catastrophes. British geologist William "Strata" Smith (1769–1839) was one of many field observers who studied the numerous geological exposures resulting from canal and railroad construction. He compiled a complicated geological table identifying geological strata and fossil animal types that appeared and disappeared at the same time everywhere on earth. He emphasized that the rocks of the earth had been formed by continuous natural geological processes. The catastrophes proposed by Cuvier and others were not needed to explain geological change. Every gale that battered the coast, every flash flood or sandstorm, and every earthquake movement were among the natural phenomena that had gradually shaped the earth into its modern form. None of the strata examined by Hutton or his colleagues showed any signs of successive regional, let alone global, cataclysms.

Hutton's theories were widely accepted by many geologists, even if many of them still favored the 6,000-year-old Ussherian chronology. His hypotheses caused immediate controversy, many respected scholars arguing that denial of catastrophism meant denial of the Biblical story of the Creation. The issue came to a head when the eminent geologist Sir Charles Lyell (1797–1875) published his three-volume *Principles of Geology* (1830–33), in which he labeled Hutton's theory the doctrine of *uniformitarianism* (Daniel, 1981). Locality by locality, stratum by stratum, Lyell summarized the meticulous findings of the new geology in a form that was intelligible not only to geologists but to the public. *Principles of Geology* became a popular bestseller, attracted dozens of newcomers to geology, and gave uniformitarianism a sturdy foundation, bolstered by solid evidence from the field gathered at hundreds of sites all over Europe. Most important, *Principles of Geology* was read by scientists in other fields, among them an obscure naturalist, Charles Darwin.

EVOLUTION AND NATURAL SELECTION

In his book, Charles Lyell had used a generalized philosophy of gradual change in describing the types of fossils found in successive strata of the earth. The *Principles of Geology* appeared just as Charles Darwin was leaving England on his five-year voyage (1831–1836) on *H.M.S. Beagle* (Moorehead, 1961). As Darwin began his classic observations in South America and elsewhere that led toward his theories of evolution and natural selection, he sat down to read Lyell. From that moment on, he looked at the earth with different eyes—as a continually changing world formed and modified by quite natural geological processes.

Upon his return to England, Darwin started the first of a series of notebooks on what he called "the species question"—ways in which species changed with timè. In 1838 he read Thomas Henry Malthus's great *Essay on the Principle of Population*, first published in 1798. Darwin immediately realized that he was near an idea of great importance. Malthus had argued that human reproductive capacity far exceeds the available food supply. In other words, people must compete with one another for the necessities of life. Competition causes famine, war, and all sorts of misery. Similar competition occurs among all living organisms. Darwin wondered if new forms had in part been formed by this "struggle for existence," in which the well-adapted individuals survive and the ill-adapted are eliminated.

The doctrine of evolution was nothing new at that time. Many scientists before Darwin, including Lamarck, Buffon, sociologist Herbert Spencer, and even Darwin's own grandfather, had suggested that animals and plants had not remained unaltered through the ages but were continuously changing. They had hinted that all organisms, including human beings, were modified descendants of previously existing forms of life. With the aid of Lyell's book, Malthus's ideas, and his own field observations of fossil and living organisms, Darwin converted evolution from speculation to active theory by showing *how* change could occur.

As Darwin delved more deeply into the "species question," he realized that his new theory would imply that accumulated favorable variations over long periods must result in emergence of new species and extinction of old ones. A timid man, Darwin procrastinated over publishing his results. To release them would bring the powerful wrath of the church down on his head. Evolution, even more than uniformitarianism, flew right in the teeth of the sacrosanct account of the Creation in Genesis. For twenty years he sat on his revolutionary ideas, agreeing to their publication only in 1858, when he found that Alfred Wallace, a colleague working in Asia, had reached the same general conclusions. A year later Charles Darwin achieved immortality with publication of *On the Origin of Species*, a preliminary sketch, he said, of the theory of evolution by natural selection.

On the Origin of Species describes the mechanisms of evolution. "As many more individuals of each species are born than can possible survive, and as consequently there is a frequently recurring struggle for existence, it follows that any being, if it vary however slightly in any manner profitable to itself . . . will have a better chance of surviving, and thus be naturally selected. . . . This . . . I have called natural selection, or the survival of the fittest" (Darwin, 1859).

Darwin's book was greeted with both acclaim and vicious criticism, as scientists and theologians took sides in a controversy that lasted for generations. Just before the *Origin* appeared, archaeological discoveries on the Somme had shown that human beings had indeed lived in Europe at the same time as long-extinct animals. Both the *Origin* and the new Somme discoveries profoundly disturbed those who believed in the Creation, for both evolution and archaeology now implied that human beings had developed far longer than 6,000 years. Not only that, but Darwin's theories made the assumption (horrifying many people) that human beings were descended from ape-like ancestors. The furor was immediate. Cartoonists lampooned the idea; clerics were horrified; parents worried about how such revelations would affect their children (Figure 2.5) (Howell, 1965). Darwin himself was well aware of the implications evolution had for the antiquity of humankind. He cautiously made but one mention of the subject. "Light," he remarked in *On the Ori-*

Mr. Bergh to the Rescue The Defrauded Gorilla. "That *Man* wants to claim my Pedigree. He says he is one of my descendants." Mr. Bergh. "Now, Mr. Darwin, how could you insult him so?"

Figure 2.5   A period cartoon by Thomas Nast lampooning Darwin's connecting apes with human beings.

gin of Species," will be thrown on the origin of man and his history" (Darwin, 1859).

Evolution by natural selection gave a theoretical explanation for the diversity of both fossil and living forms—no more relying on supernatural intervention, hypothetical catastrophes, or other improbable and undemonstrable occurrences. Evolution by means of natural selection does not, of course, entirely explain biological phenomena. But natural selection did provide one direct way of accounting for biological change as time passed. And the clear proof of great human antiquity found on the Somme in the same year was important confirmation that Darwin was on the right theoretical track.

THE ANTIQUITY OF HUMANKIND

The first of the discoveries that were to revolutionize archaeology was made by Father J. MacEnery, an English Catholic priest. Digging into the lower layers of Kent's Cavern near Torquay in Devon between 1824 and 1829 (Daniel, 1975), he found remains of extinct animals associated with stone implements. The layer in which they were found happened to be sealed by a zone of stalagmite, a cave deposit having the consistency of concrete, which takes a long time to form. MacEnery discussed his finds with some well-known Creationists. They refused to accept the contemporaneity of the bones and stones and insisted that ancient Britons had made ovens in the stalagmite, thereby introducing their implements into the older, lower levels.

MacEnery's discoveries caused high interest in scholarly circles, and were followed by new investigations in northern France. Jacques Boucher de Perthes was a customs officer at Abbeville in the Somme Valley, a region known for its fine gravels. In 1837, de Perthes began collecting stone implements and fossils from these deposits. Immediately, he began to find hand axes and bones of extinct animals in the same sealed gravel beds in such numbers that he was convinced that he had found pre-Flood people. He insisted that human beings had lived before the last catastrophic cataclysm, before the start of Ussherian time. Unfortunately, de Perthes was rather pompous, and his findings were widely ridiculed by the scientific community. But he persisted in his investigations and spent his spare time visiting quarries, acquiring a huge collection of fossil bones and stone axes, and arguing that human beings had lived before the Flood.

In 1856, a strange skull was found in a cave near Neanderthal, Germany, greatly puzzling scientists. It had huge, beetling brow ridges (Figure 2.6) and a squat skull cap that were quite unlike the smooth, rounded cranium of modern *Homo sapiens* (Huxley, 1863). The scientists were of two camps. Some regarded the Neanderthal skull as that of a pathological idiot, or even of one of Napoleon's soldiers. But a minority believed that the find was a primitive human being, perhaps one of those who made the crude stone tools that had been found from one end of Europe to the other. By this time, news of Boucher de Perthes's discoveries had drifted across the English Channel. It came to a number of eminent English scientists, among them geologist William Falconer, who was interested enough to visit the de Perthes sites. He was so impressed that he sent two colleagues, antiquarian John Evans and geologist Joseph Prestwich, to study the finds. The two men visited de Perthes at Abbeville in 1859 and examined his museum and the quarry sites. At one place John Evans actually found an axe in the same level as the bones of a hippopotamus. The sheer quantity of

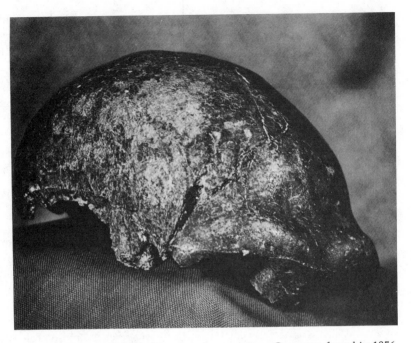

Figure 2.6   The Neanderthal cranium from western Germany, found in 1856.

finds convinced Evans and Prestwich that here, at last, was proof of great antiquity for humankind, something that the new theories of uniformitarianism and evolution had made intellectually possible. Extinct animals and human beings in existence thousands of years before the Garden of Eden were, indeed, contemporaneous (Grayson, 1983).

In June 1859, John Evans spoke to the Society of Antiquaries in London; he made this statement: "This much appears established beyond doubt, that in a period of antiquity remote beyond any of which we have hitherto found traces, this portion of the globe was peopled by man" (Evans, 1860).

There followed rapid and fairly general acceptance of the idea, as a scientific fact, that human beings had been living on this earth longer than 6,000 years. The great biologist Thomas Huxley (1825–1895), perhaps the most vigorous champion of Darwin's ideas, stated that evolution "will extend by long epochs the most liberal estimate that has yet been made of the Antiquity of Man." He also posed the "question of questions for mankind": "the problem which underlies all others, and is more deeply interesting than any other— . . . the ascertainment of the place which man occupies in nature and of his relations to the universe of things" (Huxley, 1863). At last, people were realizing that the past before written records was knowable and that it was possible to measure enormous time scales back to when people lived at the same time as animals that are now extinct. And, the "question of questions" posed by Thomas Huxley is still at the heart of all archaeological research.

HUMAN PROGRESS: EVOLUTIONISM

As we have seen, human progress was no new idea. Popular in the eighteenth century, it declined in favor during the Napoleonic wars, when civilization seemed, philosophically, to have come apart. But the spectacular social and economic changes generated by the Industrial Revolution in the nineteenth century renewed interest in progress. In 1850 the sociologist Herbert Spencer (1820–1903) was already declaring that "progress is not an accident, but a necessity. It is a fact of nature" (Spencer, 1855). Darwin's theories of evolution seemed to many a logical extension of the doctrines of social progress. The new theories opened up enormous tracts of prehistoric time for Victorian archaeologists to fill. The oldest finds were Boucher de Perthes's crude axes from the Somme Valley. Later in prehistory, apparently, other people started to live in the great caves of southwest France, at a time when reindeer, not hippopotami, were living in western Europe. And the famous "lake dwellings," abandoned prehistoric villages found below the water's edge in the Swiss lakes during the dry years 1853–1854, obviously were even more recent than the cave sites of France (Daniel, 1981). What was the best theoretical framework for all these finds? Could notions of human progress agree with the actual archaeological discoveries? Did prehistoric peoples' technology, material culture, and society develop and progress uniformly from the crude tools of the Somme Valley to the sophisticated iron technology of the much more recent La Tène culture in Europe? Had cultures evolved naturally along with the biological evolution that lifted humanity through all the stages from savagery to civilization?

Many archaeologists began to treat prehistoric peoples as geological artifacts. Intoxicated by thousands of stone tools and archaeological sites of unbelievable richness, they gaily cataloged their finds into a long series of epochs, like geological eras, stages through which every human society would ultimately pass. It was a logical step, they thought. The universal progress of humanity enjoyed the status that one French archaeologist called a "Great Law" (de Mortillet, 1867; Sackett, 1981). But, as archeological research extended beyond Europe and into the New World, the incredible diversity in early human experience became visible in the archaeological record. The great civilizations of the Near East were recovered by Henry Layard and others, and the great Mesoamerican religious complexes were described anew (Layard, 1849; Stephens, 1841). Upper Paleolithic art was accepted as authentic some years after the Altamira paintings were discovered in northern Spain in 1879 (Figure 2.7) (Cartailhac, 1901). Yet many parts of North America and Africa showed no signs of higher civilizations. Furthermore, the New World civilizations and European cave art seemed to imply that humanity sometimes "regressed." The great religious centers of Mesoamerica had been abandoned, for instance, and art equal to that from the French caves did not reappear there for many thousands of years. Scientists became less and less certain that people had a common, consistently progressing universal prehistory. Obviously, humankind had progressed considerably overall since the remote millennia of its simple origins, and life had improved for humanity—for the Victorians, at any rate.

Figure 2.7   Bison in a polychrome cave painting in Altamira, Spain. The Altamira style is the ultimate artistic achievement of the Upper Paleolithic hunter-gatherers of western Europe, about 12,000 B.C.

Edward Tylor (1832-1917). Archaeologists were not the only people thinking about human progress (Harris, 1968; Hatch, 1973). The early anthropologists, pioneers of a discipline that developed from strong Victorian interest in human institutions, were evolutionists, too. E. B. Tylor, one of the fathers of anthropology in the English-speaking world, avidly believed in human progress (Tylor, 1871). He surveyed human development in all its forms, from crude stone axes of the Somme Valley in France to Maya temples to Victorian civilization. The origins of civilized institutions, he argued, might be found in the simpler institutions of ruder peoples. If the stone axes made by Australian natives were like those found in ancient European river terraces, then perhaps marriage customs of the native Australians were similar to those among the Paleolithic inhabitants of Europe. Most of his data came from two sources: accounts of contemporary primitive peoples and archaeological findings from the past. He arranged these to reflect a three-level sequence of human development—from simple hunting *savagery,* as he called it; through a stage of simple farming, which he called *barbarism;* to *civilization,* the most complex of human conditions.

Lewis Morgan (1818-1881). American anthropologist Lewis Morgan went even further than Tylor. He outlined no fewer than seven ethnic periods of human progress in his famed book *Ancient Society* (1877). Like Tylor, however, Morgan's stages began with simple savagery and had human society reaching its highest achievements in a "state of civilization" (Willey and Sabloff, 1980). His seven stages, he said, had developed quite rationally and independently in different parts of the world.

The theories of Lewis Morgan strongly influenced Karl Marx and Friedrich Engels, Communist social philosophers. They drew on his ideas of primitive communism—the notion that people shared available resources—and proceeded to say that this type of sharing was gradually eroded by the growing forces of industrial civilization (Harris, 1968). His work was also to influence modern North American archaeology, with its strong evolutionary bias.

Such notions of human progress were easy to defend in a world whose frontiers were still being explored. There was no such thing as a "world prehistory" in the 1870s, merely thousands of scattered archaeological finds, most of them from Europe, the Mediterranean, or North America. Nearly all were from thoroughly unscientific excavations that would make a modern archaeologist shudder. Even expert scientists turned to the comfortable framework of biological and social evolution to explain the astonishing human diversity.

Guide to Further Reading

Grayson, David. *The Establishment of Human Antiquity.* New York: Academic Press, 1983.
A definitive and scholarly study of human antiquity based on contemporary sources. Strongly recommended for the advanced reader.

Daniel, Glyn. *A Short History of Archaeology.* London and New York: Thames and Hudson, 1981.
Superficial account of the major events in the history of archaeology. Somewhat dated, it provides a useful framework.

Daniel, Glyn, ed. *The Origins and Growth of Archaeology.* Baltimore: Pelican Books, 1967.
Extracts from the writings of early archaeologists that amplify the other readings in this guide.

Willey, Gordon, and Jerry Sabloff. *A History of American Archaeology,* 2nd ed. San Francisco: W. H. Freeman, 1980.
Detailed account of New World archaeology from the Spanish occupation until recent times.

CHAPTER 3 ❧

ARCHAEOLOGY COMES OF AGE

1870 TO 1950

Preview

- Unilinear evolution was recognized by early twentieth-century archaeologists as far too simple a scheme to satisfactorily explain prehistory. Some scholars began to turn to diffusionist schemes, assuming that many cultural innovations had emanated from ancient Egypt and similar centers of higher civilization.
- These diffusionist explanations proved just as unsatisfactory. Influenced by Franz Boas (1858-1942) and Vere Gordon Childe (1892-1957), archaeologists began to describe artifacts and sites much more precisely and preoccupied themselves with culture history and chronologies.
- American archaeologists extensively used the direct historical approach to prehistory, working back in time from known historical cultures to prehistoric societies. This system was first developed in the southwest, most notably by A. V. Kidder. Standard taxonomic systems also were developed in the 1930s and were widely used. Radiocarbon dating arrived in the late 1940s, coinciding with greater interest in the natural environment and study of human ecology. Anthropologist Leslie White devised a theory of multilinear evolution to explain the past, and his colleague Julian Steward formulated the principles of cultural ecology, studying the relationships between human cultures and their natural environments.

- W. W. Taylor's *A Study of Archaeology*, published in 1948, was a
landmark critique of American archaeology, chiding archaeologists for preoccupation with description and chronology rather
than with cultural change. This pioneer work and the researches
of Julian Steward and Leslie White established once and for all
the close relationship between archaeology and anthropology.

This chapter takes us from the beginnings of professional archaeology in the last decades of the nineteenth century through the
1950s, a period of tremendous strides in archaeological research.
The first professional archaeologists rejected simple evolutionary
schemes as well as the diffusionist views of prehistory representing
every significant innovation as originating in one location, then
spreading all over the world. Much influenced by such scholars as
Franz Boas and V. Gordon Childe, they concentrated on describing
sites and objects and on trying to date their finds. They used a number of well-tried approaches, including the direct historical
approach and the Midwest taxonomic system. Radiocarbon dating
became available late in the 1940s, solving a most pressing problem:
assembling chronologies for prehistoric cultures.

Most archaeologists mentioned in this chapter were content to
describe the past, rather than explain how and why cultures
changed. But after World War II new approaches took into account
environmental change and the relationships between human cultures and ecological processes. These innovations led archeology in
new directions, away from simple description and toward multilinear evolutionary frameworks for prehistoric times.

UNILINEAR EVOLUTION AND DIFFUSIONISM

The spectacular discoveries of the late nineteenth century took
place when anthropology was coming of age as one of the social
sciences. British social anthropologist Sir James Frazer laid out the
long-term objectives of anthropology in 1890. Anthropologists, he
said, were assigned the task of discovering the general laws which
regulated human history in the past and which would continue to
control human development in the future. They were to study "the

origin, or rather the rudimentary phases, infancy, and childhood of human society" (Frazer, 1890). His remarks reflected growing professional rigor among students of humanity, which coincided with gradual refinement in methods of excavation and ways of classifying the past.

Unilinear Evolution. Anthropology formed from several diverse intellectual philosophies (Harris, 1968). These included biological evolution, the notion of social progress, and the idea of cultural evolution. A most important influence was the constant contact between Western civilization and other human societies with completely different social institutions. It was easy for anthropologists, corresponding as they did with missionaries and pioneer settlers from all over the world, to argue that Victorian civilization was the pinnacle of human achievement. The huge volume of anthropological and archaeological data they collected was used to build a universal scheme of *unilinear cultural evolution.* In other words, all human societies had the potential to evolve from a simple hunter-gatherer way of life to a state of literate civilization, but many of them had never made it.

Today unilinear evolution seems far too simple an explanation for evolving society. But one must remember that every generation of archaeologists looks at the world through its own perceptions of the social and political environment around it. The early archaeologists were no exception, assuming that their own civilization was the contemporary high point of human achievement. As more and more data accumulated from anthropological researches and archaeological excavations all over the world, however, it became clear that a universal scheme of unilinear evolution was a totally unrealistic way of interpreting world history.

Diffusion and Diffusionists. As archaeological knowledge blossomed late in the nineteenth century—and in America, particularly, early in the twentieth—slowly the great human cultural diversity during prehistoric times was recognized. But scholars still faced many hard questions. What were the origins of human culture? When and where was metallurgy introduced? Who were the first farmers? If people did not develop according to universal evolutionary rules, how then *did* culture change and cultural diversity come about? Archaeologists began to expect that population movements, migrations, and invasions would explain prehistory.

The *diffusion* of ideas from one people to another was recognized early as a valid explanation for cultural change in prehistory. It was especially popular with late nineteenth-century archaeologists, who reacted against the idea that cultures changed uniformly and also realized that culture change could be explained by outside influences. The newly discovered Near Eastern civilizations raised problems that might be explained by diffusion. What were the origins, for instance, of such peoples as the Mycenaeans (found by Heinrich Schliemann in the 1870s) (Ceram, 1953)? Many archaeologists began to go along with diffusionist theories when they tried to explain why Near Eastern civilizations were so much richer than the apparently poor European cultures of the same period. Furthermore, they argued, how could the brilliant New World civilizations in Mexico and Peru have arisen if not by long-distance migration from the civilized centers in the Near East?

In its more extreme forms, diffusionism is the assumption that many major human inventions originated in one place and then diffused to other parts of the world by trade, migrating populations, cultural contact, or bold explorers. Simple diffusionist ideas were very popular late in the nineteenth and early in the twentieth centuries. They had the advantage of being easy to formulate and understand, and there was something romantic in the idea of vast migrations of adventurous people from one end of the world to the other. Early in this century British anatomist Grafton Elliot Smith became obsessed with the techniques of Egyptian mummification, sun worship, and monumental stone architecture. The achievements of ancient Egyptian civilization were so unique, he argued in *The Ancient Egyptians*, published in 1911, that all of world civilization and much of modern Western culture diffused from the Nile Valley (Smith, 1911). It was the People of the Sun who had achieved all this, people who were not afraid of voyaging all over the globe in search of gold, shells, and precious stones. Everywhere they went, they took their archaic civilization with them. Thus, the practice of sun worship and the techniques of irrigation, agriculture, metallurgy, and stone architecture—among many others— spread over the world. Although relatively few archaeologists ever took Elliot Smith too seriously, the public did. His several books enjoyed great popularity among those who were fascinated with the ancient Egyptians and who liked their prehistory simple, romantic, and exciting.

Smith's diffusionist views of human history were much oversimplified, and at least as inadequate as unilinear cultural evolution. Slowly, the first professional archaeologists of the twentieth century realized they were dealing with very complex problems. Fortunately, they set aside attempts to write universal histories and concentrated on collecting basic data from archaeological sites.

Diffusionist theories have remained popular, albeit in a modified form. In their most extreme manifestations they still reach incredible heights of absurdity, as in seeking to prove that black Africans colonized America before Columbus or that the Vikings settled Minnesota thousands of years ago.

DESCRIPTIVE ARCHAEOLOGY

The first professional archaeologists and anthropologists lived when the traditional cultures of non-Western societies were being erased by modern technological civilization. They felt their overwhelming priority to be collecting basic information about vanishing cultures. These data were an essential preliminary to the elaborate theoretical approaches used in archaeology today (Stocking, 1968; Fagan, 1984b).

Franz Boas (1858-1942).   American anthropologist Franz Boas was among those who insisted on far more detailed field research (Hatch, 1973). He and his students helped establish anthropology— and by implication, archaeology along with it—as a form of science, by applying more precise methods to collecting and classifying data. They collected an incredible quantity of data on pot designs, basketry, and thousands of other cultural details. Artifacts and customs were meticulously studied and used as the basis for explanations of the past.

Enormous inventories of cultural traits, such as types of moccasins and designs of bows and arrows, were collected by American ethnographers in the 1920s. These collections led to some quite false interpretations of American Indian culture, later disproved by archaeological research. Ethnologists of this period saw the European arrival, especially with domestic horses, as of unparalleled importance; the Great Plains quickly filled with nomadic buffalo hunters and raiders of the type made familiar to us by Hollywood films. They described the plains as sparsely populated before the horse arrived, because water was scarce and ploughs were not available to till the soil. Yet subsequent work by such archaeologists as W. D. Strong, who dug at Signal Butte, Nebraska, revealed that the

Great Plains had been inhabited by hunter-gatherers and horticulturalists for many hundreds of years before the Europeans and horses turned the plains into a macabre carnival of nomads (Strong, 1935). Archaeology, then, became a source of information against which one checked the historical reconstructions produced by ethnologists.

Vere Gordon Childe (1892-1957). Perhaps the most brilliant of these archaeologists was an Oxford-trained Australian, Vere Gordon Childe. A brilliant linguist, he acquired encyclopedic knowledge of the thousands of prehistoric finds in museums from Edinburgh to Cairo. Once he had mastered the data, a task made easier by his language skills, Childe (1925) set out to describe European prehistory in outline. He meant to distill from archaeological remains "a preliterate substitute for the conventional politico-military history with cultures, instead of statesmen, as actors and migrations instead of battles" (Childe, 1958).

Gordon Childe classified cultures by the surviving culture traits—pots, implements, house forms, ornaments—known to be characteristic because constantly found together. Such cultures were the material expression of "peoples." Not supplying a chronological record for themselves, the cultures might have widespread or limited distribution in time and space. Cultural successions were reconstructed within limited geographic areas and compared with those from neighboring regions; the culture traits—presumed to have spread from one area to another—were carefully checked. This type of methodology spread in the 1930s and 1940s, when archaeology was still mainly a descriptive discipline. But Childe went further, for he was one of the few archaeologists who realized that cataloging artfacts was useless unless conducted with some frame of reference. He therefore used data from hundreds of sites and dozens of cultures to formulate a comprehensive viewpoint of Old World prehistory that became a classic. The origins of argiculture and domestication and of urban life were, he felt, two great revolutionary turning points in world history. He thought of two major stages, the "Neolithic and Urban Revolutions." Each so-called revolution saw new and vital inventions that could be identified in the archaeological record by characteristic artifacts. The Neolithic and urban revolutions were really a technological and evolutionary model, combined with an economic one, so that the way people got their living was the criterion for comparing stages of world history. Childe dominated archaeological thinking in Europe until the late

1950s. But his ideas were less influential in the New World, because Childe himself never studied or wrote about American archaeology (for extended treatment, see McNairn, 1980; Trigger, 1981).

CULTURE HISTORY

Baos, Childe, and their disciples made collecting data a primary objective in both New and Old World archaeology. But archaeology itself evolved somewhat differently on each side of the Atlantic. The Europeans were studying their own prehistoric origins, concentrating on constructing descriptive, historical schemes tracing European society from its hunter-gatherer origins up to the threshold of recorded history. As Gordon Childe showed, the prehistoric peoples of the Near East and temperate Europe were the logical ancestors of the Greeks, Romans, and other civilizations. It was no coincidence that Arnold Toynbee and other world historians adopted Childe's universal schemes when they made prehistoric times the first chapter in their great historical syntheses.

The New World: Direct Historical Approach.   New World archaeologists were in a very different position. Their most logical way to work was from the known, historical Indian cultures backward into prehistoric times (Fagan, 1977; Willey and Sabloff, 1980). This approach was pioneered in the 1880s by Cyrus Thomas of the Bureau of American Ethnology. He and fellow archaeologists from other institutions excavated dozens of earthworks in the Ohio Valley, using pottery and other small finds to demonstrate the continuity between prehistoric and modern Indian culture. The early southwestern archaeologists adopted a similar approach in their 1890s research tracing modern Indian pottery styles centuries back into the past. This work culminated in the excavations at Pecos Pueblo carried out by Harvard archaeologist A. V. Kidder between 1915 and 1929 (Kidder, 1924). These excavations established a cultural sequence still used in modified form today. Later researchers, such as W. D. Strong, applied similar methods to Plains archaeology with great success (Strong, 1935).

This *direct historical approach*—working from known, historic sites to unknown, prehistoric settlements, preferable those of known peoples—has strict limitations, however. It works satisfactorily as long as one is dealing with the same cluster of finds, such as pottery forms. Once one excavates sites occupied by people with totally different cultures, however, continuity is lost and the direct historical approach can no longer be used.

The Midwestern Taxonomic System. Franz Boas's influence was strong from the 1920s to the 1950s among archaeologists who concentrated on collecting and classifying enormous numbers of prehistoric finds from hundreds of sites all over the Americas. They began to arrange these in increasingly elaborate regional sequences of prehistoric cultures, but ran into trouble because no two archaeologists could agree on how to classify the pottery and other objects. Thus, no one could compare one area to another using common terminology. Fortunately, a group of scholars headed by W. C. McKern prepared definitions that soon became known as the "Midwestern taxonomic system" (McKern, 1939). This system was an attempt to unify sequences of prehistoric cultures all over the Midwest by finding similarities between different collections of prehistoric artifacts. By correlating sequences of artifacts and hundreds of sites through long prehistoric periods, using seriation methods (Chapter 6), users of the system were able to compare cultural sequences throughout the Midwest and eastern United States. The system was highly effective in linking cultural sequences, but was somewhat limited as a means of interpreting the past, simply because it relied on artifacts and stratigraphic evidence, paying little attention to food remains and other lines of evidence about the past.

The Midwest taxonomic system was put to wide use over much of the central and eastern United States, partly by extensive surveys undertaken as public works during the Depression. By the 1940s James Ford, James Griffin, and Gordon Willey began to look farther afield than local regions. At their disposal was a mass of unpublished archaeological data from hundreds of sites excavated during the Depression (Ford and Willey, 1941; Griffin, 1946). Their studies in the eastern United States revealed steady development in prehistoric material culture over many thousands of years. They distinguished periods within which broad similarities in prehistoric culture could be found and designated those as developmental stages.

Just as the Midwest taxonomic system was reaching the potential limits of its effectiveness, Gordon Willey and Philip Phillips extended earlier survey work in a landmark monograph that applied essentially the same techniques to the entire New World. Most important, they devised developmental stages for the whole continent (Willey and Phillips, 1958). These proposed stages were defined by technology, economic data, settlement patterns, art traditions, and social factors rather than by chronology, which, to their way of thinking, was a less important consideration.

Chronology and Time Scales. No question worried the archaeologists of the 1920s to the 1950s more than establishing an age for their sites and finds. Once they reached the limits of direct historical ties, they had no means of dating early American cultures. The first breakthrough came in the early years of this century, when University of Arizona astronomer A. E. Douglass started his now-famous studies of annual growth rings in southwestern trees (see Chapter 6). By 1929, Douglass had developed an accurate chronology for southwestern sites that eventually was extended back from modern times into the first century B.C. Unfortunately, however, tree-ring dating could be used only in the dry areas of the Southwest, where trees had a well-defined annual growth season. (It has now been applied with some success to northern areas.)

Elsewhere, archaeological chronology was mostly done by intelligent guesswork until 1949, when University of Chicago scientists J. E. Arnold and W. F. Libby (1949) described the radiocarbon method for dating organic materials from archaeological sites (Libby, 1955). Within a few years, radiocarbon dates were processed from hundreds of sites all over the world. For the first time, a widely accepted chronological framework for New World prehistory superseded the guesswork of earlier years. Archaeologists finally could compare widely separated sites and cultures with an unbiased time scale. They could now deemphasize chronology and classification and concentrate, instead, on *why* American and Indian cultures had changed in the past. (Dating techniques are described in Chapter 7.)

CULTURAL ECOLOGY

When radiocarbon dating arrived, the new emphasis in archaeology was on interpretation, based on carefully studied regional sequences. One conclusion was obvious: Human material culture and social organization had developed from the simple to the infinitely complex. From then on, many accounts of world prehistory or broad syntheses of large culture areas allowed for the general notion of progress in prehistory. Childe with his revolutions, Robert J. Braidwood in the Near East, and Gordon Willey in North America—all attempted to look at culture history with the knowledge that human culture is constantly and dynamically related to its environment and to other factors that interact with it (Braidwood and Howe, 1962; Childe, 1942; Willey, 1966, 1971).

Julian Steward: Multilinear Evolution.   At about this time, anthropologist Julian Steward started asking himself: Are there ways of identifying common cultural features in dozens of societies distributed over many cultural areas (Steward, 1955)? Disagreeing with the ardent evolutionists, who insisted that all societies passed through similar stages of cultural development, Steward assumed that certain basic types of culture would develop in similar ways under similar conditions. Very few actual concrete features of culture, though, would appear among many human societies in a similar, regular order repeated again and again. In other words, cultural evolution was multilinear; that is, it had proceeded on many courses, not just on one universal track, as Tylor and others had believed.

Before Steward, such people as Alfred Kroeber, Lewis Morgan, and Leslie White had long thought of culture as like a layered cake, with technology as the bottom layer, social organization the middle, and ideology the top (White, 1949). Steward not only added the environment to the cake, but looked to it for causes of cultural change. To do so, he developed a method for recognizing the ways in which such change is caused by adaptation to the environment.

Calling his study of environment and culture change *cultural ecology,* Steward began by making several points:

Similar adaptations may be found in different cultures in similar environments.

No culture has ever achieved an adaptation to its environment which has remained unchanged over any length of time.

Differences and changes during periods of cultural development in any area can either add to societal complexity, or result in completely new cultural patterns. (Steward, 1955).

Steward used these principles as a basis for studying cultures and culture change in widely separated areas. To study different cultures, he would isolate and define distinguishing characteristics in each culture, a nucleus of traits he called the "cultural core." He observed that African San, Australian aborigines, and Fuegian Indians were all organized in patrilineal (descent through the father) bands, forming a cultural type. Why? Because their ecological adaptation and social organization were similar. Although their environments differed greatly, from desert to cold and rainy plains, the practical requirements of the hunting and gathering lifeway grouped all these people in small bands, each with its own territory. In each area the social structure and general organization of the bands were very similar, and their adaptation to their environment fundamentally the same, despite many differences in detail. Steward used his cultural-core device to isolate and define distinguishing characteristics of the hunter-gatherer and of other specific culture types from all the miscellaneous data he had.

Steward spent much time studying the relationships between environment and culture that form the context and reasons for critical features of culture. Though a culture trait, be it a new type of house or a form of social organization, might be found at one location because it diffused there, that did not explain why the people accepted the trait in the first place. Steward applied cultural ecology to such questions and also to problems such as why the adjustment of human societies to different environments results in certain types of behavior. To diffusion and evolution, he added a new concept—changing adaptations to the natural environment. In other words, the study of culture change involved studying human cultures and their changing environmental conditions as well.

A STUDY OF ARCHAEOLOGY

When Steward's work appeared, American archaeology was completely preoccupied with chronology and artifacts. Every issue of each archaeological journal was crowded with arid reports of pottery chronologies that seldom referred to their content or meaning as human implements. It was as if archaeologists were classifying insects or collecting postage stamps. Then, in 1948, archaeologist W. W. Taylor published his famed *Study of Archaeology*, a devastating critique of American archaeologists' preoccupation with chronology (Taylor, 1948).

Taylor called for a "conjunctive approach" to archaeology, shifting emphasis from chronological sequences and distributions to detailed, multilevel studies of individual sites and their features, such as cultural layers, floors, or hearths. The conjunctive approach brought together all possible sources of evidence on a site—technology, style, ecological evidence, architecture, and information on social life—to focus on the people who lived at the site and on the changes in their culture.

Studying the people meant seeing their artifacts in context, as products of entire cultural systems, and reconstructing these systems as completely as possible, including even the less tangible parts, such as their social organization and religious institutions. This view contrasted with that of Childe and his contemporaries on the other side of the Atlantic, who preferred to limit their study of artifacts. Taylor tried to introduce into archaeology a view of culture envisaging the discipline as integral to anthropology. He felt the disciplines should work together to arrive at general truths about human culture (Kluckhohn, 1943).

All this was a far cry from the simple evolutionary and diffusionist schemes of earlier decades. Julian Steward's and W. W. Taylor's research brought twentieth-century archaeology to the threshold of great theoretical change. They established, once and for all, the close relationship between archaeology and anthropology. *A Study of Archaeology* showed, with incisive clarity, that one of archaeology's primary goals must be to develop adequate explanations for human prehistory, an aim far more sophisticated than mere excavation, collection, and description.

Guide to Further Reading

The references for Chapter 3 will suffice, but add these:

Taylor, W. W. *A Study of Archaeology*. Menasha, Wis.: American Anthropological Association, 1948.
  The controversial pioneer statement on archaeology and a major stepping-stone for the development of processual archaeology in the 1960s.

White, Leslie. *The Evolution of Culture*. New York: McGraw-Hill, 1949.
  White's classic work on cultural evolution is one of the standards for modern archaeology and anthropology.

CHAPTER 4 ✨

TOWARD PROCESSUAL ARCHAEOLOGY

1950 TO THE 1980S

Preview

- In the 1950s, statistical methods long used in the natural and physical sciences began to be used in archaeology. With the new approaches these techniques engendered, archaeologists could form far more meticulous and detailed descriptions and manipulate larger quantities of data.
- Lewis Binford, strongly influenced by Leslie White, Julian Steward, and Albert Spaulding, formulated a new archaeological method and theory using explicitly scientific methods. He proposed that archaeological data be tested against formal hypotheses and that careful research designs be used for planning all inquiries.
- This more scientific archaeology went beyond applying the formal scientific method; one advance was a new interest in living archaeology—ethnoarchaeology. Studying surviving hunter-gatherers gives insight into prehistoric societies. Before long, it was clear, archaeology would be the only means for explaining cultural variations in nonindustrial societies.
- With the development of a more scientific archaeology, there was increasing attention paid to the works of philosophers of science, such as Thomas Kuhn, and to the principles of general systems theory. Moving away from simple explanations of the past,

archaeologists chose systems approaches to help them depict a human culture as a complicated system of interacting elements that in turn interacted with the ecological system of which it was a part.

- Systems approaches developed hand in hand with cultural ecology; that is, with studies of the changing relationship between prehistoric societies and the environments in which they flourished. Settlement archaeology depended heavily on statistical methods and computers to order large quantities of field data.
- New emphasis on scientific approaches has set off a debate as to whether archaeology is among the humanities or the sciences.

Archaeology, like the other social sciences, has changed almost beyond recognition in thirty years. The digital computer, statistical methods, and the philosophy of science have transformed archaeology from a primarily descriptive discipline into a much more comprehensive system. Chapter 4 starts with these developments and shows how much more sophisticated ecological and evolutionary approaches and a greater application of deductive scientific methods and theory building took archaeology in new directions. Scholars such as Lewis Binford, Kent Flannery, Albert Spaulding, and Julian Steward recognized the major trends in social science and began the difficult task of applying them to archaeology. The chapter ends with a brief glance at the major approaches to processual archaeology, which is described in more detail in Part VII.

SCIENCE AND ARCHAEOLOGY

Statistical Methods. Statistical methods began to change archaeology and anthropology in the 1950s. Although archaeologists had been counting tools and other finds for years, Albert Spaulding (1960), the pioneer in this field, mentioned only a few instances of people using chi-square (χ^2) and other statistical techniques in an early paper he wrote on the subject. Both changing interests among researchers and application of the digital computer to order and handle enormous numbers of tools brought about this new approach to archaeological evidence. Statistical methods rapidly came into fashion as archaeologists realized that with these they could prepare far more meticulous and detailed descriptions of finds than had ever been carried out without them. Spaulding forecast that archaeology's future depended on how successful we are in applying quantitative methods to archaeological data.

Lewis Binford and the Scientific Method. Doing graduate work at the University of Michigan, Lewis Binford came into contact with eminent scholars who had done much to develop archaeology in the 1940s and 1950s. Among them were James Griffin, who taught him descriptive archaeology; Albert Spaulding, who introduced him to statistical techniques for handling specific problems; and Leslie White, who exposed him to logic and urged him to steep himself in the philosophy of science. Binford learned that theory was a meaningful word, and saw the close links between archaeology and ethnography. The ultimate objective of archaeology, he discovered, was a search for universal laws that govern cultural change.

In the 1960s, Binford wrote closely reasoned, classic papers that caused a ferment in archaeological circles. He advocated more rigorous scientific testing: statements about the significance of the archaeological record used to be evaluated according to how far back our knowledge of contemporary peoples could be projected onto prehistoric contexts and onto our judgment of how professionally competent and honest the archaeologists interpreting the past were (Binford, 1962; 1972; 1983). Inferences about the archaeological record had been made by simple induction, along with guidance from ethnographic data and experimental archaeology. Binford argued that, although induction and inferences are perfectly sound methods for understanding the past, the real need was independent methods for testing propositions about the past, and these must be far more rigorous than the time-honored value judgments arrived at by assessing professional competence.

With a scientific approach providing interaction among old data, new ideas, and new data, we can approach a research problem from a collection of observed data that enable us to pose research hypotheses. Some general problems may have to do with change: How and why did the hunter-gatherers of the Near East turn to agriculture and domestic animals for their livelihood? Or the problems may touch on cultural relationships: Did a new pottery type suddenly appearing in a Midwest cultural sequence get there by trade, population movement, or independent invention?

Working hypotheses were nothing new in archaeology. Binford's approach was different because he advocated that these hypotheses be tested explicitly against archaeological data collected in the field and against other alternatives that have been rejected. Once a hypothesis is tested against raw data, it can join the body of reliable knowledge upon which further hypotheses can be erected. And these in turn may require additional data or even entirely new approaches to the excavation and collection of archaeological information. Binford suggested that the explicit scientific method commonly used in science should now be applied to archaeological research.

Binford's papers, lectures, and seminars provoked interest among many American archaeologists, of whom numbers joined him in reevaluating the scientific methods of archaeology. He and his disciples challenged the assumption that because the archaeological record is incomplete, reliable interpretation of the nonmaterial and perishable components of prehistoric society and culture were impossible. All artifacts found in an archaeological site functioned at one time in a particular culture and society. They occur in meaningful patterns that are systematically related to the economies, kinship systems, and other contexts within which they were used. Moreover, all these artifacts were at the mercy of transient factors such as fashion or decorative style, each of which itself has a history of acceptance, use, or rejection within the society. Thus, artifacts are far more than mere material items; rather, they reflect many of the often intangible variables that went into determining the actual form of the objects preserved. Binford argued that "data relevant to most, if not all, the components of past sociocultural systems *are* preserved in the archaeological record (Binford and Binford, 1968). The archaeologist's task is to devise methods for extracting this information that deal with *all* determinants in the society or culture being studied.

Lewis Binford was not alone in his thinking. Early in the 1960s British archaeologist David Clarke wrote a monumental critique of prehistoric archaeology, arguing for more explicit scientific methods, greater rigor, and a body of theory to replace "the murky exhalation that represents theory in archaeology" (Clarke, 1968). Clarke deeply influenced European archaeology, but unfortunately died before reaching the peak of his career (Hodder, Isaac, and Hammond, 1981).

LIVING ARCHAEOLOGY (ETHNOARCHAEOLOGY)

A spin-off from this drive for greater scientific rigor was renewed interest among archaeologists in living peoples. Lewis Binford was not, of course, the first archaeologist to look at ethnography, for many scholars were worrying about the extinction threatening preindustrial societies all over the world (Binford, 1968; Sollas, 1911; Thompson, 1956). As early as 1865, Lord Avebury had urged his archaeological colleagues to compare Stone Age cultures with modern hunter-gatherer peoples. The direct historical approach evolved from American archaeologists' recognition that modern Indian cultures had long roots in prehistory.

Binford (1977; 1978; 1983) has urged, however, that once they choose different comparisons, researchers should explicitly state the implications and then test each against archaeological data. Conditions for making such tests were best in the field, observing cultural adaptations among living hunter-gatherers and subsistence agriculturalists. Before long, he argued, archaeology would be the only source of explanations for cultural variations among nonindustrial societies. Binford really cared most about how the archaeological

Figure 4.1 An anthropologist making a plane table survey of a San camp in the Kalahari. Data from such surveys are of great value in interpreting the archaeological record.

record came into existence, and how it, as a static phenomenon, was linked to ever-changing human systems (1983).

Richard Lee was among the anthropologists who studied the !Kung San of the Kalahari Desert, realized the archaeologists' difficulties, and arranged to take a prehistorian with them to study the remains of long-abandoned campsites and compare them to modern settlements (Lee and DeVore, 1976; Yellen, 1977) (Figure 4.1). Richard Gould, an anthropologist who worked among the Australian aborigines, deliberately went out of his way to gather information on abandoned campsites that could be useful to archaeologists (Gould, 1977). Lewis Binford himself has worked among the Nunamiut Eskimo and the Navajo on variability in adaptation systems, seeking viable analogies between living cultures and archaeological materials and trying to develop workable models of culture as rigorous yardsticks for studying variability (Binford, 1978).

SYSTEMS THEORY AND ECOLOGY

Systems Theory. Another element creating a more scientific archaeology was the influence of both philosophers of science, such as Thomas Kuhn (1970), and of general systems theory (Watson, Redman, and LeBlanc, 1971; Redman, 1973). As archaeologists moved away from simple explanations and unilinear evolution toward much more elaborate theories, they began to examine the delicate and complex relationships between human societies and their ever-changing environments. Systems approaches involved thinking of human cultures as complicated systems of interacting elements, such as technology and social organization, which interacted, in turn, with the ecological systems of which they were a part (see Chapter 19). The systems approach has strongly influenced archaeology because of intense interest in relationships between prehistoric peoples and their environments. (More on systems theory in Chapter 5.)

Ecology and Archaeology. Ecological thinking about archaeology has a long history. Much of it is based on the assumption that human cultures could affect their environments, and vice versa (Trigger, 1971). One school of thought, the environmental determinists, believed that forms in nature, which are active, determined human culture, which is passive. Franz Boas and other anthropologists went so far as to argue that the environment was passive and that human culture developed because some environmental possibilities were selected and others ignored.

Modern ecology, with its distinctions among various ecosystems, caused these simple notions to be rejected in favor of more holistic views of culture and environment. In these new approaches it is assumed that cultural ecology studies the whole picture of the way in which human populations adapt to and transform their environments (Dunnell, 1980). Human cultures are thought of as open systems, because it is acknowledged that their institutions may be connected with those of other cultures and with the environment. Open-system ecology is very realistic, assuming a great deal of variation between individual modern and archaeological cultures. Any explanation of culture has to be able to handle the real patterns of variation found in living cultures, not just the artificial ones erected by classifiers of archaeological cultures. So many factors influence cultural systems that order can be sought only by understanding the system that Canadian archaeologist Bruce Trigger calls "those processes by which cultural similarities and differences are generated" (Trigger, 1971). Many complex factors are external to the culture and cannot be controlled by the archaeologist; one cannot reconstruct the whole cultural system from only one part of it (in archaeological cultures, the surviving artifacts and food residues). Every facet of the cultural system has to be reconstructed separately, using the evidence specifically relevant to that facet, making available, in time, a picture of the whole cultural system, as comprehensive as possible. The issue is a society's total adaptation to both its natural and cultural environments. Trigger points out: "Developments affecting any one aspect of the culture can ultimately produce further adjustments throughout the system and affect the system's relationship with the natural environment" (Trigger, 1971).

Studying prehistoric societies in context—in their natural environments—involves examining the relationships between prehistoric settlements and their surrounding landscape. Important studies in Mexico have assumed that the patterns of human settlement throughout time provide a reliable way of studying the changing adaptations of human cultures to an environment over a long period (Flannery, 1976; Sanders, Parsons, and Santley, 1979) (see Chapter 16). Such studies can be conducted only with detailed background knowledge of the specific environment in which the culture flouished, changed, and eventually died. One of the brightest prospects for archaeology lies in studying human cultural systems in the changing economic, demographic, and social variables interacting within an environmental setting over long periods. Some of the most sophisticated research in archaeology is being done in open-system ecology format, as archaeologists wrestle to develop a meeting ground between a broad view of cultural change and the need to look at each changing culture and its microadaptation to a dynamic environment; both clearly are needed (Flannery, 1976).

DECODING THE PAST

The emphasis on systems theory, scientific method, and new approaches to ecology changed the tactics in archaeological research in the 1960s and 1970s. The result was a state of ferment, a fascinating intellectual climate in which practically every familiar theory in archaeology was challenged. Much of the debate was about the goals of the discipline; some argued that archaeology was a science, whose objective was to study basic laws of human behavior. But other archaeologists viewed archaeology as examining the activities of past human beings, as a discipline that was less a science than a historical discipline with its own limitations, resources, and explanatory methods (Flannery, 1973; Spaulding, 1973). Everyone agrees, however, that mathematical models, statistical approaches, and rigorous scientific methods will be more and more vital in archaeology for the rest of the twentieth century. We can be certain, too, that future archaeology will incorporate the evidence and valid empirical generalizations of history (Spaulding, 1973).

The fervor of debate and controversy has quieted somewhat in the 1980s, partly because many basic tenets put forward by Lewis Binford and other scholars are now widely accepted. The pressure of demography has meant that most younger archaeologists practicing today were trained by scholars brought up in the new thinking. The scientific method is widely used; research designs are far more sophisticated than those of a generation ago; highly technical scientific techniques like remote sensing are common. But frustration remains, for most of the rich theoretical expectations of the 1960s remain unfulfilled (Dunnell, 1982). Archaeologists today seem divided into two broad groups: those who write about "theoretical" issues and concentrate on concepts, methods, and techniques, which are occasionally applied to a body of data, and those, including most archaelogists, who carry out empirical studies of the same type that have been done for generations. More "scientific" methods may be used, true, but the effect is mostly superficial. Little integration seems to link the two groups. In this sense, the "new" archaeology of the 1960s has failed. Many archaeologists wonder whether archaeology is, in fact, an atheoretical discipline. They must be wrong, for it seems to be undergoing the change that occurred in biology a generation ago, and is now taking place throughout the social sciences—a serious attempt to assemble a body of theory for archaeology as distinctive as those of physics and the other established sciences. Those who started the revolution in archaeology in the 1960s had no idea the task they were undertaking was so enormous.

What exactly has been achieved, and where do we go from here? Some of the achievements of archaeology since the 1960s are indeed impressive: an explosion in raw data, a new emphasis on regional surveys, and widespread use of quantitative methods. Ecological theory and human ecology itself are fundamental parts of archaeology in the 1980s. The "new" archaeology, not coincidentally, is no longer called that. Its most important and rigorous elements have survived. Others, like the search for general laws of human behavior, and the more extreme manifestations of general systems theory, have less significance. No one would now question that human cultures should be thought of as ever-changing systems interacting with their natural environment and each other. The difference today is that archaeologists are thinking much more profoundly about the archaeological record itself, and how it came into being. As we said in Chapter 1, archaeology is unique in depending on inference for interpreting the past. We can study that past only by means of material evidence that has been changed by centuries, even millennia, underground. How do we explain the archaeological record? This is the question that must be tackled before we try to interpret the past itself; what that record itself is may be *the* question for archaeologists in the 1980s.

Experimental archaeology and the discipline often called ethnoarchaeology grew in popularity in the 1970s. Much of this research has been focused on obvious problems like the tree-felling power of stone axes or the cultural ecology of modern hunter-gatherers in the Kalahari Desert, often referred to in these pages. But these projects have led a number of investigators to ask the question of questions: how can the present, with all its rich data on modern subsistence, climate, soil qualities, and a myriad of other phenomena, be used to interpret the past? Not only that, under our world with its varied landscape lies the archaeological record—thousands of sites and artifacts buried since they were abandoned by their makers. Theoretically at any rate, we have a wealth of data that could be used to interpret the past, to bridge the gap between sites and peoples as they were in prehistoric times, and the surviving archaeological record of the 1980s. Some people are puzzled as to why archaeologists are busy studying modern Australian aborigines or the city dump in Tucson, Arizona. The reason is that for the first time, archaeologists are investigating the relationship between the static archaeological record and the dynamic, ever-changing world in which we live—and they are doing it while simultaneously developing a new body of archaeological theory, which Binford (1983) names *Middle-Range Theory*.

Middle-Range Theory is best defined as a body of theoretical constructs designed to bridge the gap between the archaeological record in the past and the modern world (see Chapter 15). In the final analysis, archaeological research is an interaction between observed facts (the archaeological record) and research to give meaning to these observations (by means of experimental archaeology, ethnoarchaeology, and historical documents). This interaction involves the archaeologist in all manner of seemingly exotic inquiries: Eskimo subsistence in the 1980s, patterns of wear on the edges of prehistoric tools and modern replicas, and how different geological deposits affect the survival of various animal bone parts. Much of this research, dealing with basic global problems in the origins of humanity, or of more complex societies, has to be worldwide in scale. Certainly the sort of research carried out by the archaeologist in 2000 will differ from that of a colleague in the 1980s. We can be sure too that middle-range theory and studies of the contemporary world will dominate archaeology for the remainder of the twentieth century.

Archaeology has come a long way since the antiquarian digs of eighteenth-century Britain. Techniques for recovering data that were a pipe dream even a generation ago are now everyday reality. Archaeologists rely on a battery of scientific methods from dozens of scientific disciplines, and are taking the first significant steps in developing their own body of theory as a tool for interpreting the past. As the years pass, the cartoon stereotype of the pith-helmeted archaeologist digging up pyramids is bound to fade, as the prehistorian of tomorrow pursues ever more eclectic and wide-ranging research, much of it far from the familiar excavations and artifact laboratories. In the pages that follow I will describe some of the approaches that are leading the archaeologist ever more rapidly from pith helmet dusty with ancient soil to the computer and the contemporary world, still seeking to understand the past.

Guide to Further Reading

Books referred to in Chapter 2 and 3 are useful here as well.

Binford, Lewis R. *In Pursuit of the Past*. London: Thames and Hudson, 1983.
A superb, clearly written account of archaeology in the 1980s, with a personal record of intellectual developments in recent years.

Flannery, Kent V., ed. *The Early Mesoamerican Village*. New York: Seminar Press, 1976.
A volume of essays with fascinating dialogues about the different approaches to archaeology.

Redman, Charles L., ed. *Research and Theory in Current Archaeology*. New York: John Wiley Interscience, 1973.
Essays with a critique of the way in which processual archaeology evolved. Those by Kent Flannery and Albert Spaulding are especially important.

Watson, Patti Jo, Steven LeBlanc, and Charles L. Redman. *Explanation in Archaeology*. New York: Columbia University Press, 1971.
A fundamental source on the development of processual archaeology.

PART III ✦

DATA AND CONTEXT

Time which antiquates antiquities, and hath an art to make dust of all things.

SIR THOMAS BROWNE
Hydriotaphia (1658)

Part III describes the truly basic concepts behind archaeological research, those of culture and context. Every archaeological site and every find has a context, not only within some long-extinct culture but also in time and space. In this section of the text, we examine the concept of culture in archaeology, the nature of archaeological data, and the ways in which people have established archaeological contexts. Fundamental to context are methods of defining human activities in space, and especially those for measuring prehistoric time. We describe the various methods that have been devised for dating prehistoric cultures from the very earliest times.

CHAPTER 5 ✖

CULTURE, DATA, AND CONTEXT

Preview

- Culture is regarded by archaeologists as humanity's primary means of adapting to the natural environment. Human culture is made up of our behavior and its results, and is also the way in which we assign meaning to our lives. Our culture is always adjusting to both internal and external change.
- Archaeologists work with the tangible remains of human activity that survive in the ground. Archaeological finds are not culture in themselves but products of it, and they are linked to culture in a systematic way.
- Archaeologists think of human cultures as complex systems of interacting variables. This viewpoint is based loosely on principles of general systems theory, a way of searching for general relationships in the empirical world.
- A major objective of archaeology is to understand the complex linkages between human cultures and the environments in which they are found.
- Cultural process involves identifying the factors responsible for the direction and nature of change within cultural systems. Processual archaeology is the analysis of the causes behind cultural change.

· In this chapter we define the archaeological record, data, and provenience, discuss the fundamental laws of association and superposition, and examine context in archaeology.

The concepts of culture, space, and time in archaeology are insep-
arable. Accurate measuring of age in calendar years and of spatial
context lie at the very core of all archaeological research. Indeed, as
Albert Spaulding points out, a minimal definition of archaeology
describes it as the study of interrelations between the form of artifacts found in a site and their date and spatial location relative to
the problem being studied (Spaulding, 1960).

In this chapter we introduce you to some basic concepts of
archaeological research, to culture, to data in the form of artifacts,
and to the matrix, provenience, and context of the data. The provenience and context of all archaeological data are based on the two
fundamental laws, superposition and association. From basic concepts, we move on to discuss spatial context—not the limitless frontiers of the heavens, but a precisely defined location for every find
made during an archaeological survey or excavation.

THE CONCEPT OF CULTURE

In Chapter 1, I stated that "Anthropologists study human beings as
biological organisms and as people with a distinctive and unique
characteristic—culture. . . . Archaeologists are, in fact, a special type
of anthropologist, specializing in past human culture." Few concepts in anthropology have generated as much controversy and academic debate as those expressed in that statement (Kroeber and
Kluckhohn, 1952). Perhaps the best general definition of culture
was written by British anthropologist Sir Edward Tylor more than
a century ago. He stated that culture is "That complex whole which
includes knowledge, belief, art, morals, law, custom, and any other
capabilities and habits acquired by man as a member of society"
(Tylor, 1871). To that definition, modern archaeologists would add
the statement that culture is our primary means of adapting to our
environment.

Culture is a distinctively human attribute, for we are the only animals to use our culture as our *primary* means of adapting to our environment (Keesing, 1974). It is our adaptive system. Although biological evolution has protected the polar bear from Arctic cold with dense fur and has given the duck webbed feet for swimming, only human beings make thick clothes and igloos in the Arctic and live with minimal clothing under light, thatched shelters in the tropics. We use our culture as a buffer between ourselves and the environment that became more and more elaborate through the long millennia of prehistory. We are now so detached from our environment that removal of our cultural buffer would render us almost helpless and probably lead to extinction of the human race in a very short time. Thus, human cultures are made up of human behavior and its results; they obviously consist of complex and constantly interacting variables. Human culture, never static, is always adjusting to both internal and external change, whether environmental, technological, or societal (Deetz, 1967; Dunnell, 1971).

The Nature of Culture.   Culture can be subdivided in all sorts of ways—into language, economics, technology, religion, political or social organizations, and art. But human culture as a whole is a complex, structured organization in which all our categories shape one another. All cultures are made up of myriad tangible and intangible traits, the contents of which result from complex adaptation to a wide range of ecological, societal, and cultural factors. Much of human culture is transmitted from generation to generation by sophisticated communication systems that permit complex and ceaseless adaptations to aid survival and help rapid cultural change take place—as when less-advanced societies come into contact with higher civilizations.

Everyone lives within a culture of some kind, and every culture is qualified by a label, such as "middle-class American," "Eskimo," or "Masai." The qualification conjures up characteristic attributes or behavior patterns typical of those associated with the cultural label. One attribute of a middle-class American might be the hamburger; of the Eskimo, the kayak; of the Masai, a long-handled, fine-bladed spear. Our mental images of cultures are associated with popular stereotypes, too. To many Americans, Chinese culture conjures up images of paper lanterns and willow-pattern plates; French culture, good eating and fine wines. We are all familiar with the distinctive "flavor" of a culture that we encounter when dining in a foreign restaurant or arriving in a strange country. Every culture has its individuality and recognizable style, which shape its political and judicial institutions and morals (Frankfort, 1951; Renfrew, 1972). Archaeologists think of culture as possessing three components:

The individual's own version of his or her culture, the diversified individual behavior that makes up the myriad strains of a culture. Shared culture: elements of a culture shared by everyone. These can include cultural activities like human sacrifice or ritualized warfare, or any shared human activity, as well as the body of rules and prescriptions that make up the sum of the culture (Figure 5.1). Language is critical to this sharing, as is the:
Cultural system, the system of behavior in which every individual *participates*. You not only share it with other members of society, 'you participate in the cultural system.

Culture, then, can be viewed as either a blend of shared traits, or as a system that permits a society to interact with its environment. To do anything more than merely work out chronological sequences, the archaeologist has to view culture as complex, interacting components. These components remain static unless the processes that operate the system are carefully defined. Archaeologists

Figure 5.1 Palenque from the north showing the palace in the foreground and the temple of the inscriptions in the background.

are deeply involved with "cultural process," the processes by which human societies changed in the past.

A *cultural system* was well defined by archaeologist Stuart Struever (1971): "Culture and its environments represent a number of articulated [interlinked] systems in which change occurs through a series of minor, linked variations in one or more of these systems." For example, an Eskimo cultural system is part of a much larger Arctic ecosystem. The cultural system itself is made up of dozens of subsystems. There is an economic subsystem, a political subsystem, and many others. Let us say that the climate changes suddenly. The Eskimo now switch from reindeer hunting to fishing and sealing. The change triggers all sorts of linked shifts in not only the economic subsystem, but in the technological and social subsystems as well. A cultural system is in a constant state of adjustment within itself and with the ecosystem of which it is a part. The concept of cultural systems is derived from the general systems theory, a body of theoretical concepts formulated as a means of searching for general relationships in the empirical world (Watson, LeBlanc, and Redman, 1971). A system is defined as a "whole which functions by virtue of the interdependence of its parts." In other words, the relationship between the parts is the critical element that has to be described and explained. Systems theory is widely used in chemistry, physics, and biology, where relationships can be defined with great precision. It has come into use in archaeology purely as a general concept to help us understand the ever-changing relationship between human cultures and their environment. The systems approach to human culture argues that geographical distance between settlements, differences in activities conducted at various sites, and a host of other spatial differences, both large and small, have affected human culture as deeply as time has. Many archaeologists therefore use a definition of culture emphasizing cultural systems that are constantly changing in response to external and internal stimuli (Doran, 1970).

CULTURAL PROCESS

Systems theory deals with relationships and variations in relationships; in other words, it deals with precisely the phenomena involved in explaining the processes by which cultures change. Modern scientific archaeology analyzes the causes of cultural change, that is, the cultural process.

The word *process* implies a patterned sequence of events that leads one from one state of affairs to another. This patterned sequence is determined by a decision-making process that sets the order of events. A forty-foot sailing yacht starts as a pile of materials—wood, aluminum, copper, bronze—and then a patterned sequence of manufacturing events turns the material into a gleaming new ship. Archaeology is a process, too. It involves designing the research project, formulating the hypothesis, collecting and interpreting the data, testing the data, and, finally, publishing the results.

Causes are events that force people to make decisions about how to deal with new situations. As such, they are distinct from the actual process of decision making—the mechanisms that lead to any kind of change. A change in the natural environment from year-round rainfall to a seasonal pattern is a cause.

In archaeology *cultural process* refers to the "identification of the factors responsible for the direction and nature of change within cultural systems" (Sharer and Ashmore, 1979). *Processual archaeology* is analysis of the causes of culture change, which involves looking at relationships between variables that could lead to cultural change. These possible causes are then tested against actual archaeological data, sometimes in a systems-theory context.

As more and more archaeological data have become available, the older, simplistic explanations of cultural process in prehistory, such as universal evolutionism and diffusionism, fail to reflect accurately the situations as we now see them. Clearly, no one element in any cultural system is the primary cause of change; instead, a complex range of factors—rainfall, vegetation, technology, social restrictions, and population density—interact with one another and react to changes in any element in the system. It follows, then, that human culture, from the ecologist's viewpoint, is merely one element in the ecosystem, a mechanism of behavior whereby people adapt to an environment (Figure 5.2) (Dunnell, 1980).

ARCHAEOLOGICAL DATA

The cultures archaeologists study are reconstructed from archaeological data. Archaeological data consist of any material remains of human activity, whether a scatter of broken bones, a ruined house, a gold mask, or a vast temple plaza. Archaeologists have names that define these remains for research purposes.

The *archaeological record* is the general name denoting the more

Figure 5.2 A San hunter-gatherer in the Kalahari Desert searches the bole of a tree for water. " . . . Human culture is, from the ecologist's viewpoint, merely one element in the ecosystem. . . . "

or less continuous distribution of artifacts over the earth's surface, with highly variable densities, however. Variations in artifact densities reflect the character and frequency of land use, making them an important variable that the archaeologist can measure (Dunnell and Dancey, 1983). Some high-density clusters of artifacts may be subsumed under *site*. Although "archaeological record" refers specifically to distributions of artifacts, these can include:

1. *Artifacts:* in the strict sense, humanly manufactured or modified objects (Figure 5.3).
2. *Features:* artifacts that cannot be removed from the ground, such as post holes and ditches.

Figure 5.3 A magnificent Iron Age helmet from the River Thames in London (20.5 cm. diameter at base). Objects like this are useful for cross-dating archaeological sites all over Europe.

3. *Structures:* houses, granaries, temples, and other buildings that can be identified from patterns of post holes and other features in the ground.
4. *Ecofacts:* sometimes refers to food remains, such as bones, seeds, and other finds, which throw light on human activities.

Data are the materials recognized by the archaeologist as significant evidence, all of which are collected and recorded as part of the research. Archaeological data are sometimes referred to as *evidence.*

Archaeological data do not consist of artifacts, features, structures, and ecofacts alone, however; they consist also of their *context* in space and time. Lewis Binford says that "data relevant to most, if not all, the components of past sociocultural systems are preserved in the archaeological record. . . . Our task, then, is to devise means for extracting this information" (Binford, 1972).

MATRIX AND PROVENIENCE

All scientifically collected or excavated archaeological finds, be they a complete site or a lone object, occur within a matrix and have a specific provenience.

The *matrix* is the physical substance that surrounds the find. It can be gravel, sand, mud, or even water. Most archaeological matrices are of natural origin—passing time and external phenomena, such as wind and rainfall, create them. The early campsites at Olduvai Gorge in Tanzania were at the edge of a shallow and ever-fluctuating lake 1.75 million years ago. The scatter of tools and bones left by the departing inhabitants was soon covered by a layer of thin lake sand carried by advancing shallow water. This matrix preserved the tools in their original positions for thousands of millennia (Leakey, 1971). An archaeological matrix can also be humanly made, such as the huge earthen platforms of Hopewell burial mounds in the Midwest (Willey, 1966).

Provenience is the precise three-dimensional position of the find within the matrix as recorded by the archaeologist. It is derived from accurate records kept during excavations and site surveys, from evidence that is inevitably destroyed once a site is dug or artifacts collected from a surface site.

Every human artifact has a provenience in time and space. The provenience in time can range from a radiocarbon date of 1,400 ± 60 years before the present for a Mayan temple to a precise reading of A.D. 1985 for a dime released by the United States Mint. Frequently, it can simply be an exact position in an archaeological site whose general age is known. Provenience in space is based, finally, on associations between tools and other items that were results of human behavior in a culture. Provenience is determined by applying two fundamental archaeological laws: the law of association and the law of superposition.

The Law of Association. The archaeological law of association (Figure 5.4) was first stated by Danish archaeologist J. J. A. Worsaae in 1843. Working with prehistoric burials, Worsaae stated the principle clearly:

> The objects accompanying a human burial are in most cases things that were in use at the same time. When certain artifact types are found together in grave association after grave association, and when more evolved forms of the same tools are found in association with other burials, then the associations provide some basis for dividing the burials into different chronological groups on the basis of association and artifact styles.

Worsaae eventually proved the chronological validity of the law of association by stratigraphic excavations in dozens of burial sites (Harris, 1979).

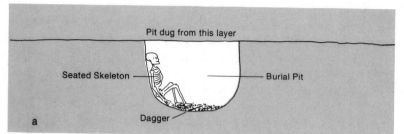

(a) The burial pit, dug from the uppermost layer, contains not only a skeleton but also a dagger that lies close to its foot. The dagger is associated with the skeleton, and both finds are associated with the burial pit and the layer from which the grave pit was cut into the subsoil.

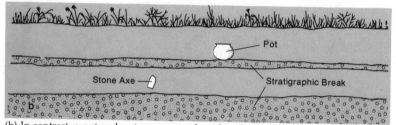

(b) In contrast, a pot and a stone axe are found in two different layers, separated by a sterile zone, a zone with no finds. The two objects are not in association.

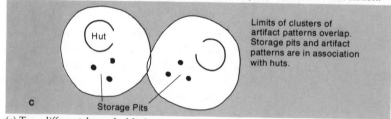

(c) Two different household clusters with associated pits and scatters of artifacts. These are in association with each other.

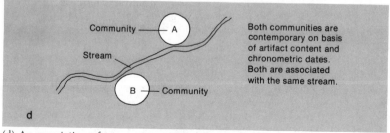

(d) An association of two contemporary communities.

Figure 5.4 Some instances of archaeological associations.

Instances of archaeological associations are legion. The first evidence of high antiquity for humankind came from associations of stone axes and the bones of extinct animals discovered in the same geological layers. Many early Mesoamerican farmers' houses are associated with storage pits for maize and other crops. In this and many other cases, it is the horizontal association between artifacts and houses, or dwellings and storage pits, or artifacts and food residues that provide the archaeological association. Unassociated artifacts, examined deprived of association with other finds, yield relatively little worthwhile information. Much of the most valuable archaeological data are derived from precise studies of associations between different finds in the ground.

The Law of Superposition.   The time dimension of archaeology is erected on basic principles of stratigraphic geology set down by the uniformitarians early in the nineteenth century. "Strata" Smith's classic studies of British geology were based on the law of superposition (Daniel, 1981). It was easy for archaeologists to adopt this law, for many of their most important finds were made within geological layers or contexts.

The law of superposition states that the geological layers of the earth are stratified one upon another, like the layers of a cake. Cliffs by the seashore and quarries are easily accessible examples. Obviously, any object found in the lowermost levels—whether a stone or something humanly made—was deposited there before the upper horizons were accumulated. In other words, the lower levels are *earlier* than the upper strata. The same law applies to archaeological sites: The tools, houses, and other finds in the layers of a site can be dated relative to the layers by their association with the stratum in which they are found (Figure 5.4).

The basis of all scientific archaeological excavation is the accurately observed and carefully recorded stratigraphic profile (Wheeler, 1954).

We will return to stratigraphy and superposition in Chapter 6.

ARCHAEOLOGICAL CONTEXT

Archaeological context is derived from careful recording of the matrix, provenience, and association of the finds. Context is far more than just a find spot, a position in time and space. It involves assessing how the find got to its position and what has happened since its original owners abandoned it. Anyone wanting to reconstruct human behavior or ancient cultural systems must pay careful attention to the context of every find.

Context is affected by these factors:

1. The manufacture and use of the object, house, or other find by its original owners. The orientation of a house may be determined by the position of the sun on summer afternoons. Because the archaeologist's objective is to reconstruct ancient *behavior*, this aspect of context is vital.
2. The way in which the find was deposited in the ground. Some discoveries, like royal burials or caches of artifacts, were deliberately buried under the ground by ancient people; others vanished as a result of natural phenomenon. Dilapidated houses that have been abandoned are slowly covered by blowing sand or rotting vegetation. The Roman city of Herculaneum in Italy, however, was buried quickly by a catastrophic eruption of Vesuvius in August A.D. 79.
3. The subsequent history of the find in the ground. Was the burial disturbed by later graves, or was the site eroded away by water?

Primary and Secondary Context.   The context of any archaeological find can be affected by two processes: the original behavior of the people who used or made it, and events that came later.

Primary context is the original context of the find, undisturbed by any factor, whether human or natural, since it was deposited by those who were involved with it. The Iron Age warrior depicted in Figure 5.5, who was buried at Maiden Castle in A.D. 43, died from his wounds in a battle against a Roman legion. The survivors buried him swiftly in a shallow grave. The skeleton survived intact in its primary context until Sir Mortimer Wheeler excavated the undisturbed burial late in the 1930s (Wheeler, 1943).

Secondary context refers to the context of a find whose primary context has been disturbed by later activity. Very frequently, excavators of a burial ground will find incomplete skeletons whose graves have been disturbed by deposition of later burials. As in the tomb of Pharaoh Tutankhamun, tomb robbers may disturb the original grave furnishings, frantically searching for gold or precious oils. The latter were highly prized as fragrances by the Egyptian nobility. In still other instances, finds can be shifted by the natural forces of wind and weather. Many of the Stone Age tools found in European river gravels have been transported by floodwaters to a

Figure 5.5   An iron arrowhead embedded in the backbone of a skeleton from a battle cemetery at Maiden Castle, England. The artifact comes from a Roman cultural context; the skeleton, from native British. Nevertheless, they are still associated in the archaeological record.

location far from their original place of use. All these disturbed finds are in a secondary context.

Spatial Context.   Spatial context is important to archaeologists because it enables them to determine the distance between different objects or features, between entire settlements, or between settlements and key vegetational zones and landmarks. Important distances can be a few inches of level ground between a dagger and the associated skeleton of its dead owner, a mile separating two seasonal camps, or a complicated series of interrelated distance measurements separating dozens of villages that are part of an elaborate trading system carrying luxury goods through several geographic regions hundreds of miles apart.

One can identify four levels of spatial context, each of them coinciding with an actual level of human behavior.

1. *Artifacts:* individual human activity.
2. *Structure:* household or group activities (structures can, of course, include public buildings, such as temples, which are used by more than one household).
3. *Site:* community activity, groups of contemporary houses, stores, temples, and other structures.
4. *Region:* the activities of groups of people reflected by sites distributed on the landscape. These are sometimes referred to as a settlement pattern.

These four levels of spatial context are closely tied to actual cultural behavior (Figure 5.6). An artifact itself can provide valuable information on technology and actual use. But to infer cultural behavior we must know the artifact's association, both with other artifacts and with the matrix in which it was found. The patterning of artifacts in space around an abandoned iron smelting furnace or near the bones of a slaughtered bison kill is tangible evidence for specific human behavior. An unassociated projectile head will never give you anything more specific than the inference that it was used as a weapon. But a patterning of projectile heads, scraping tools, and large boulders associated with a bison skeleton has a context in time and space that allows much more detailed inferences.

The basic assumption behind all studies of artifacts in space is that they were used for rational purposes and that characteristic groups of them were used for specific activities, such as ironworking, butchery, and hunting. It follows that similarly patterned groups of artifact types found on other sites resulted from similar activities, even if they show differences in detail. During the earlier millennia of the Stone Age, people enjoyed much the same level of hunting and gathering culture throughout Africa, Europe, and India. This parallel is reflected in thousands of similar-looking stone axes found in sites as widely separated as the Thames Valley in England and the Cape of Good Hope in South Africa.

ARTIFACTS, SUBASSEMBLAGES, AND ASSEMBLAGES

Artifacts. Artifacts are commonly defined as "anything which exhibits any physical attributes that can be assumed to be the result of human activity" (Dunnell, 1971). This definition implies that the term *artifact* covers every form of archaeological find, from stone

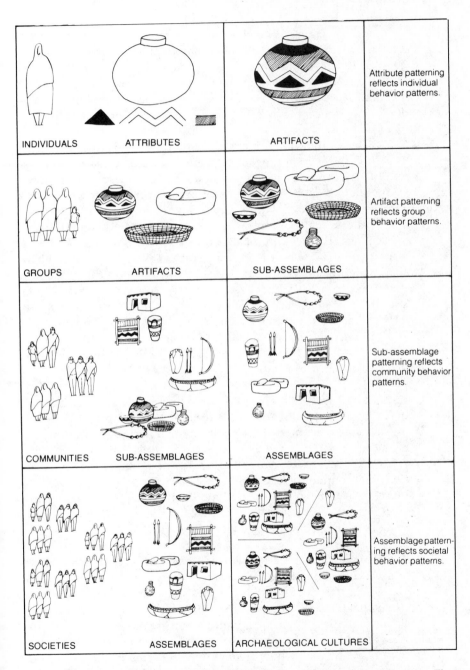

Figure 5.6 Human behavior as reflected in archaeological classifications. The hierarchy begins with attributes and artifacts and ends with entire archaeological cultures.

axes, bronze daggers, and clay pots to butchered animal bones, carbonized seeds, huts, and all other manifestations of human behavior that can be found in archaeological sites. Some archaeologists define artifacts by breaking them down into four categories: portable artifacts, features, structures, and ecofacts (forms of archaeological evidence that we will cover in more detail later in this book).

Whichever definition of artifact is preferred, it is assumed by all that any object or any event of manufacture or consumption is a product of human activity if its location or any other of its features cannot be accounted for by natural processes. In other words, artifacts are compared to natural objects and distinguished from them, not by individual features but by a patterning of different, human-caused features. It is this patterning that is important. A simple flake removed from an elaborate ceremonial obsidian knife blade may not necessarily show evidence of human modification. But the patterned, consistently repeated occurrence of several dozen or hundreds of small flakes—flakes that together formed a knife—is highly diagnostic of human activity. Normally there is no difficulty at all in telling human-made or caused artifacts from those caused by water action, fire, hyena kills, or all the other natural phenomena that one can run across.

Subassemblages.   An artifact, such as an arrowhead or a basket, is made up of a combination of attributes (see Chapter 13), which make up a constant pattern of behavior reflected in the finished artifact. When such artifacts are found in patterned associations reflecting the shared cultural behavior of minimal groups, then they are commonly classified in *subassemblages* (Deetz, 1967). A hunter uses a bow, arrows, and a quiver. A blacksmith uses hammers, tongs, and bellows to make hoes or spears, and so on. Subassemblages represent the behavior of individuals.

Assemblages.   When a number of subassemblages of artifacts, let us say a collection of hunting weapons, baskets, pounders, and digging sticks, traces of windbreaks, and stone vessels, are found in a contemporary association, they reflect in their patterning the shared activities of a total community and are known as *assemblages*. With assemblages, one is looking at the shared behavior of a community as a whole, which frequently is reflected in the remains of houses, the features associated with them, and the community settlement patterns.

ARCHAEOLOGICAL SITES

Archaeological sites are places at which traces of past human activity are to be found. Sites are normally identified by the presence of artifacts. They can range in size from a large city, such as Teotihuacán, in the Valley of Mexico, to a tiny scatter of hunter-gatherer artifacts in Death Valley, California. There are millions of archaeological sites in the world, many of them still undiscovered. Some were occupied for a few hours, days, or weeks; some were occupied for a generation or two and then abandoned forever. Other localities, such as Mesopotamian occupation mounds, or *tells*, were reoccupied again and again for hundreds, even thousands, of years and contain many stratified layers (Figure 5.7). In contrast, the occupation site may contain little more than a surface scatter of potsherds or stone tools or an occupation layer buried under a few inches of topsoil. Archaeological sites can consist of a simple association (an isolated burial and one pot), many associations making up an assemblage of artifacts representing one community, or a series of assemblages stratified one above another.

Classifying Sites. Archaeological sites can be classified in these ways:

By archaeological context. The context of artifacts in the site can be used to distinguish between sites such as surface locations, single-level occupations, and stratified settlements.

Figure 5.7   Mesopotamian *tell*, a site that was occupied over thousands of years.

By artifact content. The site is labeled according to its specific artifact content: pottery, stone tools, milling stones, and so on. The associations, assemblages, and subassemblages of artifacts in the site are used to label it as Stone Age, Mayan, and so on.

By geographical location. Most human settlements have been concentrated in well-defined types of geographical locations, and these sites can be referred to as cave sites, valley-bottom sites, foothill sites, and the like.

By artifact content related to site function. Because subassemblages reflect individual human behavior, sites can be classified by the characteristic patterning of the artifacts found in them, such as kill sites and habitations.

Common Site Functions.   These are some common site functions:

Living or *habitation sites* are the most common, for they are the places where people have lived and carried out a multitude of activities. The artifacts in living sites reflect domestic activities, such as food preparation, as well as toolmaking. Dwellings are normally present. The temporary camps of early humans at Olduvai Gorge are living sites, as are Stone Age rockshelters, southwestern pueblos, and Mesopotamian *tells*. Habitation sites of any complexity are associated with other sites that reflect specialized needs, such as agricultural systems, cemeteries, and temporary camps.

Kill sites are places where prehistoric people killed game and camped around the carcasses while butchering the meat. They are relatively common on the Great Plains; the Olsen-Chubbock site is a good example. Projectile points and butchery tools are associated with kill sites.

Ceremonial sites may or may not be integral to a living site. The Mesopotamian *ziggurat* dominated its mother city, and Mayan ceremonial sites, such as Tikal, were surrounded by habitation areas. Other famous ceremonial sites, such as Stonehenge in England or the Great Serpent Mound in Ohio, are isolated monuments. Ceremonial artifacts, such as sting-ray spines used in multilation rituals, and statuary may be associated with sacred sites.

Burial sites include both cemeteries and isolated tombs. People have been burying their dead since at least 70,000 years ago and have often taken enormous pains to prepare them for the afterlife. Perhaps the most famous burial sites of all are the Pyramids of Gizeh in Egypt. Royal burials, such as that of Egyptian pharaoh Tutankhamun, absorbed the energies of hundreds of people in their preparation. Many burials are associated with special grave furniture, jewelry, and ornaments of rank.

Trading, quarry, and art sites form a special category in that some kind of specialist activity was carried out. The special tools needed for mining copper, obsidian, and other metals identify quarry sites. Trading sites are identified by large quantities of exotic trade objects and by their strategic position near major cities. The Assyrian *karum* that flourished outside the Hittite city of Kanesh in 1900 B.C. is one of these. Art sites, which abound in southwest France, southern Africa, California, and other areas, are identified by paintings on the walls of caves and rockshelters.

CULTURES, REGIONS, AND SETTLEMENT PATTERNS

The spatial units we have referred to thus far are all confined to the boundaries of one community. They reflect the activities of the maximum number of people who occupied a settlement at some time during a cycle of settlement. Although a great deal of archaeological research is carried out on single sites, archaeologists often seek to understand the prehistory of a much wider area. Several communities or a scattered population living in a well-defined region may be linked in the same subsistence or settlement system. Such commonly held systems, and the human activities that derive from them, make up an entire culture. Culture behavior is identified by the patterning that appears in an entire assemblage. Studying an entire culture involves working with much larger bodies of archaeological information, as well as with background geographical and environmental data.

Archaeological Cultures and Other Units. A number of spatial units are in common use:

Archaeological cultures are consistent patternings of assemblages, the archaeological equivalents of human societies. Archaeological cultures consist of the material remains of human culture preserved at a specific space and time at several sites.

Culture areas are large geographical areas in which artifacts characteristic of an archaeological culture exist in a precise context of time and space. One can refer to both a Mayan cultural system and a Mayan culture area.

Archaeological regions are generally described as well-defined geographical areas bounded by conspicuous geographical features, such as ocean, lakes, or mountains. Once having defined a region geographically, the researcher will try to identify its ecological and cultural boundaries throughout prehistoric times.

Most regional approaches involve far more than comparing the artifacts from a few scattered settlements. They are based on a research strategy aimed at sampling the entire region, and on objectives intended to reconstruct many more aspects of prehistoric life than those uncovered at a single site. These include both social organization and economic strategies (see Chapter 16).

Settlement Patterns. A settlement pattern is the distribution of sites and human settlement across the natural landscape. Settlement patterns are determined by many factors: the environment, economic practices, and technological skills. Settlement archaeology is part of the analysis of interactions between people and their environment.

In determining spatial relations, the archaeologists base their studies of the behavior of a human society as a whole on models and hypotheses tested by data from many disciplines. These data bear on the ways in which communities and their associated contemporary assemblages are grouped into larger units on the landscape. They bear too on the ways in which prehistoric societies interacted with the ever-changing natural environment.

Spatial context is vital to scientific archaeology, for it provides one of the critical dimensions of archaeological data. The other critical dimension is time, which we will consider in Chapter 6.

Guide to Further Reading

The literature on basic archaeological concepts is sketchy at best, but these are some key works.

Childe, V. Gordon. *Piecing Together the Past.* London: Routledge and Kegan Paul, 1956.
A dated but still outstanding source on basic archaeological concepts, with strong European orientation.

Deetz, James. *Invitation to Archaeology.* Garden City, N.Y.: Natural History Press, 1967.
Entertaining and succinct introduction to culture in archaeology.

Hole, Frank, and Robert F. Heizer. *An Introduction to Prehistoric Archaeology,* 3rd ed. New York: Holt, Rinehart and Winston, 1973.
An advanced archaeological textbook, with superb bibliographies that give considerable coverage to the basics.

Thomas, David Hurst. *Archaeology.* New York: Holt, Rinehart and Winston, 1979.
An excellent introduction to archaeology that is especially strong on basic concepts. North American emphasis.

Watson, Patti Jo, Steven LeBlank, and Charles Redman, *Explanation in Archaeology.* New York: Columbia University Press, 1971.
A fundamental source that describes processual archaeology in rather technical language.

Wheeler, R. E. M. *Archaeology from the Earth.* Oxford: Clarendon Press, 1954.
An elegant guide to excavation that contains much of value about fundamental concepts.

Willey, Gordon R., and Philip Phillips. *Method and Theory in American Archaeology.* Chicago: Unviersity of Chicago Press, 1958.
A classic essay on basic culture history in North American archaeology.

CHAPTER 6 🐦

TIME: RELATIVE CHRONOLOGY

Preview

- Chronological ordering of prehistoric times was a major problem for early archaeologists. In an attempt to deal with this difficulty, C. J. Thomsen refined the three-age system, a technological framework that was widely used in the Old World. New World archaeologists used the direct historical approach to determine the framework for the Americas.
- Chronometric (absolute) dates are expressed in years. In contrast, relative dates represent relationships in time that are used to correlate prehistoric sites or cultures with one another. These are based on the law of superposition.
- Cultural disturbances, which result from human behavior, can affect stratigraphy. Natural disturbances, such as erosion or flooding, can change stratigraphic contexts by natural means.
- Early archaeologists studied the evolution of artifact styles throughout time. This approach has developed into formal ordering, the technique of *seriation*. This technique is based on the assumption that artifacts come into fashion, have a period of maximum popularity, and then slowly go out of style. Tested against the evidence of New England tombstones and other modern artifacts, seriation has been made into an effective way of ordering sites in chronological sequence.

- Cross-dating, which is widely applied in Europe and Mesoamerica, uses artifacts of a known age, such as coins and other items that were widely traded, to provide relative dates for sites in areas that have no historical chronology.
- The Pleistocene, or Great Ice Age, has been relative dated by such geological events as the major glaciations and interglacials as well as by fluctuations in sea level. Bones from such extinct species as Pleistocene elephants have been used to provide an approximate relative chronology for this period, a technique known as geochronology.
- Pollen analysis, or palynology, uses the fossil pollens of grasses and forest trees to study prehistoric vegetational cover with great accuracy. Pollen samples provide ecological information about glaciations and interglacials, and also insights on the environments surrounding archaeological sites. Palynology has even been used to date individual rooms in southwestern pueblos.

The measurement of time and the ordering of prehistoric cultures in chronological sequence has been one of the archaeologist's major preoccupations since the very beginnings of scientific research. In this chapter we examine the ways in which archaeologists establish chronological relationships between artifacts, sites, and other features. This type of relative chronology is based on stratigraphic principles first devised by geologists.

Early antiquarians and theologians wrestled with the enigma of the Biblical legend of the Creation and the finds of fossil animals and human artifacts. Since high antiquity was established for humankind in 1859, however, accurate measurement of time has become one of the principal preoccupations of those who study the prehistoric past. How does one classify the past and measure the age of the great events of prehistory? The time dimension of archaeology is a vital element in our description and interpretation of prehistory. Yet, our own perspectives of time and philosophies of life have taken very little account of these vast new chronological horizons (Leone, 1978).

Consider for a moment how you view time. What is the earliest date you can remember? Mine is my third birthday—I have a vague memory of balloons and lots of people. My continuous memory of people as individuals and of day-to-day events begins at age eight. Most adults have a somewhat similar span of recollection and a chronological perspective on their lives extending back into early childhood. Our sense of personal involvement in human history, too, extends only over our lifetimes. We have only indirect involvement with the lives of our parents, relatives, or other friends, some of whom may have been alive fifty to seventy years before we were born. Perhaps our profoundest involvement with time occurs toward the end of our lives, with a period covering the lives of our immediate family. But we do have, also, a marginal sense of longer chronologies and a perspective on events within them—our family ancestry, the history of our community, of our nation—and in these days of ardent internationalism, with the world as well, though few people have a sense of perspective for the whole span of human experience.

THE THREE-AGE SYSTEM

In Chapter 3, we saw how classification of the past was a major problem for early excavators. Confronted with a jumble of artifacts from burial mounds or settlements, they had no means for subdividing or measuring the past. Until the nineteenth century, the world had been comfortably secure. People had speculated freely about their origins but only within the narrow horizons of the Biblical account of the Creation. What happened before the Creation was a blank. Christians had contemplated eternity, but it was the shadowless, changeless eternity of God. Ussher's 6,000 years sufficed for all prehistory, even if subdividing these six millennia presented a problem.

As early as the late sixteenth century, some antiquarians were writing about prehistoric ages of stone, bronze, and iron. This concept was refined by Scandinavian archaeologists early in the nineteenth century. But as late as 1806, Professor Rasmus Nyerup of the University of Copenhagen complained that "everything which has come down to us from heathendom is wrapped in a thick fog; it belongs to a space of time which we cannot measure" (Daniel, 1981). Nyerup and others were responsible for setting up a Danish National Museum that housed a confusing collection of artifacts from bogs, burial chambers, and shell middens. The first curator of the Museum, Christian Jurgensen Thomsen (1788–1865), was appointed in 1816. Thomsen put the Museum collections in order by classifying them into three groups, representing ages of Stone, Bronze, and Iron, using finds in previously undisturbed graves as a basis for his classification. He claimed that his Three Ages were chronologically ranked (Thomsen, 1836).

Thomsen's bold classification was taken up by another Dane, J. J. A. Worsaae, who proved the system's basic stratigraphic validity. By studying archaeological finds from all over Europe, Worsaae demonstrated the widespread validity of the method that became known as the Three-Age System (Worsaae, 1843). This system was a technological subdividing of the prehistoric past. It gave archaeologists a broad context within which their own finds could be placed. Thus, Thomsen's Three Ages, which were a first attempt at a chronology of relationship for the prehistoric past, were widely adopted as a basis for classifying prehistoric sites in the Old World. This framework for Old World prehistory, in modified form, survives today (Table 6.1).

Table 6.1   Some nomenclature of Old World archaeology.

Approximate age	Geological epoch	Three-Age terminology	Important events
3000 B.C. – 7800 B.C. –	HOLOCENE	Iron Age Bronze Age Neolithic Mesolithic	Writing in the Near East Origins of food production
8000 B.C. – 35,000 B.P. –	END OF PLEISTOCENE	Upper Paleolithic	Origins of blade technology
70,000 B.P. – 400,000 B.P. –	PLEISTOCENE	Middle Paleolithic	
1.75 million B.P. – 5 million B.P. –		Lower Paleolithic	Hand axes in widespread use
13 million B.P. –	PLIOCENE		Origins of toolmaking
25 million B.P. –	MIOCENE		No humans
34 million B.P. –	OLIGOCENE		

Note: This table is for general reference throughout the text.

NEW WORLD CHRONOLOGY

The Three-Age System of the Scandinavians was not adopted in North America. Systematic archaeological research flourished in the New World after 1859, but early attempts to find Paleolithic sites there were unsuccessful. The complicated cultural strata of the European rivers, with their rich storehouses of hand axes, did not exist, but something that did exist—relationships between the Indian population and the finds of the archaeologist—was soon established. Stratigraphic observations and local cultural sequences did not preoccupy American archaeologists, unlike the Europeans. Few researchers bothered to apply meticulous excavation techniques to later New World archaeological sites, in which, in any case, almost no metals were found (Willey and Sabloff, 1980).

Not until 1914 did chronology and detailed stratigraphic observation of the past become important in American archaeology when N. C. Nelson (Nelson, 1914), and later A. V. Kidder, began to use potsherds in southwestern sites as stratigraphic indicators. Kidder's classic excavations at the Pecos Pueblo (Kidder, 1924) brought about a conference there in 1927, which delineated eight sequential stages of Pueblo culture. With that event the foundations of accurate stratigraphic and chronological studies in American archaeology were soundly laid in the classic archaeological laboratory of the Southwest.

As we saw in Chapter 4, the direct historical approach and the development of tree-ring dating in the southwestern United States provided at least one area of the Americas with an accurate chronological framework. Most other regions were without precise timescales in calendar years until radiocarbon dating was begun in the 1950s.

CHRONOMETRIC (ABSOLUTE) AND RELATIVE DATING

Prehistoric chronologies cover enormous periods of time—millennia and centuries. Some idea of the scale of prehistoric time can be gained by piling up a hundred quarters. If the whole pile represents the time the human race has been on earth, the length of time covered by historical records would equal considerably less than the thickness of one quarter.

Archaeologists commonly refer to dates expressed in years as chronometric or absolute dates. Julius Caesar landed in Britain in 55 B.C.; Washington, D.C., was founded in A.D. 1800. The current chronometric dates for the earliest humans begin around four million years ago. Though not nearly as precise as the date for Caesar, they are, nevertheless, expressed in years. Dating experts draw widely on techniques invented by chemists and physicists and used by geologists for chronometric dating (see Chapter 7).

Relative dates correlate prehistoric sites of cultures with one another by their relative age. They are based on the law of superposition.

Relative dates are simpler to establish than are chronometric dates. If I place a book on the table and then pile another on top of it, clearly the upper of the two was placed on the table after, at a later moment in time, than the original volume. The second book became part of the pile after the first—though how long afterward we have no means of telling.

Stratigraphy and Superposition. Most relative chronology in archaeology has its basis in large- or small-scale stratigraphic observations in archaeological sites of all ages. As the eminent British archaeologist Sir Mortimer Wheeler argues, the basis of scientific archaeological excavation is the accurately observed and carefully recorded stratigraphic profile (Wheeler, 1954).

Superposition is fundamental in studying archaeological sites, for many settlements, such as Near Eastern mounds or Indian villages in the Ohio Valley or cave sites, contain multilevel occupations whose decipherment is the key to their relative chronology. Sir Mortimer Wheeler describes the process of human occupation as applied to stratigraphy:

> The human occupation of a site normally results in the accumulation of material of one kind or another on and about the area occupied. Objects are lost or discarded and become imbedded in the earth. Floors are renewed and old ones buried. Buildings crumble and new ones are built on the ruins. A flood may destroy a building or a town and deposit a layer of alluvium on its debris and later, when the flood has subsided, the level site may be reoccupied. Sometimes, the process is in the reverse direction. Evidences of occupation may be removed as in the deepening of an unsurfaced street by traffic, or the digging of a pit for the disposal of rubbish or for burial. . . . In one way or another the surface of an ancient town or village is constantly altering in response to human effort or neglect; and it is by interpreting rightly these evidences of alteration that we may hope to reconstruct something of the vicissitudes of the site and its occupants (Wheeler, 1954).

Stratigraphy, as applied to archaeological sites, is on a much smaller scale than that of geology, but often it is correspondingly more complicated (Harris, 1979). Most archaeological relative chronology employs careful observation of sequences of occupation levels as well as correlation of these with cultural sequences at other sites in the same area. Successive occupation levels may be found at the same spot, as in a cave, fort, or mound site, where many generations of settlers lived within a circumscribed or restricted area. In other sites, however, the chronological sequence can be horizontal, as when economic or political conditions dictate regular movement of villages when fields are exhausted or residence rules modified. In this case, a cultural sequence may be scattered throughout a series of single-level occupation sites over a large area and can be put together only by judicious survey work and careful analysis of the artifacts found in the different sites.

The artifacts, food bones, or other finds recovered from the layers of a site are as critical as the stratigraphy itself. Each level in a settlement, however massive or small, has its associated artifacts, the objects that the archaeologist uses as indicators of cultural and economic change. Indeed, the finds in each layer—and their associations—often provide the basic material for relative chronology. Furthermore, the relative dating of many sites is complicated by other questions. Has the site been occupied continuously? Do stratigraphic profiles reflect continuous occupation over a long time or a sequence that has been interrupted several times by warfare or simple abandonment of the site? Such problems can be resolved by careful examination of excavated profiles (Figures 6.1, 6.2, and 6.3).

Another factor that may affect interpretation of stratigraphy is the breaks, or disruptions, in the layering caused by human activity and by natural phenomena. These disruptions in a site form a vital part of the context of archaeological data.

Cultural transformations are those resulting from human behavior. For example, later occupants of a village may dig rubbish pits or graves into earlier strata. Cattle may be kept on the site, their hooves removing the soil and disturbing the upper levels of the underlying horizons; this disturbance also may be caused by later people cultivating the rich soils of an abandoned village site. Building activities may cause foundation trenches, and even stone walls, to be sunk into earlier levels. The local inhabitants' technological level has a direct bearing on their ability to destroy evidence of earlier occupation. The inhabitants of a Near Eastern city obviously are more likely to have destroyed evidence of earlier occupation

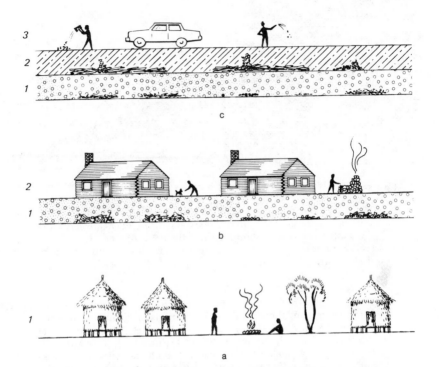

Figure 6.1 Superposition and stratigraphy: (a). A farming village built on virgin subsoil. After a time, the village is abandoned, and the huts fall into disrepair. Their ruins are covered by accumulating soil and vegetation. (b). After an interval, a second village is built on the same site, with different architectural styles. This village in turn is abandoned; the houses collapse into piles of rubble and are covered by accumulating soil. (c). Twentieth-century people park their cars on top of both village sites and drop litter and coins, which, when uncovered, reveal to the archaeologist that the top layer is modern. An archaeologist digging this site would find that the modern layer is underlain by two prehistoric occupation levels; that square houses were in use in the upper of the two, which is the later (law of superposition); and that round huts are stratigraphically earlier than square ones here. Therefore, village 1 is earlier than village 2, but when either was occupied or how many years separate village 1 from 2 cannot be known without further data.

with constant rebuilding than are a group of farmers without metal tools, who merely reoccupy earlier village sites, minimally disturbing the underlying levels. Modern construction activity, road building, or deep plowing can also disturb a site and its contents, as can depredations by pot and treasure hunters, who care not at all about scientifically collected data.

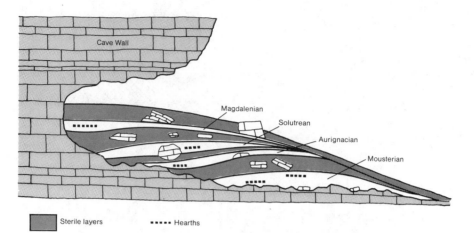

Sterile layers   ▪▪▪▪▪ Hearths

Figure 6.2   An idealized section through an Upper and Middle Paleolithic cave in France. The four archaeological culture layers are separated by sterile layers, the Mousterian being earlier than the Aurignacian, and so on. Most stratigraphic sequences are, of course, much more complicated than this hypothetical one. (After Oakley.)

Figure 6.3   A stratigraphic section through the original town nucleus in Cambridge, England, showing profiles of prehistoric and Roman enclosures and huts with a post hole (P.H.), gullies, and ditches. The complex stratigraphy is interpreted by correlating the various features with their horizontal layers, a difficult task in this case because of the jumbled layers. The lowest ditch was cut into bedrock (E) and was truncated by a later ditch. (One thirty-second actual size.)

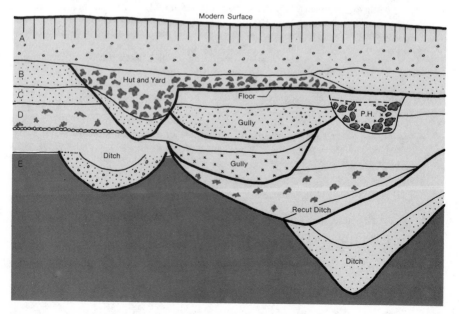

Natural transformations are those caused by natural phenomena. A sudden flood can cover an abandoned village with a thick layer of mud. Volanic ash buried Roman Herculaneum in A.D. 79. Burrowing animals, too, enjoy archaeological sites, working their way through the soft, organic soils of caves and village sites and disrupting stratigraphy over large areas of the settlement. Natural transformations are vital, for they determine the preservation of data. Preservation conditions differ widely from site to site and must be assessed carefully for each location. We must understand conditions of both cultural and natural transformation to precisely interpret archaeological data.

ARTIFACTS AND RELATIVE CHRONOLOGY

Manufactured artifacts are the fundamental data with which archaeologists study human behavior in the past. These artifacts are reflections of ancient human behavior and how it has changed throughout time. You need only look at the simple stone chopper of the earliest human beings and compare it to the latest and most sophisticated digital computer to get the point. Most artifact changes in prehistory, however, are extremely gradual. They are cumulative, minor changes in such elements as, say, shape, decoration, or lip angle of clay pots that lead ultimately to a vessel quite different in form, hardly recognizable as related.

Early Artifact Studies. Early archaeologists closely considered how objects evolved throughout time and studied minute details in these changes. If animals evolved, they argued, why not artifacts as well? As early as 1849, John Evans described the *stater* of Philip II of Macedon (Figure 6.4) and its progressive alteration in the hands of British coiners who had little interest in the Greek prototype (Evans, 1849–50). Evans noticed the degeneration in the design and used it to devise a chronological sequence for the coins. But he and others soon found that in tool design many variables affected changes, among them improved efficiency, stylistic degeneration, or simply popularity. British General Pitt-Rivers was the first to apply *typology*—a method used in natural science to work out relationships in the form and structure of organisms within an evolutionary sequence—to analysis of human-made objects (Pitt-Rivers, 1887). Pitt-Rivers's typologies were based on another important

Figure 6.4   Derivation of the British stater from the stater of Philip II of Macedon, as studied by Sir John Evans. The faces of the original Macedonian coins are at the left.

principle: some technological trends are irreversible. An obvious example is an aeronautical enthusiast who, given a series of photographs of aircraft types dating from the beginnings of aviation up to the present, could place them in approximately correct order, even if he had no idea of the dates of the photographs. It would simply be impossible to envision a typological sequence in which the earliest aircraft was a supersonic jet and the latest a 1912 Blériot monoplane: the modifications needed would be both illogical and incredible.

Another scholar, Egyptologist Sir Flinders Petrie, also contributed much to early study of artifact chronology. In 1902 he wanted to arrange a large number of pre-Dynastic tombs from the Nile Valley in chronological order. He eventually placed them in sequence by studying groups of pots found with the skeletons, so arranging the vessels that their stylistic differences reflected gradual change (Petrie, 1889). The handles on the jars were particularly informative, for they changed from functional appendages into more decorative handles and, finally, degenerated into painted lines. Petrie built up a series of pottery stages at Diospolis Parva to which he assigned "sequence dates," the fifty stages running from SD 30 to SD 80. The SD 30 was the oldest in the group. Petrie started his sequence with the number 30 because he assumed correctly that the earliest of his wares was not, in fact, the most ancient Egyptian pottery. His sequence dates were subsequently applied over wide areas of the Nile Valley, providing an admirable relative chronology for early Egyptian pottery that remained in use for many years. When one found a pot of a known type in the sequence date series, the pot itself and all objects associated with it could be dated to that stage in the sequence.

Seriation. In the past fifty years *seriation,* a technique for ordering items by their morphology, has evolved swiftly. Archaeologists generally use seriation to study relative chronology (Johnson, 1968; Marquardt, 1978). Recent studies of seriation are based on the assumption that popularity for any artifact or culture trait is transient. The miniskirt becomes the midi or maxi, dancing styles change from month to month, records hit the top forty but are forgotten in a short time, and each year's "brand-new" automobile

Figure 6.5 At the left, nine excavated sites (A to I) contain different percentages of three distinct pottery types. At the right, the nine sites have been seriated by rearranging the bars of type percentages into battleship-curve order. At the far right, later excavations are eventually fitted into the sequence.

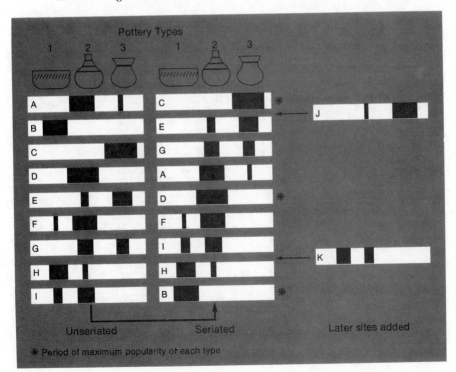

model is soon relegated to the secondhand lot. Other traits may have far longer life. The chopper tools of the earliest people were a major element in early toolkits for hundreds of thousands of years. Candles were used for centuries before kerosene and gas lamps came into fashion. But each had its period of maximum relative frequency, or popularity. Figure 6.5 shows how such popularity distributions are made up with bar graphs plotted against strata or other archaeological associations. Each distribution of artifacts or culture traits plotted has a profile that has been described as resembling a battleship's hull viewed from the air (Figure 6.6).

The technique of seriation is based on the assumption that pop-

Figure 6.6   A seriation graph in the making. Each strip of paper represents a statigraphic unit; the ten columns of black bars are different pottery types. Each strip has the pottery counts for the level plotted on it in bar-graph form. The strips, placed in position with paper clips on graph paper pinned to a backboard, produce the most viable seriated sequence. (The diagram is almost complete.)

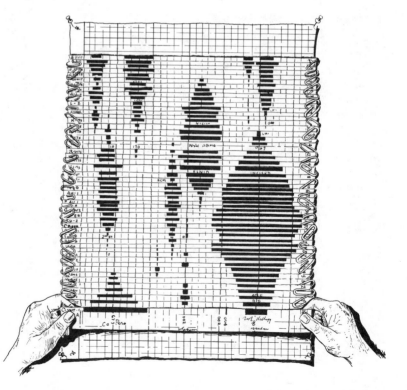

TIME: RELATIVE CHRONOLOGY

ularity of pottery types, forms of stone artifacts, and other culture traits peaks in a battleship curve, the widest part of the graph representing the period of maximum popularity. Thus, it is argued that sites within a restricted and uniform geographic area showing similar plots of pottery or other artifact types are of broadly the same relative date. A series of sites or surface collections can be linked in a relative chronology (even though, without chronometric dates, one cannot tell when they were occupied) provided that the samples of artifacts used are statistically reliable. Edwin Dethlefsen and James Deetz tested the battleship-curve assumption against some historical data, using a series of Colonial gravestones from a New England cemetery (Deetz, 1967; Dethlefsen and Deetz, 1966) (Figure 6.7). The gravestones, dated by the inscriptions on them, show three decorative styles—death's head, cherub, and urn and willow—that yield an almost perfect series of battleship curves following one upon the other. Seriation is also applied to stylistic change in a single series of artifacts that may in themselves form a battleship curve. The same principle used by Petrie with his pre-Dynastic jars applies and a battleship curve results. Once the sequence of artifact types has been established, it is possible to insert new sites or single components from multilevel settlements into the carefully correlated sequence of seriated artifact types. These are added simply by comparing the percentages of types found in the new site with those in the correlated sequence as a whole. The new site is inserted into the sequence with considerable precision, on the assumption that closely similar artifacts were made at approximately the same time and that the lifetime of these tools coincides, albeit approximately, at all sites in a restricted culture area. If the collections are radiocarbon dated, then the seriation can also be given an accurate date in years (Dunnell, 1970).

The so-called battleship-curve seriation method has been widely applied in American archaeology, especially by the late James Ford, who used it extensively in the southeastern United States (Ford, 1962). Figure 6.8 illustrates a fine example of a seriated pottery sequence, that from the Tehuacán Valley in Mexico, famed for its evidence of early cultivation of maize in Mesoamerica (MacNeish, 1970). It shows how three distinctive phases of Tehuacán culture were ordered in a relative chronology with the seriated counts of many pottery types.

You will notice that Figure 6.8 contains no absolute dates; the illustrated seriation is based on changing pottery forms and nothing else. In fact, of course, the chronological validity of the Tehu-

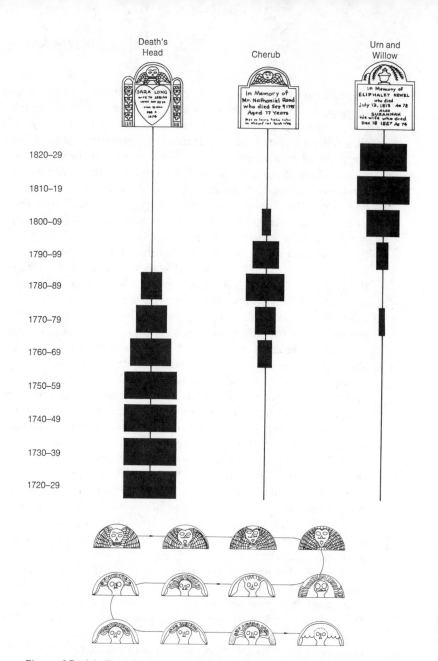

Figure 6.7 (a) Deetz's seriation of stylistic sequences of gravestones in Stoneham, Massachusetts. These dated battleship curves prove that all objects have a period of maximum popularity. (b) Seriation of a stylistic change within one New England gravestone motif. This type of seriation deals with the minute changes in a motif and shows how culture traits change very gradually throughout time.

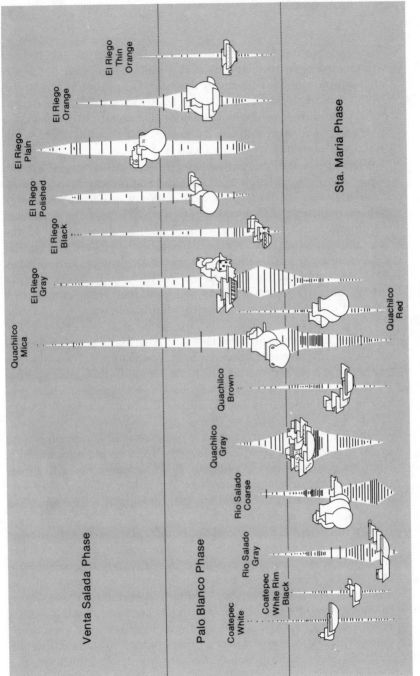

Figure 6.8 The battleship-curve principle was used to develop this seriated ceramic sequence from the Tehuacán Valley in Mexico.

acán sequence has been confirmed by radiocarbon dating. Today's seriators use sophisticated statistical techniques to produce the seriation and to test the viability of their conclusions (Hole and Shaw, 1967; Johnson, 1968; LeBlanc, 1975; Marquardt, 1978). Sound sampling procedures are obviously essential if seriation is to be used extensively and so it is necessary to establish that the samples collected were selected randomly (see Chapter 9).

Although seriation can work well with undated artifact sequences, it works even better when radiocarbon dates or other accurate dating methods are available. When artifact types change rather predictably throughout a period, and these changes are well documented and dated in such a way that the direction of change is established, then it is possible to assign undated sites with similar artifacts to an approximate relative position on the crude time scale. This is the approach pioneered by John Evans. It works well, of course, only when the artifacts being studied are of a type that changed in a distinctive and readily identifiable way.

Cross-Dating. One of the classic relative dating techniques of archaeological research, cross-dating has been applied to many sites in the New and Old worlds. In its classic application, cross-dating is based on dated objects, such as coins or pottery types, whose precise ages are known in the localities of ultimate origin (Childe, 1956).

When a dated artifact, such as a coin, turns up in an otherwise undated prehistoric occupation level far from its place of origin, it is safe to conclude that the horizon was laid down no earlier than the date of the article of known age. An Indian village site in Virginia that yielded an Elizabethan coin bearing the date A.D. 1588 obviously dates to 1588 or later.

Such items as Chinese porcelain, Roman glass vessels, faience or glass beads, cotton and flax fabrics, bronze daggers, and Greek wine amphorae were luxuries that were diffused widely throughout the Old World, often to the barbarian tribes on the fringe of the unknown. The dates of styles of Chinese porcelain or Greek vases, changing according to fashion's dictates, are firmly established in historical records. Such objects are found hundreds and even thousands of miles from the source of manufacture in undated prehistoric camps or trading centers. Because the date of the import is known at its source, the settlement in which it is found can be relatively dated to a period contemporary with, or younger than, the exotic object of known age (Garlake, 1973; Piggott, 1965).

Cross-dating has also been widely applied to sites where objects of known age are absent. In these instances, a well-studied sequence of different artifacts, whose development throughout time has been established by excavation, seriation, and stratigraphy, can be used to fit sites in neighboring areas into the master sequence simply by taking the artifacts in them and matching them with the dated collections from the central area. Perhaps the largest recent study of this type was conducted in the Tehuacán Valley in Mexico, where the excellent artifacts and seriations from Richard MacNeish's many excavations were combined with radiocarbon dates to fix the chronological time span of each cultural phase in the valley (MacNeish, 1970). Armed with the precise chronological sequence, MacNeish's team was able to fit new sites and their artifactual contents into the sequence by both radiocarbon dating and cross-dating of the seriated artifacts in the site. In some instances, the relative chronology established by cross-dated artifacts was more accurate than a radiocarbon date that was out of line with the master chronology established on the massive Tehuacán sequence. This sequence was used as a cross-dating yardstick to correlate sites and cultural sequences all over Mexico. Obviously, individual trade artifacts with a short life at Tehuacán are best for such cross-datings, for their short life gives the cross-dating considerable precision. Artifacts, such as ceramics or stone tools, give less accurate results, for entire pottery styles may be copied ony in part by others or may take time to spread from one area to another. But approximations are better than no relative chronology at all.

Readers interested in the working details of both seriation and cross-dating are referred to the specialist literature (Marquardt, 1978).

Most methods of establishing relative chronology are coarser than is desirable, especially for more complicated sites—and what archaeological site is not complicated? Some researchers have experimented with an exciting new technique, *obsidian hydration*, to sort out associations, artifact orderings, and stratigraphic layers on many kinds of sites. This method, which also has chronometric applications, is described in Chapter 7.

PLEISTOCENE GEOCHRONOLOGY

Most people have heard of the Great Ice Age, known to geologists as the Pleistocene, a period of recent geological time when much of Europe and North America experienced a bitter, arctic climate

(Butzer, 1974, 1982). It was during this period that most of human prehistory was played out—against a background of complex and often dramatic climatic change that radically affected the pattern of human settlement. A relative chronology for human evolution that links archaeological sites with major Pleistocene climatic events can be obtained by studying Pleistocene geochronology (Greek: *geos* = earth + *chronos* = time).

The Ice Age began more than two million years ago and ended, by conventional definition, 8,000 years before Christ, just shortly after the last great glacial period. During this two-million-year period, the world's climate underwent major fluctuations that saw now-temperate Europe exhibit both subtropical and arctic climates within a 100,000-year period. The Arctic and Antarctic ice sheets expanded and contracted as the Pleistocene climate fluctuated from cold to warm and back again. The expanded ice sheets locked up enormous bodies of water, causing world sea levels to fall by several hundred feet. Vast areas of the continental shelf were opened to human settlement. A land bridge joined Siberia and Alaska, a huge flat plain that was traversed by the first hunter-gatherers more than 25,000 years ago (Figure 6.9). The low-lying coastal zones of

Figure 6.9 The Bering Land Bridge as reconstructed by the latest research. (After Jason Smith.)

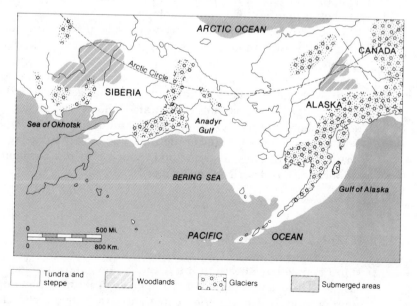

Southeast Asia were far more extensive 15,000 years ago than they are now, and they supported a thriving population of hunter-gatherers. The fluctuations and distributions of vegetation zones also affected the pattern of human settlement and the course of human history.

From the point of view of archaeology, the major climatic events of the last two million years provide an admirable framework for a relative chronology of human culture. Although almost no human beings lived on, or very close to, the great ice sheets that covered so much of the Northern Hemisphere during glacial periods, they did live in regions affected by geological phenomena associated with the ice sheets: coastal areas, long dried-up lakes, and river floodplains. When human artifacts are found in direct association with Pleistocene geological features of this type, it is sometimes possible to tie in archaeological sites with the relative chronology of Pleistocene events derived from geological strata.

Geochronology: Glaciations, Interglacials, and Sea Levels. The glaciers and ice sheets that make up the framework for geochronological studies were formed in mountainous, high-latitude areas, and on continental plains during the Pleistocene. Prolonged periods of arctic climate and abundant snowfall caused glaciers to form over enormous expanses of northern Europe, North America, and the Alpine areas of France, Italy, and Switzerland. At least four times during this period, arctic conditions prevailed over the Northern Hemisphere. These alternated with prolonged *interglacial* phases, when world climate was considerably warmer than it is today.

Every ice sheet had a *periglacial zone*, an area affected by glacial climatic influences. Twenty-five thousand years ago, the persistent glacial anticyclone centered over the northern ice sheet caused dry, frosty winds to blow over the periglacial regions. The dry winds blew fine particles of dust, known as *loess*, onto the huge, rolling plains of central and eastern Europe and northern America.

The loess plains of central and eastern Europe were inhabited by hunter-gatherers who preyed on mammoths and other big game (Klein, 1969). They lived in long houses built of bones and skins that, when excavated, were found at least partially sunk in the loess soil (Figure 6.10). The relative dates of these settlements have been established by correlating the occupation levels with the different periods of loess accumulation that took place during the Pleistocene. Much later, Danubian peoples, the first farmers of temperate

Figure 6.10 Big-game hunters' long houses in western Russia, *ca.* 25,000 years ago. At the top is the plan view of a long house from Kostenki IV, and at the bottom is a reconstruction based on finds at Push Kari. The latter was nearly 12 meters long and 3.7 meters wide and stood in a shallow depression.

Europe, settled almost exclusively on these same light loess soils, for they were eminently suitable for the simple slash-and-burn agriculture practiced by these pioneer farmers (Piggott, 1965).

The ice sheet growing on land had effects beyond formation of loess plains (Buber, 1974). The water that falls as snow to form the ice sheets and glaciers ultimately comes from the oceans. When large areas in the northern latitudes were covered with ice, enormous quantities of water—sufficient to reduce the general level of the oceans by many meters—were immobilized on land. This *eus-*

tatic effect was accompanied by an *isostatic* effect as well. The sheer dead weight of the massive ice sheets sank the loaded continental blocks of the land masses into the viscous underlying layers of the earth that lie some ten kilometers (six miles) below the surface. The isostatic effect was obviously confined to ice-covered areas, but the eustatic effect was felt all over the world. At their maximum, the sea levels of the world may have been lowered as much as 200 meters (660 feet), causing major geographic changes. Until roughly 4500 B.C., Britain was joined to the continent by a strip of marsh, covering the area that is now the North Sea and part of the English Channel (Figure 6.11).

Many prehistoric settlements occupied during periods of low sea level are, of course, buried deep beneath the modern oceans. Numerous sites on ancient beaches have been found dating to times of higher sea level. American archaeologist Richard Klein excavated a coastal cave at Nelson Bay in the Cape Province of South Africa, which now overlooks the Indian Ocean (Klein, 1977). Large quantities of shellfish and other marine animals are found in the uppermost levels of the cave. But in the lower levels, occupied roughly 11,000 to 12,000 years ago, fish bones and other marine

Figure 6.11   Great Britain and Scandinavia at the end of the Pleistocene, showing sea levels *ca.* 7000 B.C.

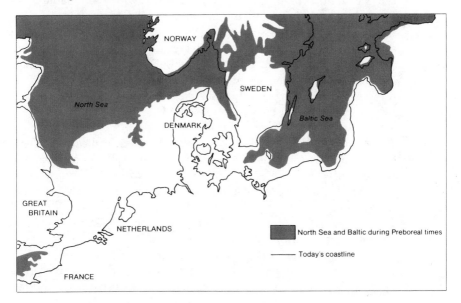

resources are very rare. Klein suspects that the seashore was many miles away at that time, for world sea levels were much lower during a long period of arctic climate in northern latitudes. Today the cave is only 45 meters (50 yards) from the sea.

Animal Bones and Human Evolution.   Stone Age hunters killed many species of large and small mammals for food, whose broken bones are often preserved in river gravels, living floors, and other sites. The animals hunted most often were species that are now extinct, such as the giant pigs and buffalo found at Olduvai Gorge in Tanzania. Paleontologists have classified Pleistocene faunas from many localities, often using the remains of these animals, and they have tried to build a very simple relative chronology of mammal types throughout the Pleistocene.

It has been found that large mammals evolved rapidly during the last five million years. Elephants, for example, changed radically during each European interglacial (Oakley, 1969). The evolving species can be distinguished by the distinctive cusp patterns of their teeth (Figure 6.12).

Unfortunately, however, the use of vertebrate fauna for dating is severely limited by the difficulty of identifying different mammal species. Animals vary in sensitivity to climatic change: some are tolerant of both cold and warm climates; others prefer warm weather but can stand exceedingly low temperatures with remarkable resilience. Furthermore, so many environmental factors affect the distribution of mammals and the success of one species at the expense of another that it is very difficult to be sure that one is dealing with a chronological, not an environmental, difference. But, with early Pleistocene sites, the uses of animal bones as chronological indicators are magnified simply because enormous time scales are involved and minor details are obscured.

Pollen Analysis.   Vegetation is one of the best indicators of ecological change, for it depends on climate and soil for survival and is a sensitive barometer of climatic alteration. Pollen analysis, or *palynology*, is a comprehensive way of studying ancient vegetation; it was developed in 1916 by a Swede, Lennart van Post, who used forest trees. Subsequently, this analysis was extended to all pollen-liberating vegetation. The principle of pollen analysis is simple (Faegri and Iverson, 1966). Large numbers of pollen grains are dispersed in the atmosphere and have remarkable preservative properties if deposited in an unaerated geological horizon. The pollen

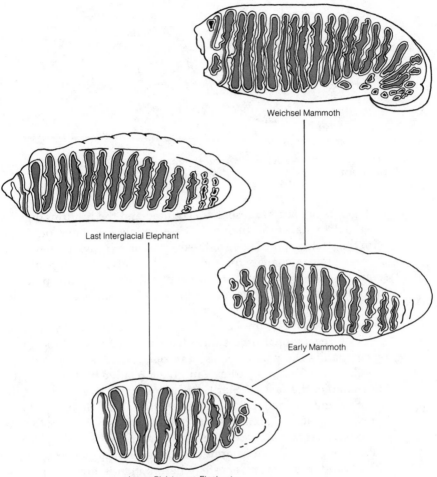

Weichsel Mammoth

Last Interglacial Elephant

Early Mammoth

Lower Pleistocene Elephant

Figure 6.12   Grinding surfaces of the third upper molars of four types of Pleistocene elephant, illustrating the differences in enamel patterns from earlier (bottom) to later (top) types. (After Oakley; one-fifth actual size.)

grains can be identified microscopically (Figure 6.13) with great accuracy and used to reconstruct a picture of the vegetation that grew near the spot where they are found.

Pollen analysis begins in the field. The botanist visits the excavation and collects a series of closely-spaced pollen samples from the stratigraphic sections at the site. Back in the laboratory, the samples are examined under a very powerful microscope. The grains of

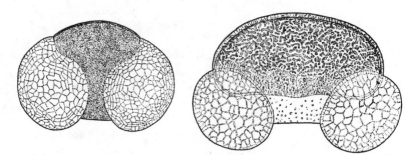

Figure 6.13   Pollen grains: left, spruce; right, silver fir. (After Oakley; both 340 times acual size.)

each genus or species present are counted and the resulting figures subjected to statistical analysis. These counts are then correlated with the stratigraphic layers of the excavation to provide a sequence of vegetational change for the site. Typically, this vegetational sequence lasts a few centuries or even millennia. It forms part of a much longer pollen sequence for the area that has been assembled from hundreds of samples from many different sites. In northern Europe, for example, the botanists have worked out a complicated series of vegetational time zones that cover the past 10,000 years. By comparing the pollen sequences from individual sites with the overall zone chronology, they can give a relative date for the site. For example, the famous Star Carr hunter-gatherer sites in northeast England yielded pollen samples that placed it in the "Pre-Boreal" vegetational zone of some 10,000 years ago. This was a time when birch trees dominated the local landscape.

Palynology has obvious applications to prehistory, for sites are often found in swampy deposits where pollen is preserved, especially fishing or fowling camps and settlements near water. Isolated artifacts, or even human corpses (such as that of Tollund man found in a Danish bog), have also been discovered in these deposits; pollen is sometimes obtained from small peat lumps adhering to crevices in such finds. Thus, botanists can assign relative dates even to isolated finds that otherwise would remain undated. An archaeological site having a pollen graph coinciding with that of a particular vegetational zone clearly belongs within that period. An example appears in Figure 6.14.

Pollen analysis has important applications for later prehistory as well. Improved recovery and excavation methods have opened up all sorts of new possibilities. Southwestern archaeologists now have

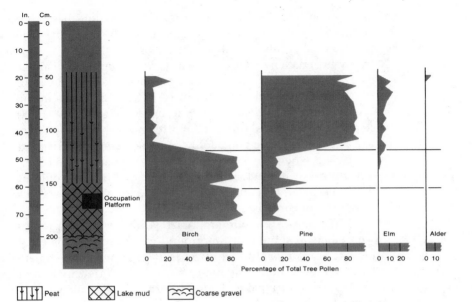

In. Cm.

Occupation Platform

Birch   Pine   Elm   Alder

0 20 40 60 80   0 20 40 60 80   0 10 20   0 10

Percentage of Total Tree Pollen

Peat   Lake mud   Coarse gravel

Figure 6.14   A simplified pollen diagram from a hunter-gatherer campsite at Star Carr, England, showing the changes in vegetational cover around the site from about 9000 B.C. up to *ca.* 6500 B.C. At the left is a vertical scale in inches and centimeters. Beside it is a column indicating the geological layers found at that spot on the site. The occupation level, which has been radiocarbon dated to about 7800 B.C., is shown at a depth of 160–170 cm. At the right are separate graphs, showing the proportions of four major tree types through the years. During the occupation of the site, birch trees were the dominant species near the lake, where the people lived. Pine trees were fairly common, too, but elm and alder, both trees associated with warmer weather, were almost non-existent. In about 7000 B.C. the proportion of birch trees fell sharply, the pine cover increased rapidly, and elms became much more common. At the end of the sequence pine trees were being supplanted by elms and a few alders, and the birch trees were much rarer.

a regional pollen sequence that provides not only climatic information but also invaluable facts about the functions of different pueblo rooms and different foods that were eaten by the Indians.

Identifying cultural activities from pollen in archaeological sites can be extremely tricky, for the tiny grains can be transported to the site in many ways—by wind, water, rodents, even people bringing ripe fruit home. Sometimes, too, people will use surface soil from neighboring areas, complete with its pollen content, to make a house floor. Some species like the sunflower have heavy pollen that can cling to ripe fruit. Such factors are likely to contaminate the pollen samples from many sites, unless one has other plant evidence, such as, say, squash rind or seeds, to confirm the palynological data (Bohrer, 1981; Gish, 1979).

Nevertheless, pollen analysis has many promising cultural applications. Pollen samples from pueblo rooms at Broken K pueblo in eastern Arizona were even used to place individual rooms in the correct chronologcial order. James Hill and Richard Hevly (1968) collected pollen samples from about fifty rooms in the pueblo, which was occupied, tree rings told them, between A.D. 1100 and 1300—a period when the area was gradually losing its tree cover. By correlating the individual pollen samples with the profile of declining tree cover, Hill and Hevly were able to place the various rooms in order of construction.

At the Lehner site in southern Arizona, three pollen profiles were combined to show that the ground cover around this early hunting site was probably that of a desert grassland. The climate seems to have been much the same as it is today (Mehringer and Haynes, 1965). So much palynological information is available from the Southwest that it may be possible to place individual sites in their correct relative chronological position in the vegetational sequence with pollen frequencies in samples taken from the undated site.

Relative chronology is an invaluable tool for archaeological research. Unfortunately, however, it does not provide accurate dates in years, the ultimate objective of all chronological research. Chapter 7 outlines the major methods used to date archaeological sites in calendar years.

Guide to Further Reading

Brothwell, D. R., and Eric Higgs, eds. *Science in Archaeology*, 2nd ed. New York: Praeger, 1969.
Essays on dating and other scientific approaches to archaeology. Some articles cover relative chronolgy.

Butzer, Karl. *Environment and Archaeology*, 2nd ed. Chicago: Aldine, 1974.
The fundamental synthesis of Pleistocene geochronology; recommended for advanced readers.

Butzer, Karl. *Archeology as Human Ecology*. Cambridge: Cambridge University Press, 1982.
Excellent on the basics of geoarchaeology, especially environmental context.

Deetz, James. *Invitation to Archaeology*. Garden City, N.Y.: Natural History Press, 1967.
The best account of seriation for the lay reader yet written, by someone closely involved with basic research in this field.

Taylor, R. E., and C. Meighan, eds. *Chronologies in New World Archaeology*. New York: Academic Press, 1978.
Articles on chronology in American archaeology; up to date and informative.

CHAPTER 7 🌿

TIME: CHRONOMETRIC DATING

Preview

- Although historical records provide a fairly accurate chronology for much of the past 5,000 years, archaeologists rely heavily on chemical and physical chronometric dating methods.
- Potassium argon methods are used for dating the earliest human beings. These can be used to determine dates from the origins of the earth up to about 400,000 years ago. This radioactive counting method is based on measuring accumulations of argon 40 in volcanic rocks. It has been used to date Olduvai Gorge and other early sites to between one and three million years ago.
- Radiocarbon dating is the most widely used method. It can be applied at sites from between 75,000 and 400 years ago. Based on the rate at which carbon 14 decays to nitrogen in organic objects, it can be used to date many such materials as charcoal and bone and even skin and leather. The accuracy of radiocarbon dating is subject to statistical errors, owing to past variations in the carbon 14 content of the atmosphere, and thus has to be calibrated against tree-ring chronologies.
- Fission track dating is done by measuring the uranium content of many minerals and volcanic glasses and examining the fission tracks left in the material by fragmentation of massive concentrations of energy-charged particles. It can be applied in sites

between a million and 100,000 years old, where volcanic rocks are found in human-occupied levels.

- The annual sedimentary layers, or varves, in melting and retreating glaciers in the Americas and Scandinavia provide a means for dating geological events at the end of the Ice Age.
- Thermoluminescence may prove to be a method for dating potsherds, in which the baked clay has trapped electrons; these are released for measurement by sudden and intense heating under controlled conditions. The visible light rays emitted during heating are known as thermoluminescence. This method is still highly experimental.
- Dendrochronology (tree-ring dating) has its principal application in the American Southwest. It provides an accurate chronology for about 2,000 years of southwestern prehistory, and has many uses on more recent sites in Europe and elsewhere. Dendrochronologists count the annual growth rings in trees such as the bristlecone pine, and correlate them into long sequences of growth years that are joined to a master chronology. Wooden beams and other archaeological wood fragments are correlated with this master chronology to provide accurate dates for pueblos and other sites.
- Archaeomagnetic dating can be used to date clay samples from furnaces and other features, by measuring the thermoremanent magnetism of the clay and correlating it with records of changes in the earth's magnetic field. It is mainly used to date pottery kilns and similar structures dating to the last 500 years, for which changes in the magnetic field have been recorded.
- Historical records and calendars developed by such people as the Ancient Egyptians and the Maya are of immense value for dating their literate civilizations. A great deal of valuable chronological information can also be obtained from objects of known age, such as clay pipe or coins. But again, these objects are confined to the most recent periods of human history.

More effort has been devoted to inventing methods of chronometric dating in archaeology than to almost any other aspect of the subject. The reason for this interest is that fundamental questions about the past are involved. How old is this tool? How long ago was that site occupied? Are these villages contemporary? These are probably the first questions asked by anyone curious about an artifact or a prehistoric village, as well as by the archaeologist. They remain among the most difficult to answer.

We now have an impressive array of chronological techniques for dating the past. Some have become well-established and are reliable. Others, after a brief vogue, have been ejected into academic

Table 7.1 Chronological spans of major chronometric methods in archaeology.

oblivion when someone discovers a fatal flaw. In practice, the huge span of human cultural history is dated by a number of scientific methods; the chronological span is shown in Table 7.1. Potassium argon dating provides a somewhat generalized chronology for the first two-thirds of human history, its recent limits reaching up to some 400,000 years ago. The other major radioactive technique, radiocarbon dating, covers a period from approximately 75,000 years ago up to as recently as A.D. 1500, when the standard errors are too large compared with the small time spans. No one has yet devised a dating method to cover the 350,000 years or so between the outer limits of radiocarbon dating and the beginnings of potassium argon chronology.

As for recent periods, historical documents provide a fairly accurate chronology for kings and political events going back more than 5,000 years in the Near East and shorter periods elsewhere in the world. In the New World, prehistory ends with European settlement of the Americas in the fifteenth century. Frequently in these more recent periods archaeology can be used in conjunction with historical documents or oral records, and they are covered by many other dating methods, including imported objects of known historical date and dendrochronology. Dates in years not only tell how old a site is, but also illuminate the relationships between communities, cultures, or larger geographic or social units.

CHEMICAL AND PHYSICAL METHODS OF DATING

Let us now look at the principal methods of chronometric dating used to develop absolute chronologies for world prehistory. Our discussion starts with the chemical and physical methods used to date the earlier millennia of prehistory and ends in modern times with objects of known age.

POTASSIUM ARGON DATING

Principles. The only viable means of chronometrically dating the earliest archaeological sites is the potassium argon method (Dalrymple and Lamphere, 1970). Geologists use this radioactive counting technique to date rocks as old as 2 billion years and as recent as

400,000 years ago. Potassium (K) is one of the most abundant elements in the earth's crust and is present in nearly every mineral. In its natural form, potassium contains a small proportion of radioactive ^{40}K atoms. For every 100 ^{40}K atoms that decay, 11 become argon 40, an inactive gas that can easily escape from its material by diffusion when lava and other igneous rocks are formed. As volcanic rock forms by crystallization, the concentration of argon 40 drops to almost nothing. But regular and reasonable decay of ^{40}K will continue, with a half-life of 1.3 billion years. It is possible, then, to measure the concentration of argon 40 that has accumulated since the rock formed with a spectrometer. Because many archaeological sites were occupied during a period when extensive volcanic activity occurred, especially in East Africa, it is possible to date them by associations of lava with human settlements.

Datable Materials and Procedures. Potassium argon dates have been obtained from many igneous minerals, of which the most resistant to later argon diffusion are biotite, muscovite, and sanidine. Microscopic examination of the rock is essential to eliminate the possibility of contamination by recrystallization and other processes. The samples are processed by crushing the rock, concentrating it, and treating it with hydrofluoric acid to remove any atmospheric argon from the sample. The various gases are then removed from the sample and the argon gas is isolated and subjected to mass spectrographic analysis. The age of the sample is then calculated using the argon 40 and ^{40}K content and a standard formula. The resulting date is quoted with a large standard deviation—for early Pleistocene sites, on the order of a quarter of a million years.

Archaeological Applications. Fortunately, many early human settlements in the Old World are found in volcanic areas, where such deposits as lava flows and tuffs are found in profusion.

The first archaeological date, and one of the most dramatic, obtained from this method came from Olduvai Gorge, Tanzania, where Louis and Mary Leakey found a long sequence of human culture extending over much of the Lower and Middle Pleistocene, associated with human fossils. Olduvai, a jagged slash in the Serengeti Plains, was formed by movement and erosion of earth, exposing the beds of a long-forgotten Pleistocene lake overlying a layer of volcanic tuff. Early humans camped around the shores of the lake; their living floors are preserved in the sides of the gorge, and their implements and broken animal bones lie where they were dropped by their owners, to be preserved under layers of fine lake silt. The remains of early humans have been found on the living floors, associated with the tools and bones, together with lumps of lava. Some layers overlying and underlying the floors have been dated by the potassium argon technique. Samples from a living floor where the first cranium of *Australopithecus boisei* was discovered were dated to about 1.75 million years (Figure 7.1) (Tobias, 1971). At the time, these and other nearly contemporary dates were a sensation, for most people had imagined that the Pleistocene began about a million years ago. With one discovery, humanity had almost doubled its antiquity. Even earlier dates have come from the Omo Valley in southern Ethiopia, where American, French, and Kenyan expeditions have investigated extensive Lower Pleistocene deposits long known for their rich fossil beds. Fragmentary Australopithecines were found at several localities, but no trace of tools; potassium argon dates gave readings between 2 and 4 million years for deposits yielding hominid fossils. Tools were found in levels between 2 and 2.5 million years. Chopper tools of undoubted human manufacture have come from Koobi Fora in northern

Figure 7.1 Skull of *Australopithecus boisei,* with reconstructed jaw, from Bed I at Olduvai Gorge, Tanzania, pottasium argon dated to about 1.75 million years ago.

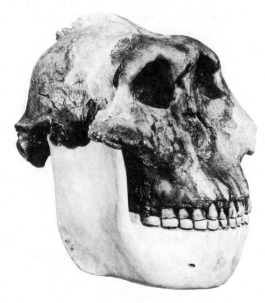

Kenya, dated to about 1.85 million years, one of the earliest for human artifacts (Curtis, 1975).

Limitations. Potassium argon dates can be taken only from volcanic rocks, and preferably from actual volcanic flows. The laboratory technique is so specialized that only a trained geologist should take the samples in the field. Archaeologically, it is obviously vital that the relationship between the lava being dated and the human settlement it purports to date be worked out carefully. The standard deviations for potassium argon dates are so large that higher accuracy is almost impossible to achieve.

Chronological Limits (Table 7.1). Potassium argon dating is accurate from the origins of the earth up to about 400,000 years before the present.

RADIOCARBON DATING

Principles. Radiocarbon dating is perhaps the best known and most widely used of all chronometric dating methods. J. R. Arnold and W. F. Libby published a paper in *Science* describing the dating of organic samples from objects of known age by their radiocarbon content (Arnold and Libby, 1949). The paper caused an archaeological furor, but once checked, it was soon applied to organic materials from prehistoric sites hitherto undatable by any reliable chronometric method. More than thirty years have elapsed since the radiocarbon dating method became a regular part of the archaeologist's toolkit. For the first time we begin to have a world chronology for prehistory, based almost entirely on dates obtained by Libby's technique.

The radiocarbon dating method is based on the fact that cosmic radiation produces neutrons that enter the earth's atmosphere and react with nitrogen. They produce carbon 14, a carbon isotope with fourteen rather than the usual twelve neutrons in the nucleus. With these additional neutrons, the nucleus is unstable and is subject to gradual radioactive decay. Willard Libby calculated that it took 5,568 years for half the carbon 14 in any sample to decay, its so-called half-life. He found that the neutrons emitted radioactive particles when they left the nucleus and arrived at a method for counting the number of emissions in a gram of carbon.

Carbon 14 is believed to behave exactly like ordinary carbon from a chemical standpoint, and together with ordinary carbon it enters into the carbon dioxide of the atmosphere, in which a constant amount of carbon 14 is to be found. The tempo of the process corresponds to the rates of supply and disintegration. Because living vegetation builds up its own organic matter by photosynthesis and by using atmospheric carbon dioxide, the proportion of radiocarbon present in it is equal to that in the atmosphere. The very short lifetime of individual plants is negligible compared with the half-life of radiocarbon. As soon as an organism dies, no further radiocarbon is incorporated into it. The radiocarbon present in the dead organism will continue to disintegrate slowly, so that after 5,568 years only half the original amount will be left; after about 11,100 years, only a quarter; and so on. Thus, if you measure the rate of disintegration of carbon 14 to carbon 12, you can get an idea of the age of the specimen being measured. The initial amount of radiocarbon in a sample is so small that the limit of detectability is soon reached. Samples earlier than 75,000 years contain only miniscule quantities of carbon 14 (Grootes, 1978).

Datable Materials and Procedures. Radiocarbon dates can be taken from samples of many organic materials. About a handful of charcoal, burnt bone, shell, hair, skin, wood, or other organic substance is needed. The samples themselves are collected with meticulous care during excavation from impeccable stratigraphic contexts, so that an exact location, specific structure, or even a hearth is dated. Several dates must be taken from each level, because one or more may have been contaminated by a variety of factors. Modern rootlets, disturbances in the stratigraphy, and even packing with cotton wool or newspaper can introduce younger carbon into an ancient sample, although some of the more obvious contaminations are eliminated by careful laboratory treatment.

The first stage in the dating procedure is physical examination of the sample. The material is then converted into gas, purified to remove radioactive contaminants, and then piped into a proportional counter (Figure 7.2). The counter itself is sheltered from background radiation by massive iron shields. The sample is counted at least twice at intervals of about a week. The results of the count are then compared to a modern count sample, and the age of the sample is computed by a formula to produce the radiocarbon date and its statistical limit of error.

Figure 7.2   A radiocarbon laboratory at the University Museum, University of Pennsylvania. Left: The equipment used to purify the sample and convert it to gas. Right: The equipment used for measuring radioactivity.

A date received from a radiocarbon dating laboratory is in this form:

3,621 ± 180 radiocarbon years before present (B.P.)

The figure 3,621 is the age of the sample (in radiocarbon years) before the present. With all radiocarbon dates, A.D. 1950, the date on which Libby announced the method, is taken as the present by international agreement. Notice that the sample reads in *radiocarbon years,* not calendar years. Corrections must be applied to make this an absolute date.

The radiocarbon age has the reading ±180 attached to it. This is the *standard deviation,* an estimate of the amount of probable error. The figure 180 years is an estimate of the 360-year range within which the date falls. Statistical theory provides that there is a 2 out of 3 chance that the correct date is between the span of one standard deviation (3441 and 3801). If we double the deviation, chances are 19 out of 20 that the span (3261 and 3981) is correct. Most dates in this book are derived from carbon 14 dated samples and should be recognized for what they are—statistical approximations.

The conventional radiocarbon method relies on measurements of a beta-ray decay rate to date the sample. A number of laboratories are now experimenting with an ultrasensitive mass spectrometer to count the individual carbon 14 atoms in a sample instead. This exciting new approach has numerous advantages and promises to overcome many disadvantages in the traditional method. One can date much smaller samples—as small as a fragment of straw in a potsherd—and the results will be more accurate than conventional readings. It takes only a few minutes to measure samples that hitherto took hours to study. The practical limits of radiocarbon dating with beta decay approaches are between 40,000 and 60,000 years. Researchers have tried enriching samples by thermal diffusion or laser excitation, and have dated organic materials at between 50,000 and 75,000 B.P., but the method is very time-consuming. An alternative is to detect carbon 14 atoms directly with a particle accelerator, a technique that could extend the limits of radiocarbon dating to as much as 100,000 years, although at present its limits, mainly because of contamination by roots, are around 70,000 years (Browman, 1981).

Archaeological Applications. Radiocarbon dates have been obtained from African hunter-gatherers' settlements as long as 50,000 years before the present, from Paleo-Indian bison kills in the American Plains, from early farming villages in the Near East and the Americas, and from cities and spectacular temples associated with early civilizations. The method can be applied to sites of almost any type where organic materials are found, provided they date to between about 75,000 years ago and A.D. 1500.

Limitations. Radiocarbon dates can be obtained only from organic materials, which means that relatively few artifacts can be dated. But associated hearths with abundant charcoal, broken animal bones, and burnt wooden structures can be dated. Artifacts contemporary with such phenomena are obviously of the same age as the dated samples. The context of any dated sample has to be established beyond all doubt, and having a block of samples from the same division is preferable, so that they can be treated statistically and tested for probable degree of accuracy. It is the moment of death of an organism that is dated. All radiocarbon dates are, of course, statistical computations, and if uncalibrated, merely the radiocarbon age that is statistically most likely.

Calibration of Radiocarbon Dates. Just when archaeologists thought they had at last found an accurate and reliable means for dating the past, radiocarbon dates for tree rings of the California bristlecone pine were published. The readings were consistently younger for trees before 1200 B.C., because Libby made a false assumption when he originally formulated the radiocarbon method. He had argued that the concentration of radiocarbon in living things remained constant as time passed, so that prehistoric samples, when alive, would have contained the same amount of radiocarbon as living things today.

In fact, changes in the strength of the earth's magnetic field and alterations in solar activity have considerably varied the concentration of radiocarbon in the atmosphere and in living things. Thus, samples of 6,000 years ago were exposed to a much higher concentration than are living things today. It is possible, fortunately, to correct radiocarbon dates by using accurate dates from tree rings. Since 1966, dendrochronology experts have been systematically applying radiocarbon analysis to tree-ring samples of known age and have plotted calibration curves, which are used for converting radiocarbon dates into actual dates in years. A task force of radiocarbon experts has recently produced tables that match radiocarbon ages with calibrated dates (Klein, Lerman, and others, 1982). This tool is likely to receive universal acceptance in coming years; it calibrates dates between A.D. 1950 and 6500 B.C. The discrepancies between radiocarbon and calibrated dates differ widely. Here is an example: 10 B.C. ± 30 has a calibrated interval of 145 B.C. to A.D. 210. British archaeologist Colin Renfrew calibrated radiocarbon dates for European prehistory some years ago. He claimed that as a result many long-accepted chronological relationships are now reversed (Renfrew, 1973). According to him, the famous megalithic stone-built tombs of western Europe are older than the pyramids of Egypt, supposedly their predecessors. The final layout of Stonehenge constructed in 1600 B.C. (the complex of prehistoric stone circles in southern Britain), was originally thought to have been inspired by Mycenaean designs. When the calibrated dates were released, it was found that the earliest stages of Stonehenge dated to before 1800 B.C., much older than the Mycenaean civilization in question. The new, calibrated radiocarbon chronology for Europe, argues Renfrew, allows us to think of distinctive European societies that developed their own institutions without the Oriental influence favored by so many archaeologists. Few prehistorians have jumped so wholeheartedly into the new chronologies as Renfrew, but widespread calibration of radiocarbon dates is certain to be a reality within a few years. In the meantime, most people think of radiocarbon dates as nothing more than *radiocarbon ages*—not dates in actual years. Earlier dates will remain radiocarbon ages of unknown accuracy, because as yet we have no means of extending dendrochronology further back into the past.

Chronological Limits (Table 7.1). Carbon 14 dating is accurate from *ca*. 75,000 years B.P. to A.D. 1500.

FISSION TRACK DATING

Principles. Fission track dating is a new chronometric method that promises to have important archaeological applications in the future. The principle of the method is that many minerals and natural glasses, such as obsidian, contain very small quantities of uranium that undergoes slow, spontaneous decay. Most uranium atoms decay by emitting alpha particles, but spontaneous fission causes the decay of about one atom in every two million. The fission decay rate and its extent are constant, and the date of any mineral containing uranium can be obtained by measuring the amount of uranium in the sample, which is done by counting the *fission tracks* in the material. These tracks are narrow trails of damage in the material caused by fragmentation of massive, energy-charged particles. The older the sample, the more tracks it has. It is possible to examine fission tracks under high magnification and to calculate the sample's age by establishing the ratio between the density of the tracks and the uranium content of the sample.

Datable Materials and Procedures. Two counts of fission tracks are needed for each sample. The materials used, which must have a high uranium content, can be either volcanic rock, as in lava flows that originated more recently than the beginnings of prehistory, or manufactured materials, such as certain types of artificial glass. In rocks, it is the time of origin of the rocks that is being dated, not the time of their utilization. An optical microscope is used to examine the tracks in the sample, which have first been etched with hydrofluoric acid. This procedure enlarges the tracks to make them more visible. The first count establishes the density of the tracks, the second, by inducing fission of uranium 235 through neutron irradiation, makes a count of the uranium content in the sample. The age of the sample is the ratio between the number of observed tracks resulting from natural fission to those resulting from induced fission.

Archaeological Applications.   The fission track dating technique is still new to archaeology, but it promises to become a fairly precise means of dating samples between 100,000 and 1,000,000 years old. The method can be used to date many mineralogical materials, but in archaeology it is applicable only to sites that were subjected to volcanic activity just before, during, or shortly after occupation. Sites overlain or underlain by lava can be given upper or lower age limits by dating the lava. Because many early sites are found in volcanic areas, such as the Great Rift Valley of East Africa, the method has obvious applications.

Few results from the fission track method have been published, but volcanic pumice from Bed I at Olduvai Gorge, where the early hominid fossils were found, was dated to 2.03 ± 0.28 million by the fission track method. This reading was in reasonably close agreement with Leakey's original date of about 1.8 million years, obtained from potassium argon readings for the same stratum. In another case, modern manufactured glass with high uranium content, used to make a nineteenth-century candlestick, was dated accurately to the last century (Brill, 1964; Fleischer, 1975).

Limitations.   The limitations of fission track dating are much the same as those of potassium argon dating. Only volcanic rocks contemporary with a human settlement and formed at the time the site was occupied can be used.

Chronological Limits (see Table 7.1).   Fission track dating is accurate from one million to 100,000 years before the present. Some limited application to historic artifacts is possible as well.

OBSIDIAN HYDRATION

Principles.   Obsidian is a natural-glass substance often formed by volcanic activity. It has long been prized for its sharp edges and other excellent qualities for toolmaking. Projectile heads, hand axes, blades, and even mirrors were made from this widely traded material in both the New World and the Old World. A new dating method makes use of the fact that a freshly made surface of obsidian (and no other known artifact material) will absorb water from its surroundings, forming a measurable *hydration layer* that is invisible to the naked eye. Because the freshly exposed surface has a strong affinity for water, it keeps absorbing until it is saturated with a layer of water molecules. These molecules then slowly diffuse into the body of the obsidian. This hydration zone contains about 3.5 percent water, increasing the density of the layer and allowing it to be measured accurately under polarized light. Each time a freshly fractured surface is prepared, as when a tool is being made, the hydration begins again from scratch. Thus, the depth of hydration achieved represents the time since the object was manufactured or used.

Hydration is observed with microscopically thin sections of obsidian sliced from artifacts and ground down to about .003 inch. The thickness of the layer is measured through the microscope at eight spots, the mean value being calibrated into units of microns. These thickness readings can be used in both absolute and relative chronologies (Taylor and Meighan, 1978; Michels and Tsong, 1980). Unfortunately, this promising dating method has some problems, mostly because we still do not fully understand hydration. Little is known about how temperature changes or chemical composition affect hydration, and so it is impossible to use the method without calibrating it against tree-ring dates or some other established archaeological procedure. Researchers are working hard to solve these problems so that obsidian hydration can become an economical and widely applicable dating method in the future.

Archaeological Applications.   Obsidian hydration is a useful way of ordering large numbers of artifacts in relative series, simply by positioning each in the series according to its micron reading, such as 1.5 or 2.0. Provided one has control over such constants as chemical composition, one can place artifacts in order with great precision. This approach was first tried at the Mammoth Junction site in Colorado, which served not only as a quarry site but as a residential settlement and hunting station. By assigning some 450 artifacts such as projectile heads and scrapers positions in a series, the investigators were able to find the order in which 37 types of projectile point came into fashion and disappeared. The chronological data could be linked to attributes like weight or length: all six of the latest styles weighed less than a gram, as if they had been used not for spears but for much ligher arrows.

Obsidian hydration is extremely useful for sorting out the cultural content of sites like shell middens, in which the stratigraphic layers are often indistinct and the site is excavated in arbitrary levels. By plotting the hydration values from obsidian artifacts against the excavated layers on a three-dimensional scatter diagram, you can sometimes identify how much the arbitrary excavation has mixed artifacts from different levels. Another possible application has researchers using hydration readings to associate artifacts found on a living surface with one another in groups. Using arbitrary ranges of hydration readings, say 1.5 to 1.9, one can group obsidian tools into units useful for analysis, with little or no possibility of contamination with other tools. This technique is particularly useful on surface sites.

Applications of obsidian hydration to chronometric chronology are still in their infancy. If one can determine the rate of hydration in a population of artifacts, then there is a chance that one can assign each artifact a date in years. More than 2,000 obsidian dates were obtained from 520 test trenches at the city of Kaminaljuyu in Guatemala. These, and a further 2,000 samples from surrounding sites, were used to piece together dozens of phases in the complicated residential history of the site and its satellite communities. Many of the dated artifacts came from surface sites, where they were the only possible source of chronological information. The same approach was used at the Aztec site of Chiconautla in the Basin of Mexico. This was known to be an important Aztec community. But the excavators were able to use obsidian hydration to show that the large numbers of rasp-ended scrapers found at Chiconautla were in fact used for maguey cactus cultivation long before the Aztec community flourished on the site (Michels and Bebrich, 1971).

Limitations.   Obsidian hydration is potentially as useful as radiocarbon dating, but it still suffers from grave limitations, especially when one is dealing with very early sites. Obsidian itself is of very limited distribution. Hydration layers more than 50 microns thick are known to "peel off," and reaching this thickness may take longer in some areas than others. Many of the world's earliest archaeological sites have yielded obsidian, and the method has been tried experimentally with East African settlements 300,000 to 780,000 years old. Should the method be validated for sites this old, then it will have far wide application than potassium argon and radiocarbon dating.

Chronological Limits. The reach of hydration dating is from recent times to (?)800,000 years ago (see Table 7.1). Until such chronometric dating methods as potassium argon, fission track, and radiocarbon were available, the chronology of major events in the Pleistocene epoch was mostly uncertain, despite many efforts to develop viable time scales.

VARVES

Accurate chronology for parts of the Pleistocene is arrived at by counting varves, the layers of silt (mud) deposited annually in glacial lakes by runoff from melting ice sheets (Zeuner, 1958). As long ago as 1878, Swedish geologist Baron Gerard DeGeer recorded this phenomenon and began a chronology for retreating ice sheets at the end of the Pleistocene, a time scale that in places now extends back as far as 17,000 years. Varve dating is applicable only where ice sheets were present during the Pleistocene and where it is possible to assemble a continuous varve chronology from modern times to link up with Pleistocene varves. Although experiments with varve chronology have been attempted in North America, Africa, and South America, the method's main application is in Scandinavia, for dating the closing stages of the Pleistocene. Archaeological sites are rarely dated by varve readings, for Pleistocene settlements near glacial lakes are very uncommon. But it is sometimes possible to correlate varve sequences with other Pleistocene features associated with human occupation.

THERMOLUMINESCENCE

Principles, Datable Materials, and Procedures. Thermoluminescence, a method for dating pottery with a formidable-sounding name, is still in the developmental stage (Aitken, 1977; Fleming, 1979). It has much promise and may one day provide absolute dating even for isolated potsherds. The principle is simple. The materials from which pottery is made have the property of storing energy by trapping electrons as atomic defects or impurity sites. This stored energy can be released by heating the pottery, at which time visible light rays, known as thermoluminescence, are emitted.

All pottery and ceramics contain some radioactive impurities at a concentration of several parts per million. These materials emit alpha particles at a known rate, depending on how densely concentrated they are in the sample. When an alpha particle is absorbed by the pottery minerals around the radioactive impurities, it causes mineral atoms to ionize. Electrons are then released from their binding to the nuclei and later settle at a metastable (relatively unstable) stage of higher energy. This energy is stored, unless the parent material is heated—as when the pot is being fired—when the trapped electrons are released and thermoluminescence occurs. After the pot is fired, alpha particles are again absorbed by the material, and the thermoluminescence increases until the pot is heated again. Thus, a clay vessel is dated by measuring the thermoluminescence of the sample, as well as its alpha-radioactivity and its potential susceptibility to producing thermoluminescence. In the laboratory, the trapped electrons are released from a powdered pottery fragment by sudden and violent heating under controlled conditions.

Archaeological Applications and Limitations. The method is still being perfected, and numerous factors affect its accuracy. As with other dating methods, results have been obtained initially from vessels of known age; because of these results, several investigators claim accuracies of ±10 percent for prehistoric dates; other proponents of the method are more cautious, however. The potential of thermoluminescence will not be fully assessed for some time; but its future use could be unlimited for later prehistory, for pottery is one of the most common archaeological finds. Theoretically, thermoluminescence will work with all previously heated objects. Experiments with accidentally and intentionally heated stones have produced results that may presage a new dating technique that could be applied directly to stone artifacts, bridging the gap between radiocarbon dating and potassium argon dating. But it is too early to say whether the method is workable, because it is still highly experimental.

DENDROCHRONOLOGY

Principles. Dendrochronology, or tree-ring dating, was originated in Arizona by Dr. A. E. Douglass in about 1913 (Bannister, 1969).

The idea of using tree rings as a method for dating archaeological sites is much older, however. As early as 1788, the Reverend Manasseh Cutler was counting the rings in trees growing on archaeological sites near Marietta, Ohio, and suggested that the site he was studying was about a thousand years old. But the prehistoric time scale established from tree rings goes back much further into the past, especially in the Southwest, where it has been applied successfully to wooden beams in ancient pueblos preserved by dry desert conditions. Both the slow-growing sequoia and the California bristlecone pine *(Pinus aristata)* provide long tree-ring sequences, the latter a continuous chronology of 8,200 years. One pine tree 4,900 years old has been reported.

Everyone is familiar with tree rings, the concentric circles, each circle representing annual growth, visible on the cross-section of a felled trunk. These rings are formed on all trees but especially where seasonal changes in weather are marked, with either a wet and dry season, or a definite alternation of summer and winter temperatures. As a rule, trees produce one growth ring a year, which is formed by the cambium or growth layer lying between the wood and the bark. When the growing season starts, large cells are added to the wood. These cells become thicker walled and smaller as the growing season progresses; by the end of the growth season, cell production has ceased altogether. This process occurs every growing year; and a distinct line is formed between the wood of the previous season, with its small cells, and the wood of the next, with its new, large cells. The thickness of each ring may vary according to the tree's age and annual climatic variations, thick rings being characteristic of good growth years.

Weather variations within a circumscribed area tend to run in cycles. A decade of wet years may be followed by five dry decades. One season may bring a forty-year rainfall record. These cycles of climate are reflected in patterns of thicker or thinner rings, which are repeated from tree to tree within a limited area. Dendrochronologists have invented sophisticated methods of correlating rings from different trees so that they build up long sequences of rings from a number of trunks that may extend over many centuries (Figure 7.3). By using modern trees, whose date of felling is known, they are able to reconstruct accurate dating as far back as 8,200 years. Actual applications to archaeological wood are much harder, but archaeological chronology for the American Southwest now goes back to 59 B.C.

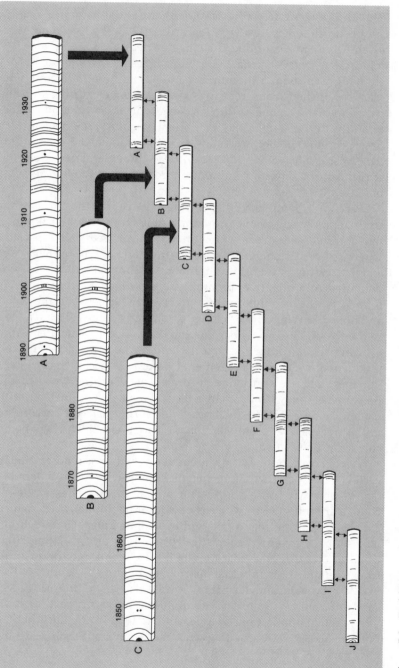

Figure 7.3   Building a tree-ring chronology: A. a radial cut taken from a living tree after the 1939 growing season; B–J. specimens taken from old houses and progressively older ruins. The ring patterns match and overlap back into pre-historic times.

Datable Materials and Procedures.   The most common dated tree is the Douglas fir. It has consistent rings that are easy to read and was much used in prehistoric buildings. Piñon and sagebrush are usable, too. Because the latter was commonly used as firewood, its charred remains are of special archaeological interest. The location of the sample tree is important. Trees growing on well-drained, gently sloping soils are best, for their rings display sufficient annual variation to make them more easily datable. The rings of trees in places with permanently abundant water supplies are too regular to be usable.

Samples are normally collected by cutting a full cross-section from an old beam no longer in a structure, by using a special core borer to obtain samples from beams still in a building, or by V-cutting exceptionally large logs. Delicate or brittle samples are impregnated with paraffin or coated with shellac before examination.

Once in the laboratory, the surface of the sample is leveled to a precise plane. Analyzing tree rings consist of recording individual ring series and then comparing them against other series. Comparisons can be made by eye or by plotting all the rings on a uniform scale, so that one series can be compared with another. The series so plotted can then be matched with the master tree-ring chronology for the region. Measuring the tree rings accurately can, also, add precision to the plottings.

Archaeological Applications.   Extremely accurate chronology for Southwestern sites has been achieved by correlating a master tree-ring sequence from felled trees and dated structures with beams from Indian pueblos. The beams in many such structures have been used again and again, and thus some are very much older than the houses in which they were most recently used for support. The earliest tree rings obtained from such settlements date to the first century B.C., but most timbers were in use between A.D. 1000 and historic times.

One of the most remarkable applications of tree-ring dating was carried out by Jeffrey Dean, who collected numerous samples from wooden beams at Betatakin, a cliff dwelling in northeastern Arizona dating to A.D. 1270. Dean ended up with no fewer than 292 samples, which he used to reconstruct a history of the cliff dwelling, room by room (Dean, 1970). He found that three room clusters were built in 1267, and a fourth was added a year later. In 1269 the inhabitants trimmed and stockpiled beams for later use. These beams were not actually used until 1275, when ten more room clusters were added to Betatakin. Dean also found that the site was abandoned between 1286 and 1300. Such intrasite datings are possible only when a large number of samples can be found.

Dendrochronology has been used widely in Alaska, the Mississippi Valley, northern Mexico, Canada, Scandinavia, England, and Germany (Bannister and Robinson, 1975; Baillie, 1982). But progress in several areas was slowed by lack of old trees and of readily cross-datable samples, as well as by evidence of irregular climatic fluctuations. In Ireland, living oaks have been dated back to A.D. 1649, and this chronology has been extended back, using beams from churches, forts, and farmhouses, to A.D. 1380. Medieval farmhouses and a Hanseatic ship buried in Bremen have taken tree-ring chronologies in Germany back to A.D. 1266. Celtic and Roman beams have been strung together in a floating chronology that has been cross-dated with archaeological data for the period ca. 717 B.C. to ca. A.D. 339. Modern oak chronologies based on Trier and Speyer cathedrals in Germany go back to A.D. 383. These two chronologies have been joined to form a tree-ring sequence going back 2,700 years. Dutch tree-ring experts have even analyzed the oak panels used by master painters to date and authenticate their paintings!

Arizona tree-ring laboratories are trying to analyze data on annual variability in rainfall from the many trees encompassed by their chronologies. A network of archaeological and modern chronologies provides a basis for reconstructing changing climatic conditions over the past two thousand years. These conditions will be compared with the complex events in southwestern prehistory over the same period (Fritts, 1976). And, as mentioned earlier, radiocarbon dates are calibrated with the aid of dendrochronology.

Limitations. Dendrochronology has traditionally been limited to areas with well-defined seasonal rainfall. Where the climate is generally humid or cold, or where trees enjoy a constant water supply, the difference in annual growth rings is either blurred or insignificant. Again, the context in which the archaeological tree-ring sample is found affects the usefulness of the sample. Many house beams are trimmed or reused several times in order to remove the outside surface of the log. The felling date cannot be established accurately without carefully observing the context and archaelogical association of the beam. For this reason, several dates must be obtained from each site. Artifacts found in a structure whose beams are dated do not necessarily belong to the same period, for the house may have been used over several generations. Like any other chronometric dating method, dendrochronology requires meticulous on-site observations and very careful collection of samples.

Chronological Range (Table 7.1). Dendrochronology is accurate from approximately 2,000 years ago to the present, with wider application possible. Non-archaeological tree-ring dates extend back 8,200 years however.

ARCHAEOMAGNETIC DATING

Principles. We know that the direction and intensity of the earth's magnetic field varied throughout prehistoric time. Many clays and clay soils contain magnetic minerals, which when heated to a dull red heat will assume the direction and intensity of the earth's magnetic field at the moment of heating. Thus, if the changes in the earth's magnetic field have been recorded over centuries, or even millennia, it is possible to date any suitable sample of clay material known to have been heated by correlating the thermoremanent magnetism of the heated clay with records of the earth's magnetic field (Figure 7.4) (Traling, 1971; 1975). Archaeologists frequently discover structures with well-baked clay floors, ovens, kilns, and iron-smelting furnaces, to name only a few, whose burned clay can be used for archaeomagnetic dating. Of course, reheated clays (clays used again after their original heating) will change their magnetic readings and are thus useless for archaeomagnetic dating.

Thermoremanent magnetism results from the ferromagnetism of magnetite and hematite, minerals found in significant quantities in most soils. When the soil containing these minerals is heated, the magnetic particles in magnetite and hematite change from a random alignment to one that conforms with that of the earth's magnetic field. In effect, the heated lump of clay becomes a very weak magnet that can be measured by a parastatic magnetometer. A record of the magnetic declination and dip similar to that of the earth's actual magnetic field at the time of heating is preserved in the clay lump. The alignment of the magnetic particles fixed by heating is called thermoremanent magnetism.

Datable Materials and Procedures. Selecting a kiln or other baked structure for magnetic dating is far from straightforward. Substantial floors of well-baked clay are best for the purpose. Tiny pillars

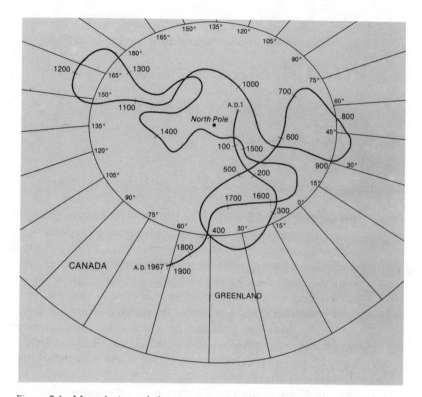

Figure 7.4   Meandering of the geomagnetic North Pole, worked out over a period of 2,000 years.

of burnt clay that will fit into a brass-framed extraction jig are extracted from the floor. The jig is oriented to present-day north–south and fitted over the pillars, which are then encapsulated in melted dental plaster. The jig and pillar are carefully removed from the floor, and then the other side of the jig is covered with dental plaster as well. The clay sample is placed under suspended magnets and rotated. The scale will record the declination and dip of the remanant magnetism in the clay.

An absolute date for the sample can then be obtained if the long-term, or *secular*, variation of the earth's field for the region is known.

Archaeological Applications and Limitations.   From the archeological point of view, archaeomagnetism has but limited application, because systematic records of the secular variation in the earth's magnetic field have been kept for only a few areas. Declination and dip have been recorded in London for 400 years, and a very accurate record of variations covers the period from A.D. 1600. France, Germany, Japan, and the southwestern United States have received some attention. From the latter, clay samples associated directly with dendrochronological or radiocarbon samples have been tested, with one set of readings from sixteen pre-Columbian villages extending back almost 2,000 years. At the moment the method is limited, but as local variation curves are recorded from more areas, archaeomagnetism is likely to be far more useful for the more recent periods of prehistory, when kilns and other burned-clay features were in use.

Chronological Range (Table 7.1). Archaeomagnetic dating is potentially useful from 2,000 years ago to the present.

CALENDARS AND OBJECTS OF KNOWN AGE

Calendars. A calendar developed by an ancient civilization provides an excellent way of dating archaeological sites, if the calendar can be linked to our own chronology. The Mesopotamians and ancient Egyptians fashioned sophisticated calendars, and the Maya of the Yucatan had a calendric system that is justly admired (Coe, 1976). Calendars were used to regulate the agricultural and religious year in Egypt and Mesoptamia and were vital in organizing secular and religious life in the Yucatan.

The Maya used both a secular 365-day calendar and a 260-day religious calendar for timing religious ceremonies (Figure 7.5). Their system of dating their own civilization in years started from a mythical date long before their own society was in being. Known as the Long Count, the system is recorded on many stelae, along with inscriptions that signal important events or transfer of priestly power. Attempts that have been made to link the Long Count and the Christian calendar place the span of the Mayan calendar from about 3113 B.C. to A.D. 889. Much of this time is, of course, long before the Maya themselves were a fully fledged state. But the Long Count stelae are a useful check on the dates of such well-known Mayan sites as Tikal and Palenque.

The most reliable chronometric dates are, of course, those obtained from historical documentation of archaeological sites. We

Figure 7.5   Many Mayan stelae (carved stone monuments) record important dates in the lives of their rulers. This stela carries a date equivalent to A.D. 771.

know that King Henry VIII began to build his palace at Nonsuch, England, in A.D. 1538, as well as the chronology of Plimoth Plantation in Massachusetts, from contemporary records, and our primary interest lies in discovering details of settlement layout or day-to-day life. Many later sites yield easily dated artifacts, such as coins dropped by the inhabitants on the floors of buildings or elsewhere in the settlement's strata. Such objects can provide accurate dates for the earliest age of the archaeological sites being investigated.

Objects of Known Age.   Objects of known age found in African, North American, and European prehistoric sites include a bewildering array of artifacts, from dated coins and glass bottles to Chinese porcelain and all manner of imported ceramics. The latter include American domestic tableware, English imported china, and Spanish majolica vessels in historic sites in North America. Ivor Noël Hume has compiled an invaluable compendium of artifacts from Colonial America that is a useful source book for anyone interested in such objects (Hume, 1969). Some of these types of finds can act as artifacts for cross-dating prehistoric sites.

One of the most useful Colonial American artifacts is the imported English kaolin pipe (Figure 7.6). Not only were pipes manufactured, imported, smoked, and thrown away within a very short cycle, but the shape of the pipe body changed in an easily recognizable evolutionary chain. Clay pipes were so cheap that everyone, however poor, used and discarded them almost like cigarettes. Not only the bowl but the length of the stem and the diameter of the hole changed between A.D. 1620 and 1800, and these characteristics have been used to date these artifacts and the sites associated with them with considerable precision (Oswald, 1975).

Stanley South and others have used statistical techniques to study the relationships betwen eighteenth-century English imported pottery and historic sites in North Carolina. They argued that once enough percentage relationships had been worked out, they would be able to date sites of unknown age by using the frequencies of imported pottery types (South, 1972). Surprisingly good correspondence was found between the calculated median dates and the known historical date of the pottery forms.

Roger Grange (1972, 1981) has taken this method a step further and applied the ceramic dating formula to the Pawnee and Loup Loup ceramic tradition of the Great Plains. This tradition was estimated, from historical data and archaeological cross-dating, to date from the period A.D. 1825 to 1846, when Pawnee potmaking died out, back to about A.D. 1500. Grange calculated median dates with archaeological data derived from seriation, which gave the range of types. He found fair correspondence between the median dates and those obtained by more conventional analyses, especially when the

Figure 7.6   Representative evolutionary changes in design of bowls of English smoking pipes dating to between 1730 and 1830.

1730-1770

1780-1820

1800-1830

greatest peaks of popularity for different pottery types were used as the basis for calculations. Formula dating of this type may have much potential in areas where tree-ring chronologies or calibrated radiocarbon dates provide a basis for accurate calculations of median age. And the advantages for cross-dating of newly discovered sites are obvious.

The potential range of historic objects that can be dated to within surprisingly narrow chronological limits is enormous. Many people collect beer cans, bottle caps, and openers, barbed wire, firearms, uniform buttons, even horseshoes. All these artifacts, to say nothing of such prosaic objects as forks, electrical switch plates, and scissors, can be dated to within a few years with mail order catalogs, U.S. patent records, and a great deal of patient detective work. Bernard Fontana points out that bottles, buckets, and horseshoes may be the unrespectable artifacts of archaeology but, unlike many of their prehistoric equivalents, they can be dated with great accuracy (Fontana, 1968). What better way to learn about archaeology than to study and date our own material culture!

Guide to Further Reading

The literature on chronometric dating is enormous, but these volumes can be of great use to the student.

Brothwell, D. R., and Eric S. Higgs. *Science in Archaeology*, 2nd ed. New York: Praeger, 1969.
Articles on major methods of dating that are admirable introductions to the subject.

Fleming, Stuart. *Dating in Archaeology*. London: St. Martin, 1977.
An introduction to archaeological chronology that is good on basic principles.

Michael, H. N., and E. K. Ralph, eds. *Dating Techniques for the Archaeologist*. Cambridge: MIT Press, 1971.
Another series of articles on basic dating methods, but the content here is highly technical.

Michel, J. W. *Dating Methods in Archaeology*. New York: Seminar Press, 1973.
Probably the most widely read book on dating presently available. A good follow-up to this chapter.

Taylor, R. E., and C. W. Meighan. *Chronologies in New World Archaeology*. New York: Academic Press, 1978.
Essays on New World chronological problems.

CHAPTER 8 ✿

PRESERVING ARCHAEOLOGICAL DATA

Preview

- Traditionally, archaeologists have argued that the archaeological record is incomplete, because many items of material culture have been lost to decay and destruction.
- Lewis Binford and others have refused to accept the assumption that archaeology yields information only on material culture. They argue that data on all components of past sociocultural systems are preserved in the archaeological record and that much depends on the methods of recovery used to obtain archaelogical data.
- Preservation conditions depend mostly on the soil and general climatic regime in the area of a site. Inorganic objects, such as stone and baked clay, often survive almost indefinitely. But organic materials, such as bone, wood, and leather survive only under exceptional conditions, such as dry climate, in permafrost areas, and when waterlogged. The surviving picture of the past obtained from excavations is often confined to inorganic materials.
- Waterlogged and peat bog conditions are especially favorable for preserving wood and vegetal remains. In this chapter we discuss the Danish bog corpses and the Ozette site in Washington State as sites of these types.

159

- Dry conditions can preserve almost the full range of human artifacts, the best examples being the remarkably complete preservation of ancient Egyptian culture and the comprehensive finds made in desert caves, such as Hogup cave in Utah, in the American West.
- Burials of horsemen at Pazyryk in Siberia show how refrigerated conditions in the soil can preserve such organic materials as human skin, horse trappings, and even woven rugs. Arctic sites in Alaska have yielded priceless information on ancient ivory carving and Eskimo material culture.
- Later human activity can radically affect archaeological preservation. People may selectively discard some types of artifacts, and many variables can affect the layout of settlements and other considerations. The Fulani compounds in West Africa demonstrate the difficulties of interpretation.
- Some people, such as the southwestern Indians, recycled wooden beams and other materials, distorting the archaeological record. Sites are reused, lower strata are often disturbed, and succeeding generations may preserve an important building, such as a temple, for centuries. Modern warfare, industrial activity, even deep agriculture and cattle grazing can affect the preservation of archaeological remains.

Modern archaelogists have assembled a battery of methods for recovering fragile objects from the soil, for preservation is a major factor both in the discovery of archaeological sites and in our reconstruction and explanation of the past. In this short chapter we review archaeologists' approaches to site preservation and give examples of unusually complete recoveries of the past. We see, too, ways in which ancient human behavior can affect preservation of archaeological data.

THE INCOMPLETE ARCHAEOLOGICAL RECORD

From the start, archaeologists have argued that the archaeological record is incomplete, for many items of material culture have been lost to decay and destruction. Wooden implements, baskets, and feather headdresses are in this category. Our interpretations of the record thus depend on how representative the surviving stone implements, pottery, or other objects are of the total material culture. It follows that the reliability of our statements about this culture also depends on how strongly we can believe that the nonmaterial elements of society and culture are reflected in the incomplete collection of finds that has come down to us.

These traditional cautionary arguments have been challenged by American archaeologist Lewis Binford and other prehistorians, who refuse to accept the assumption that archaeology yields information only on material culture. The distinction between "material culture" (artifacts, houses, and the products of human culture) and "nonmaterial" culture (kinship, social organization) is regarded as totally artificial, for every aspect of a human sociocultural system interacts with many other complex variables. According to Binford, "data relevant to most, if not all, the components of past sociocultural systems *are* preserved in the archaeological record" (Binford, 1968). The archaeologist's task, then, as he sees it, is to develop means for extracting such information from the data recovered from excavations and archaeological surveys.

This school of thought refuses to attribute the limitations in our knowledge about the past to the quality of the archaeological record and the state of its preservation in the soil. The limitations, they say, lie in our methodological naïveté, in sophisticated methodologies that many archeologists are seeking to improve by means described at intervals in this book. This approach has been shown to be simplistic, for more recent research reveals that both human beings and natural phenomena cause drastic changes in the archaeological record, disturbing the very artifact patterns that archaeologists want to study. What were the processes that modified the archaeological record after its deposition?

Formation Processes.   These are the ways in which the archaeological record itself was formed after sites, houses, and other artifacts were abandoned (Schiffer, 1983). All archaeological remains have been modified by the passage of time. These can, theoretically at any rate, cause an archaeologist to misinterpret the role of an artifact or artifacts in a prehistoric cultural system. Formation phenomena normally are local, varying from environment to environment and site to site, even from layer to layer. Many factors can affect studies of formation processes. Size of the artifacts is one. Large tools are less likely to be transported by floods or burrowing animals. Easily replaced items such as flake knives may be abandoned more readily than ceremonial items or heirlooms. Modern plowing, trampling by cattle, even human feet can shift the position of quite large artifacts in the ground (Bulzer, 1982). Wind, earthworms, carnivore activity, even the shape and orientation of objects in the ground can affect the ways in which they are preserved (Stein, 1983). All these factors, and such phenomena as size of sediments, density of artifacts in a deposit, even qualities of resistance of a soil to trampling, affect what archaeologists find in their excavations and the behavioral interpretations they make from them.

Formation processes are still imperfectly understood, for archaeologists have just begun to embark on the necessary intensive studies of the deposits in which the archaeological record is found. All this may seem remote from the interpretation of human behavior, but such interpretations clearly must not be based on data divorced from their context. Rather, the archaeologist's artifact patternings have to be recognized as not just humanly generated patterns, but distributions based also on long above- and below-ground modifications that have taken place since they were deposited.

Organic and Inorganic Materials. Preservation conditions depend mainly on the soil and the general climatic regime in the area of a site. Under highly favorable conditions, many kinds of artifactual materials are preserved, including such perishable items as leather containers, basketry, wooden arrowheads, and furniture. But under normal circumstances, only the most durable artifacts usually survive. Generally, the objects found in archaeological sites are of two broad categories: inorganic and organic materials.

Inorganic objects are of such materials as stone, metals, and clay. Prehistoric stone implements, such as the choppers of the earliest humans, made more than two million years ago, have survived in perfect condition for archaeologists to find. Their cutting edges are just as sharp as they were when abandoned by their makers. Clay pots are among the most durable human artifacts, especially if they are well fired. It is no coincidence that much of prehistory is reconstructed from chronological sequences of changing pottery styles. Fragments (potsherds) of well-fired clay vessels are practically indestructible; they have lasted as long as 10,000 years in some Japanese sites.

Organic objects are made of living substances, such as wood, leather, bone, or cotton. They rarely survive in the archaeological record. When they do, the picture of prehistoric life they give us is much more complete than that from inorganic finds. Organic materials formed a vital part of most societies' toolkits. Hunter-gatherers of southwestern France made extensive use of antler and bone for hunting tools and weapons (Grasiozi, 1960). Some of their finest artistic achievements were executed on fragments of these organic materials with flint engravers. The preservation of organic materials depends heavily on local preservation conditions. Let us examine some of the more favorable conditions that archaeologists encounter.

PRESERVING ORGANIC MATERIALS

The best way to describe different preservation conditions is to examine specific sites.

Waterlogged Environs.   Waterlogged or peat-bog conditions are particularly favorable for preserving wood or vegetal remains, whether the climate is subtropical or temperate. Tropical rain forests, such as those of the Amazon basin and Zaire, are far from kind to wooden artifacts, yet many archaeological sites are found near springs or in marshes where the water table is high and perennial waterlogging of occupation layers has occurred since they were abandoned.

Tollund man.   Danish bogs have yielded a rich harvest of wood-hafted weapons, clothing, ornaments, traps, and even complete corpses, such as that of Tollund man (Glob, 1969). This unfortunate individual's body was found by two peat cutters in 1950, lying on his side in a brown peat bed in a crouched position, a serene expression on his face and eyes tightly closed (Figure 8.1). Tollund man wore a pointed skin cap and a hide belt—nothing else. We know that he had been hanged, because a cord was found knotted tightly around his neck. The Tollund corpse has been shown to be about 2,000 years old and to belong to the Danish Iron Age. So excellent were preservation conditions in the acidic bog soil that much of his skin survives, and his peaceful portrait has been included in many archaeological volumes. A formidable team of medical experts examined his cadaver, among them a paleobotanist who established that Tollund man's last meal consisted of a gruel made from barley, linseed, and several wild grasses and weeds, eaten twelve to

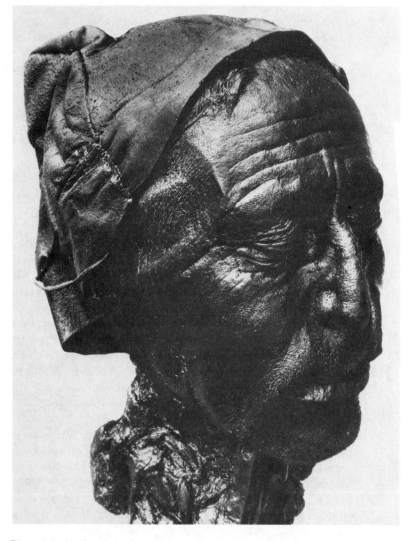

Figure 8.1   Tollund man.

twenty-four hours before his death. He is thought to have been a sacrificial victim of a fertility cult, hanged to ensure successful crops and continuation of life.

Ozette. Richard Daugherty of Washington State University worked at the Ozette site on the Olympia Peninsula in the Pacific

Northwest for more than a decade (Kirk, 1974). The site first came
to his attention in 1947, as part of a survey of coastal settlements.
Ozette had been occupied by Makah Indians until twenty or thirty
years before, and traces of their collapsed houses could be seen on
top of a large midden. It was not until 1966–1967 that Daugherty
was able to start excavations at the site, which was being threatened
with obliteration by wave action and mud slides. A trial trench
revealed large deposits of whale bones and yielded radiocarbon
samples dating back 2,500 years. Most important, the muddy deposits had preserved traces of wooden houses and the organic remains
in them. Then, in 1970, a call from the Makah Tribal Council alerted
Daugherty to a new discovery. High waves had cut into the midden
and caused the wet soil to slump, revealing traces of wooden fishhooks, boxes, and even a canoe paddle. A cursory glance showed
that the Ozette site contained the remains of collapsed wooden
houses buried under an ancient landslide.

Daugherty and his colleagues worked for over 10 years to
uncover the remains of four cedarwood longhouses and their contents (Figure 8.2). The excavations were fraught with difficulty and
high-pressure hoses and sprays were needed to clear the mud away
from the delicate woodwork. All the finds were then preserved
with chemicals before final analysis. The wet muck that mantled
the houses had engulfed them suddenly in a dense, damp blanket
that preserved everything except flesh, feathers, and skins. The
houses were perfectly preserved, one uncovered in 1972 measuring
21 meters long and 14 wide. There were separate hearths and cooking platforms and hanging mats and low walls as partitions. More
than forty thousand artifacts came from the excavations, including
conical rain hats made of spruce roots, baskets, wooden bowls still
impregnated with seal oil (Figure 8.3), mats, fishhooks, harpoons,
combs, bows and arrows, even fragments of looms, and ferns and
cedar leaves. A fine artistic tradition in wood excited the excavators:
the trove included a whale fin carved of red cedar and inlaid with
700 sea-otter teeth. No one had ever seen one of these objects
before, although Captain Cook had illustrated one in his report of
a voyage to the Northwest coast in 1778.

The Ozette site is a classic example of how much can be recovered
from an archaeological site in waterlogged conditions. But Ozette
is important in other ways, too, for the Makah Indians who lived
there had a tangible history, extending back at least two thousand
years before the whites came. Oral traditions and written records
for the Makah go back no further than A.D. 1800. The Makah aban-

Figure 8.2 Ozette, Washington. Excavation of the walls, sleeping benches, and planks of a prehistoric house uncovered by a mudslide. The waterlogged conditions preserved wood and fiber perfectly.

Figure 8.3 A bowl for oil from the Ozette site carved in the form of a man and complete, even to a braid of human hair.

doned Ozette only in modern times, to move nearer a school in the 1920s. The archaeological excavations have traced the continuity of this village of whale catchers and fisherfolk far back into prehistory, giving a new sense of identity to the Makah of today. The excavation was finally closed in 1981.

Dry Conditions. Very arid environments, such as those of the American Southwest or the Nile Valley, are even better for preservation than waterlogged localities.

The tomb of Tutankhamun. Undoubtedly one of the most famed of all archaeological discoveries is the amazing tomb of Tutankhamun (*ca.* 1345 B.C.), unearthed by Lord Carnarvon and Howard Carter in 1922 (Carter and others, 1923–33). The undisturbed burial chamber was opened, revealing the grave furniture in exactly the same state as it had been laid out by the king's mourners. Gilded wood chests, cloth, ivory caskets, models of chariots and boats, and the mummy were all perfectly preserved, together with a bewildering array of jewelry and paintings shining as brightly as the day they were painted, even showing the somewhat hasty execution accorded them by the artist. Tutankhamun's sepulchre provides as vivid a glimpse of the past as we are ever likely to obtain. Papyrus texts too have been preserved by the dry Egyptian conditions in many Nile Valley cemeteries, giving an unrivaled picture of the ancient Egyptian world (Johnson, 1978).

Hogup. C. Melvin Aikens has spent many years excavating the Hogup cave in Utah, where deep, dry deposits contain a record of human occupation that began at least 9000 B.P. and lasted into historic times (Aikens, 1970). Preservation conditions are so good that Aikens and his colleagues were able to recover stone artifacts, basketry, netting fragments, bone artifacts, and the remains of large and small animals. The early deposits of the cave were strewn with the chaff of pickleweed seeds; the seeds were also found in human feces (dung) from the site. During the earlier periods of occupation, open water and marshland lay not too far from the cave, which is known by the discovery of plentiful waterfowl bones and marsh plants in the deposits. After 3000 B.P. the waterfowl disappeared and the pickleweed declined sharply, demonstrating that the marshes were flooded by lake water. The drier environment that evolved in modern times increased exploitation of vegetable foods and small mammals. Few sites contain a wider range of evidence for hunting and food gathering than that in Hogup. And it is precisely these basically dry conditions, which have persisted over the West since the end of the Pleistocene, that have preserved this evidence so well.

Arctic Conditions.   Arctic sites, too, are excellent for preserving the human past. The circumpolar regions of Siberia and the New World have acted like a giant freezer, in which the processes of decay have been held in check for thousands of years. Close to the Arctic Sea, the carcasses of mammoths have survived thousands of winters in a state of perennial refrigeration. The Beresovka mammoth from Siberia was studied in 1901 by a Soviet expedition whose dogs ate the flesh of the Pleistocene beast as it was being dismembered (Digby, 1926). The hair was perfectly preserved, and the remains of its last meal were found on its tongue and in its stomach.

Pazyryk.   Russian archaeologist Sergei Rudenko was responsible for some remarkable excavations at the 2,300-year-old Pazyryk burial mounds in Siberia, not far from the Chinese and Mongolian borders (Rudenko, 1970). Although the mounds are south of the permafrost zones of Siberia, the sites themselves are permanently frozen because a special microclimate has been formed inside them by the heat-conducting properties of the stone cairn forming each mound's core.

The mounds covered burial shafts filled with logs and rocks. Log chambers containing the burials lay under this filling. The bodies were deposited in log coffins, usually were partly clothed, and were accompanied by wooden pillows and tables with dishes of food. Cheese and food residues still remained in the bowls. Horses were buried with their masters, having been dispatched with a poleaxe and placed in the burial shafts. Bridles, saddles, and head decorations accompanied the horses. Solid-wheeled wooden trolleys were found in each barrow, one a four-wheeled carriage with a draft pole. The horse carcasses were so well preserved in the frozen conditions that their hides could be studied: none had their winter coats. They were rather emaciated, as if they had survived a hard winter and had been slaughtered in early summer.

The refrigerated mounds preserved not only an array of wooden artifacts, horse harnesses, carpets, and even felt wall-coverings and canopies with elaborate naturalistic motifs, but also the clothes and flesh of the individuals buried there. Linen shirts adorned with braid, caftans decorated with leather and gold discs, and head-dresses of felt and leather came from the coffins, as did women's bootees, aprons, and stockings. Much of the clothing was elaborately decorated, whereas the individuals' hair was shaved. In addition to small ornaments, several bodies bore remarkable and elaborate tattooing. One chief's body showed a lively picture of a monster like a lion-griffin or some other imaginary creature. Deer, birds, and carnivores also adorned his body, with tattooing over the heart and arms and also on the legs. Presumably, the figures had some magical significance as well as a decorative intent.

The remarkable discoveries at Pazyryk have a local importance, because they show the long cultural ancestry of the modern pastoral tribes of southern Siberia. For archaeology as a whole, they reveal the potential richness of archaeological sites under the preservation conditions sometimes found in the Arctic.

Ipiutak. Eskimo archaeology has benefited enormously from the arctic cold, where permafrost, especially in Greenland and the more northern parts of the Arctic territory, has refrigerated wooden objects, bone and ivory artifacts, and the remains of animals hunted by the artifact makers. A remarkable site is the Ipiutak settlement near Point Hope on the Chukchi Sea, dated to the first few centuries A.D. (Collins, 1937). More than 60 semisubterranean dwellings were excavated out of an estimated 600–700 on the site. The floor level of the Ipiutak houses was about 50 centimeters (19 inches) below the ground, and the squarish floor between 3 and 7 meters (10 and 23 feet) in diameter. A central fireplace lay on the floor of packed gravel or logs, and sleeping benches of gravel and earth lined three walls. Vertical logs or poles, caulked with finer timbers, formed the walls; the whole structure, including the wooden roof, was covered with arctic moss. In a nearby cemetery, wooden coffins each containing a single burial were built in small pits, most of them at least a half-meter (19 inches) deep. Few grave goods were associated with these burials, in contrast to another series of skeletons deposited only a few centimeters below the surface. These bodies, when discovered, were found partially disarticulated, lying in a deposit of wood fragments, which included some flamboyant ivory carvings and midden soil. The excavators inferred that the dead had been deposited on the ground, enclosed in a wooden frame or a pile of logs. Elaborate ivory carvings were invariably associated with the surface burials at Ipiutak, preserved by the cold that has persisted at the site since its abandonment. Ipiutak art is dominated by small sculptures of bears, walruses, and other animals; composite masks and delicate spiral ornaments were probably fastened to the grave coverings. It is sobering to realize that under temperate conditions only stone artifacts and the outlines of the Ipiutak houses and bed platforms would have survived the 2,000 years since the settlement was occupied (Dumond, 1977).

Special Conditions. Geological deposits, such as oil-bearing layers in Poland or tar beds in the New World, have supplied many fossil remains of large mammals trapped in the treacherous deposits thousands of years ago. A dog corpse from a Basketmaker site in the Southwest survived so well in dry soil that the flies that fed on the putrefying corpse were found with the skeleton. Viking ships are preserved in the acid soils of temperate climates by the stones, clay, and peat packed around them by their owners. Even the wine of Roman times has come down to us. In 1867, a bottle of wine dating from the third century A.D. was found in a Roman sarcophagus at Speyer, France; the bottle was still full, and the liquid was analyzed to be wine mixed with honey. A thick layer of olive oil covered the wine, poured into the bottle by the original bottler to preserve the contents; this oil had become resinated, preventing the wine from evaporating (De Laet, 1956).

In spite of these exceptional instances, most soils are destructive. Acid soils destroy inorganic objects rapidly, but the dark discolorations of post holes and hut foundations often remain and challenge the archaeologist to reconstruct structures whose actual substance has vanished. The granitic soils of subtropical regions usually are highly destructive, but the chalk deposits of Europe preserve animal bones, burials, and metals moderately well. The great loess belts of Central Europe have mantled many Upper Paleolithic settlements, preserving the floor plans of mammoth-hunters' camps, some of the earliest human structures ever recovered (Klein, 1969).

PRESERVATION AND HUMAN ACTIVITY

The preservation of archaeological remains can, of course, be influenced by the ancient peoples themselves (Schiffer, 1976).

Discards. The patterns of artifact discard can be very subtle; understanding them often requires knowledge that is still beyond our grasp.

Cozumel. At the Mayan trading center on Cozumel, Yucatan, the people invested very little material wealth in temples, tombs, or other permanent monuments (Sabloff, 1975). Their capital was kept fluid and on hand, an investment in resources different from that found at other Mayan ceremonial centers, which invested heavily in religious monuments and tangible displays of wealth. The different investment in resources reflected the activities and significance in each type of locality. Interpreting such patterns of discard, the remains that are left for interpretation after the long centuries and millennia of natural destruction have taken place, present huge difficulties for archaeologists.

Fulani. In a fascinating discussion of thirty-six modern, inhabited Fulani compounds in North Cameroon, West Africa, Nicholas David attempted to show the "fit" between the houses in the compounds and their Fulani inhabitants (David, 1971). He found that so many variables affected the layout of the compounds that only the most general observations were possible. The huts in the compound could sometimes be used to estimate the numbers of adult women or male family heads. But what about bachelors or children? Fish-drying ovens of puddled mud and large hearths were signs of economic specialization and of evening classes for study of the Koran in the modern settlements. But had an archaeologist dug up the compound centuries after its abandonment, only the ovens would have survived. The house of the chief musician gave no clue to his profession, nor did those of many part-time specialists. The granaries used to store grain supplies were not built on stone foundations that were likely to survive: the only sign of the basic subsistence economy in the archaeological record might be the special grinding huts in the compound. Furthermore, though in prehistoric times the compounds might have reflected the status of different families—wealthy people, poor, free Fulani, and slaves—today they have no slavery and a far more homogeneous society. Above all, in earlier times wealth was not necesssarily reflected in house size. All houses were of about the same size, a dimension dictated, so David found, by white ant infestation. When insecticides became available in the late 1960s, houses started to get larger. The absolute limits of archaeological inference were soon met when David attempted to fit the material culture and houses to social structure. He found that in modern country villages people build houses to suit their precise needs. Land is abundant and free. But in modern towns, where the Fulani have to buy land and modify their property for their needs within a much tighter framework, people either have to move to new quarters or adapt their life-style to fit their limited space. The constraints are far more severe.

Any archaeologist working anywhere has to face the peculiar problems that David demonstrated with his Fulani compounds. What are the distorting effects of human discard patterns on the archaeological record, on surface site survey, and on the limits to which we can take the interpretation of sites and finds? These are questions that few archaeologists have yet tackled head-on, but they form a critical facet of the preservation question.

Recycling.   People discard artifacts, and they recycle them as well. A stone axe can be resharpened again and again, until the original, large artifact is just a small stub that has been recycled into extinction. It takes a great deal of effort to build a mud brick house from scratch. Very often, an old house is renovated again and again, its precious wooden beams used again in the same structure or in another building. Such recycling can distort the archaeological record, for what appears to be a one-time structure can in fact have been used again and again. Tree-ring dating of pueblos in the Southwest is complicated by the constant reuse of wooden beams. Sometimes too, the Indians would cut beams and stockpile them for later use.

Not only individual artifacts, but also entire archaeological sites can be recycled. A settlement flourishes on a low ridge in the Near East. After a generation or two the site is abandoned, and the inhabitants move elsewhere. Later, people return to the site, level the abandoned houses, and build their own dwellings right on top of the site. This type of recycling can result in sealing and preserving of later levels, but it can also result in reuse of building materials from earlier houses.

Heirlooms.   Successive generations may also find a structure or artifact so valuable that they consciously preserve it for the benefit of their descendants.

Eridu.   The great temple, or *ziggurat,* of the city of Eridu in Mesopotamia was first erected around 5000 B.C. This important shrine
was visible for miles around and was rebuilt on the same site time
and time again for more than 2,000 years. Tracing the complex history of this structure has consumed many hours of excavation time.
Reconstructing the sequence of mud-brick construction through
generations of recycling of successive structures involves understanding how mud brick architecture came into being and how it
decays (Lloyd, 1963).

Ceremonial artifacts.   Many prehistoric societies valued ritual
objects, such as masks, ceremonial axes, and other symbolic artifacts
that were associated with ancestor worship. These ceremonial artifacts were sometimes buried with a dead priest or leader, as with
Tutankhamun and some of the Mayan leaders. It is easy enough to
tell their age and association with a grave dug at a particular period.
In other instances, ceremonial artifacts can be treasured for generations, being displayed only on special occasions or kept in a special
relic hut. An interesting example of such heirlooms is that of the
sacred relics of the Bemba tribe in Central Africa, which included
ceremonial iron gongs and bow stands that were at least two
hundred years old (Richards, 1937). Tragically, these were
destroyed by political protestors in the early 1960s, causing great
trauma among the older Bemba. By treasuring such objects, however, the owners can unwittingly distort the archaeological record.
Fortunately, in most cases it is possible to identify instances of *curation* or preservation by the style of the artifacts. In Tutankhamun's
tomb, Carter found among the grave furniture objects that had
belonged to earlier pharaohs. Presumably, they had been placed in
the tomb to fill in gaps in the royal inventory caused by the pharaoh's unexpected death.

   The many other potential causes of human distortion of the
archaeological record can include deliberate destruction of cemeteries, erasure of inscriptions from temples at royal command, or
the ravages of warfare, both ancient and modern. The trench warfare of World War I did terrible damage to archaeological sites.
Even more destructive are depredations by treasure hunters and
antiquities dealers supplying the greed of museums and private collectors (Meyer, 1977).

   An archaeologist must always evaluate the preservation conditions at every site investigated to determine the preservation fac-

tors—both human and natural—that have affected the integrity of the archaeological record.

Guide to Further Reading

Good surveys of preservation in archaeology are few and far between. These will provide some useful reading.

Clark, J. G. D. *Archaeology and Society.* New York: Barnes and Noble, 1939. *This classic archaeological text still contains much information of value, especially on preservation of archaeological remains.*

————. *Star Carr.* Cambridge: Cambridge University Press, 1954. *A definitive monograph about a waterlogged site, which is a classic of its type.*

Glob, P. V. *The Bog People.* London: Faber and Faber, 1969. *A popular account of bog corpses found in Denmark. Includes a description of the Tollund find.*

Kirk, Ruth. *Hunters of the Whale.* New York: William Morrow, 1974. *A popular narration about the Ozette site in Washington State. Gives a summary of preservation and excavation problems.*

Rudenko, Sergei. *Frozen Tombs of Siberia: The Pazyryk Burials of Iron Age Horsemen.* Translated by M. W. Thompson. Berkeley: University of California Press, 1970

PART IV

RECOVERING ARCHAEOLOGICAL DATA

A mere hole in the ground, which of all sights is perhaps the least vivid and dramatic, is enough to grip their attention for hours at a time.

P. G. WODEHOUSE
A Damsel in Distress

Part IV deals with the ways in which archaeologists acquire data in the field. As we stressed earlier, acquiring such data depends on a sound research design and on formulating specific hypotheses before reconnaissance, site survey, or excavation can be begun. Our knowledge of the past is limited, not only by preservation in the ground but also by our own methods for recovering data. Chapters 9 through 11 describe some of the fundamental principles and processes of archaeological fieldwork, as well as some of the many special problems encountered by archaeologists in the field. And, rather than draw on a single case study, we have chosen to give many examples, relying on your instructors to use case studies derived from their own experience.

CHAPTER 9 🦋

THE PROCESS OF ARCHAEOLOGICAL RESEARCH

Preview

- Modern archaeology makes use of scientific methods devised by archaeologists and also by scientists in many other disciplines.
- A well-qualified archaeologist commands many skills, both in archaeological method and theory and in practical methodology. This expertise includes ability to select and work with specialists in other academic disciplines. Practical fieldwork experience and considerable administrative and managerial skill are also required on even the smallest research project. All archaeologists have to acquire precise analytical and writing skills that enable them to communicate their results and record them for posterity.
- Archaeologists use science as a means for acquiring knowledge and understanding about the parts of the natural world that can be observed. They do so by working with two forms of reasoning: inductive reasoning, which takes specific observations and makes a generalization from them, and deductive reasoning, which starts with a generalization and proceeds to specific implications.
- The process of archaeological research begins with formulating highly specific research designs that are flexible enough to allow changes in the overall project as field research proceeds.
- The research project is formulated to fit the problem to be investigated and the geographical area involved. Formulation means

carrying out background research and then developing hypotheses to be tested against data acquired in the field.
· Once the field team is assembled, they begin to acquire data by reconnaissance, site survey, and excavation. This acquisition requires them to record provenience, archaeological context, and a great deal of basic information about the site, its natural environment, and its archaeological finds.
· The processing of archaeological data requires analyzing and interpreting the archaeological finds, which involves sorting, classifying, and ordering the finds, and then testing the hypotheses developed as part of the research design.
· The final stage in archaeological research is publishing the results for posterity.

"The excavator without an intelligent policy may be described as an archaeological food-gatherer, master of a skill, perhaps, but not creative in the wider terms of constructive science," wrote Sir Mortimer Wheeler in his classic description of archaeological research (Wheeler, 1954). This chapter shows just how true his remarks were. Modern archaeology makes use of scientific methods developed not only by archaeologists themselves but also by scientists in many other disciplines. It is a complex process involving research design, field surveys, and actual excavation, as well as lengthy laboratory analysis of many types of finds. Above all, modern archaeological research is a multidisciplinary effort, ideally involving a closely knit group of researchers with many and diverse skills.

After discussing the qualifications of a good archaeologist, we look at the relationship between science and archaeology, at inductive and deductive reasoning, and then examine the process of archaeological research itself. This short chapter is an important preliminary to the discussions of archaeological data acquisition that follow.

THE ARCHAEOLOGIST'S SKILLS

Early archaeologists needed few qualifications beyond a liking for the past, some experience in excavation, and an ability to classify artifacts. Sir Leonard Woolley, famed excavator of Ur-of-the-Chaldees in Mesopotamia in the 1920s, was completely self-trained and learned excavation in a few seasons in the Sudan. In an interview with an Oxford college president, he was told: "*I have decided that you shall become an archaeologist!*" Fortunately for science, Woolley obeyed him (Fagan, 1979).

The archaeologists of the 1980s, however, require specialist training in administrative, technical, and academic skills of many types. Modern archaeology has become so complex that few individuals can possibly master all the skills needed to excavate a large city or even a medium-sized settlement where preservation conditions are exceptionally complete. In the 1920s Leonard Woolley excavated Ur with a handful of Europeans, three expert Syrian foremen, and several hundred workers. An expedition to an equivalent site today would consist of a carefully organized team of experts whose skills reflect the precise hypotheses about the site that were to be tested in the field.

Let us examine, then, some of the basic skills an archaeologist needs.

Theoretical Skills. The archaeologist must be able to define research problems in their context: everything that is known about them. This knowledge includes not only the current status of research on a specific problem, such as the origins of humanity or the earliest human settlement of Ohio, but also the latest theoretical and methodological advances in archaeology that could affect the definition and solution of the problem.

The research problem will be defined by the specific objectives, or goals, to be achieved. The archaeologist must have the expertise to formulate the precise hypotheses to be tested in the research. As the research proceeds, he or she will have to be able to evaluate and put together the results of the work in the context set by the original objectives.

Methodological Expertise. Every archaeologist must have the ability to plan the methods to be used in the research to achieve the theoretical goals initially laid out. Methodological skills include being able to select between methods of data collection, and to decide which analytical methods are most effective for the data being handled. Excavating sites requires a large range of methodological skills, from deciding which sampling and trenching systems to use, to devising recording methods, to dealing with special preservation conditions where fragile objects have to be removed from their matrix intact.

One important aspect of methodological expertise requires selecting and working with specialists from other disciplines. This task involves understanding of multidisciplinary research and knowing the uses and limitations of the work done by, say, geologists or zoologists, for the specific problems one is investigating.

Technical Skills. Methodological and technical skills overlap, especially in the field. The scientific excavation of any site or a large-scale field survey requires more than the ability to select a method or a recording system; one needs also to execute it under working conditions. Archaeological excavations require great precision in measurement and excavation, deployment of skilled and unskilled labor, and implementation of find-recovery systems that keep artifacts in order from the moment they are found until they are shipped to the laboratory for analysis. At issue here is provenience of the artifacts and features and of the associated ecofacts. (An ecofact consists of non-artifactual materials such as food residues and other finds that throw light on human activities). The field archaeologist has to assume the roles of supervisor, photographer, surveyor, digger, recorder, writer, and soil scientist, as well as be able to deal with any unexpected jobs, such as uncovering the delicate bones of a skeleton or setting up details of a computer program. On large sites, expertly trained students or fellow archaeologists may assume such specialist tasks as photography; on small sites, the archaeologist often must perform this and all other tasks alone.

Administrative and Managerial Skills. Modern archaeology requires—or actually demands—that its practitioners exercise high-grade administrative and managerial skills. Today's archaeologist has to be able to coordinate the activities of specialists from other disciplines, organize and deploy teams of volunteer students and paid laborers, and raise and administer research funds obtained from outside sources. He or she must always be aware of all aspects of a research project as it progresses, from arranging for permits and supplies of stationery and digging tools to doing the accounts.

Above all, anyone working on an archaeological project has to be an expert in human relations, in keeping people happy at demanding work, which is often carried out under difficult and uncomfortable conditions. The diplomatic side of archaeological excavations is often neglected. But the folklore of archaeology abounds with stories of disastrous excavations run by archaeologists with no sensitivity to their fellow workers. A truly happy excavation is a joy to work on, a dig on which people smile, argue ferociously over interpretations of stratigraphic profiles through an endless day, and enjoy the companionship of a campfire in the evenings.

Writing and Analytical Skills. If there is one basic lesson to be learned at the beginning of any archaeological endeavor, it is that all excavation is destruction of finite archives in the ground that can never be restored to their original configuration. Every archaeologist is responsible not only for analyzing his or her finds in the laboratory, but also for preparing a detailed report on the fieldwork that has been done; an important part of the permanent record of archaeological research. Regrettably, the shelves in museums all over the world are filled with finds from sites that have been excavated but never written up.

At first glance, the list of qualifications a professional archaeologist needs can be formidable. In practice though, sound classroom training combined with a great deal of fieldwork experience can give one the necessary background.

ARCHAEOLOGY, SCIENCE, AND THE SCIENTIFIC METHOD

At various places we have referred to scientific archaeology, scientific method, and testing of hypotheses against data collected in the field (Thomas, 1974). It is now time to ask the Damocletian question: Is archaeology a science? The answer is a qualified yes. In the sense that archaeologists study human societies of the past by scientifically recovering and analyzing data that consist of the material remains of these societies, it is a science. But in the sense that archaeology, as part of anthropolgy, studies the intangible philosophic and religious beliefs of a society, it is not a science.

What do we mean by "scientific"? Science is a way of acquiring knowledge and understanding about the parts of the natural world that can be measured. It is a disciplined and carefully ordered search for knowledge, carried out in a systematic manner. This is a far cry from the ways in which we acquire our personal experience of religious philosophies, social customs, or political trends. Science involves using methods of acquiring knowledge that are not only cumulative but also subject to continuous testing and retesting. Over the years, scientists have developed the general procedures for acquiring data, known as the scientific method, which have come into wide use. Even though the scientific method may be applied in somewhat different ways in botany than it is in zoology or anthropology, the basic principles are the same: the notion that knowledge of the real world is both cumulative and subject to constant rechecking. The scientific method has many applications to archaeological data, and its use classifies much of archaeology as a science.

The Scientific Method.   Science establishes facts about the natural world by observing objects, events, and phenomena. In making these observations, the scientist proceeds by using either inductive or deductive reasoning.

Inductive reasoning takes specific observations and makes a generalization from them. I once found nearly 10,000 wild vegetable remains in a 4,000-year-old hunter-gatherer camp in central Zambia. More than 42 percent of them were from the *bauhinia*, a shrub prized for its fruit and roots, which flowers from October to February. The *bauhinia* is still eaten by San hunter-gatherers in the Kalahari today. From this knowledge I induced that *bauhinia* has been a preferred seasonal food for hunter-gatherers in this general area for thousands of years (Fagan and Van Noten, 1971).

Deductive reasoning works the other way around. That is, the observer starts with a generalization and proceeds to form specific implications. In the Kalahari, I would have formulated a hypothesis (or series of hypotheses) about San and prehistoric hunter-gatherer *bauhinia* eating, and then tested it with ethnographic fieldwork and archaeological investigations. My hypothesis would then be confirmed, rejected, or refined.

A classic example of applying both inductive and deductive approaches comes from field studies done in the Great Basin in the western United States by anthropologist Julian Steward, who spent much of the 1920s and 1930s working on Shoshonean ethnography. The mass of field data that he collected led him to inductive generalizations about the ways in which the Shoshoneans moved their settlements throughout the year (Steward, 1938).

In the late 1960s this pioneer work was greatly refined by David Hurst Thomas, who approached the Shoshoneans' settlement patterns deductively. First, he took Steward's theory about the settlement patterns and devised hypotheses about the densities and distributions of artifacts in the various ecological zones of the Great

Basin. "If the late prehistoric Shoshoneans behaved in the fashion suggested by Steward, how would the artifacts have fallen on the ground?" he asked (Thomas, 1969; 1973; 1979). He constructed more than 100 hypotheses relating to Steward's original theory. Next, he devised tests to verify or invalidate his hypotheses. He expected to find specific forms of artifacts associated with particular types of activity, such as hunting, in seasonal archaeological sites where hunting was said to be important. Aware of local preservation conditions, he strongly emphasized the distribution and frequency of artifact forms. Then he collected in the field the archaeological data needed for his tests. Finally, Thomas tested each of his hypotheses against the field data and rejected about 25 percent of his original hypotheses. The remainder were supported by the data and provided a major refinement of Steward's original generalization. Later fieldwork gave him abundant opportunities to refine his original hypotheses and to collect more field data to further confirm them.

Thomas's Great Basin research is a good example of the cumulative benefits of deductive reasoning and scientific method in archaeological research.

Most early archaeological research was, and much contemporary work still is, inductive. At present, the tendency is to dismiss all inductive research as scientifically unsound, for it involves some insight or intuition rather than precise application of scientific method. Such a dismissal is totally unrealistic, however, for it means rejecting all the early archaeological knowledge acquired by scholars who did not use the scientific method.

The importance of scientific method, on the other hand, cannot be underestimated. A good statement is that "Science advances by disproof, proposing the most adequate explanations for the moment, knowing that new and better explanations will later be found. This continuous self-correcting feature is the key to the scientific method" (Sharer and Ashmore, 1979).

THE PROCESS OF ARCHAEOLOGICAL RESEARCH

The archaeology of today is becoming more and more explicitly scientific and sophisticated. To achieve this sophistication we must formulate much more specific research designs. In this section we describe the process of archaeological research, from formulation of the research design to publication of the final report.

Research Designs.   Lewis Binford was among the first archaeologists to see the necessity for highly specific research designs (Binford, 1964). To this end, he called for more regional studies, for investigations in which the archaeologist would aim at solving specific problems, and for testing of hypotheses with representative samples of data drawn from a well-defined region. Such research is so complex that without highly specific research designs it could not be executed. Under this approach, the research problem itself often determines the sites to be investigated.

A research design is a formal procedure whose purpose is to direct the carrying out of an archaeological investigation (Daniels, 1972). It has two objectives: to ensure that the results will be scientifically valid, and to carry out the research as efficiently and economically as possible. The process of archaeological research, then, is controlled by the research design, which takes the project through stages. These stages, described below, are by no means common to all research projects; for although "research design" sounds rigid and inflexible, in practice the design for any project has to be flexible enough to allow changes in the overall project as field research proceeds.

Formulation.   Any archaeological research begins with fundamental decisions about the problem or area to be studied. A research problem can be as grandiose as determining the origins of agriculture in the Southwest—a truly enormous project—or as specific as determining the date of the second phase in Stonehenge's construction. The initial decisions will identify both the problem and the geographical region in which it will be investigated. The latter can be one site or an entire geographical region. These decisions immediately limit the scope of the research design.

Once the problem and the area are identified, the researcher must do a great deal of background research, involving both library work and field investigations. He or she must read up on previous archaeological research on the problem and study the geology, climate, ecology, anthropology, and general background of the area. Several field visits are essential, both to examine fieldwork conditions and to get a feel for the region. Water supplies, campsites, and sources of labor have to be identified. Landowners' permissions to dig and survey are essential, and government permits may be needed. At least some preliminary fieldwork is needed to aid in formulating the research design, especially in areas where no archaeology has been carried out before.

The objective directing all this preliminary work is to refine the problems you are investigating until you can begin to define the specific research goals. These goals will almost invariably include testing specific hypotheses, which can be related to earlier research carried out by previous investigators, or entirely new ones that come out during the preliminary formulation of the research problem. Yet others will be added as the research work proceeds. Generating hypotheses at this stage is vital, for they determine the types of data that will be sought in the field. These types must be defined, at least in general, before one goes into the field.

Let us take two hypotheses designed as part of a research project into early food production in Egypt:

> The earliest cereal agriculture near Kom Ombo developed among hunter-gatherers who had been exploiting wild vegetable foods very intensively. The emergence of agriculture came about as a result of the intensification of gathering and rapid population growth causing shortages of wild cereals. So people began to grow wild cereals for themselves.

What sorts of data would be needed to test these hypotheses at Kom Ombo? The archaeologist formulating the project of which this hypothesis is a part would be looking for:

1. sites in areas where wild cereals could have grown, where preservation conditions would allow for survival of vegetal remains
2. food residues in the form of carbonized and discarded vegetable foods and the bones of domesticated animals
3. implements used for harvesting and processing both wild and domesticated grains—grindstones, sickles, and so on
4. evidence for such features as storage pits or baskets, indicating deliberate conservation of food supplies
5. sites that were occupied longer than the relatively short periods favored by most hunter-gatherers: farmers have to watch over their crops.

Armed with both hypotheses and lists of the types of evidence likely to be encountered in the field, the archaeologist can plan for the equipment, facilities, and people needed to carry out the job. Even more important, the project can be formulated with advice from experts, whose specialist knowledge will be needed either in the field or in the laboratory. The necessary contacts with experts are best made before the fieldwork begins and funds are obtained. A surprising number of specialists are needed for even quite simple investigations. The Kom Ombo hypothesis could ideally require the long- or short-term services of these specialists:

1. a geologist to assist in geological dating of sites in the Nile Valley
2. a soil scientist to study occupation levels and organic soils
3. a radiocarbon dating laboratory to date carbon samples
4. a botanist to supervise recovery of vegetal remains and to identify them
5. an expert on pollen analysis to work on any such samples recovered in the excavations
6. a zoologist to study the animal bones.

The larger-scale project may take an integrated team of experts from several disciplines into the field—an expensive enterprise, but it often yields important results. The study of early agriculture in the Near East was revolutionized by Robert Braidwood of the University of Chicago in the 1950s, when he took such a team of experts with him to the Zagros Mountains. The research team was able to trace agriculture and animal domestication from their beginnings among nomadic hunter-gatherers on the highlands more than 9,000 years ago (Braidwood and Howe, 1962).

Research design has a critical part in cultural resource management (Chapter 20). Regional research designs for large areas such as the San Juan Basin in Colorado provide a long-term framework for hundreds of minor environmental impact studies and research projects. These designs are not cast in concrete; they are ever-changing documents, which are brought up to date regularly to accommodate changing methodologies and new circumstances in the field (Fowler, 1983).

The final stage in formulating the research project is acquiring the necessary funding. This can be frustrating and time-consuming work, for sources of monies for archaeological fieldwork are always in short supply. Most excavations organized in the Americas are funded either by the National Science Foundation or, if within the United States, by some other government agency, such as the National Park Service. Some private organizations, such as the National Geographic Society or the Wenner Gren Foundation for Anthropological Research, support excavations. Some foundations limit their support to studies on specific topics. The L. S. B. Leakey Foundation of Pasadena supports only research into primate behavior and the origins of humankind and some types of urgent

anthropological fieldwork. Few archaeologists are expert fundrais-
ers, for it requires a great deal of time. But some excavations, such
as the Koster project at an early hunter-gatherer site in Illinois
(Brown and Struever, 1973), rely heavily on private donations. The
organizers expend considerable time on fundraising to support
each field season and the laboratory work that follows it.

Data Collection.   Once the field team is assembled and the funds
are in hand, actual implementation of the project begins. The first
stage is to acquire equipment, set up camp, and organize the
research team in the field. Once that procedure is complete, actual
collecting of archaeological data can begin.

   This collection of data involves two basic processes: locating and
surveying sites and scientifically excavating carefully selected sites.

   Locating archaeological sites is obviously the first stage in collecting data. As we will see in Chapter 10, reconnaissance can be
carried out on foot, in vehicles, or even on the back of a mule. A
variety of techniques is used to ensure that a representative sample
of sites is located and investigated before excavation. Then the surfaces of the sites are carefully examined and samples of artifacts
lying at ground level are collected, to record as much as possible
about the location without the expense of excavation. This recording can include photographs, some surveying and measurement,
and even some probing of the site with borers or remote sensing
devices. Obviously, much less information is collected from surface
surveys than from excavations.

   Archaeological excavations are ultimately a recording of subsurface features and the provenience, or precise relationships, of the
artifacts within the site. Varied techniques are used to collect and
record archaeological data from beneath the ground, as described
in Chapter 11. The scope of archaeological excavation obviously can
range from a small test pit to a large-scale investigation at a site such
as Meadowcroft rockshelter in the Ohio valley, where excavation
has gone on for many seasons (Adovasio and others, 1975).

Data Processing, Analysis, and Interpretation.   The end products
of even a month's excavation on a moderately productive site are a
daunting accumulation. Box upon box of potsherds, stone tools,
bones, and other finds are stacked in the field laboratory and must
be cleaned, labeled, and sorted. Hundreds of slides and photographs must be processed and catalogued. Rolls of drawings with

important information on the provenience of finds from the trenches must also be catalogued. Then there are radiocarbon and pollen samples, burials, and other special finds that need examination by specialists. The first stage in processing the data, then, occurs at the site, where the finds are washed, sorted, and given preservation treatment sufficient to transport them to the archaeological laboratory for more thorough examination.

The detailed analysis of the data is carried out, often for many months, in a laboratory that has the facilities for such research work. These analyses include not only classifying artifacts and identifying the materials from which they were made, but also studies of food remains, pollen samples, and other key sources of information. All these analyses are designed to provide information for interpreting the archaeological record. Some tests, such as radiocarbon dating or pollen analysis, are carried out in laboratories with the necessary technical equipment. We describe various approaches to archaeological analysis in Chapters 12–17.

Interpreting the resulting classified and thoroughly analyzed data involves not only synthesizing all the information from the investigation, but final testing of the basic hypotheses formulated at the beginning of the project. These tests produce models for reconstructing and explaining the prehistory of the site or region. We look at some of these models and interpretations in Part VII.

Publication.   The archaeologist's final responsibility is publishing the results of the research project. Archaeological excavation destroys all or part of a site; unless the investigator publishes the results, vital scientific information will be lost forever. The ideal scientific report publishes not only the research design and hypotheses that have been formulated, but also the data used to test them and to interpret the site or region, so that the same tests can be replicated by others (Grinsell, Rahtz, and Williams, 1970).

All archaeological research is cumulative, in the sense that everyone's investigations are eventually superseded by later work, which uses more refined methods of recovery and new analytical approaches. But unless every archaeologist publishes the results of his or her completed work, the chain of research is incomplete, and a fragment of human history will vanish into oblivion. It is sad that the pace of publication has been far behind that of excavation. The reason is not hard to discern: excavation is far more fun than writing reports!

Guide to Further Reading

Binford, Lewis R. "A Consideration of Archaeological Research Design." *American Antiquity* 29: 425–441.
Binford summarizes the key points about sound archaeological design.

Dancey, H. S. *Archaeological Field Methods: An Introduction.* Minneapolis: Burgess, 1981.
Probably the best and most up-to-date manual on American field methods around. Especially good on research design.

Hester, Thomas R., J. Shafer, and Robert F. Heizer, *Field Methods in Archaeology.* Menlo Park: Mayfield, 1985.
A basic field manual on survey and excavation for the beginner.

Thomas, David Hurst. *Predicting the Past: An Introduction to Anthropological Archaeology.* New York: Holt, Rinehart and Winston, 1976.
A short account of the basic methods of anthropological archaeology, which provides invaluable background for this chapter.

CHAPTER 10 🌿

FINDING
ARCHAEOLOGICAL
SITES

Preview

- Two processes are involved in locating archaeological sites: reconnaissance and site survey.
- Many archaeological sites are discovered by accident, industrial activity, modern agriculture, or natural happenings, such as floods and earthquakes.
- Many famous archaeological sites—like the Pyramids—have never been lost to human knowledge. But other, less conspicuous locations are found only by planned ground reconnaissance. Archaeological sites manifest themselves in many ways: in the form of mounds, middens, caves, and rockshelters. Many more are much less conspicuous and are located only by soil discolorations or surface finds.
- Ground reconnaissance is done at one of several levels of intensity, ranging from general surveys leading to location of only the largest sites down to precise foot surveys aimed to cover an entire area in detail. Even these are not totally effective, and all reconnaissance is, at best, a major sampling of the research area.
- In most cases, total survey is impracticable, and so archaeologists rely on probabilistic and nonprobabilistic sampling methods to obtain unbiased samples of the research area.
- Key indicators of archaeological sites include conspicuous above-

ground features, vegetational coverage, soil colors, and surface finds.

- A battery of new reconnaissance techniques involves aerial photography and remote sensing. Photographs taken from the air can be used to locate sites spread over huge areas. Pioneer efforts have been made with side-scan aerial radar and scanner imagery.
- Subsurface features are often detected with resistivity surveys, which measure the differences in electrical resistivity of the soil between disturbed and undisturbed areas. Proton magnetometers are used to locate iron objects, fired clay furnaces, and other features.
- Site survey is designed to obtain information on subsurface features at previously located sites, as well as to collect and record artifacts and other surface finds. These categories of data are used to test hypotheses about the age, significance, and function of the site.
- Site survey depends on accurate mapping. The Teotihuacán project in Mexico illustrates the results that can be obtained with a site survey.
- Surface collections may be made by gathering every artifact on the surface of the site, by selecting for diagnostic artifacts, or by random sampling. Surface collections are used to establish the activities that took place on the site, for locating major structures, and for gathering information about the most densely occupied areas of the site.
- Surface survey is much cheaper than excavation and is highly effective, provided the methods used are based on explicit research designs and the results are checked by precise excavations.

Numerous writers have spoken lyrically about time's ravages on the monuments of antiquity, some with pathos, some with humor. W. S. Gilbert, in the second act of the *Mikado*, in 1885, said:

There's a fascination frantic
In a ruin that's romantic
Do you think you are sufficiently decayed?

There was a sense of romance in the antique and the decayed, a sense experienced by every visitor to the Parthenon in Athens or to the Pyramids. Time has transformed the abandoned sites of our ancestors in many ways. Some sites, such as Stonehenge and the Pyramids of Gizeh in Egypt, have never passed into oblivion. People have always realized that they were the work of earlier human beings. Others, like the thousands of sites in the Great Basin and in Australia, have vanished almost without a trace. It takes a trained archaeological eye to identify them.

Until fairly recently, archaeologists paid relatively little attention to the techniques for locating archaeological sites and interpreting them without actual excavation. A new emphasis on regional archaeological studies, innovative remote-sensing techniques, and above all, the urgent need to save and record sites before they are destroyed by twentieth-century development has changed all this. In the pages that follow we review some of the archaeologist's techniques for locating and studying archaeological sites without digging them.

Two basic processes are involved in locating archaeological sites:

Archaeological reconnaissance, which is the systematic attempt to locate, identify, and record the distribution of archaeological sites on the ground and against the natural geographical and environmental background.

Site survey, which is the collecting of surface data and evaluating of each site's archaeological significance.

IDENTIFYING SITES

The competent fieldworker can identify archaeological sites with an ease born of experience that can astound the lay onlooker. I remember being astonished when, on a survey in the Zambezi Valley in Central Africa in 1959, my senior and very experienced colleague stopped suddenly and picked up half a stone flake from a gravel bed covered with Stone Age artifacts. "This is the other half of a flake I found here in 1938," he told me. I flatly disbelieved him. But he was right. We located the original in the local museum collections, and the two halves were reunited. My colleague's archaeological memory was astounding, but it was also a result of long experience with local conditions.

These are some key indicators of archaeological sites.

1. Conspicuous earthworks, stone ruins, or other surface features are among the most obvious indicators. Good examples are the

Adena and Hopewell burial mounds of the Ohio Valley, the pueblos of the American Southwest, and the fortified *pa*'s, or defensive earthworks built by the Maori in New Zealand (Bellwood, 1979). One of the most extensive settlement surveys ever undertaken was that in the Basin of Mexico in the 1960s and 1970s. It was designed to locate every surviving site in the area and to establish relationships between them (Sanders, Parsons, and Santley, 1979).

2. Vegetational cover is a useful indicator, for grass may grow more lushly on areas where the subsoil has been disturbed or the nitrogen content of the soil is greater. On the other hand, many California shell middens are covered with stunted vegetation caused by the artifact-filled, alkaline soil that contrasts sharply with the surrounding green grass at the end of the rainy season. They can be spotted miles away. Sometimes specific types of tree or brush are associated with archaeological sites. One is the breadnut, or *ramon*, tree, which was once cultivated by the Maya. These trees are still common near ancient sites and have been used as guides in locating many archaeological sites.

3. Soil discolorations are a sign of archaeological sites. In many cases the dark, organic soils of long-abandoned villages show up in plowed land as dark zones, often associated with potsherds and other artifacts. Burrowing animals living in such areas leave telltale traces in the form of organic earth and artifacts, which their activities bring to the surface.

4. Surface finds of artifacts, broken bones, and other materials may show up in dry areas as dense concentrations of debris that stand out from the surrounding ground. In some cases, millennia of wind erosion may remove the soil mantling the artifacts and leave them exposed on the surface.

CHANCE DISCOVERIES

The ingenious people who calculate such things estimate that something like a quarter of the world's archaeological sites have been discovered as a result of natural or human activity. Whole chapters of the past have been exposed by accidental discoveries of sites, spectacular artifacts, or skeletons. Ploughing, peat cutting, road-making, and other day-to-day activities have been a fruitful source of archaeological discoveries. Industrial activity, highway construction, airport expansion, and other destructive pastimes of twentieth-century humanity have unearthed countless archaeological sites, many of which have to be investigated hurriedly before the bulldozers remove all traces. Deep ploughing, freeway construction, and urban renewal are bitter enemies of the past. Yet dramatic discoveries have resulted from our despoiling of the environment. Some states require highway contractors to allocate a proportion of their contract budgets for investigating any archaeological sites found in the path of their freeways—this precaution at least permits some investigation of accidentally discovered settlements. But many construction programs pay little heed to the pleas of the archaeologist and bulldoze away the past with minimal sorrow (see Chapter 21).

The excavation for Mexico City's *Metro* (subway) provided a unique opportunity for accidental discoveries of archaeological sites. The shallow tunneling, which extended more than twenty-six miles under the city, yielded a wealth of archaeological material. Mexico City is built on the site of Tenochtitlán, the capital city of the Aztecs. Tenochtitlán, destroyed by the Spanish under Hernando Cortés in 1521, was a wonderful city whose markets rivaled those of most major Spanish cities in size. Little remains of Tenochtitlán on the surface today, but the contractors for the *Metro* found more than 40 tons of pottery, 380 burials, and even a small temple dedicated to the Aztec God of the Wind, Ehecatl-Quetzalcoatl (Figure 10.1). The temple is now preserved on its original site in the Pino Suárez station of the *Metro* system, part of an exhibit commemorating Mexico City's ancestor. The tunneling operations, happily, were under the constant supervision of a large group of archaeologists under the direction of Jorge Gussinyer of the world-famous National Museum of Anthropology. The archaeologists were empowered to halt digging whenever an archaeological find of importance was made. As a result, many new sculptures and artifacts were saved from destruction for the national collections.

Hydroelectric schemes and flood-control programs in North America and elsewhere have destroyed thousands upon thousands of archaeological sites without a trace—and have accelerated the discovery of others. Some of these projects have stimulated much intensive surveying. The Aswan Dam scheme in Nubia provided a rare opportunity for intensive investigation of Pleistocene geology and Stone Age sites in the area to be flooded by Lake Nasser (Wendorf and others, 1968). Nearer home, the flood-control schemes initiated by the Tennessee River Valley Authority and by the Army Corps of Engineers elsewhere in the agriculturally rich South have led to many river-basin surveys (Phillips, Ford, and Griffin, 1951).

Figure 10.1   The temple of Ehecatl-Quetzalcoatl, found during the excavations for the Pino Suarez metro station, Mexico City.

Nature itself sometimes uncovers sites for us, which may then be located by a sharp-eyed archaeologist looking for natural exposures of likely geological strata. Erosion, flooding, tidal waves, low lake levels, earthquakes, and wind action can all lead to exposure of archaeological sites. One of the most famous sites to be exposed in this manner is Olduvai Gorge in Tanzania, a great gash in the Serengeti Plains where nature, by earth movement, has sliced through hundreds of meters of Pleistocene lake bed to expose numerous living floors of early humans (Leakey, 1951). Fossil animal bones were found in the Gorge's exposed strata by Professor Wilhelm Kattwinkel as early as 1911, which led to a fossil-hunting expedition under Professor Hans Reck, and ultimately, to Louis and Mary Leakey's long and patient investigations in the Gorge. The results of their excavations are spectacular—a series of living floors stratified one above another, upon which hominid fossils, broken animal bones, stone implements, and even traces of possible structures have been found and dated to ages ranging from 400,000 years for *Homo erec-*

tus to 1,750,000 years before the present for living floors in the earliest bed of the gorge.

In late 1957, another remarkable discovery was made, this time in semiarid country in southeastern Colorado (Wheat, 1972). Wind erosion exposed what appeared to be five piles of bison bones in an arroyo near Kit Carson. Some projectile points were found with the bones. The bone bed, known as the Olsen-Chubbuck site, lay in a filled buffalo trail, of a type that crisscrossed the plains in early frontier days (Figure 10.2). The bones were carefully excavated and shown to come from *Bison occidentalis*, an extinct species. Separate piles made up of different bone types, such as limb bones, pelvic girdles, and so on, gave a clue to the hunters' butchery techniques.

Figure 10.2   A layer of excavated bison bones from the Olsen-Chubbuck site in Colorado, a kill site found by a cowboy.

They had cut up the carcasses systematically, piling the detached members in the arroyo in separate heaps, dismembering several bison at a time. The remains of nearly 200 bison came from the arroyo, but only a proportion were fully dismembered. Clearly, the arroyo was a trap into which the beasts had been stampeded. (They have a keen sense of smell but poor vision; a lumbering herd of these gregarious beasts can be readily stampeded into an abrupt declivity, and the leaders have no option but to plunge into the gully and be immobilized or disabled by the weight of those behind them.) So vivid a reconstruction of the Paleo-Indians' hunt could be made that the excavators were even able to guess at the direction of the wind on the day of the stampede. The vivid traces of this hunt of 6500 B.C. were buried in the arroyo by nature and exposed again eight thousand years later, to be discovered by the vigilant eye of an amateur archaeologist.

ARCHAEOLOGICAL RECONNAISSANCE

Famous archaeological sites like the Parthenon have never been lost. On the Acropolis at Athens, it was remembered even when Athens itself had become an obscure Medieval village. The temples of Ancient Egyptian Thebes were famous as long ago as Roman times and have never vanished from historical consciousness (Fagan, 1975). Others, such as Homeric Troy, were remembered in Classical literature, but their precise locations were rediscovered only by prolonged archaeological investigation.

Heinrich Schliemann devoted his entire career to locating the site of Homeric Troy. Born in extreme poverty, he first worked as a grocer's assistant. By the time he was thirty, Schliemann was a wealthy merchant in Russia, having made a fortune in the textile trade. Late in the 1860s he retired from business to devote the rest of his life to a search for Troy. In 1870 he started excavations at the large mound known as Hissarlik in northwest Turkey. Within a few seasons, he located the remains of several prehistoric towns, one of which, he claimed, was Priam's Troy (Ceram, 1953; Schliemann, 1881; Stone, 1975).

Of course, most of the world's archaeological sites are far less conspicuous than the Pyramids, and unlike Troy they have no historical records to testify to their existence. The early antiquarians discovered sites primarily by locating burial mounds, stone structures, hill-forts, and other conspicuous traces of prehistoric human works on the European landscape. The *tells* of the Near East, occupied by generation after generation of city dwellers, were easily recognized by early travelers, and the temples and monuments of ancient Egypt have attracted antiquarian and plunderer alike for many centuries. New World archaeological sites were described by some of the first conquistadores. Later, in 1576, Copán, the ruined Mayan city, was studied by García de Palacio. Mayan sites were vividly catalogued by John Lloyd Stephens and Frederick Catherwood in the mid-nineteenth century, and the wonders of Mesoamerican civilization were laboriously recovered from the rain forest that engulfed them (Figure 10.3.).

Archaeological reconnaissance did not become a serious part of archaeology until field archaeologists began to realize that people had enacted their lives against the background of an ever changing natural landscape, modified both by climatic and other ecological changes, and also by human activities. Thus, all that remained for archaeology to find, as expressed by Francis Bacon, was "some remnants of history which have casually escaped the shipwreck of

Figure 10.3 Copán in Honduras, a conspicuous archaeological site found by a Spanish priest in 1576 and made known by Stephens and Catherwood in the nineteenth century. This photograph shows the reconstructed ball court.

time." In the Southwest late in the nineteenth century, the immortal Adolph F. Bandelier, historian, archaeologist, ethnographer, and novelist, walked thousands of miles in search of archaeological sites. The early twentieth century brought much more of this more systematic field archaeology in Europe. J. P. Williams Freeman and O. G. S. Crawford, among others, traced Roman roads and ancient field systems, walking and bicycling over the countryside in search of known and unknown sites. In Bolivia and Peru, Max Uhle, a German, was among those who pioneered systematic field survey in the New World. The techniques these scholars pioneered form the basis for much archaeological fieldwork today (Crawford, 1953).

Most early archaeological reconnaissance sought individual sites for eventual excavation. But, as archaeologists have grown more and more intent on studying variability in the archaeological record, they have come to deal with entire regions rather than individual sites (Binford, 1964). The objectives of reconnaissance too have shifted, in part. Although archaeologists still search for sites to excavate, most do so within an entirely different theoretical framework. Those following the more traditional approaches tend to think of a survey area as a group of sites rather than a unit of space in which prehistoric peoples lived. Thus, the modern regional survey is more properly defined as "Some specified unit of space within which archaeological sites and other relevant variables are tabulated" (Dunnell and Dancey, 1983). This approach makes surface surveying a much more important component of archaeological investigation than ever before. Before considering the surface survey, let us examine the more traditional reconnaissance methods.

Ground Reconnaissance. Most archaeological sites are discovered by careful field surveying and thorough examination of the countryside for both conspicuous and inconspicuous traces of the past (Willey, 1953). A survey can vary from searching a city lot for historic structures or a tiny side valley with a few rockshelters in its walls, to a large-scale survey of an entire river basin or water catchment area—a project that would take several years to complete. For all these, the theoretical ideal is the same: to recover all traces of ancient settlement in the survey area. Often, surveys intended to recover all or nearly all sites in a region are called *complete survey* or *comprehensive reconnaissance.*

Archaeological sites manifest themselves in many ways: in the form of tells, which are mounds of occupation debris; middens,

which are mounds of food remains and occupation debris; or conspicuous caves or temples. But many others are far less easily
located, perhaps displaying no more than a small scatter of stone
tools or a patch of discolored soil. Still other sites leave no traces of
their presence above the ground and may come to light only when
the subsoil is disturbed, like the temple of Ehecatl-Quetzalcoatl,
found during excavation of Mexico City's *Metro* line (Figure 10.1).
Thus, it can be seen that no surface survey, however thorough, and
however sophisticated its remote sensing devices, will achieve complete coverage. The key to effective archaeological survey lies in
proper research designs and in rigorous sampling techniques to
provide a reliable basis of probability for extending the findings of
the survey from a sample zone to a wider region.

The comprehensiveness of any survey is affected by other factors,
too. Many surveys are carried out in intensively populated areas or
on private farmland. Some landowners may refuse access to their
lands. To their credit, most farmers or landlords do not. Indeed,
owners may recall past discoveries on their land, hitherto unsus-
pected by archaeologists. Inaccessibility can be further complicated
by such factors as dense vegetation, crops, and floodwaters. In many
parts of Mexico and California the obvious months for site survey
are at the end of the dry season, when the vegetation is dry or even
burned off. But in lush, lowland floodplains, such as those of the
American South, large tracts of the survey area may be totally inaccessible all year. Only the most conspicuous sites, like mounds,
show up under such conditions. And, of course, thousands of sites
are buried under tract housing and parking lots, or the countless
huge earthmoving operations that have radically altered the
landscape.

A great deal depends, too, on the intensity of the survey in the
field. The survey area can be traversed by automobile, horseback,
mule, camel, bicycle, or—most effectively—on foot. Most well-
known field archaeologists of this century have been avid walkers.
In fact, one used to boast that he had walked off the feet of all his
students and colleagues in pursuit of the past! Footwork is important, for it enables the archaeologist to train an eye for topography
and the relationships of human settlement to the landscape.

Michael Schiffer of the University of Arizona identifies four basic
types of intensive ground reconnaissance (Schiffer and House,
1976):

1. Conspicuous and accessible sites are located by superficial survey, such as that by Catherwood and Stephens with Mayan sites

in the Yucatan in the 1840s. The investigator visits only very conspicuous and accessible sites of great size and considerable fame. These operations, however, hardly scratch the archaeological surface.

2. In the next level of survey, assisted by local informants such as landowners, the relatively conspicuous sites at accessible locations are discovered. This type of survey was used frequently in the 1930s for the classic river-basin surveys in the lower Mississippi Valley. It can be very effective, but it gives a rather narrow view of the archaeological sites in an area.

3. Limited-area reconnaissance involves very comprehensive door-to-door inquiries, supported by actual substantiation of claims that a site exists by checking the report on the ground. This type of survey, with its built-in system of verification, may yield more comprehensive information on sites. But it still does not give the most critical information of all—data on the ratios of one site type to another—nor does it assess the percentage of accessible sites that have been found. When archaeologists need a total inventory of archaeological sites in an area, such information is vital.

4. In the last type, foot survey, a party of archaeologists covers an entire area by walking over it, perhaps with a set interval between members of the party. This is about the most rigorous method of reconnaissance, but it does work, as evidenced by the Cache River project in Arkansas. There, selected zones of the basin were surveyed by people walking sixty meters apart (Schiffer and House, 1976). When Paul Martin and Fred Plog surveyed 5.2 square miles of the Hay Hollow Valley in east-central Arizona in 1967, they supervised a team of eight people who walked back and forth over small portions of the area (Martin and Plog, 1973). Each worker was nine meters from the next, their pathways carefully laid out with compass and stakes. Two hundred and fifty sites were recorded by this survey, at the cost of thirty person-days per square mile. One would think that every site would have been recorded. Yet two entirely new sites were discovered in the same area in 1969 and 1971, prehistoric irrigation canals were spotted by an expert on some aerial photographs, and some sandstone quarry sites were found.

As we have said, the chances of any archaeological survey recording every site in even a small area are remote. Obviously, though, total survey of an area is desirable, and sometimes nearly total coverage can be achieved by combined remote sensing and ground reconnaissance. William Sanders and his colleagues carried out a long-term archaeological survey of the Basin of Mexico in which they elected to try locating every site in the area over many seasons of fieldwork. At the end of the project, Sanders argued that this approach was far more effective than any sampling of the area, for it gave a much clearer picture of site variability on the ground (Sanders, Parsons, and Santley, 1979). Undoubtedly he is right, *if* one has the time and the money. In these days of limited budgets and short-term archaeological contracts dictated by impending site destruction, the archaeologist has turned to both remote sensing and statistical sampling to achieve goals of the survey.

Remote Sensing. More and more archaeologists are relying on technology and elaborate instrumentation to help them discover the past. Some archaeologists are beginning to talk about "nondestructive archaeology," the analysis of archaeological phenomena without excavations or collecting of artifacts, both of which destroy the archaeological record. The major methods in this approach are generally labeled remote sensing (Lyon and Avery, 1977). These techniques include aerial photography, various magnetic prospecting methods, and side-scan radar.

Aerial Photography. The potential of aerial photography for archaeological reconnaissance was first recognized during World War I by O. G. S. Crawford in the American West and by German archaeologists serving in the Sinai. The latter photographed ancient fields, streets, buildings, and other features, which showed up with astonishing clarity (Crawford and Keiller, 1928). The aviation pioneer Charles Lindbergh flew Alfred Kidder over areas of Arizona and New Mexico searching for ancient village sites. These pioneer flights were followed by hundreds of later sorties. Archaeological photography has also benefited from technological advances made during World War II and by space exploration. Today, thousands of hitherto unknown sites have been plotted on maps, whole field systems and roadways have been incorporated into panoramas of prehistoric or Roman landscapes in Italy and North Africa, and well-known sites such as Stonehenge and the many Mesoamerican and South American temples have been photographed in the context of their landscapes (Figure 10.4).

Aerial photography gives an unrivaled overhead view of the past. Sites can be photographed obliquely or vertically, at different seasons or times of day, and from many directions. Numerous sites

Figure 10.4   An aerial photograph of Chan Chan in coastal Peru shows the general layout of this remarkable settlement, occupied *ca.* A.D. 1200.

that have left almost no surface traces on the ground have come to light through the all-embracing eye of the air photograph (Deuel, 1969; Vogt, 1974; Wilson, 1982).

Shadow sites.   Many earthworks and other complex structures have been leveled by plough or erosion, but their reduced topography clearly shows up from the air. The rising or setting sun can set off long shadows, emphasizing the relief of almost-vanished banks or ditches, so that the features of the site stand out in the oblique light. Such phenomena are sometimes called "shadow sites."

Crop and soil marks.   These are found in areas where the subsoil is suitable for revealing differences in soil color and in the richness of crop growth on a particular soil (Figure 10.5). Such marks cannot be detected easily on the surface, but under favorable circumstances they can be seen clearly from the air. The principle on which the crop mark is based is that the growth and color of a crop are mainly determined by the amount of moisture the plant can derive from the soil and subsoil. If the soil depth has been increased by digging features, such as pits and ditches, and then filling them in, or by heaping up additional earth to form artificial banks or mounds, crops growing over such abandoned structures are tall and well

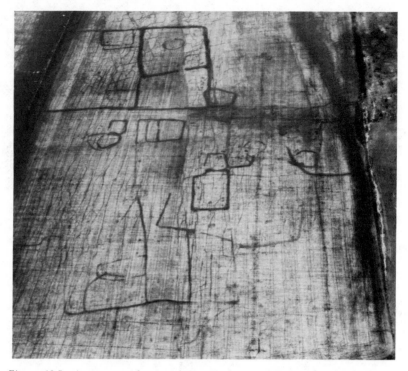

Figure 10.5 A crop mark site, from Thorpe, Achurch, Huntingdonshire, England. Under favorable circumstances, such marks can be seen clearly from the air.

nourished. The converse is true where topsoil has been removed and the infertile subsoil is near the surface, or where impenetrable surfaces, such as paved streets, are below ground level and crops are stunted. Thus a dark crop mark can be taken for a ditch or pit, and a lighter line will define a more substantial structure. Soil marks result from ploughing soil from such features as banks, and show up as a color lighter than that of the darker, deeper soil around them. Soil marks are useful in chalk country, where subsoil is a brilliant white.

Examples of aerial photography. A classic application of air photography was provided by Gordon Willey, who used a standard Peruvian Air Force mosaic of cultivated valley bottoms and margins of the Virú Valley in northern coastal Peru to survey changing set-

tlement patterns there (Willey, 1953). Employing these photographs as the basis for a master site map of the valley, Willey was
able to plot many archaeological features. Three hundred and fifteen sites in the Virú Valley were located, many of them stone
buildings, walls, or terraces that showed up quite well on the mosa-
ics. Some much less conspicuous sites were also spotted, among
them midden heaps without stone walls, refuse mounds that
appeared as low hillocks on the photographs, and small, pyramidal
mounds of insignificant proportions. Adobe houses did not show
up as clearly as stone structures. An enormous amount of time was
saved that would otherwise have been spent walking over rough
countryside. The aerial photographs enabled Willey and his team
to pinpoint many sites before going out in the field. The finds were
later investigated on the spot. The result was the fascinating story
of shifting settlement patterns in Virú over many thousands of
years, a classic of its kind.

Most aerial photographs are taken with black-and-white film,
which gives definition superior to that of color film and is much
cheaper to buy and reproduce than color. The wide range of filters
that can be used with black-and-white give the photographer great
versatility in the field.

Some valuable experiments have been made with color photography, which is useful in detecting natural rather than cultural features. But it has the disadvantage of being more expensive and less
tolerant of the photographer's errors.

Infrared film, which has three layers sensitized to green, red, and
infrared, detects reflected solar radiation at the near end of the electromagnetic spectrum, some of which is invisible to the human eye.
The different reflections from cultural and natural features are
translated by the film into distinctive "false" colors. Bedrock comes
up blue on infrared film, but vigorous grass growth on alluvial
plains shows up bright red. Experiments at the famous Snaketown
site in the American Southwest, a great Hohokam Indian pueblo,
trade, and ceremonial center, did not show up new cultural features, but tonal contrasts within a color indicated various cultural
components. Vigorous plant growth showing up red on infrared
photographs has been used to track shallow subsurface water
sources where springs were formerly used by prehistoric peoples.
The infrared data could lead the archaeologist to likely areas for
hunting camps and villages where few surface indications now
remain (Gumerman and Lyons, 1971; Harp, 1978).

No archaeological aerial photography is fully effective unless the results are checked on the ground. Even an expert can make many errors in interpreting surface features from air photographs.

Nonphotographic Methods. Archaeological sites can be detected from the air by nonphotographic techniques, as well, but they are always very expensive.

Side-scan aerial radar (SLAR). This technique is used by the military to look at the ground obliquely, and is effective even through dense cloud cover. Radar can sometimes penetrate dense vegetation as well, and can be used to show up areas where many changes in topography have taken place or subsoil of large sites has been disturbed. It has also been applied to underwater sites to locate wrecks on the sea floor.

Scanner imagery. This method can record infrared radiation beyond the practical spectral response of photographic film. A scanning system collects the emitted energy with an oscillating mirror that scans the ground surface. The radiation thus recorded is converted to an electrical signal with a cyrogenic detector. A radiation map that can be inspected on a television screen or on film is the product of this system. Infrared imagery has been used most dramatically in north-central Arizona, where prehistoric garden plots, barely visible on the ground, have shown up in sharp focus on scanning plots. The borders of the plots are enhanced on the image because the thicker volcanic ash at the edges of the gardens has a lower thermal inertia than the soil in the middle of the plots. The buried and obscure features of the field system absorb and radiate solar energy in differing amounts from the surrounding soil.

Landsat 1 and 2. Earth Resources Technology Satellites scan the earth with readers that record the intensity of reflected light and infrared radiation from the earth's surface. The data from scanning operations are converted electronically into photographic images and from these into mosaic maps. Normally, however, these maps are taken at a scale of about 1:1,000,000, far too imprecise for anything but the most general archaeological surveys. The pyramids and plazas of Teotihuacán in the Valley of Mexico might appear on such a map, but certainly not the types of minute archaeological distribution information that the average survey seeks. The Landsat imagery offers an integrated view of a large region and is made up of light reflected from many components of the earth: soil, vegetation, topography, and so on. Thus, the stratified images obtained from Landsat tell the archaeologist a great deal about the environment as a cohesive whole. Computer-enhanced Landsat images can be used to construct environmental cover maps of large survey regions that are a superb backdrop for both aerial and ground reconnaissance for archaeological resources.

Subsurface Detection.   Once sites have been located it is often possible to learn much about them by geophysical methods, most of which involve mechanical devices for subsurface detection of buried features. Many of these relatively new techniques were developed for oil or geological prospecting. Most are expensive; some are very time consuming. But their application can sometimes save many weeks of expensive excavation, and on occasion, aid in formulating an accurate research design before a dig begins.

Nonmechanical Detection.   In this method, the surface of the site is thumped with a suitable heavy pounder. The earth resonates in different ways, so much so that a practiced ear can detect the distinctive sound of a buried ditch or a subsurface stone wall. Dowsing, more an art than a geophysical method, really works—with practice. The author has used it on several occasions to detect buried walls.

The auger, or core borer.   This is a tool used to bore through subsurface deposits to find depth and consistency of archaeological deposit lying beneath the surface. This technique has its value during an excavation, but it has the obvious disadvantage that the probe may destroy valuable artifacts. Augers were used quite successfully at the Ozette site in Washington to establish the depth of midden deposits (Kirk, 1974). Some specialized augers are used to lift pollen samples. Augers with a camera attached to a periscope head are also used to investigate the interiors of Etruscan tombs (Figure 10.6). The periscope is inserted through a small hole in the roof of the tomb to inspect the interior. If the contents are undisturbed, then excavation proceeds. But if tomb robbers have emptied the chamber, many hours of labor have been saved.

Mechanical Detection.   Several types of mechanical detection are: (1) resistivity survey, (2) magnetic survey, and (3) pulse radar.

Figure 10.6   A periscope being used to investigate an Etruscan tomb.

Resistivity survey.   The electrical resistivity of the soil provides
some clues to subsurface features on archaeological sites (Coles,
1972). Rocks and minerals conduct electricity, mainly because the
deposits have moisture containing mineral salts in solution. A resistivity survey meter can be used to measure the variations in the
resistance of the ground to an electric current. Stone walls or hard
pavements obviously retain less dampness than a deep pit filled
with soft earth or a large ditch that has silted up. These differences
can be measured accurately, so that disturbed ground, stone walls,
and other subsurface features can be detected by systematic survey.
To survey a site, all that is needed is the meter, which is attached
to four or five probes. A grid of strings is laid over the site and the
readings taken from the probes are plotted as contour lines. These
show the areas of equal resistance and the presence of features, such
as ditches and walls (Figure 10.7). This method works best on well-
drained soils, and has been used more widely in Europe than
elsewhere.

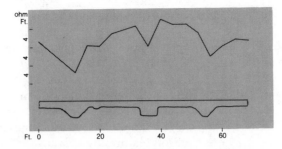

Figure 10.7   An electrical-resistance survey across a Bronze Age burial site at Dorchester, Oxford, England. The upper curve represents the traverse made across the site with the instrument, with the probes set 1.2 meters (4 feet) apart. The lower line is a schematic section across the site; the dips indicate the two outer ditches and the burial pit, the positions of which were subsequently confirmed by excavation.

Magnetic survey.   Magnetic location is used to find buried features such as iron objects, fired clay furnaces, pottery kilns, hearths, and pits filled with rubbish or softer soil. The principle is simple: Any mass of clay heated to about 700°C and then cooled acquires a weak magnetism. Rocks, boulders, and soil will also acquire magnetism if iron oxides are present when they are heated. When the remanant magnetism of fired clay or of other materials in a pit or similar feature is measured, it will give a reading different from that of the intensity of the earth's magnetic field normally obtained from undisturbed soils. The proton magnetometer is the instrument most commonly used to detect archaeological features by magnetic detection. A site is surveyed by laying out 15-meter (50-foot) square units, each of them divided into 1.5-meter (5-foot) grid squares. The measurement is taken with a staff to which are attached two small bottles filled with water or alcohol enclosed in electric coils. The magnetic intensity is measured by recording the behavior of the protons in the hydrogen atoms in the bottle's contents. The magnetometer itself amplifies the weak signals from the electrical coils. Features are traced by taking closely spaced measurements over areas where anomalies in the magnetic readings are found. Magnetic detection has been used very successfully to record pits, walls, and other features in the middle of large forts or fortified towns, where total excavation of a site is clearly uneconomical. This method has been used widely in Europe and on earthen pyramids at La Venta, Mexico, but it is subject to some error because of such modern features as barbed wire fences, electric trains, and electric cables (Steponaitis and Brain, 1976; Kaczor and Weymouth, 1981).

Pulse radar. The pulse-induction meter applies pulses of magnetic field to the soil from a transmitter coil. This instrument is very sensitive to metals and can be used to find pottery and metal objects and graves containing such objects. A soil conductivity meter can be used to detect subsoil features by measuring changes in the conductivity of the soil. Anomalies spotted by the instrument can be plotted with good accuracy, and pits as small as 30 centimeters (11.8 inches) in diameter and 10 centimeters (3.9 inches) deep have been located. Individual metal objects can also be detected by this method, which adds great promise for the future.

Application of radar and other electronic devices is proliferating in archaeology. Ken Weeks and a team of fellow Egyptologists have embarked on a long-term project to map all the royal tombs in Thebes' Valley of Kings. They are using a hot-air balloon, X rays, and sonic detectors to map subterranean features and hidden chambers in royal tombs. High technology has come to historical archaeology, too. Joel Grossman was faced with the problem of investigating a buried seventeenth- and eighteenth-century port at Raritan, New Jersey in three short months before a major sewer project butchered the site. Forced to carry out a year's worth of excavation in one-quarter the time, Grossman carried out a ground-penetrating radar survey of the site's buried features. The excavation was conducted with an infrared transit with computerized data recording that automatically provided provenience coordinates for every find. The technology used in the survey, excavation, and analysis of the site was very complicated and the excavators needed considerable technical skill to operate it smoothly (Grossman, 1982).

Recording Sites. Archaeological reconnaissance is useless unless one records the exact geographical location of the archaeological phenomena revealed by the survey. It is here that remote sensing comes into its own. Some of the larger projects in cultural resource management in the western United States make extensive use of remote sensing to record and manage archaeological sites (Chapter 20). Except for rainfall patterns, all the environmental information required for many surveys can be plotted with information obtained from aerial maps. Although large archaeological sites like road systems or major cities can be located on aerial photographs, very small phenomena like scattered artifacts or cattle enclosures are generally impossible to find on even the most detailed maps. Aerial photographs can be used, however, to mark the locations of any archaeological phenomena once they have been located on the ground. The recording was taken a stage further in the San Juan Basin, where known types of sites and locations were plotted on aerial photographs marked up with environmental data obtained from Landsat images. Density values for different types of site were then determined against each environmental zone and were used to suggest concentrations of sites in unsurveyed areas (Drager and others, 1982). The zones involved were then sampled on foot to establish their site concentrations. This method is very effective in large-scale surveys in which only parts of the region will be disturbed by agriculture, mining, oil exploration, or other activities.

The primary purpose of many remote-sensing surveys is to map concentrations of sites, and, on larger projects, to identify where maximal efforts in ground surveying and excavation should be concentrated. This decision requires not only remote-sensing data, but a comprehensive record of all sites known from the survey area as well. It is not enough, however, just to plot a site on a good map and record its precise latitude, longitude, and map grid reference. Most projects develop a site-record form as well, such as the one illustrated in Figure 10.8 (there are, of course, numerous variations on this example). Forms of this type require the investigator to record the location of the site, as well as information about surface features, the landowner, potential threats to the site, and so on. Every site in the United States is given a name and a number. Sites in Santa Barbara County, California, for example, are given the prefix CA-SBa- and are numbered sequentially.

So many sites are now known in North America that most states and many large archaeological projects have set up comprehensive computer data banks containing comprehensive information about site distributions and characteristics. Arkansas has a statewide computer bank that is in constant use for decisions on conservation and management, and the SJBRUS site file used in the San Juan Basin is a vital tool for mapping and predicting site concentrations. The project managers make their predictions by combining site data from both totally and partially surveyed two-kilometer grid squares with environmental zones, then measuring them with a digital planimeter. After arbitrarily eliminating zones in which less than 4 percent of the area had been surveyed, the project staff divided the number of sites in the data bank for each square in each zone and

Figure 10.8   Two pages of the Florida site file form, showing the standard of data now required for field surveys. This approach assumes that all sites are valuable archaeological resources, each of them a part of the total inventory of sites forming an archaeological data base that can be consulted for many purposes.

STATE OF FLORIDA DEPARTMENT OF STATE Division of Archives, History and Records Management DS-HSP-3A Rev. 4-77	FLORIDA MASTER SITE FILE	
		FDAHRM 802==
	Site No.	1009==
	Site Name	830==
Other Name(s) for Site		930==
Other Nos. for Site		906==
NR Classification Category:		916==
County		808==
Instructions for locating site (or address)		
		813==
Location: _____ subdivision name / block no. / lot no.		868==
Owner of Site: Name		;
Address		902==
Occupant, Tenant, or Manager: Name		;
Address		904==
Reporter (or local contact): Name		;
Address		816==
Recorder: Name & Title		;
Address		818==
Survey Date 820== Type Ownership		848==
Inventory Status		914==
Previous Survey(s), Excavation(s) or Collection(s): (*enter activity/title of project or survey/ name/date/respository*)		
		839==
Recording Station		804==
Specimens (Inventory Numbers)		870==
Specimens (Present Repository of Materials)		
		880==
Date of Visit to Site 828== Recording Date		832==
Photographic Record Numbers		
		860==

Location of Site (Specific):

Map Reference (incl. scale & date)_____ 809==

Township	Range	Section	¼ Sec.	¼ ¼ Sec.	¼ ¼ ¼ Sec.
					812==

LATITUDE AND LONGITUDE COORDINATES DEFINING A POLYGON LOCATING THE PROPERTY						
	LATITUDE				LONGITUDE	
Point	Degrees	Minutes	Seconds	Degrees	Minutes	Seconds
	°	′	″	°	′	″
	°	′	″	°	′	″
	°	′	″	°	′	″
	°	′	″	°	′	″
	°	′	″	°	′	″

——————————————————— OR ———————————————————

LATITUDE AND LONGITUDE COORDINATES DEFINING THE CENTER POINT OF A PROPERTY OF
LESS THAN TEN ACRES

°	′	″	°	′	″
					800==

UTM Coordinates: _____ 890==

Zone   Easting   Northing

Description of Site:

Original Use(s) of Site_____ 838==

Site Size (approx. acreage of property) _____ 833==

Condition of Site:	Integrity of Site:
Check one	Check one or more
☐ Excellent 863== ☐ Deteriorated 863==	☐ Altered 858== ☐ Restored ( )(Date:)( ) 858==
☐ Good 863== ☐ Ruins 863==	☐ Unaltered 858== ☐ Moved ( )(Date:)( ) 858==
☐ Fair 863== ☐ Unexposed 863==	☐ Destroyed 858== ☐ Original Site 858==
☐ Redeposited 863==	

Condition of Site (Remarks): ( )(_____

_____)( ) 863==

Threats to Site:

Check one or more

☐ Zoning ( )(   )( ) 878==   ☐ Transportation ( )(   )( ) 878==

☐ Development ( )(   )( ) 878==   ☐ Fill ( )(   )( ) 878==

☐ Deterioration ( )(   )( ) 878==   ☐ Dredge ( )(   )( ) 878==

☐ Borrowing ( )(   )( ) 878==

☐ Other (See Remarks below):   878==

Threats to Site (Remarks): _____

_____

_____ 879==

found a value for the number of sites per hectare for 21 of the 48 zones in the Basin. This procedure is arbitrary, but a valuable planning tool when estimating time and budget expenditures for an archaeological survey.

SAMPLING IN ARCHAEOLOGICAL SURVEY

Partly because regional studies have become more fashionable, and partly because of the growing demands of cultural resource management, archaeologists have become deeply interested in economical methods for collecting survey data. Many of them have sought refuge in statistical sampling methods. Statistical sampling theory occupies an important place in archaeological research and some statistical training is now integral to every professional's training. Unfortunately, many of the sampling applications used so far have been downright poor, so much so that one archaeologist has been moved to remark that "the literature on sampling . . . resembles in some respects a battlefield littered with pieces of machinery that have broken down" (Ammerman, 1981). It behooves us to examine sampling and archaeological survey in some detail.

Sampling has been defined as the "science of controlling and measuring the reliability of information through the theory of probability." Systematic and carefully controlled sampling of archaeological data is essential if we are to rely heavily, as we do, on statistical approaches in the reconstruction of past lifeways and cultural process. If we are interested in past adaptations to environmental conditions, we must systematically sample many types of sites in each environmental zone, not merely those which look important or likely to yield spectacular finds. Sampling techniques enable us to ensure a statistically reliable basis of archaeological data from which we can make generalizations about our research data. Because these generalizations are often estimates of probability, they must be based on unbiased data.

Sampling Terminology. Sampling design is integral in the formulation of a research project and research design, and must be fitted specifically to the problem posed by the researcher. For the data to be most useful, it is necessary to define clearly, and in highly specific words, what the sample will actually represent. Because relatively little can be known about the populations with which one is dealing, probability sampling of archaeological data can be very misleading in a strictly statistical sense. Sampling approaches are useful in reducing bias, and as aids to making decisions about data collection, but their value as precise statements of probability is much more limited.

The objectives of sampling in archaeological survey can range from such simple goals as estimating average densities of archaeological phenomena in a region or sampling area to efforts to estimate the meaning of these densities. Nance (1983) argues that the two constants, whatever the objectives of the sampling, are: The methods used must lead to *effective* discovery of cultural remains, and to efficient estimation of "the quantitative properties" in what is discovered.

Several questions arise from these constants. Effective archaeological survey is designed to locate hitherto unknown sites. How confident, then, can one be that one's sampling methods will lead to such discoveries? This doubt has led archaeologists into the concepts of discovery model sampling and discovery probability, the likelihood that archaeological remains will be detected within a sampling unit given a specified level of sampling effort (Nance, 1983). The variables influencing the probability of discovering sites are easily recited, among them the size and conspicuousness of the site (the Pyramids of Gizeh lie at one end of the spectrum; an isolated concentration of stone chips at the other, and the chances of finding the latter lie near zero). The sampler's problem is working out the probability of discovering most of the sites that lie between these extremes. To do so, one requires both several ways of assessing statistical probability and a wide range of empirical data.

Discovery model sampling deals with the problem of finding examples of the archaeological record. Statistical precision models are used to try to infer something about the total quantitative properties of a large body of information (a population) from our studies of only a statistical sample of that entity. Statistical precision methods work well when estimating the commonly occurring characteristics, such as some types of artifact or site forms. Most archaeological sampling, whether applied to site survey or to artifact analyses, requires at least some use of statistical precision models.

Some Basic Concepts.   The first stage in any sampling design is defining the boundaries of the area being investigated, the data universe.

The data universe is the unit that is chosen for investigation. It can be a single site; portions of a settlement; a well-defined geographical region, such as a river valley; or a chronological period, as between 1000 B.C. and A.D. 350 in Ohio.

Sample elements are members of a population that is of interest. Observations about a sample of elements provides a way of obtaining information about the population of which they are a part.

Sample units are the units chosen for investigating the data universe or a population (see below).

A sample element and sample unit may be the same thing, but it depends on the problems being researched. A grid of square sampling units is imposed over a river valley. To estimate the density of sites in each sampling unit, the investigator chooses a sample of grid squares (sometimes called *quadrats*) and observes the number of sites occurring in each. But if we want to examine the properties of the sites in the area—their size, for instance—then a sampling unit may contain more than one element of the population.

Nonarbitrary units are sample units that might coincide with obvious, quite natural units, such as rooms in a pueblo, graves within a cemetery, or highly distinctive local environments. *Arbitrary units* are just that—spatial units chosen to subdivide an area into convenient sections for investigation. These can be of any shape or size. Some of the most common are grid squares or quadrats; long, rectangular units, which are almost like pathways across an area, often known as *transects;* and simple site locations, or *points.* Sample units are purely a research tool, and as such, they contain archaeological data. The only assumption made, whether arbitrary or nonarbitrary units are used, is that the data in each are similar enough, or complementary enough, to allow comparison of one unit to the other.

Populations are the sum of all sampling units. They are not the same as data universes, which are a definition of a research area. Sample units may be devised to survey only the southern part of a river valley, for example. These units, perhaps transects across a densely forested plain, form a population. But the population of sample units is only a small part of the data universe. In many cases, however, the population may end up yielding data that are applicable to the universe as a whole.

The data pool is the *potential* information available to the researcher within the data universe. Sampling methods are designed to acquire as much of the data pool as possible, the data acquired coming from sample units within the populations of the data universe. Even without using formal sampling methods, the amount of information that can be obtained from a data pool is limited. Sampling methods are designed to maximize data acquisition and to do so on a statistically sound basis.

Sampling frames are the lists of chosen units that form the sample of the total population to be tested. The sample frame is compiled as a means for proceeding to the selection of units for investigation. The units are listed in order and form the *sample size*. There has been much debate about the desirable size of archaeological data samples (Asch, 1975). Obviously, the ideal sample is a total population, but in practice dictates of time and funds make samples much smaller. Obviously, too, the larger the sample, the smaller the chance of missing an important variation in the population.

Sampling the Data.   A data universe is easy enough to define on paper and in theory. But the reality of access in the field may be very different. Funds and people may be limited; and access to the area may be restricted by landowners, rugged landscape, vegetational cover, or even political events. And, in a site chosen for excavation, one should always leave a portion undisturbed so that later generations of archaeologists can check the work, using more sophisticated methods. The sampling of the data universe depends, finally, on both the amount of the universe accessible and the method used to sample the population of the sample units set up.

Nonprobabilistic sampling selects the sample units to be investigated using intuitive or pragmatic criteria chosen by the investigator. These can include such realistic considerations as access to only a few sites being possible in a dense rain forest, the precedent of generations of earlier research that lead one to concentrate on certain types of conspicuous sites, or simply the archaeologist's long experience. This type of sampling is fine for many specific tasks, *provided* that the sample units, the data universe, and the population being investigated are clearly defined ahead of time. Without such precise terms of reference, it is difficult to assess whether the sample data collected are truly representative of the data universe as a whole. Nonprobabilistic sampling often concentrates on the more conspicuous sites. Is one justified, for instance, in arguing that the burial practices in one Hopewell burial mound were similar to those at a site three miles away, and at another twenty miles away?

The answer is no, unless one's terms of reference for making generalizations are carefully defined ahead of time.

Probabilistic sampling is much more effective and appropriate where one is seeking to generalize about a large data universe from a small sample population. The discipline of statistics and statistical theory makes considerable use of probability theory, a means of relating small samples of data in mathematical ways to much larger populations. The classic example is the political opinion poll, which is based on a tiny sample (perhaps 1,500 people) used to draw much more general conclusions about national feelings on an issue. In archaeology, probabilistic sampling improves the chance that the conclusions reached on the basis of the samples are relatively reliable. This outcome depends, however, on very carefully drawn research designs and precisely defined sample units.

Probabilistic sampling involves the use of probability theory. It maximizes the probability that the site distribution in a chosen sample area is similar to that for the area as a whole. This type of approach has the advantage of allowing people not only to project the total number of sites in a research area, but also to calculate the proportion of large sites to smaller ones, and so on, information vital in the study of evolving human settlement patterns (see Chapter 16).

Probabilistic sampling in archaeology is difficult, for the peculiarities of archaeological data, compared with, say, those of physics, makes the development of sampling strategies difficult (Mueller, 1975). Once the sampling units are carefully defined and chosen, the archaeologist can elect to take a sample of individual units or of statistical clusters of them, often a decision of convenience. One example of clusters of sample units is a series of transects that lie close to one another, yet are assumed to include the range of data variability found in the entire population. It is obviously cheaper to survey such a cluster than to travel among several individual sample units scattered over a data universe of thousands of square miles.

Probabilistic Sampling Schemes.   Archaeologists rely on three basic probability sampling schemes:

1. *Simple random sampling* takes the sample frame, determines the sample size, and then randomly selects the number of units required from the frame. The actual selection of numbered units can be done by referring to a table of random numbers until the

requisite number of units has been selected. Any method, like drawing cards from a hat, will do, provided the selection is absolutely random. This method is used when it is not necessary to take into account such variables as landscape or site topography, or sometimes when an absolutely virgin area is being worked. This approach treats all samples as absolutely equal, without referring to any external variables that may affect an individual sample.

2. *Systematic sampling* is a refinement of simple random sampling. One unit is chosen, and then others are selected at equal intervals from the first one. One might excavate every fifth square on a grid of equal-sized squares laid out across a shell midden. This approach is useful for studying artifact patterning; but it is less effective when studying such situations as, say, the rooms of a pueblo, where a regular pattern of human behavior may cause one to accidentally sample only a portion of the activities at a site.

3. *Stratified sampling* is used when sample units are not uniform. The population is divided into separate groups, or strata, which reflect the observed range of variation within the population. Strata can be different ecological zones, different occupation layers or artifact classes, or groups of trenches. Such units permit intensive sampling of some units and less detailed work on others.

Charles L. Redman applied stratified sampling methods to a thirteenth-century A.D. pueblo in the El Morro Valley of west-central New Mexico (Redman, 1975). He had time to clear only about one-quarter of the 500 rooms in the pueblo, so he stratified the site into four corners and four sides—each site was divided into four sampling blocks. Redman randomly selected one corner and one block from each area for clearance. He was able to select large blocks from areas that were well separated from one another but still use random sampling methods. Fourteen rooms, in pairs selected from each side of the pueblo and from the corners, were excavated. Thus, the population was stratified to ensure testing of at least one room from each row and of compartments of different sizes, as identified during preliminary investigation. It proved possible to sample this large site systematically, with minimal expenditure of time and funds.

Sampling distribution is a fundamental concept in statistical inference. If you have a constant population and draw repeated samples of similar size from it, then you can observe what happens to some sample property of the population, say a type of enclosure wall, over these repeated samplings. The sample estimates will differ from sample to sample, are variables, and will have sampling distributions. As long as the sample size remains constant, the items are selected randomly and independently of one another, and the probability remains invariant, then you will end up with a binomial probability distribution (Nance, 1983). The sampling distribution has a number of properties important to archaeologists:

1. Is the average value of the sampling distribution equal to the population parameter, or does it consistently over- or underestimate it?
2. Is the distribution of the sample estimate symmetrical or skewed?
3. What degree of variability, or spread about the average value, is displayed by the distribution?
4. And, of paramount importance to archaeologists, what factors were responsible for producing the characteristics of the distribution?

Clusters and Elements.   Archaeological survey involves three statistical populations:
sampling units defined by area
sites
artifacts
It is of paramount importance to be highly explicit about how these populations are sampled (Mueller, 1974; Thomas, 1975). Two major types of sampling are commonly used in archaeological survey:

Element sampling.   Here you establish a sampling frame and select the sample by a random and independent selection method. This approach is used only on very large populations, typically, in archaeology, those for which arbitrary sampling units are used. You might use element sampling when estimating the density of archaeological sites over a sampling area. This is a simple approach, for the variables in this exercise would be the number of sites occurring within each of a specified number of sample units.

Cluster sampling.   Archaeologists engaged in survey work are commonly interested in populations of sites, artifacts, or features lying within a region or sample area. A survey may be made up of areal (arbitrary) survey units, a sample of which are examined for traces of archaeological remains. Any given sampling unit may contain a "cluster" of elements. One can then collect a sample of sites, artifacts, or features by means of a cluster sample, in which each sampling unit is a collection (cluster) of elements. Thus, your statistical population is made up of a number of clusters, each with a specific number of elements, the cluster size. This size can vary considerably from cluster to cluster. This type of approach is used when we wish to examine the properties of sites, not those of an arbitrary grid unit. What is the proportion of sites with seashells in the Pre-Classic Valley of Oaxaca, Mexico? What is the average site area of settlements within the sampling area, and so on?

Simple questions are tackled with single-stage cluster sampling, more complex ones with two-stage sampling, where the second stage involves selecting only a sample of elements in the cluster for closer examination. You may elect to study a river basin that you divide into 500-square-foot quadrats. Each of these units contains 250,000 potential one-foot test units. You might select 100 test units for examination out of each quadrat in your second-stage cluster sampling.

Most archaeological sampling involves simple cluster sampling designs, but the difficulties in obtaining empirical observations that are adequate for testing theoretical propositions are still enormous. We need to know more about the spatial distribution of archaeological remains, about the formation processes that affect the archaeological record, and such factors as the density of vegetational cover, the precision of dating surface sites, and the very obtrusiveness of the features, sites, and artifacts that make up the archaeological record. (For a detailed discussion of the difficulties of archaeological sampling, see Nance, 1983.) Few archaeological surveys fail to make use of sampling in the 1980s, for archaeologists are only too aware that many site distributions reflect the distribution of archaeologists rather than unbiased sampling of the archaeological record. This bias applies particularly in densely vegetated areas such as the Mesoamerican and Amazonian rain forest, where the cover is so thick that even modern roads are in constant danger of being overgrown. It is no coincidence that most archaeological sites found in rain forests are near well-trodden roads and tracks. The early archaeologists located sites by following narrow paths through the forest cut by *chicleros*, local people who collected resin from forest trees and guided them to sites. Even today, archaeologists can pass right through the middle of a large site in the forest, or within a few feet of a huge pyramid, and see nothing (Chartkoff, 1978). Some large Mayan ceremonial centers like El Mirador in the northern Peten of Guatemala have been located by air survey, but they are so difficult to get to that they have never been investigated thoroughly (Sharer and Ashmore, 1979). Sophisticated remote-sensing techniques have revolutionized survey in rain-forest areas, however, and provided new insights into the swamp agricultural techniques used by the Maya. We can expect increasing use of both remote sensing and more sophisticated sampling techniques to change survey techniques beyond recognition in the coming years, even if they never completely supersede the traditional task of the archaeologist: investigating archaeological sites on the ground.

SITE SURVEY

One objective of archaeological survey is to pinpoint site locations. Once this siting is completed, new sites normally are surveyed carefully, with these objectives in mind:

1. To collect and record information on subsurface features, such as walls, buildings, and fortifications, traces of which may be detected on the surface. Such features may include ancient roads, agricultural systems, and earthworks, which are first detected from the air and then investigated on the ground (Bradford, 1957).
2. To collect and record information on artifacts and other finds lying on the surface of the site.
3. To use both these categories of data to test hypotheses about the age, significance, and function of the site.

Teotihuacán. Site surveys can be as complex as those covering large areas. Perhaps the largest site-survey project ever undertaken was the Teotihuacán Mapping Project directed by George Cowgill and René Millon. Teotihuacán lies northeast of Mexico City and is one of the great tourist attractions of the Americas. This great pre-Columbian city flourished from about 250 B.C. until A.D. 700. Up to 150,000 people lived in Teotihuacán at the peak of its prosperity. Huge pyramids and temples, giant plazas, and an enormous market formed the core of the well-organized and well-planned city. The houses of the priests and nobles lay along the main avenues; the artisans and common people lived in crowded compounds of apartments and courtyards (Millon, 1973).

The size of Teotihaucán is overwhelming and a detailed survey of its hundreds of structures and alleyways was a monumental undertaking. Cowgill and Millon realized that the only effective way to study the city was to make a comprehensive map of all the precincts, for without it they would never have been able to study how Teotihuacán grew so huge. Fortunately, the streets and buildings lay close to the surface, unlike the vast city mounds of the Near East, where only excavation yields settlement information.

The mapping project began with a detailed ground reconnaissance, conducted with the aid of aerial photographs and large-scale survey maps. The field data were collected on 147 map data sheets of 500-meter squares at a scale of 1:2,000.

Intensive mapping and surface survey, including surface collections of artifacts, were then conducted systematically within the 20-square kilometer limits of the ancient city defined by the preliminary reconnaissance. Ultimately, the architectural interpretations of the surface features within each 500-meter square were overprinted on the base map of the site. These architectural interpretations were based not only on graphic data but also on a mass of surface data collected on special forms and through artifact collections, photographs, and drawings. Extensive use of sophisticated sampling techniques and quantitative methods was essential for successful completion of the map.

By the end of the project more than 5,000 structures and activity areas had been recorded within the city limits. The Teotihuacán maps do not, of course, convey to us the incredible majesty of this remarkable city; but they do provide, for the first time, a comprehensive view of a teeming, multifaceted community with vast public buildings, plazas, and avenues, and thousands of small apartments and courtyards, which formed individual households and pottery, figurine, and obsidian workshops, among the many diverse structures in the city. The survey also revealed that the city had been expanded over the centuries according to a comprehensive master plan. (For more on Teotihuacán, see Chapter 16.)

Mapping.   Archaeological survey on any scale depends, as in the Teotihuacán survey, on precise mapping. Maps are a convenient way of storing large quantities of archaeological information. Mapping specialists, called cartographers, have developed many effective and dramatic ways of communicating information graphically, devices that are very useful inclusions in archaeological reports (Figure 10.9).

Topographic maps. The distributions of archaeological sites are plotted on large-scale topographic maps that relate the ancient settlements to the basic features of the natural landscape (Figure 10.9, left). This master base map can be overlain with plots that show vegetational cover—either prehistoric or modern—soil types, and even prehistoric trade routes.

Planimetric maps. These are commonly used to record details of archaeological sites. They relate different archaeological features to each other and contain no topographic information (Figure 10.9, right).

Site plans. These are specially prepared maps made by archaeologists to record the horizontal provenience of artifacts, food residues, and features. Site plans are keyed to topographic and other surveys from a carefully selected point (datum point), such as a survey beacon or a landmark that appears on a large-scale map. This datum point provides a location from which a grid of squares can be laid out over the area of the site, normally open-ended so that it can be extended to cover more ground if necessary. The grid provides a system of coordinates for recording provenience. The arms of the grid are normally oriented, using true north. A site grid is

Figure 10.9 Examples of archaeological maps. Left: A topographic map that shows the relationship between sites and the landscape. Right: A planimetric map showing the features of a site. (Both maps are of Nohmul, a Maya ceremonial center.)

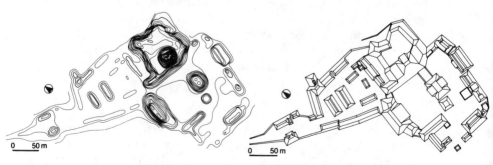

critical during excavation for use in three-dimensional recording. It is also vital in recording surface finds during the initial survey process.

Readers interested in survey and mapping techniques as they relate to archaeology are referred to the specialist literature (Hester, Shafer, and Heizer, 1985; Barker, 1977).

Surface Collection. The artifacts and other archaeological finds discovered on the surface of a site are a potentially vital source of information about the people who once lived there. Surface collection has these objectives:

1. gathering representative samples of artifacts from the surface of the site to establish the age of the area and the various periods of occupation.
2. establishing the types of activity that took place on the site.
3. gathering information on the areas of the site that were most densely occupied and that might be most productive for either total or sample excavation.
4. locating major structures that lie, for the most part, below the surface.

Limitations. Many archaeologists distrust surface collection, arguing that artifacts are easily destroyed on the surface and can be displaced from their original positions by many factors. But this viewpoint neglects a truth: *all* archaeological deposits, however deep, were once surface deposits, subject to many of the same destructive processes as those outcropping on the surface today (Dunnell and Dancey, 1983). With the increased emphasis on regional surveys and settlement archaeology in recent years, many fieldworkers have demonstrated that surface deposits can provide much information on artifact distributions and other phenomena also found underground, provided, of course, that they have not been subjected to catastrophic industrial activity, strip mining, or other drastic modifications.

Like buried deposits, surface levels contain abundant information about artifact patternings if one can separate true patternings from those caused by formation processes that have occurred since the site was abandoned. The same influences have affected both surface and buried deposits: natural weathering, erosion, rainfall, and human activity for years, which may result in the comminution (pulverizing) of potsherds, stone tools, and bone fragments. But surface data have two major advantages: they are a body of information that can be obtained on a regional scale, not site by site. And the cost of obtaining the data is but a fraction of that for excavation. Increasingly, archaeologists are thinking of surface data as primary archaeological information essential to understanding regional prehistories (Lewarch and O'Brien, 1981)

Methods. There are various ways of collecting artifacts from the surface of a site. Some archaeologists collect everything from the surface, take their finds home to the laboratory, and then analyze them at leisure. This approach is commonly used in areas where little archaeological research has been carried out before.

When dealing with a well-known area or with sites containing distinctive artifacts, it is possible to collect only diagnostic artifacts, such items as potsherds, stone artifacts, or other characteristic finds that are easily classified and identified. These key finds may enable one to assess what periods of occupation are represented at the site. Surface collections should be made, however, only in such a way that the provenience of the finds is plotted on a map at the time of collection.

Another way is random sampling. Because total collecting is impossible on sites of any size where surface finds are abundant, some type of sampling technique is used to obtain a valid random sample of the surface artifacts. A common random-sampling approach involves laying out a grid of squares on the surface of the site and then collecting everything found in randomly selected units. Once such a "controlled collection" has been made, the rest of the site is covered for highly diagnostic artifacts. Rigorous sampling techniques are essential to obtain even a minimal sample of finds at the individual site level (Baker, 1983; Jones, Grayson, and Beck, 1983). Surface collection and sampling are often combined with small test-pit excavations to get preliminary data on stratigraphic information (see also South and Widmer, 1977).

Evidence of the activities of a region's inhabitants can be obtained from surface collections, but only where the relationship between remains found on the surface and below the ground is clearly understood. Sometimes, the surface finds may accurately reflect site content; at others, they may not. This problem is compounded not only by natural erosion and other factors but also by the depth of the occupation deposits on the site. Obviously, almost no finds from the lowest levels of a thirty-foot-deep village mound will lie on the surface today, unless erosion, human activity, or animal burrows bring deeply buried artifacts to the surface.

With shallow sites, such as Teotihuacán and many prehistoric settlements in the American West, it is a reasonable assumption that the artifacts on the surface accurately reflect those slightly below the surface (Millon, 1973; Yellen, 1977). This assumption provides a basis for studying activities from surface finds. Any conclusions derived from surface collections, however, have to be verified by subsequent excavation.

Examples of effective site surveys are legion in modern archaeology. William Sanders and a team of archaeological colleagues spent many field seasons surveying the archaeological record of the

Figure 10.10   Paleo-Indian fluted projectile heads from the Plains. Judge and Dawson used such surface collections to trace changing site distributions.

Basin of Mexico. They relied heavily on surface finds for dating individual sites, and for identifying the character of individual settlements (Sanders, Parsons, and Santley, 1979). The San Juan Basin near the Four Corners region of the Southwest has been the subject of intensive regional and site surveys as part of a major cultural resource management project (Plog and Walt, 1982). James Judge and Jerry Dawson were able to study hunting and living patterns among Paleo-Indian cultures of about 8,000 years ago (Judge and Dawson, 1972). They used stone tools to define different site types, distinguishing between general localities where no diagnostic tools were found, and specific sites (Figure 10.10). In this area were found base camps and processing sites, where hunting tools were predominant. By using these site types as the basis for artifact collections, Judge and Dawson showed how older Paleo-Indian sites were much farther from large bodies of water than later settlements and campsites, which were closer to the greatly reduced streams and rivers of later, more arid times.

Site survey has the great advantage of being much cheaper than excavation, provided that the methods used are based on explicit research designs. Many of the most exciting recent studies of cultural process and changing settlement patterns have depended heavily on archaeological reconnaissance and site survey.

Guide to Further Reading

Crawford, O. G. S. *Archaeology in the Field*. New York: Praeger, 1953.
Field archaeology of the classic type, involving close observation of the ground on foot. The work has a British orientation, but is a sound, old-fashioned essay.

Deuel, Leo. *Flights into Yesterday*. London: Macdonald, 1969.
A competent introduction to aerial photography.

Lyons, Thomas R., and Thomas Avery. *Remote Sensing: A Handbook for Archaeologists and Cultural Resource Managers*. Washington, D.C.: National Park Service, 1972.
An invaluable handbook on remote sensing in all its facets, of particular value to cultural resource managers. Regular supplements keep this work up to date.

Millon, René. *The Teotihuacán Map. Urbanization at Teotihuacán, Mexico, volume I*. Austin: University of Texas, 1973.
A complicated survey and mapping project that is a prime example of a survey project.

Mueller, James A. "The Use of Sampling in Archaeological Survey." *Society for American Archaeology*. Memoir 28.
A useful study of problems in field survey sampling, for the advanced reader.

Nance, Jack D. "Regional Sampling in Archaeological Survey: The Statistical Perspective," *Advances in Archaeological Method and Theory*, 6 (1983): 289–356.
A useful survey that updates Mueller and reviews basic concepts.

Sanders, William, Jeffrey Parsons, and R. Santlay. *The Basin of Mexico: Ecological Processes in the Evolution of a Civilization*. New York: Academic Press, 1979.
The best description of a long-term survey project, and of survey problems, I have yet encountered.

Wilson, D. R. *Air Photo Interpretation for Archaeologists*. London: Batsford, 1982.
A useful, practical manual on interpreting aerial photographs for archaeologists.

CHAPTER 11 🌿
ARCHAEOLOGICAL
EXCAVATION

Preview

- Excavation is a primary way in which archaeologists acquire sub-surface data about the past. Modern archaeologists tend to carry out as little excavation as possible, however, because digging archaeological sites destroys a finite resource—the archaeological record.
- Modern excavations are often conducted by multidisciplinary research teams made up of specialists from several disciplines, who work together on a carefully formulated research design.
- All archaeological excavation is destruction of a finite resource. Accurate methods for planning, recording, and observation are essential.
- The Koster site in Illinois, where the excavators devised a sophisticated data flow system to keep their research design up to date, illustrates the essential research design.
- Sites can be excavated totally or, as is more common, selectively. Vertical excavation is used to test stratigraphy and to make deep probes of archaeological deposits. Test pits, often combined with various sampling methods, are dug to give an overall impression of an unexcavated site before major digging begins. Horizontal or area excavation is used to uncover far wider areas and especially to excavate site layouts and buildings.

- The process of archaeological excavation begins with a precise site survey and establishment of a site recording grid. A research design is formulated and hypotheses are developed for testing. Placement of trenches is determined by locating likely areas or by sampling methods. Excavation involves not only digging but also recording of stratigraphy and find proveniences, as well as observations of the processes that led to the site's formation.
- Careful stratigraphic observation in three dimensions is the basis of all good excavation and is used to demonstrate relationships among layers and between layers and artifacts.
- Three-dimensional recording methods are used to establish the provenience of artifacts and features.
- Excavation is followed by analysis and interpretation and, finally, publication of the finds to provide a permanent record of the work carried out.
- Among the special excavation problems we discuss are the recovery of fragile objects and human skeletons and the digging of postholes and structures.
- The chapter ends with a summary, using photographic and textual examples, of some of the best-known archaeological excavations throughout the world and the problems encountered in them.

Excavation! The very word conjures up romantic images of lost civilizations and royal burials, of long days in the sun digging up inscriptions and gold coins. Yet, though the image remains, the techniques of modern excavation are far less romantic than they are rigorous and demanding, requiring long training in practical field techniques. Excavation is the major way in which archaeologists acquire data about the past. Unlike reconnaissance and surface survey, excavations recover data from beneath the surface of the ground—where conditions for preservation are best—and accurate information on provenience, context, and association can be recovered intact. In this chapter we discuss some of the basic principles of archaeological excavation: the organization, planning, and execution of a scientific dig.

A SHORT HISTORY OF EXCAVATION

The earliest archaeologists were little more than treasure hunters, who thought nothing of excavating several burial mounds in one day (Daniel, 1975). At the same time, the great civilizations of the Near East and Egypt were being unearthed from millennia of oblivion by such men as Henry Layard and Heinrich Schliemann, who were hastily uncovering and removing literally tons of antiquities from their proper archaeological contexts. "Nothing was done with any uniform plan," complained Sir Flinders Petrie, an eminent Egyptologist eighty years ago. "It is sickening to see the rate at which everything is being destroyed, and the little regard paid to preservation" (Fagan, 1975).

The foundations of scientific excavation had already been laid, however, when Petrie was complaining about the work of his colleagues. A century before, Thomas Jefferson, third President of the United States and author of the Declaration of Independence, had spent time investigating Indian burial mounds in Virginia, which were rumored to be huge sepulchres. He decided to excavate one "to satisfy myself whether any and which of these opinions was just," he wrote. Here, for the first time, was a deliberate archaeological excavation undertaken to verify one of several hypotheses about Indian mounds. Jefferson cut a perpendicular trench through the mound "so that I might examine its internal structure." The trench was dug down to the natural soil and was wide enough to allow Jefferson to record the different layers of the mound. He was able to recognize at least three layers of human bones, horizons where the Indians had gathered together dozens of bones before piling stones on top of them. His *Notes on the State of Virginia*, published in 1784, contains a description of his excavations and conclusions. It is one of the first recorded instances of stratigraphic observation in archaeology (Fagan, 1977; Willey and Sabloff, 1980).

Not until nearly a century later was scientific excavation applied anywhere. The first truly scientific digs were carried out by Austrian and German archaeologists working in Greece in the 1870s. One of these was the Austrian Alexander Conze, who began excavating at the Sanctuary of the Great Gods on the island of Samothrace in 1873, with a team of scientists that included a photographer and two architects. The dig lasted two years, and the resulting monograph was beautifully illustrated and full of accurate plans. Another, the German Ernst Curtius, began excavations in 1875 at Olympia that lasted six seasons. His excavations were conducted with Teutonic thoroughness; he made careful plans of the architecture and detailed studies of the stratigraphy, and he developed new methods of digging and recording that eventually came into use in excavations all over the Near East.

The sense of purpose and discipline the Austrians and Germans introduced into the digging was also practiced by a military gentleman in England. General Augustus Lane Fox, who retired from active duty in 1880, inherited the Rivers estate in southern England and changed his name to Pitt-Rivers. He devoted the last twenty years of his life to a detailed exploration of the archaeological sites on or near his estate. Pitt-Rivers's methods were elaborate and painstaking; he recorded every object found in his trenches in such a manner that its exact find spot could be identified in the future, with reference to sections and plans of the dig. Three-dimensional recording was a cornerstone of his excavations, as were accurate stratigraphic profiles with the finds recorded on them, a large and competent staff, and prompt and meticulous publication of his results. The General is a colossus in the history of archaeological excavation; the labor involved in producing the elegant blue and gold monographs describing his excavations must have been prodigious (Thompson, 1977).

American archaeologists became involved in scientific investigation of pre-Columbian sites at about the same time. Beginning with Cyrus Thomas in the Ohio Valley and Adolph Bandelier in the Southwest, archaeologists started to design the direct historical method, working back from the known to the unknown (Fagan, 1977; Willey and Sabloff, 1980). Scientific archaeology advanced most rapidly in the Southwest. Much early research consisted of cleaning up many of the major pueblos after the massive treasure-hunting depredations late in the nineteenth century. A small team of archaeologists, including N. C. Nelson and A. V. Kidder, spent season after season preparing precise chronological and stratigraphical frameworks for the area.

N. C. Nelson, a robust and earthy Scandinavian, was the first person to use potsherds for establishing southwestern chronology. He took a cluster of sites in the Galisteo Basin of New Mexico and dug small stratigraphic trenches through their deposits. The resulting chronological sequence of pottery forms began with the Basketmaker period dating to the first millennium A.D. and ended with Spanish and historic artifacts dating to about A.D. 1680. Harvard-trained archaeologist A. V. Kidder carried Nelson's work to its logical conclusion with large-scale excavations at Pecos pueblo from

1915 to 1926. His studies of potsherds and stratigraphic profiles led him to delineate a long sequence of Southwestern prehistory that "owes to outside sources little more than the germs of its culture" (Kidder, 1924). Kidder's cultural sequence has withstood the test of time, even through detailed modifications have been made in his scheme.

It took a long time for the lessons of Pitt-Rivers, Nelson, and others to be learned by the archaeological community. European archaeologists were generally quicker to apply the rigorous principles enumerated by the General than were Americans. A great exponent of the art of scientific excavation was the Englishman Sir Mortimer Wheeler, whose short *Archaeology from the Earth* (1954) is an elegant and lively monograph in any archaeologist's library. He and his contemporaries refined and applied Pitt-Rivers's methods with consistent energy. With them, the emphasis in excavation shifted from finding objects to designing a strategy for an excavation campaign oriented toward solving archaeological problems rather than discovery for its own sake. Precise digging and recording methods invented in England and Scandinavia were soon being applied as far afield as India and South Africa (Daniel, 1981).

Modern scientific excavation owes a great deal to such people as Wheeler, who realized that good fieldwork depends on careful organization, multidisciplinary teamwork, and very accurate methods of recording and excavation.

In recent years, archaeologists have become increasingly reluctant to excavate a site except when they have a specific hypothesis to test or research problem to investigate. The reason is that the finite archaeological record is being destroyed at such a rate by industrial civilization that there is a real danger that little will be left for scientists of the future unless every effort is made to conserve undisturbed sites now. A new emphasis on regional surveys, increasing use of remote sensing to probe sites before excavation, and application of sophisticated sampling methods combined make today's excavations even more effective than those of a generation ago. They are a far cry from the popular stereotype of archaeology as a frenzied treasure hunt, as we will show in the following pages.

ORGANIZING ARCHAEOLOGICAL EXCAVATIONS

In this century there has been a total transformation of archaeology, from treasure hunting and curiosity to scientific investigation and problem-oriented excavation. As a result, organizing an excavation has become increasingly complex.

In the early days, someone like Heinrich Schliemann or Austen Henry Layard would supervise huge teams with several hundred workers. Even as late as the 1920s, Leonard Woolley excavated the ancient Mesopotamian city of Ur-of-the-Chaldees with only a handful of qualified scholars and up to three hundred unskilled laborers. Today's excavation is limited by ever-rising costs and by the sheer complexity of the data that now can be recovered from a site. Some of the more elaborate sites are dug by teams of specialists with very little unskilled help. Others are staffed by volunteer laborers, interested amateurs, and students, who gain practical experience in all aspects of excavation, from using a shovel to recording a complicated stratigraphic profile.

The director of a modern archaeological field expedition needs skills beyond those of a competent archaeologist. He or she also has to be able to fill the roles of accountant, politician, doctor, mechanic, personnel manager, and even cook. On a large dig, though manual labor may not be the director's responsibility, logistic problems are compounded, and he or she will head a large excavation team of site supervisors, artists, photographers, and numerous minor functionaries (Atkinson, 1953; Dancey, 1981; Hester, Shafer, and Heizer, 1985; Joukowsky, 1981). Above all, the field director has to be the leader of a multidisciplinary team of specialist fieldworkers.

Multidisciplinary Research Teams. Modern archaeology is so complex that all excavation projects now require multidisciplinary teams of archaeologists, botanists, geologists, zoologists, and other specialists who work together on closely integrated research problems, such as the origins of food production. The team approach is particularly important where environmental problems are most pressing, where the excavations and research seek the relationships between human cultures and the rest of the ecosystem.

A good inter- or multidisciplinary study is based on an integrated research design bringing a closely supervised team of specialists together to test carefully formulated hypotheses against data collected by all of them. Notice that we say "data collected by all of them." Many archaeologists pay lip service to the need for multidisciplinary research teams but then recruit a few experts to act as highly paid technicians on the excavation; that is, merely to do such jobs as identifying animal remains and plant fragments or recording and interpreting geological layers. There have been cases of natural scientists excavating archaeological sites that were rich in, say, vegetable remains, and then retaining an archaeologist to interpret the artifacts in the site! An effective multidisciplinary archaeological team must be just that—a team—whose combined findings are used to test specific hypotheses.

Multidisciplinary research teams have been employed with great success at early hominid campsites in East Turkana, Kenya, where geologists provided the background environmental data; zoologists, the identifications and interpretations of fossil animals found in the sites; and archaeologists, the data on surviving cultural remains; while physical anthropologists studied the human remains found in the three- to three-and-one-half-million-year-old sites. This approach is logical, but it is rarely carried to its logical extreme, where the experts would design their research together, share an integrated field mission, and communicate daily about their findings and research problems. Much of the East Turkana research has been carried out by carefully selected teams of specialist experts, whose research experience is not in, say, Pleistocene geology as a whole, but in the specific types of geological deposits and stratigraphic and ecological problems in East Turkana (Isaac and McKown, 1977).

The criteria, then, for selecting members of multidisciplinary research teams include not only academic skills, but also ability to communicate with people in other disciplines, highly specific specialist qualifications, and, above all, willingness to work closely with a group of scholars who are all committed to solving common problems. Such people are hard to find, and thus truly effective interdisciplinary research teams are few and far between. More loosely knit team approaches in which each member of a group pursues his or her own research but contributes to more general overall goals are far more common. The well-known Southwest Archaeological Group, whose members meet annually before the field season to reach consensus on approaches and research methods, is an excellent example of this approach (Brown and Struever, 1973).

Excavation Staff. Large, elaborate excavations that take several seasons to complete are staffed by a director and other specialist experts, and by several other technicians as well. Among the technicians are:

Site supervisors. Skilled excavators are responsible for excavating trenches and recording specific locations. The large-scale digs of medieval York in northern England are divided into localities, each with a skilled excavator who supervises the volunteers doing the actual digging.

Recording experts. Some very large excavations will have a full-time surveyor, who does nothing but draw and record the strati-graphic profiles and structures found in the dig. Expert archaeo-logical photographers are in great demand and will make thou-sands of slides and black-and-white prints during even a short season. Their task is to create a complete record of the excavation from beginning to end (Harp, 1975).

Artifact and small-finds staff. Even a small excavation can yield a flood of artifacts and flora and fauna remains that can overwhelm the staff of a dig. A basic laboratory staff to bag the finds and wash, rough sort, and mark them for eventual transport to the labora-tory is essential on any but the smallest excavation. Some knowl-edge of preservation techniques is essential as well. Large exca-vations, such as the Koster site in Illinois, employ computerized data processing to handle the analysis of the finds (Struever and Holton, 1979).

Foremen. Paid foremen can become skilled archaeological excavators in their own right, but their primary responsibility is managing paid laborers, especially on overseas excavations. Some devote their entire working lives to archaeology. Perhaps the most famous archaeological foremen are found in Egypt and Iraq, where successive generations of a family have served on exca-vations for decades. Sir Leonard Woolley worked with the same foreman, Sheikh Hamoudi, from 1912 to 1941. Hamoudi, who become almost a part of Woolley's family, was famous for his invective and for his sensitivity to the moods of the workmen (Fagan, 1979).

In these days of rising costs and financial stringencies, most exca-vations are conducted on a comparatively small scale. There will usually be a team of students or paid laborers under the overall supervision of the director and perhaps one or two assistants; the assistants may be graduate students with some technical training in archaeological fieldwork who can take some of the routine tasks from the director's shoulders, allowing him or her to concentrate on general supervision and interpretative problems. But, on many sites, the director will not only be in charge of the research and arrangements for the excavation but will also personally supervise all trenches excavated. On that one person, therefore, devolve the tasks of recording, photography, drawing, measurement, and supervision of labor. The director may also take a turn at recovery of fragile burials and other delicate objects that cannot be entrusted to students or workers; he or she is also responsible for maintaining the excavation diaries and find notebooks, storage and marking of artifacts, and the logistics of packing finds and shipping them to the laboratory.

So varied are the skills of the excavator that much of a professional archaeologist's training in the field is obtained as a graduate student working at routine tasks and gaining experience in the methods of excavation and site survey under experienced supervision. For the director, such students provide not only useful supervisory labor but also an admirable hone upon which to try out favorite theories and discuss in ruthless detail the interpretation of the site. Many an elaborate and much-cherished theoretical model has been demolished over a disputed profile or an evening campfire! Opportunities to gain excavation experience are always open, and notices of digs can be found on many college and university bulletin boards. You can also obtain information on field schools from the Society for American Archaeology's *Field School Catalog*, or watch issues of *Archaeology* magazine for field opportunities. The camaraderie and happiness of a well-run, student-oriented excavation is one of the more worthwhile experiences of archaeology.

PLANNING AN EXCAVATION

Excavation is the culminating step in the investigation of an archaeological site. It recovers from the earth data obtainable in no other way (Barker, 1983; Dancey, 1981). Like historical archives, the soil of an archaeological site is like a document whose pages have to be deciphered, translated, and interpreted before they can be used to write an accurate account of prehistory. If there is one general remark about the history of archaeological excavation that is applicable to all areas of the world, it is that methods of data recovery have been far too crude. Today's archaeologists are presented with the reality that their excavation methods are becoming more and more precise and slow moving, just as the destruction of archaeological sites is proceeding at a record pace.

The first lesson that budding excavators learn is that their work is potentially destructive. Excavation is destruction—the archaeological deposits so carefully dissected during any dig are destroyed forever and their contents removed. Here, again, there is a radical difference between archaeology and the sciences and history. A scientist can readily recreate the conditions for a basic experiment; the historian can return to the archives to reevaluate the complex events in a politician's life. But all that remain after an excavation are the finds from the trenches, the untouched portions of the site, and the photographs, notes, and drawings that record the excavator's observations for posterity. Thus, accurate recording and observation are overwhelmingly vital in the day-to-day work of archaeologists, not only for the sake of accuracy in their own research, but because they are creating an archive of archaeological information that may be consulted by others (Alexander, 1970). Archaeological sites are nonrenewable resources, and much of the present effort in archaeology is directed at the need to conserve most rigorously the undisturbed sites that still survive.

Austen Henry Layard, Heinrich Schliemann, and the other pioneers were looking for archaeological treasure; Thomas Jefferson, on the other hand, spent many summer days excavating for information about the inhabitants of Virginian burial mounds. Today, we follow in Jefferson's footsteps and search for the past in the widest sense, excavation being but one method at our disposal, even though it is a vital one. Thousands of observations can be made, even on a small-scale excavation. Unfocused excavation is useless, for the manageable and significant observations are buried in a mass of irrelevant trivia. A focused problem is essential for every excavation to hold the observations to a reasonable and controllable limit. Any excavation must be conducted from a sound research design intended to solve specific and well-defined problems.

Research Plans. "Problem-oriented" research has become a platitudinous catchword used by almost every archaeologist, even if his or her research designs are far from explicit. As archaeology becomes more explicitly scientific and more sophisticated, much more specific research designs are essential (Figure 11.1). Lewis Binford, who wrote about the need for sound research design in archaeological research, argues that archaeologists have no explicit criteria for selecting "important" sites. Excavations are traditionally conducted on larger sites, on sites that look more productive, or on sites that are nearest to roads. These criteria bear no resemblance to the goal that is actually required, which is representative and unbiased data to answer a particular problem—a problem whose limits

Figure 11.1   An organized horizontal-grid excavation on the Iron Age hill fort, at Danebury, England.

are ultimately defined by available money and time. Unbiased data, which do not reflect the investigator's idiosyncrasies, can properly yield probabilistic estimates of the culture from which the samples were drawn. This kind of information requires explicit sampling procedures, not only to select a few sites from an area to excavate, but also to control reliability of the information by using probability and statistics.

Excavation costs are so great that problem-oriented digging is now the rule rather than the exception, with the laboratory work forming part of the continuing evaluation of the research problem. The large piles of finds and records accumulated at the end of even a small field season contain a bewildering array of interdigitating facts that the researcher has to evaluate and reevaluate as inquiry proceeds, by constantly arranging propositions and hypotheses, correlating observations, and reevaluating interpretations of the archaeological evidence. Finds and plans are the basis of the researcher's strategy and affect fieldwork plans for the future. The days when a site was excavated because it "looked good," or because sheer lack of imagination precluded development of a research strategy, are slowly being replaced by constant reevaluation of research objectives.

The need for sound planning and design is even more acute in ecological research in archaeology, where archaeologists try to understand changes in human culture in relation to human environmental systems. Let us take the example of the Koster excavation in Illiniois, one of the largest and most complex digs ever undertaken in North America.

The Koster Site. In the lower Illinois Valley lies this site, a deep accumulation of twenty-six prehistoric occupation layers extending from about 10,000 years ago to *ca.* A.D. 1100 to 1200 (Struever and Holton, 1979). The wealth of material at Koster first came to light in 1968 and has been the subject of extremely large-scale excavation ever since. The dig has involved collaboration by three archaeologists and six specialists from such other disciplines as zoology and botany, as well as use of a computer laboratory.

Even superficial examination of the site showed that a very careful research design was needed, both to maximize use of funds and to ensure adequate control of data. In developing the Koster research design, James Brown and Stuart Struever (1973) were well aware of the numerous, complex variables that had to be controlled and the need to carefully define their sampling procedure and the size of the collecting units.

They faced a number of formidable difficulties. Thirteen of the Koster cultural horizons are isolated from their neighbors by a zone of sterile slopewash soil, which makes it possible to treat each as a separate problem in excavation and analysis—as if it were an individual site—although, in fact, the twelve are stratified one above another. Because the whole site is more than 7.1 meters (30 feet) deep, the logistical problems are formidable, as in all large-scale excavations. One possible strategy would have been to sink test pits, obtain samples from each level, and list diagnostic artifacts and cultural items. But this approach, though cheaper and commonly used, is quite inadequate to the systems model that the excavators drew up to study the origins of cultivation in the area and cultural change in the lower Illinois Valley. Large-scale excavations were needed to uncover each living surface, so that the excavators could not only understand what the living zones within each occupation were like but also, after studying in detail the sequence of differences in activities, make statements about the processes of cultural change.

From the large scale of the excavations, Brown and Struever saw the need for immediate feedback from the data flow from the site during the excavation. Changes in the excavation method would no doubt be needed during the season's fieldwork to ensure that maximum information was obtained. To accomplish this flexibility, both excavation and data-gathering activities were combined into a data-flow system (Figure 11.2) to ensure feedback to the excavators that would be as close to instantaneous as possible. The categories of data—animal bones, artifacts, vegetable remains—were processed in the field, and the information from the analyses was then fed by remote-access terminal to a computer in Evanston, Illinois, many miles away. Pollen and soil samples were sent directly to specialist laboratories for analysis. The effects of the data-flow system are highly beneficial. The tiresome analysis of artifacts and food residues is completed on the site, and the data are available to the excavators in the field in a few days, instead of months later, as is usual. The research design can be modified in the field at short notice, with ready consultation between the team members in the field. A combination of instant data retrieval; comprehensive and meticulous collecting methods involving, among other things, flotation methods (see Chapter 14); and a system approach to both excavation strategy and research planning have made the Koster project an

Figure 11.2   Data-flow system of the Koster site.

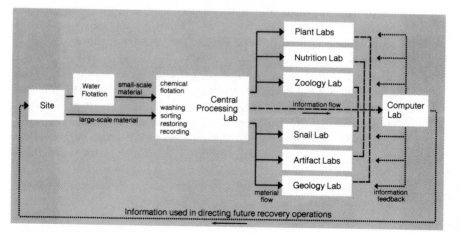

interesting example of effectively used research design in archaeology.

In many projects, excavation is only part of the overall research design. As a method, it should be used sparingly, for the end result is always destruction of a site (Barker, 1983). Under these circumstances, no one can challenge the necessity for highly specific, problem-oriented excavation at all times.

TYPES OF EXCAVATION

Archaeological excavation is designed to acquire as much raw data as possible with available financial and other resources. Its ultimate objective is to produce a three-dimensional record of an archaeological site, in which the various artifacts, structures, and other finds are placed in their correct provenience and context in time and space. The process of excavation, described below, involves the archaeologist in constant choices about the methods to be used, the types of trenches to be laid out, and the tools to be used, to mention only a few of the decisions to be made.

Total and Selective Excavation. As we saw in Chapter 9, not only the size and character of a site but also sampling techniques can be important in deciding which excavation methods are used. In the early days of archaeology, many sites were excavated completely. *Total excavation* of a site has the advantage of being comprehensive, but it is expensive and leaves none of the site intact for excavation at a later date with, perhaps, more advanced techniques. *Selective excavation* is much more common. Many prehistoric sites are simply too large for total excavation and can only be tested selectively, using sampling methods or carefully placed trenches. Selective excavation is used to obtain stratigraphic and chronological data as well as samples of pottery, stone tools, and animal bones. From this evidence, the archaeologist can decide whether or not to undertake further excavation. Some of the world's most important archaeological sites have been excavated selectively.

Vertical and Horizontal Excavation. Invariably, vertical excavation is selective digging, uncovering a limited area on a site for the purpose of recovering specific information. Most vertical excavations are probes of deep archaeological deposits, their real objective being to reveal the chronological sequence at a site. Horizontal excavation is used to expose contemporaneous settlement over a larger area.

Vertical Excavation.   *Test pits,* sometimes given the French name *sondages,* are a frequently used form of vertical excavation. They consist of small trenches just large enough to accomodate one or two diggers and are designed to penetrate to the lower strata of a site to establish the extent of archaeological deposits (Figure 11.3). Test pits are dug to obtain samples of artifacts from lower layers, and this method may be supplemented by augers or borers.

Test pits are a preliminary to larger-scale excavation, for the information they reveal is limited, at best. Some archaeologists will use them only outside the main area of a site, on the grounds that they will destroy critical strata. But carefully placed test pits can

Figure 11.3   A line of test pits on a Mesoamerican site, laid out at 15-meter intervals and aligned with the site grid.

provide invaluable insights into the stratigraphy and artifact content of a site before larger-scale excavation begins.

Test pits are also used to obtain samples from different areas of sites, such as shell middens, where dense concentrations of artifacts are found throughout the deposits. In such cases, test pits are excavated on a grid pattern, positioning of the pits being determined by probabilistic sampling or by a regular pattern such as alternate squares.

Vertical trenches are much larger, deeper cuttings used to establish such phenomena as sequences of building operations, histories of complex earthworks, and long cultural sequences in deep caves (Figure 11.4). Vertical trenches have been widely used to excavate Near Eastern mounds, such as the Tepe Yahya site in Iran (Lamberg-Karlovsky, 1970). They may be used, also, to obtain a cross-section across a site threatened by destruction or to examine outlying structures near a village or cemetery that has been dug on a large scale. Vertical excavations of this kind are almost always dug in the expectation that the most important information to come from them will be the record of layers in the walls of the trench and the finds from them. But, clearly, the amount of information to be obtained from such cuttings is of limited value compared to that from a larger excavation.

Tunneling is a form of vertical excavation done in a horizontal plane. Austen Henry Layard made use of tunneling to penetrate into the deep horizons of the Kuyunjik mound at the ancient city of Nineveh on the Tigris. Today, tunneling operations are confined to specialized excavations investigating the center of huge earthworks and other deep structures.

Horizontal, or Area, Excavation. Horizontal, or area, excavation is done on a much larger scale than vertical excavation, and is as close to total excavation as archaeology can get. An area dig implies covering wide areas to recover building plans or the layout of entire settlements (Figure 11.5). The only sites that almost invariably are totally excavated are very small hunting camps, isolated huts, and burial mounds. The Tudor palace at Nonsuch in southeastern England is a major example of this type of dig. The ground plan of the entire palace had been lost, but was recovered by horizontal excavation, adding a new portrait to the already glittering history of Henry VIII's reign (Dent, 1962).

The problems with horizontal digs are exactly the same as those with any excavation—stratigraphic control and accurate measure-

Figure 11.4   A classic example of vertical excavation from Sir Mortimer Wheeler's excavations at Maiden Castle, Dorset, England. Notice the recording posts on either side of the cutting and the workman, which give an idea of the scale of the dig.

ment. Area excavations imply exposure of large, open areas of ground to a depth of several meters. A complex network of walls or post holes may lie within the area to be investigated. Each feature relates to other structures, a relationship that must be carefully

Figure 11.5   Horizontal excavation of an open area: an Iroquois long house, Howlett Hill site, Onondaga, New York. The small stakes mark the house's wall posts; hearths and roof supports are found inside the house.

recorded so that the site can be interpreted correctly, especially if several periods of occupation are involved. If the entire area is uncovered, obviously it is difficult to measure the position of the structures in the middle of the trench, far from the walls at the excavation's edge. To achieve better control of measurement and recording, it is better to use a system that gives a network of vertical stratigraphic sections across the area to be excavated. This work is often done by laying out a grid of square or rectangular excavation units, with walls several meters thick between each square (see Figure 11.6). Such areas may average 3.7 meters (12 feet) square, or larger. As the figure shows, this system allows stratigraphic control of large areas. Large-scale excavation with grids is extremely expensive and time-consuming and is difficult to use where the ground is irregular, but it has been employed with great success at many excavations, being used to uncover structures, town plans, and fortifications. Many area digs are "open excavations," in which large tracts of a site are exposed layer by layer without a grid.

Stripping off overlying areas with no archaeological significance to expose buried subsurface features is another type of large-scale excavation. Stripping is especially useful when a site is buried only

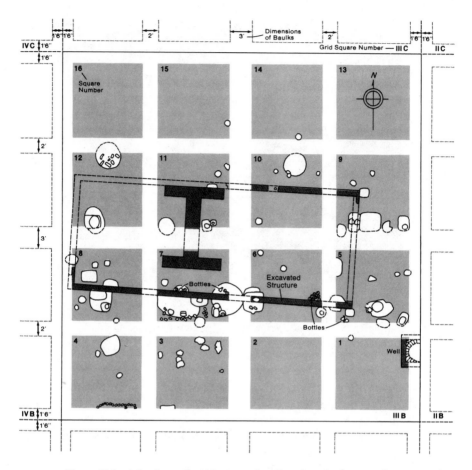

Figure 11.6 A horizontal-grid excavation showing the layout of squares relative to an excavated structure at Colonial Williamsburg.

a short distance below the surface, and the structures are preserved in the form of post holes and other discolorations in the soil.

Horizontal excavation depends, of course, on precise stratifigraphic control. It is normally combined with vertical trenches, which provide the information necessary for accurately peeling off successive horizontal layers. Many excavations involve using both vertical and horizontal excavations, with horizontal digging being the result of initial vertical trenches that reveal structures to be uncovered.

TOOLS OF THE TRADE

Every archaeological site poses different technical problems, not least of which is deciding what types of tools will be used to excavate them (Atkinson, 1953). The choice of digging tools radically affects the excavation as a whole. The following are some of the options.

Earth-moving equipment is sometimes used to remove the sterile overburden covering large areas of a site, or when speed of excavation is vital. Backhoes are sometimes used to cut crude test pits, when sites are threatened by immediate destruction. The use of mechanical equipment is always limited, however, for such devices are highly destructive of fragile archaeological remains.

Spades, shovels, mattocks, picks, and forks are used for loosening and moving large amounts of soil. The traditional archaeological symbol is the spade, which has a flat back and straight edge, and is used for cleaning walls. Shovels, with their scoop-like shape, are used for piling up earth in a trench preparatory to its being examined; they have innumerable applications in cleaning straight edges and tidying trenches, and they are the principal working tool of the archaeologist where much ground has to be uncovered.

Tools for loosening soil are the mattock, the pick, and the fork. The mattock and the pick may be considered together, because they are variants on the same type of tool; when used with care, they are a delicate gauge of soil texture, an indication used often in larger sites. The traditional Near Eastern excavation used teams of pickmen, shovelers, and basket carriers to remove the soil and dump it off the site.

The most common archaeological tool is the diamond-shaped trowel, its straight edges and tip having innumerable uses: soil can be eased from a delicate specimen; the edges can scrape a feature in sandy soil into higher relief; and as a weapon of stratigraphic recording, it can trace a scarcely visible stratum line or barely discernible feature. It is also used for clearing post holes and other minor work, so much so that it is rarely out of a digger's hand on smaller sites.

Brushes are among the most useful tools, especially for dry sites. The most commonly used is the household brush with fairly coarse bristles that can be held by the handle or the bristles. Wielded with short strokes, it effectively cleans objects found in dry and preferably hard soil. The excavator uses various paintbrushes for more delicate jobs. The one-inch or one-half-inch domestic paintbrush has wide application in cleaning animal bones and coarser specimens. Fine camel's-hair artists' brushes are best for most delicate bones, beads, and fragile ironwork.

Small tools, some improvised on the site, aid in clearing delicate finds. Six-inch nails may be filed to a point and used for delicate cleaning jobs on bones and other fragile artifacts. The needle is another tool used to clear soil from such delicate parts of skeletons as the eye sockets and cheekbones. One of the most useful digging tools is the dental pick, available in a bewildering variety of shapes. Often, dental picks can be obtained without charge from dentists, who discard them as soon as they show signs of wear. Continental European archaeologists have used a small, hooked digging tool, a *crochet,* for many years; it is widely used for excavations in which a trowel is too big but smaller tools are too slow and inefficient.

Screens are essential tools because many finds, such as coins, glass beads, shells, small tacks, nails, and other artifacts, are minuscule. Most deposits from sites where small artifacts are likely to occur are laboriously sifted through fine screens of one-quarter to one-eighth-inch openings, or smaller. Flotation techniques are also widely used (see Chapter 14).

Surveying tools normally include lines or metal tapes, plumb bobs, string, spirit levels, drawing boards, drawing instruments, a plane table, and a surveyor's level and compass—all essential for accurate recording of site plans and sections and for setting up the archaeological archive.

Storage containers are vital on any excavation to pack and transport the finds to the laboratory, as well as to store them permanently. Paper and plastic bags are essential for pottery, animal bones, and other small finds; vegetal remains and other special items may require much more delicate packaging. Cardboard cartons, supermarket bags, even large oil drums can be used for storing finds. One of the disappointments of archaeology is the gradual disappearance of the metal tobacco can, which served generations of archaeologists faithfully.

This by no means exhausts the list of equipment at the archaeologist's disposal, for much depends on conditions in the field and the types of finds encountered.

THE PROCESS OF ARCHAEOLOGICAL EXCAVATION

There is only one way to learn how to excavate and fully understand archaeological excavation, and that is to go to a field school or on a dig and learn by doing it. *In the Beginning* is not a how-to manual, and can give you only an outline summary of the process of excavation, couched in the most general terms. The interested reader is also urged to consult the specialist literature (Alexander, 1970, Atkinson, 1953; Barker, 1983; Dancey, 1981; Hester, Shafer, and Heizer, 1985).

The description of excavation that follows can be applied, generally, to any archaeological site. One must realize, however, that very few digs are conducted under ideal conditions, with unlimited time, adequate funds, and superb facilities. As Philip Barker puts it: "Just as 'all art constantly aspires toward the condition of music,' all excavation should aspire to the condition of total excavation." In other words, the ideal should always be kept in mind (Barker, 1983).

The excavator's aim should be to explain the origin of every layer and feature encountered in the site, whether natural or humanly made. It is not enough just to excavate and describe the site; one must explain, also, how the site was formed. This process is achieved by removing the superimposed layers of the site one by one. In so doing, the archaeologist records the full details of each layer and its contents as they are excavated. The process of archaeological excavation involves deciding where to dig, the actual digging, recording of the evidence contained in the excavation, and interpretation of the site and the processes by which it was formed.

Deciding Where to Dig. All archaeological excavation begins with a precise surface survey and making an accurate contour map of the site. A grid is then laid out over the site (see Chapter 10). The surface survey and the collections of artifacts made as part of it determine the working hypotheses that the archaeologist uses as a basis for deciding where to dig.

The first decision to be made is whether to carry out a total or a selective excavation. This decision depends on the size of the site, its possible imminent destruction, the hypotheses to be tested, and the time and money available. Most excavations are selective. Anyone contemplating a selective dig is faced with choosing the areas of the site to be dug. The choice can be clearcut and nonprobabilistic, or it can be based on complex sampling approaches. A selective excavation to determine the age of one of the stone uprights at Stonehenge obviously will be at the foot of the stones. But excavation of a shell midden with no surface features may be determined by probabilistic sampling and selection of random grid squares that are excavated to obtain artifact samples.

In many cases, an excavation can involve both probabilistic and nonprobabilistic choices. For the Maya ceremonial center at Tikal in Guatemala, the archaeologists were eager to learn something about the hundreds of mounds that lay in the hinterland around the main ceremonial precincts (Coe, 1967). These extended at least 10 kilometers from the center of the site and were identified along four strips of carefully surveyed ground, extending out from Tikal. Because, obviously, excavation of every mound and structure identified on the surface was impossible, a test-pit program was designed to collect random samples of datable pottery so that the chronological span of the occupation could be established. By using a proportional, stratified random sampling scheme, the investigators were able to select about 100 mound structures for testing and obtain the data they sought.

The choice of where to dig can also be determined by logistical considerations, such as access to the trench, which can present problems in small caves; by the time and funds available; or, regrettably often, by the imminent destruction of part of a site that is close to industrial activity or road construction. Ideally, though, the archaeologist will dig where the results will be maximal and the chances of acquiring data to test working hypotheses are best.

The location of some excavations may be established by test digging. When Richard MacNeish (1978) surveyed the Tehuacán valley in Mexico, he tested 39 sites with vertical trenches and selected eleven of them for more extensive excavation (see Figure 11.16). The sites chosen were those from which MacNeish felt he could obtain maximal information on different chronological periods. This strategy was brilliantly successful. The excavations enabled him to trace the early history of domesticated maize (see Chapter 20).

Stratigraphy and Sections. The actual mechanics of archaeological excavation are best learned in the field. There is an art in skillful use of the trowel, brush, and other implements to clear archaeological deposits (Atkinson, 1953; Barker, 1983). Stripping off layers exposed in a trench requires a sensitive eye for changing soil colors and textures, especially when excavating postholes and other features, and a few hours of practical experience are worth thousands of words of instructional text. Photographs at the end of this chapter will give some idea of the practical problems (Harris, 1979).

We touched briefly on archaeological stratigraphy in Chapter 6, where we said that the basis of all excavation is the properly recorded and interpreted stratigraphic profile (Wheeler, 1954). A section through a site gives one a picture of the accumulated soils and occupation levels that constitute the ancient and modern history of the locality. Obviously, anyone recording stratigraphy needs to know as much about the history of the natural processes that the site has undergone since abandonment as about the formation of the ancient site itself. The soils that cover the archaeological finds have undergone transformations that radically affect the ways in which artifacts are preserved or moved around in the soil. Burrowing animals, later human activity, erosion, wind action, grazing cattle—all can modify superimposed layers in drastic ways. Charles Darwin pointed out that even the common earthworm's activities affect the world's soils (Atkinson, 1957; Darwin, 1881).

Archaeological stratigraphy usually is much more complicated than geological layering, for the phenomena observed are much more localized, and the effects of human behavior tend to be intensive and often involve constant reuse of the same location (Adams, 1975; Drucker, 1972). Subsequent activity can radically alter the context of artifacts, structures, and other finds. A village site can be leveled and then reoccupied by a new community that digs the foundations of its structures into the lower levels, and sometimes even reuses the building materials of earlier generations. Post holes and storage pits, as well as burials, are sunk deep into older strata; their presence can be detected only by changes in soil color or the artifact content.

Anyone attempting to interpret archaeological stratigraphy has to take these points into account (Harris, 1979):

1. Human activities at the times in prehistory when the site was occupied and the effects, if any, on earlier occupations.
2. Human activities, such as plowing and industrial activity, *subsequent* to final abandonment of the site (Wood and Johnson, 1978).
3. Natural processes of deposition and erosion at the time of prehistoric occupation. Cave sites were often abandoned at times when the walls were shattered by frost and fragments of the rock face were showering down on the interior (Butzer, 1982). Such phenomena appear as dense layers of rock fragments that can separate different prehistoric occupations (McBurney, 1959; Wood and Johnson, 1978).
4. Natural phenomena that have modified the stratigraphy *after* abandonment of the site (floods, tree uprooting, animal burrowing).

Interpreting archaeological stratigraphy involves reconstructing the depositional history of the site and then interpreting the significance of the natural and occupation levels that are observed. This analysis means distinguishing between types of human activity; between deposits that result from rubbish accumulation, architectural remains, and storage pits; and between activity areas and other artifact patternings.

Vertical trenches and sections are by no means the only way of recording archaeological stratigraphy. Often—and Koster is a good example—safety considerations make it impossible to maintain vertical sections to any great depth, and the sides of the trenches are stepped. The only essential is that the section be absolutely clean when the time comes to record it with camera and pencil.

Philip Barker, English archaeologist and expert excavator, advocates a combined horizontal and vertical excavation for recording archaeological stratigraphy. He points out (1983) that a vertical profile gives a view of stratigraphy in the vertical plane only. Many important features appear in the section as a fine line and are decipherable only in the horizontal plane. The principal purpose of a stratigraphic profile is to record the information for posterity, so that later observers have an accurate impression of how it was formed. Because stratigraphy demonstrates relationships—between sites and structures, artifacts, and natural layers—he advocates cumulative recording of stratigraphy, which would enable the archaeologist to record layers in section and in plan at the same time. Such recording requires extremely skillful excavation. Various modifications of this technique are used in both Europe and North America. The Scandinavians have developed fine-tuned stratigraphic observations in which each layer is removed entirely and its surface surveyed with great accuracy. As a result, theoretically, one can reconstruct the stratigraphy at any point on the site (Biddle and Kjølbye-Biddle, 1969; Hatt, 1957).

All archaeological stratigraphy is three-dimensional; that is to say, it involves observations in both the vertical and horizontal planes. The ultimate objective of archaeological excavation is to record the three-dimensional relationships throughout a site, for these are the relationships that provide the provenience.

Archaeological Recording.   *Notebooks* are an important part of record keeping. An archaeologist maintains a number of notebooks throughout the excavation, including the site diary or daybook. In this large notebook he records all events at the site—the amount of work done, the daily schedule, the number of people on the digging team, and any labor problems that may arise. Dimensions of all sites and trenches are recorded. Any interpretations or ideas on the interpretations, even those considered and then discarded, are meticulously recorded in this book. Important finds and significant stratigraphic details are also noted carefully, as is much apparently insignificant information that may, however, prove to be vital in the laboratory. The site diary purports to be a complete record of the procedures and proceedings of the excavation. It is more than just an aid to the fallible memory of the excavator; it is a permanent record of the dig for future generations of scientists who may return to the site to amplify the original findings. Site diaries can be a most important tool in the hands of later researchers. The Knossos site diaries kept by Sir Arthur Evans as he uncovered Minoan civilization for the first time have been used again and again by later investigators in Crete (Boardman and Palmer, 1963).

A small-finds register is also important in the records on any dig. Although some artifacts, such as pottery or stone implements, may be very common, others, such as iron tools or beads, will turn out to be extremely rare and have special significance. A small-finds notebook will help in assessing their significance.

Site plans may vary from a simple contour plan for a burial mound or occupation midden to a complex plan of an entire prehistoric town or of a complicated series of structures (Hester, Shafer, and Heizer, 1985). Accurate plans are important, for they provide a record of not only the site's features but also the measurement recording grid set up prior to excavation to provide a framework for the trenching.

Stratigraphic records can be drawn in a vertical plane, or they can be drawn axonometrically (Figure 11.7). Any form of stratigraphic record is complex and requires not only skill in drawing but also considerable interpretative ability. The difficulty of recording varies with the site's complexity and with its stratigraphic conditions. Often, the different occupation levels, or geological events, are clearly delineated in the stratigraphic sections. On other sites, the layers may be much more complex and less visible, especially in drier climates where the soil's aridity has leached out colors.

Sections can be recorded with a horizontal datum string set up on the wall, with ends related to the site grid. All features on the profile are then carefully recorded with reference to the datum line.

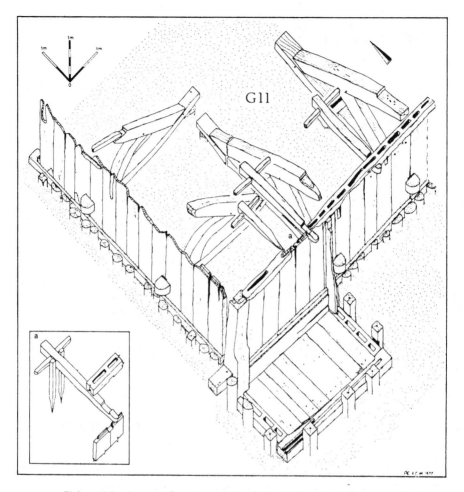

Figure 11.7   A magnificent example of cumulative recording, recorded axon-ometrically. A portion of London's pre-fifteenth-century waterfront recovered by excavation in waterlogged deposits, the particular drawing is of Triglane, Revetment G 11. shown is a projection of back-braced revetment with base of water tank (?) in SW, corner, River to S. and W. Insert, detail of junction of tie-back, top-plate, and revetment face (semi-reconstructed).

Some archaeologists have also used scaled photographs or survey-ing instruments to record sections, the latter being essential with large sections, like those through city ramparts.

Three-dimensional recording is the recording of artifacts and struc-tures in time and space. The provenience of archaeological finds is recorded with reference to the site grid (see Figure 11.8). Three-dimensional recording is carried out with a surveyor's level, or with tapes and plumb bobs. It assumes particular importance on sites where artifacts are recorded in their original positions, or on those where different periods in the construction of a building are being sorted out.

Figure 11.8   Three-dimensional recording. Top: Using a measuring square. Bottom: A close view of the square from above. The horizontal measurement is taken along the edge, perpendicular to the grid post line; the vertical measurement, from that arm with a plumb bob.

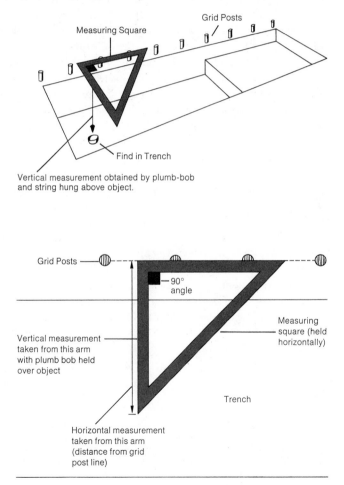

Grids, units, forms, and labels are the backbone of all recording efforts. Site grids are normally laid out with painted pegs and strings stretched over the trenches when recording is necessary. Small-scale recording of complex features may involve using an even smaller grid that covers but one square of the entire site grid.

In an interesting variant on the grid, Hallam Movius erected a permanent site grid *over* the deep deposits in the Abri Pataud rockshelter, Les Eyzies, France (Figure 11.9) (Movius, 1977). Using plumb bobs, a grid of 2-meter squares of metal pipe provided a framework for vertical and horizontal measurements on the surface of the deposits. Similar grids are sometimes erected over underwater wrecks in the Mediterranean (Bass, 1966).

The various squares in the grid and the levels of the site are designated by grid numbers (Figure 11.9, bottom), which provide the means for identifying the location of finds, as well as a basis for recording them. The labels attached to each bag or marked on the find bear the grid square numbers, which are then recorded in the site notebook. A great deal of time is saved if standardized forms are used to record site data. The forms relating to, say, radiocarbon samples can then be assembled in order in a looseleaf notebook for later reference in the laboratory and museum.

Analysis, Interpretation, and Publication. The process of archaeological excavation itself ends with filling in the trenches and transporting the finds and site records to the laboratory. The archaeologist retires from the field with a complete record of the excavations and with all the data needed to test the hypotheses that were formulated before going into the field. But with this step, the job is far from finished; in fact, the work has hardly begun. The next stage in the research process is analyzing the finds, a topic covered in Chapters 12–17. Once the analysis is completed, interpretation of the site can begin (see Chapters 18–19).

In these days of high printing costs, it is impossible to publish the finds from any but the smallest sites in complete detail. Fortunately, many data-retrieval systems enable us to store data on com-

Figure 11.9 (opposite)   The site grid at Abri Pataud. Top: The 2-meter grid-recording system at Abri Pataud, France. This permanent grid was used over many seasons of excavation. Bottom: Measuring the horizontal coordinates of a recently excavated find at Abri Pataud. Notice the small board recording the grid square number and level.

puter tape and microfilm, so that they will be available to the specialists who need them.

Beyond publication, the archaeologist has one final obligation—to place the finds and site records in a convenient repository where they will be safe and readily accessible to later generations.

SPECIAL EXCAVATION PROBLEMS

Not all excavation consists of sifting through shell mounds or uncovering huge palaces. A great deal of archaeological fieldwork is dull and monotonous; but occasionally archaeologists are confronted with unexpected and exciting challenges that require special excavation techniques. Imagine being confronted with a royal grave, such as that of Tutankhamun, which took Howard Carter nearly ten years to excavate, or with the mass of waterlogged artifacts that came from the trenches at Ozette, Washington. In both sites, the excavators had to find special techniques for dealing with these fragile discoveries.

Let us examine some of the most common problems in excavation.

Fragile Objects. Narratives of nineteenth-century excavation abound with accounts of spectacular and delicate discoveries that crumbled to dust on exposure to the air. Regrettably, similar discoveries are still made today; but many spectacular recoveries of fragile artifacts have been made. In almost every find, the archaeologist responsible has had to use great ingenuity, often with limited preservation materials on hand.

Leonard Woolley faced very difficult recovery problems when he excavated the Royal Cemetery at Ur-of-the-Chaldees in the 1920s (Woolley, 1954). In one place, he recovered an offering stand of wood, gold, and silver, portraying a he-goat with his front legs on the branches of a thicket, by pouring paraffin wax over the scattered remains. Later, he rebuilt the stand in the laboratory and restored it to a close approximation of the original.

Arthur Evans, who discovered the Palace of Minos in Crete, realized that the walls of the palace were covered with fine frescoes, of which nothing but tiny fragments still remained. Painstakingly, he recovered the fragments and then pieced together the original frescoes. Unfortunately, there was little evidence of the original, and some of his reconstructions are regarded as somewhat fanciful.

Conservation of archaeological finds has become a highly specialized field of endeavor (Dowman, 1970; Organ, 1968; Plenderleith and Werner, 1973), which covers every form of find, from textiles to leather, human skin, and basketry. Many conservation efforts, like those used to preserve the Danish bog corpses, can take months to complete (Glob, 1969).

One of the largest conservation efforts was mounted at Ozette, Washington, where the sheer volume of waterlogged wooden artifacts threatened to overwhelm the excavators. The finds that needed treatment ranged from tiny fishhooks to entire planks. A large conservation laboratory was set up nearby in Neah Bay, where the finds were processed after transportation from the site. Many objects were left to soak in polyethylene glycol to replace the water that had penetrated into the wood cells, a treatment that takes years for large objects. (A similar technique, incidentally, was used with the Swedish warship *Vasa*, which was raised from the bottom of Stockholm harbor.) The results of this major conservation effort can be seen in the Neah Bay Museum, where many of the artifacts are preserved (Kirk, 1974).

Burials. Human burials have been encountered either as isolated finds or in the midst of a settlement site. Some projects are devoted to excavating an entire cemetery. In all cases where graves are excavated, the burial and its associated grave, funerary furniture, and ornamentation are considered as a single excavation unit or grave lot.

The unearthing and recording of human burials is considered by the public to be one of the most romantic aspects of the archaeologist's job. No doubt it is true when the skeletons are adorned with an array of rich grave goods. But in fact excavation of burials is a difficult and routine task that must be performed with care, because of the delicacy and often bad state of the bones. The record of the bones' position and the placement of the grave goods and body ornaments is as important as the association of the burial, for the archaeological objective is reconstructing burial customs as much as establishing chronology (Anderson, 1969).

Although the pharaohs of Egypt were sometimes buried under great pyramids, and at Palenque, Mexico, a great burial chamber was covered by the Temple of the Inscriptions, most burials are normally located by means of a simple surface feature, such as a gravestone or a pile of stones, or by an accidental discovery during excavation. Once the grave outline has been found, the skeleton is carefully exposed from above. The first part of the skeleton to be identified will probably be the skull or one of the limb bones. The main outline of the burial is then traced before the delicate backbone, feet, and finger bones are uncovered. The greatest care is taken not to displace the bones or any of the ornaments or grave goods that surround them. In many cases the burial is in a delicate state, and the bones may be soft; therefore, they are exposed gradually, giving them time to dry before they are coated with a suitable chemical, such as polyvinyl acetate or Bedacryl. The hardened bones can then be removed to the safety of the laboratory (Bass, 1971; Brothwell, 1965). Normally, the undersurfaces of the bones are left in the soil, so that the skeleton may be recorded photographically before removal (Fig. 11.10). Photographing skeletons requires careful use of the camera to avoid parallax errors. A scale must be included in the photograph so that the relative size of the subject may be apparent to the viewer. The burial is either removed bone by bone or it is surrounded with a cocoon of plaster of paris and metal strips, the inside of which is packed with earth, and the whole structure is then transported to the laboratory, where it is cleaned at leisure. This technique is expensive and is generally used only when a skeleton is of outstanding scientific importance or when it is to be displayed in a museum. Usually, however, the bones are carefully removed, one by one, hardened with chemicals, and then packed in cardboard cartons or wooden boxes with cotton, wool, and straw for transport to the laboratory. Bones to be tested for trace elements should not, of course, be treated with chemicals.

Some burials are deposited in funerary chambers so elaborate that the contents of the tomb may reveal information not only on the funeral rites, but also, as in the Ur-of-the-Chaldees royal burials, on the social order of the royal court.

The great royal tombs of the Shang civilization of northern China are an example of complex tombs, where careful excavation made possible recording of many chariot features that otherwise would have been lost (Shang, 1977). The shaft, axle, and lower parts of the chariot wheels are visible as discolored areas in the ground. The area was dug to recover the dimensions and character of the chariots, which were found at the entrance ramps of the great Shang tombs. The charioteers were buried so as to accompany their masters.

Excavation of American Indian burials has generated furious political controversy in recent years, with Indian groups arguing that it is both illegal and unethical to dig up even the prehistoric dead. Archaeologists have sometimes been forced to rebury skele-

Figure 11.10   A classic Maya collective tomb at Guattan in the Motagua Valley, Guatemala. Note the clean excavation, the carefully cleaned-up skeletons, and the stone lining of tomb.

tons excavated many years ago. In some states like California, it is now illegal to disturb ancient Indian burial grounds.

Structures and Pits.   Excavation of houses and household clusters involves careful uncovering of the structures themselves and also of the artifacts associated with them. Humanity has constructed every type of dwelling, from simple brush shelters to elaborate palaces. Recovering the floor plans of such dwellings requires extremely sensitive methods of excavation.

Open excavations are normally used to uncover structures of considerable size (Barker, 1983). Grids allow stratigraphic control over the building site, and especially over the study of successive occupation stages. Many such structures may have been built of perishable materials like wood or matting. Wooden houses are normally recognized by the post holes of the wall timbers and, sometimes, foundation trenches. Clay walls collapse into a pile when a hut is burned or falls down; thus, the wall clay may bear impressions of matting, sticks, or thatch. Stone structures are often better preserved, especially if mortar was used, although sometimes the stone has been removed by later builders, and only foundation trenches remain (Figure 11.11). Stratigraphic cross-sections across walls give an insight into the structure's history. The dating of most stone structures is complicated, especially when successive rebuilding or occupation of the building is involved (Figure 11.12).

Some of the most spectacular buildings in the archaeological record leave few traces on the surface. Figure 11.5 shows an Iroquois long house that was identified purely from subsurface mark-

Figure 11.11   The Bronze Age palace of Nestor of Mycenaean Greece.

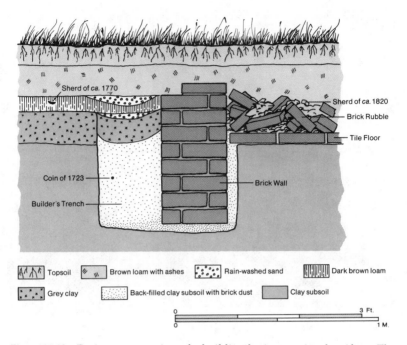

Figure 11.12   Dating construction of a building by its associated artifacts. The brick wall was built in a foundation trench that was filled with brick dust and clay. Someone dropped a coin dated 1723 into the clay as the trench was being filled. Obviously, then, the building of which the wall forms a part dates to no earlier than 1723.

ings in the soil. Numerous long houses have been identified in the same way from early farming sites in Europe (Piggott, 1965).

The pueblos of the American Southwest offer another type of problem in excavation. The many rooms of the pueblos contain complicated deposits full of occupation debris and many artifacts (Figure 11.13). Efforts have been made to record the artifact patternings in these rooms, in order to establish both the activities carried out in them and the possible residential patterns (Hill, 1970).

Storage and rubbish pits are commonly found on archaeological sites and may reach several meters in depth (Figure 11.14). Their contents furnish important information on dietary habits gleaned from food residues or caches of seeds. Trash pits are even more informative. Garbage pits and privies at Colonial Williamsburg have yielded a host of esoteric finds, including wax seals from doc-

Figure 11.13   Mesa Verde, a southwestern pueblo in Colorado.

uments that were used as toilet tissue (Noël Hume, 1969). Some historic pits can be dated from military buttons and other finds.

Storage and trash pits are normally identified by circular discolorations in the soil. The contents are then cross-sectioned, and the associated finds are analyzed as an associated unit (Figure 11.14). Large pits, which may contain thousands of seeds and other informative materials, are excavated with particular care.

Post holes are normally associated with houses and other such structures. The posts they once contained were buried in holes that were dug larger than the base of the post itself. Once the structure was abandoned, the post might be left to rot, might be removed, or might be cut off. The traces each of these outcomes leaves in the ground differ sharply and can be identified with careful excavation. Sometimes it is possible to find fragments of the post or of the charcoal from its burning, which enable one to identify the type of wood used. Some interesting experiments in Britain have shown that most small posts will last about fifteen years in damp ground (Morgan, 1975), but much depends on soil conditions.

These are but a few of the many unusual excavation problems that may confront the archaeologist in the field. Each archaeological

Figure 11.14   A double storage pit at Maiden Castle, Dorset, which was cut into the chalk subsoil.

site offers special challenges to the investigator, including preservation, recording, or interpretation. But, whatever the nature of the site, we always return again and again to stratigraphy and settlement patterns, to chronologies and cultural sequences, and to research designs, sampling, and careful surveys—principles of excavation that originated with the nineteenth-century archaeologists and have been refined progressively over the years. Though individual methods may vary from site to site and from area to area, no one denies the fundamental objective of archaeological excavation: recovering and recording data from below the ground as systematically and scientifically as possible.

SOME WELL-KNOWN ARCHAEOLOGICAL EXCAVATIONS

This section provides a summary, using photographs and text, of some types of excavation problems encountered throughout the world and the methods used to deal with them.

Hunter-Gatherer Campsites. The earliest human beings lived in small campsites that are sometimes represented in the archaeological record by little more than a scatter of broken animal bones, crude stone artifacts, and other occupation debris. Figure 11.15 shows a very early archaeological site in the Koobi Fora area of

Figure 11.15   Excavation at site FxJj50, Koobi Fora, Kenya.

northern Kenya, where a tiny scatter of animal bones and stone artifacts revealed traces of human scavenging activity. The original position of the bones was recorded before their removal. Such sites are normally excavated in their entirety, using horizontal trenching.

Interpreting campsites such as these is full of difficulties. As Lewis Binford (1981) points out, little is known of the site-formation processes that have modified the bones found on the floors. He also argues that some early living sites, notably those at Olduvai, were not base camps, and that the inhabitants were scavengers, not hunters. This is, however, a minority view, based on weak data and statistical analyses (Isaac, 1983).

Caves and Rockshelters.   Figure 11.16 shows the excavations at Coxcatlán rockshelter in the Tehuacán valley in Mexico, where

Figure 11.16   Coxcatlán, Tehuacán valley, Mexico.

important evidence for early cultivation of maize was recovered. Cave excavation like this tends to be selective and is carried out both horizontally and vertically. The Coxcatlán site was excavated in alternate squares, each of which was treated as a separate unit.

Perhaps the most meticulous rockshelter excavation ever carried out was at Abri Pataud in the Dordogne (Figure 11.9), where Hallam Movius followed on a coordinated master plan. He removed more than 6 meters (20 feet) of occupation levels over a 12-square meter (60-square foot) area, using a horizontal technique that enabled the excavators to record the exact provenience of every find and major feature.

Figure 11.17   Galatea Bay midden, North Island, New Zealand.

Middens. A midden is a dump of food remains and occupation debris. The constituents of shell middens include seashells, fish bones, ash, stone, and several other forms of food remains (Gifford, 1916). These sites are common on the world's coasts. The excavation problems are twofold; identifying stratigraphic features in the monotonous deposits, and working out adequate sampling procedures to obtain statistically reliable samples of the occupation and food residues in the site. Many modern shell-midden excavations are conducted with random sampling methods that facilitate collection of unbiased samples of midden contents for later analysis. Horizontal excavation techniques are often used, as at the Galatea Bay midden illustrated in Figure 11.17 (Shawcross, 1967; Terrell, 1967).

Mound Excavations. The great *tells*, or occupation mounds, of the Near East result from centuries, even millennia, of human occupation. Such large settlements require huge labor forces to excavate, even on a modest scale. Figures 11.18 and 11.19 contain, respectively, a stratigraphic profile through the ramparts of the ancient city of Harappa in the Indus Valley, Pakistan, and a photograph of the actual excavation, a deep probe into the depths of the city's citadel. Here, vertical excavation provided the history of the defenses (Wheeler, 1967).

Figure 11.18 A section through the defenses of the citadel at Harappa, Pakistan.

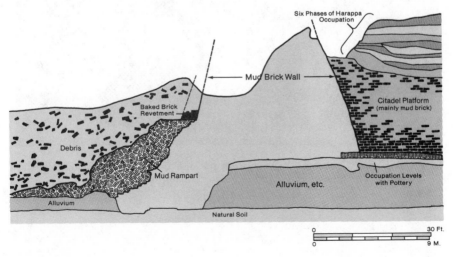

Figure 11.19 Wheeler's excavation through the mud-brick rampart at Harappa. The lower figure stands on the original ground surface.

Clearly, with sites of such great dimensions, only a sampling of the deposits can be made. The most important primary objective is to obtain details of the stratigraphy of the settlement (Figure 11.20). Mound stratigraphy is rarely simple, for both humans and animals complicate it: burrowing animals saunter through the soft soil of the occupation levels, disturbing burials, huts, and hearths; rubbish, burial, and storage pits are dug into lower levels; drains, new street levels, and house foundations disturb natural accumulations. As Braidwood and Howe remark about early farming village mounds in the Near East: "The . . . strata of the archaeological sites may pitch and toss in ways their surface contours seldom suggest. . . ." (Braidwood and Howe, 1962).

Small burial mounds may be excavated in their entirety, using a quadrant method of excavation that removes the mound to its foundations while leaving unexcavated control sections across the site (Figure 11.21).

Village and Town Sites. Larger habitation sites, such as farming villages, complete prehistoric towns, or even Medieval cities, are

Figure 11.20 Two approaches to mound trenching: (a) A stepped trench from the summit exposes a small amount of the original occupation, if this is the mound's center. All earth must be lifted out. (b) A stepped cutting at the mound's edge may miss the core, but soil is easily disposed of. In both approaches, stepping the walls prevents collapse.

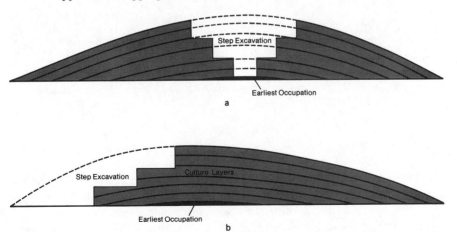

Figure 11.21   A quadrant excavation on a round barrow in Wiltshire, England, photographed from above.

best investigated by area excavation, if resources are available and the deposits are shallow enough.

A remarkable example of this type of archaeology came from Winchester, England, where the history of a row of cottages, eleven houses, and two churches was re-created from documents and archaeological research (Selkirk and Selkirk, 1970). The Brooks area of Winchester was formerly a cloth-working area, where dyeing and fulling was done (Figure 11.22). The Brooks houses had workrooms and shops facing the street, with the water channels for the dyeing process penetrating the front walls; working and living quarters were behind or on top of the shop. A title deed to one house shows that by 1366 it was owned by Richard Bosynton, a leading fuller of his day, who became City Cofferer (treasurer) in 1380–1381. Bosynton appears to have been a strong character, who was fined sixpence in 1390 for polluting the stream that ran by the Brooks houses with dyer's waste. He sold part of his house in 1407 when he retired, and the surviving deed describes the house of that time in detail. Another house was owned by William Bolt, a vigorous businessman, who evicted a feckless tenant named John Shovelar in 1402 after a complex law case. Shovelar had been in trouble with the courts for, among other offenses, erecting a public urinal on his property—urine was a vital ingredient in the fulling

Figure 11.22   A view of the Brooks site, Winchester, England. The outlines of the thirteenth-century cottage walls and of small rooms are clear, as is the narrow lane in front of the dwellings.

process, acting as a type of soap. In this and other instances at Winchester, documents and excavations were linked to provide a remarkably graphic picture of life in a Medieval town.

Guide to Further Reading

Some of the best excavation manuals are from Britain, which is no surprise because of the long tradition of fieldwork and excavation there. The British are lucky in having a wide range of very challenging excavation problems to confront, and the literature reflects this breadth. These are the major publications on excavation.

Alexander, John. *The Directing of Archaeological Excavations*. London: John Baker, 1970.
Provides very wide coverage of different site problems.

Atkinson, R. J. C. *Field Archaeology*. London: Methuen, 1953.
An older manual, but superb in its clear exposition of basic approaches.

Barker, Philip. *The Techniques of Archaeological Excavation*, 2nd ed. London: Batsford, 1983.
An expert guide to excavation that can be used in conjunction with Alexander and Atkinson. Strong European orientation.

Dancey, H. S. *Archaeological Field Methods: An Introduction*. Minneapolis: Burgess, 1981.
An excellent brief survey of American fieldwork approaches.

Hester, Thomas N., J. Shafer, and R. F. Heizer. *Field Methods in Archaeology*, 6th ed. Palo Alto: Mayfield, 1985.
The American manual used widely in field schools.

Joukowsky, Martha. *Complete Manual of Field Archaeology*. Englewood Cliffs: Prentice-Hall, 1981.
A comprehensive survey of excavation methods in both New and Old World contexts. Recommended for general reading.

Wheeler, R. E. M. *Archaeology from the Earth*. Oxford: Clarendon Press, 1954.
An archaeological classic that describes excavation on a grand scale with verve and elegance. A must for every archaeologist's bookshelf, if only for its commonsense information.

PART V ⚜

ANALYZING THE PAST

ARTIFACTS AND TECHNOLOGY

"Intelligence . . . is the faculty of making artificial objects, especially tools to make tools."

HENRI BERGSON,
L'Évolution Créatrice (1907)

Part V begins our exploration of archaeology's ultimate objectives: constructing culture history, reconstructing past lifeways, and studying cultural process. Upon returning from the field, we begin by sorting the data that came from the excavation into categories. From there, we concentrate on artifacts and prehistoric technology. We outline the basic principles of archaeological classification and examine the ways in which ancient peoples used organic and inorganic raw materials. Proper understanding of technology and its uses and limitations is an essential preliminary to any discussion of prehistoric lifeways and culture change in the past.

CHAPTER 12 🌿

IDENTIFYING AND CLASSIFYING DATA

Preview

- The first stage in laboratory analysis is processing field data into a form that will enable one to analyze and interpret them. The basic processing of data takes place as excavation proceeds: finds are washed, conserved, labeled, and sorted into basic categories, such as bone (animal and human), stone, shell, wood, and so on. The finds are also inventoried during this stage.
- Classifying artifacts in archaeology is somewhat different from our day-to-day classifying of the objects around us.
- Two systems of classification are taxonomy and systematics. Taxonomy is a classification system of concepts and terms used by many sciences, among them archaeology. Systematics is a way of creating units that can be used to categorize things as a basis for explaining archaeological or other phenomena. It is a means of creating units of classification within a scientific discipline.
- The objectives of archaeological classification are to organize data into manageable units, to describe types, and to identify relationships between types.
- Archaeological classification begins with identifying artifact attributes, the characteristics that distinguish one artifact from another. Form attributes are such features as the shape of an artifact, and technological attributes include the materials used to make an artifact and the way in which it was manufactured.

Attributes can be selected either by closely examining a collection of artifacts, or they can be derived statistically.

• Modes are attributes that define types; that is, they are clusters of attributes that have been placed in a cultural context.

• Archaeological types are groupings of artifacts created for comparison with other groups. This grouping may or may not coincide with the actual tool types designed by the manufacturers.

• Types are based on modes, or clusters of attributes.

• Natural types are those which are identified with reference to our own cultural background. They are based on the assumption that all artifacts are the result of human behavior, the products of society and culture that placed complex limitations and technological boundaries around the artifacts. These are functional types, designed to coincide closely with actual categories established by the original owners. It is difficult to achieve this goal in archaeology, except where there is cultural continuity between prehistoric and recent societies in areas such as the American Southwest.

• Analytical types are purely arbitrary categories set up by archaeologists for their own specific research purposes. One commonly used system is the convenience type, by which artifacts are divided according to their obvious characteristics. This approach relies heavily on the archaeologist's experience. Another is classification according to norms; that is, two or three obvious attributes that are found in a wide range of artifacts. Norms are assumed to represent the normal range of variation based on visual inspection, as well as on measurements and statistical calculations, and are often designed to identify the "average" artifact. Convenience types and norms are both intuitive approaches.

• Statistical types are based on probability techniques, which rely on computer analysis of individual attributes to determine clusters of attributes. The cluster patterns are then tested for random and nonrandom significance. A statistical type may be defined as a group of artifacts displaying a consistent assemblage of attributes whose combined properties give a characteristic pattern.

Once the excavations and surveys are completed, the archaeologist is confronted with the enormous task of organizing, analyzing, and interpreting the data. This chapter describes the first stage in the long work of identifying and classifying artifacts.

PROCESSING ARCHAEOLOGICAL DATA

The first stage in any laboratory analysis starts in the field—processing and organizing the data so that they can be analyzed and interpreted. The basic processing of archaeological data goes on simultaneously with excavation, for the excavator needs to know where the data are weak and where they are strong. The objective of data collection is to test working hypotheses, and the data acquired for these purposes normally are highly specific. It would be nothing less than stupid to discover in the laboratory that you failed to collect data needed to verify part of your hypothesis simply because you did not monitor it. The wise excavator keeps an eye on the data flowing from the trenches and plans further excavation to obtain larger samples, if they are required.

Preliminary Processing. An essential part of preliminary data processing is the packing, conservation, and marking of the artifacts and other finds. As we stressed in Chapter 5, the provenience of archaeological finds is a major key to understanding their significance. It is no coincidence, then, that most archaeologists develop a careful sequence of stages for processing artifacts and other small finds.

The field laboratory. The first stages in processing newly excavated archaeological data are entirely routine and are common to all finds (Figure 12.1). Most excavations maintain some form of field laboratory, where the finds are taken for preliminary examination. It is here that the major site records are kept and developed, stratigraphic profile drawings are kept up to date, and radiocarbon samples and other special finds are packed for examination by specialists. The field laboratory is staffed by a small group of people whose job is to ensure that all data are processed promptly, packed carefully, and labeled and recorded precisely. The successful laboratory is organized to cope with a steady flow of finds, all of which are handled promptly, thus enabling the director of the excavation to evaluate the available data daily—even hourly.

Cleaning. The laboratory staff's first task is to clean the newly excavated finds. For stone implements or potsherds, fresh water is used for cleaning. More delicate artifacts may have to wait for special laboratory treatment, or they may simply be brushed clean with a fine brush. Cleaning the artifacts is essential, for it permits at least

Figure 12.1   Preliminary data processing: archaeologists sorting pottery finds at a site.

a superficial examination of the find a short time after its discovery, which is part of the process of evaluating the data.

Labeling.   "Never let the sun set on an unmarked artifact," one of my professors used to say. He was right, for an artifact without provenience is almost useless. The finds should arrive in the laboratory in a bag or other container with a label attached, and they should never be separated from this label throughout cleaning and conservation. Sometimes special drying trays are used, with an individual compartment for each batch of finds. With these, the label is pinned to the side of the compartment while the finds dry out. Large or especially important artifacts normally are marked with black ink and the mark is covered with clear lacquer. A large number of potsherds or stone waste flakes are placed in labeled bags, with labels inside and outside the bag.

Conservation.   Fragile artifacts, animal or human bones, or very small finds may need special conservation work, which begins as soon as the find reaches the laboratory—sometimes even in the trench itself. Entire burials can be lifted out of a trench in their original matrix if they are encased in plaster of paris. But most conservation work is carried out in the laboratory. Some sites, such as Ozette, Washington, require a special laboratory for treating thousands of waterlogged wooden finds, often for months on end. Much of the wood was lifted in a waterlogged state and slowly dried out in the laboratory.

Conservation can involve many activities: reassembling fragmented pots, a time-consuming and delicate process; hardening bones, using such chemicals as polyvinyl acetate; or treatment of iron objects. Most field conservation measures are designed to transport the find to the laboratory safely, where it will be examined and preserved at leisure.

Sorting and inventorying. These procedures begin with a rough sorting of the finds, which is based, normally, on the raw material involved.

Finds are counted and recorded in broad categories—bone, stone tools, and so on—to give a general impression of the data and to record the numbers in each category and within each level. These count data are carefully related to provenience and context. Subsequently, the artifact counts may be refined by cataloging each specimen individually. Some excavations maintain looseleaf catalogue books. Others, such as the Koster dig in Illinois, record their artifact data on a computer terminal hooked up to data banks hundreds of miles away (Struever and Holton, 1979). Cataloguing is very time-consuming, and therefore normally it is reserved for highly significant artifacts and for special lots, such as the contents of storage pits or inventories from house floors. Data of this type are vital for studies of household and other activities.

Packing and storage. These make up the final stage of preliminary data processing. Potsherds, animal bones, and stone tools are placed in bags and taken to the laboratory in cartons. Radiocarbon samples, soil specimens, vegetable remains, and other such materials are packed separately, ready for shipment to specialists. Such delicate finds as burials are packed with great care, using tissue paper and special packing materials to prevent breakage in transit. Packing, like all preliminary processing, requires great skill and patience, far more than that accorded your china by a moving company! A complex site can devour huge quantities of packing materials. Howard Carter used several miles of wadding to pack the wooden finds from Tutankhamun's tomb (Carter and others, 1923–33).

The preliminary data processing ends with storing the finds in the permanent laboratory. Days, months, and sometimes even years later the long tasks of classification and analysis begin. In the remainder of this chapter we will discuss objectives and methods of classifying and ordering artifacts.

CLASSIFYING ARTIFACTS

Our attitude toward life and our surroundings involves constant classification and sorting of massive quantities of data. We classify types of eating utensils: knives, forks, and spoons—each type has a different use and is kept in a separate compartment in the drawer. We group roads according to their surface, finish, and size. A station wagon is classified separately from a truck. In addition to classifying artifacts, life-styles, and cultures, we make choices among them. If we are eating soup, we choose to use a spoon. Some people eat rice with a fork, some use chopsticks, and others have decided that a spoon is more suitable. A variety of choices are available, the final decision often being dictated by cultural usage rather than functional pragmatism.

Everyone "classifies," because doing so is a requirement for abstract thought and language. But everyday classes are not often best for archaeological purposes. In our daily life we habitually use classification as a tool for and a part of our life-style. Like the computer, however, it should be a servant rather than a master. Sometimes our classifications of good and bad—those based on color of skin or on our definitions of what is moral or immoral, pornographic or acceptable—are made and then adhered to as binding principles of life without ever being questioned or modified, no matter how much our circumstances may change. Dogmatism and rigidity result from these attitudes and are as dangerous in archaeology as they are in daily life. In archaeology, classification is a research tool, a means for ordering data. All classifications used by archaeologists follow directly from the problems that they are studying. Let us say that our prehistorian is studying changes in pottery designs over a five-hundred-year period in the Southwest. The classification he or she uses will follow not only from what other people have done, but also from the problems being studied. How, and even what, you classify stems directly from the research questions asked of the data. Because the objectives of classifications may change according to the problems being investigated, archaeologists must be sensitive to the need for revising their classifications when circumstances require it.

Taxonomy and Systematics. Taxonomy is the name given to the system of classifying concepts and terms used in many sciences, including archaeology. The taxonomies of biology, botany, geology, and some other disciplines are highly sophisticated and often very rigid systems that were created in the nineteenth and early twentieth centuries, and many are now outgrown. In contrast, archaeology has built its own taxonomy of specialist terminologies and concepts quite haphazardly. Universal comparisons and classifications have been a virtual impossibility. British archaeologists refer to cultures, North American scholars refer to phases, and the French to periods. Each term has basically the same meaning, but the subtle differences stem from cultural attitudes and from different field situations (Goggin, 1949; McKern, 1939; Rouse, 1939).

Systematics is essentially a way of creating units that can be used to *categorize* things as a basis for explaining archaeological or other phenomena (Dunnell, 1971). It is a means of creating units of classification within a scientific discipline. Biologists classify human beings within a hierarchy of classification developed by Carl Linnaeus in the eighteenth century. It begins with the *Kingdom* Animalia, the *Phylum* Chordata (animals with notochords and gill slits), the *Subphylum* Vertebrata (animals with backbones), the *Class* Mammalia, the *Subclass* Eutheria, the *Order* Primates, the *Suborder* Hominoidea (apes and hominidae), the *Family* Hominidae, the *Genus* Homo, the *Species Homo sapiens*, and, finally, the *Subspecies Homo sapiens sapiens*. This hierarchy is gradually fined down until only *Homo sapiens* remains in its own taxonomic niche. The biological classification just described is somewhat arbitrary and is based on each form having common progenitors. It consists of empirically defined units arranged in the form of a hierarchy. Each element in the hierarchy is precisely defined and related to the others. Again, classification in archaeology is a matter of using a classification closely related to the problem being studied.

Objectives of Classification. Classification in archaeology depends greatly on the problems to be studied. Clearly, the culture historian, dealing with space and time, will have very different classificatory needs than the processual archaeologist looking at cultural variability in six contemporary hunter-gatherer sites. But a number of major objectives can be identified:

1. *Organizing data into manageable units.* This is part of the preliminary data-processing operation, and it commonly involves separating finds on the basis of raw material (stone, bone, and so on) or artifacts from food remains. This preliminary ordering allows much more detailed classification later on.
2. *Describing types.* By identifying the individual attributes of hundreds of artifacts, or clusters of artifacts, the archaeologist can group them, by common attributes, into relatively few types. These types are economical ways of describing large numbers of artifacts.
3. *Identifying relationships between types.* This procedure is done to provide a basis for formulating hypotheses about the meaning of the classification. The hierarchy of types orders the relationships between artifacts, which stem, in part, from the use of a variety of raw materials, manufacturing techniques, and functions.

These three objectives are much used in culture-historical research. Processual archaeologists may use classification for:

4. *Studying assemblage variability* in the archaeological record. These studies are often combined with middle-range research on dynamic, living cultural systems (See Chapter 15).

Archaeological classifications are artificial formulations that are based on criteria set up by archaeologists. These classificatory systems, however, do not necessarily coincide with those developed by the people who made the original artifacts (Willey and Phillips, 1958).

Typology.   The system of classification that is based on comparison of types is *typology.* It is a search for structure among either objects or the variables that define these objects, a search that has taken on added meaning and complexity as archaeologists have begun to use computer technology and sophisticated statistical methods. This kind of typology is totally different from arbitrarily dividing up the objects and variables. Such an arbitrary proceeding breaks up the underlying patterning from which the structure is created, so that you lose the opportunity to examine underlying patterns of human design and behavior (Brown, 1982). The value of typology is that it enables one to *compare* what has been found at two sites or in different levels of the same site. Typology, as James Deetz puts it (1967), has one main aim: "classification which permits comparison. . . . Such a comparison allows the archaeologist to align his assemblage with others in time and space." Let's look over a group of archaeologists' shoulders as they sort through a large pile of potsherds, from one occupation level, on the laboratory table.

First the sherds are separated by decoration or lack of it, paste, temper, firing methods, and vessel shape. Once the undecorated or shapeless potsherds have been counted and weighed, they are put to one side, unless they have some special significance. Then the remaining sherds are examined individually and divided into types, according to the features they display. Soon, a number of piles are on the table: one consists of sherds painted with black designs; a second, of red-painted fragments; a third, a group of plain sherds that come from shallow platters. Once the preliminary sort is completed, the archaeologists look over each pile in turn. They have already identified three broad types in the pottery collection. But when they examine the first pile more closely, they find that the black-painted sherds can be divided into several smaller groupings: one with square, black panels; another with diamond designs; and a third with black-dotted decoration. The other two major piles also yield several subtypes. Eventually, the original three types become nine, as the archaeologists study the collection in minute detail, identifying dozens, if not hundreds of attributes, conspicuous and inconspicuous, stylistic or dimensional, even some based on chemical analyses. These data are programmed into a computer in preparing for the quantitative analyses that will help sort out discrete types and variations between them. This is the process of typology, classifying artifacts so that you can compare one type with another. Obviously, the nine types from this one site can be compared with other arbitrary types found during laboratory sorting of collections from nearby sites.

For accurate and meaningful comparisons to be made, rigorous definitions of analytical types are needed, to define not only the "norm" of the artifact type but also its approximate range of variation, at either end of which one type becomes one of two others. Conventional analytical definitions are usually couched in terms of one or more attributes that indicate how the artifact was made, or the shape, or the decoration, or some other feature that the maker wanted the finished product to display. These definitions are set up following carefully defined technological differences, often bolstered by measurements or statistical clusterings of attributes. Most often, the average artifact, rather than the variation between individual examples, is the ultimate objective of the definition. A classifier who finds a group, or even an individual artifact, which deviates at all conspicuously from the norm, often erects a new analytical type. Those who are splitters tend to proliferate types, and those who are lumpers do the opposite. The whole operation is more or less intuitive (Dunnell, 1971).

PROCESS OF ARCHAEOLOGICAL CLASSIFICATION

As we have emphasized, archaeological classification is the ordering of data on the basis of shared characteristics. But how do archaeologists go about this process, and what procedures do they use to do so (Rouse, 1972)?

Typology is based on the archaeologist's "concept of types," subject of one of the great controversies in archaeology. On a formal level, a *type* can be defined as "a group or class of items that was internally cohesive and separated from other groups by one or more discontinuities" (Whallon and Brown, 1982). Beyond this distinction there is profound disagreement among the experts. Most argue that types are identified by combinations of attributes that distinguish and isolate one artifact type from another (Spaulding, 1982). A minority believe that artifacts should be classified by their overall similarity to one another, the so-called object-clustering view of types (Hodson, 1982). Whatever the approach, however, everyone using quantitative approaches to typology agrees that the conceptual setting is organization of data to reveal continuities and breaks between groups of artifacts that display internal cohesion and are isolated from other such groups.

Attributes. The characteristics used to distinguish one artifact from another are known as *attributes* (for a detailed discussion, see Whallon and Brown, 1982). As archaeologists work out their typologies, they find themselves examining hundreds of individual fragments, each of which bears several distinctive attributes (Figure 12.2). To return to our hypothetical laboratory, fifty sherds bear black-painted designs, eighty have red panels on the neck, ten are flattened bowls, and so on. A single potsherd may bear an everted lip, incised decoration applied in a cross-hatched motif, and a red-painted surface. It may have a grit temper, bright red paste, and a

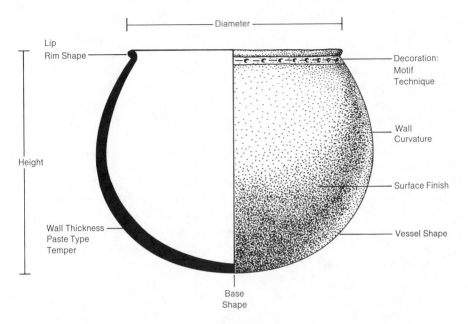

Figure 12.2   Some common attributes of a clay vessel. Specific attributes that could be listed for this pot are concave shoulder, dot and drag decoration, mica temper, round base, and thickness of wall at base.

slipped interior surface. Each of these many individual features is an attribute, most of them obvious enough. Only a critically selected few of these attributes, however, will be used in classifying the artifacts. (If all were used, then no classification would be possible: each artifact would be an individual object identified by several trivial manufacturing or design idiosyncrasies.) The point to remember about attributes is that there is an infinite range of them on any artifact, and the archaeologist works with those considered most appropriate for the classificatory task at hand. All attributes are defined very specifically, often by a measurement. A number of broad groups of attributes are commonly recognized.

Form attributes are features like the shape of the artifact, its measurable dimensions, and its components. Normally, they are fairly obvious.

Stylistic attributes include decoration, color, surface finish, and so on. (Sackett, 1977, 1982).

Technological attributes are those covering the material used to make an artifact and the way it was made.

The selection of attributes normally proceeds through a close examination of a collection of artifacts. A group of potsherds can be divided into different decorative styles based on shapes, surfaces, and colors. The selected attributes are then hand-recorded, and a series of artifact types erected from them. The definition of the type here can depend on the order in which the attributes are examined (see Figure 12.2), and on the researcher's decision as to which are important.

Statistical typologies are derived from attribute clusters that are identified by a computer.

Types. All of us have feelings and reactions about any artifact, whether it is a magnificent wooden helmet from the Pacific Northwest coast (Figure 12.3), or a simple acorn pounder from the southern California interior. Our immediate instinct is to look at and clas-

Figure 12.3   Tlingit carved wood helmet from the Northwest Coast, a "natural" type, classified as such when found in an archaeological context. This artifact would obviously be classified as a helmet from the perspective of our cultural experience. (Height, 9 inches; width, 10 inches.)

sify these and other prehistoric artifacts from our own cultural standpoint. That is, of course, what prehistoric peoples did as well. The owners of the tools archaeologists study classified them into groups for themselves, each one having a definite role in their society. We assign different roles in eating to a knife, fork, and spoon. Knives cut meat, steak knives are used in eating steaks. The prehistoric arrowhead is employed in the chase; one type of missile head is used to hunt deer, another to shoot birds, and so on. The use of an artifact may be determined not only by convenience and practical considerations, but by custom or regulation. The light-barbed spearheads used by some Australian hunting bands to catch fish are too fragile for dispatching kangaroo; with the special barbs the impaled fish can be lifted out of the water. Pots are made by women in most African or American Indian societies, which have division of labor by sex; each has formed complicated customs, regulations, or taboos, which, functional considerations apart, categorize clay pots into different types with varying uses and rules in the culture (Fig. 12.4).

Furthermore, each society has its own conception of what a particular artifact should look like. Americans have generally preferred larger cars, Europeans small ones. These preferences reflect not only pragmatic considerations of road width and longer distances in the New World, but also differing attitudes toward traveling, and, for many Americans, a preoccupation with prestige and driveway display manifested in chromium plate, knock-off wheel covers, and style changes. We think that a car should have a color-coordinated interior and a long hood to look "right." The steering wheel is on the left, and it is equipped with turn signals and seatbelts by law. In other words, we know what we want and expect an automobile to look like, even though minor design details change—as do the length of women's skirts and the width of men's ties.

The problem that confronts the archaeologist is to develop archaeological types that are appropriate to the research problems they are tackling, an extremely difficult task. The concept of archaeological type has generated a large and often controversial academic literature (Ford, 1954a,b; Kreiger, 1944; Rouse, 1960; Spaulding, 1960; Steward, 1954). In archaeology, a type is a grouping of artifacts created for comparison with other groups. This grouping may or may not coincide with the actual tool types designed by the original manufacturers. Everyone agrees that a type is based on clusters of attributes, or on clusters of objects (Whallon and Brown, 1982).

Figure 12.4   A Chumash parching tray.
A good example of the difficulties in archaeological classification. This finely made basket was produced by the Chumash Indians of southern California (Deetz, 1967). It was made by weaving plant fibers. The design was formed in the maker's mind by several factors, most important of which is the tremendous reservoir of inherited cultural experience that the Chumash have learned, generation by generation, through the several thousand years they lived in southern California. The designs of their baskets are almost unconscious, and relate to the feeling that such and such a form and color are "correct" and traditionally acceptable. But there are more pragmatic and complex reasons, too, including the flat, circular shape that enables the user to roast seeds by tossing them with red embers.

Each attribute of the basket has a good reason for its presence—whether traditional, innovative, functional, or imposed by the technology used to make it. The band of decoration around the rim is a feature of the decorative tradition of the Chumash and occurs on most of their baskets. It has a rich red-brown color from the species of reed used to make it. The steplike decoration was dictated by the sewing and weaving techniques, but the diamond pattern is unique and the innovative stamp of one weaver, which might or might not be adopted by other craftspeople in later generations. The problem for the archaeologist is to measure the variations in human artifacts, and to establish the causes behind, and directions of, change, and to find what these variations can be used to measure. This fine parching tray is a warning that variations in human artifacts are both complex and subtle.

Though patterns of attributes may be fairly easy to identify, how do archaeologists know what is a type and what is not? Should they try to reproduce the categories of pot that the makers themselves conceived? Or should they just go ahead and create quite arbitrary "archaeological" types designed purely for analytical purposes? This is the nub of the controversy about types in archaeology.

Julian Steward (1954) distinguishes three "types of types" that are still widely used today (Figure 12.5):

Descriptive types are the most elementary, descriptions based solely on the form of the artifact—physical or external properties. The descriptive type is used when the use of cultural significance of an object or practice is unknown. The excavations at Snaketown in Arizona revealed a "large, basin-like depression." This descriptive "type" was subsequently proven to be a ball court, and so the noncommittal descriptive classification was abandoned in favor of a functional one that defined the structure's role in Hohokam culture. Descriptive types are commonly used in the earlier periods of archaeology, when functional interpretation is much harder to arrive at.

Chronological types are defined by form, but are time markers. They are types with chronological significance. Like descriptive

Figure 12.5 Nine-thousand-year-old Mesolithic artifacts from Star Carr, England (actual size). You can classify these by—Descriptive type: geometric stone tools; Chronological type: Mesolithic microliths, Star Carr forms; Functional type: microlithic arrowhead barbs.

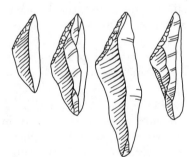
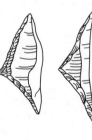

a Obliquely blunted   b Triangular

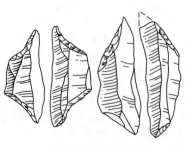

c Elongated trapeze

types, they are part of a culture's inventory as reflected in the archaeological record, but are widely used to distinguish chronological and spatial differences. Pottery is probably the most common form of chronological type, for the clay, shape, decoration, and so on change, and are assumed to have noncultural significance and to be significant and historical indices. Thus pottery, stone artifacts, and other chronological types have become vital elements in building the cultural sequences constructed by culture historians.

The great Egyptologist Flinders Petrie used chronological types when he studied the pre-Dynastic jars from Diospolis Parva on the Nile. He based his chronological indices on the changing handle designs, which degenerated from a fully functional handle for lifting the vessel down to a meaningless squiggle painted on the pot (Petrie, 1899). Chronological types figure prominently in southwestern archaeology, and were used by Alfred Kidder (1924) in his classic excavations at Pecos. Chronological types have the disadvantage that they are often hard for an archaeologist other than their originator to duplicate, except under favorable conditions, or when all in a group of archaeologists have received the same training over a long period (Sackett, 1977).

Functional types are based on cultural use or role rather than on outward form or chronological position. The same artifacts can be treated as of the functional type or the descriptive one. You can classify an assemblage in broad categories: "wood," "bone," "stone," and so on. But equally well, you may adopt a functional classification: "weapons," "clothing," "food preparation," and so on.

Ideally, functional types should reflect the precise roles and functional classifications made by the members of the society from which they came. Needless to say, such an objective is very difficult to achieve, because of incomplete preservation and lack of written records. We have no means of visualizing the complex roles that some artifacts achieved in prehistoric society, or of establishing the restrictions placed on their use by the society. Although in some cases obvious functional roles, such as that of an arrowhead for hunting or warfare or of a pot for carrying water, can be correctly established in the laboratory, functional classifications are necessarily restricted and limited. Let us consider a Scandinavian flint dagger (Figure 12.6)—a beautifully made, pressure-flaked tool, a copy of the bronze daggers so fashionable at the time in central Europe. This tool has been classified by generations of archaeologists as a dagger, by implication of a weapon of war and defense, worn by

Figure 12.6 A pressure-flaked Scandinavian flint dagger. (After Oakley; one-half actual size.)

Scandinavian farmers who still had no metals and made a slavish imitation of a more advanced metal tool. This instinctive designation may be correct, but we really do not know if our functional classification was correct. Was the dagger actually used in warfare and for personal defense? Was it a weapon, or was it purely an object or prestige for the owner, perhaps with some religious function?

It is in cases like this that we are confronted with the truth that the archaeological record is static (Fig. 12.6), and that it is very difficult to make analogies between material culture of modern people and that of the past (Chapter 15). Middle-range research and theory, also described in Chapter 15, offers some opportunities for making more meaningful artifact and assemblage classifications.

Stylistic types are best exemplified by items like dress, because style is often used to convey information by displaying it in public. The Aztecs of central Mexico lived in a ranked society where everyone's dress was carefully regulated by sumptuary laws (Anawalt, 1982). Thus, a glance at the noble in the marketplace could reveal not only his rank but the number of prisoners he had taken in battle and many other subtle differences. Even the gods had their own regalia and costumes that reflected their roles in the pantheon (Fagan, 1984a). Stylistic types can be expected, theoretically at any rate, to have a structure entirely different from that of functional ones. As such, they are not used often in archaeological classification, except when historical records are available.

Statistical techniques and clustering of artifacts.   The researchers of the past thirty years have produced such massive quantities of new archaeological data that it is a full-time job to keep track of the myriad records and artifacts from old and new excavations and surveys. Fortunately, the digital computer and a battery of statistical techniques have come to our aid. Computers can be used to store information and to identify patterns of regularity on the artifacts. A computer data bank can be manipulated in such a way as to tell you the percentage in a collection of projectile points in a Paleo-Indian collection stored in the computer that have notched bases and chisel-like tips, or the percentage of painted bowls from an Anasazi assemblage that have turned-in rims (Figure 12.7).

Modern archaeology relies heavily on statistical methods as well as sampling techniques. Statistical procedures have two objectives in archaeology. The first of these, *descriptive statistics*, is a battery of standard procedures with which large bodies of data are reduced to manageable proportions. These include frequency distributions of artifact attributes and types, various forms of graphs, and measures (central tendency and dispersion; that is, means, modes, and medians). These enable one to establish clustering or dispersion of variables and measurement of degrees of variability.

The second objective, *inferential statistics*, provides systematic procedures for generating sensible conclusions about the whole when only a part is known. Archaeologists most often work with only samples of data, and therefore face a fundamental problem: How far can one generalize from sample findings? Common-sense inferences have been used for generations, but the great bodies of data

Figure 12.7   Still Life with Hand Axes, 1968. A pleasing group by Derek Roe symbolizing the quantitative approach to classification of artifacts.

now available make such approaches much less effective than before. A body of statistical tools has been developed that forms a process of reasoning from a sample statistic to a population as a whole. At issue here is the need to determine the chances of error when making inferences about a population as a whole. In other words, what are the probabilities that statistical decisions based on small samples of data are reliable? Probability statistics involves a battery of well-defined statistical tests that assess the significance of distributions obtained from descriptive procedures, such as binomial distributions, normal curves, and chi-square tests. (For a more technical description of these, see Thomas, 1976.) It is important to realize that statistical methods enable archaeologists to organize their data in an intelligible way, and also to attempt predictions as to the probability that their inferences from small samples are valid for larger populations.

Assemblages and Patternings.   Culture history in archaeology is based on classification of artifacts and assemblages, defined as associations of artifacts that are thought to be contemporary. This was the approach espoused by V. Gordon Childe in the 1930s and 1940s, and was also popular in North America. "We find certain types of remains . . . constantly recurring together," Childe wrote (1929): "Such a complex of regularly associated traits we shall term . . . a 'culture.' We may assume that such a complex is the material expression of what would today be called a 'people.'" This assumption was virtually archaeological law until the 1950s, when a number of prehistorians began using statistical methods to look at assemblages of artifacts. Among them was French archaeologist François Bordes, who worked out methods for classifying Paleolithic tools found together in excavated levels that became primary means of comparing not individual artifacts, but *assemblage-based* components of the archaeological record. He also argued that the techniques used in manufacturing stone tools should be treated independently of the form of the same artifacts. Bordes spent years applying his new classification system to both existing collections and material he excavated from deep Middle and Upper Paleolithic rockshelters in southwest France. He compared the frequencies of tool types from dozens of layers, producing cumulative graphs showing several repetitive patterns for the Middle Paleolithic Mousterian period of some 70,000 to 35,000 years ago. There appeared to be no fewer than four basic forms of graph, which Bordes identified as four distinct types of Mousterian assemblage (the names he gave them, shown in Figure 13.8, p. 314 do not affect us here). The artifact assemblages identified by Bordes persisted for a long time, appearing in one level at Bordes' Combe Grenal excavations in southwestern France, then vanishing, only to reappear millennia later. The same alternating patterns were repeated at dozens of other locations. What did these empirical data, patterns of artifacts in the archaeological record gathered and analyzed with meticulous care, really mean? Earlier archaeologists had assumed a steady, almost inevitable progress of human culture through the ages. They assumed that artifact assemblages with recurring patterns like these were merely traces of contemporary cultural "species" that extended far back into antiquity. This "organic" view of culture history saw assemblages of artifacts as distinct categories like organic species that did not modify their form from one context to the next (Sackett, 1981). The argument went on to assume that a specific cultural tradition leads to only one characteristic type of industry in the archaeological record that is circumscribed in time and space.

    This view of the past, and the classifications that go with it, is almost like the famous "tree-of-life" view of living things in biology, where everything has its place. American archaeologists have generally preferred a more "cultural" view, in which assemblages of artifacts and other traits from living societies have been studied over vast areas of North America. They admit a strong correlation between the distribution of distinctive cultural forms and different environments. These observations based on living societies have shown that it is almost impossible to distinguish between ethnic and social groups from artifact assemblages alone. If this is cultural reality, what exactly do Bordes' empirical data mean? Were conditions in the past different from those of today? Did the Mousterian archaeological record chronicle alternate occupations by different cultural groups, or seasonal occupations, or what? Lewis Binford (1983) is among those who have thought about the problem. For the Mousterian, he could work with extremely rigorous classifications. The archaeological record was exceptionally well studied, and so Binford tried more sophisticated methods of analysis, but still meanings eluded him. When the facts did not speak for themselves, Binford turned to living caribou hunters, the Nunamiut Eskimo of northern Alaska (1978). There, he learned that the only way to understand a living society's subsistence and material culture was to conceive of all their sites as part of a larger system. The Nunamiut had residential sites, and many other kinds of sites used for specialized purposes. Thus, he argued, archaeologists have to identify the specific function of each site they examine, then fit the sites into a much larger, overall pattern of land use. Archaeology's basic unit is the site; the artifacts in it are part of an assemblage pattern that reveals the different behaviors that took place there. If archaeologists want to understand the dynamics of cultural systems like that of the Mousterian in the past, they will have to study and interpret prehistoric living conditions, using such classificatory devices as typology, tool frequencies, and the relationships between tool debris and finished artifacts, as just some of their methods of doing so. Thus, the role of classification in archaeology is shifting away from "organic" viewpoints that see artifacts and cultures as finite in time and space, to new means of problem-oriented classification that concentrate not only on individual tools, but on entire assemblages and their patternings. But the data for interpreting these patterns must finally come from sources other than stone tools or potsherds. In other words, classification alone is meaningless, unless the classifications are interpreted in terms of other data. And here is where the study of contemporary societies, "middle-range research," is coming into its own (Chapter 15).

CLASSIFICATION AND PROCESSUAL ARCHAEOLOGY: EVOLUTION, FUNCTION, AND STYLE

Artifact classifications are still carried out, for the most part, using approaches meant for reconstructing culture history, formulations of time and space that owed much to functional classifications of artifacts based on common sense. Robert Dunnell (1978) points out that relatively few new classificatory concepts are relevant to the new interest in processual archaeology. In classifying artifacts, archaeologists usually have made use of functional units or stylistic types that have their basis in their historical significance through time. More recently archaeologists have adopted inductive, statistical procedures (Spaulding, 1953; Doran and Hudson, 1975) that are technically more rigorous and of great use within an assemblage, but less applicable on a wider canvas. Thus, the same classificatory units have remained in use, while archaeologists pay lip service to newer approaches. As Dunnell (1978) points out, the question of questions is a simple one: Can style be explained within a scientific and evolutionary framework, using laws of cultural change?

Evolutionary Archaeology is an explanatory framework for the past that accounts for the "structure and change" Dunnell finds evident in the archaeological record in terms of such evolutionary processes as natural selection and mutation. This is not, of course, to say that cultural and genetic phenomena are similar. Quite the contrary, for archaeologists are going to have to redefine the processes considerably. Let us examine some of these more closely.

First, it no longer matters when a new element in human culture is invented or appears. Rather, the question is how and why it becomes accepted and visible in the archaeological record. As in biology, impelling forces of natural selection operate in this process, for people are likely to accept the most effective and suitable artifacts or innovations. Invention, on the other hand, is somewhat equivalent to biological mutation, perhaps a random phenomenon. Millions of inventions were made over the millennia of prehistory, but only a tiny proportion of them were widely accepted, partly because there are so many people in the world, a major constraint on a rapid rate of cultural change. Inevitably, though, as the world population rose, so too the complexity of human culture increased at a logarithmic rate. It may be that biological change or environmental circumstances exert some influence on cultural change, but our estimates of these influences are too imprecise to enable us to

say much more than that increased numbers of people are correlated with accelerating complexity.

We must now ask what cultural as opposed to biological laws are
operating on human evolution. Dunnell (1978) points out that the
archaeological record of human culture extends back about three
million years, but only within the last 50,000 years or so has there
been an explosion in both population and cultural complexity. Ever
since the first hominids appeared, human beings have been trans-
mitting culture from one generation to the next, a process that
could be called somewhat analogous to sexual reproduction. The
latter is thought to have been a major factor in the explosion of life
on earth after the Cambrian epoch. In an analogous manner, argues
Dunnell, cultural transmission increased cultural diversity, short-
ened adaptive response time, and increased the range of options
open to humanity. Such an argument may cause one to take a radically different look at explanations of such major events as the
emergence of states and civilizations. Perhaps these should be
viewed not as unique environmental phenomena, but as the logarithmic progression of natural growth curves that began as long ago
as the very beginnings of human existence.

If this evolutionary approach does apply to the archaeological
record, then one must recognize that two distinct elements are
involved in any evolving cultural system:

Traits with selective values over measurable amounts of time: these values
   can be accounted for by processes of natural selection and those
   imposed by external conditions.
Traits that are adaptively neutral, whose frequencies in a population
   cannot be accounted for by natural selection or external
   conditions.

In the context of these evolutionary processes, both function and
style can be redefined:

Function in an evolutionary context refers to forms that directly
   affect the Darwinian fitness of the populations in which they
   occur. Under this title, an archaeologist would use *form* only for
   artificial attributes. This definition of form differs radically from
   that traditionally adopted by archaeologists, a definition based on
   the perceived "use" of tools, which relied heavily on analogies
   with modern artifacts like axes and hoes.
Style in the same context describes forms that do not have detectable selective values. This definition is fairly close to that already

used by culture historians, for stylistic similarities in pottery shapes and so on result directly from cultural transmission from one potter to another, from veteran to novice, and so on. Stylistic variables are independent of external conditions, and are homologous, so that one can use them as a tool for identifying interaction between neighboring sites, culture areas, and so on, just as archaeologists have been doing for generations. By the same token, they are useless for explanations in terms of natural selection.

Stylistic variations have served as the primary means for archaeologists to identify the classic cultural processes beloved of culture historians: diffusion, acculturation, migration, and so on. All these processes go little further than demonstrating the source and space-time context of an artifact or stylistic form. Only independent invention lies outside this framework, and even it has been invoked to explain such phenomena as the appearance of pottery. To explain the archaeological record in an evolutionary framework when it is structured in stylistic terms is almost impossible. Explaining changes in style is, and always has been, a mostly conjectural pastime.

Archaeological evolutionary theory will have to be written in forms that can be identified in the archaeological record (Dunnell, 1980). Integral to this process are new definitions of style and form in archaeology that are, as yet, still in their infancy.

Guide to Further Reading

The literature on archaeological classification is both complex and enormous. I strongly advise you to obtain expert advice before delving into even key references. Here, however, are some useful starting points.

Dunnell, Robert. *Systematics in Prehistory.* Seattle: University of Washington Press, 1971.
A highly technical introduction to systematic classification in archaeology.

Rouse, Irving. *An Introduction to Prehistory: A Systematic Approach.* New York: McGraw-Hill, 1972.
Describes a basic approach to archaeological classification that has fairly wide application.

Spaulding, Albert C. "Statistical Techniques for the Study of Artifact Types." *American Antiquity* 18,4: 305–13.

————. "Statistical Descriptions and Comparison of Artifact Assemblages,"in R. F. Heizer and S. F. Cook, eds. *Quantitative Methods in Archaeology*. New York: Viking Fund, 1960, pp. 60–92.
Two widely read papers on statistical approaches to classification of artifacts. A reaction to these articles appeared in a series of papers reprinted in American Antiquity *in 1977.*

Thomas, David Hurst. *Figuring Anthropology: First Principles of Probability and Statistics*. New York: Holt, Rinehart and Winston, 1976.
A basic text on quantitative methods that can be strongly recommended to serious students of the past.

Whallon, Robert, and James A. Brown, eds. *Essays on Archaeological Typology*. Evanston: Center for American Archaeology, 1982.
Thought-provoking essays on the theory behind archaeological typology by the authorities in the field. Updates the earlier literature.

Willey, Gordon R., and Philip Phillips. *Method and Theory in American Archaeology*. Chicago: University of Chicago Press, 1958.
The classic work on construction of culture history in New World archaeology. Every advanced student reads this book.

CHAPTER 13 ✿

TECHNOLOGY AND ARTIFACTS

Preview

- One of the main inorganic materials used by prehistoric people was stone, especially siliceous rock, which fractures according to the conchoidal principle.
- We describe the basic techniques for manufacturing stone tools, starting with the stone-on-stone technique, the cylinder-hammer method, and the prepared cores used to produce blanks for Middle Paleolithic artifacts. Blade technology came into use about 35,000 years ago, and the first use of pressure flaking was identified among the Solutrean people of some 17,000 years ago.
- Stone technology and artifacts were first studied by means of rigid "type fossil" concepts, which were superseded by functional analyses: artifacts were classified according to shape, dimensions, and assumed use. Attribute analysis has, in turn, replaced functional approaches, and it involves the study of finished artifacts and also of the by-products of their manufacture.
- Lithic experimentation and ethnoarchaeology have leading roles in the study of stone technologies; edge wear and petrological studies throw light on the trade in raw materials and the uses to which tools were put.
- Ceramics (clay objects) are a major preoccupation of archaeologists and date to the last 10,000 years of prehistory. We describe

the process of pottery manufacture, the various methods used, and the surface finishes employed.

- Ceramic analysis proceeds by analogy and experiment, research in which controlled experiments with firing and the properties of clay have had leading parts. The vessels themselves are studied by form and functional analyses, on the assumption that the shape of a vessel directly reflects its function. This assumption can be a dangerous one, however, and many archaeologists prefer to use stylistic analyses. Clusters of attributes are used now, also, in attempts to standardize stylistic classifications.
- Prehistoric metallurgy is a phenomenon of the past 6,000 years. We describe the basic properties of copper, bronze, gold, and iron and some of the cultural contexts in which metallurgy developed. Typological and technological analyses are used to study prehistoric metallurgy, with European archaeologists emphasizing typological comparisons based on minute stylistic variations.
- Bone tools are thought to be among the earliest of all artifacts. The so-called osteodontokeratic culture of the Australopithecines has, however, been shown to be of natural origin. They are important in some areas—noticeably, the Arctic—as indicators of typological change. The functional analysis of bone tools is somewhat easier than that of stone tools or ceramics, for the uses of bone objects are often easier to determine. Technological analyses of bone artifacts have concentrated on the ways in which the tools were made. Ethnographic analogy also is important in bone studies.
- Wood artifacts are a mine of information on prehistoric life. The manufacture of wood tools involves well-understood mechanical processes, such as cutting and whittling, and these can often be identified even from unfinished artifacts. Stone artifacts and other materials have been found mounted in wood handles and this provides insights into the uses of composite artifacts.
- Basketry and textiles are among the least understood of prehistoric technologies, but they offer unique opportunities for studying individual idiosyncrasies in the archaeological record, as well as providing useful chronological markers. We cite an innovative computer mapping project on basketry styles at Ozette, Washington.

"Whatever the ultimate inspiration or the intermediate cause, it was by their hands that the early Europeans dragged themselves out of the primeval mist of savagery, struggled up the long slopes of barbarism and ultimately attained to some kind of civilized existence." wrote Grahame Clark (1952) about prehistoric Europe. His words provide us with ample justification for studying the technology of the ancients.

The tools that people have manufactured throughout their long history have been the means by which they augmented their limbs and extended the use of their environment. The technological achievements of humanity over the past three million years of cultural evolution have been both impressive and terrifying. Today we can land an astronaut on the moon, transplant human hearts, and build sophisticated computers. Yet, in the final analysis, our contemporary armory of lasers, atomic bombs, household appliances, and every conceivable artifact designed for a multitude of specialized needs has evolved in a direct, albeit branching, way from the first simple tools made by the earliest human beings. In this chapter, we examine some of the main technologies used by prehistoric people to adapt to their natural environments and look at some of the ways in which archaeologists study them. We emphasize, however, that the study of artifacts and technologies is only a small part of the total archaeological process. The data that come from these studies are designed to verify specific research hypotheses formulated before collection of data began.

STONE

Certain categories of rock have, with bone and wood, been the primary raw materials for human technology for most of human existence. Metallurgy is but a recent development, and stone tools have provided the foundation for classification of many prehistoric cultures since scientific archaeology began. The raw material itself has set severe limits on people's technological achievements for much of their history, and the evolution of stoneworking over the millions of years during which it has been practiced has been infinitely slow. Nonetheless, people eventually exploited almost every possibility afforded by suitable rocks for making implements.

How People Worked Stone. The simplest way of producing a stone that will cut or chop, surely the basic tool produced by prehistoric people, is simply to break off a piece and use the resulting sharp edge (Figure 13.1). But to produce a tool which has a more specialized use or which can be employed for several purposes requires a slightly more sophisticated flaking technique. First, an angular fragment or smooth pebble of suitable rock can be brought

Figure 13.1 These chopping tools from Olduvai Gorge, Tanzania, are some of the earliest human tool forms. Arrows show the working edges. (Three-fifths actual size.)

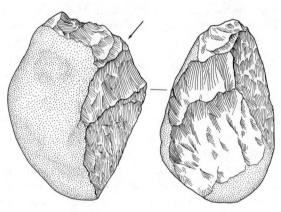

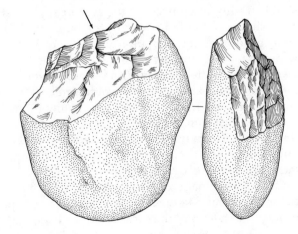

to the desired shape by systematically flaking it with another stone. The flakes removed from this core, or lump, are then primarily waste products, whereas the core becomes the implement that is the intentional end product of the toolmaker. Furthermore, the flakes struck from the core can themselves be used as sharp-edged knives, or they can be further modified to make other artifacts. From this simple beginning, many and complex stone industries have evolved, the earliest tools being simple—many of them virtually indistinguishable from naturally fractured rock.

Principles of manufacture. Identifying human-made implements as distinct from naturally broken rocks can be learned only by experience in handling many artifacts. Here is a generalized description of the principles of stone-implement manufacture (Hester and Heizer, 1973; Howell, 1965). Generally, Stone Age people and other makers of stone tools chose flint, obsidian, and other hard homogeneous rocks to fashion their artifacts. All these rocks break in a systematic way, like industrial glass. A sharp blow directed vertically at a point on the surface of a suitable stone dislodges a flake, with its apex at the point where the hammer hit the stone. This blow effects a *conchoidal fracture* (Figure 13.2). When a blow is directed at a stone slab obliquely from the edge, however, and the break occurs conchoidally, a flake is detached. The fractured face of the flake has a characteristic shape, with a bulge extending from the surface of the piece outward down the side. This is known as the *bulb of percussion;* there is a corresponding hollow or flake scar on the core from which the flake has been struck. The bulb of percussion is readily recognized, as the accompanying text figure (Figure 13.3) shows, not only because of the bulge itself but also from the concentric rings that radiate from the center of the impact point, widening gradually away from it. Such deliberate human-made fractures are quite different from those produced by such natural means as frost, extreme heat or cold, water action, or stones falling from a cliff and fracturing boulders below (Clark, 1958). In these types the rock sometimes breaks in a similar manner, but most of the flake scars are irregular, and instead of concentric rings and a bulb of percussion, often a rough depressed area is left on the surface with concentric rings formed around it.

Careful examination is needed to distinguish human-worked and naturally fractured stones from one another, a particularly acute problem with tools of the earliest human beings. Many of their artifacts were made by the simplest of hammerstone techniques,

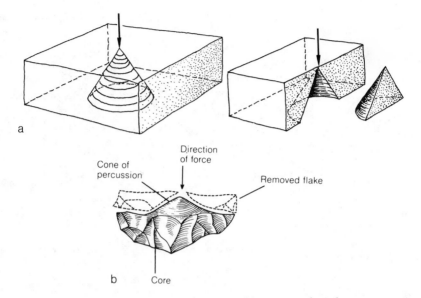

Figure 13.2 How stone fractures: (a) when a blow is struck on homogeneous types of rock, a cone of percussion is formed by the shock waves rippling through the stone. At the right a flake is chipped when the block (or core) is hit at the edge and the stone fractures along the edge of the ripple. (b.) Looking down on the surface of a Stone Age core. The arrow shows the point of impact, where the hammerstone fell. This is the summit of the bulb of percussion. Two removed flakes are shown in dotted lines.

removing two or three flakes from the pebble (Figure 13.3). This work produced a jagged edge that was effective, so experiment shows, in dismembering carcasses of game. Several famous controversies have raged over alleged "artifacts" found in Lower Pleistocene deposits in Europe and Africa that are contemporary with periods when hominids were already flourishing elsewhere. A celebrated furor arose over alleged tools, named "eoliths," found early in this century in Lower Pleistocene horizons in eastern England (Burkitt, 1955). These were championed for many years as early evidence of human occupation until reexamination of the geological contexts and accurate measurements of the flaking angles on the "eoliths" demonstrated that they were probably of natural origin (Barnes, 1938). Under such circumstances, the only sure identification of human-fractured stone implements is to find them in association with fossil human remains and broken animal bones, preferably on living sites.

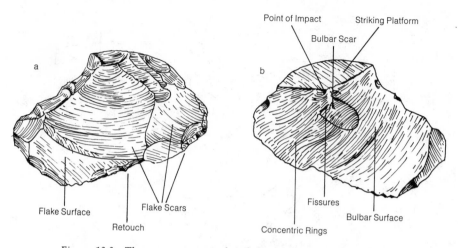

Figure 13.3 The components of a flake tool: (a) flake surface; (b) bulbar surface.

Methods. Figures 13.4–13.7 show some of the major stone-flaking methods used by prehistoric peoples. The simplest and earliest used was direct fracturing of the stone with a hammerstone (Figure 13.4). After thousands of years, people began to make tools flaked on both surfaces, such as Acheulian hand axes (Figure 13.5). As time went on, the stoneworkers began to use bone hammers to trim the edges of their hand axes. The hand axe of 150,000 years ago had a symmetrical shape, sharp, tough working edges, and a beautiful finish.

As people became more skillful and specialized, such as the hunter-gatherers of about 100,000 years ago, they began to develop stone technologies producing artifacts for highly specific purposes. They shaped special cores that were carefully prepared to provide one flake or two of a standard size and shape (Figure 13.6). About 35,000 years ago, some stoneworkers developed a new technology based on preparing cylindrical cores from which long, parallel-sided blades were removed with a punch and hammerstone (Holmes, 1919) (Figure 13.7). These regular blanks were then trimmed into knives, scraping tools, and other specialized artifacts (Figure 13.8). Blade technology was so successful that it spread all over the world. It was the first stone technology introduced into the Americas (Clark, 1970).

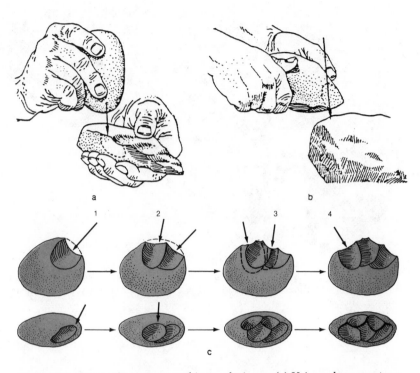

Figure 13.4 The earliest stoneworking techniques: (a) Using a hammerstone. (b) A variant on the hammerstone, striking a core against a stone block, the so-called anvil technique. (c) The earliest stone tools, often crude choppers, were made by a simple method. The top row shows the side view: first, two flakes were struck off (1 and 2); second, the stone was turned over, and two more flakes were removed (3); and third, a fifth flake completed the tool (4), giving it a sharp edge. The bottom row shows the process from above.

Once blades had been removed from their cores, they were trimmed into shape using a variety of techniques. In some, the blade's side was flaked with an antler or piece of wood to sharpen or blunt it. Sometimes the flake would be pressed against another stone, a bone, or a piece of wood to produce a steep, stepped edge or a notch (Figure 13.8a and b). The Australian aborigines and some Plains Indians sometimes nibbled the edges of their tools with their teeth.

The best-known and most common technique used in the later periods of prehistory, especially in the New World, was pressure

Figure 13.5   An Acheulian hand axe from Wolvercote, Oxford, England, with finely trimmed edges made with a bone hammer. (Approximate length, 5 inches.)

Figure 13.6   A special core shaped to produce one thin flake that was turned into a knife. Arrow indicates where flake was removed. (One-half actual size.)

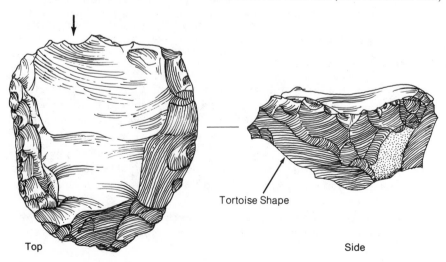

Tortoise Shape

Top

Side

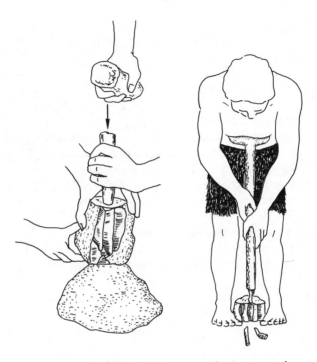

Figure 13.7 Two uses of the blade technique, employing a punch.

flaking (Figure 13.8c and d). The stoneworker used a small billet of wood or antler pressed against the working edge so as to exert pressure in a limited direction and remove a fine, shallow, parallel-sided flake. This formed one of many flake scars that eventually covered most of the implement's surfaces. The advantage of pressure flaking is that it facilitates production of many standardized tools with extremely effective working edges in a comparatively short time.

In southwest Asia, Europe, and many parts of Africa and southern and eastern Asia, small blades were fashioned into minute arrowheads, barbs, and adzes, known as *microliths*, often made by a characteristic notching technique (Clark, 1932). These also evolved in arctic America and Australia.

The blade technologies of later times could produce far more tools per pound of material than earlier methods. Even tougher working edges were developed by later Stone Age peoples, who began to grind and polish stone when they needed a sharp and highly durable blade. The edges were shaped by rough flaking and then laboriously polished and ground against a coarser rock, such as sandstone, to produce a sharp, tough working edge. Modern experiments have demonstrated the greater effectiveness of polished stone axes in felling forest trees, the toughened working edge taking longer to blunt than that of a flaked axe (Townsend, 1969; White and Thomas, 1972). Polished stone axes became important in many early farming societies, especially in Europe, Asia, Mesoamerica, and parts of temperate North America. They were used in New Guinea as early as 20,000 years ago and in Melanesia and Polynesia for the manufacture of canoes, which were essential for fishing and trade (Clark, 1978; Fagan, 1980).

Stone-Tool Analysis. Early attempts at stone-tool analysis were based on the classification of finished tools, or "type fossils," which were thought to be representative of different human cultures. The

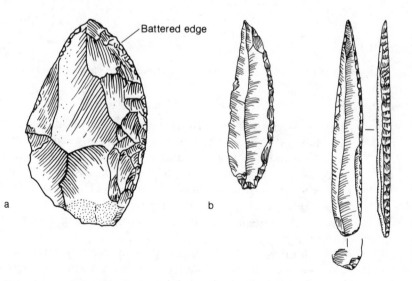

Figure 13.8 Some methods of trimming stone tools: (a) Steep retouch by battering, on a Mousterian side scraper. (One-half actual size.) (b) Specialized blade tools made by pressing and sharpening the edges. These are backed blades used as spearpoints about 22,000 years ago. (Actual size.) Opposite: (c) The pressure-flaking technique. (d) Paleo-Indian pressure-flaked points: (1) Clovis point, (2) Folsom point, (3) Scottsbluff point, (4) Eden point. (All actual size; used with permission of McGraw-Hill Book Company and Thames and Hudson Ltd.)

French prehistorian Gabriel de Mortillet formulated a sequence of Paleolithic cultures in 1881 that was also based on stratified type fossils. He and others argued that human progress was inevitable and that, therefore, slow development of stone tools was inevitable as well. This type of fossil approach was abandoned gradually, as more sophisticated typological methods came into use.

Functional analysis was first used by nineteenth-century archaeologists. With this approach, well-defined artifact types were

c

d

1   2   3   4

named according to their shape, dimensions, and assumed use, such
as the Acheulian hand axe (Figure 13.5) and the Mousterian side
scraper (see Figure 13.8a). This approach led to the use of type fossils and to a tendency to look for the perfect, typical artifact. Many
functional labels remain in use in modern archaeology, but they are
no longer thought of as anything more than a generalized description of the form of an artifact. Functional analysis has reached great
refinement in western Europe, where many varieties of Stone Age
artifacts are to be found (Bordaz, 1970; Bordes, 1968; Sackett, 1977).

Attribute analysis has replaced the functional approach in recent
years (Clay, 1976). Attribute analyses are based on selection of many
artifact features, which can range from technological attributes such
as the form of striking platform to a functional attribute such as a
steep scraping edge (Figure 13.8a). Stone tools are a revealing
source of information on both uses and processes of manufacture.
Any attribute analysis, however, requires studying not only finished artifacts but also the waste products, or *débitage* (French:
throwaway waste), that were created during stoneworking activity.
Sophisticated cluster analyses and probability tests are part of the
statistical armory that stone tool experts use to derive classes of artifacts from statistically significant clusterings of attributes. (For
details of statistical methods and relevant literature, see Redman,
1978; Spaulding, 1953, 1960; Thomas, 1976, 1978; Whallon and
Brown, 1982).

Archaeologists rely on three other approaches to stone-tool
analysis:

1. *Lithic experimentation.* Many archaeology laboratories ring to the
   sound of people trying to make stone tools—and cutting their
   fingers in doing so (Johnson, 1978). The study of prehistoric
   stone tools began with ethnographers comparing the stone toolmaking methods of peoples like the Tasmanians with those of
   prehistoric artisans (Figure 13.9). Modern experimenters have
   drawn on both experimentation and ethnographic observation
   to work out prehistoric techniques (Swanton, 1975). Another
   fruitful source of analytical data has been professional gunflint
   makers, such as those at Brandon, in Suffolk, England (R. Clark,
   1935; Phillipson, 1969). Obsidian flake and blade edges are so
   sharp that they are sometimes used today for delicate eye
   surgery.

Figure 13.9   Australian aborigines making stone tools.

2. *Use-wear analysis* involves both microscopic examination of artifact working edges and actual experiments with using stone
tools (Hayden, 1979; Keeley, 1980). Soviet archaeologist S. A.
Semenov (1964) used a high-magnification microscope to study
the working edges of hundreds of Upper Paleolithic tools. He
found that the scraping edges of so-called end scrapers bore clear
signs not only of scratches but of luster from wear as well. He
experimented with such scrapers and found that identical marks
could be obtained by using the scraper both as a graver and a
scraping tool. Many researchers have experimented with both
low- and high-power magnification in recent years, and are now
able to distinguish with considerable confidence between the
wear polishes associated with different materials like wood,
bone, and hide (Keeley and Newcomer, 1977). The approach is
now reliable enough to allow one to state whether a tool was
used to slice wood, cut up vegetables, or strip meat from bones,
but relatively few archaeologists are trained in using the microscopes and photographic techniques required for analyzing
wear. David Cahen and Lawrence Keeley (1980) have also used
wear analysis to study the activities of individuals. They studied

a scatter of stone tools from the 9,000-year-old Meer II site in northern Belgium. By reassembling some of the stone flakes and cores, studying the wear patterns on tool working edges, and examining distribution of the stone fragments throughout the site, they were able to show that two people, one of them left-handed, had made some tools that they then used to bore and grave fragments of bone. In instances like this, tool-wear analysis offers exciting opportunities for studying the behavior of individual stoneworkers thousands of years ago. There are many examples of distinctive microwear patterns, among them polishes that can be identified with high-powered microscopes (Anderson, 1980). One instance is the flint sickle blade used for harvesting wild or domesticated grasses, which often shows a gloss caused by the silica in the grass stems (Garrod and Bate, 1937).

3. *Petrological analyses* have been applied with great success to the rocks from which stone tools are made, especially ground stone axes in Europe. Petrology is the study of rocks (Greek: *petros* = stone). A thin section of the axe is prepared and examined under a microscope. The minerals in the rock can then be identified and compared with samples from quarry sites. British archaeologists have had remarkable success with this approach and have identified more than twenty sources of axe-blade stone (Clark, 1952; Phillips, 1980). Such researches can lead to vital information on prehistoric trade (see Chapter 18). Spectrographic analysis of distinctive trace elements in obsidian has yielded remarkable results in the Near East and Mesoamerica, where this distinctive volcanic rock was traded widely from several quarry centers (Cann and Renfrew, 1964; Flannery and Winter, 1976).

4. *Refitting.* Watch someone making stone tools and you will find that they are sitting in the middle of a pile of ever-accumulating debris—chips, flakes, abandoned cores, and discarded hammerstones. Prehistoric stoneworkers produced the same sort of debris—hundreds, if not thousands of small waste fragments, by-products of toolmaking that are buried on archaeological sites of all ages. A fascinating and important approach to lithic technology is to collect all these waste fragments with special care, then to try to fit the pieces together, to reconstruct the procedures by which the artisan made his tools. Refitting taxes the patience of even the most even-tempered archaeologist, but can yield remarkable results. At the 9,000-year-old Meer II site in Belgium, Cahen and Keeley (1980) combined edge-wear analysis

with refitting to reconstruct a fascinating scenario. They used the evidence from three borers that were turned counterclockwise to show that a right-handed artisan walked away from the settlement and made some tools, using some prepared blanks and cores he brought with him. Later a *left-handed* artisan came and sat next to him, bringing a previously prepared core, from which he proceeded to strike some blanks that he turned into tools. Reconstruction in this sort of fine detail is often impossible, but has the advantage that the artifact patterning revealed in the archaeological record can be interpreted with extreme precision, because the refitting shows that no modification has affected the evidence displayed in the archaeological record.

CLAY (CERAMICS)

Objects made of clay are among the most imperishable of all archaeological finds; but pottery is a relatively recent innovation. From the very earliest times, people used animal skins, bark trays, ostrich eggshells, and wild gourds for carrying loads beyond the immediate surroundings of their settlements. Such informal vessels were ideal for hunter-gatherers, who were constantly on the move. At one time, it was thought that pottery's beginnings coincided with the origins of food production. We now know, however, that both agriculture and domesticated animals existed in the Near East from the eighth millennium B.C., if not earlier. Pottery did not appear until slightly before 6000 B.C. at such early agricultural settlements in the Near East as Jarmo and Jericho (Braidwood and Howe, 1962; Mellaart, 1975). In contrast, in Japan pottery was made by hunter-gatherers as early as 8000 B.C. (Hayashi, 1968; Morlan, 1967). The inhabitants of the Tehuacán Valley in highland Mexico began cultivating crops several thousand years before the first pottery appeared in North America in about 2500 B.C. (MacNeish, 1978).

The invention of pottery seems to have coincided with the beginnings of more lasting settlement. Clay receptacles have the advantage of being both durable and long-lived. We can assume that the first clay vessels were used for domestic purposes: for cooking, carrying water, and storing food. They soon assumed more specialized roles in salt making, oil lamps, burial urns, and ceremonial activities. Broken ceramic vessels are among the most common archaeological finds. Their shape, style, and form have provided the foundations for thousands of archaeological analyses.

Pottery Technology. Modern industrial potters turn out dinnerware by the millions, using mass-production methods and automated technology. Prehistoric artisans created each of their pieces individually, using the simplest of technology but attaining astonishing skill in shaping and adorning their vessels.

The clay used in pot making was invariably selected with the utmost care; often, it was even traded over considerable distances. The consistency of the clay is critical; it is pounded meticulously and mixed with water to make it entirely even in texture. By careful kneading, the potter removes the air bubbles and makes the clay as plastic as possible, allowing it to be moulded into shape as the pot is built up. When the clay is fired it loses its water content and can crack, so that the potter adds a *temper* to the clay, a substance that helps reduce shrinkage and cracking. Although some pot clays contain a suitable temper in their natural state, pot makers commonly add fine sand, powdered shell, or even mica as artificial temper.

Pot making (ceramics) is a highly skilled art, with three major methods:

1. *Coil.* The vessel is built up with long coils or wedges of clay that are shaped and joined together with a mixture of clay and water (Figure 13.10). Sometimes the pot is built up from a lump of clay. Hand methods were common everywhere that pot making was a part-time activity satisfying local needs.

2. *Mold.* The vessel is made from a lump of clay that is either pressed into a concave mold or placed over the top of a convex shape. Molding techniques were used to make large numbers of vessels of the same size and shape, as well as figurines, fishing-net weights, and spindle whorls. Sometimes several molds were used to make the different parts of a vessel.

3. *Potter's wheel.* Wheel-made pots came into wide use after the first invention of potters' wheels in Mesopotamia about 5,000 years ago. The vessel is formed by placing a lump of clay on a rotating platform turned by the potter's hands or feet. The wheel method has the advantage of speed and standardization and was used to mass produce thousands of similar vessels, such as the bright red Roman Samian ware (Shepard, 1971). Wheel-made pots can sometimes be identified by the parallel rotation marks on their interior surface.

Figure 13.10   Making pots by the coil method.

Surface finishes provided a pleasing appearance and also improved the durability of the vessel in day-to-day use. The potter smoothed the exterior surface of the pot with wet hands. Often a wet clay solution, known as a *slip*, was applied to the smooth surface. Brightly colored slips were often used and formed painted decorations on the vessel (Figure 13.11). In later times, *glazes* came into use in some areas. A glaze is a form of slip that turns to a glasslike finish during high-temperature firing. When a slip was not applied, the vessel was allowed to dry slowly until the external surface was almost like leather in texture. It was then burnished with a round stone or similar object to give it a shiny, hard surface. Some pots were decorated with incised or stamped decorations, using shells, combs, stamps, and other tools. Some were even modeled into human effigies or given decorations imitating the cords used to suspend the pot from the roof (Figure 13.12).

Figure 13.11   A painted Zuñi pot of the 1880s. (Height 9¾ inches.)

The firing of clay objects requires careful judgment on the part of the potter. Most early pottery was fired over open hearths. The vessels were covered with fast-burning wood, whose ash would fall around the vessels and bake them evenly over a few hours. Far higher temperatures were attained in special ovens, known as *kilns*, which would not only bake the clay and remove its plasticity, but also dissolve carbons and iron compounds. Kilns were used to fire vessels at high temperatures and also in glazing, when two firings were needed. Once fired, the pots were allowed to cool slowly and small cracks were repaired before they were ready for use.

The making of clay vessels was circumscribed by all manner of social and other variables. Archaeological literature is rich in descriptions of pot-making techniques among people all over the world. Unfortunately, however, few of these studies go beyond technology and processes of manufacture. They may tell us something about the division of labor in making pots, but they reveal little about the potters' status in their own society, their artistic attitudes, or the changing ceramic fashions. In many societies, pottery

Figure 13.12   A spouted Mochica bottle from Peru.

has a well-defined economic role, and the training of potters is long and elaborate. The analysis of ceramics in archaeology must, however, depend on an understanding of the cultural influences that lie behind the variations in pottery in the archaeological record (Fontana, Robinson, Cormack, and Leavitt, 1962; Matson, 1965). Although recent research has been focused on the significance of the variations, it also deals with the role of the individual potter (Hardin, 1977).

Ceramic Analysis. Serious potsherd archaeology began in the New World with N. C. Nelson in 1914, and A. V. Kidder a few years later. Within a generation, regional pottery sequences were available for most parts of North America. An enormous expenditure of archaeological energy has gone into ceramic analysis since these pioneer studies, and a sophisticated literature covers the common analytical methods (Bennet, 1974; Matson, 1965; Shepard, 1971; Bishop and others, 1982).

Analogy and experiment. Controlled experiments to replicate prehistoric ceramic technology have been undertaken to acquire data on firing temperatures, properties of tempers, and glazing techniques (Coles, 1973; Shepard, 1971). Ethnographic analogy has been a fruitful source of basic information on potters and their techniques, and the direct historical approach traces modern pottery styles back to the prehistoric past.

Form and function analysis. Two features of prehistoric pottery are immediately obvious when we examine a collection of vessels — the shape and decoration. Generations of archaeologists have used ethnographic analogy to assign specific functions to different vessel forms. Bowls are commonly used for cooking and eating, but globular vessels are most suitable for storing liquids. Sometimes associations of clay vessels and other artifacts, such as cooking utensils, leave no doubt as to their function. But such instances are rare, and one usually has to rely on analysis of the vessel form to infer its function.

Form analysis depends on the common assumption that the shape of a vessel directly reflects its function. This assumption, which is based on ethnographic analogies, can be dangerous for many intangibles affect the function of pottery. Intangibles include the properties of the clay used, the technological devices available, and perhaps most important, the cultural values that constrain not only the technology but also the uses and fashions of the vessels. Changes in vessel form can sometimes reflect a change in economic activities, but the economic evidence must be complete before such conclusions can be drawn. At the Isamu Pati mound village in Zambia, occupied intermittently from the seventh to the thirteenth centuries A.D., the uppermost levels contained a much higher proportion of cattle bones than the lower horizons (Fagan, 1967). At the same time, the pottery changed dramatically from a preponderance

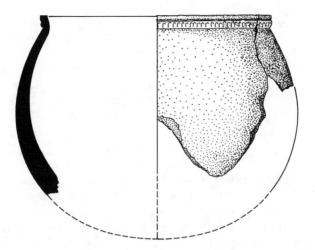

Figure 13.13   A utilitarian clay vessel: an Iron Age pot from the Kalomo culture of Zambia. (One-third actual size.)

of simple bag-shaped vessels (Figure 13.13) to an overwhelming dominance of spherical pots with out-turned lips. These could only have contained liquid and were interpreted tentatively as reflecting a change in dietary habits, perhaps an increase in consumption of milk. The functional distinction between utilitarian and ceremonial vessels is one of the most evident, but it must be supported not only by vessel form but also by direct association. For example, ceremonial pots were commonly buried with important people in many parts of the world, especially Mesoamerica.

Form analysis depends on careful classification of clusters of different vessel shapes. These shapes can be derived from complete vessels, or from potsherds that preserve the rim and shoulder profiles of the vessel. It is possible to reconstruct the pot form from these pieces by projecting measurements of diameter and vessel height. Such analyses produce broad categories of vessel form that are capable of considerable refinement. (For an excellent example, see Sabloff, 1975.)

Stylistic analysis.   This form of analysis is much more commonly used, for it concentrates not on the form and function of the vessel, but on the decorative styles used by the potters. These are assumed to be independent of functional considerations and so more accurately reflect the cultural choices made by the makers. In areas like the American Southwest, pottery styles have been used to trace cultural variations over thousands of years.

Even a cursory glance of pottery reports from different parts of the world will show you that archaeologists have used dozens of different stylistic classifications to study their potsherds. Only in recent years have people tried to standardize stylistic classifications, using clusters of easily recognized attributes to produce hierarchies of types, varieties, and modes.

With this approach, small numbers of distinctive attributes from different pottery assemblages are recorded. These attributes commonly appear in associated sets of features that provide the basis for erecting types, varieties, and modes of pottery styles. In Chapter 12 we defined these three classifications, which are assumed to represent the social system behind the pots studied. Although a *variety* may represent only the activities of one family of potters, a *type* can represent the work of several villages or an entire community. Thus, goes the argument, standardized pottery types reflect a fairly rigid social system that prescribes what pottery styles are used, but less formal designs are characteristic of a less restrictive society. James Gifford studied the ceramics from Barton Ramie in the Belize valley and traced the development of Maya pottery from 800 B.C. onward. He argued that the highly localized styles of earlier times reflected a much more flexible social system than in the Late Preclassic period, after 300 B.C., when pottery designs were standardized over large areas and their designs were controlled, perhaps by rigid cultural values (Gifford, 1976).

Gifford's analysis is based on behavioral assumptions that have yet to be tested. Can one really assume that pottery styles reflect social behavior? The answer must await the day when many more standardized typologies from different areas of the world are available.

Technological analyses. The manufacturing process used by prehistoric potters is the subject of technological analysis. Anna Shepard of the Smithsonian Institution was a pioneer in this work and spent a lifetime analyzing the constituents of pottery clays and firing techniques (Shepard, 1971). Trace-element analyses of mineral elements in clays have provided invaluable evidence for local trading of finished vessels across Lake Malawi in Central Africa (Asaro and Perlman, 1967). Technological analyses of pottery are in their infancy but they nevertheless provide an important means of amplifying manufacturing data obtained from archaeological analyses and ethnographic analogy (Bishop and others, 1982).

METALS AND METALLURGY

The study of metallurgy and metals found in archaeological sites is limited both by the state of preservation and by our knowledge of prehistoric metallurgy as a whole (Tylecote, 1972; Wertime and Muhly, 1980). Preservation of metal tools in archaeological horizons depends entirely on the soil's acidity. In some circumstances, iron tools are preserved perfectly and can be studied in great detail; in other cases, soil acids have reduced the iron to a rusty mass that is almost entirely useless. Copper and gold normally survive somewhat better.

Metals first became familiar to people in the form of rocks in their environment. Properties of metal-bearing rocks—color, luster, and weight—made them attractive for use in the natural state. Eventually, people realized that heat made some stone like flint and chert easier to work. When this knowledge was applied to metallic rocks, stoneworkers discovered that native copper and other rocks could be formed into tools by a sequence of hammering and heating (Wheeler and Maddin, 1980). Of the seventy or so metallic elements on earth, only eight, iron, copper, arsenic, tin, silver, gold, lead, and mercury, were worked before the eighteenth century A.D. Properties of these metals that were important to ancient metalworkers were, among others, color, luster, reflecting abilities (for mirrors), acoustic quality, ease of casting and welding, and degrees of hardness, strength, and malleability. Metal that was easily recyclable had obvious advantages. Almost every prehistoric metal was prized initially for its decorative qualities.

We know much about ancient metallurgy because prehistoric artifacts preserve traces of their thermal and mechanical history in their metallic microstructure. This structure can be studied under an optical microscope. Each grain of the metal is a crystal that forms as the metal solidifies. The shape and size of the grains can reveal whether alloys were used and indicate the cooling conditions and the type of mold used. At first, prehistoric metallurgists used "pure" metals, which could be easily worked, but produced only soft tools. Then they discovered how to alloy each of these metals with a second one to produce stronger, harder objects with lower melting points. The basic data for studying prehistoric alloys comes from *phase diagrams*, which relate temperature and alloy composition, showing how soluble metals are in one another. Phase diagrams were developed under controlled conditions in a laboratory, and tend to reflect ideal conditions. By examining the object under an optical microscope, one can often spot differences in chemical composition, such as the cored, treelike structure that is characteristic of cast copper-tin alloys. Metals contain insoluble particles that can give clues to the smelting procedures and types of ores used. An energy-dispersive x-ray spectrometer and a scanning electron microscope are used to identify the particles. This impressive battery of analytical techniques has enabled archaeologists to study how 6,000 years of experimentation took humanity from simple manipulation of rocks to production of steel in about 1000 B.C. The record of these millenia is read in the lenses of the microscope, which reveals the triumphs and frustrations of the ancient smith. (Tylecote, 1980, is an excellent review of our knowledge of prehistoric smelting techniques).

Copper.   The earliest metal tools were made by cold-hammering copper into simple artifacts. Such objects were fairly common in Near Eastern villages by 6000 B.C. Eventually, some people began to melt the copper. They may have achieved sufficiently high temperatures with established methods used to fire pottery in clay kilns. The copper was usually melted or smelted into shapes and ingots within the furnace hearth itself. Copper metallurgy was widespread about 4000 B.C. (Mallowan, 1965), although European smiths were working copper in the Balkans as early as 3500 B.C. (Cernych, 1978; Coles and Harding, 1979; Tringham, 1971). In contrast to high-quality stone and iron, copper ores are rare, and concentrated in well-defined regions. The metal was normally, but not invariably, alloyed with tin, which is even rarer. In the New World, copperworking was well developed among the Aztecs and the Inca. The Hopewell Indians of Lake Superior exploited the native deposits of copper ore on the southern shores of the lake, and the metal was widely traded and cold-hammered into artifacts from Archaic to Woodland times (Figure 13.14).

Bronze.   But the real explosion—it was nothing less—in copper metallurgy took place midway through the fourth millennium B.C., when the smiths of both the Near East and southeast Asia discov-

Figure 13.14   Hopewell hammered copper ornaments, found in 1920 in Ross County, Ohio: a bird and a cut-out breast plate.

ered that they could improve the properties of copper by alloying it with a second metal such as arsenic, lead, or tin (Coles and Harding, 1979; Bayard, 1972). Perhaps the first alloys came about when smiths tried to produce different colors and textures in ornaments. But they soon realized the advantages of tin, zinc, and other alloys that led to stronger, harder, and more easily worked artifacts. There is reason to believe that they experimented with the proportions of tin for some time, but most early bronzes contain about 5 to 10 percent (10 percent is the optimum for hardness). An extraordinary development of metallurgical technology occurred during the third millennium B.C., perhaps in part resulting from the evolution of writing (Muhly, 1980). By 2500 B.C., practically every type of metallurgical phenomenon except hardening of steel was known and used regularly. The use of tin alloying may have stimulated much trading activity, for the metal is relatively rare, especially in the Near East.

Chinese workers in bronze, laboring for the rulers of Shang urban centers in the Huangho Valley, were responsible for some of the most sophisticated bronze vessels of prehistoric times. Clay molds were used to cast elaborate legged cauldrons and smaller vessels with distinctive shapes and decoration. Casting was used to produce not only weapons but also elaborate works of art that were valued by early Chinese antiquarians as well as modern collectors (Chang, 1977).

Gold.   Gold-decked burials fascinate many people, but in fact they are rare finds in archaeological excavations. Gold did, however, have a vital part in prestige and ornament in many prehistoric societies. It is not without reason that Tutankhamun is sometimes

Figure 13.15 Gold beaker with repoussé decoration and turquoise inlay, attributed to Chimú goldsmiths of Peru. (About two-thirds actual size.)

described as the "Golden Pharaoh": his grave was rich in spectacular gold finds. The Chimú peoples of coastal Peru were master goldsmiths of pre-Columbian Latin America (Figure 13.15). The Aztec and Inca also were talented goldsmiths, whose magnificent products were shipped off to Europe and melted down for royal treasuries. The famous artist Albrecht Dürer saw a storeroom full of Aztec gold in Brussels in 1520, in which was included, as he described it: "A Sun all in gold, as much as six feet in diameter . . . there were two chambers full of armor used by these people, and all kinds of weapons, cuirasses, wonderful shields . . ." (Fagan, 1984a).

Gold is a metal that rarely forms compounds in its natural state. It was collected in this form, or in grains gathered by crushing quartz and concentrating the fine gold by washing. The melting point of gold is about the same as that of copper, and so no elaborate technology was needed. Gold is easily hammered into thin sheets without annealing. Prehistoric smiths frequently used such sheets to sheath wooden objects such as statuettes. They also cast it and used appliqué techniques, as well as alloying it with silver and other ores. Gold was worked in the Near East almost as early as copper, and it was soon associated with royal prestige. The metal was widely traded in dust, ornament, and bead form in many parts of the New and Old World (Phillips, 1980; Fagan, 1984a).

Iron.   Bronze Age smiths certainly knew about iron. It was a curiosity, of little apparent use. They knew where to find the ore and how to fashion iron objects by hammering and heating. But the crucial process in iron production is carburization, in which iron is converted into steel. The result is a much harder object, far tougher than bronze tools. To carburize an iron object, it is heated in close contact with charcoal for a considerable period of time. The solubility of carbon in iron is very small at room temperature, but increases dramatically at temperatures above 910 degrees Celsius, which could easily be achieved with charcoal and good Bronze Age bellows. It was this technological development that led to the widespread adoption of iron technologies in the eastern Mediterranean area at least by 1000 B.C.

Iron tools are found occasionally in some sites as early as 3000 B.C., but widespread smelting does not seem to have begun until the second millennium B.C. Use of iron was sporadic at first, for objects made of the metal were still curiosities. Iron tools were not common until around 1200 B.C., when the first weapons made of it appear in eastern Mediterranean tombs (Waldbaum, 1980). The new metal was slow to catch on, partly because of the difficulty of smelting it. Its widespread adoption may coincide with a period of disruption in eastern Mediterranean trade routes as a result of the collapse of several major kingdoms, among them that of the Hittites, after 1200 B.C. Deprived of tin, the smiths turned to a much more readily available substitute—iron. It was soon in use even for utilitarian tools and was first established on a large scale in continental Europe in the seventh century B.C. by the Hallstatt peoples. In earlier times iron had a comparatively limited economic role, most artifacts being slavish copies of bronze tools before the metal's full potentials were realized. Weapons like swords and spears were the first artifacts to be modified to make use of the new material. Specialized ironworking tools, such as tongs, as well as woodworking artifacts, began to be used as soon as the qualities of iron were recognized.

Iron ore is much more abundant in the natural state than copper ore. It is readily obtainable from surface outcrops and bog deposits. Once its potential had been realized it became much more widespread in use, and stone and bronze were relegated to subsidiary, often ornamental uses.

The influence of iron was immense, for it made available abundant supplies of tough cutting edges for agriculture. With iron tools, clearing forests became easier, and people achieved even greater mastery over their environment. Ironworking profoundly influenced the development of literate civilizations. Some people, such as the Australian aborigines and the pre-Columbian Americans, did not develop iron metallurgy until they came into contact with European explorers.

Metal Technologies.   Copper technology began with the cold-hammering of the ore into simple artifacts. Copper smelting may have originated in accidental melting of some copper ore in a domestic hearth or oven. In smelting, the ore is melted at a high temperature in a small kiln and the molten metal is allowed to trickle down through the charcoal fuel into a vessel at the base of the furnace. The copper is further reduced at a high temperature and then cooled slowly and hammered into shape. This *annealing* (heating, cooling, and hammering) adds strength to the metal. Molten copper was poured into molds and cast into widely varied shapes.

Copper ores were obtained from weathered surface outcrops, but the best material came from subsurface ores, which were mined by expert diggers. Copper mines were in many parts of the Old World and provide a fruitful field for the student of metallurgy to investigate. The most elaborate European workings were in the Tyrol and Salzburg areas, where many oval workings were entered by a shaft from above (Clark, 1952). At Mitterburg, Austria, the miners drove shafts into the hillside with bronze picks and extracted the copper by elaborate fire-setting techniques. Many early copper workings have been found in southern Africa, where the miners followed surface lodes under the ground (Figure 13.16) (Bisson, 1977; Summers, 1969). Fortunately, the traditional Central African processes of copper smelting have been recorded. The ore was

Figure 13.16   Excavation in a prehistoric copper mine at Kansanshi, Zambia. The miners followed outcrops of copper ore deep into the ground with narrow shafts, the earth fillings of which yield both radiocarbon samples and artifacts abandoned by the miners.

placed in a small furnace with alternating layers of charcoal and smelted for several hours at high heat maintained with goatskin bellows (Figure 13.17). After each firing, the furnace was destroyed and the molten copper dripped onto the top of a sand-filled pot buried under the fire (Chaplin, 1961).

Figure 13.17   An African ironworker using a goatskin bellows. Similar bellows were used for copper smelting.

Bronze technology depended on alloying, the mingling of small quantities of such substances as arsenic and tin with copper. With its lower melting point, bronze soon superseded copper for much metalwork. Some of the most sophisticated bronzeworking was created by Chinese smiths, who cast elaborate vessels in clay molds using the so-called lost-wax method. In this method the mold was assembled with wax in the place of metal, then the wax was replaced with molten bronze, and a cast vessel would emerge from the mold (Figure 13.18).

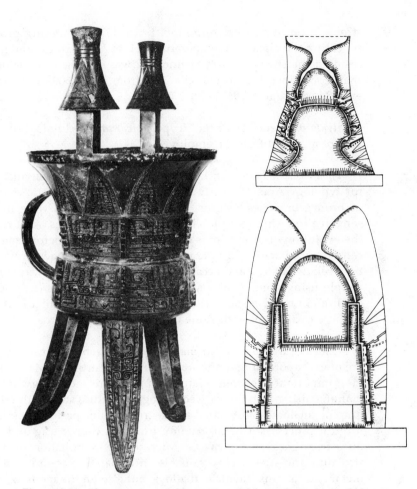

Figure 13.18   Shang ceremonial bronze vessel from about the twelfth century
B.C., and diagrams of clay molds for casting such vessels.

Ironworking is a much more elaborate technology that requires
a melting temperature of at least 1,537 degrees centigrade. Prehistoric smiths normally used an elaborate furnace filled with alternate layers of charcoal and iron ore that was maintained at a high
temperature for many hours with bellows. A single firing often
yielded only a spongy lump of iron, called a bloom, which then had
to be forged and hammered into artifacts. It took some time for the
metallurgists to learn that they could strengthen working edges by
quenching the tool in cold water. This process gave greater

strength, but it also made the tool brittle. The tempering process, reheating the blade to a temperature below 727 degrees centigrade, restored the strength. Iron technology was so slow in developing that it remained basically unchanged from about 600 B.C. to Medieval times (Piggott, 1965).

Analysis of Metal Artifacts.   Typological and technological analyses of metal artifacts are employed.

Typological analyses.   In Europe, metal tools have been analyzed for typology since the early nineteenth century. Stylistic changes in bronze brooches, swords, axes, and iron artifacts were highly sensitive to fashion and to changing trading patterns. As a result, the evolution of bronze pins or iron slashing swords, for example, can be traced across Europe, with small design changes providing both relative dating and occasional insights into the lifeways of the people using them. (Coles and Harding, 1979, summarize the literature.) In many respects these types of study are similar in intent to those carried out with stone implements or potsherds.

Technological analyses.   In many respects, technological analyses are more important than the study of finished artifacts. Many of the most important questions relating to prehistoric metallurgy involve manufacturing techniques. Technological studies start with ethnographic analogies and actual reconstructions of prehistoric metallurgical processes. Chemists study iron and copper slag and residues from excavated furnaces. Microscopic examination of metal structure and ores yields valuable information not only on the metal and its constituents and alloys, but also on the methods used to produce the finished tool. The ultimate objective of the technological analyses is to reconstruct the entire process of metal tool production, from the mining of the ore to the production of the finished artifact.

BONE

Bone as a material for toolmaking probably dates to the very beginnings of human history, but the earliest artifacts apparently consisted of little more than fragments of fractured animal bone used for purposes that could not be fulfilled by wood or stone implements. South African anatomist Raymond Dart has alleged that *Australopithecus* had a fully fledged bone culture and systematically fractured such bones as jaws and limb bones to form clubs, scrapers, and other artifacts. Dart's "osteodontokeratic"—bone, teeth, horn— culture has been the subject of much controversy, and most scholars reject his hypothesis on the grounds that other, natural factors could have caused such systematic bone fractures (Brain, 1981; Dart, 1957). Formal bone tools are rare on the Olduvai living floors, but several bone fragments show systematic utilization, as though they were used for scraping skins and similar purposes (M. D. Leakey, 1973).

The earliest standardized bone tools date from later prehistoric times. Splinters of bone were sharpened and used as points in many societies, but bone and antler artifacts were especially favored by the Upper Paleolithic peoples of southwestern France from 30,000 to 12,000 years ago and by postglacial hunter-gatherers in Scandinavia (Bordes, 1968). Bone artifacts as old as 40,000 B.P. may have been located at Old Crow Flats, Alaska (Morlan, 1978). In later times, splinters from long bones were ground and scraped, as well as hardened in the fire and polished with beeswax, to produce arrowheads, spearpoints, needles, and other artifacts. Bone was also carved and engraved, especially during Upper Paleolithic times in western Europe, as was reindeer antler (Grasiozi, 1960).

Deer antler was an even more important material than bone for some later hunter-gatherers. Fully grown deer antler is particularly suitable for making barbed or simple harpoons and spearpoints. Bone and antler were much used in prehistoric times for harpoons for fishing and for conventional hunting. Numerous harpoons are found in Magdalenian sites in western Europe (Figure 13.19) and also in Eskimo settlements in the Arctic, where they form an invaluable index of cultural development, analogous to that of pottery in the American Southwest.

Bone-Tool Analysis. In the Arctic, where bone and ivory are critical materials, elaborate typological studies have been made of the stylistic and functional changes in such diverse items as the harpoons, the winged ivory objects fastened to the butts of harpoons, and other objects (Figure 13.20). Other artifacts include picks made of walrus tusk and snow shovels and wedges of ivory and bone— as well as drills and domestic utensils. Studying such a range of bone artifacts is complicated by the elaborate and variable engraved designs applied to some, but H. B. Collins and others have been

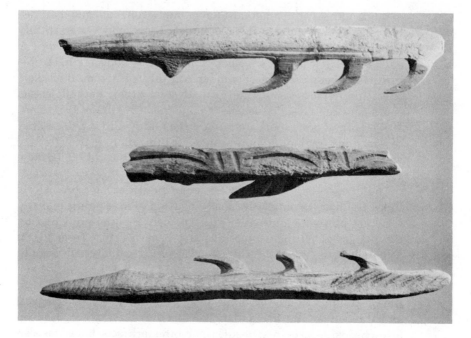

Figure 13.19   Magdalenian harpoons from France, *ca.* 14,000 years B.P. (About two-thirds actual size.)

able to trace the development of the harpoon of the Northern Maritime Eskimo, from the elaborate types of the Okvik and Old Bering Sea phases to the simpler forms characteristic of the Punuk phase and the modern Eskimo weapons (Collins, 1937; Dumond, 1977).

Functional analysis.   In some areas like the Arctic and Southern Africa, contemporary ethnographic accounts can be used for fruitful analogies with prehistoric tools. There are, however, dangers to this approach. Although no one can seriously doubt the functional classification of the Old Bering Sea harpoon socket in Figure 13.20, a classification based firmly in analogies, the situation is more complex for the remote past. The Magdalenian peoples who lived in Southwest France 15,000 years ago made extensive use of bone and antler to produce a wide range of artifacts, ranging from spearthrowers to harpoons and thong straighteners.

Figure 13.20   Bone and ivory artifacts. Left: Harpoon socket piece, Old Bering
Sea style. (9.5 centimeters long.) Right: Turreted ivory object of the Punuk
phase. (7 centimeters wide.) From the University of Alaska Museum. Used by
permission.

Technological analysis.   The way in which the tool was made is the
subject of technological analysis. The simplest bone technologies
involved splitting and flaking bones. Fine points were produced by
polishing slivers of bone against grinding surfaces. The Magdalenians used fine lengths of reindeer antler, which they removed from
the beam by grooving through the hard outer core of the antler
with stone burins or engraving tools. It is no coincidence that their
material culture includes a wide range of scraping and graving
tools (Clark, 1954).

As with all technological analyses, ethnographic analogy and
experimentation with prehistoric boneworking methods under
controlled modern conditions provide the best insights into early
tool making (Coles, 1973).

WOOD

Nonhuman primates sometimes use sticks to obtain grubs, or for other purposes, and so it is logical to assume that since the earliest times humans may have used sticks also. Wood implements form a major part of many modern hunter-gatherer toolkits; occasional tantalizing glimpses of prehistoric wood artifacts have come down to us where preservation conditions have been favorable. One of the earliest is a fire-hardened spearpoint found in the Clacton Channel, England, which dates to the Holstein interglacial (ca. ?150,000 B.P.) (Clark, 1970). Numerous wood artifacts, as well as basketry, have come from dry sites in western North America (Jennings, 1978).

The Ozette prehistoric village on the Olympia Peninsula in Washington was buried by a prehistoric landslide that covered up not only several wood long houses, but many domestic artifacts, baskets, boxes, and other fine wooden tools as well. The waterlogged preservation conditions preserved fibers and delicate halibut fish hooks complete with their bindings. Richard Daugherty's most important wooden find was a ritual whale fin carved in cedar wood, decorated with 700 sea otter teeth (Figure 13.21). One of Captain Cook's artists drew a similar artifact during his voyage of exploration to the Northwest coast in 1778, but no modern examples survive (Kirk, 1974).

Wood Technology and Analysis.   The manufacture of wood tools involves such well-understood mechanical processes as cutting, whittling, scraping, planing, carving, and polishing. Fire was often used to harden sharpened spearpoints, and oil and paint imparted a fine sheen and appearance to all kinds of wood artifacts. On the rare occasions when wood artifacts are preserved, important clues to their manufacture can be obtained by closely examining the object itself. Unfinished tools are very useful, especially handles and weapons that have been blocked out but not finished (Coles, Heal, and Orme, 1978). Even more revealing are wood fragments from abandoned buildings, fortifications, and even track walkways that survive in post holes and other such locations. Microscopic analysis of wood fragments and charcoals can provide information on the woods used to build houses, canoes, and other such objects. On very rare occasions, stone projectile heads and axes have been recovered in both waterlogged and dry conditions where their wood handles and shafts have survived, together with the thongs

Figure 13.21 A whale fin carved from cedar wood and inlaid with more than 700 sea otter teeth, found at Ozette, Washington. The teeth at the base are set in the design of a mythical bird with a whale in its talons.

used to bind stone to wood. The Ozette excavations yielded complete house planks, and even some wood boxes that had been assembled by skillful grooving and bending of planks (Kirk, 1974).

In many instances, the only clues to the use of wood come from stone artifacts, such as spokeshaves and scrapers used to work it, or from stone axe blades and other tools that were once mounted in wood handles (Figure 13.22). Only the form of the artifact and occasional ethnographic analogies allow one to reconstruct the nature of the perishable mount that once made the artifact an effective tool.

One often forgets just how important wood was to prehistoric societies. The thousands upon thousands of ground stone axes in the archaeological record all once had wood handles. Wood was used for house building, fortifications, fuel, canoes, and containers.

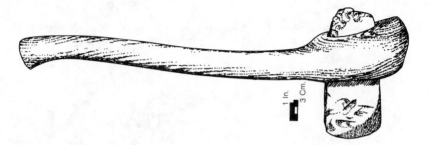

Figure 13.22   Artifacts as evidence for subsistence: a reconstructed Neolithic stone axe with a handle of ash wood. The handle is a copy of an example found in a Danish bog; only the stone is original, which illustrates how little of an artifact survives under normal conditions. (Approximate length, 30 inches.)

Most skilled woodworking societies used the simplest technology to produce both utilitarian and ceremonial objects. They used fire and the ringing of bark to fell trees, stone wedges to split logs, and shells and stones to scrape spear shafts (Drucker, 1968). Wood was probably the most important raw material available to our ancestors. It is a tragedy that it rarely survives in the archaeological record. But, as John Coles points out (Coles, Heal, and Orme, 1978), wooden artifacts do occur, with greater frequency than has been believed, and very often locating them is simply a matter of investigating the localities where they are likely to occur.

BASKETRY AND TEXTILES

We do not have the space to discuss basketry in detail, but production of baskets is estimated to be one of the oldest crafts (Adovasio and Gunn, 1977). Basketry includes such items as containers, matting, bags, and a wide range of fiber objects. Textiles are found in many later, dry sites, and they are especially evident among prehistoric Peruvian artifacts (King, 1978).

Some scholars believe that basketry and textiles are among the most sensitive artifacts for the archaeologist to work with, culturally speaking, on the grounds that people lived in much more intimate association with baskets and textiles than with clay vessels, stone tools, or houses. Furthermore, even small fragments of basketry and textiles display remarkable idiosyncrasies of individual manufacture. Much research has concentrated on methods of manufacture and on raw materials, and it is only in recent years that people have realized their great value as time markers and as potential sources of information on social organization, subsistence activities, and technology.

In a remarkable experiment, Dale Croes and Jonathan Davis (1977) used a computer mapping program to study the baskets made by several families occupying a large house at the waterlogged Ozette site in Washington. They compiled a computer plot of the distribution of basket types, and found that basketry activities were concentrated near the walls of the house. Using the computer, they then plotted and compared different attributes throughout the structure. The clusters that resulted from these analyses were used to show that basketry styles differed from family to family within the group who lived in the house. This is highly experimental research, but it does show the great potential for computer-aided studies of basketry and other artifacts. When preserved, baskets are amenable to the same kind of functional and stylistic analyses as other artifacts.

It is easy for archaeologists to become preoccupied with technology and artifacts, but as the Ozette experiment and other recent studies have emphasized, the potential is great for insights into prehistoric society and subsistence from such research, provided that the ultimate objective is to study people rather than inanimate objects.

Guide to Further Reading

Binford, Lewis R. *Bones*. New York: Academic Press, 1981.
A provocative and far-ranging discussion of faunal analysis and bone technology in prehistoric times that draws on ethnographic analogy.

Bordaz, J. *Tools of the Old and New Stone Age*. Garden City, N. Y.: Doubleday Natural History Press, 1970.
A simple manual on stone technology for the beginner.

Clark, J. G. D. *Prehistoric Europe: The Economic Basis*. Palo Alto: Stanford University Press, 1952.
A classic essay on European prehistory that covers the relationship between technology and economic life.

Hill, James, and Joel Gunn. *The Individual in Prehistory.* New York: Academic Press, 1977.
Essays on ways in which one might identify the work of one human being in the archaeological record. Especially strong on pottery and basketry. For the more advanced reader.

Matson, F. R. *Ceramics and Man.* New York: Viking Fund, 1965.
A set of conference papers dealing with ceramics. Somewhat dated, but a thought-provoking beginning for further reading.

Shepard, Anna O. *Ceramics for the Archaeologist.* Washington, D. C.: Smithsonian Institution, 1971.
The definitive work on ceramics in the New World. Highly technical and informative.

Tylecote, R. F. *Metallurgy in Antiquity.* London: Edward Arnold, 1962.
An introduction to prehistoric metallurgy that is widely respected as a source book.

PART VI ✒

RECONSTRUCTING PAST LIFEWAYS

And I prophesied as I was commanded; and as I prophesied, there was a noise, and behold, a rattling; and the bones came together, bone to its bone. And as I looked, there were sinews on them, and flesh had come upon them, and skin had covered them. . . .

EZEKIEL 37:10

A major objective of archaeology is to study the ways in which people have solved the problems of making a living and adapting to their environment. In Part VI we look more closely at this objective, at research into prehistoric subsistence, settlement archaeology, and the study of religious beliefs and social organization in prehistoric societies. Chapter 14 describes the analysis of food remains, animal bones, vegetable foods, and evidence for prehistoric diet. Archaeologists rely very heavily on ethnographic analogies for interpreting prehistoric subsistence and past lifeways. In Chapter 15, we examine some of the latest work in experimental archaeology and ethnoarchaeology, approaches that involve both controlled experiments and observations in the field. Human settlements changed radically through prehistory. In Chapter 16 we examine the ways in which archaeologists study ancient settlement patterns, with special reference to recent research in Mesoamerica. We give special attention to methods for reconstructing ancient environments. Trade, social organization, and religious beliefs are the special matters of Chapter 17, which makes the point that much information on these subjects can be obtained with careful research design and meticulous analysis of field data. The study of prehistoric lifeways is an essential preliminary to interpretation of cultural process, discussed in Part VII.

CHAPTER 14 🌿

SUBSISTENCE
AND DIET

Preview

- Archaeologists rely on many sources to reconstruct prehistoric subsistence methods. These include environmental data, animal bones, vegetable remains, human feces, artifacts, and prehistoric art.
- Zooarchaeology involves the study of animal bones. We describe the sorting of teeth, horns, and some limb bones. Bone identification is carried out by direct comparison between modern and ancient bones.
- Game animal remains can give insights into prehistoric hunting practices. The proportions of animals present can be affected by cultural taboos, the relative meat yields of different species, and hunting preferences. Overhunting and extinction can also affect the numbers of animals in a site.
- Early domesticated animals are very difficult to identify from their wild ancestors. Domestication alters both the characteristics of an animal and its bone structure.
- Slaughtering and butchery practices can be derived from the frequency and distribution of animal bones in the ground. Teeth can be used to establish the age of animals slaughtered, but hunting and slaughter patterns are subject to all manner of subtle variables, including convenience, season of the year, and so on.

Understanding the cultural systems of which the food remains are a part is essential for interpreting slaughter and butchery patterns.

· Carbonized and unburned vegetable remains are recovered from hearths and pits, often using a flotation method with water to separate seeds from the matrix around them. Dry sites, such as the rockshelters and camps in the Tehuacán Valley, Mexico, provide abundant evidence for early crop domestication; grain impressions on European pots are studied to reconstruct prehistoric agriculture in the Old World. Danish archaeologists have used pollen analysis to study forest clearance in temperate zones during early farming times.

· Bird bones have been much neglected, but they provide invaluable information on seasonal occupation; fish remains reflect specialized coastal adaptations that became common in later prehistoric times. Hooks, nets, and other artifacts, as well as fish remains themselves, provide insights into both coastal and offshore fishing practices.

· Fresh- and saltwater molluscs were both consumed as food and traded over enormous distances as prestigious luxuries or ornaments. We cite the African *Conus* shell, which was an important trade commodity in southern Africa.

· Prehistoric diet and nutrition must be studied together, for they are distinct from subsistence, which is the actual process of obtaining food. It is difficult to estimate the caloric needs of modern peoples, let alone those of prehistoric groups. Despite such recovery methods as flotation, archaeological data can indicate only some of the foods eaten by prehistoric communities and show their importance in general. But this is far from ascribing their true caloric importance to prehistoric peoples.

· Human skeletal remains, stomach contents, and feces, are the few direct sources available to us of information on prehistoric diet. The information they yield is limited, at best.

Archaeologists and anthropologists have long been fascinated by the ways in which people have obtained food and essential raw materials. As early as the mid-nineteenth century, Danish scientists were identifying seashells and animals bones from coastal shell middens to see what their inhabitants lived on (Lubbock, 1865). The study of prehistoric subsistence—subsistence being the means of supporting life with food supplies—has developed in sophisticated ways since the 1860s.

Greater understanding of ecology and its implications for archaeology has led people to view humans and their culture as merely one element in a complex ecosystem. The study of prehistoric subsistence, then, has developed hand-in-hand with attempts to understand the complex interrelationships between the way people make their living and their environment.

EVIDENCE FOR SUBSISTENCE

Archaeologists rely on many sources of data to reconstruct prehistoric subsistence. These include the following (Gabel, 1967):

1. *Environmental data.* Background data on the natural environment are a prerequisite for studying subsistence. Such data can include information such as animal distributions, ancient and modern flora, and soils, a range of potential resources to be exploited.

2. *Faunal remains.* Animal bones are a major source of information on hunting practices and domestic animals. The identification and interpretation of such finds depends on detailed knowledge of mammalian anatomy, as well as on ethnographic data relating to butchery practices.

3. *Vegetable remains.* These can include both wild and domestic species, obtained by flotation methods or from carbonized contexts. Such materials are less frequently preserved in the archaeological record than animal bones. Sometimes pollen analysis will throw light on prehistoric agriculture and collecting habits.

4. *Human feces.* These yield both tiny fragments of ecofacts and pollen grains and are preserved in dry caves. They are vital evidence for reconstructing prehistoric diet (Bryant, 1974).

5. *Artifacts.* The picture of human subsistence yelded by artifacts is necessarily limited. Flint axes, pressure-flaked arrowheads, iron hoes, or digging-stick weights may indicate the outlines of the picture, but they hardly clothe it with substance and intricate detail. Many critical artifacts used in the chase or for gardening were made from perishable materials, such as basketry, wood, or fiber.

6. *Prehistoric art.* Artists sometimes depicted scenes of the chase and fishing, as well as food-gathering.

ANIMAL BONES (ZOOARCHAEOLOGY)

Zooarchaeology is the study of animal remains found in the archaeological record. Although some zoologists have specialized in the study of animal bones from archaeological sites, most zooarchaeologists receive training in archaeology and engage in the study of prehistoric faunas as a specialty (Chaplin, 1971; Cornwall, 1956; Binford, 1981).

Taphonomy. The word *taphonomy* (Greek: *taphnos*, tomb; *nomos*, law) is used to describe the processes that operate on organic remains after the organism dies, to form fossil deposits. Simply put, it is the study of the transition in animal remains from the biosphere to the lithosphere. Taphonomy involves two related avenues of investigation. The first is actual observation of recently dead organic remains as they are transformed gradually into fossils, the other the study of fossil remains in the light of this evidence (Gifford, 1981). This new field of investigation came into fashion during the 1960s and 1970s, when archaeologists became interested in the meaning of animal bone scatters at such early sites as Olduvai Gorge and Ismailia in East Africa, and especially in the celebrated *Australopithecus* caves of South Africa.

In the 1950s, South African anatomist Raymond Dart (1957) had studied the fragmentary bones from the South African caves and argued that the bone fragments had been fractured systematically by *Australopithecus*, an early hominid. *Australopithecus*, he argued, had not used stone, but had relied on an "osteodontokeratic" culture of bone and horn to satisfy daily needs. Dart's research was based on little more than study of the bones alone, and on the assumption that the caves were typical inhabitable caverns rather than refuges. Then biologist C. K. Brain questioned Dart's assumptions with long-term observations of bone fractures made by nonhuman primates. He showed that the uninhabitable caves were filled with the remains of hyena kills, and that the bone fractures were not the result of human toolmaking. Brain also pointed out that different skeletal parts had different preservation qualities, that some more-delicate bones might vanish sooner than, say, robust limb bones. Therefore the "archaeological animals," say the fragmentary remains of oxen you find in a site, may well not coincide with the actual animal population that was slaughtered at the original settlement. Bridging this gap, between the living beast and the fossilized animal, is the primary aim of taphonomy.

Many questions about the processes that transform living organisms into "archaeological" bones remain unanswered, despite some research into such topics as ways in which bones can be transported and disarticulated by both carnivores and natural agents such as water. Humans disarticulate animals with tools long before the carcasses are dispersed by natural phenomena or by carnivores, and so their systematic activities are at least a baseline for examining patterns of damage on archaeological bones. Some controlled experiments with open-air weathering of bone in both New World and Old suggest that smaller bones, and those with a high ratio of surface area to volume, break down faster, but data to support these impressions are scarce. Even roots and burrowing animals can transform buried bones. Interpretation of prehistoric living floors and kill sites has to be undertaken with great care, for the apparent patterns of bones and artifacts on such a prehistoric land surface represent not only human activity but complex and little-understood taphonomic processes as well. (Gifford, 1981 has an excellent summary of taphonomy.)

Sorting and Identification.   Broken food bones are probably the most tangible remains of human subsistence patterns to survive from the past. Bone is one of the more durable raw materials and survives in various environments, either fossilized or in fresh form. Most people think skeletal remains occur in a more or less complete state, but rarely does an animal obligingly lie down and die in an archaeological site. Indeed, about the only mammals to do so are small rodents who have died in their burrows or such domestic animals as dogs that normally were not eaten.

Faunal remains are usually fragmentary, coming from dismembered carcasses butchered either at the archaeological site or at the hunting grounds. To some degree, how much of the carcass is carried back to camp depends on the animal's size. Small deer may be taken back whole, slung from the shoulder. Hunter-gatherers sometimes camped at the site of the kill of a large animal, where they both ate and dried parts of the carcass for later use. Almost invariably, however, the bones found in occupation sites have been cut to splinters. Every piece of usable meat was stripped from the bones; sinews were made into thongs, and the skin into clothing, containers, or sometimes, housing. Even the entrails were eaten. Limb bones were split for their delicious marrow; some bones were made into such tools as harpoon heads, arrow tips, or mattocks (Figure 14.1).

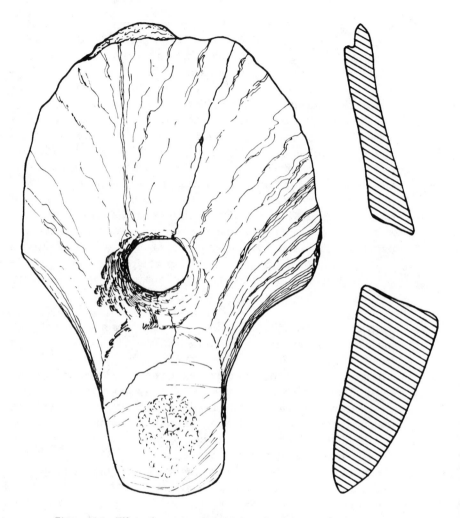

Figure 14.1   Elk antler mattock from Star Carr, England.

It would be a mistake to assume that the fragmentary bones found in an archaeological deposit will give you either an accurate count of the number of animals killed by the inhabitants, or accurate insights into the environment at the time of occupation (Grayson, 1979, 1981). The fragmentary bones found in an archaeological deposit have been subjected to many diverse processes since their deposition. Taphonomic processes often result in major changes in buried bone, perhaps even destroying the bones of smaller animals though not of larger ones. Then there are human factors: people may carry in some game from far away, yet kill all their goats at the village. We have no means of knowing what spiritual role some animals possessed in ancient societies, or of studying taboos and other prohibitions that may have caused certain animals to be hunted, others to be ignored. Furthermore, we have no means of knowing precisely what the abundances of different animal species were in the prehistoric environment. Certainly one cannot use animal bones from archaeological sites for this purpose. The difference between what one might call the "actual animal" and the "archaeological animal" identified by the archaeologist is always unknown (Binford, 1978, 1981b; Grayson, 1981). The archaeological animal consists of a scatter of broken bones that have been shattered by a butcher, then subjected to hundreds if not thousands of years of gradual deterioration in the soil. The most one can normally do is to record the presence of a species in an archaeological deposit, or data on seasonal occupation of a settlement.

Most bone identification is done by direct comparison. It is fairly simple, easily learned by anyone with sharp eyes (Cornwall, 1956). But only a small proportion of the bones in a collection are sufficiently characteristic for this purpose. As an example, only 2,128 fragments of a collection of 195,415 from a Stone Age campsite in Zambia could be identified as to species; another 9,207 could be assigned to a body part; the remainder of the collection had been smashed into small pieces by hunters in search of marrow, sinew, or meat (Fagan and Van Noten, 1971).

The drawing of a dog in Figure 14.2 illustrates a typical mammalian skeleton. Small skull fragments, vertebrae, ribs, scapulae, and pelvic bones are normally of little use in identifying a domestic as opposed to a wild animal, or to differentiate one species of antelope from another. Upper and lower jaws and their dentition, individual teeth, the bony cores of horns, and sometimes the articular surfaces of long bones are susceptible to identification (Olsen, 1978). Teeth are identified by comparing the cusp patterns on their surfaces with those on comparative collections carefully taken from the site area (Figure 14.3). In some parts of the world, the articular ends of long bones can be used as well, especially in such regions as the Near East or parts of North America, where the indigenous mammalian fauna is somewhat restricted (Hole, Flannery, Kent, and Neely, 1969). It is even possible to distinguish the fragmentary long bones of domestic stock from those of wild animals of the

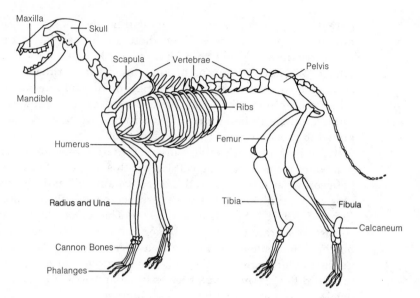

Figure 14.2   Skeleton of a dog, showing the most important body parts, from the osteological viewpoint.

same size in the Near East, provided that the collections are large enough, and the comparative material sufficiently complete and representative of all ages of individuals and of variations in size from male to female. But in other areas, such as sub-Saharan Africa, the indigenous fauna is so rich and varied, with such small variations in skeletal geography, that only horn cores or teeth can help distinguish between species of antelope and separate domestic stock from game animals. Even the dentition is confusing, for the cusp patterns of buffalo and domestic cattle are remarkably similar, often distinguishable only by the smaller size of the latter.

The identification stage of a bone analysis is the most important for several fundamental questions need answering: Are domestic and wild species present? If so, what are the proportions of each group? What types of domestic stock were kept by the inhabitants? Did they have any hunting preferences that are reflected in the proportions of game animals found in the occupation levels? Are any wild species characteristic of vegetational associations no longer found in the area today?

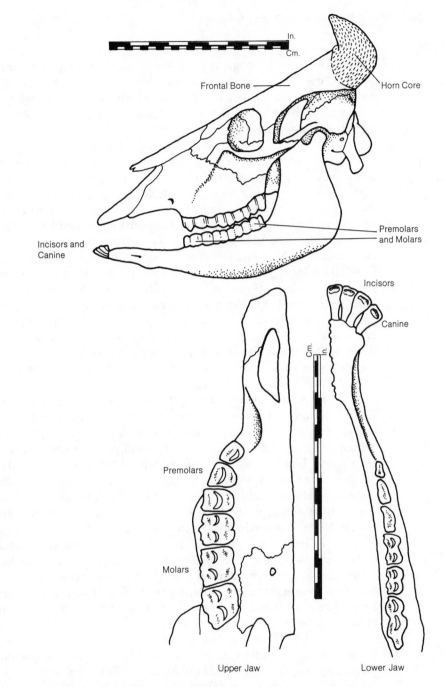

Frontal Bone

Horn Core

Premolars
and Molars

Incisors and
Canine

Incisors

Canine

Premolars

Molars

Upper Jaw

Lower Jaw

Figure 14.3 The skull and mandible of a domestic ox, showing important osteological features. (One-fourth actual size.)

Game Animals. Though the listing of game animals and their habits gives an insight into hunting practices, in many cases, the content of the faunal list gains particular significance when we seek to explain why the hunters concentrated on certain species and apparently ignored others.

Taboos. Dominance by one game species can result from economic necessity or convenience or it can simply be a matter of cultural preference. Many societies restrict hunting of particular animals or consumption of certain game meat to one or the other sex. The !Kung San of the Dobe area of Botswana have complicated personal and age- and sex-specific taboos on eating mammals (Lee and DeVore, 1976). No one can eat all twenty-nine game animals regularly taken by the San; indeed, no two individuals will have the same set of taboos. Some mammals can be eaten by everyone but with restrictions on what part they may eat. Ritual curers will set personal dietary restrictions on other animals; no one eats primates and some carnivores. Such complicated taboos are repeated with innumerable variations in other hunter-gatherer and agricultural societies and have undoubtedly affected the proportions of game animals found in archaeological sites.

Examples of specialized hunting are common, even if the reasons for the attention given to one or more species are rarely explained. Upper Paleolithic hunters of Solutré in southwestern France concentrated on wild horses, apparently driving them over cliffs in large herds (Smith, 1966). At the eighth millennium B.C. hunting camp of Star Carr in northeast England, Grahame Clark found the remains of at least eighty red deer in the occupation levels, and roe deer—thirty-three individuals—were the most common game (Clark, 1954). The Archaic Riverton culture peoples of the central Wabash Valley, Illinois, hunted the white-tailed deer as the basic meat staple in their diet to such an extent that the remains of this mammal were more numerous than those of any other species in the sites, except, in most cases, birds, fish, and turtles (Winters, 1969). The specialized big-game hunting economies of the Plains Indians are well known (Frison, 1974).

Overhunting. Another factor is overhunting, or the gradual extinction of a favorite species (Grayson, 1980). One well-known example is *Bos primigenius* (Figure 14.4), the European aurochs, or wild ox, which was a major quarry of Upper Paleolithic hunters in western Europe and was still hunted in postglacial times and after

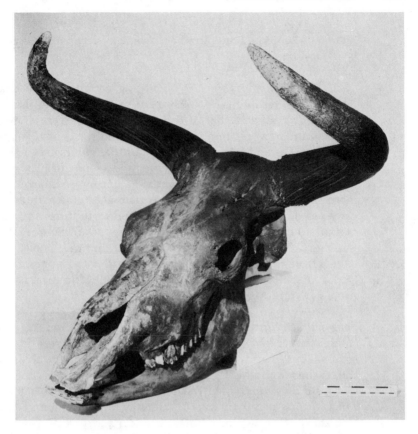

Figure 14.4   A *Bos primigenius* skull from Cambridgeshire, England.

food production began (Zeuner, 1963). The last aurochs died in a
Polish park in 1627. We know from illustrations and contemporary
descriptions what these massive animals looked like. The bulls
were large, up to six and a half feet at the shoulder, and often had
very long horns. The male coat was black with a white stripe along
the back and white curly hair between the horns. Professor Lutz
Heck of Berlin has tried to reconstitute the aurochs by crossing
breeds of cattle that exhibit characteristics of the wild ancestor.
Heck's experiments were most successful—forty "reconstituted
aurochsen" were living by 1951. The mental characteristics of the
aurochs reappeared along with the physical appearance. "Reconstituted aurochsen" are fierce, temperamental, and extremely agile if
allowed to run wild. The German experiments have provided a far
more convincing reconstruction of a most formidable Pleistocene

mammal than could any number of skeletal reconstructions or artists' impressions.

Changes in hunting activities. Hunting activities have changed drastically in recent times. Richard Lee records how the older members of the San state that in earlier times there were more game animals and a bigger hunting population in the central interior of Botswana (Lee and DeVore, 1976). Their forefathers used to hunt in large groups, killing buffalo, giraffe, and elephants. Today, their descendants have a predominantly gathering economy, supplemented by the meat of twenty-nine mammals, mostly those whose carcasses have a relatively high meat yield. Hunting is a common pursuit, the warthog being the most important source of meat, together with small game. This change in hunting habits directly results from the importation of Victorian rifles and from early hunting safaris, which decimated the wonderful African fauna within three generations.

Seasonal Occupation. Many prehistoric, and indeed modern hunter-gatherers and farmers lived, or live, their lives on regular, seasonal cycles, in which subsistence activities change according to the seasons of the year. The Pacific Northwest Indians congregated near salmon rivers when the seasonal runs upstream took place. They would catch thousands of salmon and dry them for consumption during the winter months. The early dry season in Central Africa brings an abundance of wild fruit into season, which formed an important part of early farmers' diet 1,500 years ago. How do archaeologists study seasonal activities, reconstruct the "economic seasons" of the year (Jochim, 1976)? Every aspect of prehistoric life was affected by seasonal movements. The Northwest Indians enjoyed a complex ceremonial life during the sedentary winter months, and the settlement pattern of the Khoi Khoi pastoralists of the Cape of Good Hope changed radically between dry and wet seasons. During the dry months they would congregate at the few permanent water holes and near perennial rivers. When the rains came, the cattle herders spread out over the neighboring arid lands, watering their herds in the standing waters left by rainstorms.

How do archaeologists study seasonality? A variety of approaches have been used with some success (Monks, 1981). The simplest method uses bones or plant remains. To illustrate this technique, in one case bird bones were used to establish that a San Francisco Bay site was visited about June 28, when cormorants were young (Howard, 1929). Grahame Clark has argued that the presence of cod bones in Norwegian sites indicates they were occupied during the winter and early spring (Clark, 1952). This type of analysis is fine, provided that the habits of the animals or of the plant remains being examined are well known. Some plant remains are available for much of the year, but are edible only during a few short weeks. Knowledge about the ecology of both animals and plants is essential, for the "scheduling" of resource exploitation, though perhaps not explicit, was certainly a major factor in the evolution of cultural systems. Some species such as deer are relatively insensitive to seasonal changes, but people sometimes exploited them in different ways at different times of the year. The Coast Salish of the Pacific Northwest took bucks in the spring, and does in the fall (Monks, 1981).

Then there are physiological events in an animal's life that can sometimes be used to establish seasonal occupation. The epiphyses at the end of limb bones are slowly joined to the main bone by ossification as an animal ages. This approach can certainly give some clues as to the general age of an animal population in, say, a hunting camp, but such variables as nutrition, even castration in domesticated animals, can affect the rate of fusion. Some species, such as ducks, mature much faster than others, such as deer. Clearly, knowledge of the different ages at which epiphyses fuse is essential to this approach.

Everyone knows that teeth erupt from upper and lower jaws as one grows into adulthood, often causing problems with wisdom teeth in people. Teeth are such durable animal remains that many archaeologists have tried to use them to age game and domestic animal populations. It is easy enough to study tooth eruption from complete or even fragmentary upper and lower jaws, and it has been done with domesticated sheep, goats, and wild deer. Again, factors of nutrition, even domestication, can affect eruption rates, and the rate at which teeth wear can vary dramatically between one population and another (Monks, 1981). Figure 14.6 shows some simple aging graphs derived from an African farming village (Fagan, 1967). Though simplistic, they at least show the potential of the approach.

In some cases, too, archaeologists have used reindeer and deer antlers to study seasonal occupations. The males of the deer family shed their antlers after the fall breeding season. By studying the antlers in a site, it is sometimes possible to establish the general season at which the settlement was in use (Clark, 1954).

Interpretation of seasonal occupation depends heavily on ethnographic analogies. One classic example is wild wheat. Botanist Jack Harlan (1967) has studied the gathering of wild wheat in the Near East, and has shown that the collectors have to schedule their collecting activities very precisely if they are to gather the harvest before the ears fall off the stems or the grain is consumed by birds and other animals. It is reasonable to assume that the same precise scheduling was essential during prehistoric times, an analogy that has enabled Near Eastern archaeologists to interpret seasonal occupations on sites in Syria and elsewhere.

Seasonality is still a surprisingly neglected subject in the archaeological literature, but it has great potential. By studying not only large mammals and obvious plant remains, but also tiny molluscs, and even fish bones and fish scales, it may be possible to narrow the "window" of seasonal occupation at many sites to surprisingly tight limits. (Interested readers should consult Monks, 1981, for an extended discussion of different approaches.)

Domestic Animals.   Nearly all domestic animals originated from a wild species with an inclination to be sociable, facilitating an association with humans (Ucko and Dimbelby, 1969). Domestic animals did not all originate in the same part of the world; they were domesticated in their natural area of distribution in the wild. Scholars have assumed that domestication of wild animals takes place when a certain level of cultural achievement is reached. Domestication everywhere seems to begin when a growing population needs a more regular food supply to feed larger groups of people; domestication is dependent on such conditions and is a prerequisite for further population growth.

Wild animals lack many characteristics that are valuable in their domestic counterparts. Thus, wild sheep have hairy coats, but their wool is not the type produced by domestic sheep, which is suitable for spinning; aurochs, ancestors of the domestic ox, and wild goats produce sufficient milk for their young, but not in the quantities so important to man. Considerable changes have taken place during domestication, as people develop characteristics in their animals that often render them unfit for survival in the wild (Olsen, 1979b).

The history of the domestic species is based on fragmentary animal bones found in the deposits of innumerable caves, rockshelters, and open sites (Reed, 1977). Osteological studies of wild and domesticated animals are inhibited both by fragmentation of the bones in most sites and by the much greater range of sexual and growth variation in domestic than in wild populations. Nevertheless, a number of sites have produced evidence of gradual osteological change toward domesticated animals (Redman, 1978). If the bones of the wild species of prehistoric domesticated animals are compared with those of the domestic animals throughout time, the range of size variations first increases, and eventually, selection in favor of smaller animals and less variation in size appears. This transition is fluid, however, and it is difficult to identify wild or domestic individuals from single bones or small collections.

The bones of domestic animals demonstrate that a high degree of adaptability is inherent in wild animals. People have found it necessary to change the size and qualities of animals according to their needs, with corresponding effects on their skeletal remains. Different breeds of cattle, sheep, and other domestic animals have been developed since the beginning of domestication.

Slaughtering and Butchery. Some insights into peoples' exploitation of wild and domestic animals can be obtained by studying not only animal bones themselves, but also their frequency and distribution in the ground. As Lewis Binford (1978) points out, however, the problem is not to record distributions and frequencies alone, but to establish what they mean in terms of human behavior. His recent studies of caribou hunting and exploitation by the Nunamiut Eskimo of Alaska have provided a mass of new data on the ways in which people exploit animals, and are directly relevant to interpretation of faunal remains (see Chapter 15).

Aging and Slaughtering. Clearly, the age at which an animal was killed can give valuable insights into the hunting habits of those who pursued them. Archaeologists have used a variety of methods for establishing animal ages from fragmentary bones. One general way is to examine the articular ends and cross-sections of limb bones. The epiphyses at the end of long bones may be unfused or partially joined in immature animals. Some Near Eastern sites have yielded such large collections that higher proportions of immature epiphyses were used to show the threshold of domestication. Early goat herders such as the inhabitants of Belt Cave in Iran systematically began to kill goats younger than they did when they were hunting the wild species (Reed, 1977). Immature epiphyses are of only marginal use in many areas of the world, for almost nothing is known about the osteology of long bones among, say, African mammals.

Most aging is determined by dentition or horn cores. The latter are ideal for the purpose, but are rarely preserved. Complete upper or lower jaws are excellent, too, for one can study the eruption formulas of the teeth and identify the proportion of the jaws that retain their immature milk teeth. But in most instances the archaeologist has to fall back on measuring wear on single teeth, a somewhat chancy approach, because little is known about tooth eruption and dental wear in most wild mammals. Richard Klein, an expert on African bones, has measured crown heights on Stone Age mammal teeth found at Klassies River Mouth and Nelson's Bay caves in the Cape Province of South Africa. Taken as two groups, the teeth measurements probably give interesting general impressions of the hunting habits of Middle and Later Stone Age peoples in this area (Klein, 1978). He compared the mortality distributions from the Cape buffalo and other large and medium-sized species to mortality curves from modern mammal populations. He identified two basic distributions (Klein and Cruz-Uribe, 1983):

The *catastrophic age profile* is stable in size and structure, and has progressively fewer older individuals. This is the normal distribution for living ungulate populations (Figure 14.5a) and is that normally found in mass game kills achieved by driving herds into swamps or over cliffs.

The *attritional age profile* (Figure 14.5b), shows an underrepresentation of prime-age animals relative to their abundance in living populations, but young and old are overrepresented. This profile is thought to result from scavenging or simple spear hunting.

Klein found that the Cape buffalo age distributions from both sites were close to those observed on modern buffalo killed by lions, where both young and old males are vulnerable to attack because they are isolated from the large herds of formidable prime animals. Thus, he argued, the Stone Age hunters at both caves were enjoying a lasting, stable relationship with their prey populations of buffalo. The distribution for eland and bastard hartebeest (smaller, gregarious antelopes) were much more similar to the catastrophic profile. Klein speculates that they were similar because these species were hunted in large game drives, like the bison on the Great Plains. Thus, entire populations would be killed at one time. Age distributions can reflect all kinds of other activities as well. The Star Carr site in northeast England contains no young red deer. Most of the animals were in their prime, perhaps because the

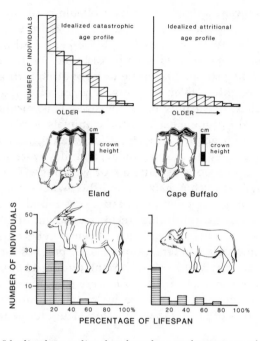

Figure 14.5   Idealized mortality data based on molar crowns of two common South African mammals, the eland and the Cape buffalo. (a) Idealized catastrophic age profile. (b) Idealized attritional age profile (for explanations see text).

place was a hide- and antler-processing station (Clark, 1954; Pitts, 1979).

Hunting and slaughter patterns are subject to all manner of subtle variables; many of which are described by Lewis Binford (1978; 1981b). When studying hunting practices among the Nunamiut Eskimo of Alaska, he found that the hunters butchered animals as part of a much broader subsistence strategy. The Nunamiut rely heavily on stored meat for most of the year and thus orient their hunting practices toward storage objectives, as well as many other considerations. In the fall, they may hunt caribou calves to obtain skins for winter clothing, and the heads and tongues of these animals provide the meat for the people who process the skins. Binford stresses that it is difficult to interpret slaughter patterns without closely understanding the cultural systems of which hunting was a part.

Domestic animals are a controllable meat supply, and subject to quite different selection criteria. In more advanced agricultural societies, cattle or horses might be kept until old age for draught purposes, surplus males being castrated and females being retained until they stopped lactating or were of no further use for breeding or ploughing. Even if riding or work animals were not kept, the problem of surplus males persists. This surplus is an abundant source of prime meat, and these animals were often slaughtered in early adulthood. Cattle stood for wealth in many traditional societies, as they do in some today; and they were slaughtered on such special occasions as funerals or weddings. The herd surplus was consumed in this manner, and the owner's obligations were satisfied. Thus, a population of cattle jaws found on a site may reveal a characteristic graph (Figure 14.6a), showing that the animals were slaughtered at different ages. This may reflect distinct slaughtering ages for male and female animals. Or perhaps the remains of a herd of goats may yield a simple graph (Figure 14.6b), reflecting circumstances in which small stock were slaughtered in their prime for meat. These situations are by no means universal, but they are examples of factors that can affect slaughter pattern data.

Butchery.   The fragmentary bones in an occupation level are the end product of the killing, cutting up, and consumption of domestic or wild animals. To understand the butchery process, the articulation of animal bones must be examined in the levels where they are found, or a close study must be made of fragmentary body parts. The Olsen-Chubbock kill site in Colorado yielded evidence of a slaughtered bison herd. The hunters camped beside their kill, removing the skin and meat from the carcass of a large mammal, and perhaps drying some surplus meat for later consumption. The butchering tools used by the skinners are found in direct association with the bones, so that the excavations preserve the moment of butchery for posterity (Wheat, 1972).

Interpreting butchery techniques is a complicated matter, for many variables affect the way in which carcasses were dismembered. The Nunamiut relied heavily on stored meat, and the way they dismembered a caribou varied according to storage needs, meat yield of different body parts, and proximity of the base camp. The animal's size may affect the number of bones found at a base site: goats, chickens, or small deer could have been carried to the village as complete carcasses; but often only small portions of larger

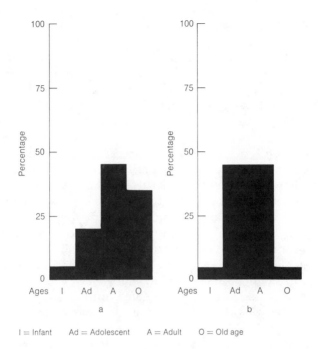

Figure 14.6 Aging graphs derived from domestic animal skeletal remains for ideal hypothetical cases. (a) Typical domestic cattle population. (b) Typical domestic goat population. Notice that these graphs are purely hypothetical and take no account of actual systems.

beasts were brought in. Sometimes, animals with high meat yield were consumed where they were killed and every scrap of flesh and entrails utilized. Theodore White (1953) developed a method for studying the distribution of body parts by reducing them to proportions of the most common bone present. He applied the method with success to bison kills in the Great Plains. But his technique, though useful, does not solve the problem of interpretation. Once again, the problem is to establish the meaning of archaeological distributions in terms of human behavior. Just how complicated this is in the context of butchery can be appreciated from Binford's comment (1978) that the Nunamiut criteria for selecting meat for consumption are the amount of usable meat, the time required to process it, and the quality of the flesh. The only way to interpret archaeological distributions is with detailed understanding of the cultural systems that generated them (see Chapter 15).

VEGETAL REMAINS

Gathering and agriculture are two major components of prehistoric subsistence that are almost invariably underrepresented in the archaeological record. Seeds, fruits, grasses, and leaves are among the most fragile of organic materials and do not survive long unless they are carbonized or preserved under very wet or arid conditions.

Carbonized and Unburned Seeds. These are normally found in cooking pots, midden deposits, or among the ashes of hearths, where they were dropped by accident. Though the preservation conditions are not ideal, it is possible to identify both domestic and wild plant species from such discoveries (Ford, 1979; Helbaek, 1969; J. Renfrew, 1973). Much early evidence for cereal cultivation in the Near East comes from carbonized seeds. Many more unburned vegetable remains occur in waterlogged sites and in dry caves. The Star Carr site in northeastern England yielded a range of fungi and wild seeds, some of which were eaten until recently by European peasants (Clark, 1954). A Stone Age campsite at Gwisho hot springs in central Zambia, on the edge of a tract of savannah woodland rich in vegetal foods, contained quantities of seeds and fruit preserved by the high water table in the spring (Fagan and Van Noten, 1971). Ten thousand identifiable vegetal fragments came from the occupation levels at Gwisho, many of them from six species still eaten by southern African hunters, a remarkable continuity of subsistence patterns over more than 4,000 years.

The dry caves of the western United States and Mexico have provided a great quantity of dried vegetable remains. The inhabitants of Tularosa Cave in New Mexico were harvesting primitive corn by 2000 B.C., and their successors employed horticulture fully. The lower levels, occupied by hunter-gatherers, yielded the remains of no fewer than thirty-nine species of wild flora that were used for food, tools, and raw materials; edible plants included yucca seeds, cacti, walnuts, and various grasses (Jennings, 1973).

Tehuacán. The Tehuacán Valley in the state of Puebla, Mexico, has provided a record of continuous human occupation from the earliest times to the Spanish conquest (Byers, 1967; MacNeish, 1978). Early inhabitants of the valley lived mainly by hunting rabbits, birds, and turtles. Later, about 6700–5000 B.C., their successors subsisted mostly on wild plants such as beans and amaranth. These people, who lived in caves during the dry season, began to cultivate squashes and avocados; pollens from a plant that some botanists believe is transitional between wild teosinte and corn, through human selection, occur in the cave deposits. Grinding stones, pestles, and mortars were in use for the first time, indicating that seeds were being ground for food.

Richard MacNeish has excavated more than a dozen sites in Tehuacán, five of which contained the remains of ancient corn; 80,000 wild plant remains and 25,000 specimens of corn came from the sites, providing a detailed picture of agriculture's origins in highland Mexico. The transitional pollens and cobs came from the lowest occupation level in San Marcos Cave, and the cobs were no more than twenty millimeters (0.78 inch) long. Coxcatlán Cave contained important botanical evidence, too, for by 5000 B.C., although the inhabitants of this and other sites were still gathering most of their vegetal food, 10 percent of the diet came from domestic cultivation—gourds, squashes, beans, chili peppers, and corn. One-third of Tehuacán subsistence was based on agriculture by 3400 B.C., a period when the domestic dog first appeared; permanent settlement began soon after that. Pottery was being manufactured by 2300 B.C., and more hybrid types of corn came into use.

So many vegetal remains were found in the settlements of Tehuacán that the history of domestic corn in this area can be written in quite astonishing detail (Figure 14.7). Much controversy surrounds the ultimate ancestry of the maize. One school of thought regards teosinte, a native annual grass, as the ancestor. Another, a long-lived theory, contends that the wild ancestor of maize became extinct some 2,000 years ago, as did the early cultivated varieties, which were superseded by more modern forms (Flannery, 1973). Botanical evidence of this completeness is unique in the archaeological record.

Flotation Recovery.   Flotation techniques have been employed systematically to recover seeds in central Illinois, and also at Ali Kosh in Iran. The method uses water or chemicals to free the seeds, which are often microscopic, from the fine earth or occupation residue that masks them: the vegetal remains usually float and the residue sinks. Although this technique enables us to recover seeds from many sites where it was impossible before, by no means can it be applied universally, for its effectiveness depends on soil conditions. By flotation, Stuart Struever and his colleagues recovered more than 36,000 fragments of carbonized hickory nut shell from ovens, hearths, and storage-refuse pits in the Apple Creek site in

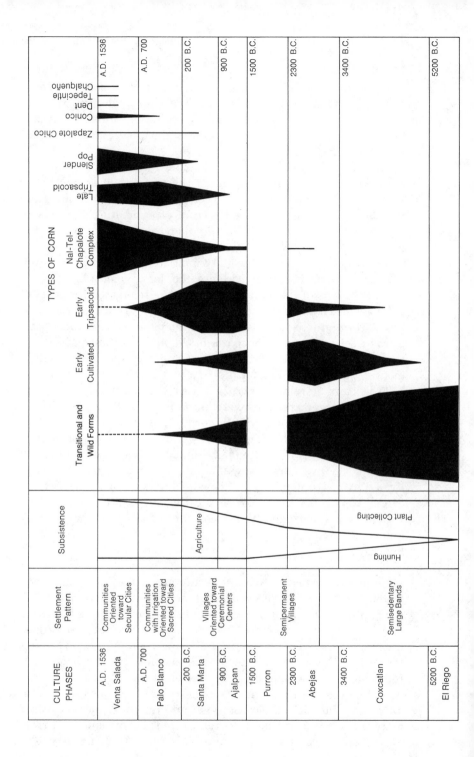

the Lower Illinois Valley (Struever, 1968). This settlement also yielded 4,200 fragments of acorn shell, as well as more than 2,000 other seeds from at least three species. Few cultivated seeds were found, indicating that the inhabitants relied on hickory nuts and acorns for much of their vegetable diet (Asch, Asch, and Ford, 1972).

Kent Flannery's experiments with flotation at the Ali Kosh site in Iran were also successful—indeed, the results were dramatic (Hole, Flannery, and Neely, 1969). After the first season of excavations, Flannery and his colleagues stated confidently that "plant remains were scarce at Ali Kosh." Two years later they used a modified version of Struever's flotation technique and recovered more than 40,000 seeds stratified throughout the cultural sequence at the Ali Kosh mound. The data gave a startlingly complete botanical history for the site, showing the increasing importance of emmer wheat and two-row hulled barley and the effects of irrigation (Figure 14.8).

Flotation is slowly revolutionizing the study of prehistoric vegetal remains. The methods used are being refined as more experience is gained with them under varied field conditions. Simple hand flotation systems were used at Ali Kosh and Apple Creek, where the deposit was hand sorted and passed through fine meshes immersed in water. A variation on this method was used in dry areas. The samples were poured into mesh-lined sieves suspended in water-filled oil drums, and fine seeds were carefully removed and dried in newspaper before study.

A major goal of excavators has been speed, to recover large quantities of seeds in a relatively short time (Watson, 1976). A number of ingenious machines have been developed to carry out large-scale flotation: These include a device known as a froth flotation machine, which separates the archaeological material from its matrix in a special flotation chamber, with a mixture of water and chemicals to aid the process (Jarman, Legge, and Charles, 1972). This is an expensive machine to assemble and operate compared with a much simpler device that was assembled for the Mammoth Cave excavations in Kentucky, in which water is forced through a pressure hose and a shower head onto the bottom of a screened container that sits inside the oil drum (Figure 14.9). The sample of earth is poured into the screened container and agitated by the water pouring into the screen. The light plant remains and other fine materials float on the water and are carried out of the container

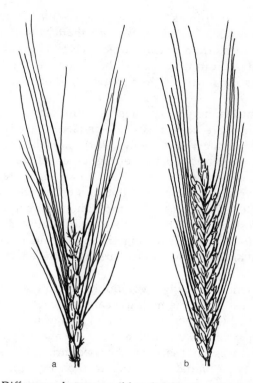

Figure 14.8 Differences between wild and domesticated wheat: (a) the wild ancestor of one-grained wheat (einkorn: *Triticum boeoticum*); (b) cultivated einkorn *(T. monococum).*

by a sluiceway that leads to fine mesh screens, where the finds are caught, wrapped in fine cloth, and preserved for the botanists to study. The heavy sludge, in the meantime, sinks to the bottom of the container inside the oil drum. This Mammoth Cave system has the advantage of being cheap to make and easy to operate. It is estimated to process about 0.50 cubic meter of deposit a working day. To work most effectively, the system has to be close to a source of running water, whether a river or a faucet.

Flotation, though still in its infancy, promises to rewrite the early history of domestic crops in the New and Old worlds. Recent flotation operations have revealed domestic sunflowers in a site in Tennessee dating to about 900 ± 85 B.C., and finds on Kentucky sites may well push the origins of horticulture in eastern North America as far back as the late third millennium B.C. (Watson, 1974,

Figure 14.9 A simple flotation device used at Mammoth Cave in western Kentucky.

1976). And in the Near East wild einkorn and barley seeds have come from the Mureybit site in Syria, dating to the eighth millennium B.C. (Redman, 1978). These preliminary results have the advantage of being empirical results that can be treated statistically, and—provided that the flotation methods used are carefully defined in each instance—compared to one another.

Grain Impressions. Apart from the seeds themselves, which reveal what the food plants were, grain impressions in the walls of clay vessels or adobe brick help uncover the history of agriculture or gathering. The microscopic casts of grains that adhered to the wet clay of a pot while it was being made are preserved in the firing and can be identified with a microscope. Numerous grain impressions have been found in European handmade pottery from the end of the Stone Age (Figure 14.10). Indeed, a remarkably complete crop

Figure 14.10   A grain impression from a Neolithic pot at Hurst Fen, Cambridgeshire, England.

history of prehistoric Europe has been pieced together from grain impressions. The most abundantly cultivated cereal in prehistoric Europe was emmer wheat *(Triticum dicoccum);* wheat was the most important grain during early farming times, but barley rose into prominence during the Bronze Age (Clark, 1952; J. Renfrew, 1973). Grain impressions have been studied in the Near East and the western Sahara, whereas some related work on adobe bricks has been carried out in the western United States (Darrah, 1938).

Palynology. The study of pollen has been an invaluable tool for studying European forest clearance (Figure 14.11). Many years ago, Danish botanist Johannes Iversen was studying pollen diagrams from Scandinavian peat sequences when he noticed a remarkably sudden change in the composition of the forests at the beginning of the sub-Boreal period (Blytt and Sernander, zones VII–VIII) (Iversen, 1941). The elements of high forest—oak, ash, beech, and elm—simultaneously declined, while the pollens of grasses increased sharply. At one locality he found a charcoal layer immediately underlying the zone where forest trees declined. The increase in grass pollens was also associated with the appearance of several cultivation weeds, including *Plantago,* which is characteristically associated with cereal agriculture in Europe and went with European farmers throughout the world, even to North America. Iversen concluded that the tree cover vanished as a direct result of farming activity—humanity's first major imprint on the environment. Similar pollen curves have been plotted from data gathered elsewhere in Europe.

Figure 14.11 Fluctuation in frequencies of charcoal and fossil pollen brought by Neolithic colonization: Ordrup Mose, Denmark. The amount of grass pollen rises sharply as the forest decreases. (After Iversen.)

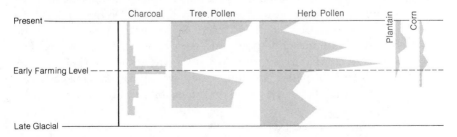

Plant Phytolith Analysis. Opal phytoliths are created from hydrated silica dissolved in groundwater that is absorbed through a plant's roots and carried through its vascular system (Rovner, 1983). Silica production is continuous throughout the growth of a plant. Phytolith samples are collected in much the same way as pollen samples, then studied by identifying individual species. Most research in the field has been with grasses, and so the archaeological applications are obvious, especially in the study of prehistoric agriculture.

Archaeological applications of phytolith research have hardly begun, but the method shows great promise. A study of phytoliths from two sites in north central Wyoming, one dating to about 9000 B.C., the other occupied from 5000 B.C. to the present, revealed that the earlier location was occupied during a warmer climatic period. The earliest inhabitants of the later site also lived in a warmer climate, but the weather cooled off around 1000 B.C. Other studies of this type have been conducted, but the research is still isolated. More has been attempted with prehistoric agriculture. Anna Roosevelt (1978) used phytolith analysis on sites in the Orinoco River Valley, Venezuela. She found that the percentages of grass phytoliths increased dramatically at the very moment when carbon 13 and carbon 12 analysis of skeletal material and actual seeds indicated that maize was introduced to the area. A similar result was obtained at the Early Preclassic site of Cuello in Belize, where carbonized seeds came from a level where phytolith quantities also suggested the presence of maize (Hammond and Miksicek, 1981).

Phytolith analysis has many potential applications in archaeology in the study of diet, by using coprolites and even phytoliths embedded in jawbones, but research is still in its infancy. It is likely to become as important as palynology in the next decade.

Interpreting Evidence. No matter how effective the recovery techniques used for vegetal remains, the picture of either food gathering or agriculture is bound to be incomplete. A look at modern hunter-gatherers reveals the problem (Lee and DeVore, 1976). The !Kung San of the Kalahari Desert in southern Africa are classic hunter-gatherers who appear in every book on ethnography, and yet, until comparatively recently, little was known of their ecology or subsistence patterns. Many early writers on hunter-gatherers assumed that the !Kung relied on game alone and lived in perennial starvation that was relieved periodically by meat-eating orgies. Nothing, in fact, could be further from the truth. Much subsistence activity of the San and other hunter-gatherers is conducted by the women, who gather the wild vegetable foods that comprise a substantial part of their diet. Many early observers were naturally preoccupied with hunting techniques and more spectacular subsistence activities, for in former times, many peoples pursued larger game, often cooperating with other bands in the chase.

Today, vegetable foods have a leading part in the San diet and have presumably increased in importance as the large game herds have diminished. The San know of at least eighty-five species of edible fruit, seeds, and plants; of this enormous subsistence base, they eat regularly only some nine species, noticeably the *Bauhinia*. In a famine year or when prime vegetable food sources are exhausted, they turn to other species, having an excellent cushion of edible food to fall back on when their conventional diet staple is scarce. Theoretically, therefore, the San can never starve, even if food is scarce at times. Their territory, of course, is delineated in part by available sources of vegetable foods as well as by water supplies; its frontiers in many cases represent a day's walking distance out to the gathering grounds and back to the base camp.

AGRICULTURE AND DOMESTIC AND WILD ANIMALS

Very few subsistence-farming peoples have ever relied on agricultural products or their herds alone to provide them with food the year around. Hunting, fishing, and gathering have always supplemented the diet, and in famine years or times of epidemic the people have fallen back on the natural resources of their environment for survival.

Since food production has led to increased population densities, however, famine often ensues because the resource base of wild foods for farmers is smaller than that which may have supported a smaller hunter-gatherer population in comfort (Scudder, 1962). Even in times of plenty, most food producers rely on game for some of their meat, as evidenced by the bones of wild animals in faunal collections where cattle and small stock are also present. The proportions of domestic and wild species in such a collection are important in assessing the roles of hunting and pastoralism in the economy. If such figures are based on how many individuals are represented in the collection, or on some sound formulas, the results can be revealing, especially when a series of collections are available from a cultural sequence extending over several hundred years.

Deh Luran. Just how important an influence domesticated animals had on prehistoric agriculture is well documented on the Deh Luran Plain in Iran (Hole, Neely, and Flannery, 1969). The inhabitants first cultivated cereal crops and kept goats sometime before 7000 B.C. Their first food production involved plants and animals introduced from the mountains to the rolling steppe of the Plain. As the excavators point out, "What man did, before 7000 B.C., was to domesticate the annuals he could eat, and then domesticate the animals who lived on the perennials." The cultivation system was expanded so that domestic grains increased from 5 percent of the vegetal remains to about 40 percent between 7000 and 6000 B.C. But this early domestic plant and animal complex, based as it was on upland-mountain environmental adaptations, inhibited rapid population growth. Even so, the vegetational pattern of the steppe was altered as field weeds were established and land clearance and grazing removed the natural grass covering.

Between 5500 and 5000 B.C., some simple irrigation techniques were introduced that took advantage of the local drainage pattern. Barley cultivation became of prime importance, and the cultivation areas expanded. Sheep increased in importance, and cattle were introduced, the latter assuming a vital role in the economy only when plows began to be used around 2000 B.C. Each gradual or rapid change in the subsistence pattern or environment of Deh Luran instituted by humans led to a complicated chain reaction affecting every sector of the inhabitants' culture.

The rate of herd growth is affected by many factors, among them endemic stock disease, nutrient qualities of grazing grass, availability of water supplies, and in some areas, distribution of the dreaded tsetse fly, carrier of *trypanosomiasis*, which is fatal to cattle and harmful to humanity (Lambrecht, 1964). Similar factors also affect the growth rate of domestic stock, because the size of cattle or smaller stock can vary widely from one environment to another.

BIRDS, FISH, AND MOLLUSCS

Birds. Bird bones have been sadly neglected in archaeology, although some early investigators did realize their significance.

Japetus Steenstrup and other early investigators of Danish shell middens took care to identify bird bones, including those of migrant birds (Lubbock, 1865). In 1902 the famous Peruvianist Max Uhle dug a large Indian mound on the eastern shores of San Francisco Bay. The site was excavated again in 1926, and Dr. Hildegarde Howard studied a large collection of bird remains from the dig. Her report illustrates the potential importance of bird faunas in archaeology (Howard, 1929). She found that water birds were the predominant species, especially ducks, geese, and cormorants, and that land birds distinctive of hill country were absent. All the geese were winter visitors, mostly found in the Bay area between January and April of each year. The cormorant bones were nearly all immature, suggesting that the Indians had been robbing cormorant rookeries; most of the cormorant bones equaled an adult bird's in size, but ossification was less complete, equivalent to that in modern birds about five to six weeks old. Dr. Howard examined rookery records and estimated that a date of June 28 each year would be the approximate time when the rookeries could be raided. Thus, from the evidence, she concluded that the Emeryville mound was occupied both during the winter and the early summer, and probably all year.

Bird hunting has often been a sideline in the struggle for subsistence. In many societies, boys have hunted winged prey with bow and arrows, while training for hunting larger game. A specialized bird-hunting kit is found in several cultures, among them the postglacial hunter-gatherer cultures of northern Europe. Though bows and spears were used in the chase, snaring obviously was practiced regularly. The birds found in some African hunting and farming sites are almost invariably species like guinea fowl, which fly rarely and are easily snared (Dawson, 1969; Fagan, 1967). No traces of the snares have been found in excavations, for they would have been made of perishable materials. Surprisingly little has been written on prehistoric fowling, perhaps because bird bones are fragile and present tricky identification problems.

Fish.   Fishing, like fowling, became increasingly important as people began to specialize in different and distinctive economies and as their environmental adaptations became more sophisticated and their technological abilities improved. Evidence for this activity comes from both artifacts and fish bones.

Freshwater and ocean fish can be caught in various ways. Nets, basket traps, and dams were methods in wide use from postglacial times on, but their remains rarely survive in the archaeological record, except in dry sites or waterlogged deposits. Basket fish traps have been found in Danish peat bogs, dating to the Atlantic vegetational period (Clark, 1975). The ancient Egyptians employed somewhat similar traps, depicted in Old Kingdom tomb paintings (2600–2180 B.C.). Nets remain the most popular fishing device and were used in northern Europe in postglacial times, too. A larger fish weir, constructed of vertical sticks 1.2 to 4.9 meters long (4 to 16 feet), sharpened at one end with a stone axe, enclosed an area of two acres at Boylston Street, Boston (Jennings, 1973). The weir was built about 2500 B.C. and was probably the work of coastal Archaic people. Such traps were evidently widely used along the Atlantic Coast, built in estuary areas where tidal currents were strong. In the Boston weir, brush and flexible withes were placed between the stakes; fish were diverted into the enclosure by "leaders," also made of brush, leading to the trap mouth. Some days' work must have been necessary to build this weir, which provided an almost inexhaustible food supply for its designers.

Fishhooks, harpoons, and barbed spearheads are frequent finds in lake- or riverside encampments. The earliest fishhooks had no barbs, but they did have a U-shaped profile (Figure 14.12). Postglacial hunting peoples, such as the Maglemose folk of Denmark, used

Figure 14.12   Bone fishhooks of the Maglemose culture in northern Europe. (After Clark; two-thirds actual size.)

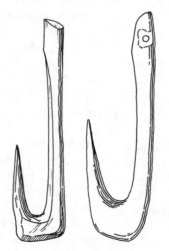

such artifacts in the seventh millennium B.C., in all probability to hunt the pike, a prized freshwater fish in prehistoric times (Clark, 1952).

Artifacts alone tell us little about the role of fish in prehistoric economy or about the fishing techniques of prehistoric peoples. Did they fish all year or only when salmon were running? Did they concentrate on bottom fish or rely on stranded whales for protein? Such questions can be answered only by examining the surviving fish bones themselves, or if they survive, which is unusual, actual fish scales. Perhaps the most effective method of collecting fish remains is by taking samples from each level, an approach advocated by Richard Casteel, who found that it was nine times less time-consuming than normal collection methods. Furthermore, he succeeded in identifying 30 percent more fish types from his column samples. This type of approach is particularly important on sites like the Glen Cannery site in British Columbia, where fishing was the major economic activity (Casteel, 1976).

The Chumash Indians of Southern California were remarkably skillful fishermen, venturing far offshore in frameless plank canoes and fishing with hook and line, basket, net, and harpoon. Their piscatory skill is reflected in the archaeological sites of Century Ranch, Los Angeles, where the bones of such deep-sea fish as the albacore and oceanic skipjack were found, together with the remains of large deep-water rockfish that live near the sea bottom in water too deep to be fished from the shore (King, Blackburn, and Chandonet, 1968). Five other species normally occurring offshore, including the barracuda, were found in the same midden. The bones of shallow-water fish, among them the leopard shark and California halibut, were discovered on the same sites, indicating that both surf fishing and canoe fishing in estuaries with hook and line, basket, or net were also practiced.

The degree to which a community depends on fishing can be impressive. Lake- or seaside fishing encampments tend to be occupied longer than hunting camps, for the food supply, especially when combined with collection of shellfish, is both reliable and nourishing.

Molluscs.   Shellfish from seashore, lake, or river formed an important part of the prehistoric diet for many thousands of years. Augustin de Beaulieu, who visited the Cape of Good Hope in 1620 with a fleet of ships from Honfleur, France, was a curious and perceptive observer whose wanderings over the Cape Peninsula enabled him to describe the Khoi Khoi, the indigenous cattle herders and gatherers: "Also they go along the seashore where they find certain shell fish, or some dead whale or other fish, however putrefied it may be, and this they put on the fire for a little and make a good meal of it" (Raven-Hart, 1967). The identification of the molluscs in shell middens is a matter for expert conchologists, who possess a mine of information on the edibility and seasons of shellfish. With such data, it was determined that the Khoi Khoi seem to have depended on shellfish at dry times of the year, when inland pastures were parched and vegetable foods in short supply.

Freshwater molluscs were important to many Archaic bands living in the southeastern United States, but because each mollusk in itself has limited food value, the amount of molluscs needed to feed even a small band of about twenty-five people must have been enormous. It has been calculated that such a band would need between 1,900 and 2,250 mussels from the Meramec River each day, and a colossal accumulation of between 57,000 and 67,000 each month (Parmalee and Klippel, 1974). A group of 100 persons would need at least three tons of mussels each month. Confronted with such figures, no one can believe that molluscs were the staple diet of any prehistoric peoples. Rather, they were an invaluable supplemental food at scarce times of the year or a source of variety in a staple diet of fish, game, or vegetable foods.

When fresh- or seawater molluscs were collected, the collectors soon accumulated huge piles of shells at strategic places on the coast or on the shores of lakes, near rocky outcrops or tidal pools where molluscs were commonly found. Modern midden analysis involves systematic sampling of the deposits and counting and weighing the various constituents of the soil. The proportions of different shells are readily calculated, and their size, which sometimes changes through time, is easily measured. California shell middens have long been the subject of intensive research, with the changes in frequency of molluscs projected against ecological changes in the site areas.

The La Jolla culture middens of La Batiquitos Lagoon in San Diego are a notable example of such analysis. Claude N. Warren (Crabtree, 1963) took column samples from one shell mound and found that the remains of five species of shellfish were the dominant elements in the molluscan diet of the inhabitants. The changes in the major species of shellfish were then calculated for each excavated level. They found that *Mytilus*, the bay mussel, was the most common in the lower levels, gradually being replaced by *Chione*, the Venus shell, and *Pecten*, the scallop, both of which assumed greater importance in the later phases of the site's occupation, which has been radiocarbon-dated from the fifth to the second millennia B.C. Warren found that *Ostrea*, the oyster, a species characteristic of a rocky coast, was also most common in the lower levels, indicating that the San Diego shore was rocky beach at that time, with extensive colonies of shellfish. By about 6300 years ago La Batiquitos Lagoon was silted to the extent that it was ecologically more suitable for *Pecten* than the rock-loving *Mytilus*. Soon afterward, however, the lagoons became so silted that even *Pecten* and *Chione* could no longer support a large population dependent on shellfish. The inhabitants then had to move elsewhere. Similar investigations elsewhere in California have also shown the great potential of molluscs in studying prehistoric ecology.

Many peoples collected molluscs seasonally, but it is difficult to identify such practices from the archaeological record. Growth bands in mollusc shells have been used to measure seasonality, but the most promising approach is to measure the oxygen isotopic ratio of its shell carbonate, which is a function of the water temperature from which precipitation occurred. Using a mass spectrometer, you can measure the oxygen 18 composition at the edge of a shell, obtaining the temperature of the water at the time of the mollusc's death. It is difficult to obtain actual temperature readings, but you can gain an idea of seasonal fluctuations, thereby establishing whether a mollusc was taken in winter or summer (Killingley, 1981).

Both fresh water and seawater shells had ornamental roles as well. Favored species were traded over great distances in North America. Millions of *Mercenaria* and *Busycon* shells were turned into wampum belts in New England in early Colonial times. *Spondylus gaederopus*, a mussel native to the Black Sea, the Sea of Marmora, and the Aegean, was widely distributed as far north and west as Poland and the Rhineland by European farmers in the fifth millennium B.C. The *Conus* shell, common on the East African coast, was widely traded, finding its way into the African interior and becoming a traditional prerequisite of chieftainly prestige. The nineteenth-century missionary and explorer David Livingstone records his visit to Chief Shinte in Western Zambia in 1855: the going price for two *Conus* shells at that time was a slave, or five for a tusk of elephant ivory. Archaeological digs have indicated that *Conus* shells were used in the Zambezi Valley 700 years earlier, reflecting a long history of trade in such prestigious ornaments (Figure 14.13) (Fagan, 1969). Indeed, as late as 1910, enterprising merchants were trading china replicas of *Conus* shells to the tribesmen of Central Africa.

Rock Art.   Rock art is a major source of information on economic activities. Some years ago, African archaeologist J. Desmond Clark

Figure 14.13   Ingombe Ilede burial with *Conus* shells, *ca.* fifteenth century A.D. The shells are the circular objects around the neck numbered 1–4.

published an account of late Stone Age hunting and gathering practices in southern Africa, in which he drew heavily on the rock art of Zimbabwe and South Africa. The paintings depict the chase, weapons, collecting, and camp life. Clark remarked, "In the rock art there is preserved an invaluable record of the people's hunting methods, the different kinds of weapons and domestic equipment they used, their customs and ceremonies" (Clark, 1959).

The rock paintings of Natal, South Africa, provide fascinating information on fishing practices and the boats associated with them. Patricia Vinnecombe recorded a fishing scene in the Tsoelike River rockshelter in Lesotho, southern Africa (Figure 14.14) (Vinnecombe, 1960). The fishermen, armed with long spears, are massed in boats, apparently cornering a shoal of fish that are swimming around in confusion. Some boats have lines under their hulls that may represent anchors; the fish cannot be identified with certainty, but they may be freshwater catfish or yellowfish. Vinnecombe's paper generated much discussion—some authorities argued that the boats in the paintings were probably made of bark (Clark, 1960). Another famous scene from the Cape Province of South Africa depicts a group of ostriches feeding peacefully; among them lurks a hunter wearing an ostrich skin, his legs and bow protruding beneath the belly of an apparently harmless bird. Such vignettes of prehistoric hunting life add insight into data obtained from the

Figure 14.14   A rock drawing depicting a fishing scene from Lesotho, southern Africa.

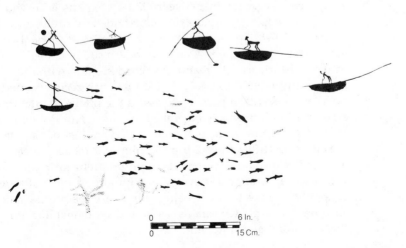

food residues recovered from caves and rockshelters, but the actual interpretation of the art is subject to many sophisticated variables, among them the symbolic meaning of the paintings (see Lewis-Williams, 1981).

PREHISTORIC DIET

So far, the only information on prehistoric subsistence has been gleaned from various archaeological finds. The ultimate objective of economic archaeology is not only to establish how people obtained their food but also to reconstruct their actual diet. Dietary reconstruction is difficult, mainly because of incomplete economic information. Yet the problems involved are fundamental. What proportion of the diet was meat? How diverse were dietary sources? Did the principal sources of diet change from season to season? To what extent did the people rely on food from neighboring areas? Was food stored? What limitations or restrictions did technology or society place on diet? All these questions lie behind any inquiry into prehistoric subsistence.

Diet (what is eaten) and *nutrition* (measure of the ability of a diet to maintain the body in its environment) have to be studied in close conjunction, for they are quite distinct from subsistence, the actual process of obtaining resources. The baseline for any study of prehistoric diet and nutrition must be surveys of modern hunter-gatherers, subsistence cultivators, and pastoralists. Unfortunately, however, lack of agreement between dietary experts is so widespread that it is difficult to estimate the caloric needs of prehistoric peoples (Dennell, 1979). So many cultural, medical, and physiological factors have to be weighed—even in modern situations—that research into prehistoric nutrition and food consumption will often be little more than inspired guesswork. Despite such recovery methods as flotation, it is still impossible to assess the intake of vitamins, minerals, and milk products in prehistoric diets. Nor do we have adequate data on the wastage of food in preparation and storage or on the effects of different cooking techniques. Archaeological data can only indicate some of the foods eaten by prehistoric communities, and show, at least qualitatively, how important some of them were generally. We are far from being able to ascribe precise food value to animal and plant remains, as would be demanded for precise studies of diet and nutrition.

Sources of Data on Diet and Nutrition. There are only a few sources of data on prehistoric diet and nutrition, and these are subject to serious limitations (Begler and Keatinge, 1979; Dennell, 1979). *Human skeletal remains* can sometimes provide evidence of ancient malnutrition and other dietary conditions (Huss-Ashmore and others, 1982). Some diseases, such as caries, leprosy, and even rickets, leave traces on the human skeleton (Brothwell, 1965; Wells, 1964). Unfortunately, meaningful statements about nutrition and nutritional stress depend on demonstrating that normal growth patterns in the skeleton were disturbed. Some of the best evidence comes from juvenile skeletons, where the bones are more easily imprinted by nutritional disturbance.

One promising technique involves identifying types of plant foods from the isotopic analysis of prehistoric bone and hair. By using the ratio between two stable carbon isotopes—carbon 12 and carbon 13 in animal tissue—one can establish the diet of the organism. Research on controlled animal populations has shown that as carbon is passed along the food chain, the carbon composition of animals continues to reflect the relative isotopic composition of their diet (Huss-Ashmore and others, 1982). Carbon is metabolized in plants through three major pathways: carbon$_3$, carbon$_4$, and by Crassulacean acid metabolism. The plants that make up the diet of animals have distinct carbon 13 values. Maize, for example, is a carbon$_4$ plant. In contrast, most indigenous temperate flora in North America is composed of carbon$_3$ varieties. Thus, a population that shifts its diet from wild vegetable foods to maize will also experience a shift in dietary isotopic values. Because carbon 13 and carbon 12 values do not change after death, you can study archaeological carbon from food remains, soil humus, and skeletal remains to gain insight into ancient diet.

This approach is of great importance to archaeologists studying the introduction of agriculture in different areas. N. J. van der Merwe and J. C. Vogel (1978) studied 52 skeletons from ten Midwestern sites dating from 300 B.C. to A.D. 1300. The δ carbon 13 value (reflecting the immediate carbon source of the skeleton) for pre-maize skeletons averaged −21.4 ± .78%, whereas those from agricultural settlements averaged −11.8 ± 1.3%. Another study on skeletal material from the Viru Valley in Peru revealed an increase in the use of maize in a diet that had earlier relied heavily on shellfish (DeNiro and Epstein, 1978). These isotopic studies are in an early stage of development, but may provide vital information on the dates when cultivation began. The Viru isotopic analyses suggest that maize was introduced in the valley at least 200 years before archaeological evidence suggests that it appeared.

Stomach contents and feces provide unrivaled momentary insights into meals eaten by individual members of a prehistoric society. Dietary reconstructions based on these sources, however, suffer from the disadvantage that they are rare, and represent one person's food intake. Furthermore, some foods are more rapidly digested than others. But even these insights are better than no data at all. The stomach of Tollund man, who was executed around the time of Christ, contained the vegetable remains of a finely ground meal made from barley, linseed, and several wild grasses; no meat was found in the stomach contents (Glob, 1969).

Many American scholars have studied *coprolites* (human droppings) from dry caves in the United States and Mexico. Most analyses have consisted of dry sorting and microscopic analysis, but more advanced techniques are being developed. Robert Heizer and his colleagues analyzed numerous coprolites from the Lovelock Cave in central Nevada (Heizer, 1969). Most of the 101 coprolites analyzed contained bulrush and cattail seeds; they also showed that Lahontan chub from the waters of nearby Humboldt Lake were regularly eaten. Undoubtedly caught with fiber dip nets found in the cave, they were eaten raw or roasted. One coprolite contained the remains of at least fifty-one chub, calculated by a fish expert to represent a total fish weight of 3.65 pounds. Adult and baby birds, the water tiger beetle, and possibly freshwater gastropods were also eaten. Collecting vegetable foods seems to have been done casually. The remains of large mammals were not found in the feces. Identifying large mammals is particularly difficult, except from hairs or splinters of heavy mammal bones.

Coprolites have been analyzed, also, from stratified cave sequences in the Tehuacán Valley. A diet of grass seeds and a starchy root known as *Ceiba*, eaten as a starvation food, came into vogue at the beginning of the incipient agriculture stage; this diet continued in sporadic use almost up to the time of the Spanish conquest (Bryant and Williams-Dean, 1975). Maize is conspicuously absent from the Tehuacán Valley cave coprolites, as though the crop was grown for tribute purposes and not eaten by the inhabitants—or ground so finely that the meal was digested without a trace. There is always the possibility, too, that the cave dwellers were living in a marginal area where maize cultivation was impossible.

Recent coprolite studies in North America have analyzed pollen grains and parasites found in human feces. Fifty-four samples from Glen Canyon in Utah showed that the pollen ingested by their owners could yield valuable information on plants eaten, seasonal occupation, and even on the medicinal use of juniper stem tea (Bryant, 1974). Vaughn Bryant has recently analyzed coprolite pollen from a site near the mouth of the Pecos River in southwest Texas. He found that the inhabitants of the site between 800 B.C. and A.D. 500 spent the spring and summer months at this locality. During their stay they ate many vegetable foods, including several flowers. One danger of using pollen grains is that of contamination from the background pollen "rain" that is always with us. But Bryant was able to show that all but two of the species represented in the pollen were local plants. French archaeologist Henry de Lumley used pollen data from 400,000-year-old coprolites to determine that the Terra Amata Stone Age campsite near Nice was occupied in spring and summer (Lumley, 1969). In all these instances, too, valuable insights were obtained into minor details of prehistoric diet.

Basically, information on prehistoric diets comes from the analysis and the identification procedures described in this chapter. Because the ultimate objective is explaining how people lived in the past, new theoretical frameworks, systematic use of ethnographic analogy, and quantitative methods will, it is hoped, intensify research on the dietary requirements of prehistoric peoples.

In this chapter we have focused on food remains and subsistence, and not on the manufactured artifacts that also reflect the economic practices of prehistoric peoples. The next chapters deal almost exclusively with artifacts and with the patterning of artifacts. These often reflect specific human activities in the past, including ancient subsistence activities, and we will provide examples of those from time to time in the text that follows.

Guide to Further Reading

Binford, Lewis R. *Bones.* New York: Academic Press, 1981.
   A provocative essay on animal bones concentrating both on analysis and ethnographic analogy and faunal analysis.

Chaplin, R. E. *The Study of Animal Bones from Archaeological Sites.* New York: Seminar Press, 1971.
A summary of faunal analysis. Of wide general use.

Hole, Frank, Kent V. Flannery, and J. A. Neely. *Prehistoric Human Ecology of the Deh Luran Plain.* Ann Arbor: Memoirs of the Museum of Anthropology, 1969.
An exemplary report on human ecology among early agriculturalists in the Near East.

Olsen, Stanley J. *Osteology for the Archaeologist.* Cambridge: Peabody Museum, 1979.
A primer for archaeologists on bone identification and analysis, oriented toward the New World.

Renfrew, Jane. *Paleoethnobotany.* London: Methuen, 1973.
A primer on prehistoric vegetal remains that is oriented toward the Old World but has wide application. A useful introduction to this complex subject.

CHAPTER 15

ANALOGY, MIDDLE-RANGE THEORY, AND THE LIVING PAST

Preview

- The diversity of modern human societies provides us with a unique source of interpretative information about the past. For this reason, archaeologists have been studying living cultures as a means for better interpreting the archaeological record.
- Ethnographic analogy helps in ascribing meaning to the prehistoric past. Analogy itself is a form of reasoning that assumes that if objects have some similar attributes, they will share other similarities as well. It involves using a known, identifiable phenomenon to identify unknown ones of a broadly similar type.
- Early analogies were based on unilinear evolutionary schemes and involved direct comparisons between entire living and prehistoric societies. Today, most simple analogies are based on technology, style, and function of artifacts, as they are defined archaeologically. Such analogies, however, based as they are on people's beliefs, can be unreliable.
- Direct historical analogies and comparisons made with the aid of texts are common, but meaningful analogies for American and Paleolithic sites are much harder to achieve. One approach has been to devise test implications, using several analogies. This technique is based on the functional approach assuming that cultures are not made up of random traits but are integrated in various ways. Thus, analogies are made between recent and prehistoric societies with closely similar general characteristics.
- Middle-range research is carried out on living societies, using ethnoarchaeology, by experimental archaeology, and with historical documents. It is designed to create a body of middle-range

theory, objective theoretical devices for forging a link between the dynamic living systems of today and the static archaeological record of the past.

- Ethnoarchaeology is ethnographic archaeology with a strongly materialist bias. Archaeologists engage in ethnoarchaeology as part of middle-range research, in attempts to make meaningful interpretations of artifact patternings in the archaeological record. We examine examples of this research among the San, Australian aborigines, and Nunamiut Eskimo.

- Experimental archaeology seeks to replicate prehistoric technology and lifeways under carefully controlled conditions. As such, it is a form of archaeological analogy. Experiments have been conducted on every aspect of prehistoric culture, from lithics to housing. Archaeology by experiment rarely produces conclusive answers, but does provide insights into the methods and techniques used by prehistoric cultures.

In chapter 1, we described a new and exciting goal of archaeology: decoding the archaeological record, using the present in the service of the past, as Binford (1983) puts it. So far, we have considered the processes of archaeological research—data acquisition, analysis, and interpretation. It is now time to look more closely at the relationship between past and present, at what Lewis Binford calls "Middle-Range Theory," at analogy, ethnoarchaeology, and experimental archaeology. These are the tools archaeologists use to bridge the gap between the world of the past and the archaeological record of the present.

EARLY COMPARISONS

For well over a century, anthropologists have been working among non-Western peoples. They have recovered a mass of information of great interpretative value, much of it still buried in museum storerooms and archives. For their part, archaeologists have long recognized the value of comparisons between prehistoric and modern cultures. In Part I, we discussed the evolutionists of the late nineteenth century, who considered living tribes to be good examples of successive stages of development in culture history. Each stage of cultural development was correlated with a stage of technology, a form of the family, a kind of religious belief, and a type of political control that could be observed in some living group of people. Thus, the Australian aborigines, the Eskimo, and the San, who retained a hunter-gatherer lifeway, manufactured stone tools, and had no knowledge of metallurgy, were considered to be living representatives of Paleolithic peoples. British geologist W. J. Sollas wrote a bestseller entitled *Ancient Hunters* in 1911. In this famed work, he went so far as to equate the living Eskimo with the Magdalenians of Upper Paleolithic France, who had lived more than 14,000 years earlier. Many early investigators thought that the most primitive Stone Age peoples were matriarchal, had no government, and believed in numerous spirits. They believed it was perfectly in order to turn to the literature on Eskimos, or other living hunter-gatherers, for the "correct" interpretation of artifacts in the archaeological record.

This kind of simplistic comparison has been abandoned by Western archaeologists, who no longer believe in unilineal evolution. In the Soviet Union, however, unilineal schemes of evolution form an important part of Marxist-Leninist doctrine. Even recent Soviet archaeological monographs refer to the "correct stage of development" in order to interpret the social structure of archaeologically known peoples (Rudenko, 1961). For them, the first stage of prehistoric Eskimo culture was characterized by primitive communism and a matriarchal form of the family, when in fact modern anthropological observations record all known Eskimo groups as patrilocal. American sailors traded with the Eskimo, argues Rudenko, and so they became patrilocal!

ANALOGY

Analogy is a process of reasoning assuming that if objects have some similar attributes, they will share other similarities as well. It involves using a known, identifiable phenomenon to identify unknown ones of broadly similar type. It implies that a particular relationship exists between two or more phenomena, because the same relationship may be observed in a similar situation. Our abilities to reason by analogy are often tested in aptitude examinations by such questions as: "A fish is to water as a bird is to: (a) a tree (b) a house (c) air (d) grass seed." Obviously, if we grasp the relationship between fish and water, we will have no trouble completing the question. Analogy in archaeology involves inferring that the relationship between various traces of human activity in the archaeological record is the same as, or similar to, those of similar phenomena found among modern "primitive" peoples.

Archaeologists use analogy on many levels. In a simple one, someone infers that small, pointed pieces of stone are projectile points, because there are ethnographic records of peoples making small, pointed pieces of stone for the tips of lances or arrows. People often make use of an ethnographic name, such as *arrowhead*, as a label for an artifact. In doing so, they are assuming that their artifact type, which they recognize by attributes whose presence cannot be explained by natural processes, is identical in form to other, known arrowheads used by the people who made the artifact in question (Figure 15.1). But this simple analogy is a far cry from claiming similarities—or analogies—between the ways in which the prehistoric culture referred to used the arrowhead and the ways in which a living society uses it. To do the latter is to assume that the relationship between the form and function of the artifact have remained static through the ages. If you explain the past simply by analogy with the present, then you are assuming that nothing new has been learned.

Many archaeologists make use of analogies based on the technology, style, and function of cultures as they are defined archaeologically. Grahame Clark wrote an economic prehistory of Europe in which he made systematic and judicious use of analogy to interpret such artifacts as freshwater fish spears that were still common in historical European folk culture (Clark, 1952). This type of analogy is secure enough, as are those about small, pointed pieces of stone claimed to be arrowheads. Enough of these have been found embedded in the bones of animals and people for us to safely acknowledge that such tools were most likely to be projectile points. Still, we have no way of knowing if the points were part of ritual activity as well as the hunt. Similarly, the archaeologist will have information about how houses were constructed and what they looked like, what plants were grown and how these were prepared for food, and perhaps some facts on grave furniture. But the archaeologist will not know what the people who lived at this site *thought* a proper house should look like, or which relatives would be invited to help build a house, or what spirits were responsible

Figure 15.1 Eskimo demonstrating a sinew-backed bow and ivory-tipped arrow at Chicago's Columbian Exposition in 1893. Archaeologists often make use of an ethnographic name, such as *arrowhead*, assuming that their artifact type is identical to arrowheads used by the people who made the artifact. A simple example of analogy.

for making crops grow, and who in the house customarily prepared the food, or whether or not the people believed in life after death. Most analogies drawn from the ideas and beliefs of present-day people are probably inadequate (Thompson, 1956).

Archaeologists develop analogies in many ways. One approach is *direct historical analogy*, using the simple principle of working from the known to the unknown. In archaeological problems, the known are the living people with written records of their way of life, and the unknown are their ancestors for whom we have no written records. Text-aided analogies involve using written records to interpret archaeological data. Ivor Noël Hume, working at the Colonial settlement on Martin's Hundred, Virginia, found some short strands of gold and silver wire in the cellar filling of one of the houses. Each was as thick as sewing thread, the kind of wire used in the early seventeenth century for decorating clothing. Hume turned to historical records for analogies. He found European paintings showing military captains wearing clothes adorned with gold and silver wire, and a resolution of the Virginia Governor and his Council in 1621, forbidding "any but ye Council & heads of hundreds to wear gold in their cloaths" (Noël Hume, 1982). Using this and other historical analogies, he was able to identify the owner of the house as William Harewood, a member of the Council and the head of Martin's Hundred.

Then there are analogies for settlements occupied by peoples who had no knowledge of writing themselves but who were contemporary with literate societies. Their customs or affiliations may be mentioned in the written records of their literate neighbors. The Iron Age inhabitants of Maiden Castle in Dorset, England, although illiterate themselves, were subdued by the legions of a thoroughly literate Roman Empire; the conquerors left numerous traces of their campaigns, both in documentary records and in the archaeological record. Sir Mortimer Wheeler's classic account of the investment of Maiden Castle in the first century A.D. owes much to the Roman records of the conquest (Wheeler, 1943) (Figure 15.2).

According to the proponents of the direct historical approach, confidence in interpretation of past lifeways diminishes as we move from historic to prehistoric times. Analogies to living peoples become less and less secure as we grow remote from written records. Furthermore, the earlier the site, the more likely it is that site-formation processes and other variables have affected the patterning of artifacts, food remains, and structures in the ground.

Figure 15.2   Aerial photograph of Maiden Castle, Dorset, England, stormed by the Romans in A.D. 43, an event described through excavation by Mortimer Wheeler.

Nevertheless, many archaeologists have taken a *functionalist* approach to analogy.

Functionalist ethnographies integrate various aspects of culture with one another and with the adaptation of the culture as a whole to its environment. Functionalism stresses the notion that cultures are not made up of random selections of traits but that cultural traits are integrated in various ways and influence each other in fairly predictable ways. Much of processual archaeology, with its emphasis on adaptation and cultural systems, falls under the general title of functionalist archaeology. Functionalist thinking is evident in the way in which many archaeologists select analogies from the ethnographic data to help them interpret their archaeological finds. Because several ethnologically known cultures might provide reasonable analogies, functionally oriented scholars suggest selecting those which most resemble the archaeological culture in subsistence, technology, and environment—and those which are least removed from the archaeological culture in time and space.

We might want to know about the role of sandal making among the Great Basin Indians of 6,000 years ago. Were sandals produced by men, women, individuals on their own initiative, or by formal groups working together? If we consider sandal making an aspect of technology, we might turn to the ethnographic literature on Australian and San material, in which sandals are sometimes featured. Among both the San and the Australian aborigines, domestic tasks are generally done by women working alone or with one or two helpers. The analogy might lead us to argue that sandal making was regarded as a domestic task by Great Basin people and carried out by women who usually worked alone. On the other hand, weaving is men's work among the Pueblo Indians and is carried out in special ceremonial rooms; because much ritual performed there today reflects very ancient Pueblo Indian practices, we might be led to infer by analogy that the Great Basin people of 6,000 years ago did not regard weaving as domestic work, and so it was carried out by men. No matter what alternative we chose, we would probably not have much confidence in our choice.

The selection of possibly appropriate analogies from the ethnographic literature is increasingly being seen as only the first step toward interpretation. Once several analogies are chosen, the implications of each are explicitly stated and then are tested against the archaeological data. In our example of sandal making among Great Basin peoples, the ethnographic literature provided conflicting analogies. If we want to gain confidence in selecting one analogy or the other, we must state explicitly the implications each would have for the archaeological data and then examine the latter again in the light of each implication. If sandal making were a domestic task done by women working alone, we might expect to find the raw materials for sandal manufacture associated with tools that more surely represent women's work, such as grinding stones for food preparation. We might also expect to find tools for sandal making (such as awls and scrapers for preparing fiber) among the debris of more domestic sites. We could anticipate that women working alone might introduce more variation into the finished product than might be done in products made by group effort or by individuals working in the company of other specialists. A contrasting list of implications for the possibility that men produced sandals could also be made, and both sets could be tested against the archaeological data.

Devising test implications is not an easy task. To find a measure for the amount of variation in a finished product that one would expect under specific production conditions requires sophisticated measurements, various statistical tests, and often experimentation among groups of people. Archaeologists willing to make the effort entailed in this approach, however, have found that they are able to discover more about ancient societies than was previously thought possible. Reasoning by analogy is, of course, an important part of this process, but it is only one step in the archaeologist's task. Analogies provide the material from which test implications are drawn; they are no longer ends in themselves. James Hill used this approach at Broken K. Pueblo in Hay Hollow Valley, Arizona (1970). He analyzed the functions of the ninety-five rooms of the pueblo using sampling techniques and artifact patterning for the purpose. Then he turned to the ethnography of living Pueblo peoples, identified three room functions, and hypothesized that the different artifact patternings in Broken K. reflected the same three room functions. Hill now listed sixteen test implications based on the ethnographic data that could be tested against the excavated material. Testing suggested that most of his implications were confirmed.

Or were they? Although there can be no doubt that simple analogy is a highly effective method of interpreting sites with written records or artifacts that have a long tradition of use right into historic times, many centuries and millennia separate most prehistoric sites from the ethnographic present. Did the artifact patternings at Broken K. Pueblo actually reflect functions similar to those of modern pueblos? Recently, more and more archaeologists have been questioning the validity of ethnographic comparisons for the remote past.

TOWARD MIDDLE-RANGE THEORY

A great deal of archaeological analogy is based on guesswork, on the assumption that because an artifact is used in a specific way today, it was used in that way millennia before. The great contribution of the processual archaeologists has been not in their search for general laws, but in their insistence that independent data should be used to test and verify conclusions from surveys, excavations, and laboratory analyses. The basic objective in using hypotheses and deductions—scientific method if you will—is not to formulate laws, but to explore the relationship between past and present. This relationship is assumed to have two parts. The first is that the past is dead and knowable only through the present. The second is that accurate knowledge of the past is essential to understanding the present (Leone, 1982). Lewis Binford (1977, 1978, 1981b, 1983) has argued that conventional analogy based on guesses or hunches constitutes projection of the present into the past. By turning these guesses into testable hypotheses associated with theory, the projections into the past could be sorted out, according to their match against evidence that might represent their presence in the past. In other words, how do the image or images of the past we create match up against reality?

The great European archaeologist V. Gordon Childe was a past master in the use of analogy. His magnificent syntheses of European prehistory presented the progress of humanity from simple hunter-gatherers to farmers, and created a rich tie between prehistoric past and historic present. Childe wrote a historical narrative, full of generalized ethnographic analogy and based on Marxist assumptions about the rise of classes and their conflicts. It was possible for him to treat of European prehistory as though it was tied directly to the present, and many of his analogies stand. American scholars are dealing with an archaeological record that has a much more tenuous connection with the present. Childe looked back at the past with a Marxist perspective, in which ideology created and sustained the link between past and present. He realized that archaeology creates an image of the past, which is not necessarily inaccurate, but is a tie to the modern world, informed, Mark Leone says, "by modern uses." Students of American archaeology, and of the Paleolithic, which is remote from all of us, are faced with the same problem, but there are no ties with us. Thus the past is far harder to know. The only way in which this can be achieved is with rigorously tested analogies, based on thorough knowledge of the modern world. The hypothetico-deductive methods of processual archaeology are the scientific substitute for political ties created between past and present by Childe, and also for the human imagination's ability to make the past into any form of the present—as Childe did with his Marxist thinking. But whatever one's approach, the leading problem in archaeological analogy is to let the present serve the past. Processual archaeologists achieve this bargain by using middle-range theory, ethnoarchaeology, and controlled experiment.

The archaeological record is a static and contemporary phenomenon, but what archaeologists are interested in from the past is *dynamics*. As Binford (1983) wrote in one of his notebooks: "The archaeological record is contemporary; it exists with me today and any observation I make about it is a contemporary observation." How can one make inferences about the past unless one knows "the necessary and determinant linkages between dynamic causes and static consequences"? The dynamic elements of the past are long gone. Some of the answers could be obtained from ethnoarchaeology, the study of living peoples.

Ethnoarchaeology is the study of living societies to aid in the understanding and interpreting of the archaeological record. By living in, say, an Eskimo hunting camp and observing the activities of its occupants, the archaeologist hopes to record archaeologically observable patterns, knowing what activities brought them into existence. Sometimes historical documents can be used to amplify observations in the field. Archaeologists have actually lived on San campsites, then gone back later and recorded the scatter of artifacts on them or excavated them (Yellen, 1977). The earliest ethnoarchaeological work focused on specific artifact patternings, and on studies of hunter-gatherer encampments that might provide ways of interpreting the very earliest human encampments at Olduvai Gorge and elsewhere. But a major focus of later work has been to develop archaeological methods of inference that bridge the gap between past and present.

MIDDLE-RANGE THEORY

Binford (1977) coined the name *Middle-Range Theory*—a term already used in sociology—to characterize this new search. This theory seeks accurate means of identifying and measuring specified properties in past cultural systems. "We are seeking reliable cognitive devices; we are looking for 'Rosetta stones' that permit the accurate conversion from observation on statics to statement about dynamics," writes Binford (1981b). Proponents of middle-range theory are trying to build a frame of reference to give meaning to selected characteristics in the archaeological record, not simply by guesswork or folk analogy, but by theoretically grounded research.

Middle-range theory begins with these fundamental assumptions:

The archaeological record is a static contemporary phenomenon—static information preserved in structured arrangements of matter.

Once energy ceased to power the cultural system preserved in the archaeological record, a static condition was achieved. Thus, the contents of the archaeological record are a complex mechanical system, created both by long-dead human interaction and by subsequent mechanical forces, formation processes if you wish (Chapter 8)—lower-level theory (Schiffer, 1976).

To understand and explain the past, we must comprehend the relationship between static, material properties common to both past and present, and the long-extinct dynamic properties of the past.

This new body of theory is often described as "actualistic," and is designed to treat of the relationship between statics and dynamics, between behavior and material derivatives. It is actualistic because it studies the coincidence of both static and dynamic in cultural systems in the only time frame in which it can be achieved—in the present. Archaeologists have long wrestled with a body of general theory for observing and conveying meaning to the archaeological record. Middle-range theory is quite distinct from this body of theory, for it is tested with living cultural systems, and provides the instruments for testing the variables identified in archaeological theory. In other words, middle-range theory provides the conceptual tools for explaining artifact patternings and other material phenomena from the archaeological record. Michael Schiffer (1976) argues, in contrast, that the subject matter of archaeology is the relationship between human behavior and material culture in all times and places. Binford considers that the archaeological record is static and material, containing no *direct* information on the subject whatsoever (1981a, b). For a critique, see Raab and Goodyear, 1984.

ETHNOARCHAEOLOGY

Middle-range research is crucial to archaeology, whether one believes that this research is meant to specify the relationships between behavior and material remains or to understand the determinants of patterning and structural properties of the archaeological record. It is conducted by studying living systems (ethnoarchaeology), or by using historical documents or controlled experiments.

A few people are still uncomfortable with archaeologists going out to live with Australian aborigines, Eskimo, or San. Some prehistorians are even studying modern urban garbage, looking at contemporary rubbish-disposal practices of city dwellers. It is not that anthropologists are doing a bad job, it is simply that archaeology is beginning to think about the bases of the inferences it makes about the past.

Ethnoarchaeology is a form of ethnography that has a strongly materialist bias (Gould, 1978). Many archaeologists regard it as simply a mass of observed data on human behavior from which they can draw up suitable hypotheses to compare to the finds from their excavations and laboratory analyses. This interpretation is totally wrong, for in fact ethnoarchaeological research deals with dynamic processes in the modern world. Brain's study of the Australopithecine bone accumulations in South Africa was based on controlled observations of the dynamics of modern hyena lairs. He was able to show that Dart was wrong in assuming that the Australopithecines used bone tools: in fact, the bones had been fractured by predators. Several archaeologists have used modern predator data to try to identify the processes responsible for a bone deposit before they can interpret it. Wolves, hyenas, and lions seem to break up and accumulate bone assemblages in very similar ways. What varies is the frequency and amount of bone that they bring to their sleeping places. Studies like these permit much more accurate and informed inferences about ancient bone accumulations (Binford, 1983; Brain, 1981).

Ethnoarchaeology Among the San.   One interesting example of ethnoarchaeology comes from the Kalahari Desert of southern Africa, where Richard Lee has spent many years studying the human ecology of the !Kung San hunter-gatherers (Lee and DeVore, 1976). Lee spent a great deal of time observing the food-collecting and hunting habits of the San and accumulated a mass of information of great use to archaeologists. In one of his later expeditions, an archaeologist accompanied the research team and made detailed studies of butchery techniques and fractured animal bones and also drew plans of abandoned settlements of known age. John Yellen's research has yielded a wealth of facts on house and camp arrangements, hearth locations, census information, and bone refuse, all of which is fundamentally important to archaeologists in southern Africa (Yellen, 1977). He points out that a !Kung camp develops through conscious acts, such as the construction of windbreaks and hearths, as well as through such incidental deeds as the discarding of refuse and manufacturing debris (Figure 15.3). He recognized communal areas in the campsites, often in the middle of

Figure 15.3 A San camp in the ≠ Tum = /toa grove, Botswana, Africa, as plotted by John Yellen to show the layout of activity areas and artifacts. (After Lee and DeVore, 1976.)

Hut (circles show hut poles)   Firewood   Charcoal   Cracked mongongo nuts

Bone   Wild orange shells   Stone for cracking mongongo nuts   Smoking pipe

the settlement, which belonged to no one in particular, and family areas focused on hearths that belonged to individual families. The communal activities of the camp members, such as dancing and the first distribution of meat, take place in the open spaces that belong to no one family. Such activities leave few traces in the archaeological record. Cooking and food processing as well as manufacturing of artifacts normally take place around family hearths. Yellen points out some interesting variations on this pattern: manufacturing activities taking place at one hearth will sometimes involve people from other families; large skins will normally be pegged out for treatment away from main living areas because of vermin and carnivores. And activity areas are sometimes shifted around on hot days to take advantage of patches of heavy shade. Such activity areas can be identified on recently abandoned sites where a scatter of discarded mugongo nuts and charcoal fragments lies outside the encampment. The !Kung study showed that it is dangerous to assume that activities with the greatest archaeological visibility, such as meat preparation or cracking of nuts, take place in special places. In most !Kung instances, except for some small, temporary encampments where some specific and temporary food-gathering activities took place, manufacturing, food preparation, and other such activities went on within the family residence area of the campsite. The activity patterning at !Kung campsites relates, for the most part, diirectly to family groups. And, hypothetically, argues Yellen, it should be possible to use artifact clusters through time to study the development and evolution of such social structures.

Ethnoarchaeology in Australia.   A pioneer study of systematic ethnoarchaeology was carried out by Richard Gould in the Western Desert of Australia. He pointed out (1978) that most ethnographers study first the nature and transformation of whole cultures, but that the archaeologist as ethnographer considers sites as particular instances of patterned behavior. Gould observed some of the few remaining bands of nomadic, foraging aborigines in an area where he was searching for archaeological sites. Most of the sites were found with the help of aboriginal informants, who supplied valuable information on the people who had lived at the sites, their activities, and the sacred traditions associated with the settlements.

One such locality was Puntutjarpa Rockshelter, where excavations revealed a record of human occupation extending from modern times back to about 6,800 years ago (Gould, 1977). Indeed, the site is still visited by aborigines, although they no longer live there.

The stone implements at the site consisted of cores, flake tools, and smaller artifacts, which in their later forms were indistinguishable from modern Ngatatjara implements still in use today. Gould made detailed comparisons between the tools found in the rockshelter and modern examples. The local people use a simple technology of hafted and unhafted tools for cutting meat and skin and for wood-working. By examining traces of edge wear on modern stone tools and artifacts found at Puntutjarpa, Gould was able to demonstrate remarkable continuity between prehistoric and modern tools, and he could say that some of the implements that were more than 5,000 years old had been hafted, when no traces of the wooden handle survived. He also compared modern living surfaces with equivalent features found in the rockshelter (Figure 15.4). He attempted some tentative population estimates and came up with a figure of 3.55 persons per camp in the area. In the Western Desert, living archaeology could be brought to bear on at least three levels of archaeo-

Figure 15.4   Comparison of a prehistoric campsite at Puntutjarpa Rockshelter, Australia, at the right, with a modern aborigine campsite.

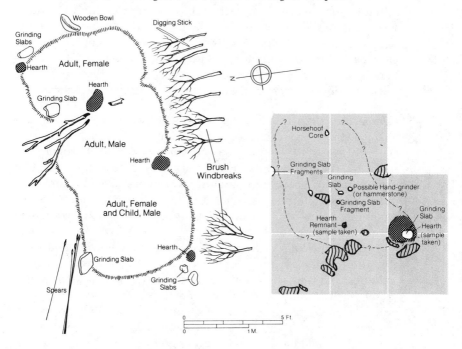

logical research. The first was the practical level, where the local people were able to direct Gould to sites and give him information on them. The second was the specific, functional interpretation of artifacts and living surfaces. The final level was that of general interpretation, where broad interpretations of culture history were attempted, taking form as general hypotheses about an Australian desert culture. Gould's work was successful because he combined archaeology and ethnography into a holistic, site-oriented approach, working with a site at which direct connections with modern peoples were still possible.

"Le Project de Garbage," Tucson.   Another form of middle-range research is being conducted on modern urban garbage in Tucson, Arizona, focusing on the relationship between material culture and social organization. University of Arizona archaeologist William Rathje has used the latest archaeological methods and research designs to investigate the relationships between resource management, urban demography, and social and economic stratification in a modern context, where some control data from interviews and other perspectives are available to amplify an archaeological study of the type that is conducted at an ancient urban center. The project has yielded remarkable results, showing how resource management varies from one segment of the city's population to another. Patterns of waste and consumption can be studied for different households, and the various trends show up clearly in the discarded food residues and artifacts.

Rathje and his colleagues found, for example, that the average middle-class Tuscon household wasted $100 of edible beef a year. White middle-class families ate proportionately more ham, lamb, pork, and chicken than black, American Indian, and Asian families. In contrast, lower-income groups consumed much more vitamins, liquor, and bread. The recently discarded refuse in Tucson revealed the surprising fact that high-income residences were associated with relatively little waste of food or artifacts and that it was the middle-income families that were the most wasteful (Rathje, 1979).

Most of the Tucson garbage research is based on modern artifact patterning, and its conclusions may have bearing on the study of prehistoric social organization. Rathje's work, however, does throw light on social organization within one society, whereas much other effort has gone into examining the evolution of social organization on a much larger scale.

Nunamiut Eskimo. Lewis Binford and his students undertook ethnoarchaeological studies to help begin construction of middle-range theory. He decided to study the Nunamiut Eskimo of Alaska, 80 percent of whose subsistence comes from hunting caribou. His aims were to find out as much as he could about "all aspects of the procurement, processing, and consumption strategies of the Nunamiut Eskimo and relate these behaviors directly to their faunal consequences" (Binford, 1978). He chose to concentrate on animal bones rather than artifacts, because although the bones were not human-manufactured, the patterns of their use were the result of cultural activity.

The Nunamiut depend more heavily on meat than any other hunter-gatherers known. Indeed, Binford estimates that each adult eats around a cup and a half of vegetable foods a year, supplemented by the partially digested stomach contents of caribou. In an environment that has a growing season of only twenty-two days, the Eskimo relies on stored food entirely for eight and a half months a year, and partially on it for an additional month and a half. Fresh meat is freely available for only two months a year. Binford soon realized that the strategies they used to feed themselves were based not only on game distributions but on other considerations as well. With such a heavy reliance on stored food, the problem of bulk was always important. Was it easier to move people to where fresh meat was available, or to carry the meat back to a base camp where precious stored food was kept? It is no coincidence that the Nunamiut move around most in late summer and early fall, when stored foods are at their lowest levels. The Nunamiut's lifeway involved complicated and interacting decisions that were related to the distribution of food resources at different seasons, the storage potential of different animals and of different parts of an animal, and also the logistics of procuring, carrying, and storing meat. All these and many other variables make up the cultural system of the Nunamiut. Binford points out that the linkage between the facts of animal anatomy and the realities of lifeway strategies among the people are the keys to any meaningful analysis of animal bones.

By close study, not only of the Nunamiuts' annual round of activities, but also of their butchery and storage strategies, Binford was able to develop indices that measured, in exhaustive detail, the utility of different body parts of caribou and described the butchering techniques, distribution of body parts, and methods of food preparation used. He showed that the people have an intimate knowledge of caribou anatomy, which is related to meat yield, storage potential, and consumption needs relative to the logistical, storage, and social needs of the moment. The field study also included analysis of forty-two archaeologically known locations that dated to earlier times.

The Nunamiut adaptation depended on long-term storage strategies that were keyed to two aggressive periods of caribou hunting in spring and fall. That they were able to hunt the caribou twice a year was a factor of the topography in their homeland, which lies close to the borders of both summer and winter caribou feeding ranges (Figure 15.5). The movement of the people was keyed to seasonal game movements and to storage and other needs. Fall hunting was directed toward calves, whose skins were used to make winter clothing. Small, mobile parties of Nunamiut would pursue them, knowing that their prey would yield not only skins but the added bonus of heads and tongues to feed the people who processed the skins. Without taking account of this fact, the Nunamiut were unable to maintain a viable cultural system.

What is the importance of the Nunamiut research? First, it provides a mass of empirical data on human exploitation of animals that is applicable not only to the Nunamiut and other caribou hunters, but also to the interpretation of different types of archaeological sites in many parts of the world. Binford showed how local any cultural adaptation is, that of the Nunamiut depending on interacting topographic, climatic, logistical, and other realities. These adaptations are so local that he was able to draw a number of important conclusions:

1. The continuing dynamics of a local adaptation can result in considerable variation in archaeological sites.
2. There may be considerable interregional variations within a culture, which are reflected in different archaeological remains. Yet the inhabitants of one site were well aware of the general cultural variations displayed at other sites nearby.
3. The adaptive strategies and the factors affecting the peoples' decision making may remain constant, even if the archaeological remains show great variability.
4. Perhaps most important, changes in stone-tool frequencies or pottery forms may reflect no significant change in adaptation at all. It is impossible to tell without understanding the strategies

Figure 15.5   The Mask site, a Nunamiut Eskimo hunting stand: (a) the hunting stand in its environmental setting; (b) caribou remains at the stand.

behind the local adaptation through time. And such understanding can be obtained only from sites where food remains and other such data are available.

"There is an unrelenting demonstration that the Nunamiut behave rationally in their treatment of animal foods," says Binford. "This rationality is facilitated by a truly remarkable knowledge of animal anatomy. It is facilitated by an outlook that is future-oriented. . . . The Eskimo are pragmatic, they are empiricists, and they are very skeptical of statements as to the 'right' way to do something."At the center of the Nunamiut's and, we may suspect, most other prehistoric peoples' lives, are judgments about their present situation relative to some desired end in the future.

The Nunamiut and other ethnoarchaeological studies show that archaeologists can no longer assume that all variability in the archaeological record is directly related to cultural similarity and difference. Binford's ethnoarchaeological work, and that of most other researchers in this field, is predominantly functional, behavioral, and ecological in its general approach. It has profoundly affected archaeological studies of prehistoric hunter-gatherers, not only the earliest hominids, but in areas like the Great Basin (O'Connell, 1975). It has led to such fundamental cross-cultural statements of possible predictive value as "Optimal Foraging Strategy" (Chapter 16). So far, the main influence of middle-range theory and ethnoarchaeology has been on the archaeology of hunter-gatherers (but see Kramer, 1982).

Ian Hodder (1982b) has taken a somewhat different structural and symbolic tack in ethnoarchaeological studies of farming and hunter-gatherer societies in tropical Africa. He studied the Nuba farmers of the Sudan and the Lozi of western Zambia, among other peoples. "Symbols are actively involved in social strategies," he writes. Every society, he believes, has a set of general conceptual principles that form a "structure" that runs through each society. Structuralism has long been debated in anthropology, but is new to archaeology. Under this approach, Hodder would have archaeologists looking for the principles and concepts that played a part in all social and ecological actions in individual ancient societies, a structure that affected the patterning of the material culture found in the archaeological record. It still too early to say what effect structural and symbolic approaches will have on archaeological research and the search for middle-range theory (for tentative examples, see

Hodder, 1982a), but it is certainly a healthy reaction away from the functional approach that dominated thinking in the late 1970s.

EXPERIMENTAL ARCHAEOLOGY

Controlled experiments with the dynamics of material culture can be a fruitful source of data to test middle-range theory. Experimental archaeology began in Europe during the eighteenth century, when people tried to blow the spectacular bronze horns recovered from peat bogs in Scandinavia and Britain. The exaggerated claims for the qualities of the horns fascinated the gullible public. One ardent experimenter, a Dr. Robert Ball of Dublin, Ireland, blew an Irish horn so hard that he was able to produce "a deep bass note, resembling the bellowing of a bull." Sadly, a subsquent experiment with a trumpet caused him to burst a blood vessel, and he died several days later. Dr. Ball is the only recorded casualty of experimental archaeology, for most modern experiments have been conducted with greater precision and perhaps less gusto (Coles, 1973).

Scientific archaeologists have been interested in experimenting with prehistoric technologies and lifeways ever since the early days of anthropology. As we showed earlier, much experimental effort went into stone toolmaking and the study of prehistoric stone technology by replication. One French archaeologist even went so far as to make stone tools by casting pebbles into a cement mixer! In a sense, the early stoneworking experiments were the product of academic curiosity, and it was not until the early years of this century that experimental archaeology involving stone tools took on more immediate relevance. One reason that it did was the capture and observation of Ishi, one of the last California Indians to follow a traditional lifeway.

Ishi. Ishi, the last "wild" Yahi Indian, was captured near Oroville, California, in 1913 (Kroeber, 1965). Fortunately, the story of his capture came to the notice of University of California anthropologists Alfred Kroeber and Thomas Waterman. They managed to assume responsibility for Ishi, who resided at the University Museum at Berkeley for four and a half years before he died of tuberculosis. Ishi became a local attraction, a living museum exhibit that brought hundreds of visitors to the campus. But he was far more than an exhibit; he proved to be a mine of information about the hunter-gatherer lifeway and about the simple technology that the Yahi had enjoyed. Kroeber, Waterman, and a doctor named Saxon Pope from the University of California Medical School accompanied Ishi to his homeland, and observed him as he stalked game and used his bow and snares. They acquired a mass of vital anthropological and linguistic information that would otherwise have been lost forever. Pope, an archery expert, not only apprenticed himself to Ishi, but also spent years studying bows and arrows in the museum collections. He subsequently published a monograph on the subject, which did much to make archery the popular sport it is today (Pope, 1923).

Stone Technology.   Ishi left a wonderful legacy to archaeologists, a mass of data that made people realize just how ignorant we were about prehistoric technologies. Only the sketchiest historical accounts of stoneworking and other craft activities survived in the records of early explorers. Some of the Spanish friars, notably Juan de Torquemada, saw Indian stoneworkers flaking obsidian knives. In 1615, he described how the Indians would take a stick and press it against a stone core with their "brest." "With the force of the knife there flies off a knife," he wrote. But, until recently, no one knew just how pressure flaking, as it is called, was done.

It was an Idaho rancher named Don Crabtree, who worked out some of the ways in which the Paleo-Indians had made the beautiful Folsom projectile points found on the Plains. He experimented for more than forty years and was able to describe no fewer than eleven methods of reproducing the "flute" at the base of the artifact (1966, 1972). Eventually, he came across Torquemada's account of pressure flaking and used a chest punch to remove flakes from the base of unfinished points gripped in a vise on the ground. The result was points that were almost indistinguishable from the prehistoric artifacts. Many others have followed in Crabtree's footsteps and have successfully replicated almost every kind of stone artifact made by pre-Columbian Indians. Stone tool edges can be so sharp that they are better than steel for delicate surgery. Some eye surgeons use commercially produced obsidian blades for this purpose, made under the quality-control supervision of an archaeologist!

Crabtree's long-term experiments raise a basic question: Does the production of an exact replica mean, in fact, that modern experimentation has recovered the original technique? The answer, of course, is that we can never be certain. Our hypotheses about prehistoric technology, however, are now on a firmer footing than ever before.

Criteria for Experimental Archaeology. Experimental archaeology can rarely provide conclusive answers. It can merely provide some possible insights into the methods and techniques used in prehistory; for many of the behaviors involved in, say, prehistoric agriculture have left no tangible traces in the archaeological record. But some general rules must be applied to all experimental archaeology. First, the materials used in the experiment must be those available locally to the prehistoric society one is studying. Second, the methods must conform with the society's technological abilities. Obviously, modern technology must not be allowed to interfere with the experiment. Experiments with a prehistoric plough must be conducted with a ploughshare made correctly, with careful reference to the direction of wood grain, the shape and method of manufacture of working edges, and all other specifications. If the plough is drawn by a tractor, the experiment's efficiency will be radically affected; thus, for accuracy, you will need a pair of trained, paired oxen. The results of the experiment must be replicable and consist of tests that lead to suggested conclusions.

Some Examples of Experimental Archaeology. One of the best-known instances of experimental archaeology is the *Kon-Tiki* expedition, on which Thor Heyerdahl attempted to prove that Polynesia had been settled by adventurous Peruvians who sailed balsa-log rafts across thousands of miles of ocean (Heyerdahl, 1950). He did succeed in reaching Polynesia, but his expedition merely showed that long ocean voyages in *Kon-Tiki* rafts were possible; he did not prove that the Peruvians settled Polynesia.

Most experimental archaeology is far more limited in scope. Many experiments have been done on clearance of forests in Europe and elsewhere. Stone axes have been surprisingly effective at clearing woodland, one Danish experiment yielding estimates that a man could clear 0.2 hectare of forest in a week. Tree-ringing and fire have been shown to be effective tree-felling techniques in West Africa and Mesoamerica (Shaw, 1969). Experiments with agriculture over eight or more years have been conducted in the southern Maya lowlands and the Mesa Verde National Park. The latter experiment lasted seventeen years. A hectare of heavy red clay soil was cultivated and planted with maize, beans, and other small

crops. Good crop yields were obtained in all but two of the seventeen years, when drought killed the young crop. The test revealed
how important careful crop rotation is to preserve the land's carrying capacity.

Housing experiments.   Houses of poles and thatch, logs, or hut clay
normally survive in the form of post holes, foundation trenches, or
collapsed rubble. Traces of the roof and information on wall and
roof heights, unfortunately, normally are lacking. But this absence
has not deterred experiments from building replicas of Mississippian houses in Tennessee, using excavated floor plans associated
with charred poles, thatching grass, and wall-clay fragments (Nash,
1968) (Figure 15.6). Two types of house, dating to A.D. 1000–1600,
were rebuilt. One of these was a "small pole" type with slender
poles bent over to form an inverted basketlike rectangular structure
with clay plaster on the exterior. Later houses were given log walls,
which supported a steep, peaked roof. In this, as in many other
instances, many details of the rafter and roof design are probably
lost forever. A logical next stage in housing experiments is to
observe how the structure decays. The Danes have carried out valuable observations on the decay of reconstructed "Neolithic" houses
at Allerslev, where they found that rising dampness was a major

Figure 15.6   Reconstruction of a Mississippian house.

cause of decay. Eventually, a house burned down by accident, and they excavated the pile of poles and rubble that resulted. The success of this experiment prompted the Danish Television Service to finance the reconstruction and destruction by fire of an Iron Age long house near Roskilde (Hansen, 1962). The foundation plan of a house excavated in 1937 was chosen as a model, and the complete structure was reconstructed. Thermocouples were placed at key locations to record fire temperatures, the timbers were marked with metal numbers, and domestic objects were placed inside the house. It was then burned on a windy day, with spectacular results. After thirty-five minutes nothing was left of the hut, which disintegrated completely except for the large upright posts. Six months later the archaeologists returned and excavated the remains. They recovered a floor plan that coincided remarkably closely with that of the original Iron Age house, as well as valuable information on the types of features, such as door frames, which could be identified by careful excavation and analogy with the Roskilde experiment.

Overton Down.   One of the longest experiments in archaeological interpretation is that of the Overton Down earthwork in England, which will last as long as 128 years. In 1960 the British Association for the Advancement of Science built an experimental earthwork at Overton Down, Wiltshire (Jewell and Dimbleby, 1966). The earthwork and its associated ditch were built on chalk subsoil, with profiles approximating those of prehistoric monuments. Archaeological materials including textiles, leather, wood, animal and human bones, as well as pottery were buried within and on the earthwork. The Overton Down earthwork was partly built with modern picks, shovels, and hatchets and partly with red deer antlers, ox shoulder blades, wicker baskets, and other prehistoric digging tools, in an attempt to establish relative work rates for different technologies. The difference was about 1.3:1.0 in favor of modern tools, mostly because modern shovels were more efficient. Overton Down was then abandoned, but small and very precise excavations of the ditch and bank were to take place at intervals of 2, 4, 8, 16, 32, 64, and 128 years. The digs were to be used to check the decay and attrition of the earthwork and the silting of the ditch over a lengthening period. The project will yield invaluable information of great use for interpreting archaeological sites of a similar type on chalk soils.

These are but a few of the classic examples of experimental archaeology, many of them long-term efforts that will yield valuable interpretative data for archaeologists well into the next century. It is these sorts of controlled experiments that will give archaeologists the objective data that will be needed to understand the static archaeological record, as studied in the dynamic present.

In this chapter we have described "living archaeology," a new and accelerating search for reliable methods of inferring past conditions from the archaeological record. Middle-range research is a quest for a scientifically built language that gives meaning to the archaeological observations, for methods that will enable us to evaluate our ideas about the past, and one day to make progress in answering the question of questions, not "what happened," but "why."

Guide to Further Reading

Binford, Lewis R. *In Pursuit of the Past.* New York: Thames and Hudson, 1981.
An account of living archaeology and "middle-range theory" for a more general audience. Strongly recommended for beginners.

———. *Nunamiut Ethnoarchaeology.* New York: Academic Press, 1978.
A descriptive monograph about ethnoarchaeology among caribou hunters. A must for the serious student.

Coles, John. *Archaeology by Experiment.* London: Heinemann, 1973.
An introduction to experimental archaeology with numerous examples, mainly from the Old World.

Gould, Richard A., ed. *Explorations in Ethnoarchaeology.* Albuquerque: University of New Mexico Press, 1978.
A volume containing many useful articles on ethnoarchaeology in many parts of the world.

Hodder, Ian, ed. *Symbols in Action.* Cambridge: Cambridge University Press, 1982.
Ethnoarchaeological studies in tropical Africa that are used to support a structural and symbolic approach to archaeology.

Yellen, John E. *Archaeological Approaches to the Present.* New York: Academic Press, 1977.
Ethnoarchaeology among the San of the Kalahari Desert. A technical work with broad implications.

CHAPTER 16 ✌

SETTLEMENT ARCHAEOLOGY AND SPATIAL ANALYSIS

Preview

- Settlement archaeology, the study of changing human settlement patterns, is part of the analysis of adaptive interactions between people and their environment.
- Settlement patterns are determined by many factors, among them, the environment, economic practices, and technological skills. Learned cultural skills and established networks of human behavior also affect settlement, as do practical political considerations, population growth, and social organization. Settlement archaeology involves examining the complex relationships between parts of a cultural system and the natural environment.
- Bruce Trigger defines three levels of settlement: the single building, the arrangement of structures within individual communities, and the distribution of communities across the landscape.
- Single structures can be studied from the perspective of form and material or from a functional viewpoint. Social and political institutions also affect the design of individual houses.
- A community is a maximal group of people that normally resides in face-to-face associations. The layout of communities is much affected by political and social considerations. The archaeologist looks for clusters of settlement attributes that may indicate a grouping of social units. Estimates of population are very difficult to obtain from even comprehensive archaeological data—there simply are too many intangible variables that affect the archaeological record.
- Prehistoric environmental data are obtained from both Pleistocene geology and from animal bones, especially those of small

mammals. Pollen analysis is one of the most effective methods of reconstructing ancient environments. We cite examples from Star Carr and Kalambo Falls to show how people adapted to environments that were very different from those of today.

- Site-catchment analysis is a method used to inventory resources within range of prehistoric sites. It is a study of the relationships between technology and available natural resources. We use examples from Israel and Oaxaca to demonstrate its applications.

- Site-distribution maps are used to study prehistoric settlement patterns; these are analyzed using rigorous, objective criteria, which take into account sampling errors and other variables. The objective of such analyses is to establish the factors that governed human settlement in prehistoric times.

- Spatial analyses in archaeology make use of a variety of techniques that were developed by geographers. They include central place theory, cluster analysis, and other concepts.

- Population estimates for prehistoric sites have been made by subjective guesswork, mathematical formulas, and sophisticated estimates of carrying capacity of the land. Such estimates rarely are precise.

- Population growth was a major factor in later prehistory. Most archaeologists agree with Thomas Henry Malthus that humanity's reproductive capacity far exceeds available food supplies. But Ester Boserup and her colleagues disagree, arguing that people intensify their food gathering or production efforts in the face of rising population. This controversy highlights the necessity for archaeologists to examine the many intangible variables that affect cultural change over long periods of prehistoric time.

In the preceding chapters we examined the ways in which archaeologists study artifacts and prehistoric subsistence and the various technologies that people developed to adapt to their environments. We also glanced briefly at some methods used to reconstruct the prehistoric environment itself. But what about the relationships between different prehistoric settlements and the environment? In this chapter we examine some of the ways in which archaeologists have studied changing settlement patterns in prehistoric times.

One of the pervasive theoretical frameworks for archaeology is that of cultural ecology, the study of the interrelationships between people and their environment. But "environment" covers not only the natural environment, but the social environment as well (Jochim, 1979). Technology and subsistence have leading roles in the study of prehistoric settlement patterns, and the research methods used rely heavily on both systems models and cultural ecology, as well as on large bodies of information manipulated by computers and quantitative methods.

SETTLEMENT ARCHAEOLOGY AND SETTLEMENT PATTERNS

Settlement archaeology, the study of changing human settlement patterns, is part of the analysis of adaptive interactions between people and their external environment, both natural and cultural (Chang, 1968).

Settlement patterns, the layout of human settlements on the landscape, are the result of relationships between people who decided, from practical, political, economic, and social considerations, to place their houses, settlements, and religious structures where they did. Thus, settlement archaeology offers the archaeologist a chance to examine not only relationships between different communities, but trading networks, the ways in which people exploited the resources in their environment, and social organization as well. The study of settlement patterns involves examining the degree to which human settlement reflects a society and its technology's adaptation to a specific environment.

Determinants of Settlement Patterns. Settlement patterns are determined by many factors: the environment, economic practices, and technological skills. Inherited cultural patterns and established networks of human behavior have an impelling influence on settlement patterns in some societies. The distribution of San camps in the Kalahari Desert depends on the availability of water supplies and vegetable foods; and ancient Maya settlements in Mexico were laid out in segments dictated by political and religious considerations.

Village layout may be determined by the need to protect one's herds against animal predators or war parties. Other settlements may be strung out at regular intervals along an important trade artery, such as a river. Even the positioning of individual houses is dictated by a complex variety of social, economic, and even personal factors that can defy explanation.

The determinants of settlement patterns operate on at least three levels, each formed by factors that differ in quality or degree from those which shape other levels (Trigger, 1968).

1. *The single building, or structure.* Houses, household clusters, and activity areas are minimal units of archaeological analysis.
2. *Communities.* The arrangement of single structures within a single group constitutes a community. The term community is defined as a "maximal group of persons who normally reside in face-to-face association" (Murdock, 1949).
3. *Distribution of communities.* The density and distribution of communities, whatever their size, is determined, to a considerable extent, by the natural resources in their environment and by the economy, nutritional requirements, and technological level of the population, as well as by social and religious constraints.

A critical part of settlement archaeology is understanding the factors that interact to determine a settlement pattern at any of these three levels. These factors can best be understood by referring to anthropological analogy with modern societies (see Chapter 15). And the ultimate objective of the exercise is to study prehistoric settlement systems as an aspect of the whole picture of a prehistoric society.

STRUCTURES AND COMMUNITIES

Structures.   Human dwelling places occur in infinite size and variety, from the crude windbreak of the Tasmanian aborigine to the magnificent palaces of King Henry VIII. Temples, fortifications, and even cattle pens are all forms of standardized structures. Domestic architecture may be standardized, or it may differ according to strict modes of variation dictated by a number of factors. The study of individual structures can be approached from several standpoints.

Form and material are among the major determinants of house design. For example, 20,000 years ago the mammoth hunters of the western Russian plains lived in semisubterranean dwellings with roofs made of skins and mammoth bones and with interior hearths (Klein, 1969). Theirs was a treeless, arctic environment, where protection from icy cold winds was vital. The people made use of the only abundant raw materials available to them—the bones and skins of the huge mammoths they hunted. In contrast, the Tonga peoples of the Middle Zambezi Valley in Central Africa, where the midday temperature is often over 100° Fahrenheit, and the nights are hot through most of the year, spend more of their lives in the shade of their pole-and-mud huts than they do inside them. Their dwellings therefore have thatched roofs that project far from the walls to form large and shady verandas (Reynolds, 1967) (Figure 16.1).

The nature of the raw materials used to build a structure affect not only its form but also its preservation in the archaeological record. Unfired mud brick was used throughout the Near East for house building, and it is still employed today. Once a house is abandoned, the unmaintained brick melts and reverts to clay. It took archaeologists generations to learn how to recover traces of mud brick houses from their matrix (Lloyd, 1963). As we saw in Chapter 11, wooden structures often leave no trace in the soil except, perhaps, post holes or foundation trenches.

Function radically affects house design, too. The earliest human

Figure 16.1   Tonga hut from the Middle Zambezi Valley, Central Africa.

beings lived in temporary brush shelters that reflected their mobile life-style and the fact that the nights were rarely cold. More sedentary communities, such as subsistence farmers in the Near East, built houses that combined a need for shelter with a need for storage and cooking facilities for each family.

Social and political organization can affect the design of structures also, for the size and layout of a dwelling can reflect the family organization of the occupants, as well as their social standing. A polygamous family may live in a house with several kitchen areas, each owned by a different wife. Sometimes, with controlled use of anthropological data, particular house types in the archaeological record can be related to specific forms of family organization. Within one house, a family unit can be distinguished only by interpreting the use of the artifacts found in it, in order to identify different rooms, especially cooking areas.

Many societies developed special architectural styles and structures that were associated with political or religious activities or with leadership. Classic Maya temples, exemplified by the pyramids at Tikal (Figure 16.2), provide an excellent instance of such structures. The plazas and pyramids were designed to create a sense of awe. Artisans' houses can be identified by distinctive artifact clusters, such as the potters' workshops found by James Mellaart at the early town of Hacilar in Turkey, dating to about 5300 B.C. (Mellaart, 1975).

Recovering Houses and Households. Evidence for individual houses and households is obtained by carefully excavating features, household clusters, and activity sets in the archaeological record. In many societies, limited economic opportunities and even distribution of wealth resulted in standardized floor plans. Such houses, which served as shelters for their occupants, provide the archaeologist, centuries afterward, with convenient analytic units, provided the house remains isolated from surrounding occupation debris. The variations between houses may reflect a variation between families in subsistence activities, social status, manufacturing activity, wealth, and so on.

Early Mesoamerican houses.   Between 1350 and 850 B.C. the one-room, thatched wattle and daub house became the most common dwelling type in Early Formative Mesoamerican villages. In the Valley of Oaxaca, Early Formative houses were generally rectangular. The floors were sand-covered and dug out from the subsoil,

Figure 16.2   Temple I at Tikal, Guatemala, which dates to about A.D. 700, an example of a ceremonial structure.

and the thatched roof was supported by pine posts. The puddled clay walls were smoothed and sometimes whitewashed (Flannery, 1976).

House contents.   In studying such houses, Kent Flannery and his colleagues distinguished carefully between the households themselves, the household cluster of associated features, such as storage pits and graves, and the various activity areas sometimes associated with them (Winter, 1976) (Figure 16.3). Many of the houses were swept clean before abandonment, but several contained accumulations of debris that included not only potsherds and bone tools but food remains as well. Marcus Winter broke down the house contents into at least five possible activities, including sewing and basketry (needles), cooking and food consumption (pots and food remains), and cutting and scraping (stone tools). He plotted the

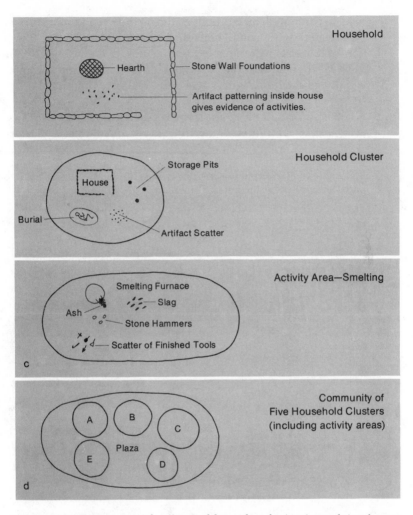

Figure 16.3 Various spatial units used by archaeologists in studying human settlement: (a) household; (b) household cluster; (c) activity area; (d) community.

house contents (Figure 16.3c) in an attempt to distinguish the craft activities of the family who occupied each dwelling.

Household cluster. It was possible for the archaeologists to isolate the household clusters in Oaxaca. These included bell-shaped storage pits large enough to hold a metric tone of maize; and some of them contained maize pollen and grinders. Human burials were associated with some houses, perhaps those of the family, but archaeologists were unable to prove it. The Oaxaca household clusters also included various types of ovens, refuse middens, and drainage ditches (Figures 16.4 and 16.5).

Activity sets (a set of artifacts associated with specific activities, i.e., a bow and arrow with hunting). Twenty-two household clusters were

Figure 16.4 Plan of a house at Tierras Largas, Oaxaca, *ca.* 900 B.C., with selected artifacts plotted on the floor.

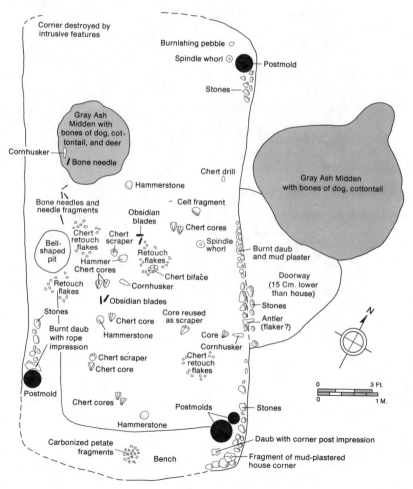

Figure 16.5 Features near houses at San José Mogote: storage pits, drainage canals, and a large cistern.

analyzed for traces of specialist activities. Food procurement, preparation, and food storage activities were common to all households; these were identified by grindstone fragments, storage pits, and jars, as well as by food remains. Every household chipped local stone and made baskets; but there were also signs of specialist activities. One large pit at Tierras Largas contained large quantities of pressure-flaking debris, while other household clusters yielded no such fine debitage. Perhaps this household boasted a part-time specialist who made fine stone artifacts for others.

The Oaxacan study offered some potential for identifying division of labor within a household and artifacts used by children rather than adults. Unfortunately, the excavated samples were too small for definitive study, but Figure 16.6, from Evon Vogt's classic study of the Maya of Zinacantan in Chiapas, shows some of the long-term possibilities (Vogt, 1967).

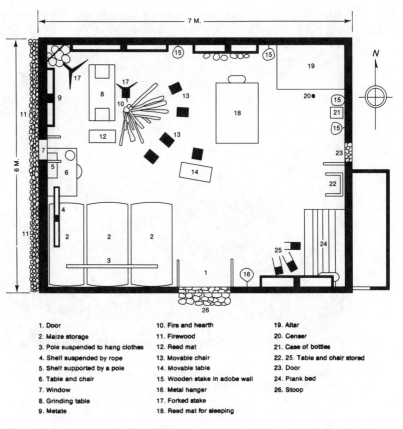

1. Door
2. Maize storage
3. Pole suspended to hang clothes
4. Shelf suspended by rope
5. Shelf supported by a pole
6. Table and chair
7. Window
8. Grinding table
9. Metate

10. Fire and hearth
11. Firewood
12. Reed mat
13. Movable chair
14. Movable table
15. Wooden stake in adobe wall
16. Metal hanger
17. Forked stake
18. Reed mat for sleeping

19. Altar
20. Censer
21. Case of bottles
22, 25. Table and chair stored
23. Door
24. Plank bed
26. Stoop

Figure 16.6   Modern highland Maya house from Zinacantan, Chiapas, Mexico, conceptually divided into male and female work spaces.

Communities.   Many variables act to determine the layout of communities, both large and small (Figure 16.7).

Environment and economy   limit the size and permanence of a settlement, because the ability to gather and store food is as important as the technology necessary to transport and process it into edible form. These two factors are vital, because they determine whether a community lives in one place permanently or must shift camp at regular intervals during the year. Preliterate 'Ubaid farmers in Mesopotamia (*ca.* 4500 B.C.) relied on simple irrigation agriculture. Because they had no need to move in order to achieve a stable subsistence cycle, they lived at the same location for centuries, forming large *tells* (Redman, 1978).

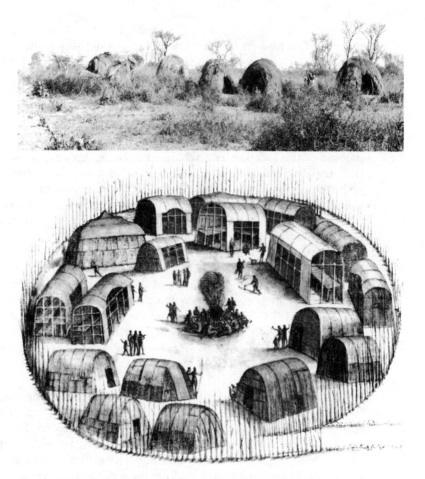

Figure 16.7   Examples of communities. Top: !Kung San winter camp at a water hole; Bottom: Algonquin village in North Carolina, painted by John White in 1585.

Social and political factors are also strong determinants, even in simple societies. Family and kinship considerations are important in camps and small villages. State-organized societies reserved special precincts for ceremonial centers, palaces, and official buildings where the business of the state was conducted (see Figure 16.2). Whole sectors of towns were sometimes reserved for minority religious groups or foreign traders living under the protection of the local ruler. These quarters may be reflected in the archaeological record by exotic objects, unusual architecture, or religious objects. At the trading port of Kilwa on the Tanzanian coast, the Sultan lived in a magnificent palace, a special precinct with its own mosque. The fine artifacts in the palace are not duplicated in any numbers elsewhere in the site, where a cosmopolitan population of Arabs and Africans lived and traded (Chittick, 1974).

Studying a Community: Teotihuacán. The behavior of a complete community, insofar as it can be discerned as having a pattern, is reflected in its artifact grouping and in the characteristic settlement pattern of the location as a whole—house design and layout, and the distribution of household clusters and activity areas. The archaeologist uses site survey and selective excavation, as well as sampling techniques, to look for systematic and statistical associations of settlement attributes—in the same way as for artifact attributes—that may reflect a grouping of social units.

The most ambitious settlement-pattern study of a community ever undertaken was really a study of many communities—George Cowgill and René Millon's survey of the Classic city of Teotihuacán in the Valley of Mexico, which flourished from *ca.* 250 B.C. to A.D. 700 (Millon, 1973). Their objective was to examine the changing settlement pattern of the urban complex during the vital period when the city was growing rapidly. How large was the population? How did it come into being? What was the social composition of the city, and how was it organized?

Cowgill and Millon spent years mapping and sampling the city (see Chapter 10). They found that it was built in four quadrants, following a master plan that was adhered to for centuries. The basic cruciform layout was established very early, when the great Street of the Dead (Figure 16.8) was laid out. The oldest part of the city lies in the northern quadrant, where most of the city's craftspeople lived. It contains many more structures than the southern quadrants, where exceptionally fertile soils, ideal for irrigation agriculture, are located. The archaeologists found that the city spread southward from the northern quadrant and that it was organized into neighborhoods, or *barrios*, groups of apartment compounds separated from one another. Teotihuacán's population may have reached a peak of more than 150,000 people in A.D. 600. More than 2,000 compounds contained thousands of standardized, one-story apartments sharing courtyards and temples with their neighbors. Some of these compounds contained large concentrations of obsidian flakes or potters' artifacts, and were identified as specialist precincts or groups of workshops.

There were foreign traders' quarters, too. One Oaxacan *barrio*

Figure 16.8   Teotihuacán, Mexico, Pyramid of the Sun.

seems to have flourished in the western part of the city, a compound where Oaxacan pottery and artifacts were common. The percentage of Oaxacan wares was very high in this area compared with other precincts, and Millon hypothesizes that there may have been an Oaxacan quarter in Teotihuacán for centuries.

A major objective of the Teotihuacán research is to understand the diverse internal workings of this remarkable city as a going organization throughout its long history. This result can be won only by comprehensive surveys that rely heavily on samples of artifact patternings and analyses of house contents and entire neighborhoods conducted all over this enormous site.

Analysis of Smaller Communities.   Communities much smaller than Teotihuacán can be investigated somewhat more easily, but

large amounts of archaeological data are still involved. Early Formative villages in the Valley of Oaxaca were investigated to test a
number of hypotheses about the relationships between parts of the
settlement. Were the villages subdivided into a number of *barrios*,
which are still an organizational unit in modern Indian communities that have well-defined communal and ceremonial responsibilities (Flannery, 1976)? By studying artifact patterns and inventories,
the archaeologists found traces of at least four residential wards at
San José Mogote, each separated from its neighbors by an erosion
gully where the trash was dumped. This larger village displayed
some different craft specializations between the wards.

In many smaller communities, the distinctions between zones of
the settlement may be inconspicuous. At Santo Domingo Tomalte-
pec in Oaxaca, Michael Whallon (1976) managed to isolate three
distinct zones in the village of four or five households, occupied
between 1150–1000 B.C. He found a cemetery, a zone with two
houses containing more trade goods, perhaps a "higher status residential area," and another zone with almost no imports. There was,
however, little separation between the zones. Unlike Teotihuacán,
the village had no formal layout, nor were any public buildings
discernible.

Population Estimates for Communities.   How does one estimate
community populations? Obviously, as in the Algonquin historical
villages (see Figure 16.6), written records can sometimes provide a
fairly accurate estimate. Modern censuses of villages and towns,
however, are of only marginal use, for many variables affect even
nineteenth-century population densities relative to those of prehistoric times. Some investigators have attempted to estimate population sizes with mathematical formulas that allocate so much living
space to each individual and each family. But again, one is dealing
with so many intangible variables, such as social restrictions, that it
is difficult to be accurate. Estimates of the rates at which people
accumulate refuse middens over long periods have also been used
to calculate population size (Cook, 1972; Zubrow, 1976), but this
method has the same serious disadvantages as the others
mentioned.

About the only reliable estimates of population are based on the
number of households at any one moment in a community's history. Millon's guesses about Teotihuacán's population are based on
such house counts. Using samples of early Mesoamerican village
households, Joyce Marcus (1976) showed that perhaps 90 percent

were small hamlets with from one to ten or twelve households and up to sixty people. But some villages were much larger than this average. The contemporary Olmec site of San Lorenzo in Vera Cruz may have housed as many as 1,200 people. Thus, you can see that this method, too, is far from accurate.

Community population estimates are important, because they can give insights into the maximum size that a settlement can achieve. What, for example, was the maximum size that early Mesoamerican hamlets and villages could reach before further growth was impossible? Characteristically, societies that were not organized in large states tended to live in small villages, which frequently split off from one another as further growth at the mother settlement was cut off. This process is straightforward enough, and in Formative Mesoamerica many villages split off in just this manner. But others, such as the Olmec settlement at San Lorenzo, were able to grow larger and still remain viable settlements. Why was this growth possible? The search for explanations of evolving settlement patterns takes us on to a broader area of research, the layout of communities against the background of their natural environment.

RECONSTRUCTING THE NATURAL ENVIRONMENT

The density and distribution of communities, whatever their size, are determined, to a considerable extent, by the natural resources of the region in which they flourish and by cultural factors. The requirements of hunter-gatherers, for example, differ from those of agriculturalists, and those of cattle herders are different from both. In Africa, the distribution of cattle is determined by zones of tsetse-fly infested country, for the insect's bite is fatal to stock and dangerous to humans. Pastoral populations tend to concentrate their settlements in grassland areas that are free from these flies and where good fodder and abundant standing water are available (Clark, 1967).

By the same token, the settlement patterns of agricultural populations are determined by equally critical factors. Such shifting cultivators as the Bemba farmers of northern Zambia have an understanding of their environment that is astonishingly detailed. They can rate a garden's fertility and its suitability for different crops by examining the vegetational cover and the soil's physical characteristics. Critical factors are the land's staying power, the number of seasons during which it can be cropped with satisfactory results, and the fallow period required before it can be reused. As land is exhausted, the Bemba use new or regenerated plots and move their settlements accordingly (Allan, 1965). Like the Bemba, the archaeologist has to achieve detailed understanding of the environmental variables that affected prehistoric settlement patterns.

The dynamics of human behavior are closely tied to those of the natural environment, the dynamics of such resources as soils, plants, and animals. The changes and patterns of behavior in these resources are just as variable as those of human populations, and they condition the way in which people plan their hunting-and-gathering activities and plant their crops. Increasingly, archaeologists are becoming involved not only with cultural ecology but also with modern ecological research on feeding activities, energy inputs and outputs, and data on the ways in which modern populations utilize natural resources (Hardesty, 1977; Jochim, 1979).

By way of illustration, the hunter-gatherers of the Tehuacán Valley in Mexico are known to have concentrated in larger camps during the wet season and to have dispersed over a much wider area in smaller settlements during the months of the dry season. Their food-procurement activities were scheduled carefully from season to season (MacNeish, 1978). These activities, in terms of energy maximization and specialization and clustering of population, are much better understood now that archaeologists are beginning to use the concepts of modern ecology.

A viable concept of environment that an archaeologist can adopt is that it must be considered a dynamic factor in the analysis of archaeological context (Butzer, 1982). Archaeology has a four-dimensional spatial and temporal context that consists of both a cultural and a noncultural environment. The ultimate goal of environmental archaeology is to understand the relationship between culture and environment. The primary goal of environmental archaeology is to define the characteristics and processes of the biophysical environment. This environment is the matrix for the interaction that occurs between socioeconomic systems and the natural environment. Another objective is to understand the human ecosystem that is defined by the interaction between the environmental and human systems. Archaeological sites, or distributions of them, are part of the human ecosystem, a useful conceptual framework for examining such interactions (Butzer, 1982).

Butzer (1982) considers that environmental archaeology has five major themes, which are common to geography and biology as well, but are especially important in the study of prehistoric human ecology:

Spatial patterning, both of natural and human phenomena, is amenable to spatial analysis.

The *size* and *scale* of both environmental and human phenomena can be measured, also through spatial analysis.

The *complexity* of both environments and human communities can vary greatly and must be defined and delimited.

Human and *nonhuman communities interact* in any complex environment where the distribution of resources is uneven. They interact internally and with one another, as well as with the nonliving environment. This interaction takes place on many levels and at changing or unequal rates.

Equilibrium between human societies and their environments are an ideal that is almost never achieved. Thanks to constant negative feedback resulting from both internal and external processes and inputs, they are constantly in a state of environmental readjustment.

Environmental Systems.   Environmental systems provide the spatial and temporal frameworks within which human societies flourish. These are some key ecological concepts.

Human societies are part of the *biosphere,* which encompasses all the earth's living organisms interacting with the physical environment. The biosphere is organized both vertically and horizontally, with genes and cells at the base and organisms, populations, and communities above them. The community, all the biological populations in an area, functions together with the nonliving environment in an ecosystem.

Biomes are the largest terrestrial communities, major biotic landscapes on earth in which distinctive plant and animal groups live in harmony. *Habitats* are the areas within a biome where different populations and communities flourish, each with hundreds of individual *sites,* specific locales each with its own immediate setting. There are often transition zones between habitats that are areas of considerable importance to human communities exploiting specific resources such as obsidian or salt. These are known as *ecotones.*

Ecology is a study of functional relationships rather than genetic or phylogenetic ones. This difference is reflected in the concept of the ecological *niche,* the physical space occupied by an organism, its functional role in the community, and how it is constrained by other species and external factors.

Every ecosystem is maintained by the regulation of trophic levels (vertical food chains) and by patterns of energy flow (Figure 16.9). The complexities of even modern ecosystems make them difficult to study empirically; prehistoric ones are impossible to reconstruct. But the broad conceptual framework of the ecosystem serves as a very useful research tool for archaeologists.

Figure 16.9 A simplified energy cycle for an environmental system. After Butzer, 1982.

Perspectives

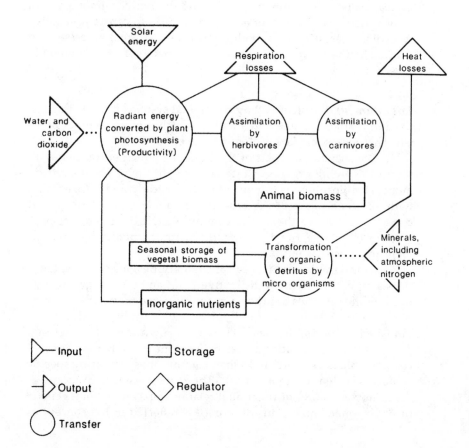

Human ecosystems differ from biological ecosystems in many ways. Information, technology, and social organization all have much greater roles. Human beings, both as individuals and as groups, have unique capacities for matching resources with specific objectives. They not only think objectively about such matching, but also transform the natural environment to meet their objectives. As Figure 16.10 shows, value systems and goal orientation are important to human ecosystems, as are group attitudes and decision-making institutions, especially in more complex societies. Any attempt to reconstruct prehistoric environments must take account not only of environmental resources and constraints, but of the ways in which human beings utilized resources and intervened in the environment and changed it.

Geoarchaeology and Other Approaches.   Archaeological research using the methods and concepts of the early sciences, or *geoarchaeology*, is a cornerstone of environmental reconstruction (Butzer, 1982). This is a far wider enterprise than merely geology, is deeply

Figure 16.10 A much-simplified energy cycle for a human ecosystem. This chart does not include provisions for storage of food and other resources. After Butzer, 1982.

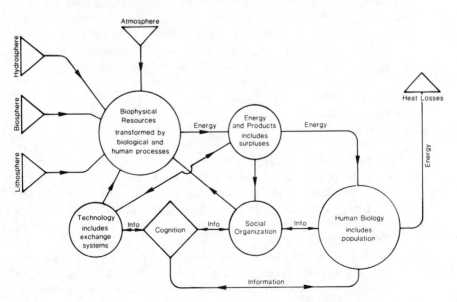

enmeshed in the planning and execution of both surveys and excavations, and encompasses at least five major approaches:

1. Geochemical, electromagnetic, and other remote-sensing techniques to locate sites and features (Chapter 10).
2. Studies of site-formation processes and of the spatial context of
   a site within its habitat (Chapter 8).
3. Development of methods for differentiating cultural from natural features. This distinction includes disturbances due to biological, geological, and pedological processes since sites were
   occupied.
4. Relative and chronometric dating to establish chronological contexts both in and outside a site (Chapters 6 and 7).
5. Reconstructing the ancient landscape by a variety of paleogeo-
   graphic and biological methods. These include pollen analysis
   and phytolith studies (Chapters 6, 14).

Until recently, geoarchaeology was little more than a battery of
techniques, many of them either developed and used by nonarchaeologists or used as a sideline. This was an ineffective approach,
for nonarchaeologists have little appreciation of prehistoric human
activities. People are geomorphic agents, just like the wind is. Accidentally or deliberately, they carry inorganic and organic materials
to their homes. They remove rubbish, make tools, build houses,
abandon tools. All these mineral and organic materials are subjected to all manner of mechanical and biochemical processes during occupation and after the site is occupied. The controlling geomorphic system at a site, whatever its size, is made up not only of
natural elements, but of a vital cultural component as well. And the
geoarchaeologist is involved with archaeological investigations
from the very beginning, and deals not only with formation of
sites, and with the changes they underwent during occupation, but
also with what happened to them after abandonment.

In the field, the geoarchaeologist is part of the multidisciplinary
research team, recording vertical profiles within the excavation and
in special pits close by, to obtain information on soil sediment
sequences (Butzer, 1982). At the same time, he or she takes soil samples for pollen and sediment analyses, and relates the site to its
landscape by topographic survey. Working closely with survey
archaeologists, geoarchaeologists locate sites and other cultural features on the natural landscape using aerial photographs, satellite
images, and even geophysical prospecting on individual sites. As
part of this process, they examine dozens of natural geological

exposures, where they study the stratigraphic and sedimentary history of the entire region as a wider context for the sites found within it. Back in the laboratory, maps and soil samples are analyzed. Studying the sediments in the site, they work out the microstratigraphy of the site relative to that of the surrounding area (Figure 16.11), and analyze the deposits for such properties as pH and organic content to establish the effects of human activity on the sedimentary sequence at the site. The ultimate objective is to identify not only the microenvironment of the site, but that of the region as a whole—to establish ecological and spatial frameworks for the socioeconomic and settlement patterns that are revealed by archaeological excavations and surveys.

Geoarchaeology is a highly technical field, requiring expert skill in many procedures ranging from palynology to isotopic analysis. But it is far more than geology in the service of archaeology, or merely a collection of scientific methods used to study prehistoric remains. It is an integral part of the settlement archaeology process, even if many of its research procedures are the province of specialists.

In addition to geoarchaeology, both animal bones and paleobotanical finds can yield important information on prehistoric environments, especially if combined with other approaches. Pollen analysis has proved useful for this purpose, and has sometimes provided reconstructions of the surroundings of prehistoric sites, as well as measures of the effects of human activities like agriculture on the natural vegetation (Iversen, 1941). Thousands of tiny pollen grains and waterlogged wood fragments found in the deposits of the 10,000-year-old hunter-gatherer site at Star Carr, England, showed that the occupants had thrown down a tiny birch platform in some lakeside reeds. The site was surrounded by birch trees that came down to the water's edge. Some pine and willow trees grew nearby, and water plants and fungi were common (Clark, 1954, 1972) (Figure 16.12).

(Readers interested in a detailed summary of geoarchaeology should read Butzer, 1982.)

Inventorying Environmental Resources. Cultural adaptation to any environment can be understood only in the context of two categories of data: the ancient environment and resources available therein, and the technology of the culture being studied. Once these data are on hand, the archaeologist can proceed to establish which subsistence and economic options the people chose, given

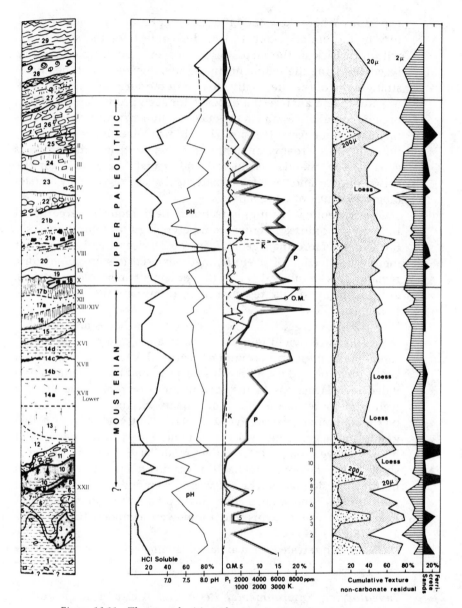

Figure 16.11   The complexities of microstratigraphy. A composite archaeose-dimentary profile for Cueva Morin, a Paleolithic cave in northern Spain. The different sedimentary classes form the vertical columns; the actual strati-graphic layers appear at the left. After Butzer, 1982.

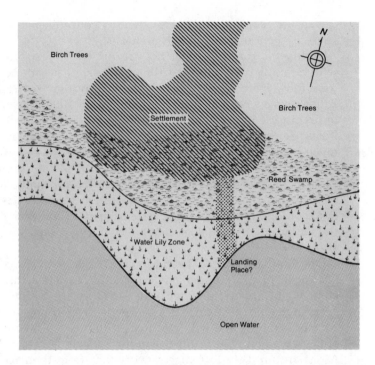

Figure 16.12   Reconstruction of the vegetational surroundings of the Star Carr site in England.

the available resources and their technological ability to exploit them.

It is easy enough to make an inventory of the natural resources available in any area, but it is not sufficient merely to list them, for it is the ways in which they can be exploited—the seasons of availability of vegetable foods, the migration patterns of game, and the months when salmon runs take place—and not just the resources themselves that are significant. These many variables, to say nothing of soil distributions, rainfall patterns, and distributions of valuable raw materials, determine the critical element of a settlement pattern—the carrying capacity of the land.

Carrying capacity is the number and density of people that any tract of land can support. It is a flexible statistic that can be affected by factors other than those of the available resources in an area. People can alter the carrying capacity of their land by taking up agriculture, or by cultivating a new crop that needs deeper plowing and thus exhausts the land faster. Or the introduction of fertilizer can enable people to settle permanently in one village because their lands are kept fertile by artificial means.

Prehistoric carrying capacities are difficult to establish, except with carefully controlled experimental data, such as those obtained for southwestern agriculture and Maya cultivation (see Chapter 15). Attempts have been made to measure the amount of meat available to prehistoric hunters in the Mississippi Valley (Smith, 1974), and it has been clear for some time that Classic Maya populations were much larger than those which could be supported from the felling and burning of forest gardens (Adams, 1977). One problem has been that earlier settlement models were far too simple to accommodate the complexity of the data. Recent research has concentrated on resource inventories, systems models, and even computer simulation of the variables that affect carrying capacity (Hodder, 1978).

One approach that has been tried is *site-catchment analysis*, which is difficult to apply under modern conditions when the environment is not greatly modified. It is based on the assumption that every human settlement has a *catchment area* around it. This is a zone of domestic and wild resources within easy walking distance of the settlement. The !Kung San of the Kalahari Desert in Southern Africa are unlikely to forage much father from their base camps than 10 kilometers, a comfortable day's walking distance. The fundamental assumption then is simple: the farther the resources in an area are from a site, the less likely they are to be exploited.

Most site-catchment studies, like those done in the Mount Carmel area of Israel in the 1960s, were rather generalized, little more than broad statements about resource availability (Vita-Finzi and Higgs, 1970). More recent studies, like those by Kent Flannery and others in the Valley of Oaxaca, Mexico, have focused on individual sites where rigorously analyzed data from households and communities are available for comparison. At San José Mogote, a village occupied between 1150 and 850 B.C., Flannery wanted to know from how far away the villagers obtained their animal and plant resources. He tested the various resources: those from within the village (turkeys, stored maize, edible fruit); those from the river, 1 kilometer away (reeds, sand, mud turtles); those on the high alluvium, within 2 to 5 kilometers (maize and other crops); those on the piedmont, 0 to 5 kilometers away (seasonal vegetable foods); and those in the mountains, 5 to 15 kilometers distant (hut timbers, game, and firewood). Mineral resources—essentials such as salt, chert, and pottery clay—were obtained from 3 to 50 kilometers away. Pacific marine shells, freshwater mussels, jadeite, and other exotic substances and objects came from distant regions, perhaps as far as 200 kilometers away.

San José Mogote thus needed a circle of under 2 to 5 kilometers to satisfy its basic agricultural needs, 5 kilometers to supply basic minerals and seasonal wild vegetable foods, and 15 kilometers for game meat and construction materials. Exotic trade materials and ceremonial life required occasional collecting trips of up to 50 kilometers from the settlement and some contacts with even greater distances. When Flannery plotted the San José Mogote catchment areas relative to those of the neighboring Early Formative villages, he found that the innermost circles (2 to 5 kilometers) of one village did not overlap those of any other village, but that wider circles did, as the exclusive possession of catchment areas was progressively reduced. Once the 50-kilometer ring was reached, all the villages of Oaxaca shared a common catchment area. Seasonal campsites were placed at strategic points on the outer rings, places where hut timbers, game, and trade materials were collected, perhaps by three or four villages sharing the same area. Such temporary camps were annexes to the main villages, providing more ready access to resources, which were, in their way, as important as those in the inner rings.

Site-catchment analysis is a very general way of assessing resources, but not one that can provide fine-tuned data, except where the environment has been unchanged for many centuries (Roper, 1979).

SITE DISTRIBUTIONS AND INTERACTIONS

The distribution of natural resources in the environment was but one determinant of settlement patterns. As human societies became more complex, so too did the interactions between them; and these interactions were reflected in evolving settlement patterns. The study of entire settlement patterns brings into play a number of basic research methods that require large quantities of archaeological data.

Distribution Maps. The distribution map, which plots site distributions against the environmental background, has been used by archaeologists for a long time. One of the early pioneers in this field was the Englishman Sir Cyril Fox, whose classic monograph, *The Personality of Britain* (1932), plotted archaeological sites against base maps of the reconstructed prehistoric vegetation and modern topography. Other studies soon followed, as people found that prehistoric settlement patterns did tend to coincide with many environmental zones.

Distribution maps, and the settlement patterns plotted on them, are normally derived from aerial photographs and ground reconnaissance. As such, they are subject to several obvious sources of error, among them the location of archaeologists in the field, site destruction by modern construction, and the difficulties of dating sites without excavation. Most early interpretations of distribution maps were based on "eyeballing" distributions to show, using radiocarbon dates, the direction of spread of a culture trait, such as a sword type, or to explain how a scatter of site clusters came to take shape on the landscape. Obviously, however, such impressionistic interpretations are far too superficial.

Ultimately, the objective is not only to describe the distribution or settlement pattern itself, but to look at the factors that generated the settlement pattern in the first place. These factors cannot be deduced from archaeological evidence alone, but they can be deduced by computer simulations or statistical techniques of probability.

SPATIAL ANALYSIS

Any attempt to analyze a settlement pattern must begin with development of a site typology. Such a classification should provide objective criteria for separating sites on the basis of size, function, and other features. Archaeologists in the Valley of Mexico, for example, use a local classification that distinguishes between primary and secondary regional centers, nucleated and dispersed villages, hamlets, camps, and residences, on the basis of population size, architecture, and other specific criteria. Each of these site types has a relationship to the others; the sites form a constellation that makes up a settlement pattern on a local, regional, and even a continental level. And the precise definitions of site types—ceremonial centers, villages, and so on—supply us with an explicit administrative hierarchy, a series of successive levels of settlement that organizes our patterns of dots on the map hierarchically (Figure 16.13).

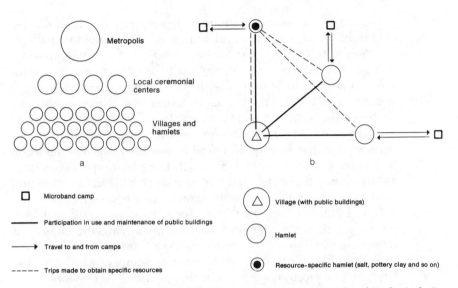

Figure 16.13 (a) A hypothetical population pyramid of archaeological site types. (b) A simplified diagram showing possible and hypothetical interactions between different Early Formative settlement types in the Valley of Oaxaca.

This hierarchy raises the fundamental question: What were the rules that shaped it on the landscape?

Site-Distribution Analyses. Our thinking about site hierarchies, settlement spacing, and hypothetical rules of settlement patterning depends on accurate distribution information, and even more important, on one's evaluation of the significance of the various "clusters" of sites that can be discerned on the map. Are these clusterings accidental, the result of deliberate human planning, or due to modern factors?

A number of statistical techniques can be used to analyze site distributions, most of them borrowed from geographers. David Thomas used a method called *cluster analysis* to study socioeconomic patterns in the Great Basin, where he found striking differences in site distributions. He discovered that "harvesting village and rabbit-driving implements are in a clumped distribution, while hunting artifacts tend to be distributed over piñon-juniper and upper sagebrush-grass zones." He was able to compare the theoretical distributions of the artifacts with his observed patterns (Thomas, 1969, 1976).

Other approaches include *point-pattern analysis,* in which site distributions are plotted on a grid and tested for nonrandom patterning (Figure 16.14). The *nearest-neighbor statistic* of the geographers is another. It has been used experimentally on Olmec sites as a test for measuring the intensity of a settlement pattern (Earle, 1976; Earle and Ericson, 1977). Timothy Earle found that Olmec ceremonial centers were spaced at regular intervals in territories that were 44 kilometers in diameter, with lesser centers within each territory. He tried to use that statistic to examine the intensity of interaction between major and minor centers. All these techniques are still in an experimental stage, and all require sophisticated statistical manipulations and data of meticulous quality to be effective.

One essential ingredient for understanding settlement patterns—which Earle attempted to find in studying the Olmec—is knowledge of how site hierarchies came into being and of the intensity of interaction between the inhabitants of each site type. One useful concept for this end is that of *central-place theory.*

Central-Place Theory. Central-place theory, which was first developed by the German geographer Walter Christaller (1933) in a study of southern German communities, is a series of statements about the relationship between settlement systems. Christaller

Figure 16.14 Three possible models for archaeological distributions: (a) A random distribution, with the points scattered at random. All points have an equal probability of being located at any given place on what is assumed to be a featureless landscape. (b) Clusters of points, representing artifacts or sites grouped in clumps. Distributions in clumps can occur when people are attracted toward a valuable resource or when a village, for example, generates new settlements that are located nearby. An extreme example is, of course, a distribution in which everyone is located at the same point. (c) A spaced distribution, which has the sites or artifacts at more-or-less regular intervals. Here, people are spaced at regular intervals because they are competing with each other for resources or in some other way.

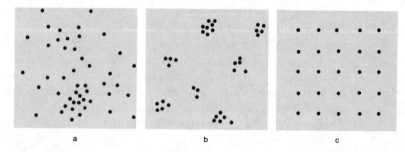

a   b   c

stated that "if the population distribution and its purchasing power, as well as the topography, its resources, and transport facilities, are all uniform, then all central places providing similar services, performing similar functions, and serving areas of equal size, will be spaced at an equal distance from one another."

After this general definition, Christaller went on to develop a hierarchy of central places, which divided groups of centers of decreasing size and facilities into various hierarchical groups. In these hierarchies it was assumed that there were fewer large places than small ones, which provided the widest range of services possible. The largest places performed not only the services of the smaller ones, but they also performed central functions that distinguish them from their lesser neighbors.

The simple Christaller model has been modified by later research to allow the size of a service area to vary with the size of the central place that services it. Under this arrangement, the central-place function of Teotihuacán, for example, affects a much larger area than that serviced by smaller service centers lying within, say, twenty miles of the city. The latter merely duplicate services available at Teotihuacán and are less likely to develop close to the city than they are to develop close to one another. Behind these modifications is the assumption that the location of any form of center will be determined, at least in part, by convenience to its clients. It will be located where it can be reached with minimal effort.

Ideally, a single service center that provides multiple services to a surrounding population situated on a flat plain will service a circular area, with the center located in the middle. But, when there are several types of central place, each fulfilling different functions within a region, then the most logical shape of service territory would be a hexagon.

The hexagon is a theoretical configuration, to be sure, but it does reflect the essential regularity of service areas. This shape of territory minimizes the distance to the centers from the boundaries of the area and keeps population movement to a minimum (Figure 16.15). This model has been tested using southern English market towns, which were spaced 6 to 10 kilometers (4 to 6 miles) apart in medieval times, a convenient day's journey by cart from the surrounding rural villages. Indeed, a twelfth-century law expressly forbade placement of markets closer than 10 kilometers apart. Although Ian Hodder and Mark Hassall (1972) have shown that a hexagonal model works relatively well when applied to Romano-British towns, this spacing cannot be claimed as a universal law, for

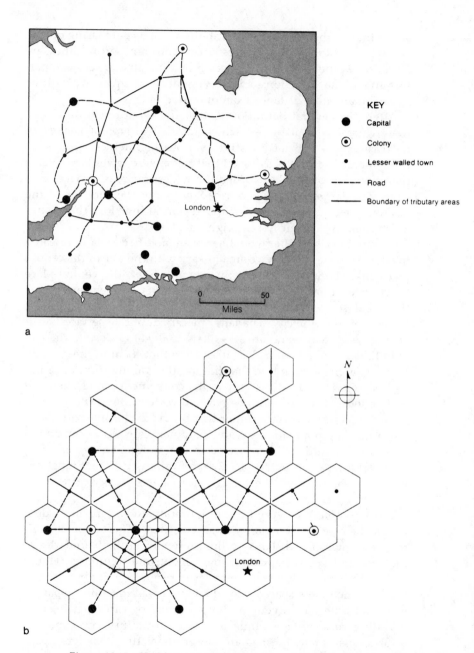

KEY

●   Capital

⊙   Colony

•   Lesser walled town

------   Road

———   Boundary of tributary areas

Figure 16.15 Hodder and Hassall's map of Romano-British settlement in southern Britain during the third centruy A.D. (a) The site hierarchy plotted on a conventional map. (b) The hexagonal lattice that they erected over the hierarchy.

many factors, such as terrain or population density, can still act on even the most seemingly regular patterns.

Central-place theory's main use to archaeologists is as a descriptive device for regional settlement patterns. Richard Blanton (1978) has used it to document the rise of Teotihuacán, showing how this rapidly burgeoning central place took over the functions of nearby secondary centers and affected the entire settlement hierarchy at the same time. The central-place model provides a means of suggesting hypotheses as to what economic moves and organizational decisions were needed. These can then be tested against field data. In addition, the notion of a hierarchy of central places serving areas of different sizes—that is, in an interlocking relationship in space— is vital to archaeology. A number of attempts have been made to show that the distribution of specific prehistoric sites was patterned on a centralized or hierarchical system. The Hopewell people of the Midwest are an example. Famous traders, their cult objects were traded over the length and breadth of Ohio, Illinois, Michigan, and Wisconsin, as well as wider afield. Stuart Struever and Gail Houart (1972) examined the relationships between Hopewell sites in the Midwest and were able to suggest that the large mound sites found were regional centers, where important trading was focused. They assembled a picture of the hierarchy of sites through which the Hopewell trade objects were handled, the levels of the hierarchy being defined by site size, similarity of construction, location, and distance apart.

SOCIOECOLOGICAL MODELS

The formal methods of spatial analysis used by archaeologists are little more than general perspectives, part of a wider examination of archaeological sites considering the spaced resources available to their inhabitants and the constraints placed upon them by such variables as perception, information, and technology (Butzer, 1982).

Hunter-Gatherer Sites. The implicit models used by archaeologists to model the spatial behavior of hunter-gatherers have a distinct evolutionary undertone. The assumption seems to be that human beings progressed from a simple, unspecialized, freewheeling lifeway to a more and more specialized existence circumscribed within a scheduled annual round, and then on to a farming life with more lasting settlement. This approach was used by Richard MacNeish to describe the gradual changes in human settlement that took place in the Tehuacán Valley of Mexico during the past 10,000 years (MacNeish, 1972). During this long period, the inhabitants progressed gradually from simple, nomadic hunter-gatherers, to living in seasonal villages and scheduling hunting and gathering activities carefully through the year. MacNeish measured the changes in settlement that resulted from agriculture, and later the birth of city-states in the region.

Karl Butzer (1977, 1982) made another assumption when he studied the Lower Paleolithic Acheulian sites of Ambrona and Torralba in central Spain. He argued that early hunter-gatherers shared the ability of large grazing animals like elephants to adopt different feeding habits and seasonal movements according to the abundance of resources through the year. Ambrona and Torralba lie along the only low-altitude mountain pass dividing the plains of Castile. This was the route through which large mammals migrated in spring and fall from winter to summer pastures and back again. The Acheulians preyed on these migrating beasts. During other seasons of the year, they spread over the neighboring country in temporary camps near water and constantly moving herds (Figure 16.16). This settlement pattern is suggested not only by site distributions, but by such phenomena as migratory bird bones in the archaeological deposits.

These Mexican and Spanish examples suggest that the movements of hunter-gatherers were related to different ways of exploiting local resources that can be detected in the archaeological record. The first requirement in establishing spatial and temporal variables is to find the span of time during which individual sites were used (Binford, 1971; Butzer, 1982). They can be ephemeral, occupied for a few hours or days; temporary, places used for several days or weeks; seasonal; or semipermanent. Functional and social considerations affect the duration of occupation, too, but these cannot always be inferred from the archaeological record. Armed with these data, you can prepare "mobility models" for hunter-gatherers, samples of which are shown in Figure 16.17.

Sufficient research has been carried out among both living and prehistoric hunter-gatherers to suggest some normative models for their spatial behavior that can be posed as hypotheses (Butzer, 1982). A sampling of these:

The shapes of hunter-gatherer territories will depend on the distribution of resources, topography, and mobility patterns.

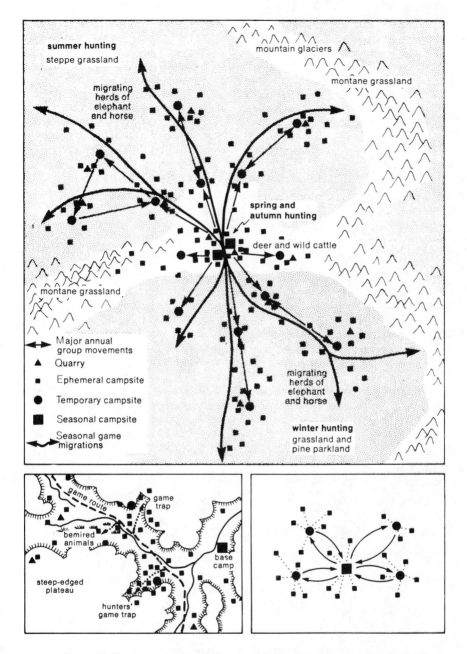

Figure 16.16 A seasonal mobility model for Acheulian hunter-gatherers in central Spain, based in part on data from Ambrona and Torralba. During spring and fall, the hunters preyed on herds migrating through the mountain passes (lower-left map). In summer and winter, the hunters divided into smaller groups and lived in temporary sites near to water, animal herds, and stone outcrops. After Butzer, 1982.

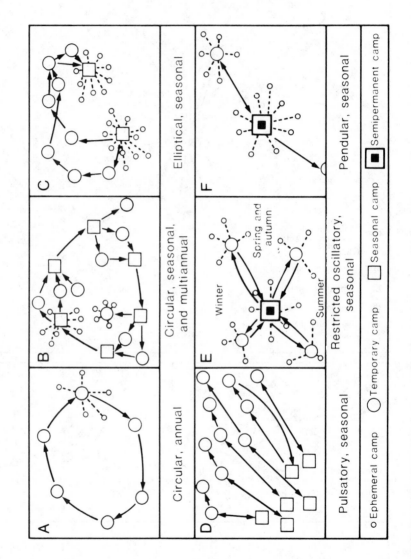

Hunter-gatherers will probably choose a reasonably broad-based diet whenever possible, to reduce their dependence on one food source that may fluctuate in availability. This strategy usually means less time is spent in procuring food.

Every band will tend to optimize their use of resources by coming together in larger settlements and dispersing at others. The dispersal may be designed to exploit scattered resources. The Khoi Khoi at the Cape of Good Hope were cattle herders, who fanned out over the neighboring desert floor during the rainy months when grass and water were abundant, then concentrated in fertile enclaves during the dry months. Alternatively, dispersal was a strategy to combat extreme scarcity of food at "hungry" times of the year. This notion of "optimal foraging strategy" has received much attention in recent years, especially as a means of predicting the effects of such technological changes as introduction of new weapons, even firearms. (For more information, see Winterhalder and Smith, 1981. More normative models for hunter-gatherer behavior are to be found in Butzer, 1982.)

Agricultural Settlements. The clustering and patterning of agricultural settlements are affected by cultural and environmental factors combined. Some key variables are:

The distribution of economic resources such as different types of land with separate uses for grazing, cultivation, and so on. Soil distributions are also vital, for different depths, textures, and subsoils can impose severe limitations for grazing and other uses. The earliest European farmers concentrated on well-drained, easily dug soils, because they lacked the heavy plows that enabled cultivators to turn over heavier clay soils. The distribution of game and vegetable food resources are also vital.

Figure 16.17 (*left*) Hypothetical mobility models for hunter-gatherers. (a) Seasonal camps on a semirandom annual circular movement. (b) Seasonal aggregation and dispersal to optimize use of scattered, less predictable resources. Over the years, the pattern will be roughly circular. (c) Elliptical nomadic pattern, such as one might find along a perennial river, with the inhabitants moving out into less well-watered areas during the rainy season. (d) Pulsatory seasonal movement, as might occur when lowland herders venture into the highlands at certain seasons of the year. (e) Oscillatory pattern, where people use one base at certain times of the year, then disperse outward at other seasons. This is the Ambrona-Torralba model. (f) Pendular model, which might apply when people were experimenting with crops, and were living in one place for much of the year, dispersing at others; can be likened to a seasonal pendulum effect. After Butzer, 1982.

Available technology, land-clearance techniques, available transport or *draft animals, crop types exploited,* and other such factors within the site itself are critical. So too is the socioeconomic organization that schedules planting and harvest, determines who works with whom, and copes with the obligations among members of the community. A wide range of symbolic and social values also place their imprint on settlement patterns, for they determine not only perceptions of resources but attitudes toward the environment, as well as toward one's neighbors.

Topography influences the placement of agricultural sites in relation to their neighbors, affects direction of trade routes, and encourages or inhibits communication. The Ancient Egyptians depended on the Nile for transportation and water; their modern successors do so still. The same topography can profoundly affect the ways in which agricultural settlement fills in areas that were not settled at first, for spacing of new communities will be affected by location of the original settlements with their continuing needs for land. Defense, too, can radically affect agricultural site distributions. Everyone may elect to live on hilltops, simply to guard against surprise attack.

Trade networks play a leading role in the emergence of central places, such as great cities like the Aztec capital of Tenochtitlán, which attracted trade from all over Mesoamerica (Fagan, 1984a). Originally a settlement pattern based on trade may be determined in part by environment or social considerations, but eventually a vertical hierarchy of sites may grow, as technological, demographic, social, and religious forces come into play. Eventually, as society becomes more complex, site networks may be modified by overriding religious or political considerations. This change happened in Colonial Mexico, where the incoming Spanish authorities resettled thousands of Indians into small towns that were under direct control of the central government.

Agricultural settlements on any scale are affected by so many environmental, economic, social, and other factors that simple propositions like those developed for hunter-gatherers are impracticable. Any approach to the study of agricultural settlements has to emphasize not only the distribution patterns, so critical in interpreting hunter-gatherer subsistence patterns, but the interactions between sites that made them occur, for agricultural settlements were far more dependent on one another than those of hunter-gatherers.

How Did People Perceive the Environment? We have discussed prehistoric settlements rather scientifically, and ignored some of the most important factors, the ways in which prehistoric peoples themselves conceived of the earth around them. The early European explorers in the Age of Discovery came into contact with non-Western societies that had a view of the world quite different from their own (Fagan, 1984b). They conceived of their environment as something communally owned, as something not to be exploited but to be held in trust for future generations. Every field, every headland, every tree had meaning within this environment, was part of the environment in which they lived. This is the entity some archaeologists call the "perceived environment," the areas of the environment around them of which a band or society is aware. The Acheulians probably conceptualized a world that was little more than a few hundred square miles in area, a world perhaps in which few other people lived. In contrast, the Aztecs of Mexico were familiar not only with the Basin of Mexico, but with the Gulf of Mexico and the Pacific. Their intensely symbolic world encompassed not only city-states and resources, but their own articulated values of how the world should be organized—into cardinal directions, layers of the heavens, and so on. Only the parts of the world that were relevant to San life were part of their perceived environment. For thousands of years, the San hunted and gathered food on the highlands of the Transvaal in South Africa, yet they were totally unaware of the rich gold fields that lay beneath their feet; indeed those were useless to them, for they lacked the technology to exploit the metal.

Studying perceived environments is almost impossible except with descriptive simulations tested on the basis of assumptions that prehistoric peoples made optimal use of their environment. Such an approach is dangerous, for human beings are not necessarily rational or even logical in their attitudes toward their environment.

Prehistoric settlement patterns are quite well documented in some areas of the world, notably Roman Britain, the Basin of Mexico, and parts of the American Southwest. The data may still be incomplete, but frameworks for regional analyses do exist, and these call for development and testing of new spatial models. As we have shown in this chapter, these should be applied to explaining the patterns of site locations and the utilization and modification of resource spaces, as well as interactions between sites and areas. To do so effectively requires examining not only site distributions, but the human landscape as a whole, so that the archaeological record is seen within its wider environmental context.

POPULATION

Settlement patterns evolve in response to three broad variables: environmental change, alterations in population density, and interaction among people. One major factor in the later cultural evolution of humanity undoubtedly has been rapidly growing population densities. Many of the classic arguments of archaeology have revolved around the role of population growth in the origins of agriculture, urban life, and civilization. Unfortunately, however, as mentioned previously, estimating population densities is a task fraught with difficulty.

Estimating Populations. As yet, no one has devised a foolproof method of estimating prehistoric population densities: there are simply too many variables to contend with, many of them impossible to reconstruct from archaeological data.

Methods based on settlement data rely on information from excavated household clusters and ethnographic information to provide an estimate of the amount of floor space or living area needed by an individual. The average family size is first calculated and then multiplied by the available living space. Efforts have been made to estimate the amount of living space required by individuals in many societies. R. Naroll (1962), conducted one such experiment that produced a figure of 10 square meters per person. Clearly, however, such estimates could not possibly apply to all societies, let alone to both hunter-gatherers and city dwellers. Others, such as Millon at Teotihuacán, have used as the formula the amount of sleeping area required. Although there may be instances where a relatively reliable population estimate can be obtained, much depends on precise ethnographic analogy, very careful control of the archaeological data, and excavation of considerable areas of the site.

Methods based on *food consumption* have been used to calculate populations of hunter-gatherer camps in Europe and of shell middens in the western United States. A clever but mainly theoretical calculation—but one that may give a reasonable estimate of general population size—was made by a group of California archaeologists, who estimated that about 30 people occupied the Scripps Estate in southern California between about 5500 and 3500 B.C. (Cook, 1972). They based their estimates on the amount of shell refuse and the number of grindstones found there.

Cemeteries and burial grounds have been used to estimate population also, but this evidence has the disadvantage that it is seldom representative of the population as a whole. Most cemeteries are used for a long time, and represent a cumulative population rather than the number of people living at a given moment.

Most demographic figures from large geographic areas clearly are little more than feasible guesses. One estimate places the average population of the early Sumerian states in Mesopotamia at about 17,000 souls (Sanders and Price, 1968); and the Late Glacial population of Britain at about 10,000 people (Clark, 1952).

Population Growth. Although accurate population estimates, settlement-by-settlement, are obviously of great interest, especially if one assumes that the growing size of a village represents a growing population, the consequences of population growth and decline are even more important. Population is a key element in cultural process, for there is a clear cause-and-effect relationship between population and the potential carrying capacity and productivity of agricultural land. Competition and cooperation between communities may result from a shortage of resources engendered by population growth, and these interactions may, in turn, affect both settlement patterns and population density (Hassan, 1982).

The classic hypothesis on world population was formulated by Thomas Henry Malthus late in the eighteenth century. Malthus believed that humankind's reproductive capacity far exceeds available food supplies; in other words, people must compete for the necessities of life. Competition causes famine, war, and misery. The Malthusian thesis has so dominated archaeological thinking for generations that many scholars believed that the capacity of land and other resources, as well as that of technology, places limits on population growth.

The Malthusian viewpoint has been challenged by economist Ester Boserup, who stated the thesis that population growth should be treated as a quite independent variable when studying technological and cultural change. "As population grows," she argued, "more people per unit of land are faced with the necessity of providing more food per unit of land, and they are able to do this by intensifying their relationship with the land—technology—moving from hunting and gathering through stages of cultivation with ever-shorter fallow periods up to the final stage of intensification, which is multicropping with no fallowing." She went on to argue that people intensify their agricultural efforts only when forced by population pressure to do so. The implication is that more intensive land use is accompanied by parallel intensification of other aspects of culture and society (Spooner, 1972).

Boserup's theoretical viewpoint highlights population as another variable in settlement archaeology. Unfortunately, few regions have been surveyed in sufficient archaeological detail to enable population estimates or data on intensity of agriculture to be made with any statistical confidence. Elizabeth Brumfiel (1976) used site-catchment analysis and modern agricultural data to study population growth in Formative villages in the Valley of Mexico. She recorded a slight increase in the settlement area at the end of the Formative, but the ratio of productive potential of the agricultural land to site size remained almost the same as before, and climatic conditions also had remained the same. But three of the larger sites had a much higher population-to-productivity ratio than the smaller settlements. From this difference she concluded that there were political and social reasons why this situation developed. Conceivably, she argued, the smaller villages had to pay taxes for services to larger settlements. Therefore, the smaller settlements boosted their agricultural production, while the larger centers enjoyed greater population densities but did not have to raise their own agricultural production.

The Brumfiel research, and that of other investigators, such as Jeffrey Parsons, in the same region (Sanders, Parsons, and Santley, 1979), and Robert Adams (1974), on irrigation in Mesopotamia, clearly demonstrate the complex economic and social variables that could affect population growth in prehistory. Much of the time, settlement archaeology involves hypothesizing about intangibles, those aspects of human society that are never preserved in the archaeological record. But, as Chapter 17 shows, much of our understanding of cultural evolution and changing settlement patterns comes from the insights we can obtain into the interactions between different communities reflected in their trading, social, and religious practices.

Guide to Further Reading

Butzer, Karl W. *Archaeology as Human Ecology: Method and Theory for a Contextual Approach.* Cambridge: Cambridge University Press, 1982.
  An authoritative description of basic environmental and spatial concepts in archaeology. Strongly recommended as a starting point.

Chang, K. C., ed. *Settlement Archaeology*. Palo Alto: National Press, 1968.
Fundamental essays on settlement archaeology that cover both general theory and specific examples.

Flannery, Kent V., ed. *The Early Mesoamerican Village*. New York: Academic Press, 1976.
A modern classic, a study by a team of Michigan archaeologists of settlement patterns in the Valley of Oaxaca. Enlivened by some hypothetical but highly entertaining debates between fictitious archaeologists of different theoretical viewpoints.

Hodder, Ian, and Clive Orton. *Spatial Analysis in Archaeology*. Cambridge: Cambridge University Press, 1976.
A study of this new field, rather technical but full of useful concepts and ideas.

Sanders, William T., Jeffrey R. Parsons, and Robert S. Santley. *The Basin of Mexico: Ecological Processes in the Evolution of a Civilization*, 2 vols. New York: Academic Press, 1979.
A settlement-ecological study that gives an admirable impression of the state-of-the-art research in this field.

Winterhalder, Bruce, and Eric Alden Smith, eds. *Hunter-Gatherer Foraging Strategies*. Chicago: University of Chicago Press, 1981.
Essays for the advanced reader that concentrate on analyses of hunter-gatherer societies. A strong emphasis on optimal foraging strategy.

CHAPTER 17 ✺

TRADE, SOCIAL ORGANIZATION, AND RELIGIOUS LIFE

Preview

- Human subsistence is based on natural resources and on exploitation of the environment, whether or not people produce food. Trade may have had its beginnings when people moved to a new territory where a previously available raw material was no longer abundant. Much early trade probably took the form of gift exchanges and the bartering of food and other commodities between neighboring settlements. The pattern of the trade was established by the distance between settlements and available sources of raw material.

- Trade is normally recognized in the archaeological record by the discovery of objects exotic to the material culture of the economy of the host society. Prehistoric trade networks are studied by examining the distributions of such objects and of tool patterns in individual households and household clusters.

- Trading activity is closely tied to growing complexity in social and political organization among prehistoric peoples. It is not enough simply to identify trading activity in the archaeological record; one also has to understand the exchange processes that lay behind the trading.

- We cite two examples of prehistoric trading to show how trade cannot be studied except by referring to the cultural systems of which it was a part. Our first example is Maya trade in the lowlands, where trade in *metates*, jadeite, and other raw materials was essential for survival. At Tepe Yahya in Iran, steatite trading assumed great importance, but it was controlled by middlemen and depended on a demand for luxury objects in Mesopotamia, hundreds of miles away.

· Redistribution of trade objects through a society is often controlled politically by chiefs and other leaders. We use obsidian trading in Mesoamerica to show how such redistribution mechanisms can be studied in the archaeological record.

· Social organization is difficult to study from archaeological evidence, although a systematic view of human culture makes it possible to examine it as one variable among the many that affect cultural change. The Tucson Garbage Project suggests that the use of artifacts and food remains for the study of ancient social organization has great potential.

· Leslie White and other anthropologists have developed an evolutionary model of social organization that envisages four broad levels: bands, tribes, chiefdoms, and state-organized societies.

· Social organization can be studied in the archaeological record by using burials and associated grave furniture, as at Ur-of-the-Chaldees, and by using structures or artifact patternings.

· The use of artifact patternings to study prehistoric social organization is still at an experimental stage. We cite William Longacre's study of Carter Ranch, Arizona, to exemplify some of the difficulties.

· Religion has been studied traditionally through burials, burial rites, and sacred buildings. Organized religions were a feature of many of the more complex prehistoric societies, and they were often centers of elaborate ceremonial areas that were a focus for state-organized societies. The rituals that ensured the continuity of religious belief are reflected in architecture and art, and the presence or absence of sacred artifacts in the archaeological record may reveal valuable information on prehistoric religion, provided careful research designs are carefully made.

So far, we have discussed human cultures as more-or-less self-sufficient entities, each with its own territory and constellation of natural resources. Very few human societies have lived in complete isolation from their neighbors, however. One major theme of world prehistory is the increasing interdependence and competition between communities, the culmination of which is the highly interdependent, industrialized world we live in today. In this chapter we examine the ways in which archaeologists study these evolving interactions, which are reflected in the exchange of resources and trading and in kinship, marriage, and more complex social structures, as well as in shared religious beliefs.

TRADE AND EXCHANGE SYSTEMS

Trade has been defined as the "mutually appropriative movement of goods between hands" (Renfrew, 1975). People make trade connections and the exchange systems that handle trade goods when they need to acquire goods and services that are not available to them within their own site-catchment area. The movement of goods need not be over any great distance, and it can operate internally, within a society, or externally, across cultural boundaries. Trade always involves two elements: the goods and commodities being exchanged, and the people doing the exchanging. Thus, any form of trading activity implies both procurement and handling of tools and raw materials and some form of social system that provides the people-to-people relationships within which the trade flourishes.

Trade is recognized in the archaeological record by the discovery of objects exotic to the material culture or economy of the host society. Glass was never manufactured in sub-Saharan Africa during prehistoric times, yet imported glass beads are widespread finds in archaeological sites of the first millennium A.D. (Beck and Schofield, 1958). Prehistoric exchange networks can be studied in the distribution of exotic artifacts and materials, using the artifacts and also trace elements and other characteristic features of such raw materials as obsidian, the volcanic glass so highly prized for ceremonial and utilitarian artifacts in Mesoamerica, North America, and the Near East (Figure 17.1).

Pioneer studies of obsidian were made by Colin Renfrew and others in the Near East, where spectroscopic analysis was used to identify no fewer than twelve early farming villages that had obtained obsidian from the Ciftlik area of central Turkey (Renfrew, Dixon, and Cann, 1966). The study showed that 80 percent of the

Figure 17.1   An obsidian mirror from Mesoamerica, reflecting a figurine.

chipped stone in villages within 300 kilometers of Ciftlik was obsidian. Outside this "supply zone," the percentages of obsidian dropped away sharply with distance, to 5 percent in a Syrian village, and 0.1 percent in the Jordan Valley. Renfrew and his colleagues argued that regularly spaced villages were passing about half the obsidian they received to their more distant neighbors (Figure 17.2).

The study of prehistoric trade through artifacts and raw materials is critical to archaeology, for it provides a unique opportunity to examine the mechanics of trading networks and the changing social institutions that regulated them.

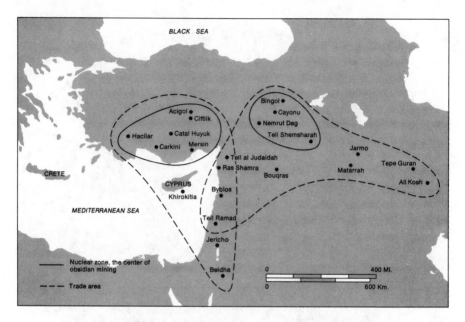

Figure 17.2   Obsidian trade routes in the Neolithic Near East. The nuclear zone was the center of obsidian mining.

Social Interaction and Organization.   *Gift giving* is a common medium of exchange and trade in societies that are relatively self-supporting. The exchange of gifts is primarily designed to reinforce a social relationship, both of an individual and of a group as a whole. This form of trade is common in New Guinea and the Pacific, widespread in Africa during the past 2,000 years, and in the Americas as well. Much depends on the types of commodity being exchanged. The exchange of seashells may have involved individuals of higher status, and that of foodstuffs and hut poles was a more common form of transaction involving many individuals and families. And, of course, not only objects but also information can be exchanged, which may lead to technological innovation or social change. Gift giving and bartering formed a basic trading mechanism for millennia, a simple means of exchanging basic commodities. But this sporadic interaction between individuals and communities reduced people's self-sufficiency, and eventually made them part of a larger, functioning society whose members were no longer so self-sufficient and who depended on one another not only for basic commodities but also for social purposes.

The decision to engage in trading—to acquire commodities from afar—depends on both how urgent the need for the goods is and the difficulties in acquiring and transporting them. Clearly, such items as cattle or slaves are more easily transported than tons of iron ore or salt cakes. The former move on their own, but metals require human or animal carriers or wheeled carts. To ignore these differences is to oversimplify the study of prehistoric trade.

Reciprocity, the exchange of goods between two individuals or groups, is at the heart of much gift giving and barter trade. It can happen at the same place year after year and be focused on a central place, which can be as humble as someone's house. Such central places become the focus of gift giving and trade. When a village becomes involved in both the production of trade goods and their exchange with other communities, it will probably become an even more important center, a place to which people will travel to trade.

Redistribution of trade goods from a central place throughout a culture requires some form of organization to ensure that the redistribution is equitable. A redistributive mechanism may be controlled by a chief, a religious leader, or some form of management organization. Such an organization might control production of copper ornaments, or it might simply control distribution and delivery of trade objects. Redistribution of any commodity requires someone to both collect and redistribute it, which requires considerable social organization for collection, storage, and redistribution for grain and other commodities. The chief, whose position is perhaps reinforced by religious power, has a serious responsibility to his community that can extend over several villages, as his lines of redistribution stretch out through people of lesser rank to the individual villager. A chief will negotiate exchanges with other chiefs, substituting the regulatory elements of reciprocal trading for a redistributive economy in which less trading in exotic materials is carried out by individual households.

Prehistoric trade was an important variable that developed in conjunction with sociopolitical organization. It has been assumed that trade proceeded from simple reciprocal exchange to the more complex redistribution of goods under a redistributor. In other words, trading is closely tied to growing complexity in social and political organization.

Markets are both places and particular styles of trading administration and organization that encourage people to set aside one place for trading and relatively stable, almost fixed prices for staple commodities. This stability does not mean regulated prices, but some regulation is needed in a network of markets in which commodities from an area of abundant supplies are sold to one with strong demand for the same materials. The mechanisms of the exchange relationship particularly require some regulation. Markets are normally associated with more complex societies. No literate civilization ever developed without strong central places, where trading activities were regulated and monopolies developed over both sources of materials and trade routes themselves.

Successful market trading required predictable supplies of basic commodities and adequate policing of trade routes. It is significant that most early Mesopotamian and Egyptian trade was riverine, where policing was easier. With the great caravan routes opened, the political and military issues—tribute, control of trade routes, and tolls—became paramount. The caravan, predating the great empires, was a form of organized trading that kept to carefully defined routes set up and maintained by state authorities. The travelers moved along set routes, looking neither left nor right, bent only on delivering and exchanging imports and exports. These caravans were a far cry from the huge economic complex that accompanied Alexander the Great's army across Asia, or the Grand Mogul's annual summer progress from the heat in Delhi in India to the mountains, which moved a half million people, including the entire Delhi bazaar.

Studying Market Networks. Emphasis on these mechanisms has led Johnson, Lamberg-Karlovsky, Rathje, and others to study market networks and the mechanisms by which suppliers are channeled down well-defined routes and by which profits are regulated and fed back to the source, providing further incentive for more supplies (Sabloff and Lamberg-Karlovsky, 1975) (Figure 17.3). There may or may not be a physical marketplace; it is the state of affairs surrounding the trade that forms the focus of the trading system and the mechanisms by means of which trade interacts with other parts of the culture. Taking a systems approach to trading activity means emphasizing the role of archaeological finds as the material expressions of interdependent factors. These factors include the need for goods—which prompts a search for supplies. The supplies themselves represent production above local needs and are created to satisfy external demands. Other factors are the logistics of transportation and the extent of the trading network, as well as the social and political environment. With all these variables, no one aspect of trade can be reasonably viewed as an overriding cause of cultural

Figure 17.3   A ceremonial Maya *metate*, a carved stone slab used for grinding corn and other materials, an artifact widely traded in the Maya lowlands 1,500 years ago. Stela of the *Visor Paser*, 1303–1287 B.C. Limestone. 46.5 × 50.8 × 8.0 cm. 09.287, gift of Mrs. Frank E. Peabody. Courtesy, Museum of Fine Arts, Boston.

change or of evolution in trading practices. Hitherto, archaeologists have concentrated on the objects of trade or on trade as an abstraction—trade as a cause of civilization; but they have had no profound knowledge about the workings of even one trading network from which to build more theoretical abstractions.

TEPE YAHYA: TRADE IN PREHISTORY

Trading was integral in early Sumerian civilization in the Near East, too, a many-faceted operation that absorbed the energies of thousands of people. Sumerian trade was much more tightly organized and controlled than, say, Hopewell trading. The redistribution systems of the cities combined many activities, all controlled by the central authority that ruled the settlements. Food surpluses were redistributed and raw materials were obtained from far away for the manufacture of ornaments, weapons, and prestigious luxuries. Demands for raw materials appear to have risen steadily, spreading market networks into territories remote from the home state. For these long-distance routes to succeed, political stability at both ends of the route was essential. An intricate system of political, financial, and logistical checks and balances had to be kept up, requiring an efficient and alert administrative organization.

The raw materials traded by the Sumerians included metals, timber, skins, ivory, and such precious stones as malachite. Many could be found only in the remote highlands to the north and east of Mesopotamia. The trade in steatite (soapstone—an easy-to-work material) shows how far-flung Mesopotamian trade became (Lamberg-Karlovsky, 1973, 1975). Steatite was used to make stone bowls as early as 10,000 B.C., but it suddenly became a highly fashionable material abound 2750 B.C. Steatite bowls are found in Early Dynastic Mesopotamian tells and also occur at Moenjo-daro in the Indus Valley, one of the great cities of the Indus civilization, and at contemporaneous sites on islands in the Persian Gulf. Objects of the same materials are also common in settlements near today's Iran-Pakistan border, the hinterland between Indus and Mesopotamian civilizations. Most of the steatite objects are stone bowls bearing intricate designs, the same designs being found all over the area where steatite is found.

Experiments with physiochemical analysis have identified at least a dozen sources for the stone, but so far only Tepe Yahya in Iran is known to have been a center of steatite bowl production (Figure 17.4). Abundant steatite deposits occur near the site. The bowls produced at Tepe Yahya and elsewhere were definitely items

Figure 17.4   The tell at Tepe Yahya, Iran, an important center of steatite trade.

of luxury; they were so prized in Mesopotamia that they may have caused keen competition among those rich enough to afford them. The competition for luxury goods generally may have been intense enough to affect production rates in the source areas, with political vicissitudes in the Mesopotamian city-states constantly shifting production rates of steatite centers and making profits from the trade fluctuate. Interestingly, the demand for steatite around Tepe Yahya was minimal, and the occurrence of few finds in the Indus Valley contrasts sharply with the very large quantities found in Mesopotamia. Most of the trade was with the west, depending on the demand for luxuries among the increasingly wealthy elites of the Mesopotamian cities. Local artisans seem to have produced the steatite near Tepe Yahya, perhaps working part-time or at selected seasons. But the trade itself was not in the artisans' hands; it was run by middlemen and ultimately by the exploitative elite of Mesopotamia. C. C. Lamberg-Karlovsky calls this trade a form of economic imperialism: "Economic exploitation of foreign areas without political control."

The study of prehistoric trade is a vital source of information on social organization and the ways in which societies became more complex. Trade itself developed a great complexity, in both goods traded and the interactions of people involved. Colin Renfrew (1975) identified no fewer than ten types of interaction between people that can result from trading, ranging from simple contact between individuals to trading by professional traders, such as the *pochteca* of the Maya and the Aztec, who were not above acting as spies (Figure 17.5) (Fagan, 1984a).

SOCIAL ORGANIZATION

"Data relevant to most, if not all, components of past sociocultural systems *are* preserved in the archaeological record," argued Lewis Binford some years ago (Binford, 1968). Traditionally, archaeologists had regarded the more intangible aspects of human society, such as religious and social organization, as particularly difficult to infer from archaeological data. Many minor differences between prehistoric peoples—speech, religion, and social organization among them—are, it is true, seldom obvious in the archaeological record, and traditional definitions of culture help us to recognize differences only when they are detectable in the data obtained by

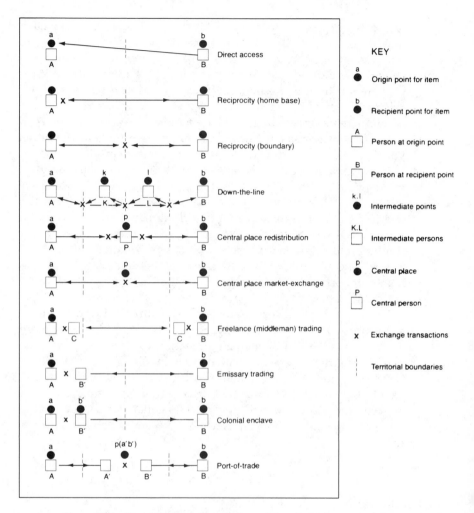

Figure 17.5 The ten ways in which prehistoric trade can operate, as determined by Colin Renfrew. The diagram illustrates the wide variety of means by which trade goods are exchanged, each of which has specific implications for settlement patterns.

excavation, analysis, and induction. But Binford's approach sees human cultures in archaeology as sociocultural systems that enable one to think of social and religious factors as vital subsystems in regulating cultural change. These intangibles can be reconstructed, at least partially, he believes, by studying artifact patterning and stylistic changes in material culture, as well as by use of middle-range theory (Chapter 16). Other archaeologists have pointed out that material culture is extremely sensitive to changes in ideology, as reflected in stylistic changes in such items as New England Colonial tombstones (Deetz, 1967). As we saw in Chapter 16, other archaeologists disagree with this notion.

Stages of Social Organization. Archaeologists look at social organization in prehistory with the aid of general conceptual schemes drawn up by anthropologists. Such schemes are particularly important when one is examining human cultural evolution. Edward Tylor, Lewis Morgan, and more recently, V. Gordon Childe and Leslie White, were among those who realized that it was a mistake to consider human cultural evolution as divorced from social organization. Childe recognized this truth with his formulations of Neolithic and Urban Revolutions; Leslie White, Elman Service, and others developed a simple model of societal evolution through prehistory that attracted, and still attracts, wide attention among archaeologists. In his classic *Profiles in Ethnology*, Elman Service (1971) defined several broad levels of sociocultural evolution, which provided a framework for tracing the evolution of human social organization from the first simple, primitive family structures of the earliest hunter-gatherers to the highly complex state-organized societies of the early civilizations.

Bands. For most of its long prehistory, humanity flourished in small bands, associations of families that may have been no larger than twenty-five to sixty people. These bands were knit by close kinship ties. This highly viable form of social organization is extremely effective for hunter-gatherers and survives into modern times among the !Kung San, the Australian aborigines, and other groups. The tight organization of the band encourages cooperative hunting and gathering and sharing of resources.

Tribes. The social level of the band proved effective as long as human beings were hunter-gatherers. But once they began to cultivate the soil and domesticate animals, the more sedentary life and demanding requirements of food production caused people to associate in aggregates of bands that were linked by class into tribes. A clan unites families within an organization in which all its members claim descent from a common ancestor. Tribal societies are essentially democratic, for the leadership of this much larger social unit is normally conducted through a tribal council of some type whose membership consists of band and clan representatives. A tribe may also possess nonkinship social units that transcend kinship ties, often units that foster a particular activity, such as canoe navigation or potmaking. These sodalities are but one of several new forms of social organization that tribes employ to manipulate their growing populations. At the core of tribal life is the notion that all resources are owned by the tribe as a whole and are to be controlled in a basically egalitarian manner.

Chiefdoms. Tribal societies develop chiefdoms in situations where the egalitarian principles of the society are replaced by a new order, where different kin groups assume a form of ranking within society as a whole. One kin group may achieve prominence because its members, all descended from a common ancestor, are associated with extraordinary deeds, or are believed to have unusual religious or other abilities. This lineage may soon enjoy a special status in society, which gives its leaders organizational powers to cater to the needs of society as a whole. The lineage chieftains do not actually control or own the products or services of the society that they manipulate or redistribute. Rather, they act as the social instrument for the redistribution of goods and services for their society as a whole. These chiefdoms are headed by lineage leaders who coordinate the management of food surpluses and the products of the diverse part-time specialist craftspeople that even a tribal society possesses.

Once food supplies are regularly produced and the division of labor within a society has diversified far beyond that of simple male-female roles, then the leaders of the principal lineage or lineages assume an important role in redistributing specialist products throughout the tribe fairly, keeping a proportion of the supplies for their own use and for storage in communal food reserves. The authority of such leaders is commonly backed by their spiritual powers, their intermediary role with the society's deities, and their abilities at regulating the cycles of planting, harvesting, and even rainmaking. The leaders of chiefdoms may even be specialists themselves, priests with extraordinary spiritual powers, who were the only people permitted access to certain types of exotic cult objects, certain clothing, and even certain types of food. Chiefdoms, such as those of the Hopewell people of the Midwest, are really a transitional stage between tribal society and the much more organized state societies of the early civilizations.

The state-organized society.   This stage developed out of the chiefdom. Lineage chieftains enjoyed a social and economic status that relieved them of many of the day-to-day burdens of agriculture or stock breeding. Their authority was based on spiritual and managerial roles bolstered by the wealth of their possessions, visible signs of their immense prestige. A state-organized society, on the other hand, is governed by a full-fledged ruling class, whose privileges and powers are bolstered by a hierarchic secular and religious bureaucracy; at least a rudimentary system of justice; and a system of ranked classes of nobility, warriors, traders, priests, bureaucrats, peasants, and perhaps slaves. The ruler enjoys great wealth and is often regarded as semidivine. Ancient Egyptian pharaohs were divine monarchs with absolute powers. Ownership of land and administration of state religion were vested in their hands

Figure 17.6   Rameses II, seated upon a cushioned chair, receives a foreign dignitary. Rameses II and Queen in Audience, stela from eighteenth dynasty (09.287). Gift of Mrs. Frank E. Peabody. Courtesy of the Museum of Fine Arts, Boston.

(Figure 17.6). The pharaohs ruled by centuries of legal precedent, through an elaborate hierarchy of bureaucrats, whose principal officials represented practically hereditary dynasties (Aldred, 1961). Many state societies, such as those of the Maya and the Inca, were organized along rigid lines, with strict classes of nobles, craftsmen, and others. Only the most extraordinary act of military skill or religious devotion would allow a few lucky people entry into the highest classes of society.

When French explorers visited the Natchez people of the Mississippi Valley early in the eighteenth century, they found a state society so rigid that the Great Sun and his noblemen at the pinnacle of Natchez society referred to the commoners as "stinkards" (Swanton, 1911). Yet all noblemen, even the Great Sun, were required to marry stinkards. Everyone knew exactly where they stood in society, even slaves. State-organized societies were the foundation of the early civilizations of the Near East, China, and the Americas; indeed, they were precursors of the Classical civilization of Greece and Rome.

SOCIAL ORGANIZATION IN THE ARCHAEOLOGICAL RECORD

The archaeological evidence that bears directly on prehistoric social organization comes from several sources, each of which can give us insights into the general level of social organization of a prehistoric society and into much more specific social details as well.

Burials. Human burials are one important source of information about prehistoric social organization (Brown, 1971). The actual disposal of the corpse is really a minimal part of the sequence of mortuary practice within a society. Funerary rites are a ritual of passage, and are usually reflected not only in the position of the body in the grave but also by the ornaments and grave furniture that accompany it. The contents of a grave, whether spectacular or extremely simple, are useful barometers of social ranking. In some, the differing status of burials may indicate that a society was rigidly ranked.

When Leonard Woolley excavated the Early Dynastic royal burials of Ur-of-the-Chaldees in Mesopotamia (Figure 17.7), he found a great cemetery containing 1,850 graves (Woolley, 1943). Sixteen of them stood out by virtue of their remarkable grave furniture. The royal tombs were sunk into the earlier levels of the mound, and a

Figure 17.7   The Royal Cemetery at Ur-of-the-Chaldees, excavated by Leonard Woolley.

sepulchre consisting of several rooms was erected in the middle of a huge pit. The royal corpses were decked out in a cascade of gold and semiprecious stone ornaments; gold and silver ornaments were placed next to the biers; and several attendants were slaughtered to accompany the dead. Once the royal sepulchre was closed, the entire court filed into the grave pit, drank poison, and lay down to die in correct order of protocol. Wooley was able to identify the different rankings of the courtiers from their ornaments. In contrast to all this luxury, the average person was buried in a matting roll or a humble coffin.

In burials like this, or with pharaohs' graves, or even the burials of Iron Age chieftains in Europe, the ranking of society is obvious. But what about less affluent societies, in which differences in rank and social status are often more muted? It is very important for archaeologists to be able to recognize such inequalities, for the degree of social ranking is often a measure of the size and complexity of a society. Very often, too, rank appears when centuries-old ties of kin and family are being replaced by rulers who preside over much more elaborate social systems. Brown (1981) points out that such variables as age, sex, personal ability, personality, even circumstances of death can affect the way in which one is buried. The evidence for ranking comes not only from grave furniture and insignia of rank deposited with the deceased, but from the positions of graves in a settlement or cemetery, and even from symbolic distinctions that are hard to find in the archaeological record. Generally, however, the greater and more secure a ruler's authority becomes, the more effort and wealth is expended on burial. This lavishness may also extend to immediate relatives and friends. (For essays on the archaeology of death, read Chapman, Kinnes, and Randsborg, 1981).

Physical anthropologists have just begun to look at groups of skeletons as another means of identifying the family relationships between groups of burials. The minute study of skeletal geography is an approach that is still in its infancy.

Structures. Evidence of social organization can sometimes be inferred from buildings. Teotihuacán shows every sign of having been an elaborately planned city, with special precincts for markets and craftspeople, and the houses of the leading priests and nobles were near the Street of the Dead, which bisected the city. In instances like this, it is easy enough to locate the houses belonging to each class in the society, both by their architecture and by the distinctive artifacts found in them.

Some civilizations seem to have regulated the houses occupied by the various classes of society with almost stultifying monotony. A classic example is the Harappan civilization of the Indus Valley. Both Harappa and Moenjo-daro were dominated by great citadels, with rectangular grids of monotonous workers' houses surrounding them. Special quarters of the city were reserved for craftspeople and for storage purposes. In these, and many other cases, one can study the relationships between different segments of society by examining the spacing between the structures within the site.

Artifact Patterning: Houses and Settlement Patterns. Theoretically, at any rate, distinctive artifact patternings within houses, household clusters, and communities should provide data on prehistoric social organization. Few archaeologists have ventured into this difficult research field, partly because no one has yet invented a battery of tested methods for studying and manipulating the many pottery-design elements that form the basis of most studies of prehistoric organization.

At issue, too, is the role of the individual potter and artifact user.

Can one use artifact styles to identify individual fashions and social groupings in the archaeological record? Some stylistic attributes of basketry or pottery could be the result of individual effort, and others could be the work of a group of craftspeople or a social unit. The study of social organization from artifacts depends on making such distinctions (Hill and Gunn, 1977). Only recently, however, have archaeologists confronted the problem with rigorous methodology.

James Hill argues that it should sometimes be possible to identify the work of individual craftspeople, and has experimented with assemblages of painted pottery from the Southwest. He suggests that there are five areas in which progress can be made:

1. Studying artifact classes closely to see if one can identify the number of people making the objects and calculating the degree of craft specialization. Do we find fewer people making such artifacts throughout time? Does this shrinkage reflect increased craft specialization? And, by studying the tools, can we identify the individual tasks assigned to specialists within the group?
2. Studying trade and identifying specific artifact classes that were exchanged outside the community. Can we identify objects made by an individual and establish their distribution in space and their maximum concentration at, presumably, the place of manufacture?
3. Examining residence units and pottery styles associated with them in minute detail, as has been done with southwestern pueblos (Longacre, 1970). If one could identify individual craftspeople, then perhaps one could say something about social organization.
4. Examining burials, which are a potential source of information about relationships between individuals and groups of individuals. Graves may be clustered in different places, and can be associated with artifacts found in nearby communities.
5. Finding artifacts made by the same individual in more than one community, we may be able to identify population movements.

This type of research is highly complex, and involves methodologies that may not even exist yet. The problem is not only identifying the work of individuals, but also controlling the many variables affecting, say, pottery making. As Margaret Ann Hardin points out, variables such as the choice of paintbrush and paint composition have to be controlled before individual variations can be identified (Hill and Gunn, 1977).

Example: Carter Ranch Pueblo.   The Carter Ranch Pueblo in the Hay Hollow Valley, Arizona, was occupied for 150 years from around A.D. 1050 or 1100. William Longacre was confronted with the problem of untangling five periods of occupation and the contents of 39 rooms and several subterranean ceremonial structures, known as *kivas*. But he wanted to go even further; he sought to isolate and explain the social systems of the occupants as a means of better understanding their adaptive changes to environmental stress (Longacre, 1970).

Longacre began by setting up testable hypotheses based on the assumption that the occupants of the pueblo had lived according to residence rules that led to related families living in the same place for generations. Thus, he argued, pottery styles would be passed down from mother to daughter within the household. He also assumed that the potsherds found in the rooms were the result of the "patterned behavior" of the occupants. Using 175 design elements identified on more than 6,000 potsherds, he applied computer-calculated statistical studies not only to identify groups of elements but also to correlate these groups with occupation floors in the pueblo rooms.

The Carter Ranch rooms were in two distinct clusters, one at the south end of the Pueblo and the second associated with a *kiva* at the north end. When a burial area on the east side of the site was subjected to similar analysis, Longacre found that the northern graves contained pottery designs from the northern group, and those at the south end contained designs from the southern rooms. The archaeological evidence, in the form of *kivas*, associated burial practices, and jointly owned storage areas, favored a corporate residential area maintained by a social unit larger than a family.

Longacre found it far harder to identify households, the basic economic and landholding unit in a pueblo. They probably consisted of groups of adjoining rooms that formed residence areas. After lengthy analyses of room contents, Longacre concluded that they had many functions, ranging from cooking to sleeping and storage, even though different structures had varying purposes—a pattern found in pueblo architecture today. As a result, the household unit is hard to delimit at this site, in contrast to settlements where the rooms' activities tend to be more specialized.

The Longacre study has been criticized on the grounds that the research fails to demonstrate the "asymmetry between presumed products of the two sexes" (Dumond, 1977). Dumond also feels that Longacre's data patterns reflect variations in occupation during the

150-year life of the site rather than a coincidence of pottery design elements and residence units. (For another example of this type of research, see Hill, 1970). The average archaeologist will probably be daunted at the sophisticated statistical methods needed to test archaeological data for their possible social implications. Several of the pioneer studies in this field, regarded as modern classics by many people, have been shown to be inadequate measures of social phenomena (Dunnell, 1977). However, relatively simple statistical tests can be used to correlate artifact patternings with sites on the basis of objects whose exact provenance is accurately established.

RELIGION AND RITUAL

An anonymous archaeologist wrote cynically that "religion is the last resort of troubled excavators." At one time archaeologists ascribed any artifact or structure with even vaguely religious associations to a category broadly named "ritual." In many famous instances the religious associations of an artifact or a structure can be determined readily enough. The Pyramid of the Sun at Teotihuacán is clearly a structure of religious significance; so too are the Temple of Amun at Karnak in Egypt and the famous stone circles at Stonehenge in England (Atkinson, 1969; Hawkins, 1965; Thom, 1974). The "Venus" figurines of the European Upper Paleolithic have been widely interpreted as fertility symbols, and later human figures have received similar interpretation; but the ritual associations of such objects are still in doubt (Grasiozi, 1960) (Figure 17.8). The cave art of Altamira and Lascaux has been called a manifestation of "sympathetic hunting magic" by many observers, and new investigative methods are dealing with this interpretation (Leroi-Gourhan, 1967; Marshak, 1972). Burial mutilations, oral tradition, and even astronomy have been used to infer religious activities from archaeological data. Mother Goddess cults, Baal-Astarte rituals, and earth worship are only a few of the fascinating manifestations of ritual found in archaeological literature—a delight to the eccentric and entertainment for the serious student of prehistory (Ucko, 1962).

Religion and Burials. The traditional archaeological evidence for religious rituals has come from burials. The first human beings to

Figure 17.8   A Venus figurine from Dolní Věstonice, Czechoslovakia.

deliberately bury their dead were the Neanderthal peoples of 70,000 years ago. The bodies of Neanderthal families have been found in French caves, such as La Ferrassie, buried in shallow pits, the skeletons covered with the red ochre powder that was scattered over their corpses. Ralph Solecki found Neanderthal burials in the Shanidar Cave in Iraq. One deformed individual had been killed in a rockfall from the cave roof and was buried with some choice cuts of game meat. Another skeleton was found in association with many pollens of some brightly colored wild flowers and a piney shrub. Perhaps, Solecki felt, this individual was covered with wild flowers before his grave was filled in. "No longer," he wrote, "can we deny the early men the full range of human feelings" (Solecki, 1972). The validity of this assertion has recently been challenged.

There are clear signs that highly organized religions were a feature of many of the more complex prehistoric societies. We have only to mention the Chavín and Olmec art styles and religious beliefs that spread so widely in Peru and Mesoamerica just before the emergence of state-organized societies to verify this. Such organized religions can be detected by the patterning of characteristic art objects or other artifacts clearly associated with religious rituals or by the appearance of public temples or ceremonial centers in small villages and towns. The ceremonial centers of the Mesopotamians were towering ziggurats that gave rise to the legend of the Tower of Babel, and Maya centers consisted of pyramids and other large strutures grouped around huge open plazas. The ceremonial center became a focus for a group of independent settlements, "the sanctified terrain where were manifested those hierophanies that guaranteed the seasonal renewal of cyclic time, and where the splendor, potency, and wealth of their rulers symbolized the well being of the whole community" (Wheatley, 1971). According to Mircea Eliade, the ceremonial center ensured the continuity of cultural traditions; the religious and moral models of society were laid down in sacred canons recited in temples in reassuring chants passed from generation to generation (Eliade, 1954).

The distinctive religious art and architecture of Teotihuacán reflects such interest in cultural continuity and ritual; so too do the cult objects of the Hopewell and the endless religious friezes and inscriptions of the ancient Egyptians. Maya calendars, too, are convincing evidence that the priests of one generation considered it their responsibility to ensure the continuity of religion for future generations.

Religious Systems.   Religious beliefs have often linked large areas of the world into gigantic spheres of common cosmology and ritual practices, even if the many peoples unified under a common religious banner enjoy widely disparate governmental, societal, and economic institutions. One has only to look at the distribution of Christianity and Islam to realize the importance of religion as an integrative force. Yet the many peoples who follow either religion are linked merely by a very general common belief, by some religious practices, and perhaps by some shared artistic or architectural traditions. Thousands of prehistoric societies, too, were linked by common beliefs and cosmologies, which are reflected in the archaeological record by common artistic traditions, temple and ceremonial center architecture, wall paintings, and even trade in cult objects. The Adena and Hopewell preoccupation with burial and death spread far beyond their Illinois and Ohio heartlands. The megalithic (large-stone) monuments of western Europe (Daniel, 1973), Mapungubwe and Zimbabwe in southern Africa, ceremonial centers connected with the Shona peoples—all are archaeological manifestations of widely distributed religious cults and beliefs (Garlake, 1973).

Until recently, religion and ritual have been thought of in isolation, not as integral to social organization, economic life, and political systems; but the ideas and beliefs, the core of all religions, are reflected in many aspects of human life, especially in art and architecture. Ethnologist Roy Rappaport has examined this problem of integration (Rappaport, 1968, 1971). His conceptual framework ties religion to other aspects of human life (Figure 17.9). Every society has its own model of how the world is put together, its own ultimate beliefs. An origin myth and other sacred propositions can shape the entire world of a society.

Rappaport argues that these sacred propositions are interpreted for the faithful through a body of theology and rituals associated with it. The rituals are more or less standardized, religious acts often repeated at regular times of the year—harvests, plantings, and other key times. Others are performed when needed: marriages, funerals, and the like. Some societies, such as those of the ancient Egyptians and the Maya, made regular calendars to time religious events and astronomical cycles. These regular ceremonies performed important functions not only in integrating society but also in such activities as redistributing food, population control by infanticide, and dispersing of surplus male cattle in the form of rit-

Figure 17.9 The circular relationship between Rappaport's ultimate sacred propositions, ritual, and religious experience. Ritual is also an articulation point between religion and socioenvironmental processes.

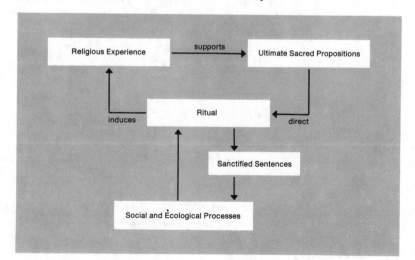

ually accumulated wealth. Any ritual, according to Rappaport, is designed to produce in the believer a religious experience that reinforces beliefs and ensures maintenance of belief. Religious experiences are predominantly emotional, often supernatural and awe-inspiring. Each aspect of religion—sacred propositions, ritual, experience—supports the others. A religion will operate through sanctified attitudes, values, and messages, an ethic that adds a sacred blessing, derived from the ultimate sacred propositions of the society, to elicit responses that ensure predictable responses from the people. Such predictability, sparked by directives from some central religious authority, ensures orderly operation of society. In time, as in Mesopotamia, that authority can become secular as well. The institutions and individuals associated with these messages can become sanctified, for they are associated with the very sacred propositions that lie at the heart of the society's beliefs. As societies became more complex, so too did the need for a stable framework to administer the needs of the many increasingly specialized subgroups that made up society as a whole.

By 3000 B.C. in Egypt and Mesopotamia, and between 1150 and 850 B.C. in Mesoamerica, there are signs that administrative authority became more institutionalized, dealing with all manner of social and economic problems, such as new rankings in society (reflected in burials), specialists' communities and households of specialists in each village, and an increased need for predictable social behavior and mutual interdependence. It is during these periods that the first of the more elaborate public buildings appear in the near East and, independently, in Mexico, temples and monumental works that reflect not only the involvement of individual communities but also that of other villages without ceremonial structures of their own. The emergence of such ceremonial buildings, and presumably, administrative centers had, as we showed earlier, a major effect on the hierarchies and spacing of settlements. Thus, in a sense, a circular relationship links the ultimate sacred beliefs and rituals of a society with the processes of social and environmental change that act upon them. And the link between administrative policy and belief is in ritual and the sanctified message.

To attempt to detect religion and ritual in the archaeological record without a careful research design is to invite disaster. As we have seen frequently, religious beliefs are intangible and survive only in the form of temples, ritual paraphernalia, and art. Viewed in isolation, the study of ancient religion seems a hopeless task, if archaeological finds are the only source of information available.

But if one views religion and ritual as integral in a society closely tied to all other aspects of its activities, then there is some hope that, armed with a theoretical framework, such as that of Rappaport, we may be able to look at ritual and religious artifacts in the context of a society as a whole.

Formative Oaxaca.   The presence or absence of distinctive ritual artifacts or buildings in a site or society may be significant. In Formative Oaxaca, public buildings appear between 1400 and 1150 B.C., many of them oriented eight degrees west of north and built on adobe and earth platforms (Flannery, 1976). Rare conch-shell trumpets and turtle-shell drums traded from the coastal lowlands were apparently used in public ceremonies in such buildings. Clay figurines of dancers wearing costumes and masks that make them look like fantastic creatures and animals, as well as pottery masks, are also signs of communal ritual (Figure 17.10). The personal ritual of self-mutilation by bloodletting was widespread in early Mesoamerica. The Spanish described how the Aztec nobles would gash themselves with knives or fish and stingray spines in acts of mutilation that were penances before the gods imposed by religion (Valliant, 1941). A few stingray spines have come from Middle Formative villages, probably traded into the far interior for the specific use of community leaders. Marine fish spines have been found in public buildings, houses, and even in refuse heaps of the Early Formative. Kent Flannery suggests that bloodletting fish spines were kept and used at home and that they were also used in public buildings. The ritual artifacts in the Oaxacan villages enabled Flannery and his colleagues to identify three levels of religious ceremony: personal bloodletting; dances run by sodalities, which cut across household lines; and public rituals in ceremonial buildings, involving a region wider than one village.

The Olmec Religion.   Robert Drennan, in studying the Olmec religion, used Rappaport's scheme to look closely at the role of religion in social change in early Mesoamerica. He argued that the sudden diffusion of the Olmec art style through Mesoamerica resulted from "the increased need for mechanisms of sanctification in various regions owing to internal social evolution" (Drennan, 1976). This diffusion occurred after the exchange networks for handling ritual objects, such as stingray spines, had been in operation for centuries. This interaction between lowlands and highlands was disrupted by the sudden collapse of Olmec society in the first millennium B.C.

Figure 17.10   Four clay figurines grouped deliberately to form a scene, found buried beneath an Early Formative house at San José Mogote in Oaxaca, Mexico. (No scale given.)

Drennan looked at the accumulated evidence on settlement patterns, population, and prehistoric agriculture in Olmec country. At the height of their prosperity, the two great Olmec centers of San Lorenzo and La Venta would have been strong magnets for increased human settlement, for drawing goods and services into the immediate vicinity of the ceremonial center. On the other hand, the outlying villages were dependent on tropical rain-forest agriculture, a shifting form of cultivation that tends to make people spread outward from their home base as their fields are exhausted and new forest is cleared. The land around San Lorenzo may have supported a peak population of 2,500 people living in those villages within 2 to 8 kilometers of each other. This occupation would have left little margin of land to cover fluctuations in productivity caused by flooding and other environmental phenomena. And, if the continued concentration of population and overuse of land continued, the resistance of society as a whole to environmental fluctuations would be drastically reduced. The result could be desanctification, the populace at large being unable to support the burden of a ritual system that regulated the checks and balances of their entire society. A social calamity ensued, resulting in the collapse not only of San Lorenzo and La Venta but also of the socioeconomic system and beliefs behind them. Perhaps many of the large Olmec statues at both sites were mutilated because such disfigurement was the final defiant act of desanctification of the entire belief system upon which the Olmec once thought their very existence depended.

Drennan's desanctification hypothesis is highly tentative. It does, however, demonstrate the importance of considering religious beliefs and the rituals that go with them as a part of the many complex regulatory mechanisms affecting not only prehistoric societies but our own as well.

The study of prehistoric religion depends heavily on the study of sacred artifacts and temples and also on careful research design. The most effective way to study such intangibles as social organization or religious beliefs and rituals is to consider them as integral to a society, closely tied to all other aspects of its activities.

Guide to Further Reading

Chapman, Robert, Ian Kinnes, and Klavs Randsborg, eds. *The Archaeology of Death*. Cambridge: Cambridge University Press, 1981.
A series of essays on the interpretation of mortuary practices. For the serious reader.

Earle, T. K., and J. E. Ericson, eds. *Exchange Systems in Prehistory*. New York: Academic Press, 1977.
Articles dealing with method and theory in the study of prehistoric trade. For the more advanced reader.

Rappaport, Roy A. *Pigs for the Ancestors*. New Haven: Yale University Press, 1968.
A fascinating study of the role of ritual in the cultural ecology of a New Guinea tribe. Essential reading for anyone interested in ritual as integral to a cultural system.

Sabloff, Jeremy A., and C. C. Lamberg-Karlovsky. *Ancient Civilizations and Trade.* Albuquerque: University of New Mexico Press, 1975.
Conference papers that cover a wide range of problems in the study of prehistoric trade. Strong on theory and actual case studies.

Woolley, C. L. *Ur Excavations, vol 2: The Royal Cemetery.* London and Philadelphia: British Museum and University of Pennsylvania Museum, 1943.
This detailed description of the pre-Dynastic royal cemetry is a classic of archaeology and provides fascinating insight into the study of prehistoric social organization.

PART VII

INTERPRETING CULTURE CHANGE IN THE PAST

Is it too late for salvation? If not, please let me have the analytical expertise of the New Archaeology—and the humility and common sense of the Old.

KENT V. FLANNERY
The Early Mesoamerican Village, 1976

Only in recent years have archaeologists become preoccupied with describing the past and also explaining it. In Part VII we look at the explanation of the past from two perspectives: the culture-historical perspective, which is an inductive form of archaeological research; and the processual perspective, which is based on deductive research. Neither of these two approaches to archaeological explanation is mutually exclusive. Much processual archaeology, for example, is based on data derived from inductive research.

Part VII shows what an amazing battery of powerful analytical tools is being brought to bear on archaeological interpretation. Archaeology is on the threshold of a quantum jump in analytical sophistication, in which the work of mathematicians, statisticians, and scientists will have a leading part. As Colin Renfrew (1979) observed, archaeologists are "replacing anecdote by analysis."

CHAPTER 18 ❧

CONSTRUCTING CULTURE HISTORY

Preview

- The study of culture history is based on inductive research methods and on a normative view of culture, which assumes that abstract rules govern what a given culture considers normal behavior.
- The process of constructing culture history begins with identifying a research area, with reconnaissance and surface survey. These efforts yield at least a tentative chronological sequence for the area, which is based on attributes and artifact types that have been seriated in their correct order. Then, carefully selected excavations are made to test, refine, and expand the sequence. The data are then analyzed and classified. Artifacts and structures are used as sensitive barometers of cultural change; they are divided into complexes, each of which is used to chronicle one aspect of technological and cultural change.
- The process of synthesis in culture history is based on constructing precise chronological sequences. Expanding these chronologies beyond one site or occupation layer is a cumulative process, in which seriation and cross-dating have key roles.
- A series of arbitrary archaeological units are used to aid in this synthesis. Local chronological sequences lie at the core of all culture-historical research. These are based on phases, which are cultural units in a local sequence that possess culture traits sufficient to distinguish them from all other phases. Normally, the boundaries of a phase are set arbitrarily. The term *component* describes a single manifestation of a phase at a single site.
- Archaeological regions are normally defined by natural geographic boundaries, but culture areas are much larger and coincide with major ethnographic culture areas—such as the Southwest.

- Horizons link a number of phases in neighboring areas, containing rather general cultural patterns, which are often distinguished by characteristic art styles, as the Chavín of Peru. The term *tradition* describes a lasting artifact type—assemblages of tools, architectural styles, and so on—which last much longer than a phase, or even a horizon.
- The interpretation of culture history depends on analogy and descriptive cultural models that are used to identify variables that operate when culture change takes place.
- Some commonly accepted descriptive models of cultural change are inevitable variation, cultural selection, diffusion, and migration. These in themselves, however, do not describe the factors that led to cultural change in the first place.

In Part II, we discussed how reconstruction of culture history was a major preoccupation of archaeologists from the early years of this century. Culture history itself describes human cultures in the past, and it is based on chronological and spatial ordering of archaeological data. This approach is a sound way of describing the past, based as it is on the chronological and spatial ordering of archaeological data. But it is of minimal use for explaining variability in the archaeological record or cultural process. As we shall see, some of the mechanisms, like diffusion, which culture historians have used to explain the past are, in fact, not even explanations at all. In this chapter we describe the culture-historical approach and some of its limitations.

THE CULTURE-HISTORICAL METHOD

The study of culture history is based on two fundamental principles that were enumerated as long ago as the early years of this century by Franz Boas, N.C. Nelson, and A. V. Kidder (Willey and Sabloff, 1975). These principles are: *inductive research methods*, the development of generalizations about a research problem that are based on numerous specific observations (see Chapter 9); and *a normative view of culture*, which is based on the notion that abstract rules govern what the culture considers normal behavior. The normative view is a descriptive approach to culture, which can be used to describe culture during one time period or throughout time. Archaeologists base it on the assumption that surviving artifacts, such as potsherds, display stylistic and other changes that represent the changing norms of human behavior throughout time.

Most archaeological interpretation in the New and Old Worlds has been based on normative models. The culture-historical approach has resulted in a descriptive outline of prehistory in time and space for much of the world. The interpretation of culture-historical data is based on simple analogies from historical and ethnographic data, far simpler than those envisaged by archaeologists studying living societies today (Chapter 15). Within its limitations, culture-historical reconstruction is a useful organizational tool that has added some descriptive order to world prehistory.

Constructing Culture History. All culture-history research is based on inductive methods, which acquire specific data from one or many archaeological sites that are not only accumulated but also subjected to a gradual synthesis that leads to generalizations based on the data.

The sequence of research begins with identifying a research area, with reconnaissance and surface survey. These surveys yield a mass of surface collections, which allow the researcher to develop at least a tentative chronological sequence for the area, based on attributes and artifact types that are seriated according to the principles outlined in Chapter 13. The research continues with carefully selected excavations designed to test the validity of the sequence and to refine and expand it as well. Although the excavations may be meant, ultimately, to recover structures and village layouts, their primary goals are always stratigraphic—observing and recording occupation layers and developing relative and absolute chronologies. The data from the excavations are then analyzed and classified and used to refine the preliminary classifications and chronologies put together before digging began.

This data base consists of artifacts and structures and of food remains and other information. The process of classification involves analyzing all these categories of data. Artifacts and structures are the primary interest of culture historians, for they provide a sensitive barometer for studying technological and cultural change throughout time and space. Often, artifacts and structures are divided into *complexes*, chronological subdivisions of artifact forms, such as stone tools, pottery, and bone objects, each of which can be used to chronicle an aspect of technological and cultural change. Some artifact complexes, such as pottery, are more sensitive than others, and these are the ones that are used for correlating cultural sequences with one another. Archaeologists have developed arbitrary time-space units to aid them in this process.

SYNTHESIS: ARCHAEOLOGICAL UNITS

The basis of all culture-historical reconstruction is the precise and carefully described site chronology. The synthesis of these chronologies beyond the confines of one site or local area involves not only repeating the same descriptive processes at other sites, but also constantly refining the original cultural sequence from the original excavations. The synthesis is cumulative, for some new excavations may yield cultural materials that are not represented in the early digs. It is here that the techniques of seriation and cross-dating come into play. This is, of course, an entirely descriptive exercise, which yields no explanations whatsoever. It is a site-oriented procedure, too, very different from the regional surveys that have dominated archaeological research in recent years.

The archaeological units used to aid the synthesis form an arbitrary, hierarchic classification for this purpose. They represent the combining of the formal content of a site or sites with its distribution in time and space. Three occupation levels in a Utah cave each have distinctive artifact assemblages that have been sorted into types. Occupation levels at a dozen nearby sites contain examples of these three assemblages. What arbitrary units can we use to help us compare these various sites and occupation levels with their different contents? What arbitrary units will assist us to study cultural change as well? The archaeological units used most widely in the Americas are those developed by Gordon Willey and Philip Phillips (1958), and we describe some of these below.

Components and Phases.   The basis of culture history is the local chronological sequence, whether at one site or many. Once chronological types are identified, they are studied closely to see how they cluster to reflect the cultural chronology of the site as a whole. It is here that you use the first in the hierarchy of archaeological units:

Components are culturally homogeneous stratigraphic units within a site. An occupation site like Martin's Hundred, Virginia, will consist of a single component, but a settlement occupied at three different times will contain three distinct components. Each may belong to a separate cultural phase. The Koster site in Illinois could be described as an excellent example of a multicomponent site, with its various layers representing different components separated by sterile layers of soil (Struever and Holton, 1979).

"Cultural homogeneity" is, of course, an intangible, so that the definition of a component depends very much on stratigraphic observation and the archaeologist's observational skills. Some cave sites in southwest France contain many occupation levels separated by sterile layers. These can, of course, be isolated stratigraphically and be grouped on the basis of shared chronological types like antler harpoons or side scrapers. In other sites, as in San Cristobal in the Great Basin, the midden deposits were so churned up that the various components had to be separated by quantitative artifact analysis rather than stratigraphic observation (Thomas, 1979).

Components occur at one location. To produce a regional chronology, one must synthesize them with components from other sites, using the next analytical step:

Phases consist of similar components from more than one site. They are limited to a specific locality or region and span a relatively limited period of chronological time (Willey and Phillips, 1958). Distinctive culture traits distinguish one phase from another; in themselves these are characteristic of the phase, and the passage of a relatively brief time. Again, the phase is somewhat subjective in its application, and much depends on the judgment of the archaeologist.

Thomas (1979) uses the Gatecliff shelter in Nevada to show how components and phases mesh. He found five components at the site, each defined by chronological types. As long as he was excavating just one site, this procedure was fine. But he wanted to compare the Gatecliff findings with those from other excavated sites in central Nevada. He found that a number of these sites contained late components with artifacts like projectile points and Shoshoni pottery similar to those found in equivalent stratigraphic contexts at Gatecliff. He brought together the components from Gatecliff and the other sites into a phase, which he named Yellow Blade. This period dates from about A.D. 1300 to 1850, the moment of European contact. The phase term applies not only to Gatecliff, but to the entire region. It is the basic unit of area synthesis. Some phases are but a few years long, others span centuries, even millennia. All the phase really does is to break up long, continuous periods of prehistoric time into discrete chronological and spatial units, each with their specific artifacts. The Gatecliff site was occupied for about 8,000 years, divided by chronological types into five components stacked one upon the other. Each of these components has its own dates and characteristic artifacts. The components can be compared to those from other sites and be used to build up a regional chronology. The phase enables us to establish regional contemporaneity. At first a phase may embrace, as the Yellow Blade phase does, as much as 550 years or more. But, as research proceeds, chronologies become more refined, and artifact classifications become finer, the original phase may be broken down even further into more and more chronologically precise subphases.

Regions and Culture Areas. Culture-historical synthesis involves working with much larger areas in time and space than those covered by phases or local sequences. The two major divisions are archaeological regions and culture areas.

Archaeological regions are normally defined by natural geographic boundaries. They may also be defined, however, by a heavy concentration of archaeological sites. Normally, a region will display some cultural homogeneity. Examples are the Santa Barbara channel region and the valley of Oaxaca in Mexico.

Culture areas define much larger tracts of land, and they often coincide with the broad ethnographic culture areas identified by early anthropologists. Many areas tend to coincide with the various physiographic divisions of the world. The southwestern United States is one such area, as it is defined, in part, by its history of research, and in part, by cultural and environmental associations that lasted more than 2,000 years. Such large areas can be divided into subareas, where differences within the culture of an area are sufficiently distinctive to separate one subarea from another. The Southwest was divided by Gordon Willey (1966) into the Anasazi, Hohokam, and Mogollon subareas, among others (Figure 18.1). But *area* implies nothing more than a very general and widespread cultural homogeneity. Within any large area, societies will adapt to new circumstances—some evolving more quickly than others—and enjoy quite different economies.

Stages, Periods, Horizons, and Traditions. In Chapter 6 we described the three-age system, an evolutionary framework of cultural stages that still provides a broad framework for Old World prehistory. This evolutionary scheme has no exact counterpart in the Americas, where the early archaeologists deliberately avoided

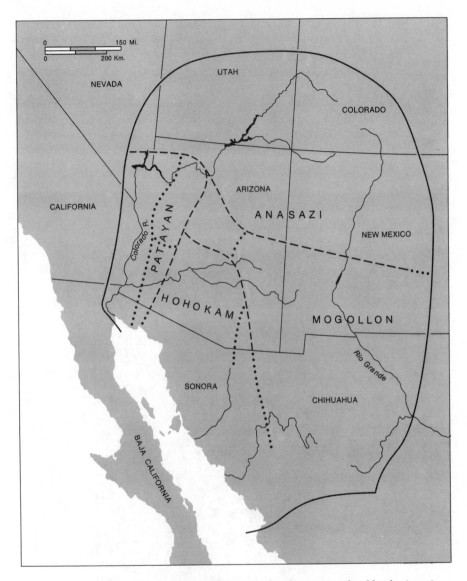

Figure 18.1 Archaeological regions and subareas in the North American Southwest. (After Gordon Willey.)

evolutionary models. For generations, Old World archaeologists have been filling in details of the three-age framework. The Stone Age, the Bronze Age, and the Iron Age are the broadest of technological stages. All are purely arbitrary technological labels, which in no way coincide exactly with any levels of social evolution. Periods, on the other hand, are units of time, during which specific cultural phenomena are observed. The Stone Age is a technological stage that, although it ended in Mesopotamia about 6,000 years ago,

Figure 18.2   Chavín carving on a pillar in the temple interior at Chavín de Huantar, Peru. The Chavín art style formed one of the bases for identifying the Chavín horizon in Peruvian prehistory.

is still in progress in parts of the Amazon Basin. In contrast, the Inca period in Peru lasted from about A.D. 1200 to 1534.

New World archaeologists have two units that synthesize archaeological data over wide areas: horizons and traditions.

Horizons link a number of phases in neighboring areas that contain rather general cultural patterns in common. In some parts of the world, an all-embracing religious cult may transcend cultural boundaries and spread over an enormous area. Such cults are often associated with characteristic religious artifacts or art styles that can be identified in phases hundreds of miles apart—in well-defined chronological contexts. The Chavín art style of coastal Peru, for example, was associated with distinctive religious beliefs and rituals shared by many Peruvian societies in the highlands and lowlands between 900 B.C. and 200 B.C. (Willey, 1971). This commonality of belief is manifested in the archaeological record by Chavín art, a style that stresses savage, jaguarlike motifs; hence the use of the term *Chavín Horizon* (Figure 18.2).

The term *tradition* has widespread application in archaeology. It is used to describe a lasting artifact type, assemblages of tools, architectural styles, economic practices, or art styles that last much longer than one phase or even the duration of a horizon. The toolmaking tradition, for example, may continue in use while the many cultures that share it develop in entirely different ways. Tradition implies a degree of cultural continuity, even if shifts in cultural adaptation have taken place in the meantime. A good example of such a tradition is the so-called Arctic small-tool tradition of Alaska, which originated at least as early as 4000 B.C. (Dumond, 1977). The small tools made by these hunter-gatherers were so effective that they continued in use until recent times and led to the modern Eskimo cultures of the far north.

INTERPRETATION

The interpretation of culture history depends on analogy and descriptive cultural models, which are used to identify the variables that are in operation when culture change takes place. These models are used to account for changes in the archaeological record. This record, however, does not invariably show a smooth and orderly chronicle of culture change. A seriated pottery sequence from six sites may display the sudden arrival of a new ware that is

radically different from others in the sequence. An entire new artifact inventory may suddenly appear in components at eight sites,
while the toolkits of earlier centuries rapidly vanish. The economy
of sites in a local sequence may change completely within fifty
years as the plow comes into use in the locality. Such changes are
readily observed in the thousands of local sequences found in the
archaeological record. But how did these changes come about?
What processes of cultural change were at work to cause major and
minor alterations in the archaeological record? A number of
descriptive models have been formulated to characterize culture
change: some of these are cultural models, others noncultural; several involve internal change, others external influence.

Cultural Models.   The widely used models of culture change in
archaeology are inevitable variation, cultural selection, and the
three classic processes—invention, diffusion, and migration (Trigger, 1968).

Inevitable variation.   This is somewhat similar to the well-known
biological phenomenon of genetic drift. As people learn the behavior patterns of their society, inevitably some minor differences in
learned behavior will appear from generation to generation;
although minor in themselves, these differences accumulate over a
long time, especially if the populations are isolated. Today we live
in a far more complex society than people did even thirty years ago.
The "snowballing" effect of inevitable variation and slow-moving
cultural evolution can be detected in dozens of prehistoric societies,
not least among them the Adena and Hopewell cultures of the
American Midwest, whose burial customs and religious beliefs
gradually assumed great complexity between 1000 B.C. and the early
centuries of the Christian era (Snow, 1976). The story of culture
change in prehistory has been one of gradual acceleration in cultural evolution, with an attendant increase in the rate of technological invention, population movements, and the spread of new ideas.

Cultural selection.   This concept is somewhat analogous to that of
natural selection in biological evolutions. It is the notion that
human cultures accept or reject new traits—whether technological,
economic, or intangible—on the basis of whether or not they are
advantageous to society as a whole. Cultural selection results in
cumulative cultural change, and it operates within the prevailing
values of the society. This condition tends to make it harder for a

society to accept social change as opposed to technological advance, which is less circumscribed by restrictive values. The state-organized societies in Mesopotamia and Mexico resulted from centuries of gradual social evolution, where centralized political and religious authority was perceived to be advantageous.

Invention. The first of the three classic processes that contribute to culture change involves creating a new idea and transforming it—in archaeological contexts—into an artifact or other tangible innovation. Unfortunately, many inventions, such as new religions or ideas, leave little tangible trace in the archaeological record. An invention implies either the modifying of an old idea or series of ideas, or the creation of a completely new concept; it may come about by accident or by intentional research. The atom was split by long and patient investigation, with the ultimate objective of fragmentation; fire was probably the result of an accident. Inventions spread, and if they are sufficiently important, they spread widely and rapidly. The transistor is in almost universal use because it is an effective advance in electronic technology; plows had an equally dramatic effect on agriculture in prehistoric Europe. How inventions spread has been studied extensively by archaeologists and anthropologists, for the quality of inventiveness is an essential part of the human genius, as our society defines it.

In the early study of prehistory, people assumed that metallurgy and other major innovations were invented in only one place, a notion that led to the great diffusionist theories of fifty years ago (Figure 18.3). But as people have come to understand the impor-

Figure 18.3 Iron-bladed dagger of the Egyptian pharaoh Tutankhamun, *ca.* 1340 B.C. This weapon was probably made of native hammered iron. The Egyptians tried, without success, to obtain iron tools from the Hittites after hearing of the revolutionary new metal.

tance of environment and adaptation in prehistory, they have realized that many inventions have been made in several parts of the world, where identical adaptive processes occurred. Agriculture is known to have developed quite independently in the Near East, southeast Asia, Mesoamerica, and Peru, quite apart from its supposed origins in northern China.

Diffusion. This model is defined as the processes by which new ideas or cultural traits spread from one person to another or from one group to another—often over long distances. Much modern research on diffusion is about how innovations that are new to the recipients spread to other areas. Diffusion can proceed through such diverse mechanisms as trade, warfare, frequent visits between neighboring communities, and migrations of entire communities. A key issue here is the formal or informal mechanisms of contact between the members of separate groups that account for the spread and acceptance of a new idea.

Just how are patterned stylistic trait distributions diffused from one area to another? The subject is rich in controversy and invalid assumptions (Davis, 1983). The growing popularity of evolutionary explanations in recent years has led to wholesale rejections of diffusion as a way of interpreting the past, so much so that archaeologists have tended to neglect it. Diffusion is, however, assuming new importance as large bodies of regional data are produced by large-scale CRM surveys in such areas as the San Juan and Great Basins.

Current archaeological thinking about diffusion stems from pioneer work by early anthropologists like Franz Boas and Alfred Kroeber. They were interested in diffusion, but argued that the symbolic value or prestige of a culture trait were major factors in determining whether it was accepted and diffused to other societies. Archaeologists borrowed some of this thinking in the 1930s, but found it impossible to establish the social context of culture traits from the archaeological record alone. They therefore assumed that acceptance of culture traits was directly proportional to the frequency with which people learned about an innovation. This simplistic approach, which often talked of culture "contact" instead of diffusion, collapsed in the face of more sophisticated archaeological and ethnographic studies showing that knowledge of an innovation did not necessarily mean that it would be adopted (Schiffer, 1979). A classic example occurs among the aborigines of northern

Australia, who are well aware of agriculture among their neighbors, but still remain hunter-gatherers themselves.

Diffusion of this type is still found among some archaeologists,
including those who study possible trans-Atlantic and trans-Pacific
contacts between Old World and New (Riley, 1971). Were European
or African crops diffused to the Americas? The researchers interested in this kind of topic concentrate not so much, as they should,
on the social context of the innovations, as on the archaeological
criteria for establishing diffusion in the archaeological record.

Let us look at this sort of approach to diffusion more closely. Figure 18.4 diagrams a culture trait in space and time. Let us say that a
new type of painted pot is invented in a village in about A.D. 1400.
The advantages of this new pot are so great that villagers ten miles
away learn about the vessel at a beer party five years later. Within
ten years, potters are making similar receptacles. In a short time the
pot form is found not only in one village but in three within a ten-
mile radius. By A.D. 1450, the pot form is so widely used that dozens
of villages within a fifty-mile circle of the original settlement are
making the same vessels. Plotting this development on paper yields
the cone effect shown in Figure 18.4, and it is this effect that is the
principle applied by culture historians looking at diffusion.

Under this topic, several criteria have to be satisfied before one
can decide whether a series of artifacts in archaeological sites dis-

Figure 18.4   The spread of a culture trait in time and space: the *cone effect.*

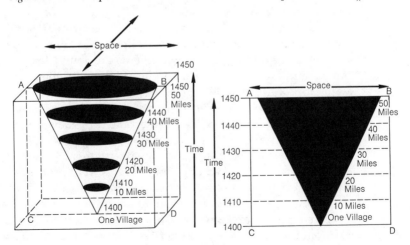

tant from one another are related to each other in a historically meaningful way. First, the traits or objects must be sufficiently similar in design and typological attributes to indicate that they probably have a common origin. Second, it must be shown that the traits did not result from convergent evolution. The earlier development of the trait, perhaps as general as a form of architecture or a domestic animal, must be carefully traced in both cultures. Third, distributions of the surviving traits must be carefully studied, as well as those of their antecedents. The only acceptable evidence for diffusion of a trait is a series of sites that show, when plotted on a map, continuous distribution for the trait or, perhaps, a route along which it spread. Accurate chronological control is essential, with a time-gradient from either end of the distribution, or one from the middle. For many traits, the archaeological criteria may be difficult to establish; indeed, they are rarely satisfied, but the importance of reliable evidence is obvious. Theoretical speculations are all very well, but they may result in completely false conclusions, sometimes supported by uncritical use of scanty archaeological evidence (Thompson, 1956).

Instances of diffusion in prehistory are legion. There are innumerable cases wherein ideas or new technologies have spread widely from their place of origin, although none are as grandiose as Elliot Smith's schemes or Thor Heyerdahl's attempts to prove that the Egyptians colonized Mesoamerica. A well-documented instance is the religious beliefs of the Adena and Hopewell peoples of the Midwest, who enjoyed beliefs associated with death that spread far beyond the relatively narrow confines of the Midwest. Religious beliefs are expressed in the form of distinctive rituals, which for the Adena and Hopewell involved extensive earthwork and mound building. Such monuments are found far outside the Adena and Hopewell heartlands, as are the cult objects associated with Hopewell ritual. For the Hopewell, we know that widespread exchange networks carried raw materials and fine cult objects all over the Midwest, as well as farther afield (Struever and Houart, 1972). These networks were the means by which religions and rituals and the material culture associated with them were transmitted to other groups. The exchange transactions were probably handled through kin connections that involved individual bonds of friendship between people in different communities. These friendships involved regular exchange of luxury goods, in situations where the gift could not be refused. These ties not only cemented friendships but aided diffusion as well (Figure 18.5).

Figure 18.5   A Hopewell craftsman cut this human hand from a sheet of mica. It was found in an Ohio burial mound with the body of its owner, who lived 370 miles from the nearest mica source. An example of the consequence of diffusion of religious beliefs, this hand probably had powerful shamanistic associations in Hopewell society.

During the 1960s and 1970s, the move away from normative explanations led to research into a number of basic assumptions about diffusion. Ethnoarchaeological studies of pottery making have shown just how important informal communication between potters is in spreading technological and stylistic changes (Longacre, 1974). Some basic research into the role of artifact style in reinforcing social identity and solidarity is important, because it identifies factors that may have accelerated or rejected adoption of culture traits (Plog, 1980). Despite these efforts, and a large body of diffusion research in other social sciences, many archaeologists are deeply suspicious of diffusion research, partly because a body of archaeological theory on the subject still does not exist. (For a valuable and comprehensive discussion, see Davis, 1983.)

Much of the unpopularity of diffusion stems from archaeologists using the term wrongly. Diffusion itself is not a cause of the spread or adoption of culture traits, it is a way of referring to a set of phenomena that have been caused by a wide range of cultural factors. To say that bronze swordmaking diffused from one society to another is merely a label describing what has happened. It does not describe *how* the spread occurred. Under the culture-history title, diffusion has been invoked as a satisfactory explanation for distribution patterns of culture traits, when in fact the factors behind the diffusion are still unexplained.

Migration. Migration as an explanatory concept suffers from many of the same disadvantages as diffusion. But this type of cultural change involves movement of entire populations, both large and small. Migration can be peaceful, or it can be the result of deliberate aggression, ending in invasion and conquest.

In every case, people deliberately decide to expand their sphere of influence into new areas. English settlers moved to the North American continent, taking their own culture and society with them; the Spanish occupied Mexico. Such population movements result not only in diffusion of ideas but also in a mass shift of people, with extensive social and cultural changes accompanying it.

For migration to be recognized in the archaeological record, one would need to find local sequences where the phases show a complete disruption of earlier cultural patterns by an intrusive new phase—not just of one tool type, or even several. Of course, some elements in earlier cultural traditions might survive and become an acculturated part of the peoples' new culture. Perhaps the classic instance of migration in world prehistory is that of the Polynesians, who settled the remote islands of the Pacific by deliberate voyaging from archipelago to archipelago (Bellwood, 1979). Each time, the islands were discovered by an act of deliberate exploration, by voyagers who set out with every intention of returning. Hawaii, Easter Island, and Tahiti were first settled by deliberate colonization that was perforce a migration of a small number of people to a new, uninhabited land mass. The kind of total population movement, or in some cases, population replacement, which occurs with mass migrations of this type is rare in human prehistory. It will be reflected in the archaeological record either by totally new components and phases of artifacts or by skeletal evidence. When a total replacement is violent, a result of widespread warfare, the occurrence of such an event must be proved by excavation. It is not sufficient to find a few skeletons lying in confusion and then claim that a city was sacked, as Mortimer Wheeler did at Moenjo-daro in the Indus Valley (Wheeler, 1963).

A second type of migration, on a much smaller scale, occurs when a small group of foreigners move into another region and settle there as an organized group. A group of Oaxacans may have done just that at Teotihuacán in the Valley of Mexico (Millon, 1973). They settled in their own special precinct of the city, tentatively identified by a concentration of Oaxacan potsherds and ornaments. The Oaxacan enclave lasted for centuries.

There are other forms of migration, too. Slaves and artisans wander as unorganized migrants. Artisans are an important source of diffusion of techniques and ideas. This type of unorganized migration is difficult to discern in the form of culture traits, for the individual migrant leaves little behind except, perhaps, some specialist artifacts, as bronzeworking migrant artisans did in prehistoric Europe. Finally, there are great warrior migrations, such as those of the Eastern nomads in temperate Europe and the warlike Nguni tribes of southern Africa (Omer-Cooper, 1966). Both of these warrior bands swept over an indigenous, sedentary population, causing widespread disruption and population shifts. But, within a few generations the warrior newcomers had adopted the sedentary way of life of their neighbors and were virtually indistinguishable from them. Such migrations leave few traces in archaeological sites.

Noncultural Models.   Cultural change triggered by alterations in the natural environment is an integral part of culture history. The model for this type of change is a simple one. Earlier models for the origins of agriculture in the Near East were based on the notion that the climate became progressively drier. Animal and human populations were forced into oases, where people started to domesticate animals and grow wild cereal grasses so that they could survive (Redman, 1978). In other words, climatic changes caused cultural modifications. More recent research has shown, however, that actually a large number of highly complex variables were involved in the development of food production in this area, environmental change being only one of them.

Of course, human cultures can modify their environments, either accidentally or deliberately. Enormous areas of the Sahel regions of the southern Sahara have been stripped of vegetation by the overgrazing of goats and other domestic animals. These areas are now deserts, and the local people are starving as a result of their long-term cultural practices. One should emphasize the words "long-term," for such modifications are not simply a phenomenon of recent times.

The most recent research in archaeology has focused heavily on specific details of the relationship between the environment and prehistoric cultures. The complex models that are growing from this research show that earlier models were far too general to explain these complex and ever-changing environment-culture relationships.

Reconstruction of culture history is a descriptive process, which is very difficult and complex and which depends on the availability of large amounts of basic data to be effective. In itself, inductive research of the type involved in culture history takes little account of the role of artifacts in the whole cultural system. Thus, the explanation of cultural process requires far more complex models based on quite a different approach to archaeology. These are described in Chapter 19.

Guide to Further Reading

Childe, V. G. *Piecing Together the Past.* London: Routledge and Kegan Paul, 1956.
Although dated, this is still an eloquent and easy-to-understand exposition of the basic principles of constructing culture history—European style.

Rouse, Irving. *Introduction to Prehistory: A Systematic Approach.* New York: McGraw-Hill, 1972.
A basic account, which is widely quoted, of archaeological units at the synthetic level.

Willey, Gordon R., and Philip Phillips. *Method and Theory in American Archaeology.* Chicago: University of Chicago Press, 1958.
I have heard this work described as the culture historian's bible. Certainly it is a fundamental source on the methods of culture history, which forms part of the training of every professional archaeologist.

CHAPTER 19 ✍

STUDY OF
CULTURAL PROCESS
PROCESSUAL ARCHAEOLOGY

Preview

- Processual archaeology is based on deductive research methodology that employs formal research design, explicit research hypotheses, and the testing of these against basic data. Its methods are cumulative; that is, synthesized archaeological data are interpreted on the basis of successive generations of working hypotheses that are tested again and again.
- The processual approach is based firmly on culture history and on data obtained from inductive research. The differences between it and the inductive approach lie in the orientation of the research, which is deductive rather than inductive.
- Processual archaeologists who use the deductive nomological approach are committed to a highly formal, scientific methodology that is based on the study of general laws and the work of philosophers of science. They who consider the world to be composed of observable phenomena that act in an orderly way. In other words, the world can be explained by predicting when a set of phenomena, that indicate a particular law is in operation, will occur.
- General laws governing human behavior are derived from anthropology and other social sciences. But many archaeologists reject the assumption that such general laws exist and believe that the highly specific, deductive scientific methods of physics and other sciences are inappropriate to archaeological data. They do, however, recognize the value of deductive research.

- Most processual archaeology embraces a systems-ecological approach that deals with the ways in which cultural systems function, both internally and in relation to external factors, such as the environment. This approach is based on general systems theory, cultural ecology, and multilinear cultural evolution.
- The systems approach provides a way of looking at relationships between different traits within a cultural system. In contrast to closed systems, such as a heating thermostat, which is self-regulating, archaeologists deal with open systems that are regulated, at least in part, by external stimuli. In cultural systems, these stimuli are the elements in the environment. The regulatory mechanisms that govern the system keep it in equilibrium and sometimes trigger further cultural change through positive feedback.
- Cultural ecologists see human cultures as subsystems interacting with other subsystems, all of which are part of a total ecosystem. Under this rubric, human culture is, ecologically speaking, a way in which human beings compete successfully with other plants, animals, and human beings.
- Multilinear cultural evolution recognizes that cultural adaptations are complex processes, fine-tuned to local conditions, with long-term cumulative effects. The four stages of the evolution of social organization described in Chapter 17 are defined in terms of social complexity, subsistence strategy, and population size, among other factors.
- Processual archaeology has proved effective in studying the origins of literate civilization, for explanations for cultural change are now couched in terms of multiple causes rather than single prime movers. The new multicausal models resulting from the systems-ecological approach will require development of new, rigorous methodologies for data collection, comparative studies of cultural variables in the archaeological record, and the tracing of the development of these variables in the millennia immediately preceding the origins of civilization.
- Future research in processual archaeology undoubtedly will make much use of mathematical models, for biologists and archaeologists are facing the same problem: How do forms, whether living or cultural, emerge and stabilize? The research problems being faced are very complex, and the sciences provide archaeologists with new and sophisticated tools with which to solve them.

Processual archaeology, defined in Chapter 4, is a phenomenon of the 1960s and 1970s that stemmed from the research of W. W. Taylor, Albert Spaulding, and Lewis Binford, among many others (Binford, 1972). It provides a vehicle for closely examining cultural process and a viable means of searching for explanations of culture change in prehistory (Plog, 1974). This chapter describes some of the applications of processual archaeology.

PROCESSUAL APPROACH

Processual archaeology is based on deductive research methodology that employs research design, formulation of explicit research hypotheses, and testing of these against basic data. Its methods are cumulative; that is, initial hypotheses are designed that propose a working model to explain culture change. These hypotheses are tested against basic data, and some are discarded, while others are retested again and again, until the factors that affect cultural change are isolated in highly specific form. The synthesized archaeological data are interpreted on the basis of successive generations of working hypotheses that are tested many times.

The processual approach is firmly based on culture history and data obtained from inductive research. It has to be, for the chronological and spatial frameworks for prehistory come from descriptive methods developed over many years of arduous fieldwork and analysis. The difference between the two approaches lies in the *orientation* of the research. Processual archaeologists rely on deductive strategies that begin with formulating testable hypotheses and proceed to the gathering of data to test them. Very often, however, the initial hypotheses are based on data derived from inductive culture history.

The early days of processual archaeology were marked by furious academic controversy between not only culture historians and those espousing processual methodology but also between proponents of different approaches to the study of cultural process (Flannery, 1973). Two methods are commonly espoused: the dedutive nomological approach and the systems-ecological approach.

Deductive-Nomological Approach. Archaeologists who use this approach are firmly committed to a highly formal, scientific methodology, which is based on the work of Carl Hempel and other philosophers of science (Watson, Redman, and Le Blanc, 1971). Nomology is the study of general laws; a deductive-nomological approach is based on the philosophy of logical positivism. This philosophy considers the world to be composed of observable phenomena that act in an orderly way. It views the world as governed by general laws that can be identified by rigorous research methods. In other words, the world can be explained by predicting when a set of phenomena occurs that indicate that a particular law is in operation.

In archaeology, these general laws are derived from anthropology and other social sciences. Laws have been formulated about the relationships between human cultures and the environment, about ecological adaptation, and about cultural evolution (Sahlins and Service, 1960). Most of them are so generalized, however, that it is difficult to test them with specific data. Nevertheless, some archaeologists believe that archaeological data can be used to formulate and test hypotheses that identify the general and universal laws governing cultural process.

At the heart of this approach to processual archaeology is the notion that there actually are general laws that govern human behavior. Proponents of the deductive-nomological approach also assume that formal scientific experiments, which can be repeated and can produce predictable results, can be used to identify instances when a particular law is in operation. Their explanations of cultural change are based on the predictability of these results. In other words, the hypothesis that allows accurate prediction of similar phenomena in one area under the same circumstances elsewhere is the one that can be justified as the best explanation.

The trouble is that archaeology just is not that sort of science. The deductive-nomological approach came to archaeology late in the 1960s, when to become a science was a desirable goal for archaeology. Physics had a theoretical rigor that was attractive to people who wanted more scientific rigor in archaeology. But physics has an essential metaphysic and spacelike conception of reality that is quite different from that of archaeology, which concentrates so on change through time (Dunnell, 1982). The highly specific deductive methods applied to physics and other hard sciences are far less applicable to archaeological data, which are governed mainly by intangible variables such as values and beliefs. Deductive research is extremely valuable for study of the past, provided that realistic account is taken of the uniqueness of archaeological data. If there is one scientific discipline that archaeology lies closest to, it is biology, for biologists are struggling with many similar theoretical problems connected with change (for a prolonged discussion, see Dunnell, 1982).

Systems-Ecological Approach. The second and more common processual approach deals with the ways in which cultural systems function, both internally and in relation to external factors, such as the natural environment. It involves three basic models of cultural change: *systems models,* which are based on general systems theory; *cultural ecology,* which provides complicated models of the interactions between human cultures and their environments; and *multilinear cultural evolution,* which combines both systems approaches and cultural ecology in a theory of the cumulative evolution of culture over long periods through complex adaptations to the environment.

The argument for using the systems-ecological approach was summarized by Kent Flannery some years ago (1973), when he wrote that archaeologists using these models are intent on "the search for the ways human populations (in their own way) do the things that other systems do."

General systems theory was first constructed in the sciences in the 1950s. It is a body of theoretical concepts that provides a way of searching for "general relationships" in the empirical world. By the same token, a system is defined as "a whole which functions as a whole by virtue of the interdependence of its parts" (Rapoport, 1968). Systems theory has been widely applied in physics and other "hard" sciences, where relationships between parts of a system can be defined with great precision. It has obvious appeal to archaeologists, for its believers assume that any organization, however simple or complex, can be studied as a system of interrelated concepts (Salmon, 1982). A change in one of these components will trigger reactions in many of the other parts. The notion of cultural systems, which was described in Chapter 5, is derived, in part, from systems theory.

Archaeologists took to systems theory with great enthusiasm as part of the great borrowing of concepts from the sciences that took hold in the 1960s and 1970s. They thought of human cultures as "open" systems, regulated in part by external stimuli. This general concept is most applicable to human cultures that interact intimately with the natural environment. For a while, everything was interpreted within rigid systems frameworks, as if human cultures were like systems in physics. So many intangibles affect the operation of human cultural systems, however, that the initial enthusiasm soon evaporated, to be replaced by the realization that systems theory was valuable as a general concept, and little more. The advantage of systems theory is that it frees one from having to look at only one agent of cultural change, such as irrigation or diffusion; and it allows one to focus instead on regulatory mechanisms and on the relationships between different components of a cultural system and the system as a whole and its environment. The systems approach is invaluable to archaeology as it is to the study of ecology—as a general concept. But we must keep in mind that the data used to test the hypotheses derived to validate this model are acquired by the same methods used to acquire valuable culture-historical information.

CULTURAL ECOLOGY

As we saw in Chapter 4, processual archaeology relies not only on the concepts of systems theory but also on the study of cultural ecology (Netting, 1977). Cultural ecology is a way of obtaining a total picture of how human populations adapt to and transform their environments. These environments include not only the natural landscape but also vegetational and animal populations as well as other cultures.

This method is being hailed widely as a possible explanation for many major cultural changes in prehistory. Cultural ecologists see human cultures as subsystems interacting with other subsystems, all forming part of a total ecosystem with three major subsystems: human culture, the biotic community, and the physical environment. Thus the key to cultural process lies in understanding the interactive relationships between the various subsystems. William Sanders has pointed out that every biological and physical environment offers problems for human utilization (Sanders and Price, 1968). Furthermore, the human response to diverse environments will be different and distinctive. Although the possibilities for human adaptation to an environment are almost unlimited, the number of probable adaptations to a specific environment is limited. Thus, communities with highly differing cultures may occupy the same or similar environments and the level of technological achievement and effectiveness of the hunting-gathering or food-producing economy involved naturally affects their varied responses in other aspects of culture. Some environments are inherently less productive than others, a factor that can limit population growth as well as other cultural responses.

The adaptation of any population is achieved primarily by effective subsistence strategies and technological artifices, but social organization and religious beliefs are important in ensuring cooperative exploitation of the environment as well as technological cooperation. Religious life provided an integrating force in many societies, not least among them the Maya and Sumerians. Human cultures are as dynamic as all other components of an ecological system, and any human culture can be thought of as what William Sanders and Barbara Price call "a complex of techniques adaptive to the problems of survival in a particular geographical region." Human culture is, ecologically speaking, a way in which human beings compete successfully with animals, plants, and other human beings. Sanders and Price point out that "The product of plant and animal evolution is more effective utilization of the landscape in competition with individuals of the same and other species. This effectiveness is usually expressed in population growth, and this growth can therefore be taken as a measure of success in a given area at a given point."

There are obvious difficulties in studying the interactions between people and their environment, especially when preservation conditions limit the artifacts and other data available for study. Fortunately, however, artifacts and other elements of the technological subsystem often survive. Because technology is a primary way in which different cultures adapt to their environment, detailed models of technological subsystems allow archaeologists to obtain a relatively comprehensive picture of the cultural system as a whole. It is in research of this type that the storage capacity of the digital computer has come into play. Cultural-ecological studies depend for their effectiveness on enormous quantities of basic data. Once these data are stored on the computer, one can use simulation techniques to model possible cultural outcomes, by inserting hypothetical variables into the surviving cultural system. The techniques are somewhat like those used for business forecasting, but they are still in a highly experimental stage.

MULTILINEAR CULTURAL EVOLUTION

Anthropologist Julian Steward argued many years ago (1955) that people living in similar environments tend to solve the problem of adaptation in similar ways. This argument led him and others to develop the concept of *multilinear cultural evolution*. This is not the single-line evolutionary theory of the early evolutionists, but a branching, cumulative process, which results from cultural adaptations over long periods.

There was a stultifying inevitability about the earlier unilinear theories that put twentieth-century civilization at the pinnacle of human achievement. Multilinear evolutionary theory is far more flexible; it recognizes that there are many evolutionary tracks, from simple to complex, the differences resulting from individual adaptative solutions (Mill, 1977). Despite these variations, some broad evolutionary developmental stages can be recognized in the world's societies. The four-stage evolutionary classification of bands, tribes, chiefdoms, and state-organized societies was described in Chapter 17 (Service, 1971). These highly flexible stages are defined with reference to social complexity, subsistence strategy, and population size. None of them are rigidly defined, for multilinear evolutionary theory recognizes that cultural adaptations are complex processes that are fine-tuned to local conditions, with long-term, cumulative effects.

Multilinear cultural evolution, then, is the vital integrative force that brings systems theory and cultural ecology together into a closely knit, highly flexible way of studying and explaining cultural process (Sanders and Webster, 1978).

PROCESSUAL ARCHAEOLOGY APPLIED: ORIGINS OF LITERATE CIVILIZATION

Theoretical approaches are meaningless unless they are tested against actual field data. The models of processual archaeology have been applied successfully to many small-scale problems, and they have provided new means of studying major developments in world prehistory. The origins of literate civilization in the Near East some 5,000 years ago illustrate the effectiveness of the processual approach very clearly.

Prime Movers.   Early theories on the origins of cities and civilization in the Near East assumed that Sumerian civilization developed as a result of a major invention or technological advance, often called a *prime mover,* which was the ultimate cause of dramatic cultural change. Many people believed that the development of irrigation, with all its complex administrative problems, caused the growth of early civilization; others believed that population growth was the cause of the major changes in settlement patterns and agriculture that resulted in civilization. Warfare, trade, religious beliefs—all have been claimed as prime movers of early civilization. In truth, however, none of these prime-mover hypotheses is adequate to explain the complex cultural changes that preceded the emergence of the first civilizations. As Kent Flannery pointed out,"complex societies are simply not amenable to the simple types of structural, functional, or 'culturological' analyses that anthropologists have traditionally carried out" (Flannery, 1972).

Multicausal Explanations.   To replace the prime-mover hypotheses, Flannery proposed a many-sided approach to the origins of literate civilization. Instead of prime movers, he argued that there was a "whole series of important variables with complex interrelationships and variations between them." He said that, for example, the behavior of the people living in Mesopotamia at the time when the first city-states were formed was "a point of overlap (or articulation) between a vast number of systems, each of which encompasses both cultural and non-cultural phenomena—often much more of the latter."

Under this rubric, the rise of civilization should be thought of as a series of interacting and cumulative processes, which were triggered by favorable cultural and ecological conditions and which continued to develop cumulatively, as a result of continual positive feedback. Just how complex the interactions may have been is shown in Figure 19.1 (Redman, 1978b). The process began with establishment of agricultural communities in the Mesopotamian delta about 7,300 years ago. These settlements triggered three processes that set up critical positive feedback relationships:

1. slow but steady population growth within the delta region
2. increased specialization in food production by different groups within the society
3. a demand for and acquisition of raw materials from outside the delta.

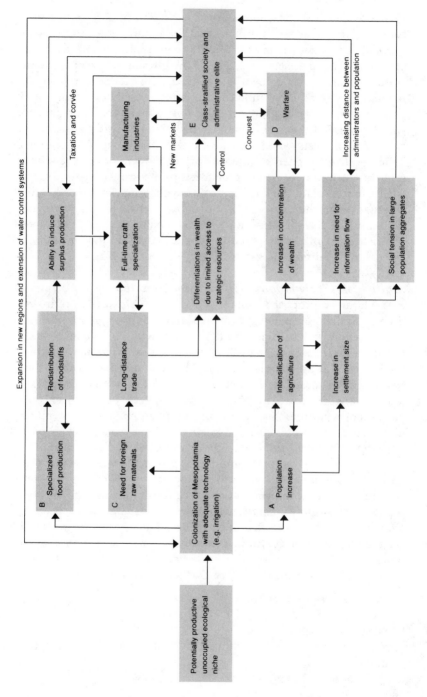

Figure 19.1 A tentative systems model that is an attempt to document the interrelationships among cultural and environmental variables leading to increasing stratification of class structure in Mesopotamian society between

Each of these processes set off feedback reactions that became more and more complex as time went on. An increase in population led to either more extensive fields or more intensive cultivation of existing acreage. The need for increased agricultural production leads to more centralized planning and administration of irrigation works and other communal food-producing activities. The inhabitants of the delta lived within a restricted area, and as populations rose, were forced to live in larger, more densely populated settlements that took up the minimum of agricultural land and required extremely intensive exploitation of the closest fields. And finally, an administrative elite that controlled people's access to strategic agricultural resources eventually emerged. As Figure 19.1 shows, it is possible to develop a highly complex, multicausal model for emergence of Mesopotamian civilization that is based on logical, interlocking hypotheses. The problem is to test this model and its many hypotheses in the field.

Testing such a multicausal model is a difficult task, involving not only developing rigorous methodologies for identifying the variables in the archaeological record, but also comparative studies of these variables in regions where civilization emerged and where it did not, and also in societies that flourished immediately before this development. Only in this way could one identify the crucial variables for the appearance of early civilization (Redman, 1978).

William Sanders and David Webster (1978) point out that Flannery's approach relies heavily on cultural evolution and invokes a variety of universal processes that affected the formation of complex societies (see also Binford, 1983). They argue that it seems a paradox to try to explain variability within human cultures by using universal, evolutionary processes that are, in themselves, ever-unchanging. The one component of the scheme that does vary is that of environmental stimuli. In his classic study of the civilizations in the Basin of Mexico, Sanders shows how the Aztecs created and organized agricultural systems, huge acreages of swamp gardens that spread over the shallow waters of the Basin's lakes. The variability of the Basin environment meant that the Aztecs had to exploit every environmental opportunity afforded them; the state therefore organized large-scale swamp agriculture. By the time of the Spanish Conquest (1519–1521), their agricultural systems were supporting a population of up to 250,000 people just in the Aztec capital, Tenochtitlán (Sanders, Parsons, and Santley, 1979).

FUNCTIONALISM AND STRUCTURAL ARCHAEOLOGY

Functionalism, the notion that a social institution within a society has a "function" in fulfilling all the needs of a social organism, is a concept that has been integral to much anthropological thinking since late in the nineteenth century. Hodder (1982a) uses the analogy of the stomach, which provides a function for the human body as a whole. Thus, functionalists assess any aspect of a society according to its contribution to the total working of society. Functionalism has long been a controversial topic among anthropologists, but is inextricable from the notion of systems and cultural systems, concepts that are fundamental tenets of processual archaeology. As Renfrew (1972) points out, to examine connections between cultural subsystems is to look at ancient society through a functionalist perspective. Processual archaeology proposes to identify relationships between variables in cultural systems, a concept of archaeological explanation that tries to predict relationships between variables, such as those which contributed to the beginnings of urban civilization (Flannery, 1972; Salmons, 1978).

The "functionalist" approach of what was once called the "New" archaeology has been criticized by some archaeologists, who attack processual archaeologists of this school for their emphasis on equilibrium and the idea that most change has to come from outside the system (Hodder, 1982a). Function and utility are inadequate ways of explaining social and cultural systems, for many archaeologists distinguished between culture on the one hand and adaptive utility on the other. More extreme viewpoints reject any normative descriptions of cultural variation and seek to explain everything in terms of adaptive expedience. Under this title, material culture is simply seen as functioning at the interface between human organisms and the social and physical environment, as a means of allowing adaptation. Ian Hodder (1982a) writes: "There is much more to culture than functions and activities. Behind functioning and doing there is a structure and content which has partly to be understood in its own terms, with its own logic and coherence. This applies as much to refuse distributions and 'the economy' as it does to burial, pot decoration and art." Not only that, but the processual school has stressed identification of variability in human culture, and in so doing has tended to think of adaptation in general rather than adaptation in individual historical context. Systems are seen as in equilibrium or disequilibrium, populated by human beings, who, as individuals, are minimally important. An impersonality about this form of processual archaeology is inclined to see things as cross-cultural statements of predictable value, even with the notion of predicting the past (Thomas, 1974). It is within this context that ethnoarchaeology and concepts like middle-range theory have become fashionable. Prehistoric institutions were rational in dealing with their environments, assume archaeologists of this persuasion. Although there can be little doubt that they are partly right, recent theoretical argument has moved beyond functionalism into the realm of what is becoming known as "structural archaeology."

Structure in an archaeological context is defined by Ian Hodder (1982a) not as a set of relationships between components of a cultural system (a way in which it could be used, interchangeably with "system"), but as "the codes and rules according to which observed systems of interrelations are produced." Hodder argues that many studies of areas like the Peruvian coast or the Southwest have explained the structure of human societies in terms of social functions and adaptive values. But they also hint that there is more to culture than observable relationships and functional utility. Hodder writes of a set of rules, a code, as it were, which he likens to those operating in chess or Monopoly, which are followed as people go about the business of survival, adaptation, and making a living.

Hodder calls this approach structural (or cognitive) archaeology. He associates his definition of a set of rules with three essential concepts:

The *artifacts, features, and other items*—signs in the archaeological record—occur in relation to one another to create patterns. The patterns resulting from this *interrelatedness* are the important thing, not the "signs" themselves.

Language is how the meaning of the world is communicated, in a sense the *code* to the structure.

Transformation, the notion that the patterns in the archaeological record are *generated* by underlying logic. Another important aspect of transformation is change through time. Cultural change is seen by Hodder as manipulation of this logic by people through their intentional, behavioral strategies.

Structural archaeology is an attempt to get at the active, social manipulation of *symbols*, objects as they are perceived by their owners, not merely at their use. Hodder himself studied the Nuba agriculturalists of the Sudan, and showed that all aspects of their material culture, including burial customs, settlement pattern, and artifact styles, could be understood in the context of a set of rules that perpetuated their beliefs in "purity, boundedness, and categorization" (Hodder, 1982b). Thus, Nuba society is the result of structured, symbolizing behavior, and has fundamental utility. But it also has a logic of its own, which generated the material culture that is observed by the archaeologist. Structural archaeologists believe that, although functionalist analyses can yield information on the underlying codes, explanations for them must be based not on function but on the logic behind them.

Structural archaeology at its most general is the analysis of patterns and their transformations. It has probably arisen through frustration with the problems and limitations of spatial analysis (Chapter 16), where one confronts head-on the difficulties and frustrations of interpreting spatial patterns and the variables that affected their distribution. The concept is all very well in theory, but few archaeological studies have yet provided convincing accounts of the relationships between the "codes" and social and ecological organization. One reason is that we still lack a sound theory of structural archaeology, another that structural approaches deal with ideas that are separate from those of adaptation. Burial patterns in a cemetery are not just a reflection of human behavior and social patterns; they are structured in a highly emotional symbolic and social context. By the same token, pottery shapes and decoration can be used by their makers not just to distinguish different functional uses for pots, but also to play out all manner of subtle social relationships.

On superficial examination, the notion of structural archaeology is not very different from the more traditional, normative approaches used by older generations of archaeologists in both the New and Old World. Many of them realized that the material remains they studied had a little-understood social context. But it was difficult for them to move beyond chronology and artifacts, partly because they lacked the large bodies of data that are now available, and also because they had no detailed descriptions of ethnographic contexts that would help them develop historical explanations. The new fascination with structural archaeology has flared at a time when these data are becoming available, when archaeologists are beginning to wrestle with the problems of developing a theory of social practice for understanding the relationships among structure, belief, action, and the material remains they ultimately generate (Hodder, 1982a). To some extent, structural archaeology is a reaction against the logico-deductive approach of much processual archaeology. But it is far more than that; it is an extension of the functionalist approach of processualists in that it reconsiders many of the basic issues about culture, ideology, and structure that worried earlier archaeologists just as much as their successors. Little more than a beginning has been made in developing the theory, or carrying out the field studies, to validate this new approach, but it is clear that the "new archaeology," with its systems and explicitly scientific approach, is about to undergo further exciting and radical change as archaeology begins to be a cultural and historical discipline that has the potential not only to contribute to our understanding of the past, but to contribute some highly original ideas to humanity's thinking about itself. (For examples of this approach, see Hodder, 1982b).

WHAT LIES AHEAD?

Where does the future lie? Clearly, both evolutionary theory and ecology will be important in the study of cultural change and the birth of complex societies. As Robert Dunnell (1980) points out, evolutionary theory has yet to be systematically explored in archaeology, for Flannery's models are still fundamentally based on the concept of cultural evolution as perceived by anthropologists. The functional, monocausal approach has long been shown to be inadequate, and so we see promise in evolutionary approaches. Archaeologists have done little to explore the thinking of modern evolutionary biologists, where giant strides have been made in recent years in accounting for the behavior of animal species. Processual archaeologists have long understood that individual human actions and decisions are an important part of human history. But these actions and decisions were made within a framework of checks and balances that were not only cultural and biological but also environmental. They regard the understanding of these frameworks to establish the circumstances under which cultural process takes place as one of their primary tasks. In recent years, mathematicians have developed some approaches and techniques that are very suitable to the study of the evolution and change of structures and frameworks. In many ways, the biologist and the archaeologist are facing the same problem: How do forms, whether living or cultural, emerge and stabilize?

At first glance, the problems of applying mathematical models to archaeology seem daunting (Doran and Hodson, 1975). Few archaeologists have a sophisticated understanding of mathematics, and the inevitable feeling is that the use of such models will dehumanize archaeology (Renfrew, 1979). There can be only one reply to such suggestions: The problems we are trying to solve are very complex and difficult; so too are the concepts needed to solve them.

Our knowledge of world prehistory grows more complex every day. We can discern some regularities, yet the more general relationships and processes that have led to these regularities are still little understood. "We may glimpse," writes Colin Renfrew, "that there are relationships which may one day find formal expression, just like those of chemistry have done . . . we may aspire to express them by means of the precision and generality of mathematics."

The few general experiments in this fascinating area that have appeared are tantalizing and highly technical contributions that lie beyond the scope of this book, and indeed, the technical competence of many professional archaeologists. But one can predict that future processual archaeologists will rely heavily on mathematical studies of relationships, forms, and processes that enable us to explain how and why human societies have taken the forms and followed the courses they have. (For technical information, read Renfrew and Cooke, 1979.)

Dunnell says that "archaeology badly needs a general theory capable of generating scientific explanations in an historical framework and integrating these explanations into a systematic, coherent body of knowledge" (1980). We cannot yet formulate even the outline of such a theory, nor are we likely to be able to do so in the near future. The problems are too fundamental, the research still too inadequate. Some progress has been made. The new insistence on systemic description emphasizes the sort of empirical studies of variability within human culture that are needed as a basis for new theorical approaches. But this theory will have to be constructed by drawing both on the consequences of research into evolutionary theory in biology, and on ethnographic data for artifacts and what Dunnell calls "frequency distributions." The new theory will draw on explanations of the archaeological record based on strictly cultural terms as well. Archaeologists have hardly begun this ambitious project, which is likely to be the major aim of research for the remainder of this century.

Guide to Further Reading

Binford, Lewis R. *An Archaeological Perspective*. New York: Seminar Press, 1972.
Binford's autobiographical account of how he developed his ideas on processual archaeology. Polemical, but essential reading; the volume contains Binford's early papers.

————. *In Pursuit of the Past*. London and New York: Thames and Hudson, 1983.
An essay on the archaeological record and archaeological interpretation by the same author.

Clarke, David L. *Analytical Archaeology*. London: Methuen, 1968.
A massive discussion of processual archaeology written by an archaeologist regarded by many scholars as a genius. European orientation, but worth close attention by the serious student.

Flannery, Kent V., ed. *The Early Mesoamerican Village*. New York: Academic Press, 1976.
The "dialogues" that introduce each paper in this volume on settlement archaeology are a mine of entertaining and frank information on the uses and limitations of processual archaeology.

Hodder, Ian, ed. *Symbolic and Structural Archaeology*. Cambridge: Cambridge University Press, 1982.
Essays on symbolic and structural archaeology that grapple with the problems of reconciling normative and processual archaeology.

Redman, Charles L., ed. *Research and Theory in Current Archaeology*. New York: John Wiley Interscience, 1973.
Useful articles on processual archaeology, especially those by Kent Flannery and Albert Spaulding, which offer a perceptive critique.

Watson, Patti Jo, Steven LeBlanc, and Charles L. Redman. *Explanation in Archaeology*. New York: Columbia University Press, 1971.
A primer on processual archaeology. Good on the deductive-nomological approach.

PART VIII

CULTURAL
RESOURCE
MANAGEMENT

We have now completed our journey through the complexities of contemporary archaeology, a journey that should leave you with some insights into the processes of archaeological research. Our discussion of contemporary archaeology would be incomplete, however, without considering cultural resource management, one of the most pressing and complex aspects of the discipline. A major crisis confronts archaeologists: destruction of finite resources. In the two chapters that follow we survey the problems of managing the world's archaeological resources and look at the various ways in which one can become involved in archaeology, both as a pastime and as a professional career.

CHAPTER 20 ✤

MANAGEMENT
OF THE PAST

Preview

- In this chapter we survey the destruction of archaeological sites in the United States and outline the history of federal legislation designed to protect antiquities and archaeological sites. One of the key pieces of legislation was the Historic Preservation Act of 1966, which called for a National Register of Historic Places and appropriated funds for state-level planning for inventorying sites. Another, the Reservoir Salvage Act of 1960, authorized salvage archaeology and led to some valuable large-scale surveys, such as the Navajo Reservoir project.

- The 1960s saw the development of the concept of cultural resource management, overall strategies for conservation priorities and management of a finite resource—the archaeological record. The National Environmental Policy Act of 1969 laid down comprehensive government land-use and resource policies that require environmental impact reports on all federally owned land that was to be developed or modified. Executive Order 11593 brought historians and archaeologists together with the common goal of managing cultural resources and developing long-term goals. These new laws had an immediate effect on archaeology and led to a dramatic expansion of cultural resource management activity on thousands of acres.

- The Archaeological Resources Protection Act of 1979 defines an archaeological resource as any artifact more than one century old, but it still offers very limited protection to antiquities on privately owned land. Despite this and other laws, archaeology still faces a severe crisis.

- There are important sources of conflict between cultural resource management archaeologists and academic scholars, the former often considering archaeology to be an inductive rather than a deductive science. The tendency was to assume that each site threatened with destruction should be investigated and described, on the assumption that it would one day become part of a wider synthesis. Relatively few cultural resource management projects were based on specific research designs, until federal agencies began to take a stronger interest in land-use management, and state historic preservation plans began to take effect.

- As a result of these conflicts, and of the crisis in general, the Society of Professional Archaeologists has developed a set of ethics for people engaged in field research. These guidelines have drawn criticism, especially from people who have failed to realize that archaeology, as an academic discipine, is adapting to completely new conditions; under these conditions, most research in North America is funded as part of a cultural resource management project.

- Archaeologists have an obligation to police unethical operators, to keep charges for contract work within reasonable bounds, and to develop strategies for making the public aware of the importance of cultural resource management and of the results and benefits obtained from it. The Alexandria, Virginia, project is cited as an excellent example of public involvement in archaeology.

All archaeological excavation is destruction, the destruction of a finite resource. But, though archaeologists themselves have destroyed thousands of sites in their research, far more damage has resulted from looting, treasure hunting, and modern agricultural and industrial activity (Gumerman and Schiffer, 1977; King, Hickman, and Berg, 1977; Fowler, 1982). In this chapter we look at ways in which archaeologists have sought to halt the destruction of sites by legislative means and at the practical problems of managing cultural resources.

The inexorable destruction of archaeological sites has accelerated rapidly in the past twenty years. Deep plowing, freeway construction, water control schemes, and unprecedented urban development have all played havoc with the archaeological record. In many areas, the situation has reached crisis proportions. It is estimated that less than 5 percent of archaeological sites in Los Angeles

County are still undisturbed. Charles McGimsey (1972) estimated that at least 25 percent of the sites in Arkansas have been destroyed by agricultural and other land use, to say nothing of looters, in the previous ten years. Archaeologists in Britain, worried about the wanton destruction of archaeological sites by industrial development and by treasure hunters using metal detectors, have formed an organization named RESCUE that helps fight to save key sites and to prevent looting (Rahtz, 1974) (Figure 20.1). Perhaps the most famous example of "rescue" archaeology was the international effort, sponsored by UNESCO, that resulted in moving the Abu Simbel temples in Egypt from the banks of the Nile behind the Aswan High Dam to a new site clear of the rising waters of Lake Nasser. The Aswan project also resulted in the discovery of hundreds of additional sites in the area to be flooded (Macquilty, 1965).

In this chapter we examine a vital branch of archaeology, the multifarious activities that come under the title "cultural resource management" (CRM). Because much of this work is done under

Figure 20.1   Rescue speaks for itself: "Tomorrow may be too late."

Tomorrow maybe too late.

Rescue

contract to government agencies or private companies, it is sometimes called "contract archaeology," to distinguish it from the management of the actual resources.

Cultural resources refers to both human-made and natural physical
features associated with human activity. They are unique and nonrenewable resources and can include sites, structures, and artifacts
significant in history or archaeology. Cultural resource management is the application of management skills to preserve important
parts of our cultural heritage for the benefit of the public. The concept of cultural resource management came into being in the mid-
1970s, but stemmed from long anxiety of archaeologists and others
over the destruction of archaeological sites and historic buildings.
For a survey covering both Americas, see Wilson and Layda (1982).

EARLY ANTIQUITIES LEGISLATION

People have worried about the destruction of archaeological sites
for a long time. There were loud outcries in 1801 when Lord Elgin
removed the stunning marbles that now bear his name from the
Parthenon and bore them away to chilly London (Bracken, 1975).
When the British built a dam across the Nile at the First Cataract in
1898, they flooded the temples on the island of Philae, one of the
most glorious legacies of ancient Egypt (Fagan, 1975). The furious
protests of the archaeologists were ignored in the interest of industrial progress. Only now, three-quarters of a century later, have the
temples been rescued from the waters of the Nile, with the help of
UNESCO. Apart from their enormous historical value, the temples
are simply too lucrative a tourist attraction to remain partially
submerged.

Archaeological preservation has a long and respectable history in
the Americas, too. The earliest proponents of historic preservation
included late-nineteenth-century architects, archaeologists, anthropologists, and historians, who realized that a valuable part of America's heritage was slipping away in the face of colonization and vigorous industrial development (Lee, 1970). John Wesley Powell, the
famed explorer of the Colorado, and later director of the newly
formed Bureau of American Ethnology attached to the Smithsonian, was one eminent American who spent years organizing the
preservation of American Indian artifacts, customs, and languages.
An early triumph of archaeological conservation occurred in 1886,

when Frederick Putnam of Harvard's Peabody Museum managed to save the Serpent Mound in Ohio, by the simple expedient of buying it with subscriptions contributed by wealthy ladies of Boston and Cambridge (Fagan, 1977). This unique effigy monument (Figure 20.2) was then restored and fenced for posterity.

But even by the 1880s the damage done to America's prehistoric past was incalculable. Thousands of Adena and Hopewell mounds in the Midwest had been quarried away for topsoil or razed to make way for the streets of Cincinnati and other cities. In the Southwest, pioneer farmers, who settled near the same streams as their prehistoric predecessors, soon found that the painted pots and other artifacts from abandoned pueblos fetched a ready price in Chicago and other cities. Within a few years the farmers had dug into the Aztec site, Pueblo Bonito, the Mesa Verde region, and other famous sites

Figure 20.2   The Great Serpent Mound, Ohio.

with abandon, destroying many of the Southwest's most precious cultural resources. So many collectors and pot hunters, many of them actively encouraged by large museums, descended on the Southwest that many sites soon resembled a battleground. The few professional archaeologists working in the region, such as Edgar Hewitt and Nels Nelson, pooled their efforts and formed an archaeological field school; they lobbied in Washington for passage of an antiquities law to protect at least well-known sites.

The early preservation movement, if one can call it that, although somewhat involved with archaeology, primarily dealt with historic landmarks, acquisition of the homes and birthplaces of founding fathers and famous pioneers, and architectural preservation. The efforts of this loosely knit group of influential citizens and scholars resulted in the passage of the Antiquities Act of 1906, the so-called Lacey Law. This was an important first step, for it extended some protection to America's embattled archaeological sites—though only those on land owned or controlled by the United States government.

By the 1930s, preservation of America's past had become a far more complex business, one whose impetus was accelerated by the "make-work" programs of the Depression. Hundreds of architects and historians were employed documenting, interpreting, and restoring old buildings, occasionally with the collaboration of archaeologists. The La Purisima mission near Lompoc, California, is an example. Founded in 1813, it remained in active use until 1844, when it gradually went into disuse. During the Depression a team of experts aided by large numbers of Works Progress Administration (WPA) and Civilian Conservation Corps (CCC) laborers descended on the ruined buildings and slowly restored them to a state approaching that of the original mission. La Purisima is now a state park, one that gives the visitor a perception of life at the early Spanish missions. The experts who restored La Purisima spent a great deal of time researching many topics, from Spanish tile-making methods, adobe brick construction, and ecclesiastical furniture, to archival information on the missionaries themselves. Much of this information has formed the basis for historical preservation in California ever since.

Although some archaeologists were employed in historic preservation, many more became involved in archaeological salvage, excavating sites with WPA labor in river basins and other areas where federal dams were being constructed. The Tennessee Valley Authority (TVA) employed many archaeologists, whose published reports recorded vast quantities of data on site distributions and key cultural sequences before they vanished forever. Some of these publications are now classics of North American archaeology (Thomas and Lewis, 1961; Webb, 1939).

LEGISLATION AND SALVAGE ARCHAEOLOGY

The lobbying efforts of the historic preservationists gave rise to the Historic Sites Act of 1935. This legislation gave the National Park Service a broad mandate to identify, protect, and preserve cultural properties fundamentally important to Americans *in situ*, such as Gettysburg. The Historic Sites Act stressed permanent physical preservation of actual "living" properties. It meant that the federal government acknowledged broad responsibility for the nation's historic properties (including archaeological sites) both on and off federally owned land. Archaeologists, meanwhile, continued their increasingly deep involvement in salvage, both in reservoir areas and elsewhere. Two Federal Aid to Highway acts (1956 and 1958) authorized use of highway funds for archaeological salvage. In 1960 the Reservoir Salvage Act was passed, directing the Secretary of the Interior to oversee salvage operations in the river basins that were still being flooded with abandon. The funds provided the Secretary never really matched the need, however, and great losses continued to occur.

Historic Preservation Act of 1966. Theoretically, the ultimate goal and philosophic assumption of historic preservation is that everything of historical value should be preserved. This aim is obviously impracticable, so that one has to develop strategies that maximize preservation. This is what historical preservationists have done, especially through the Historic Preservation Act of 1966, a complex but carefully assembled piece of legislation that required the federal government to establish a nationwide system for identifying, protecting, and rehabilitating what are commonly called "historic places" (Gumerman and Schiffer, 1977). The Act called for a National Register of Historic Places (a "historic place" could include archaeological sites), and it appropriated funds for historic preservation organizations to carry out surveys and planning in each state. It required federal agencies to protect Register properties when development projects were planned, and it established a

National Advisory Council to oversee compliance with this requirement. This Act set up a national framework for historic
preservation.

Reservoir Salvage Act of 1960.   In contrast, the Reservoir Salvage
Act merely authorized archaeologists to dig and salvage sites that
were in immediate danger of destruction. Although the Historic
Preservation Act was a first attempt at cultural resource management, the Reservoir Salvage Act was merely a "last-ditch" measure.
Its enactment did, however, make possible some fairly substantial
surveys that were not only valuable salvage operations but useful
pieces of archaeological research as well. Salvage archaeology rapidly became a watchcry among archaeologists in the 1960s, as thousands of sites were excavated hastily and then lost in the face of
bulldozers and deep plowing. Rough-and-ready methods often had
to suffice, for there was little time for sophisticated research designs
or leisurely excavation. Such archaeology was—and still is—practiced all over North America, as well as in Britain and Europe.
Many of these projects consisted of wide-ranging surveys that
yielded much information on site distributions. But only a small,
arbitrarily selected sample of sites could be excavated, chosen in the
hope they were representative of many others (Figure 20.3). One
early large-scale salvage operation in the late 1950s resulted from
excavation for construction of the Navajo Reservoir in New Mexico
(Dittert, Hester, and Eddy, 1961). The area of the 34-mile-long lake
was divided into nine sections and surveyed on foot and by jeep.
The archaeologists inventoried as many sites as possible, reconstructing a cultural sequence for the area. But they were not asked
to recommend mitigation measures that might have saved some of
the sites for the future, nor were they involved in the planning and
siting of this water project, when archaeological considerations
could have been taken into account.

The archaeologists who surveyed Glen Canyon on the Upper
Colorado River in Utah and Arizona before Lake Powell came into
being had more time for their surveys. They made a "total sampling
of all cultures and all the periods to be found in the area" the first
priority (Jennings, 1966). They placed great emphasis on accurate
records and publication of results—for no one would be able to
check their results in the field later. This was a highly effective form
of salvage, but here again the archaeologists were not expected to
make recommendations about *management* of resources.

Figure 20.3 Salvage archaeology. Top: In Arkansas, four land-leveling machines work while archaeologists try to salvage the bottoms of trash pits and crushed burials exposed by the machines. Bottom: In California, emergency salvage in the wake of huge machinery recovers only scattered remnants of occupation.

MANAGING ARCHAEOLOGICAL SITES

The rate of destruction of archaeological sites still accelerated, and it still does, far faster than the expansion of even the most superficial salvage archaeology efforts. By the mid- to late 1960s, important historic places were being destroyed faster than they could be placed on the National Register of Historic Places, and the philosophical and practical concept of salvage archaeology was becoming outmoded. The idea of salvage archaeology appealed to archaeologists of what one authority has called the "have trowel, will travel" mentality, people who lived from contract to contract job, working in advance of bulldozers and contractors. The reports from much of this work were so sketchy as to be almost useless. All too frequently, there was no report at all. Clearly, the problem of site destruction had many more aspects than merely that of salvage. Like the historic preservationists, archaeologists had to think of overall strategies, conservation priorities, and field research designs that ensured close marriage between the latest methodological and theoretical approaches and practical salvage excavation in the field.

National Environmental Policy Act of 1969. The changing attitudes toward historical preservation in the widest sense during the 1960s led to new federal legislation that, again, affected the course of American archaeology radically. The National Environmental Policy Act (NEPA) of 1969 laid down a comprehensive policy for government land-use planning and resource management. This Act, and accompanying regulations, required federal agencies to consider the environmental, historical, and cultural values to be weighed whenever federally owned land is modified or private land modified with federal funds. The regulations required documented environmental impact statements and reports that considered the impact of any project on the environment, an environment that included archaeological sites. The idea was that information on the nature, extent, and significance of archaeological resources should be inventoried, on the assumption that this information would affect planning of land use in the future. But, although impact reports were required, there was no guarantee that either preservation of a site or measures to gentle the effect of new land-use projects on the area would be taken.

Executive Order 11593. In 1971, President Nixon issued Executive Order 11593, which helped tie NEPA, the National Historic Preservation Act, and other legislation into a sensible federal policy on archaeological and historic preservation. The executive order directed all federal agencies to take the lead in historic preservation; they were to study lands under their jurisdiction to locate properties that might qualify for the National Register and nominate them; they were to exercise caution to make sure that such properties were not inadvertently damaged; and they were to develop programs to contribute to protection of important historic properties on nonfederal lands. By this time, the Advisory Council on Historic Preservation, authorized by the Historic Preservation Act, had become fully operational. At the same time, the programs of the National Park Service that monitored historic preservation outside the parks were consolidated, together with the Interagency Archaeological Salvage program, into the Office of Archaeology and Historic Preservation. In addition, the states had begun to develop historic preservation programs of their own, each headed by a state historic preservation officer designated by the governor and partly funded by the National Park Service. Each state's historic preservation office was required to have a professional archaeologist (as well as an architectural historian and an historian) on its staff. Thus, archaeologists and historic preservationists were brought back together after years of division to begin to work toward a common goal—preserving the nation's historical environment.

Effects of Legislation. The new laws and programs immediately and profoundly affected not only salvage archaeology but also North American archaeology as a whole. The NEPA and Executive Order 11593 made it essential for archaeologists to prepare and maintain extremely comprehensive information on archaeological resources on federal, state, and privately owned land that would enable them to assess, often on short notice, the effect of many projects on these resources. Research strategies to meet the requirements of NEPA alone are still being worked out. Federal agencies are now contracting for archaeological surveys on a scale never undertaken before. Indeed, the major sources of support for North American archaeology in the 1970s were such federal agencies as the Forest Service, the National Park Service, and the Army Corps of Engineers, as well as some private companies that were funding research on a contract basis (Wendorf, 1979).

This dramatic expansion of archaeological effort was hailed by some as the greatest opportunity for scientific advance in archaeology in this century, provided that archaeologists could adjust to the new situation. But others feared that rapid expansion in survey and contract research would result in catastrophic declines in the quality of field research and research designs. One thing was certain: any archaeological work conducted under the general rubric of cultural resource management must have more sophisticated objectives than merely production of site-distribution maps. Key issues, such as the significance of sites and priorities of preservation and excavation, are obviously critical to any research designs for cultural resource management.

Archaeological and Historical Preservation Act of 1974. The NEPA and Executive Order 11593 are but a small part of an elaborate framework of laws, regulations, and statutes that the archaeologist in cultural resource management now works with. There are state, county, city, and Indian tribal laws to amplify federal legislation and adapt it to local conditions. Keeping abreast of changes in the laws is itself practically a full-time job.

One final piece of federal legislation in 1974 added a new dimension to NEPA and EO 11593, neither of which provided special funds for preservation or recovery of archaeological and historical resources when these are endangered by federal projects. An amendment to the Reservoir Salvage Act in 1974 (The Archaeological and Historical Preservation Act) authorized federal agencies to provide such funds, either by contract, by allocating up to 1 percent of the cost of a project to the National Park Service, or by trying to persuade the Service to do the work from its own funds. Most important, the 1974 amendment provided funds for digging and also for analysis of finds and publication of results.

Archaeological Resources Protection Act of 1979. The latest piece of federal legislation gives somewhat more stringent protection to archaeological sites on federal lands. Archaeological resources under this act are defined as at least 100 years old, a serious loophole that affects many historic sites. People removing archaeological materials from federal lands without a valid permit are subject to fines of up to $10,000 and one year in prison, unless the objects removed have a commercial value of more than $5,000, in which case the penalties rise sharply. Fines can reach $100,000 for repeated offenses. The Act bans assessment of civil penalties on individuals removing arrowheads "located on the surface of the ground," and tightens up much of the earlier legislation. This legislation is aimed at commercial vandals, and tightens earlier laws. Unfortunately it offers no protection to archaeological resources on privately owned land.

COMPLIANCE PROCESS

A morass of laws and regulations at all levels and a growing body of legal opinions and court decisions provide an elaborate framework for long-term cultural resource management in American archaeology. The "compliance process" on even a medium-sized federal project is an attempt to see that cultural resources threatened by the project are properly "managed"—recorded, evaluated, protected, or if necessary salvaged (Fowler, 1982). The management of cultural resources is carried out by federal, state, and local agencies, among them the National Park Service, the Bureau of Land Management, the Department of Defense, and the Bureau of Reclamation, which builds major dams and irrigation projects. Each employs personnel who carry out the necessary management tasks, which include inventorying, evaluating resource significance for possible inclusion in the National Register of Historic Places, and protecting and managing the sites under their jurisdiction. All this work is carried out to meet the requirements of Executive Order 11593.

This procedure of identification and management has three phases:

An overview of cultural resources in an area is compiled, ideally a description of the environment and ethnographic background, a history of previous research, and a description of the known culture history of the area. Then the authors assess the research potential of the area, identify important research problems, and make management recommendations.

An Archaeological Assessment Report involves further inventory and assessment, including reexamination of known sites and surveys for new ones. These reports are especially important for areas where substantial modification of the land is likely to take place as a result of strip mining, dam building, and other such developments. The finished document discusses known cultural resources in the area, and recommends additional research needed to evaluate their significance and to establish suitable mitigation measures to protect them. The Assessment Report often forms a preliminary environmental impact report on the area.

A *Management Plan*, which proposes measures for protecting, preserving, interpreting, and using cultural resources. This is a formal part of the final environmental impact report. To be effective, a management plan should be regarded as a constantly evolving document, maintained and changed as archaeologists continue to manage and monitor the area.

Management plans are very difficult to implement, especially in large areas where the land may be subjected to a multitude of uses. The California Desert Conservation Area is an example. It covers nearly a quarter of California and is under the jurisdiction of the Bureau of Land Management.

The compliance process, even on simple projects, can be a nightmare, and involves the archaeologist both in management and in delicate negotiations with several government agencies at once. One of the most interesting examples of a management plan in action is that for the San Juan Basin in the Four Corners area of the Southwest.

The San Juan Basin has been occupied since around 10,000 B.C. right up to modern times. Several pueblo groups and Navajo, Apache, and Ute live in the region, which has been subjected to extensive energy development, including strip mining. Still more exploration and mining is planned. Not only that, large numbers of people will start depending on the area for recreation—and archaeological sites are part of that recreation. At least seven federal, state, and local agencies have some CRM jurisdiction in the area, and several of them have joined in a cooperative management effort. The National Park Service carried out a preliminary assessment study in 1980. Now the agencies are developing a dynamic management program that makes use of a huge computerized data base of more than 15,000 sites, with 15 categories of information for each one. An additional 4,000 entries comprise a survey file (Plog and Wait, 1982) that is estimated to contain about 70 percent of known sites in the San Juan Basin. Unlike the general data bases maintained by the State of Arkansas, this is thought of as a tool for formulating research designs and management strategies. From the beginning "SJBRUS" was designed as a management tool, with the categories of information in it limited to those conceived of as having management potential. This arrangement made it both cost effective and highly specific in its application. This data base is combined with extensive remote-sensing surveys, for ground-based methods of data collection cannot collect enough information in the short time often allowed before development occurs. Remote sensing is mainly used to relate various types of environmental information to the locations of archaeological sites. Correlations between known site locations and environmental variations could then be used to prepare predictions about possible concentrations of sites in hitherto unsurveyed areas.

This sort of multiagency approach is fine, provided that the federal, state, and local organizations cooperate with one another. Alaska has an Alaska Land Managers' Cooperative Task Force, which brings together every federal, state, and local agency in the state involved with land planning. A Cultural Resources Subcommittee of the Task Force deals with the full range of cultural resources in the state, covering everything from early prehistoric sites to historical monuments.

The compliance process involves both federal and state agencies in other management duties as well. They have the responsibility for protecting sites against vandalism, a major problem in some areas. Then the value of each individual resource has to be assessed, either on account of its scientific value, established within the context of a valid research design, or because it merits preservation *in situ*. Agencies also have to consider how a site can be utilized for the public good. This responsibility means interpreting them for the public, who may either visit the location, as they do at, say, Mesa Verde, or through books, television programs, popular articles, and so on.

The main goal of Cultural Resource Management in the United States has been preserving sites and artifacts for the information they have yielded or may yield. Experts in the field have been confronted with a number of management problems:

Because archaeological sites are a nonrenewable resource, which should be saved for future research rather than being investigated now?

Should data from sites acquired for conservation and planning be used for pure research as well?

How is the significance of archaeological resources to be established for legal compliance purposes?

MANAGEMENT PROBLEMS

Conservation. Obviously the basic ethics of archaeology demand that as many sites as possible be preserved. Under ideal circumstances the sites are not threatened by development, and the investigator can develop a research design based on purely scientific considerations. However, many other variables—budget, possible design alternatives in the development project, and mitigation costs, to mention only a few—come into play when sites are threatened by imminent destruction. Then there is the problem of "secondary impacts," when unexpected spin-offs of the main project destroy resources outside the main project area. Don Fowler (1982) cites the monstrous MX Missile Project in the Great Basin that would have affected archaeological resources in no less than twenty-three valleys in the region. Although the project would have primarily affected sites in the lowlands, the archaeologists pointed out that most of the sites lay in the foothills and uplands nearby. These would have been disastrously affected by secondary activities such as seismic testing, survey work, and the sheer numbers of construction workers and military personnel brought into the area during the MX project. Whether effective ways of mitigating these secondary impacts would have been possible is questionable. Few, if any agencies consider such impacts, often critical to archaeologists.

Management versus Academic Research. The apparent conflict between resource management on the one hand and academic research in archaeology on the other comes down to a dilemma. Most CRM contracts involve collecting or developing scientifically useful data from a highly specific area like the site of an oil drilling pad, or the sites of pylons along a 100-mile power line. Are such activities meaningful unless tied to other cultural resources in the region? Though compliance requirements may be satisfied, scholarly needs often most emphatically are not.

One reason for the conflict between contract archaeology, with its emphasis on compliance and management, and "academic" archaeology, which concentrates on basic research, is that most contracting parties assume that archaeology is an inductive science (see Hester, 1981; Longacre, 1981). Certainly the traditional methods of archaeological research have been inductive. That is, they assume that sufficient facts can be collected to eventually provide enough data for synthesis and inference from the data. Of course, inductive research is useful, especially in the sort of general exploratory work that is carried out in many large survey areas, such as the Cache River Valley in Arkansas (Schiffer and House, 1976). Until recently, most contracting agencies thought of archaeology as a discipline able to conduct piecemeal research. They assumed that the results from each small project would, somehow, eventually become part of a grand, final synthesis. This type of archaeology was, in fact, attractive to those with some command of excavation techniques, whose final objective was to produce a descriptive site report. Sites or areas were preselected by such criteria as imminence of destruction or availability of salvage funds.

In fact, the 1970s saw much archaeological research become deductive, and archaeologists were now viewing fieldwork and excavation as activities to be carried out only when a specific problem needed solution, or a hypothesis needed testing. To these scholars, salvage archaeology for its own sake was an entirely inconsistent activity that simply did not mesh with the specific problem orientation of deductive research. There was a real danger that archaeology would divide into camps: the deductive researchers taking on specific problems on the one hand, the contract archaeologists involved with salvage, management, and compliance on the other.

Can management and research needs be reconciled? The answer is probably a qualified yes. The academic archaeologists point out that there is little point in conserving and managing sites if their research significance is not a primary part of this activity. The solution leading to reconciliation seems to be development of adequate regional research designs, within which research data gathered from dozens, even hundreds, of contract projects is synthesized into scholarly sense (Fowler, 1982; Gumerman and Schiffer, 1977; Powell and Rice, 1981). But for such research designs to work requires very careful writing of contract statements by contracting agencies.

Research Designs. In the context of contract archaeology, the research design is best described as a "frame of reference," plans in which basic assumptions, research goals, hypotheses, methodologies, and operating procedures are laid out (Fowler, 1982). Ideally, there should be a hierarchy of research designs. The Historic Preservation Act of 1966 required all states to prepare historic preservation plans. In 1976 the Secretary of the Interior developed regulations formulating these plans under professional supervision. The surveys, still incomplete, are to include nominations for the Register of Historic Places and also inventories and *predictions* of where all forms of cultural resources may exist.

States are, of course, political rather than cultural entities, and so the best overall research designs are those for regions, whether defined topographically, ecologically, or culturally. A good example of a region is the San Juan Basin in the Four Corners region.

Fowler (1982) lists six key elements for a successful research design:

1. A description of the resource base—an outline of current knowledge about the area and its culture history.
2. A statement of basic assumptions, of the investigators' theoretical approach, whether ecological, materialist, or some other.
3. A statement of general areas of research interest, both general and specific problems to be worked upon. These questions are the basis for future hypotheses.
4. A description of the kinds of data needed to complete the research design, and specifics on maintaining the quality of the data, and on the standards of data required.
5. A formulation of investigative strategies to acquire data of the quality needed. The vital element here is sampling strategies that reflect the realities of time, contract requirements, available funding, and size of the research area.
6. For specific project design, a statement of operating procedures from preliminary fieldwork right up to completion of the final report must be specified.

Research designs may be laid out in many ways, but the critical point is that they must be dynamic, ever-changing statements, not rigid dogma but state-of-the-art designs that keep up with new methodological advances and changing circumstances in the field and out of it. Large-scale research designs are becoming more common for such well-known CRM projects as the Dolores Archaeological Program in Colorado, and that developed for the MX Missile Project in Utah and Nevada (Fowler, 1982). A good CRM research design is far more than a plan for archaeological research; it is a management document, an administrative manifesto, and a high-quality control manual in the bargain. The administrative and legal skills required of a contract archaeologist are much further-ranging than anything envisaged by an academic researcher.

Training and the Crisis of Quality.   An archaeologist in contract archaeology and management of cultural resources requires training in a battery of skills far from the halls of academe. Not only must a contract archaeologist be thoroughly versed in academic archaeology, he or she must also have a background in the legal requirements of CRM, in antiquities and historic-preservation legislation, and in methods of administration and conservation as well. Even the beginning contract manager requires formidable archaeological and bureaucratic skills—and a few institutions still offer training programs in contract archaeology. The situation is somewhat similar to that undergone by geology some years ago. Archaeology is changing from a wholly academic discipline to what Fowler calls a "real-world" profession. But unlike geology, its "product" is not energy or more water, but knowledge, much of which is not critical to the national interest by any stretch of the imagination.

No one is happy about the quality of training given contract archaeologists at this time. There are some master's and doctorate programs which cater to fledgling contract archaeologists, but none which achieve an ideal balance between academic and business and management skills. It remains uncomfortably true that many of the archaeologists involved in cultural resource management projects have received little or no formal training in anything more than basic archaeological method and theory—and that is simply not enough. We can, however, expect the situation to improve in the future, as archaeology completes the transition undergone by academic geology some years ago. The curricula of the future should blend academic and practical management skills in graduate programs reflecting an employment picture that has most archaeologists working in government or business rather than in universities, colleges, and museums.

A number of organizations, among them the Society of Professional Archaeologists (SOPA) and the American Society for Conservation Archaeology, have started to work on the thorny question of professional qualifications. The SOPA has drawn up basic ethical guidelines that focus on training and qualifications for carrying out cultural resource management. But these ethical guidelines have drawn fire, partly on the grounds that they do not reflect the reality of carrying out archaeology under commercial conditions (Fitting and Goodyear, 1979). The SOPA guidelines have appeared at a time when the academic discipline of archaeology is busy adjusting to a completely new environment, in which most financial support comes from federal and state agencies and private companies involved with projects on government land (Wendorf, 1979). One authority estimates that no less than $200,000,000 was spent on archaeology by federal agencies alone in 1979 (King, 1979). The severe recession of 1982–1983 cut deeply into this figure, but the expenditure has been enough to widen the gap between academic and contract archaeologists.

The rise in contract archaeology has come while university and college curricula are shifting perceptibly into directions that are called, euphemistically, "more pragmatic," with students flocking into majors that offer the best prospects of employment in later life. To some degree, archaeology has been caught up in this trend. With most archaeological jobs in contract rather than academic archaeology, graduate curricula, and some undergraduate curricula as well, have become more and more "practical," designed to turn out people with at least some background in the realities of contract archaeology. This compromise is fine, if you believe that archaeology is merely a service to government agencies. That, of course, it is not. It is the way in which we achieve an understanding of the remote past, a discipline with far more to offer humanity than mere environmental impact reports. Regrettably, many contract archaeologists think more about management and conservation for conservation's sake than they do about the wider goals of archaeology. Despite heroic efforts by many archaeologists, the question of questions is still unanswered: Is contract archaeology, with its emphasis on conservation and management, to be considered distinct from academic archaeology? The answer undoubtedly lies in just how effective research designs prove to be at the regional and local level.

Then there is a crisis of quality. The poorly documented salvage archaeology of the 1950s and 1960s is now a small industry, whose products are often worse than useless. In 1975 Michael Schiffer wrote that "a glance at the bibliography of any compendium of method and theory will attest to the negligible impact of contract 'research' on modern archaeological thought" (Schiffer and House, 1976). Not all archaeologists would agree with him—and the situation has improved somewhat in recent years. In fact, contract archaeology has brought extensive methodological benefits to basic research, among them much greater emphasis on prehistoric settlement patterns, sampling procedures, computer applications, and, above all, remote sensing. The San Juan Basin project and others are excellent examples of how sophisticated research designs and theoretical constructs are blended into a multitude of small contract projects. But among contract archaeology's worst products is that some agencies and contractors are, even today, quietly accepting second-rate reports and claiming that even minimal surveys are fulfilling both the requirements and the spirit of legislation. Work of such poor quality led both the Society for American Archaeology and SOPA to prepare ethical guidelines for contract research, as well as a registration procedure for contract archaeologists. These steps have helped mitigate the problem of quality somewhat. But the problem is so large and the amount of activity so great, even in times of recession, that the only long-term solution to the crisis of quality lies in a close relationship between the goals and research techniques of a sophisticated scientific archaeology, on the one hand, and the realities and demands of cultural management and contract archaeology on the other.

The crisis of quality has taken a new twist in recent years. Proliferating contract archaeology and CRM have caused an explosion not only of raw data, but also of publications and reports on completed projects (see Longacre, 1981; Hester, 1981). The essence of publishing archaeological data is, of course, to make them available to as wide an audience of archaeologists as need access to it. This distribution is achieved with many books and national or international journals, even with regional periodicals like *Plains Anthropologist*, most of which are little concerned with CRM. But most contract archaeology reports are either privately circulated documents buried in the files of government agencies or private companies, or, at best, mimeographed publications that have the most limited circulation. Within a few years, even months, they are forgotten, even destroyed, and the vital data in them are as good as lost to science. The problem of failure to publish is of epidemic size. Although efforts have been made to abstract CRM reports, the results have been patchy at best. Ironically, now that awareness about destruction of the archaeological record is greater than ever before, the results of much of this anxiety are being buried almost as effectively as if they had been destroyed—in inaccessible or temporary publications. The only solution appears to be some form of organization like a national microfilm archive, where copies of all reports are required to be deposited—by law. As yet, there is no sign that such an organization will be created.

Protection and the Public.   Although expenditures on contract archaeology may no longer be at the $200 million level, arguments rage about the worth of even a tenth of such expenditure. While one can argue that knowledge is intangible, and as such is worth spending money on, one has to show at least something for the money beyond an abundance of technical and often inaccessible reports. To begin with, one has to convince people that the sites are worth preserving. Archaeologists may wax lyrical about the scientific significance of a site within a specific research design, but the public is much more interested in sites with humanistic significance. Gettysburg has a supreme place in our national heritage, as Mesa Verde does. Both are visited by tens of thousands of people a year. The protection afforded by the National Register of Historic Places covers both sites as in the "significant" category, a significance that provides a basis for management decisions about cultural resources.

Protection of archaeological sites proceeds through legislation, but until 1979 the United States had no legislation forbidding the export of antiquities. Rapid acceleration in grave looting, especially in the Southwest, prompted passage of the Archaeological Resources Protection Act in 1979. This long-overdue legislation gives federal resource managers and prosecutors access to stringent criminal and civil penalties that may slow the destruction of sites on public lands. Even so, it is doubtful whether the Act will be completely effective. The situation is even more complicated with underwater sites like Spanish galleons, where a plethora of jurisdictions cover shipwrecks, and massive lobbying by sports-diver interests has impeded protective legislation.

Legislation is not the only protective tool available to archaeologists. The power of eminent domain, zoning, easements, even tax incentives are tools that may be used to protect cultural resources on private land. The aim of the recently formed Archaeological Conservancy is to protect important cultural resources on private property, but its effect will, perforce, be somewhat limited. A great deal of the effectiveness in protection of archaeological sites depends on public attitudes toward the past. The basic question is easily stated: Is the public benefiting in practical ways from the expenditure of enormous sums on archaeology?

The only people who can answer that question are the archaeologists themselves, who have several immediate obligations. The first is to police unethical archaeologists and to keep charges for contract work within limits that are realistic and not exorbitant. The second is to develop strategies for making the public aware of the importance of their work (Lipe and Lindsay, 1974). And the third is to see to it that much greater attention is paid to research planning and to developing carefully formulated research designs before excavation begins.

Public Involvement.   Many people think of archaeology as a luxury, and wonder why so much taxpayers' money is spent on cultural resource management. Almost none of the vast sums spent on the past go to public education and involvement in archaeology. A few projects around the nation have made efforts to reach the public. For example, the Alexandria Urban Archaeology Project was founded in Alexandria, Virginia, in 1977, with the specific objective of integrating academic and archaeological needs under the auspices of one organization. The project conceives of itself as having four major activities: research, conservation, interpretation, and education. It has developed a research design for survey and excavation within the city that includes investigating nineteenth-century ethnic neighborhoods. Sample excavations have been conducted, and are used for drawing up a data base of archaeologically sensitive areas and to establish conservation priorities. Along with its technical activities, the project maintains a museum area, where interested people are trained to assist in archaeological work and the public can learn about Alexandria's past. This closely integrated project, one of the few urban archaeology centers in the United States, provides a possible blueprint for great public participation in, and appreciation of, archaeological research (Cressey, 1980).

American Indians.   The American Indian Religious Freedom Act of 1978 states that it is "the policy of the United States to protect and preserve for American Indians their inherent freedom to believe, express, and exercise the traditional religions of the American Indian . . . including but not limited to access to sites, use and possession of sacred objects and the freedom to worship through ceremonials and traditional rites" (Fowler, 1982). The Act guarantees access to sacred sites, requires federal agencies to adjust management policies to reflect its provisions, and recognizes the existence of sacred sites. This legislation already is profoundly affecting American archaeology, for it often involves consultation with tribal and religious leaders if religious sites are to be disturbed.

In recent years, American Indians have protested strongly not only about excavation of prehistoric graves, but also about archaeological excavations and surveys on sacred areas in many parts of the West and Southwest. The 1978 Act gives American Indians considerable say in the conduct of CRM on public lands, and they have reacted strongly to development projects destined for sacred, privately owned lands as well. American archaeologists have long regarded their work as a way of studying ancient American Indian lifeways, but the Indians themselves have displayed little interest in archaeology. As Fowler (1982) points out, Western intellectual traditions regard scholarly research as beneficial to the public good. Other societies have entirely different cultural values, prohibiting desecration of sacred sites if they are studied by outsiders, even if this activity adds to the common knowledge of the outside world (Johnson, E., and others, 1977). For the first time, archaeologists have to forge a working partnership with American Indians. The influence of this change on archaeology remains to be seen.

Contract archaeology and cultural resource management have come of age. They dominate American archaeology, and will continue to do so for the foreseeable future. Many of the prospective archaeologists who read this book will end up in contract archaeology. The problems of CRM are a leading issue in contemporary archaeology, and will never disappear. All archaeologists are managers of a finite resource, which is banked in various ways—in the ground, within the pages of a report, or by finds and records in a museum storeroom. We as a nation have two alternatives for the future: collect and interpret information about our cultural resources in a useful manner as an activity that contributes to the public good, or take the easy way out and abandon the archaeological record to extinction.

Guide to Further Reading

Contract archaeologists and resource managers are still wrestling with the basic issues of their work, and have yet to generate an extensive methodological and theoretical literature. Many of the best field reports are, to all intents and purposes, inaccessible to the general reader. Listed here are useful signpost publications to a complicated literature:

Fowler, Don. "Cultural Resources Management," *Advances in Archaeological Method and Theory*, 5: 1–50, 1982.
   A superb essay on the basic issues of CRM in the early 1980s. Recommended also for its clear exposition and comprehensive references.

Gumerman, George J., and Michael Schiffer, eds. *Conservation Archaeology.* New York: Academic Press, 1977.
   Basic essays of variable quality on the beginning of the art. Some very useful case studies and theoretical arguments are included.

King, T. F., Patricia P. Hickman, and Gary Berg, eds. *Anthropology in Historic Preservation: Caring for Culture's Clutter*. New York: Academic Press, 1977.
More articles on the state of the art, with both case-study and theoretical orientation.

McGimsey, Charles. *Public Archaeology*. New York: Seminar Press, 1972.
An eloquent essay drawing attention to the destruction of sites, with hard data from Arkansas. A landmark book.

McGimsey, Charles, and Hester Davis, eds. *The Management of Archaeological Resources*. Washington, D.C.: National Park Service, 1977.
Proceedings of a conference on various aspects of cultural resource management and public archaeology. Useful essays to read as a starting point.

CHAPTER 21 ༄

ARCHAEOLOGY AND YOU

Preview

- Career opportunities for professional archaeologists can be found in universities, colleges, museums, government service, and private business both in the United States and overseas. Most archaeological jobs require at least an M.A., and very often a Ph.D.
- Do not consider becoming a professional archaeologist unless you have an above-average academic record, some field experience, strong support from your professors, and a moral commitment not to collect artifacts for profit.
- Even people who have no intention of becoming professional archaeologists can gain digging experience by attending a field school or by digging overseas.
- Archaeology can give you insight into the past and the potential for involvement as an informed layperson. It will also enable you to enjoy the major achaeological sites of the world in a unique way and to aid in archaeologists' attempts to preserve the past.
- All of us have ethical responsibilities to the past: *not to collect artifacts;* to report new finds; and to obey federal, state, and tribal laws that protect archaeological sites. Unless we all take our responsibility to the past seriously, the past has no future.

We have two final questions to answer: How can I become an archaeologist? Even if I do not become one, what are my responsibilities as an informed citizen?

ARCHAEOLOGY AS A PROFESSION

Professional archaeologists are much more common than they were even a generation ago, mostly because the discipline now has many more career tracks. Archaeology is changing rapidly, from a purely academic discipline into more of a profession, with archaeologists performing a multitude of management, conservation, and environmental tasks. Until recently, most American archaeologists taught in universities and colleges, and a few in high schools. Others headed archaeology departments of national, state, city, or local museums all over the country, or directed state archaeological surveys. But today, the majority of America's archaeologists work for the National Park Service or other federal, state, or local agencies in many activities that can be labeled loosely as cultural resource management. Others are employed by private firms undertaking environmental impact projects, both large and small, or are in business on their own doing similar work. The specialties of these archaeologists range from early Indian Plains settlement to historical sites in New England; from theoretical models of early agriculture to computer simulations. Although most American archaeologists now work on the "applied" side of archaeology, a considerable number of academic archaeologists work overseas—in Africa, Europe, Mesoamerica, Peru, and even farther afield.

But, a word of warning! Jobs in archaeology, except those involved in cultural resource management, are often hard to come by, even with a doctoral degree.

Qualifications. Most archaeological jobs, whether in a college, museum, or university, require a minimum of an M.A. degree, but most often, a Ph.D. is needed. The doctorate is a research degree requiring comprehensive seminar, course, and field training in graduate school followed by a period of intensive fieldwork that, in written form, constitutes the Ph.D. thesis. The average doctoral program takes between four and seven years to complete. The M.A. degree is normally completed in one or two years and gives you broad, general training in the basic methods and theory of archaeology and world prehistory. In addition to this general knowledge, you will specialize in a local area or in cultural resource management. You may have to write a library thesis and obtain some digging experience as well. The M.A. qualifies you to teach at two-year colleges and some state universities. Although it does not give you as much access to research funds and opportunities as a Ph.D., you can do invaluable work in cultural resource management or local archaeology.

Do *not* consider becoming a professional archaeologist unless you have these qualifications:

1. An academic record well above average with in-depth coverage of anthropology and archaeology. An A-minus grade-point average is a minimal requirement for good graduate schools.
2. Some field experience on a dig or survey.
3. Strong and *meaningful* support from at least two qualified archaeologists, who are able to write letters for you.
4. Strong motivation to become an archaeologist, and, for the Ph.D., a specific research interest.
5. The type of personality that thrives on hard work and some discomfort, a mass of detail, and long hours of routine laboratory work.
6. Ability to face up to a very tight employment situation.
7. Interest in teaching or resource management.
8. A moral commitment not to collect artifacts for profit or personal gratification.

Gaining Digging Experience. Many people want to gain some digging experience, whether or not they intend to go to graduate school. The best way to learn is to take a course in field methods and then volunteer to dig for a time on a summer excavation. Details of these excavations are normally posted on anthropology department bulletin boards or at local museums. Some people elect to go on a university-sponsored field school and to obtain academic credit for their work. Many such schools are designed mainly for graduate students, but again, you should consult your own department. General field schools, like the Koster dig in Illinois, are worthwhile because they combine excavation, laboratory analysis, and academic instruction into one intensive experience. And the camaraderie among participants in such digs can be a memorable experience.

Some people venture farther and join an excavation overseas for several weeks. By contacting such organizations as the Council for British Archaeology in London, it is possible to obtain details of excavations in progress where volunteers are needed. (Very few digs, either in this country or overseas, pay you to be an excavator.) At the other end of the spectrum are package travel tours that take students to such places as Israel to dig and learn archaeology under close supervision. These can be expensive experiences, often of variable academic quality. Whatever type of dig you choose, an excavation experience is a good way of testing your commitment to archaeology.

What an Undergraduate Degree Gives You. It is possible to get a low-level job in archaeology with a B.A.—a job—either as a fieldworker or a laboratory assistant. Some day, however, you will probably need further qualifications, and it is best to acquire these as soon as possible.

Most people who take a B.A. with a major in or emphasis on archaeology never become professionals. Nevertheless, they can enjoy the achievements and perspectives derived from archaeology for the rest of their lives. There are many ways to enjoy archaeology as a lay person. You can join a local archaeological society, participate in excavations and volunteer museum programs, and keep an eye on endangered sites in your neighborhood. Your background in archaeology will enable you to visit famous sites all over the world as an informed observer and to enjoy the achievements of prehistoric peoples to the fullest. I received a postcard mailed from Stonehenge by a former student: "Thank you for introducing me to archaeology," it read. "I enjoyed Stonehenge so much more after taking your course." His postcard made my day, for archaeology cannot survive without the involvement and interest of many people beyond professional archaeologists. And, as an interested lay person, you have responsibilities.

WHAT ARE OUR RESPONSIBILITIES TO THE PAST?

Professional archaeologists have ethical responsibilities as members of a demanding profession. But everyone interested in archaeology has responsibilities, too. The world's archaeological sites are under attack from many sources: from industrial development, mining, and agriculture, as well as from treasure hunters, collectors, and professional tomb robbers. In these inflated times, even modest antiquities fetch high prices on the antiquarian market. No government can hope to free the necessary funds to protect its antiquities adequately. And countries like Egypt, Guatemala, and Mexico, with rich archaeological heritages, have almost overwhelming problems protecting even their well-known sites. As long as there is a demand for antiquities among collectors and we maintain our materialistic values about personal possessions, destruction of archaeological sites will continue unabated. Even the necessary legal controls to prevent destruction of archaeological sites are just barely in force in most parts of the world.

Yet there is still hope, which stems from the enormous numbers of informed people who have gained an interest in archaeology from university and college courses or from chance encounters with archaeologists or the prehistoric past. If sufficient numbers of lay people can influence public behavior and attitudes toward archaeological sites and the morality of collecting, then there is still hope that our descendants will have archaeological sites to study and enjoy.

Is there a future for the past? Yes, but only if *we all* help, not only by influencing other people's attitudes toward archaeology, but also by obeying this simple code of ethics:

1. To treat all archaeological sites and artifacts as a finite resource.
2. Never to dig an archaeological site.
3. Never to collect artifacts for ourselves or to buy and sell them for personal gain.
4. To adhere to all federal, state, local, or tribal laws that affect the archaeological record.
5. To report all accidental archaeological discoveries.
6. To avoid disturbing any archaeological site, and to respect the sanctity of Indian burial sites.

Some Useful Addresses

Here are three addresses from which you can obtain information about archaeological activities and excavations that need volunteers:

> Archaeological Institute of America
> Box 1901, Kenmore Station
> Boston, MA 02215

Members receive the journal *Archaeology*.

> Society for American Archaeology
> 1511 K Street NW, Suite 716
> Washington, D.C. 20005

Members receive *American Antiquity*, a more technical journal.

For excavation opportunities overseas, contact:

> The Council for British Archaeology
> 112 Kennington Road
> London SE11 6RE
> England

This admirable organization publishes a monthly *Calendar of Excavations*, which you can obtain by airmail subscription. It contains complete details of volunteer excavations in Britain and sometimes in other parts of the world.

Information on Archaeological Field Schools can be obtained from fliers that are posted on university department bulletin boards, and also from the Society for American Archaeology.

BIBLIOGRAPHY 🦋

This Bibliography is not intended as a comprehensive reference guide to method and theory in archaeology. Rather, it is a compilation of both the majority of the sources used to compile this book and a cross-section of the most important methodological and theoretical research. Readers interested in probing even more deeply into the literature should consult the references in the text.

Adams, R. E. W. 1975. "Stratigraphy," in Thomas R. Hester, Robert F. Heizer, and John A. Graham, eds., *Field Methods in Archaeology*, 6th ed. Palo Alto: Mayfield, pp. 147–162.

———. 1977. *Prehistoric Mesoamerica*. Boston: Little, Brown.

Adams, Robert M. 1974. *The Uruk Landscape*. Chicago: University of Chicago Press.

Adovasio, J. M. 1979. *Basketry Technology: A Guide to Identification and Analysis*. Chicago: Aldine.

Adovasio, J. M., J. D. Gunn, J. Donahue, and R. Stuckenrath, 1975. "Excavations at Meadowcroft Rockshelter, 1973–74," *Pennsylvania Archaeologist* 45: 1–30.

Adovasio, J. M., and Joel Gunn, 1977. "Style, Basketry, and Basketmakers," in James Hill and Joel Gunn, eds., *The Individual in Prehistory*. New York: Academic Press, pp. 137–154.

Aikens, C. Melvin. 1970. *Hogup Cave*. University of Utah Anthropological Papers, no. 93.

———. 1978. "The Far West," in Jesse D. Jennings, ed., *Ancient Native Americans*. San Francisco: W. H. Freeman, pp. 131–182.

Aitken, Mark. 1977. "Thermoluminescence and the Archaeologist," *Antiquity* 51: 11–19.

Aldred, Cyril. 1961. *The Egyptians*. New York: Praeger.

Alexander, John. 1970. *The Directing of Archaeological Excavations*. London: John Baker.

Allan, William. 1965. *The African Husbandman*. Edinburgh: Oliver and Boyd.

Ammerman, A. J. 1981. "Surveys and Archaeological Research," *Annual Review of Anthropology* 10: 63–88.

Ammerman, A. J., and G. D. Schaffer. 1981. "Neolithic Settlement Patterns in Calabria," *Current Anthropology* 22: 430–432.

Anawalt, Patricia. 1981. *Indian Clothing Before Cortés*. Norman: University of Oklahoma Press.

Anderson, J. E. 1969. *The Human Skeleton: A Manual for Archaeologists*. Ottawa: National Museum of Canada.

Anderson, Patricia C. 1960. "A Testimony of Prehistoric Tasks: Design Residues on Stone Tool Edges," *World Archaeology*, 12, 2: 181–194.

Arnold, J. R., and W. F. Libby, 1949. "Age Determinations by Radiocarbon Content," *Science* 110: 678–680.

Asaro, Fred, and I. Perlman. 1967. *Determination of Provenience of Pottery from Trace Element Analysis*. Berkeley: Lawrence Radiation Laboratory.

Asch, David L. 1975. "On Sample Size Problems and the Uses of Non-Probabilistic Sampling," in James W. Mueller, ed., *Sampling in Archaeology*. New York: Academic Press, pp. 170–191.

Asch, Nancy B., Richard I. Ford, and David L. Asch. 1972. *The Paleoethnobotany of the Koster Site: The Archaic Horizon*. Springfield: Illinois State Museum.

Atkinson, R. J. C. 1953. *Field Archaeology*. London: Methuen.

———. 1957. "Worms and Weathering," *Antiquity* 31: 46–52.

———. 1969. "Moonshine on Stonehenge," *Antiquity* 43: 212–216.

Avebury, Lord (Sir John Lubbock). 1865. *Prehistoric Times*. London: Williams and Norgate.

Bailey, Geoffrey N., Margaret R. Deith, and Nicholas J. Shackleton. 1982. "Oxygen Isotope Analysis and Seasonality Determinants: Limits and Potential of a New Technique," *American Antiquity*, 48, 2: 390–398.

Baillie, M. G. L. 1982. *Tree-Ring Dating and Archaeology*. Chicago: University of Chicago Press.

Baker, C. M. 1978. "The Size Effect: An Explanation of Variability in Surface Artifact and Assemblage Content," *American Antiquity* 43: 288–293.

Bannister, Bryant, and William J. Robinson. 1975. "Tree Dating In Archaeology," *World Archaeology* 7, 2: 210–225.

Bannister, R. 1969. "Dendrochronology," in D. R. Brothwell and Eric Higgs, eds., *Science in Archaeology*. London: Thames and Hudson, pp. 191–205.

Barker, Philip. 1983. *Techniques of Archaeological Excavation*. New York: Humanities Press.

Barnes, A. S. 1938. "Les Outils de l'Homme Tertiaire en Angleterre: étude critique," *L'Anthropologie* 47: 1–31.

Bartel, Brad. 1982. "A Historical Review of Ethnological and Archaeological Analyses of Mortuary Practice," *Journal of Anthropological Archaeology*. 1, 1: 32–58.

Bass, G. F. 1966. *Archaeology Under Water*. New York: Praeger.

———. 1970. *A History of Seafaring from Underwater Archaeology*. London: Thames and Hudson.

Bass, W. M. 1971. *Human Osteology: A Laboratory and Field Manual of the Human Skeleton*. Columbia: Missouri Archaeological Society.

Bayard, D. T. 1972. "Early Thai Bronze: Analysis and New Dates," *Science* 196: 1411–1412.

Beck, Horace, and J. F. Schoefield. 1958. "Beads," in Roger Summers, ed., *Inyanga*. Cambridge: Cambridge University Press.

Begler, Elsie B., and Richard W. Keatinge. 1979. "Theoretical Goals and Methodological Realities: Problems in the Reconstruction of Prehistoric Subsistence Economies," *World Archaeology* 11, 2: 208–226.

Bellwood, Peter. 1979. *Man's Conquest of the Pacific*. New York: Oxford University Press.

Bennett, W. J. 1974. *Basic Ceramic Analysis*. Eastern New Mexico University Contributions in Anthropology, vol. 6, no. 1.

Bettinger, Robert L. 1980. "Explanatory/Predictive Models of Hunter-Gatherer Adaptations," *Advances in Archaeological Method and Theory* 3: 189–256.

Biddle, Martin. 1961. "Nonsuch Palace, 1959–60: An Interim Report," *Surrey Archaeological Collections* 58: 1–20.

Biddle, M., and B. Kjølbye-Biddle. 1969. "Metres, Areas, and Robbing," *World Archaeology* 2: 208–219.

Binford, Lewis R. 1962. "Archaeology as Anthropology," *American Antiquity* 28: 217–225.

———. 1964. "A Consideration of Archaeological Research Design," *American Antiquity* 29: 425–441.

———. 1980. "Willow Smoke and Dog's Tails: Hunter-Gatherer Settlement Systems and Archaeological Site Formation," *American Antiquity* 45, 1: 4–20.

———. 1968. "Archaeological Perspectives," in Sally R. Binford and Lewis R. Binford, eds., *New Perspectives in Archaeology*. Chicago: Aldine, pp. 5–32.

———. 1972. *An Archaeological Perspective*. New York: Seminar Press.

———, ed. 1977. *For Theory Building in Archaeology*. New York: Academic Press.

———. 1978. *Nunamiut Ethnoarchaeology*. New York: Academic Press.

———. 1981a. "Behavioral Archaeology and the Pompeii Premise," *Journal of Archaeological Research* 37: 195–208.

———. 1981b. *Bones: Ancient Men and Modern Myths*. New York: Academic Press.

———. 1983. *In Pursuit of the Past*. London and New York: Thames and Hudson.

Binford, Lewis R., and Jeremy A. Sabloff. "Paradigms, Systematics, and Archaeology," *Journal of Anthropological Research* 38, 2: 137–153.

Bishop, Ronald L., Robert L. Rands, and George R. Hedley. 1982. "Ceramic Compositional Analysis in Archaeological Perspectives," *Advances in Archaeological Method and Theory* 5: 275-331.

Bisson, Michael S. 1977. "Prehistoric Copper Mining in North West Zambia," *Archaeology* 29: 242-247.

Blanton, Richard E. 1978. *Monte Alban: Settlement Patterns at the Ancient Zatopec Capital*. New York: Academic Press.

Boardman, J., and L. R. Palmer. 1963. *On the Knossos Tablets*. Oxford: Clarendon Press.

Bohrer, Vorsila L. 1981. "Methods of Recognizing Cultural Activity from Pollen in Archaeological Sites," *The Kiva*, 46, 3: 13.

Bordaz, J. 1970. *Tools of the Old and New Stone Age*. Garden City, N.Y.: Natural History Press.

Bordes, F. 1968. *The Old Stone Age*. New York: McGraw-Hill.

Boserup, Ester, 1965. *Conditions of Agricultural Growth: The Economics of Agrarian Change under Population Pressure*. Chicago: Aldine.

Bracken, C. P. 1975. *Antiquities Acquired*. Newton Abbott: David and Charles.

Bradford, John. 1957. *Ancient Landscapes: Studies in Field Archaeology*. London: G. Bell.

Braidwood, Robert J., and Bruce Howe. 1962. "Southwestern Asia Beyond the Lands of the Mediterranean Littoral," in Robert J. Braidwood and Gordon R. Willey, eds., *Courses Toward Urban Life*. New York: Viking Fund, pp. 132-146.

Brain, C. K. 1967. "Hottentot Food Remains and Their Bearing on the Interpretation of Fossil Bone Assemblages," *Scientific Papers of the Namib Desert Research Station* 32, 6: 1-7.

———. 1981. *The Hunters or the Hunted: An Introduction to African Cave Taphonomy*. Chicago: University of Chicago Press.

Brill, R. H. 1964. "Applications of Fission-Track Dating to Historic and Prehistoric Glasses," *Archaeometry* 7: 51-57.

Brothwell, D. R. 1965. *Digging Up Bones*. London: British Museum (Natural History).

Brothwell, D. R., and Eric Higgs. eds. 1969. *Science in Archaeology*. London: Thames and Hudson.

Browman, David L. 1981. "Isotopic Discrimination and Correction Factors in Radiocarbon Dating," *Advances in Archaeological Method and Theory* 4: 241-295.

Brown, James A., ed. 1971. *Approaches to the Social Dimensions of Mortuary Practices*. Memoirs of the Society for American Archaeology, vol. 25.

———. 1981. "The Search for Rank in Prehistoric Burials," in Robert Chapman and others, eds., *The Archaeology of Death*. Cambridge: Cambridge University Press, pp. 25-38.

———. 1982. "On the Structure of Artifact Typologies," in Robert Whallon and James A. Brown. *Essays on Archaeological Typology*. Evanston: Center for American Archaeology, pp. 176-190.

Brown, James A., and Stuart Struever. 1973. "The Organization of Archaeological Research: An Illinois Example," in Charles L. Redman, ed., *Method and Theory in Current Archaeology*. New York: John Wiley Interscience, pp. 261-280.

Brumfiel, Elizabeth O. 1976. "Regional Growth in the Eastern Valley of Mexico," in Kent V. Flannery, ed., *The Early Mesoamerican Village*. New York: Academic Press, pp. 243-247.

Bryant, Vaughn, 1974. "Prehistoric Diet in Southwest Texas: The Coprolite Evidence," *American Antiquity* 39: 407-420.

Bryant, Vaughn, and Glenna Williams-Dean. 1975. "The Coprolites of Man," *Scientific American* 232: 100-109.

Buchanon, R. A. 1972. *Industrial Archaeology in Britain*. Baltimore: Pelican Books.

Burghardt, Andrew F. 1959. "The Location of Towns in the Central Lowland of the United States," *Annals of the Association of American Geographers* 49: 305-323.

Burkitt, Miles C. 1955. *The Old Stone Age*. Cambridge: Cambridge University Press.

Burleigh, R., and D. R. Brothwell. 1978. "Studies on Amerindian Dogs," *Journal of Archaeological Science* 5: 355-362.

Butzer, Karl. 1974. *Environment and Archaeology*, 3rd ed. Chicago: Aldine.

———. 1982. *Archaeology as Human Ecology*. Cambridge: Cambridge University Press.

Byers, Douglas S., ed. 1967. *The Prehistory of the Tehuacán Valley*. Austin: University of Texas Press.

Cahen, D., and Lawrence H. Keeley. 1980. "Not Less Than Two, Not More Than Three," *World Archaeology*, 12, 2: 166-180.

Campbell, John B. 1977. *The Upper Palaeolithic of Britain*. Oxford: Oxford University Press.

Cann, J. R., and Colin Renfrew. 1964. "The Characterization of Obsidian and Its Application to the Mediterranean Region," *Proceedings of the Prehistoric Society* 30: 111-133.

Cartailhac, Emil. 1901. "Les Cavernes Ornées de Dessins: La Grotte d'Altamira. Mea Culpa d'un Sceptique," *L'Anthropologie* 12: 671.

Carter, Howard, and others. 1923-33. *The Tomb of Tutankhamun*. London: Cassell.

Casteel, Richard W. 1976. *Fish Remains in Archaeology and Paleo-Environmental Studies*. New York: Academic Press.

Ceram, C. W. 1953. *Gods, Graves, and Scholars*. New York: Alfred A. Knopf.

Cernych, E. N. 1978. "Aibunar—A Balkan Copper Mine of the Fourth Millennium B.C.," *Proceedings of the Prehistoric Society* 44: 203-218.

Chang, K. C., ed. 1968. *Settlement Archaeology*. Palo Alto: National Press.

———. 1977. *The Archaeology of Ancient China*, 3rd ed. New Haven: Yale University Press.

Chaplin, J. H. 1961. "Notes on Traditional Smelting in Northern Rhodesia," *South African Archaeological Bulletin* 16, 63: 53-60.

Chaplin, R. E. 1971. *The Study of Animal Bones from Archaeological Sites*. New York: Seminar Press.

Chapman, Robert, Ian Kinnes, and Klavs Randsborg, eds. 1981. *The Archaeology of Death*. Cambridge: Cambridge University Press.

Chartkoff, J. L. 1978. "Transect Interval Sampling in Forests." *American Antiquity* 43: 46-53.

Charton, Thomas H. 1981. "Archaeology, Ethnohistory, and Ethnology: Interpretative Interfaces," *Advances in Archaeological Method and Theory* 4: 129-176.

Childe, V. G. 1925. *The Dawn of European Civilization*. London: Routledge and Kegan Paul.

———. 1942. *What Happened in History*. Baltimore: Pelican Books.

———. 1956. *Piecing Together the Past*. London: Routledge and Kegan Paul.

———. 1958. "Retrospect," *Antiquity* 32: 69-74.

Chisholm, Michael. 1968. *Rural Settlement and Land Use*. London: Hutchinson.

Chittick, H. N. 1974. *Kilwa*. Nairobi: British Institute in Eastern Africa.

Christaller, Walter. 1933. *Die Zentralen Orte in Süddeutschland*. Jena: Karl Zeiss.

Clark, G. A. 1982. "Quantifying Archaeological Research," *Advances in Archaeological Method and Theory* 5: 217-274.

Clark, J. Desmond. 1958. "The Natural Fracturing of Pebbles from the Batoka Gorge, Northern Rhodesia, and Its Bearing on the Kafuan Industries of Africa," *Proceedings of the Prehistoric Society* 24: 64-77.

———. 1959. *The Prehistory of Southern Africa*. Baltimore: Pelican Books.

———. 1960. "A Note on Early Fishing-Craft and Fishing Practices in Southeast Africa," *South African Archaeological Bulletin* 15: 77-79.

———, ed. 1967. *Atlas of African Prehistory*. Chicago: University of Chicago Press.

Clark, J. G. D. 1932. *The Mesolithic Age in Britain*. Cambridge: Cambridge University Press.

———. 1939. *Archaeology and Society*. New York: Barnes and Noble.

———. 1952. *Prehistoric Europe: The Economic Basis*. Palo Alto: Stanford University Press.

Clark, J. G. D. 1954. *Star Carr*. Cambridge: Cambridge University Press.

———. 1970. *Aspects of Prehistory*. Berkeley: University of California Press.

———. 1972. *Star Carr: A Case Study in Bioarchaeology*. Reading: Addison-Wesley Modules in Anthropology, no. 10.

———. 1975. *The Early Stone Age Settlement of Scandinavia*. Cambridge: Cambridge University Press.

———. 1978. *World Prehistory in New Perspective*, 3rd ed. Cambridge: Cambridge University Press.

Clark, Rainbird. 1935. "The Flint Knapping Industry at Brandon," *Antiquity* 9: 38–56.

Clark, R. M. 1975. "A Calibration Curve for Radiocarbon Dates," *Antiquity* 49: 251–266.

Clarke, David L. 1968. *Analytical Archaeology*. London: Methuen.

———, ed. 1977. *Spatial Archaeology*. New York: Academic Press.

Clarke, John E. 1982. "Manufacture of Mesoamerican Prismatic Blades: An Alternative Technique," *American Antiquity* 47, 2: 355–375.

Clay, R. B. 1976. "Typological Classification, Attribute Analysis, and Lithic Variability," *Journal of Field Archaeology* 3: 303–311.

Coe, Michael D. 1962. *Mexico*. New York: Praeger.

———. 1967. *Tikal: A Handbook of the Ancient Maya Ruins*. Philadelphia: University Museum.

———. 1976. *The Maya*, 2nd ed. New York: Praeger.

Cole, John H. 1980. "Cult Archaeology and Unscientific Method and Theory," *Advances in Archaeological Method and Theory* 3: 4–37.

Coles, John M. 1972. *Field Archaeology in Britain*. London: Heinemann.

———. 1973. *Archaeology by Experiment*. London: Heinemann.

Coles, J. M., and A. F. Harding. 1979. *The Bronze Age in Europe*. London: Methuen.

Coles, J. M., S. V. E. Heal, and B. J. Orme. 1978. "The Use and Character of Wood in Prehistoric Britain and Ireland," *Proceedings of the Prehistoric Society* 44: 1–45.

Coles J. M., and B. J. Orme. 1983. "*Homo sapiens* or *Caster Fiber?*" *Antiquity* 57: 95–102.

Collins, H. B. 1937. *The Archaeology of St. Lawrence Island*. Smithsonian Miscellaneous Collections, no. 96.

Cook, S. F. 1972. *Prehistoric Demography*. Reading: Addison-Wesley Modules in Anthropology.

Cornwall, I. W. 1956. *Bones for the Archaeologist*. London: Phoenix.

Crabtree, Don E. 1966. "An Introduction to Flintworking, Part I: An Introduction to the Technology of Stone Tools," *Occasional Papers of the Idaho State University*, vol. 28.

———. 1972. "A Stoneworker's Approach to Analysing and Replicating the Lindenmeier Folsom," *Tebiwa* 9: 3–39.

Crabtree, Robert M. 1963. "Archaeological Investigations at Batiquitos Lagoon, San Diego County," *California Archaeological Survey Annual Report*, pp. 319–462.

Crawford, O. G. S. 1953. *Archaeology in the Field*. New York: Praeger.

Crawford, O. G. S., and Alexander Keiller. 1928. *Wessex from the Air*. Oxford: Clarendon Press.

Cressey, Pamela J. 1980. "Studying the American City: The Alexandria Urban Archaeology Project," Unpublished paper read at the Society for American Archaeology meetings, Philadelphia, 1980.

Croes, Dale R., and Jonathan O. Davis. 1977. "Computer Mapping of Idiosyncratic Basketry Manufacturing Techniques in the Prehistoric Ozette House, Cape Alava, Washington," in James Hill and Joel Gunn, eds., *The Individual in Prehistory*. New York: Academic Press, pp. 155–166.

Curtis, Garniss H. 1975. "Improvements in Potassium-Argon Dating, 1962–1975," *World Archaeology* 7, 2: 198–209.

Dalrymple, G. Brett, and Mason A. Lamphere. 1970. *Potassium Argon Dating*. San Francisco: W. H. Freeman.

Dancey, H. S. 1981. *Archaeological Field Methods: An Introduction.* Minneapolis: Burgess.

Daniel, Glyn. 1962. *The Idea of Prehistory.* London: Watts.

————, ed. 1967. *The Origins and Growth of Archaeology.* Baltimore: Pelican Books.

————. 1973. *Megaliths in History.* London: Thames and Hudson.

————. 1976. "Stone, Bronze, and Iron," in J. V. S. Megaw, ed., *To Illustrate the Monuments.* London: Thames and Hudson, pp. 35–42.

————. 1981. *A Short History of Archaeology.* London and New York: Thames and Hudson.

Daniels, S. G. H. 1972. "Research Design Models," in David L. Clarke, ed., *Models in Archaeology.* London: Methuen, pp. 201–229.

Däniken, Erich von. 1970. *Chariots of the Gods?* New York: Bantam Books.

————. 1971. *Gods from Outer Space.* New York: Bantam Books.

Darrah, W. C. 1938. "Technical Contributions to the Study of Archaeological Materials," *American Antiquity* 3: 269–270.

Dart, R. A. 1957. *The Osteodontokeratic Culture of Australopithecus Prometheus.* Pretoria: Transvaal Museum.

Darwin, Charles. 1859. *On the Origin of Species.* London: John Murray.

————. 1881. *The Formation of Vegetable Mould Through the Actions of Worms with Observations on Their Habits.* London: Faber and Faber. (Republished in 1945.)

David, N. C. 1971. "The Fulani Compound and the Archaeologist," *World Archaeology* 3, 2: 111–131.

Davis, Dave D. 1983. "Investigating the Diffusion of Stylistic Innovations," *Advances in Archaeological Method and Theory* 6: 53–89.

Dawson, Elliot W. 1969. "Bird Remains in Archaeology," in D. R. Brothwell and Eric Higgs, eds., *Science in Archaeology.* London: Thames and Hudson, pp. 359–375.

Deagan, Kathleen. 1982. "Avenues of Inquiry in Historical Archaeology," *Advances in Archaeological Method and Theory* 5: 151–178.

Dean, Jeffrey S. 1970. "Aspects of Tsegi Phase Soil Organization," in W. A. Longacre, ed., *Reconstructing Prehistoric Pueblo Societies.* Albuquerque: University of New Mexico Press.

Deetz, James. 1967. *Invitation to Archaeology.* Garden City, N.Y.: Natural History Press.

De Laet, S. J. 1956. *Archaeology and Its Problems.* London: Phoenix.

De Mortillet, Gabriel. 1867. *Promenades Préhistoriques á L'Exposition Universelle.* Paris.

Dennell, R. W. 1979. "Prehistoric Diet and Nutrition: Some Food for Thought," *World Archaeology* 11, 2: 121–135.

Dent, John. 1962. *The Quest for Nonsuch.* London: Pall Mall Press.

De Perthes, Boucher. 1841. *De La Création: Essai Sur L'Origine et la Progression des Êtres.* Abbeville.

Dethlefsen, Edwin, and James Deetz. 1966. "Death's Heads, Cherubs, and Willow Trees: Experimental Archaeology in Colonial Cemeteries," *American Antiquity* 31: 502–510.

Deuel, Leo. 1969. *Flights into Yesterday.* London: Macdonald.

————. 1977. *Memoirs of Heinrich Schliemann.* New York: Harper and Row.

De Viro, B., and S. Epstein. 1978. "Dietary Analysis from $^{12}C/^{13}C$ Ratios of Carbonate and Collagen Fractions of Bone," *U.S. Geological Survey Open File Report,* 78-701: 90–91.

Digby, Bernard. 1926. *The Mammoth and Mammoth-Hunting in North-East Siberia.* London: Macmillan.

Dittert, Alfred E., Jr., Jim J. Hester, and Frank W. Eddy. 1961. *An Archaeological Survey of the Navajo Reservoir District of Northwestern New Mexico.* Monographs of the School of American Research and Museum of New Mexico, no. 23.

Doran, James. 1970. "Systems Theory, Computer Simulations, and Archaeology," *World Archaeology* 1, 3: 289–298.

Doran, J. E., and F. R. Hodson. 1975. *Mathematics and Computers in Archaeology.* Cambridge: Harvard University Press.

Dowman, Elizabeth A. 1970. *Conservation in Field Archaeology.* London: Methuen.

Drennan, Robert D. 1976. "Religion and Social Evolution in Formative Mesoamerica," in Kent V. Flannery, ed., *The Early Mesoamerican Village.* New York: Academic Press, pp. 345–363.

Drucker, Philip. 1966. *Cultures of the North Pacific Coast.* San Francisco: Chandler.

———. 1972. *Stratigraphy in Archaeology: An Introduction.* Reading: Addison-Wesley Modules in Anthropology, no. 30.

Dumond, Don E. 1977. *The Eskimos and Aleuts.* London: Thames and Hudson.

Dunnell, Robert C. 1970. "The Seriation Method and Its Evaluation," *American Antiquity* 35, 3: 305–319.

———. 1971. *Systematics in Prehistory.* New York: Free Press.

———. 1977. "Science and Archaeology: When the Saints Go Marching in," *American Antiquity* 42: 33–49.

———. 1978. "Style and Function: A Fundamental Dichotomy," *American Antiquity* 43, 2: 192–202.

———. 1980. "Evolutionary Theory and Archaeology," *Advances in Archaeological Method and Theory* 3: 38–99.

———. 1982. "Science, Social Science, and Common Sense: The Agonizing Dilemma of Modern Archaeology," *Journal of Anthropological Research* 38, 1: 1–25.

Dunnell, Robert C., and William S. Dancey. 1983. "The Siteless Survey: A Regional Scale Data Collection," *Advances in Archaeological Method and Theory* 6: 267–288.

Dymond, D. P. 1974. *Archaeology and History.* London: Thames and Hudson.

Earle, Timothy. 1976. "A Nearest Neighbor Analysis of Two Formative Settlement Systems," in Kent V. Flannery, ed., *The Early Mesoamerican Village.* New York: Academic Press, pp. 196–224.

Earle, Timothy, and J. E. Ericson, eds. 1977. *Exchange Systems in Prehistory.* New York: Academic Press.

Eliade, Mercea. 1954. *The Myth of the Eternal Return.* New York: Pantheon.

Evans, John. 1849–50. "On the Date of British Coins," *Numismatic Chronicle* 12: 127.

———. 1860. "On the Occurrence of Flint Implements in Undisturbed Beds of Gravel, Sand, and Clay," *Archaeologia* 38: 280–308.

Evans, John D. 1978. *An Introduction to Environmental Archaeology.* London: Paul Elek.

Faegri, K., and J. Iverson. 1975. *Textbook of Pollen Analysis.* New York: Hafner.

Fagan, Brian M. 1967. *Iron Age Cultures in Zambia,* vol. 1. New York: Humanities Press.

———. 1969. "Early Trade and Raw Materials in South Central Africa," *Journal of African History* 10: 1–26.

———. 1975. *The Rape of the Nile.* New York: Charles Scribner's.

———. 1977. *Elusive Treasure.* New York: Charles Scribner's.

———. 1978a. *Quest for the Past.* Reading: Addison-Wesley.

———. 1978b. *Archaeology: A Brief Introduction.* Boston: Little, Brown.

———. 1979. *Return to Babylon.* Boston: Little, Brown.

———. 1982. *People of the Earth,* 3rd ed. Boston: Little, Brown.

———. 1983. *Archaeology: A Brief Introduction,* 2nd ed. Boston: Little, Brown.

———. 1984a. *The Aztecs.* New York: W. H. Freeman.

———. 1984b. *Clash of Cultures.* New York: W. H. Freeman.

Fagan, Brian M., and F. Van Noten. 1971. *The Hunter-Gatherers of Gwisho.* Tervuren: Musée Royal de l'Afrique Centrale.

Fell, Barry. 1977. *America B. C.* New York: Viking.

Finley, M. I. 1971. "Archaeology and History," *Daedalus* 100: 168–186.

Fitting, James F., and Albert C. Goodyear. 1979. "Client Oriented Archaeology: An Exchange of Views," *Journal of Field Archaeology* 6: 352–360.

Flannery, Kent V. 1968. "Archaeological Systems Theory and Early Mesoamerica," in Betty J. Meggers, ed., *Anthropological Archaeology in the Americas*. Washington: Anthropological Society of Washington, pp. 67–87.

————. 1972. "The Cultural Evolution of Civilizations," *Biennial Review of Ecology and Systematics*, pp. 399–426.

————. 1973a. "Archaeology with a Capital A," in Charles L. Redman, ed., *Research and Theory in Current Archaeology*. New York: John Wiley Interscience, pp. 337–354.

————. 1973b. "The Origins of Agriculture," *Biennial Review of Anthropology* 12: 271–310.

————, ed. 1976. *The Early Mesoamerican Village*. New York: Academic Press.

Flannery, Kent V., and Marcus C. Winter. 1976. "Analyzing Village Activities," in Kent V. Flannery, ed., *The Early Mesoamerican Village*. New York: Academic Press, pp. 34–44.

Fleischer, Robert L. 1975. "Advances in Fission Track Dating," *World Archaeology* 7, 2: 136–150.

Fleming, Stuart. 1976. *Dating in Archaeology*. London: Dent.

Fontana, Bernard L. 1968. "Bottles, Buckets, and Horseshoes: The Unrespectable in American Archaeology," *Keystone Folklore Quarterly* 13, 3: 171–184.

Fontana, Bernard, W. J. Robinson, C. W. Cormack, and E. E. Leavitt. 1962. *Papago Indian Pottery*. Seattle: University of Washington Press.

Forbes, R. J. 1955–58. *Studies in Ancient Technology*. The Hague: Brill.

Ford, J. A. 1954a. "A Comment on A. C. Spaulding 'Statistical Techniques,'" *American Antiquity* 19: 390–391.

————. 1954b. "On the Concept of Types," *American Antiquity* 56: 42–54.

————. 1962. *A Quantitative Method for Deriving Cultural Chronology*. Washington, D.C.: Pan American Union.

Ford, J. A., and Gordon R. Willey. 1941. "An Interpretation of the Prehistory of the Eastern United States," *American Anthropologist* 43, 3: 325–363.

Ford, Richard I. 1979. "Paleoethnobotany in American Archaeology," *Advances in Archaeological Method and Theory* 2: 286–336.

Fowler, Don. 1982. "Cultural Resources Management," *Advances in Archaeological Method and Theory* 5: 1–50.

Fox, Sir Cyril. 1932. *The Personality of Britain*. Cambridge: Cambridge University Press.

Frankfort, Henri. 1951. *The Birth of Civilization in the Near East*. New York: Doubleday.

Frazer, James. 1890. *The Golden Bough*. London: Macmillan.

Friedman, I., D. Clark, and R. L. Smith. 1969. "Obsidian Dating," in D. R. Brothwell and Eric Higgs, eds., *Science in Archaeology*. London: Thames and Hudson.

Frison, George. 1974. *The Casper Site: A Hell Gap Bison Kill on the High Plains*. New York: Academic Press.

Fritts, H. C. 1976. *Tree Rings and Climate*. New York: Academic Press.

Gabel, Creighton. 1967. *Analysis of Prehistoric Economic Patterns*. New York: Holt, Rinehart and Winston.

Garlake, Peter. 1973. *Great Zimbabwe*. London: Thames and Hudson.

Garrod, D. A. E., and Dorothea Bate. 1937. *The Stone Age of Mount Carmel*, vol. 1. Cambridge: Cambridge University Press.

Gifford, Diane P. 1981. "Taphonomy and Paleoecology: A Critical Review of Archaeology's Sister Discipline," *Advances in Archaeological Method and Theory* 4: 365–437.

Gifford, E. W. 1916. "Composition of California Shell Middens," *University of California Publications in Archaeology and Anthropology* 12: 1–29.

Gifford, J. C. 1976. *Prehistoric Pottery Analysis and the Ceramics of Barton Ramie in the Belize Valley.* Memoirs of the Peabody Museum, no. 18. Harvard University, Cambridge, Mass.

Gish, Janifer W. 1979. "Palynological Research at Pueblo Grande Ruin," *The Kiva* 44, 2–3: 159–177.

Glob, P. V. 1969. *The Bog People.* London: Faber and Faber.

Goggin, J. W., ed. 1949. *The Florida Indian and His Neighbors.* Winter Park, Fla.: Rollins College.

Goodyear, A. C., L. A. Raab, and T. C. Klinger. 1978. "The Status of Archaeological Research Design in Cultural Resource Management," *American Antiquity* 43: 159–173.

Gould, Richard. 1977. *Puntutjarpa Rockshelter.* New York: American Museum of Natural History.

———, ed. 1978. *Explorations in Ethnoarchaeology.* Albuquerque: University of New Mexico Press.

Gould, Richard H., and M. B. Schiffer. 1981. *Modern Material Culture: The Archaeology of Us.* New York: Academic Press.

Grange, Roger T. 1972. "Pawnee Potsherds Revisited: Formula Dating of a Non-European Ceramic Tradition," *The Conference on Historic Site Archaeology Papers* 7: 318–336.

———. 1981. "Ceramic Dating Formula of the Arikara," in Alfred E. Johnson and Larry J. Zimmerman. 1981. *Method and Theory in Plains Archaeology.* Vermillion: South Dakota Archaeological Society.

Grasiozi, Paolo. 1960. *Palaeolithic Art.* New York: McGraw-Hill.

Graybill, Don. 1978. "The Destruction of Archaeological Sites," *Journal of Field Archaeology* 3: 25–38.

Grayson, Donald K. 1979. "On the Quantification of Vertebrate Archaeofaunas," *Advances in Archaeological Method and Theory* 2: 200–238.

———. 1980. "Vicissitudes and Overkill: The Development of Explanations of Pleistocene Extinctions," *Advances in Archaeological Method and Theory* 3: 357–404.

———. 1981. "A Critical View of the Use of Archaeological Vertebrates in Paleoenvironmental Reconstruction," *Journal of Ethnobiology* 1, 1: 28–38.

———. 1983. *The Search for Human Antiquity.* New York: Academic Press.

Griffin, J. B. 1946. "Culture Change and Continuity in the Eastern United States, in F. Johnson, ed., *Man in Northeastern North America.* Andover: Peabody Foundation.

Grinsell, L. V., P. Rahtz, and D. P. Williams. 1970. *The Preparation of Archaeological Reports.* London: John Baker.

Grootes, P. M. 1978. "Carbon-14 Time Scale Extended: Comparison of Chronologies," *Science* 200, 4337: 11–15.

Grossman, Joel W. 1982. *Raritan Landing: The Archaeology of a Buried Port,* 2 vols. New Brunswick, N.J.: Rutgers Archaeological Survey Office.

Gumerman, George J., and Robert C. Euler. 1976. *Papers on the Archaeology of Black Mesa, Arizona.* Carbondale: Southern Illinois University Press.

Gumerman, George J., and T. R. Lyons, 1971. "Archaeological Methodology and Remote Sensing," *Science* 210: 11–15.

Gumerman, George J., and M. Schiffer, eds. 1977. *Conservation Archaeology.* New York: Academic Press.

Hally, D. J. 1981. "Plant Preservation and the Content of Paleobotanical Samples: A Case Study," *American Antiquity* 46: 723–742.

Hamblin, Dora Jane. 1970. *Pots and Robbers.* New York: Simon and Schuster.

Hammond, Norman. 1982. *Ancient Maya Civilization*. New Brunswick: Rutgers University Press.

Hammond, Norman, and C. H. Miksicek. 1981. "Ecology and Economy of a Formative Maya Site at Cuello, Belize," *Journal of Field Archaeology* 8, 3: 259–269.

Hanson, H. O. 1962. *I Built a Stone Age House*. London: Phoenix.

Hardesty, Donald. 1977. *Ecological Anthropology*. New York: John Wiley.

————. 1980. "The Use of General Ecological Principles in Archaeology," *Advances in Archaeological Method and Theory* 3: 158–188.

Hardin, Margaret Ann. 1977. "Individual Style in San José Pottery Painting: The Role of Deliberate Choice," in James Hill and Joel Gunn, eds., *The Individual in Prehistory*. New York: Academic Press, pp. 109–136.

Harp, Elmer. 1978. *Photography for Archaeologists*. New York: Academic Press.

Harp, E., Jr., ed. 1975. *Photography in Archaeological Research*. Albuquerque: University of New Mexico Press.

Harrington, J. C. 1948. "Evidence of Manual Reckoning in the Cittie of Raleigh," *North Carolina Historical Review* 33, 1: 1–8.

Harris, Edward C. 1979. *Principles of Archaeological Stratigraphy*. New York: Academic Press.

Harris, Marvin, 1968. *The Rise of Anthropological Theory*. New York: Thomas Crowell.

Hassan, Fekri. 1981. *Demographic Archaeology*. New York: Academic Press.

Hatch, Elvin. 1973. *Theories of Man and Culture*. New York: Columbia University Press.

Hatt, C. 1957. "Norre Fjord, an Early Iron Age Village in West Jutland," *Archaeologiske Kunsthistorische* 2, 2: 1–25.

Hawkins, Gerald. 1965. *Stonehenge Decoded*. New York: Doubleday.

Hayashi, Kensaku. 1968. "The Fukui Microblade Technology and Its Relationships in Northeast Asia and North America," *Arctic Anthropology* 5: 128–190.

Hayden, Brian, ed. 1979. *Lithic Wear Analysis*. New York: Academic Press.

Heizer, Robert F. 1969. "The Archaeology of Great Basin Coprolites," in D. R. Brothwell and Eric Higgs, eds., *Science in Archaeology*. London: Thames and Hudson, pp. 244–250.

Helbaek, Hans. 1969. "Plant Collecting, Dry-Farming, and Irrigation Agriculture," in Frank Hole, Kent V. Flannery, and James Neely, eds., *The Prehistoric Human Ecology of the Deh Luran Plain*. Ann Arbor: Memoirs of the Museum of Anthropology, no. 1.

Hess, John L. 1974. *The Grand Acquisitors*. Boston: Houghton Mifflin.

Hester, Thomas R. 1981. "CRM Publication: Dealing with Reality." *Journal of Field Archaeology*, 8: 493–496.

Hester, Thomas, and Robert F. Heizer. 1973. *Bibliography of Archaeology—I: Lithic Technology and Petrography*. Reading: Addison-Wesley Modules in Anthropology, no. 29.

Hester, Thomas, Harry J. Shafer, and Robert F. Heizer. 1985. *Field Methods in Archaeology*, Palo Alto: Mayfield.

Heyerdahl, Thor. 1950. *The Kon Tiki Expedition*. London: George Unwin.

Hill, James N. 1970. *Broken K Pueblo: Prehistoric Social Organization in the American Southwest*. Tucson: University of Arizona Press.

————, ed. 1977. *Explanation of Prehistoric Change*. Albuquerque: University of New Mexico Press.

Hill, James, and Joel Gunn, eds. 1977. *The Individual in Prehistory*. New York: Academic Press.

Hill, James N., and Richard H. Hevly. 1968. "Pollen at Broken K: Some New Interpretations," *American Antiquity* 33: 200–210.

Hodder, Ian, ed. 1978. *Simulation Studies in Archaeology*. Cambridge: Cambridge University Press.

————. 1982a. *The Present Past: An Introduction to Anthropology for Archaeologists*. London: Batsford.

————. 1982b. *Symbolic and Structural Archaeology*. Cambridge: Cambridge University Press.

————. 1982c. *Symbols in Action*. Cambridge: Cambridge University Press.

Hodder, Ian, and M. Hassall. 1972. "The Non-random Spacing of Romano-British Walled Towns," *Man* 6: 391–407.

Hodder, Ian, and Clive Orton. 1976. *Spatial Analysis in Archaeology*. Cambridge: Cambridge University Press.

Hodder, Ian, Glynn L. Isaac, and Norman Hammond. 1981. *Patterns in the Past: Studies in Honor of David Clarke*. Cambridge: Cambridge University Press.

Hogg, A. H. A. 1980. *Surveying for Archaeologists and Other Professionals*. New York: St. Martin's Press.

Hole, Frank, Kent V. Flannery, and J. A. Neely. 1969. *The Prehistory and Human Ecology of the Deh Luran Plain*. Ann Arbor: Memoirs of the Museum of Anthropology, no. 1.

Hole, Frank, and R. F. Heizer. 1973. *An Introduction to Prehistoric Archaeology*, 3rd ed. New York: Holt, Rinehart and Winston.

Hole, Frank, and M. Shaw. 1967. "Computer Analysis of Chronological Seriation," *Rice University Studies* vol. 53, no. 3.

Holly, Gerald, A., and Terry A. Del Bene. 1981. "An Evaluation of Keeley's Microwear Approach," *Journal of Archaeological Science*, 8: 337–352.

Holmes, W. H. 1919. *Handbook of Aboriginal American Antiquities, Part I: Introductory: The Lithic Industry*. Bureau of American Ethnology, Bulletin no. 60.

Howard, Hildegaard. 1929. "The Avifauna of Emeryville Shellmound," *University of California Publications in Zoology* 23: 378–383.

Howell, F. Clark. 1965. *Early Man*. New York: Time-Life Books.

Hudson, Kenneth. 1982. *World Industrial Archaeology*. Cambridge: Cambridge University Press.

Huss-Ashmore, Rebecca, Alan H. Goodman, and George J. Armelagos. 1982. "Nutritional Inference from Paleopathology" *Advances in Archaeological Method and Theory* 5: 395–476.

Huxley, Thomas. 1863. *Man's Place in Nature*. London: Macmillan.

Ingersoll, Daniel, John E. Yellen, and William Macdonald, eds. 1977. *Experimental Archaeology*. New York: Columbia University Press.

Issac, Glynn L. 1983. "Review: *Ancient Men and Modern Myths*," *American Antiquity*, 48, 2: 416–419.

Isaac, Glynn L., and Elizabeth McKown, eds. 1977. *Human Origins: Louis Leakey and the East African Evidence*. Menlo Park: W. A. Benjamin.

Iversen, Johannes. 1941. "Land Occupation in Denmark's Stone Age," *Danmarks Geologiske Undersøgelse*, II Raekke 66: 70–76.

Jarman, H. N., A. J. Legge, and J. A. Charles. 1972. "Retrieval of Plant Remains from Archaeological Sites by Froth Flotation," in E. S. Higgs, ed., *Essays in Economic Prehistory*. Cambridge: Cambridge University Press, pp. 39–48.

Jennings, Jesse D. 1966. *Glen Canyon: A Summary*. Salt Lake City: University of Utah Anthropological Papers.

————. 1973. *The Prehistory of North America*, 2nd ed. New York: McGraw-Hill.

————, ed. 1978. *Ancient Native Americans*. San Francisco: W. H. Freeman.

Jewell, P. A., and G. W. Dimbleby. 1966. "The Experimental Earthwork at Overton Down, Wiltshire, England," *Proceedings of the Prehistoric Society* 32: 313–342.

Jochim, Michael A. 1979. "Breaking Down the System: Recent Ecological Approaches in Archaeology," *Advances in Archaeological Method and Theory* 2: 77–119.

Johnson, E. and others. 1977. "Archaeology and Native Americans," in C. R. McGimsey and H. A. Davis, eds. *The Management of Archaeological Resources*, Washington, D.C.: Society for American Archaeology, pp. 90–96.

Johnson, L. 1968. *Item Seriation as an Aid for Elementary Scale and Cluster Analysis*. Bulletin of the Museum of Natural History, no. 15. University of Oregon, Eugene.

Johnson, L. L. 1978. "A History of Flint Knapping Experimentation, 1838–1976," *Current Anthropology* 19: 337–372.

Johnson, Paul. 1968. *The Civilization of Ancient Egypt*. London: Weidenfeld and Nicholson.

Jones, Peter R. 1980. "Experimental butchery with modern stone tools and its relevance for Palaeolithic Archaeology," *World Archaeology* 12, 2: 153–165.

Joukowsky, Martha. 1981. *Complete Manual of Field Archaeology*. Englewood Cliffs: Prentice-Hall.

Judge, James W., and J. Dawson. 1972. "Paleo-Indian Settlement Technology in New Mexico," *Science* 176: 1210–1216.

Kaczor, M. J., and J. Weymouth. 1981. "Magnetic Prospecting: Results of the 1980 Field Season at the Toltec Site, 3LN42," *Proceedings of the South-East Archaeological Conference* 24: 118–123.

Keesing, R. M. 1974. "Theories of Culture," *Annual Review of Anthropology* 3: 71–97.

Kidder, A. V. 1924. *An Introduction to the Study of Southwestern Archaeology*. New Haven: Yale University Press.

Killingley, John S. 1981. "Seasonality of Mollusk Collecting Determined from 0-18 Profiles of Midden Shells," *American Antiquity* 46: 152–158.

King, Chester, Thomas Blackburn, and Ernest Chandonet. 1968. "The Archaeological Inventory of Three Sites on the Century Ranch, Western Los Angeles County, California," *California Archaeological Survey Annual Report* 10: 12–161.

King, M. E. 1978. "Analytical Methods and Prehistoric Textiles," *American Antiquity* 43: 89–96.

King, T. F. 1971. "Resolving a Conflict of Values in American Archaeology," *American Antiquity* 36: 255–262.

———. 1979. "Preservation and Rescue: Challenges and Controversies in the Protection of Archaeological Resources," *Journal of Field Archaeology* 6: 351–352.

King, T. F., Patricia Hickman, and Gary Berg, eds. 1977. *Anthropology in Historic Preservation: Caring for Culture's Clutter*. New York: Academic Press.

Kirch, Patrick V. 1980. "The Archaeological Study of Adaptation: Theoretical and Methodological Issues," *Advances in Archaeological Method and Theory* 3: 101–155.

Kirk, Ruth 1974. *Hunters of the Whale*. New York: Morrow.

Klein, Jeffrey, and others. 1982. "Calibration of Radiocarbon Dating: Tables based on the consensus data of the workshop on calibrating the Radiocarbon Time Scale," *Radiocarbon* 22: 103–153.

Klein, Richard, 1969. *Man and Culture in the Late Pleistocene*. San Francisco: Chandler.

———. 1977. "Environment and Subsistence of Prehistoric Man in the Southern Cape Province, South Africa," *World Archaeology* 5: 249–284.

Klein, Richard G., and Kathryne Cruz-Uribe. 1983. "The computation of ungulate age (mortality) profiles from dental crown heights," *Paleobiology* 9, 1: 70–78.

Kluckhohn, Clyde. 1940. "The Conceptual Structure in Middle American Studies," in A. M. Tozzer, ed., *The Maya and Their Neighbors*. New York: Appleton-Century-Crofts.

———. 1943. "Bronislaw Malinowski, 1884–1942," *Journal of American Folklore* 56: 208–219.

Kramer, Carol. 1982. *Village Ethnoarchaeology: Rural Iran in Archaeological Perspective*. New York: Academic Press.

Kreiger, A. D. 1944. "The Typological Concept," *American Antiquity* 9: 271-288.

Kroeber, Alfred L., and Clyde Kluckhohn. 1952. *Culture: A Critical Review of Concepts and Definitions*. Papers of the Peabody Museum of American Archaeology and Ethnology. Cambridge: Harvard University.

Kroeber, Theodora. 1965. *Ishi in Two Worlds*. Berkeley: University of California Press.

Kuhn, T. S. 1970. *The Structure of Scientific Revolutions*, 2nd ed. Chicago: University of Chicago Press.

Lamberg-Karlovsky, C. C. 1970. *Excavations at Tepe Yahya, Iran, 1967–1969*. Cambridge: Bulletin of the American School of Prehistoric Research.

———. 1975. "Third Millennium Modes of Exchange and Modes of Production," in Jeremy A. Sabloff and C. C. Lamberg-Karlovsky, eds., *Early Civilization and Trade*. Albuquerque: University of New Mexico Press, pp. 341–368.

Lambrecht, Frank L. 1964. "Aspects of the Evolution and Ecology of Tsetse Flies and Trypanosomiasis in the Prehistoric African Environment," *Journal of African History* 5: 1–24.

Layard, A. H. 1849. *Nineveh and Its Remains*. London: John Murray.

Leakey, L. S. B. 1951. *Olduvai Gorge, 1931–1951*. Cambridge: Cambridge University Press.

———. 1971. *Olduvai Gorge*, vol. 1. Cambridge: Cambridge University Press.

Leakey, M. D. 1973. *Olduvai Gorge*, vol. 3. Cambridge: Cambridge University Press.

LeBlanc, Steven A. 1975. "Microseriation: A Method for Fine Chronologic Differentiation," *American Antiquity* 40: 22–30.

Lee, Richard B., and Irven DeVore, eds. 1976. *Kalahari Hunter-Gatherers*. Cambridge: Harvard University Press.

Lee, Ronald F. 1970. *The Antiquities Act of 1906*. Washington, D.C.: National Park Service.

Leone, Mark P. 1978. "Time in American Archaeology," in Charles L. Redman and others, eds., *Social Archaeology*. New York: Academic Press, pp. 25–36.

Leone, Mark. 1982. "Childe's Offspring," in Ian Hodder, ed. *Structural Archaeology*. Cambridge: Cambridge University Press, pp. 179–184.

Lepper, Bradley T. 1983. "Fluted point distributional patterns in the Eastern United States," *Midcontinental Journal of Archaeology* 8: 269–285.

Leroi-Gourhan, André. 1967. *Treasures of Prehistoric Art*. New York: Abrams.

Lewarch, Dennis E., and Michael J. O'Brien. 1981. "The Expanding Role of Surface Assemblages in Archaeological Research," *Advances in Archaeological Method and Theory* 4: 297–343.

Lewis-Williams, J. D. 1981. *Believing and Seeing: Symbolic Meanings in Southern San Rock Paintings*. New York: Academic Press.

Libby, W. F. 1955. *Radiocarbon Dating*. Chicago: University of Chicago Press.

Limbrey, Susan. 1972. *Soil Science in Archaeology*. New York: Seminar Press.

Lipe, William D. 1970. "A Conservation Model for American Archaeology," *The Kiva* 3, 4: 213–243.

Lipe, William D., and Alexander J. Lindsay, Jr. 1974. *Proceedings of the 1974 Cultural Resource Management Conference*. Flagstaff: Museum of Northern Arizona.

Lloyd, Seton. 1963. *Mounds of the Near East*. Chicago: Aldine.

Longacre, W. 1970. *Archaeology as Anthropology*. Tucson: University of Arizona Press.

———. 1974. "Kalinga Pottery Making: The Evolution of a Research Design," in M. J. Leaf, ed. *Frontiers of Anthropology*. New York: Van Nostrand, pp. 51–67.

———. 1981. "CRM Publication: a Review Essay." *Journal of Field Archaeology*, 8: 487–490.

———. 1981. "Kalinga Pottery: An Ethnoarchaeological Study," in Ian Hodder, Glynn Isaac, and Norman Hammond, eds., *Patterns in the Past*. Cambridge: Cambridge University Press, pp. 232–249.

Lubbock, Sir John (Lord Avebury). 1865. *Prehistoric Times.* London: Williams and Norgate.
Lumley, Henry de. 1969. "A Palaeolithic Camp at Nice," *Scientific American* 220: 42–50.
Lyman, R. Lee. 1982. "Archaeofaunas and Subsistence Studies," *Advances in Archaeological Method and Theory* 5: 332–394.
Lyons, T. R., ed. 1981. *Remote Sensing: Multispectral Analysis of Cultural Resources in Chaco Canyon and Bandelier National Monument.* Washington, D.C.: National Park Service.
Lyons, Thomas R., and Thomas Avery. 1977. *Remote Sensing: A Handbook for Archaeologists and Cultural Resource Managers.* Washington, D.C.: National Park Service.

McBurney, C. B. M. 1959. "First Season's Fieldwork on British Upper Palaeolithic Cave Deposits," *Proceedings of the Prehistoric Society* 25: 260–269.
McGimsey, Charles. 1972. *Public Archaeology.* New York: Seminar Press.
McGimsey, Charles, and Hester Davis. 1977. *The Management of Archaeological Resources.* Washington, D.C.: National Park Service.
McHargue, George, and Michael Roberts. 1977. *A Field Guide to Conservation Archaeology in North America.* Philadelphia: Lippincott.
McKern, W. C. 1939. "The Midwestern Taxonomic System as an Aid to Archaeological Culture Study," *American Antiquity* 4, 4: 301–313.
McNairn, Barbara. 1980. *The Theory and Method of V. Gordon Childe.* Edinburgh: Edinburgh University Press.
MacNeish, Richard S., ed. 1970. *The Prehistory of the Tehuacán Valley,* vol. 3. Austin: University of Texas Press.
———. 1978. *The Science of Archaeology?* North Scituate, Mass.: Duxbury Press.
Macquilty, William. 1965. *Abu Simbel.* London: Macmillan.
Mallowan, Max L. 1965. *Early Mesopotamia and Iran.* New York: McGraw-Hill.
Marcus, Joyce. 1976. "The Size of the Early Mesoamerican Village," in Kent V. Flannery, ed., *The Early Mesoamerican Village.* New York: Academic Press, pp. 79–88.
Marquardt, William H. 1978. "Advances in Archaeological Seriation," *Advances in Archaeological Method and Theory,* vol. 1.
Marshack, Alexander. 1972. *The Roots of Civilization.* New York: McGraw-Hill.
Martin, Paul S., and Fred Plog. 1973. *The Archaeology of Arizona.* Garden City, N.Y.: Doubleday Natural History Press.
Matson, F. R. 1965. *Ceramics and Man.* New York: Viking Fund.
Meeke, N. D., and others. 1982. "Gloss and Use-Wear Traces on Flint Sickles and Similar Phenomena," *Journal of Archaeological Science* 9: 317–340.
Mehringer, Peter J., and Vance Haynes. 1965. "The Pollen Evidence for the Environment of Early Man and Extinct Animals at the Lehner Mammoth Site, Southeastern Arizona," *American Antiquity* 31: 11–23.
Mellaart, James. 1975. *The Neolithic of the Near East.* London: Thames and Hudson.
Mercati, Michael. 1717. *Metallotheca Vaticana.* Rome.
Mewhinney, H. 1957. *A Manual for Neanderthalers.* Austin: University of Texas Press.
Meyer, Karl. 1977. *The Plundered Past,* 2nd ed. Baltimore: Pelican Books.
Michael, H. N., and E. K. Ralph, eds. 1971. *Dating Techniques for the Archaeologist.* Cambridge: MIT Press.
Michels, J. W. 1973. *Dating Methods in Archaeology.* New York: Seminar Press.
Michels, J. W., and R. Tsong. 1980. "Obsidian Hydration," *Advances in Archaeological Method and Theory* 3: 233–271.
Millon, René. 1973. *The Teotihuacán Map: Urbanization at Teotihuacán, Mexico,* vol. 1. Austin: University of Texas Press.
Moorehead, Alan. 1961. *Darwin and the Beagle.* London: Hamish Hamilton.

Morgan, J. W. W. 1975. "The Preservation of Timber," *Timber Grower* 8: 55.

Morgan, Lewis. 1877. *Ancient Society*. New York: Holt, Rinehart and Winston.

Morlan, Richard E. 1967. "The Preceramic Period of Hokkaido: An Outline" *Arctic Anthropology* 4: 164–220.

——. 1978. "Early Man in Northern Yukon Territory: Perspectives as of 1977," in Alan L. Bryan, ed., *Early Man in America*. Edmonton: Archaeological Research International, pp. 78–95.

Movius, H. L. 1974. "The Abri Pataud Program of the French Upper Paleolithic in Retrospect." in Gordon R. Willey, ed., *Archaeological Researches in Retrospect*. Cambridge: Winthrop.

——. 1977. *Excavation of the Abri Pataud, Les Eyzies (Dordogne)*. Cambridge: Peabody Museum.

Muckelroy, Keith. 1978. *Maritime Archaeology*. Cambridge: Cambridge University Press.

Mueller, James A. 1974. *The Use of Sampling in Archaeological Survey*. Memoirs of the Society for American Archaeology, no. 28, Washington, D.C.: U.S. Government Printing Office.

——, ed. 1975. *Sampling in Archaeology*. Tucson: University of Arizona Press.

Muhly, James D. 1980. "The Bronze Age Setting," in James D. Muhly and Theodore A. Wertime, eds., *The Coming of the Age of Iron*. New Haven: Yale University Press, pp. 25–68.

Murdock, George P. 1949. *Social Structure*. New York: Macmillan.

Nance, Jack D. 1983. "Regional Sampling in Archaeological Survey: The Statistical Perspective," *Advances in Archaeological Method and Theory* 6: 289–356.

Naroll, R. 1962. "Floor Size and Settlement Population," *American Antiquity* 27: 587–588.

Nash, C. H. 1968. *Residence Mounds: An Intermediate Middle Mississippian Settlement Pattern*. Memphis: Memphis State University Anthropological Research Center, Occasional Paper no. 2.

Nelson, N. C. 1914. *Pueblo Ruins of the Galisteo Basin, New Mexico*. New York: Macmillan.

Netting, R. McC. 1977. *Cultural Ecology*. Menlo Park: Cummings.

Noël Hume, Ivor. 1969. *Historical Archaeology*. New York: Alfred A. Knopf.

——. 1982. *Martin's Hundred*. New York: Alfred Knopf.

Oakley, K. P. 1969. *Frameworks for Dating Fossil Man*, 2nd ed. Chicago: Aldine.

O'Connell, James. 1975. *The Prehistory of Surprise Valley*. Ramona, Calif: Ballena Press.

Odell, George H., and Frieda Odell-Vereechea. 1980. "Verifying the Reliability of Lithic Use-Wear: The Lower Power Approach," *Journal of Field Archaeology* 7: 87–120.

Olsen, S. J. 1972. *Zooarchaeology: Animal Bones in Archaeology and Their Interpretation*. Reading: Addison-Wesley Modules in Anthropology, no. 12.

——. 1978. *Fish, Amphibians, and Reptile Remains from Archaeological Sites*. Cambridge: Peabody Museum.

——. 1979a. *Osteology for the Archaeologist*, rev. ed. Cambridge: Peabody Museum.

——. 1979b. "Osteologically, What Constitutes an Early Domesticated Animal?" *Advances in Archaeological Method and Theory* 2: 175–197.

Omer-Cooper, John. 1966. *The Zulu Aftermath*. London: Heinemann.

Organ, R. M. 1968. *Design for Scientific Conservation of Antiquities*. Washington, D.C.: Smithsonian Institution Press.

Orme, B. 1979. *Thermoluminescence Techniques in Archaeology*. Oxford: Clarendon Press.

——. 1981. *Anthropology for Archaeologists*. Ithaca: Cornell University Press.

Ortner, Donald J., and Walter G. J. Putschar. 1982. *Identification of Pathological Conditions in Human Remains*. Washington, D.C.: Smithsonian Contributions to Anthropology, no. 28.

Pallottino, Massimo. 1968. *The Meaning of Archaeology.* New York: Abrams.

Parmalee, Paul, and Walter E. Klippel. 1974. "Freshwater Mollusca as a Prehistoric Food Resource," *American Antiquity* 39: 421–434.

Parsons, J. A., and B. J. Price. 1971. *Mesoamerican Trade and Its Role in the Emergence of Civilization.* University of California Archaeological Research Facility Contribution, no. 11, Berkeley.

Pavlish, L. A., and E. B. Banning. 1980. "Revolutionary Developments in Carbon 14 Dating," *American Antiquity* 45, 2: 290–296.

Petrie, Flinders. 1889. "Sequences in Prehistoric Remains," *Journal of the Royal Anthropological Institute* 29: 295–301.

Phillips, Patricia. 1980. *The Prehistory of Europe.* London: Alan Lane Books.

Phillips, P., J. A. Ford, and J. A. Griffin. 1951. *Archaeological Survey in the Lower Mississippi, 1940–1947.* Papers of the Peabody Museum of American Archaeology and Ethnology, no. 25. Cambridge: Harvard University.

Phillipson, D. W. 1969. "Gunflint Manufacture in North-Western Zambia," *Antiquity* 43: 301–304.

Piggott, Stuart. 1965. *Ancient Europe.* Chicago: Aldine.

———. 1968. *The Druids.* London: Thames and Hudson.

———. 1979. *Ruins in a Landscape.* Edinburgh: Edinburgh University Press.

Pires-Ferreira, Jane. 1976. "Obsidian Exchange in Formative Mesoamerica," in Kent V. Flannery, ed., *The Early Mesoamerican Village.* New York: Academic Press, pp. 293–305.

Plenderleith, H. J., and A. E. A. Werner. 1973. *The Conservation of Antiquities and Works of Art,* 2nd ed. London: Oxford University Press.

Plog, F. T., ed. 1974. *The Study of Prehistoric Change.* New York: Academic Press.

———. 1978. "Cultural Resource Management and the 'New Archaeology,'" in Charles L. Redman and others, eds., *Social Archaeology.* New York: Academic Press, pp. 421–429.

Plog, F., and Walter Wait, eds. 1982. *The San Juan Tomorrow.* Santa Fe: National Park Service, SW Region.

Plog, S. 1976a. "Relative Efficiencies of Sampling Techniques for Archaeological Surveys," in Kent V. Flannery, ed., *The Early Mesoamerican Village.* New York: Academic Press, pp. 136–158.

———. 1976b. "Measurement of Prehistoric Interaction between Communities," in Kent V. Flannery, ed., *The Early Mesoamerican Village.* New York: Academic Press, pp. 255–272.

———. 1980. *Stylistic Variation in Prehistoric Ceramics.* New York: Cambridge University Press.

Plumb, J. H. 1969. *The Death of the Past.* London: Macmillan.

Polyani, Karl. 1975. "Traders and Trade," in Jeremy A. Sabloff and C. C. Lamberg-Karlovsky, eds., *Early Civilization and Trade.* Albuquerque: University of New Mexico Press, pp. 133–154.

Pope, Saxton T. 1923. *Hunting with the Bow and Arrow.* San Francisco: James H. Barry.

Powell, S., and G. E. Rice. 1981. "The Inclusion of Small Contract Projects Within a Regional Sampling Design," *American Antiquity* 46: 602–610.

Raab, L. Mark and Abbot C. Goodyear, 1984. "Middle Range Theory in Archaeology: A Critical Review of Origins and Applications," *American Antiquity* 49: 255–268.

Rahtz, P. A. 1974. *RESCUE Archaeology.* Baltimore: Pelican Books.

Rapoport, Anatol. 1968. "Foreword," in W. Buckley, ed., *Modern Systems Research for the Behavioral Sciences.* Chicago: Aldine.

Rappoport, Roy A. 1968. *Pigs for the Ancestors.* New Haven: Yale University Press.

———. 1971. "Ritual, Sanctity, and Cybernetics," *Current Anthropology* 73: 59–76.

Rathje, William. 1970. "Socio-Political Implications of Maya Lowland Burials," *World Archaeology* 1: 359–374.

———. 1971. "The Origin and Development of Lowland Classic Mayan Civilization," *American Antiquity* 36, 3: 275–285.

———. 1974. "The Garbage Project: A New Way of Looking at the Problems of Archaeology," *Archaeology* 27, 4: 236–241.

———. 1978. "Le Project de Garbage 1978: Historical Trade Offs," in Charles L. Redman and others, eds. *Social Archaeology.* New York: Academic Press, pp. 124–135.

———. 1979. "Modern Material Culture Studies," *Advances in Archaeological Method and Theory,* 2: 1–38.

Rathje, W. H., and W. McCarthy. 1977. "Regularity and Variability in Contemporary Garbage," in Stanley A. South, ed., *Method and Theory in Historical Archaeology.* New York: Academic Press.

Rathje, W. H., and Michael Schiffer. 1982. *Archaeology.* New York: Harcourt, Brace.

Raven-Hart, R. 1967. *Before Van Riebeeck.* Capetown: Struik.

Read, D. W., and Steven A. LeBlanc. 1978. "Descriptive Statistics, Covering Laws, and Theories in Archaeology," *Current Anthropology* 19: 307–335.

Redman, Charles L., ed. 1973. *Research and Theory in Current Archaeology.* New York: John Wiley Interscience.

———. 1974. *Archaeological Sampling Strategies.* Reading: Addison-Wesley Modules in Anthropology, no. 55.

———. 1975. "Productive Sampling Strategies for Archaeological Sites," in James Mueller, ed., *Sampling in Archaeology.* Tucson: University of Arizona Press, pp. 147–154.

———. 1978a. *The Rise of Civilization.* San Francisco: W. H. Freeman.

———. 1978b. "Multivariate Artifact Analysis: A Basis for Multidimensional Interpretations," in Charles L. Redman and others, eds., *Social Archaeology.* New York: Academic Press, pp. 159–192.

———. 1978c. "Mesopotamian Urban Ecology: The Systemic Context of the Emergence of Urbanism," in Charles L. Redman and others, eds., *Social Archaeology.* New York: Academic Press, pp. 329–348.

Redman, C. L., and P. J. Watson. 1970. "Systematic, Intensive Surface Collection," *American Antiquity* 35: 279–291.

Redman, Charles L., and others, eds. *Social Archaeology.* New York: Academic Press.

Reed, Charles A., ed. 1977. *The Origins of Agriculture.* The Hague: Mouton.

Renfrew, A. C., J. E. Dixon, and J. R. Cann. 1966. "Obsidian and Early Cultural Contact in the Near East," *Proceedings of the Prehistoric Society* 32: 1–29.

Renfrew, Colin. 1971. *Before Civilization.* New York: Alfred A. Knopf.

———. 1975. *The Emergence of Civilization.* London: Methuen.

———. 1979. "Transformations," in Colin Renfrew and Keith L. Cooke, eds., *Transformations: Mathematical Applications to Cultural Change.* New York: Academic Press, pp. 3–44.

Renfrew, Colin, and Keith L. Cooke, eds. 1979. *Transformations: Mathematical Applications to Cultural Change.* New York: Academic Press.

Renfrew, Jane. 1973. *Paleoethnobotany.* London: Methuen.

Reynolds, Barrie. 1967. *The Material Culture of the Gwembe Tonga.* Manchester: Manchester University Press.

Riley, C. L. 1971. *Man Across the Sea.* Austin: University of Texas Press.

Roper, D. C. 1979. "The Method and Theory of Site Catchment Analysis: A Review," *Advances in Archaeological Method and Theory* 2: 120–142.

Rouse, Irving. 1939. *Prehistory in Haiti: A Study in Method.* New Haven: Yale University Press.

———. 1960. "The Classification of Artifacts in Archaeology," *American Antiquity* 25: 313–323.

———. 1972. *Introduction to Prehistory: A Systematic Approach.* New York: McGraw-Hill.
Rovner, Irwin. 1983. "Plant Opal Phytolith Research: Major Advances in Archaeobotanical Research," *Advances in Archaeological Method and Theory,* 6: 225–266.
Rudenko, S. I. 1961. "The Ancient Cultures of the Bering Sea and the Eskimo Problem," *Arctic Institute of North America: Anthropology of the North, Translations from Russian Sources,* no. 1. Toronto: University of Toronto Press, pp. 163–164.
———. 1970. *Frozen Tombs of Siberia: The Pazyryk Burials of Iron Age Horsemen.* Trans. by M. W. Thompson. Berkeley: University of California Press.
Rudwick, J. 1972. *The Meaning of Fossils.* New York: Elsevier.

Sabloff, Jeremy A. 1975. *Excavations at Seibal: Ceramics. Memoirs of the Peabody Museum of American Archaeology and Ethnology,* vol. 13, no. 2, Cambridge: Harvard University.
———, ed. 1981. *Simulation in Archaeology.* Albuquerque: University of New Mexico Press.
Sabloff, Jeremy A., and C. C. Lamberg-Karlovsky, eds. 1975. *Early Civilization and Trade.* Albuquerque: University of New Mexico Press.
Sabloff, Jeremy A., and W. L. Rathje, eds. 1975. *A Study of Pre-Columbian Commercial Systems: The 1972–1973 Seasons at Cozumel, Mexico.* Memoirs of the Peabody Museum, no. 3. Cambridge: Harvard University.
Sackett, James, 1966. "Quantitative Analysis of Upper Paleolithic Stone Tools," *American Anthropologist* 68, 2: 356–394.
———. 1977. "The Meaning of Style in Archaeology," *American Antiquity* 43: 369–382.
———. 1981. "From de Mortillet to Bordes: A Century of French Upper Paleolithic Research," in Glyn Daniel, ed., *Towards a History of Archaeology.* London: Thames and Hudson, pp. 85–99.
———. 1982. "Approaches to Style in Lithic Archaeology," *Journal of Anthropological Archaeology* 1, 1: 59–112.
Sahlins, Marshall, and Elman Service, eds., 1960. *Evolution and Culture.* Ann Arbor, Mich.: University of Michigan Press.
Salmon, M. 1978. "What Can Systems Theory Do for Archaeology?" *American Antiquity* 43: 174–183.
———. 1982. *The Philosophy of Archaeology.* New York: Academic Press.
Sanders, W. T., and Barbara J. Price. 1968. *Mesoamerica: Evolution of a Civilization.* New York: Random House.
Sanders, W. T., Jeffrey R. Parsons, and Robert S. Santley. 1979. *The Basin of Mexico: Ecological Processes in the Evolution of a Civilization.* New York: Academic Press.
Sanders, W. T., and David Webster. 1978. "Unilinealism, Multilinealism, and the Evolution of Complex Societies," in Charles L. Redman and others, eds., *Social Archaeology.* New York: Academic Press, pp. 249–302.
Schiffer, Michael. 1976. *Behavioral Archaeology.* New York: Academic Press.
———. 1979. "A Preliminary Consideration of Behavioral Change," in Colin Renfrew, ed., *Transformations: Mathematical Approaches to Culture Change.* New York: Academic Press, pp. 353–368.
———. 1983. "Towards the Identification of Site Formation Processes," *American Antiquity* 48, 4: 675–706.
Schiffer, Michael, and John H. House. 1976. *The Cache River Archaeological Project.* Fayetteville: Arkansas Archaeological Survey.
———. 1977. "Cultural Resource Management and Archaeological Research: The Cache Project," *Current Anthropology* 18: 43–68.
Schiffer, M. B., A. P. Sullivan, and T. C. Klinger. 1978. "The Design of Archaeological Surveys," *World Archaeology* 10: 1–28.

Schuyler, Robert L., ed. 1978. *Historical Archaeology: A Guide to Substantive and Theoretical Contributions*. Farmingdale, N.Y.: Baywood.

Scudder, Thayer. 1962. *The Ecology of the Gwembe Tonga*. Manchester: Manchester University Press.

Selkirk, Andrew, and Wendy Selkirk. 1970. "Winchester: The Brooks," *Current Archaeology* 2: 250–255.

Semenov, S. A. 1964. *Prehistoric Technology*. Trans. by M. W. Thompson. London: Cory, Adams, and MacKay.

Service, Elman. 1971. *Primitive Social Organization*. New York: Random House.

Shackley, M. L. 1975. *Archaeological Sediments*. New York: John Wiley.

Sharer, Robert J., and Wendy Ashmore. 1979. *Fundamentals of Archaeology*. Menlo Park: Cummings.

Shaw, Thurstan. 1960. "Early Smoking Pipes in Africa, Europe, and America," *Journal of the Royal Anthropological Institute* 90: 272–305.

———. 1969. "Tree Felling by Fire," *Antiquity* 43: 52.

Shawcross, F. C. 1967. "Prehistoric Diet and Economy on a Coastal Site at Galatea Bay, New Zealand," *Proceedings of the Prehistoric Society* 33, 7: 125–130.

Shepard, Anna O. 1971. *Ceramics for the Archaeologist*, 2nd ed. Washington, D.C.: Smithsonian Institution.

Silverberg, Robert. 1968. *The Mound Builders of Ancient America*. New York: New York Graphic Society.

Slotkin, J. S., ed. 1965. *Readings in Early Anthropology*. New York: Viking Fund.

Smith, B. D. 1974. "Middle Mississippian Exploitation of Animal Populations: A Predictive Model," *American Antiquity* 39: 274–291.

Smith, Eliot Grafton. 1911. *The Ancient Egyptians*. London: Macmillan.

Smith, Philip E. L. 1966. *Le Solutréen en France*. Paris: Payot.

Snow, Dean. 1976. *The North American Indians*. New York: Viking.

Solecki, Ralph. 1972. *Shanidar: The Humanity of Neanderthal Man*. New York: Penguin Press.

Sollas, W. J. *Ancient Hunters*. London: Macmillan, 1911.

South, Stanley. 1972. "Evolution and Horizon as Revealed in Ceramic Analysis in Historical Archaeology," *Conference on Historic Sites Archaeology Papers* 6, 2: 71–106.

———, ed. 1977. *Method and Theory in Historical Archaeology*. New York: Academic Press.

South, Stanley, and Randolph Widmer. 1977. "A Subsurface Strategy for Archaeological Reconnaissance," in Stanley South, ed., *Method and Theory in Historical Archaeology*. New York: Academic Press.

Spaulding, A. C. 1953. "Statistical Techniques for the Study of Artifact Types," *American Antiquity* 18, 4: 305–313.

———. 1960a. "The Dimensions of Archaeology," in G. E. Dole and R. L. Carneiro, eds., *Essays in the Science of Culture in Honor of Leslie A. White*. New York: Crowell, pp. 437–456.

———. 1960b. "Statistical Description and Comparison of Artifact Assemblages," in Robert F. Heizer and S. F. Cook, eds., *Quantitative Methods in Archaeology*. New York: Viking Fund, pp. 60–92.

———. 1973. "Archaeology in the Active Voice: The New Anthropology," in Charles L. Redman, ed., *Research and Theory in Current Archaeology*. New York: John Wiley Interscience, pp. 337–354.

Spencer, Herbert. 1855. *Social Statistics*. London: Macmillan.

Spooner, Brian, ed. 1972. *Population Growth: Anthropological Implications*. Cambridge: MIT Press.

Starki, Edward. 1982. "Advances in Urban Archaeology," *Advances in Archaeological Method and Theory* 5: 97–150.

Stein, Julia K. 1983. "Earthworm Activity: A Source of Potential Disturbance of Archaeological Sediments," *American Antiquity* 48, 2: 277–289.

Stephens, John Lloyd. 1841. *Incidents of Travel in Central America, Chiapas, and Yucatan.* New York: Harper and Brothers.

Steponaitis, V. P., and J. P. Brain. 1976. "A Portable Differential Proton Magnetometer," *Journal of Field Archaeology* 3: 455–463.

Steward, Julian. 1938. *Basin-Plateau Aboriginal Sociopolitical Groups.* Bureau of American Ethnology, Bulletin no. 120. Washington, D.C.: Smithsonian Institution.

———. 1955. *A Theory of Culture Change.* Urbana: University of Illinois Press.

Steward, Julian, and F. M. Setzler, eds. 1977. *Evolution and Ecology.* Urbana: University of Illinois Press.

Stocking, George. 1968. *Race, Culture, and Evolution.* New York: Free Press.

Stone, Irving. 1975. *The Greek Treasure.* New York: Doubleday.

Story, Ron. 1976. *The Space Gods Revisited.* New York: Harper and Row.

Strong, W. D. 1935. *An Introduction to Nebraska Archaeology.* Washington, D.C.: Smithsonian Institution Miscellaneous Collections, vol. 93, no. 10.

Struever, Stuart. 1968. "Woodland Subsistence-Settlement Systems in the Lower Illinois Valley," in Sally R. Binford and Lewis R. Binford, eds., *New Perspectives in Archaeology.* Chicago: Aldine, pp. 285–312.

———. 1971. "Comments on Archaeological Data Requirements and Research Strategy," *American Antiquity* 36: 10.

Struever, Stuart, and F. A. Holton. 1979. *Koster.* New York: Anchor Press/Doubleday.

Struever, Stuart, and Gail L. Houart. 1972. "An Analysis of the Hopewell Interaction Sphere," *Anthropological Papers of the University of Michigan* 46: 47–79.

Suess, Hans E. 1965. "Secular Variations of the Cosmic-Ray-Produced Carbon 14 in the Atmosphere and Their Interpretations," *Journal of Geophysical Research* 70: 23–31.

Summers, Roger. 1969. *Ancient Mining in Rhodesia.* Salisbury: National Museums of Rhodesia.

Swanton, E., ed. 1975. *Lithic Technology: Making and Using Stone Tools.* Chicago: Aldine.

Swanton, John R. 1911. "Le Page de Pratz's *Histoire de Louisiane,*" *Bureau of American Ethnology Bulletin* 41: 144–149.

Taylor, R. E., and C. W. Meighan, eds. 1978. *Chronologies in New World Archaeology.* New York: Academic Press.

Taylor, W. W. 1948. *A Study of Archaeology.* Menasha, Wis.: American Anthropological Association.

Terrell, J. 1967. "Galatea Bay: The Excavation of a Beach-Stream Midden Site on Ponju Island in the Hauraki Gulf, New Zealand," *Transactions of the Royal Society of New Zealand* 2, 3: 31–70.

Thom, Alexander, and others. 1974. "Stonehenge," *Journal for the Study of Astronomy* 5: 71–90.

Thomas, David Hurst. 1969. "Regional Sampling in Archaeology: A Pilot Great Basin Research Design," *UCLA Archaeological Survey Annual Report* 11: 87–100.

———. 1973. "An Empirical Test for Steward's Model of Great Basin Settlement Patterns," *American Antiquity* 38: 155–176.

———. 1974. *Predicting the Past.* New York: Holt, Rinehart and Winston.

———. 1976. *Figuring Anthropology: First Principles of Probability and Statistics.* New York: Holt, Rinehart and Winston.

———. 1978. "The Awful Truth about Statistics in Archaeology," *American Antiquity* 43: 231–244.

————. 1979. *Archaeology.* New York: Holt, Rinehart and Winston.

Thomas, M. N. and Madeleine K. Lewis. 1961. *Eva: An Archaic Site.* Knoxville: University of Tennessee Press.

Thompson, J. E. S. 1972. *Maya Hieroglyphs without Tears.* London: British Museum.

Thompson, M. W. 1977. *General Pitt Rivers.* London: Moonraker Press.

Thompson, R. H. 1956. "The Subjective Element in Archaeological Inference," *Southwestern Journal of Anthropology* 12, 3: 327–332.

Thomsen, C. J. 1836. *Ledestraad til Nordisk Oldkyndighed.* Trans. by Lord Ellesmere in 1848 as *A Guide to the Northern Antiquities.* Copenhagen.

Tite, M. S. 1972. *Methods of Physical Examination in Archaeology.* New York: Academic Press.

Townsend, William H. 1969. "Stone and Steel Tool Use in a New Guinea Society," *Ethnology* 8, 2: 199–205.

Traling, D. H. 1971. *Principles and Applications of Paleomagnetism.* London: Chapman and Hall.

————. 1975. "Archaeomagnetism: The Dating of Archaeological Materials by Their Magnetic Properties," *World Archaeology* 7, 2: 198–209.

Trigger, Bruce. 1968a. *Beyond History: The Methods of Prehistory.* New York: Holt, Rinehart and Winston.

————. 1968b. "The Determinants of Settlement Patterns," in K. C. Chang, ed., *Settlement Archaeology.* Palo Alto: National Press, pp. 53–78.

————. 1971. "Archaeology and Ecology," *World Archaeology* 2, 3: 321–336.

————. 1978. *Time and Tradition.* Edinburgh: Edinburgh University Press.

————. 1980. *Gordon Childe: Revolutions in Archaeology.* London: Thames and Hudson.

Tringham, Ruth. 1971. *Hunters, Fishers, and Farmers of Southeastern Europe, 6000 to 3000 B.C.* London: Hutchinson.

Tylecote, R. F. 1972. *Metallurgy in Antiquity.* London: Edward Arnold.

————. 1980. "Furnaces, Crucibles, and Slags," in James Muhly and Theodore Wertime. eds., *The Coming of the Age of Iron.* New Haven: Yale University Press, pp. 183–228.

Tylor, Edward. 1871. *Primitive Culture.* London: John Murray.

Ucko, Peter J. 1962. "The Interpretation of Prehistoric Anthropomorphic Figurines," *Journal of the Royal Anthropological Institute* 92: 38–54.

Ucko, Peter J., and G. W. Dimbleby, eds. 1969. *The Domestication and Exploitation of Plants and Animals.* London: Duckworth.

United States Department of the Interior. 1976. "National Register of Historic Places: Criteria for Statewide Surveys and Plans," *Code of Federal Regulations, Title 36.* Chapter 1, Part 60.

Valliant, C. G. 1941. *The Aztecs of Mexico.* New York: Doubleday.

van der Merwe, Nikolaas J. 1982. "Carbon Isotopes, Photosynthesis and Archaeology," *American Scientist* 70: 596–606.

Valliant, C. G. and J. C. Vogel. 1978. "^{13}C Content of Human Collagen as a Measure of Prehistoric Diet in Woodland North America," *Nature* 276: 815–816.

Villa, Paola. 1982. "Conjoinable Pieces and Site Formation Processes," *American Antiquity* 47, 2: 276–290.

————. 1983. *Terra Amata and the Middle Pleistocene Archaeological Record of Southern France.* Berkeley: University of California Press.

Vinnecombe, Patricia. 1960. "A Fishing Scene from the Tsoelike River, Southwestern Basutoland," *South African Archaeological Bulletin* 15: 15–19.

Vita-Finzi, Claudio. 1978. *Archaeological Sites in Their Setting.* London: Thames and Hudson.

Vita-Finzi, Claudio, and E. S. Higgs. 1970. "Prehistoric Ecology in the Mount Carmel Area of Palestine: Site Catchment Analysis," *Proceedings of the Prehistoric Society* 36: 1–37.

Vogt, Evon Z. 1967. *A Maya Community in the Highlands of Chiapas*. Cambridge, Eng.: Belknap Press.
————, ed. 1974. *Aerial Photography in Anthropological Field Research*. Cambridge: Harvard University Press.

Watson, Patti Jo. 1974. *Archaeology of the Mammoth Cave Area*. New York: Academic Press.
————. 1976. "In Pursuit of Prehistoric Subsistence: A Comparative Account of Some Contemporary Flotation Techniques," *Mid-Continental Journal of Archaeology* 1, 1: 77–100.
Watson, Patti Jo, Steven A. LeBlanc, and Charles A. Redman. 1971. *Explanation in Archaeology*. Columbia: Columbia University Press.
Watson, R. A. 1976. "Inference in Archaeology," *American Antiquity* 41: 58–66.
Wauchope, Robert. 1972. *Lost Tribes and Sunken Continents*. Chicago: University of Chicago Press.
Webb, William S. 1939. *An Archaeological Survey of Wheeler Basin on the Tennessee River in Northern Alabama*. Bureau of American Ethnology, no. 122. Washington, D.C.: Smithsonian Institution.
Wells, Calvin. 1964. *Bones, Bodies, and Disease*. London: Thames and Hudson.
Wendorf, Fred. 1979. "Changing Values in Archaeology," *American Antiquity* 44, 4: 641–643.
Wendorf, Fred, and others. 1968. *The Prehistory of Nubia*. Dallas: Southern Methodist University Press.
Wenke, Robert J. 1981. "Explaining the Evolution of Cultural Complexity: A Review," *Advances in Archaeological Method and Theory* 4: 979–1028.
Whalen, Michael A. 1976. "Zoning within an Early Formative Community in the Valley of Oaxaca," in Kent V. Flannery, ed., *The Early Mesoamerican Village*. New York: Academic Press, pp. 75–78.
Whallon, Robert, and James A. Brown, eds. 1982. *Essays in Archaeological Typology*. Evanston: Center for American Archaeology.
Wheat, Joe Ben. 1972. *The Olsen-Chubbock Site: A Paleo-Indian Bison Kill*. Society for American Archaeology, Memoir 26. Washington, D.C.: Smithsonian Institution.
Wheatley, Paul. 1971. *The Pivot of the Four Quarters*. Chicago: Aldine.
Wheeler, R. E. M. 1943. *Maiden Castle*. London: Society of Antiquaries.
————. 1954. *Archaeology from the Earth*. Oxford: Clarendon Press.
————. 1967. *The Indus Civilization*. Cambridge: Cambridge University Press.
Wheeler, Tamara S., and Robert Madden. 1980. "Metallurgy and Ancient Man," in James Muhly and Theodore Wertime, eds., *The Coming of the Age of Iron*. New Haven: Yale University Press, pp. 99–126.
White, J. Peter. 1974. *The Past Is Human*. New York: Taplinger.
White, J. Peter, and David Hurst Thomas. 1972. "What Mean These Stones?" in D. L. Clarke, ed., *Models in Archaeology*. London: Methuen, pp. 275–308.
White, Leslie, 1949. *The Evolution of Culture*. New York: McGraw-Hill.
White, Theodore. 1953. "Observations on the Butchery Techniques of Some Aboriginal Peoples," *American Antiquity* 19, 2: 160–164.
Wildeson, Leslie E. 1982. "The Study of Impacts on Archaeological Sites," *Advances in Archaeological Method and Theory* 5: 51–96.
Willey, Gordon R. 1953. *Prehistoric Settlement Patterns in the Virú Valley, Peru*. Bureau of American Ethnology, Bulletin 155. Washington, D.C.: Smithsonian Institution.
————. 1962. "The Early Great Styles and the Rise of the Pre-Columbian Civilizations," *American Anthropologist* 64: 1–14.
————. 1966. *An Introduction to American Archaeology, Vol. 1: North America*. Englewood Cliffs, N.J.: Prentice-Hall.

————. 1971. *An Introduction to American Archaeology, Vol. 2: Middle and South America.* Englewood Cliffs, N.J.: Prentice-Hall.

————, ed. 1974. *Archaeological Researches in Retrospect.* Cambridge: Winthrop.

Willey, Gordon R., and Philip Phillips. 1958. *Method and Theory in American Archaeology.* Chicago: University of Chicago Press.

Willey, Gordon R., and Jeremy A. Sabloff. 1980. *A History of American Archaeology,* 2nd ed. San Francisco: W. H. Freeman.

Wilson, D. R. 1982. *Air Photo Interpretation for Archaeologists.* London: Batsford.

Wilson, Rex, and Gloria Loyola, (eds). 1982, *Rescue Archaeology: Paper from the First New World Conference on Rescue Archaeology.* Washington D.C.: The Preservation Press.

Winter, Marcus C. 1976. "The Archaeological Household Cluster in the Valley of Oaxaca," in Kent V. Flannery, ed., *The Early Mesoamerican Village.* New York: Academic Press, pp. 25–30.

Winters, Howard D. 1969. *The Riverton Culture.* Urbana: Illinois Archaeological Survey.

Wood, J. J. 1978. "Optimal Location in Settlement Space: A Model for Describing Location Strategies," *American Antiquity* 43: 258–270.

Wood, W. Raymond, and Donald Lee Johnson. 1978. "A Survey of the Disturbance Processes in Archaeological Site Formation," *Advances in Archaeological Method and Theory,* vol. 1.

Woodbury, Jane C. 1980. "The First Archaeological Appearance of Iron," in James Muhly and Theodore Wertime, *The Coming of the Age of Iron.* New Haven: Yale University Press, pp. 69–98.

Woolley, C. L. 1943. *Ur Excavations,* Volume II: *The Royal Cemetery.* London and Philadelphia: British Museum and University Museum.

————. 1954. *Excavations at Ur.* New York: Barnes and Noble.

Worsaae, J. J. A. 1843. *Danmarks Oldtid.* Copenhagen.

Wright, Thomas. 1852. "Wanderings of an Antiquary: Part VII," *Gentleman's Magazine,* p. 569.

Yellen, John E. 1977. *Archaeological Approaches to the Present: Models for Predicting the Past.* New York: Academic Press.

Zeuner, F. E. 1958. *Dating the Past,* 3rd ed. London: Methuen.

————. 1963. *A History of the Domesticated Animals.* London: Hutchinson.

Zubrow, Ezra. 1976. *Demographic Anthropology: Quantitative Approaches.* Albuquerque: University of New Mexico.

GLOSSARY ✍

This glossary is designed to give informal definitions of words and ideas in the text, particularly those which are theoretical. It is not a comprehensive dictionary of archaeology. Jargon is kept to a minimum, but a few technical expressions are inevitable. Terms such as *adaptation* and *mutation*, which are common in contexts other than archaeology, are not listed; a good dictionary will clarify these.

Absolute dating: dating in calendar years before the present; chronometric dating.

Activity area: a patterning of artifacts in a site indicating that a specific activity, such as stone toolmaking, took place.

Activity set: a set of artifacts that reveals the activities of an individual.

Alluvium: geological deposit laid down by the action of a river or stream.

Analogy: a process of reasoning whereby two entities that share some similarities are assumed to share many others.

Analysis: a stage of archaeological research that involves describing and classifying artifactual and nonartifactual data.

Analytical type: arbitrary groupings that an archaeologist defines for classifying human-manufactured artifacts. Analytical types consist of groups of attributes that define convenient types of artifacts for comparing sites in space and time. They do not necessarily coincide with actual tool types used by prehistoric people.

Anthropology: the study of humanity in the widest possible sense. Anthropology studies humanity from the earliest times up to the present, and it includes cultural and physical anthropology and archaeology.

Antiquarian: someone interested in the past who collects and digs up antiquities unscientifically, in contrast to the scientific archaeologist.

Arbitrary sample unit: a carefully defined unit of a total population of artifacts, or whatever is being sampled, selected by absolutely artificial criteria, without referring to cultural yardsticks. A typical example is a grid of squares laid out over a site.

Archaeological context: see Context.

Archaeological culture: a group of assemblages representing the surviving remains of an extinct culture.

Archaeological data: material recognized as significant as evidence by the archaeologist and collected and recorded as part of the research. The four main classes of archaeological data are artifacts, features, structures, and food remains.

Archaeological reconnaissance: systematic attempts to locate, identify, and record the distribution of archaeological sites on the ground and against the natural geographic and environmental background.

Archaeological theory: a body of theoretical concepts providing both a framework and a means for archaeologists to look beyond the facts and material objects for explanations of events that took place in prehistory.

Archaeological unit: arbitrary unit of classification set up by archaeologists to separate conveniently one grouping of artifacts in time and space from another.

Archaeologist: someone who studies the past using scientific methods, with the motive of recording and interpreting ancient cultures rather than collecting artifacts for profit or display.

Archaeology: a special form of anthropology studying extinct human societies using the material remains of their behavior. The objectives of archaeology are to construct culture history, reconstruct past lifeways, and study cultural process.

Archaeomagnetic dating: chronometric dating using magnetic alignments from buried features, such as pottery kilns, which can be compared to known fluctuations in the earth's magnetic field to produce a date in years.

Archaic: in the New World, a period when hunter-gatherers were exploiting a broad spectrum of resources and may have been experimenting with agriculture.

Area excavation: excavation of a large, horizontal area, normally used to uncover houses and prehistoric settlement patterns.

Artifact: any object manufactured or modified by human beings.

Assemblage: all the artifacts found at a site, including the sum of all subassemblages at the site.

Association: the relationship between an artifact and other archaeological finds and a site level, or other artifact, structure, or feature in the site.

Assyriologist: a student of the Assyrian civilization of Mesopotamia.

Attribute: a well-defined feature of an artifact that cannot be further subdivided. Archaeologists identify types of attributes, including form, style, and technology, in order to classify and interpret artifacts.

Attribute analysis: analyzing artifacts using many of their features. Normally these attributes are studied statistically to produce clusters of attributes that can be used to identify statistical classes of artifacts.

Attritional age profile: the distribution of ages in an animal population that results from selective hunting or predation.

Auger: a drill, either hand or power driven, used to probe subsurface deposits.

Australopithecus: primates whose fossil remains have been found mainly in East and southern Africa. They are thought to be closely related to the first human beings, who may, indeed, have evolved among them.

Band: the simple form of human social organization that flourished for most of prehistory. Bands consist of a family or a series of families normally with twenty to fifty people.

Battleship curve: shape on a seriation graph formed by plotted points representing, for instance, the rise in popularity of an artifact, its period of maximum popularity, and its eventual decline.

Biome: major biotic landscapes in which distinctive plant and animal communities live in harmony together.

Biosphere: all the earth's living organisms interacting with the physical environment.

Blades: parallel-sided stone flakes, normally removed from a carefully prepared core, often by means of a punch.

Bowsing: technique for detecting buried features by thumping the ground and sensing the differences between compacted and undisturbed earth.

Bulb of percussion: the conelike effect caused by conchoidal fracture on siliceous rocks.

Bulbar surface: the surface upon which the bulb of percussion occurs.

Burin: blade tool, flaked on either or both ends to form a small chisel or grooving tool.

Cambium: a viscid substance under the bark of trees, in which the annual growth of wood and bark takes place.

Carrying capacity: the number and density of people per square mile that a specified area of land can support, given a particular subsistence level.

Catastrophic ageing profile: distribution of ages in an animal population as a result of death by natural causes.

Causes: in archaeology, events that force people to make decisions about how to deal with new situations.

Central-place theory: a geographical theory applied to archaeology, stating that human settlements will space themselves evenly across a landscape depending on availability of natural resources and other factors. Eventually, these will evolve into a hierarchy of settlements of different size that depend on one another.

Ceramics: objects of fired clay.

Chiefdom: a form of social organization more complex than a tribal society, which has evolved some form of leadership structure and some mechanisms for distributing goods and services throughout society. The chief who heads such a society, and the specialists who work for the chief, are supported by the voluntary contributions of the people.

Chronological types: types defined by form that are time markers.

Chronometric dating: dating in years before the present; absolute dating.

Clan: group of people from many lineages who live in one place and have a common line of descent—a kin grouping.

Class: a general group of artifacts, like "hand axes," which will be broken down into specific types, like "ovates," and so on.

Classic: in both Mesoamerica and Peru, the period of vigorous civilization characterized by numerous ceremonial centers and small states.

Classical archaeologist: a student of the Classical civilizations of Greece and Rome.

Classification: the ordering of archaeological data into groups and classes, using various ordering systems.

Closed system: a system that is internally self-regulating and receives no feedback from external sources (a good example is a household heating and cooling system).

Cluster analysis: the process of analyzing clusters of sites in space.

Cognitive archaeology: see Structural archaeology.

Community: in archaeology, the tangible remains of the activities of the maximum number of people who together occupy a settlement at any one period.

Complex: in archaeology, a chronological subdivision of different artifact types like stone tools, pottery, etc.

Component: an association of all the artifacts from one occupation level at a site.

Conchoidal fracture: characteristic fracture pattern that occurs in siliceous rocks, such as obsidian and flint.

Conchologist: one who studies shells.

Conservation archaeology: another name for cultural resource management.

Context: the position of an archaeological find in time and space, established by measuring and assessing its associations, matrix, and provenience. The assessment includes study of what has happened to the find since it was buried in the ground.

Coprolite: excrement preserved by desiccation or fossilization.

Core: in archaeology, a lump of stone from which human-struck flakes have been removed.

Core borer: a hollow tubelike instrument used to collect samples of soils, pollens, and other materials from below the surface.

Cranial: of or pertaining to the skull (cranium).

Crop marks: differential growth in crops and vegetational cover that reveals the outlines of archaeological sites from the air.

Cross-dating: dating of sites by objects of known age, or artifact associations of known age.

Cultural anthropology: the aspects of anthropology focusing on cultural facets of human societies (a term widely used in the United States).

Cultural ecology: study of the dynamic interactions between human societies and their environments. Under this approach, culture is the primary adaptive mechanism used by human societies.

Cultural evolution: a theory similar to that of biological evolution, which argues that human cultures change gradually throughout time, as a result of a number of cultural processes.

Cultural process: a deductive approach to archaeological research that is designed to study the changes and interactions in cultural systems and the processes by which human cultures change throughout time. Processual archaeologists use both descriptive and explanatory models.

Cultural resource management: the conservation and management of archaeological sites and artifacts as a means of protecting the past.

Cultural selection: the process that leads to the acceptance of some cultural traits and innovations that make a culture more adaptive to its environment; somewhat akin to natural selection in biological evolution.

Cultural system: a perspective on culture that thinks of culture and its environment as a number of linked systems in which change occurs through a series of minor, linked variations in one or more of these systems.

Cultural tradition: in archaeology, a distinctive toolkit or technology that lasts a long time, longer than the duration of one culture, at one locality or several localities.

Cultural transformations: changes in the archaeological record resulting from later human behavior, such as digging a rubbish pit into earlier levels.

Culture: human culture is a set of designs for living that help mold our responses to different situations. It is our primary means of adapting to our environment. A "culture" in archaeology is an arbitrary unit meaning similar assemblages of artifacts found at several sites, defined in a precise context of time and space.

Culture area: an arbitrary geographic or research area in which general cultural homogeneity is to be found.

Culture history: an approach to archaeology assuming that artifacts can be used to build up a generalized picture of human culture and descriptive models in time and space and that these can be interpreted.

Cumulative recording: stratigraphic recording in excavation that involves excavating and recording a trench in three dimensions, using both horizontal and vertical observations to reconstruct events at the site.

Cuneiform: from the Greek word *cuneus,* meaning a wedge. The earliest known, wedgelike script from Mesopotamia.

Curation: deliberate attempts by prehistoric peoples to preserve key artifacts and structures for posterity.

Cybernetics: general systems theory.

Cylinder hammer technique: stone-flaking technique using a bone hammer that removes small, flat flakes from a core.

Data universe: a defined area of archaeological investigation, bounded in time and space, often a geographic region or an archaeological site.

Datum point: a location from which all measurements on a site are made. The datum point is tied into local survey maps.

Debitage: waste byproducts resulting from the manufacture of stone tools.

Deduction: a process of reasoning that involves testing generalizations by generating hypotheses and testing them with data. Deductive research is cumulative and involves constant refining of hypotheses. Contrasts with inductive approaches where one proceeds from specific observations to general conclusions.

Deductive-nomological reasoning: a way of explaining observable phenomena by means of formal scientific methods, testing hypotheses generated from general laws governing human behavior. Some archaeologists believe this is the appropriate way to explain cultural process.

Demography: the study of population.

Dendrochronology: tree-ring chronology.

Descriptive types: types based on the physical or external properties of an artifact.

Detritus: debris or droppings.

Diffusion: the spread of a culture trait from one area to another by means of contact between people.

Direct historical analogy: analogy using historical records or historical ethnographic data.

Direct historical approach: archaeological technique of working backward in time from historic sites of known age into earlier times.

Drift: a glacial deposit laid down by ice or water in glacial streams, lakes, or arctic oceans.

Ecofact: archaeological finds which are of cultural significance but which were not manufactured by humans, such as bones and vegetal remains. Not a commonly used term.

Ecosystem: an environmental system maintained by the regulation of trophic levels (vertical food chains) and by patterns of energy flow.

Ecotone: a transition zone between habitats.

Egyptologist: a student of the cultures of Ancient Egypt.

Epigrapher: one who studies inscriptions.

Epiphysis: the articular end of a long bone, a process that fuses at adulthood.

Escarpment: a hill range or cliff (a geological term).

Eolith: a controversial artifact, identified by European archaeologists early in the twentieth century and claimed to be the earliest human tools. Eoliths are now considered to be of natural origin.

Ethnoarchaeology: living archaeology, a form of ethnography that deals mainly with material remains. Archaeologists carry out living archaeology to document the relationships between human behavior and the patterns of artifacts and food remains in the archaeological record.

Ethnography: a descriptive study, normally an in-depth examination of a culture.

Ethnohistory: study of the past using non-Western, indigenous historical records, and especially oral traditions.

Ethnology: A cross-cultural study of aspects of various cultures, usually based on theory.

Evolutionary archaeology: an explanatory framework for the past that accounts for the structure and change in the archaeological record.

Excavation: the digging of archaeological sites, removing the matrix and observing the provenience and context of the finds therein, and recording them in a three-dimensional way.

Exchange system: a system for exchanging goods and services between individuals and communities.

Exogamy: a rule requiring marriage outside a social or cultural unit (*endogamy* means the opposite).

Experimental archaeology: the use of carefully controlled modern experiments to provide data to aid in interpretation of the archaeological record.

Extrasomatic: outside the body.

Faience: glazed terracotta.

Feature: an artifact such as a house or storage pit, which cannot be removed from a site; normally, it is recorded only.

Feces: excrement.

Feedback: a concept in archaeological applications of systems theory reflecting the continually changing relationship between cultural variables and their environment.

Fire setting: quarrying stone by using fire to shatter the outcrops of rock.

Fission-track dating: observing accumulations of radioactivity in glass and volcanic rocks to produce absolute dates.

Flake tools: stone tools made of flakes removed from cores.

Flotation: in archaeology, recovering plant remains by using water to separate seeds from their surrounding deposit.

Focus: approximately equivalent to a phase.

Form: the physical characteristics—size and shape or composition—of any archaeological find. Form is an essential part of attribute analysis.

Form analysis: analysis of artifacts based on the assumption that the shape of a pot or other tool directly reflects its function.

Formation processes: humanly caused or natural processes by which an archaeological site is modified during or after occupation and abandonment.

Formative: in Mesoamerica, the period when more complex societies and settlement patterns were coming into being; these led to the complex states of later times (contemporary with the rise of agriculture).

Form types: artifact types based on the shape of an artifact.

Formulation: in archaeology, the process of making decisions about a research project as a preliminary to formal research design.

Foot survey: archaeological reconnaissance on foot, often with a set interval between members of the survey team.

Fuller: a clothmaker.

Function: in an evolutionary context, the forms that directly affect the Darwinian fitness of the populations in which they occur.

Functionalism: the notion that a social institution within a society has a function in fulfilling all the needs of a social organism.

Functional type: type based on cultural use or function rather than on outward form or chronological position.

General systems theory: the notion that any organism or organization can be studied as a system broken down into many interacting subsystems, or parts; sometimes called cybernetics.

Geoarchaeology: archaeological research using the methods and concepts of the earth sciences.

Geochronology: geological dating.

Glacial eustasy: the adjustments in sea levels and the earth's crust resulting from expansion and contraction of Pleistocene ice sheets.

Habitat: an area in the biome where different communities and populations flourish, each with specific locales.

Half-life: the time required for one half of a radioactive isotope to decay into a stable element. Used as a basis for radiocarbon and other dating methods.

Heuristic: serving to find out; a means of discovery.

Hieroglyphs: ancient writing form with pictographic or ideographic symbols; used in Egypt, Mesoamerica, and elsewhere.

Historical archaeology: the study of archaeological sites in conjunction with historical records. It is sometimes called historic sites archaeology.

Historiography: the process of studying history.

History: study of the past through written records.

Hominid: a member of the family *Hominidae,* represented today by one species, *Homo sapiens.*

Homo erectus: human beings who evolved from Lower Pleistocene hominids. They possessed larger brains and made more elaborate stone tools than their predecessors and settled in much more extreme environments, as far apart as western Europe, Asia, and tropical Africa.

Homotaxial: strata or cultures that have the same relationship to one another but are not necessarily contemporaneous.

Horizon: a widely distributed set of culture traits and artifact assemblages whose distribution and chronology allow one to assume that they spread rapidly. Often, horizons are formed of artifacts that were associated with widespread, distinctive religious beliefs.

Horizontal (area) excavation: archaeological excavation designed to uncover large areas of a site, especially settlement layouts.

Household cluster: an arbitrary archaeological unit defining artifact patterns reflecting the activities that take place around a house and assumed to belong to one household.

Hydrology: the scientific study of water—its properties and laws.

Ideology: the knowledge or beliefs developed by human societies as part of their cultural adaptation.

Induction: reasoning by which one proceeds from specific observations to general conclusions.

Industrial archaeology: the study of sites of the Industrial Revolution and later.

Industry: the industry at a site is all the particular artifacts (bone, stone, wood) found at that site and made at the same time by the same population.

Inevitable variation: the notion that cultures change and vary with time, cumulatively. The reasons for these changes are little understood.

Inorganic materials: material objects that are not part of the animal or vegetable kingdoms.

Interpretation: the stage in research at which the results of archaeological analyses are synthesized and we attempt to explain their meaning.

Interstadial: a period of slightly warmer climate between two cold periods during a major glaciation.

Kinship: in anthropology, relationships between people that are based on real or imagined descent, or, sometimes, on marriage. Kinship ties impose mutual obligations on all members of a kin group; these ties were at the core of most prehistoric societies.

Knapper: someone who manufactures stone artifacts.

Leaching: water seeping through the soil and removing from it the soluble materials.

Levallois technique: stoneworking technique that involves preparing a bun-shaped core from which one preshaped flake is removed.

Limited-area reconnaissance: comprehensive door-to-door inquiries, supported by actual substantiation of claims that sites exist by checking on the ground. This method fails to give information on proportions of different sites in an area.

Lineage: a kinship that traces descent through either the male or female members.

Lithic: of or pertaining to stone, as in *lithic technology.*

Lithic experimentation: experimenting with the manufacture of stone tools. A useful analytical approach to the interpretation of prehistoric artifacts.

Loess: windblown glacial soil.

Lost-wax technique: a method of bronzeworking in which a wax model of the object is made. The mold is assembled with wax in place of the artifact. The wax is then melted and replaced with molten bronze. This technique was much used by the Shang bronzeworkers of China.

Lower-level theory: a means of identifying site-formation processes.

Magnetometer: a subsurface detection device that measures minor variations in the earth's magnetic field and locates archaeological features before excavation.

Material culture: normally refers to technology and artifacts.

Matriarchal: family authority rests with the woman's family.

Matrilineal: descent reckoned through the female line only.

Matrilocal: married couples live with or near the wife's mother.

Matrix: the surrounding deposit in which archaeological finds are situated.

Mesolithic: rather dated name sometimes applied by Old World archaeologists to the period of transition between the Paleolithic and Neolithic eras. No precise economic or technological definition has ever been formulated.

Mica: a mineral that occurs in a glittering scaly form, widely prized for ornament.

Midden: a deposit of occupation debris, rubbish, or other by-products of human activity.

Middle-range theory: a way of seeking accurate means for identifying and measuring specified properties of past cultural systems.

Midwestern taxonomic system: system of archaeological units developed before World War II to organize artifacts and sites in North America; still in widespread use in modified form.

Mitigation: in archaeology, measures taken to minimize destruction on archaeological sites.

Model: a theoretical reconstruction of a set of phenomena, devised to understand them better. Archaeological models can be descriptive or explanatory.

Modified diffusionism: form of diffusionist theory, espoused by Gordon Childe and others, which allowed for some local cultural evolution.

Monotheistic: religion recognizing one god.

Moraine: deposit of debris left by an advancing or retreating glacier.

Multilinear cultural evolution: a theory of cultural evolution that sees each human culture evolving in its own way by adaptations to diverse environments. Sometimes divided into four broad stages of evolving of social organization (band, tribe, chiefdom, and state-organized society).

Natural transformations: changes in the archaeological record resulting from natural phenomena that occur after the artifacts are deposited in the ground.

Natural type: an archaeological type coinciding with an actual category recognized by the original toolmaker.

Negative feedback: a response to a system that lessens the chance of change.

Neolithic: a dated Old World term referring to that period of the Stone Age when people were cultivating without metals.

Niche: the physical space occupied by an organism, its functional role in the community, and how it is constrained by other species and external forces.

Nonarbitrary sample unit: a sample unit chosen to conform with cultural and other factors, such as geographic proximity or layout of rooms in a pueblo. These types of sample unit are often clustered.

Nonprobablistic sampling: sampling using instinctual criteria, such as the archaeologist's experience, or factors affecting access to a research area.

Normative view: a view of human culture arguing that one can identify the abstract rules regulating a particular culture: a commonly used basis for studying archaeological cultures throughout time.

Object-clustering: an approach to typology based on clusters of human artifacts that are seen as specific classificatory types.

Obsidian: black volcanic glass.

Obsidian hydration: a dating method that measures the thickness of the hydration layer in osbidian artifacts. The hydration layer is caused by absorption of water on exposed surfaces of the rock.

Open system: in archaeology, cultural systems that interchange both energy and information with their environment.

Oral tradition: historical traditions, often genealogies, passed down from generation to generation by word of mouth.

Ordering: in archaeology, the arranging of artifacts in logical classes and in chronological order.

Organic materials: materials like bone, wood, horn, or hide, which were once living organisms.

Ossification: fusion of a limb bone with its articular end. Implies the stagnation, or calcification, of soft tissue into bonelike material.

Osteologist: one who studies bones.

Paleoanthropologist: an archaeologist who studies the archaeology of the earliest human beings.

Paleobotanist: one who studies prehistoric botany.

Paleoecology: the modern study of past ecology.

Paleolithic: the Old Stone Age.

Paleontology: the study of fossil (or ancient) bones.

Palynology: pollen analysis.

Parahistoric sites: archaeological sites of preliterate peoples who were contemporary with cultures that had writing.

Palination: natural weathering on the surface of rocks and artifacts.

Patrilineal: descent reckoned through the male line only.

Patrilocal: married couples live with or near the husband's father.

Patterns of discard: Remains left for investigation after natural destructive forces have affected artifacts and food remains abandoned by their original users.

Pedology: scientific study of soil.

Perceived environment: the physical environment as perceived by a human society; does not coincide with the archaeologist's perception of the same phenomenon.

Periglacial: surrounding a glacial area.

Period: an archaeological unit defining a major unit of prehistoric time; it contains several phases and pertains to a wide area.

Permafrost: permanently frozen subsoil.

Petrological analysis: examining thin sections of stone artifacts to determine provenience of the rock used to make them.

Petrology: the study of rocks; in archaeology, normally refers to analysis of trace elements and other characteristics of rocks used to make such artifacts as axe blades, which were traded over long distances.

Phase: an archaeological unit defined by characteristic groupings of culture traits that can be identified precisely in time and space. It lasts for a relatively short time and is found at one or more sites in a locality or region. Its culture traits are clear enough to distinguish it from other phases.

Physical anthropology: basically, biological anthropology, which includes the study of fossil human beings, genetics, primates, and blood groups.

Planimetric maps: maps used to record details of archaeological sites; they contain no topographic information.

Pleistocene: the last major geological epoch, extending from about two million years ago until about 11,500 B.P. It is sometimes called the Quaternary, or the Great Ice Age.

Population: in sampling methods, the sum of sampling units selected within a data universe.

Positive feedback: a system's response to external stimuli that leads to further change and reinforces it.

Postclassic: a stage in Mesoamerican and Andean prehistory, during which militarism arose, such as that of the Aztec and the Inca.

Potassium argon dating: an absolute dating technique based on the decay rate of potassium ^{40}K, which becomes ^{40}Ar.

Potsherd: a fragment of a clay vessel.

Preclassic: see Formative.

Prehistory: the millennia of human history preceding written records. Prehistorians study prehistoric archaeology.

Pressure flaking: a stoneworking technique in which thin flakes are removed from a core or artifact by applying hand or chest pressure.

Primary context: an undisturbed association, matrix, and provenience.

Prime movers: an early concept in the study of the origins of civilization, meaning a single, primary cause generating urban societies; many considered irrigation a prime mover of Egyptian civilization.

Probabilistic sampling: archaeological sampling based on formal statistical criteria. This method enables one to use probability statistics in analyzing data.

Process: in archaeology, the process of cultural change that takes place as a result of interactions between a cultural system's elements and the system and its environment.

Provenience: the position of an archaeological find in time and space, recorded three-dimensionally.

Proximal: opposite to distal: the end of a bone nearest to the skeleton's center line.

Pulse radar: use of a pulse-induction meter that applies pulses of magnetic field to the soil; this method can be used to find graves, metals, and pottery.

Quadrat: a unit of spatial analysis used to divide up an area into cells for analysis.

Quaternary: geological time since the beginning of the Pleistocene up to recent times. The exact date of its commencement is uncertain, but it is more than two million years old.

Radiocarbon dating: an absolute dating method based on measuring the decay rate of the carbon isotope, carbon 14, to stable nitrogen. The resulting dates are calibrated with tree-ring chronologies, from radiocarbon ages into dates in calendar years.

Random sampling: sampling techniques based on totally random selection of sample units to be investigated.

Reciprocity: in archaeology, the exchange of goods between two parties.

Redistribution: the dispersing of trade goods from a central place throughout a society, a complex process that was a critical part of the evolution of civilization.

Refitting: the reassembling of stone debitage and cores to reconstruct ancient lithic technologies.

Region: a geographically defined area in which ecological adaptations are basically similar.

Relative chronology: time scale developed by the law of superposition or artifact ordering.

Remote sensing: reconnaissance and site survey methods using such devices as aerial photography to detect subsurface features and sites.

Research design: a carefully formulated and systematic plan for executing archaeological research.

Resistivity survey: measurement of differences in electrical conductivity in soils, used to detect buried features such as walls and ditches.

Sample unit: an arbitrary or nonarbitrary unit of the data universe, used for sampling archaeological data.

Sampling frame: lists of chosen sampling units that form the sample of the population to be tested. Compiling as a means of proceeding to selection of units for investigation.

Scanner imagery: a method of recording sites from the air using infrared radiation that is beyond the practical spectral response of photographic film. Useful for tracing prehistoric agricultural systems that have disturbed the topsoil over wide areas.

Science: a way of acquiring knowledge and understanding about the parts of the natural world that can be observed. A disciplined and highly ordered search for knowledge carried out systematically.

Seasonality: seasonal occupation.

Secondary context: a context of an archaeological find that has been disturbed by subsequent human activity or natural phenomena.

Selective excavation: archaeological excavation of parts of a site using sampling methods or carefully placed trenches that do not uncover the entire site.

Seriation: methods used to place artifacts in chronological order; artifacts closely similar in form or style are placed close to one another.

Settlement pattern: distribution of human settlement on the landscape and within archaeological communities.

Shadow sites: archaeological sites identified from the air, where oblique light can show up reduced topography of sites invisible on the ground.

Site: any place where objects, features, or ecofacts manufactured or modified by human beings are found. A site can range from a living site to a quarry site, and it can be defined in functional and other ways.

Site-catchment analysis: inventorying natural resources within a given distance of a site.

Site plans: specially prepared maps for recording the horizontal provenience of artifacts, food remains, and features. They are keyed to topographic maps.

Site survey: collection of surface data and evaluation of each site's archaeological significance.

Slip: fine, wet clay finish applied to the surface of a clay vessel prior to its firing and decoration.

Social anthropology: the British equivalent of cultural anthropology, but emphasizing sociological factors.

Sociocultural: combining social and cultural factors.

Sodality: a nonkinship organization within a society that cuts across kinship groups and lineages for specific purposes that add to the cohesiveness of that society.

Sondage: see Test pit.

Spectographic analysis: chemical analysis that involves passing the light from a number of trace elements through a prism or diffraction grating that spreads out the wavelengths in a spectrum. This enables one to separate the emissions and identify different trace elements. A useful approach for studying metal objects and obsidian artifacts.

Stage: a technological subdivison of prehistoric time that has little chronological meaning but denotes the level of technological achievement of societies within it, such as the Stone Age.

Stela (or stele): a column or stone slab, often with inscribed or sculptured surface.

Stratified sampling: a probabilistic sampling technique used to cluster and isolate sample units, when regular spacing is inappropriate for cultural reasons.

Stratigraphy: observing of the superimposed layers in an archaeological site.

Stratum: a single-deposited or cultural level.

Structural archaeology: theoretical approach to archaeology based on the assumption that codes and rules produce observed systems of relations in human culture.

Style: in an evolutionary context, a means of describing forms that do not have detectable selective values.

Stylistic analysis: artifact analysis that concentrates not only on form and function, but on the decorative styles used by the makers—a much-used approach to ceramic analysis.

Stylistic attributes and types: such phenomena based on stylistic features.

Stylistic type: type based on stylistic distinctions.

Subarea: subdivision of an archaeological area, normally defined by geographic or cultural considerations.

Subassemblage: association of artifacts denoting a particular form of prehistoric activity practiced by a group of people.

Surface survey: the collecting of archaeological finds from sites, with the objective of gathering representative samples of artifacts from the surface. Surface survey also establishes the types of activity on the site, locates major structures, and gathers information on the most densely occupied areas of the site that could be most productive for total or sample excavation.

Synthesis: the assembling and analyzing of data preparatory to interpretation.

Systematics: in archaeology, procedures for creating sets of archaeological units derived from a logical system for a particular purpose.

Systematic sampling: a refinement of random sampling in which one unit is chosen, then others at regular intervals from the first. Useful for studying artifact patterning.

Taphonomy: study of the processes by which animal bones and other fossil remains are transformed after deposition.

Taxonomy: an ordered set of operations that results in the subdividing of objects into ordered classifications.

Technological analysis: study of technological methods used to make an artifact.

Technological attributes (technological types): attributes based on technological features of an object.

Tectonic: a term referring to the earth's crust; a tectonic movement is an earthquake.

Telehistoric sites: sites far removed from written records: prehistoric sites.

Tell: a mound; a term referring to archaeological sites of this type in the Near East.

Temper: coarse material such as sand or shell added to fine potclay to make it bond during firing.

Tempering: a process for hardening iron blades, involving heating and rapid cooling. Also, material added to potters' clay.

Test pit: an excavation unit used to sample or probe a site before large-scale excavation or to check surface surveys.

Thermoluminescence: a chronometric dating method that measures the amount of light energy released by a baked clay object when heated rapidly. Gives an indication of the time elapsed since the object was last heated.

Three-age system: a technological subdivision of the prehistoric past developed for Old World prehistory in 1806.

Topographic maps: maps that can be used to relate archaeological sites to basic features of the natural landscape.

Total excavation: complete excavation of an archaeological site. Normally confined to smaller sites, such as burial mounds or campsites.

Trace elements: minute elements found in rocks that emit characteristic wavelengths of light when heated to incandescence. Trace-element analysis is used to study the sources of obsidian and other materials traded over long distances.

Tradition: persistent technological or cultural patterns identified by characteristic artifact forms. These persistent forms outlast a single phase and can occur over a wide area.

Transformational processes: processes that transform an abandoned prehistoric settlement into an archaeological site through the passage of time. These processes can be initiated by natural phenomena or human activity.

Tribe: a larger group of bands unified by sodalities and governed by a council of representatives from the bands, kin groups, or sodalities within it.

Trypanosomiasis: sleeping sickness.

Tsetse: a fly that carries trypanosomiasis. Because of belts of tsetse fly country in Africa, inhabitants are prevented from raising cattle.

Tuff: solidified volcanic ash.

Type: in archaeology, a grouping of artifacts created for comparison with other groups. This grouping may or may not coincide with the actual tool types designed by the original manufacturers.

Type fossil: a tool characteristic of a particular "archaeological era," a dated concept borrowed from geology.

Typology: the classification of types.

Unaerated: not exposed to the open air.

Underwater archaeology: study of archaelogocal sites and shipwrecks beneath the surface of the water.

Uniformitarianism: doctrine that states the earth was formed by the same natural geological processes that are operating today.

Unilinear cultural evolution: a late-nineteenth-century evolutionary theory envisaging all human societies as evolving along one track of cultural evolution, from simple hunting and gathering to literate civilization.

Unit: in archaeology, an artificial grouping used for describing artifacts.

Use-wear analysis: microscopic analysis of artifacts to detect signs of wear through their use on their working edges.

Varves: annual clay deposits made by retreating and melting glaciers. Used to measure recent Pleistocene geological events.

Vertical excavation: excavation undertaken to establish a chronological sequence, normally covering a limited area.

Votive: intended as an offering as a result of a vow.

Zooarchaeology: study of animal remains in archaeology.

Illustration Credits (*continued*)

Reproduced by permission of Doubleday & Company, Inc.; *Fig. 5.7*, Courtesy of The University Museum, University of Pennsylvania.

Chapter 6: *Fig. 6.2*, Redrawn from John Alexander, *The Directing of Archaeological Excavations.* London: John Baker Publishers, Ltd., 1970, Fig. 16a. After Kenneth P. Oakley, *Frameworks for Dating Fossil Man,* Chicago: Aldine Publishing Co., 1964; *Fig. 6.3,* from John Alexander, *The Directing of Archaeological Excavations.* London: A & C Black (Publishers) Ltd., 1970, Fig. 36. Reprinted by courtesy of John Alexander; *Fig. 6.4,* After Sir John Evans from J. G. D. Clark, *Archaeology and Society,* London: Methuen and Company, 1939, Fig. 18, reprinted by Barnes and Noble, New York; *Fig. 6.6,* Adapted from James A. Ford, *A Quantitative Method for Deriving Cultural Chronology.* Washington, D.C.: General Secretariat of the Organization of American States, 1962, by permission of the publisher; *Fig. 6.7,* From James Deetz, *Invitation to Archaeology,* illustrated by Eric G. Engstrom. Copyright © 1967 by James Deetz. Reproduced by permission of Doubleday & Company, Inc.; *Fig. 6.8,* Adapted from R. S. MacNeish, *The Prehistory of the Tehuacan Valley,* Vol. 3, Figs. 2 and 3. Copyright © 1970 by The University of Texas Press, Austin; *Fig. 6.9,* From Jason W. Smith, *Foundations of Archaeology.* Copyright © 1976 by Jason W. Smith. Reprinted with permission of Glencoe Publishing Co., Inc., division of Macmillan Publishing Co, Inc.; *Fig. 6.10,* From A. L. Mongait, *The Archaeology of the USSR.* Courtesy of VAAP the USSR Copyright Agency. Reprinted with permission; *Fig. 6.11,* after J. G. D. Clark, *Star Carr.* New York: Cambridge University Press, 1954, Fig. 27b. Reprinted by permission; *Fig. 6.12,* adapted from Kenneth P. Oakley, *Frameworks for Dating Fossil Man,* Chicago: Aldine Publishers and London: Weidenfeld & Nicholson Publishing Co., Ltd., 1964, Fig. 22; *Fig. 6.13,* adapted from Kenneth P. Oakley, *Frameworks for Dating Fossil Man,* Chicago: Aldine Publishers and London: Weidenfeld & Nicholson Publishing Co., Ltd., 1964, Fig. 7; *Fig. 6.14,* After J. G. D. Clark, *Star Carr,* New York: Cambridge University Press, 1954, Fig. 27b. Reprinted by permission.

Chapter 7: *Fig. 7.1,* By permission of Phillip V. Tobias, University of the Witwatersrand Medical School, Johannesburg, South Africa; *Fig. 7.2,* Courtesy of the University Museum, University of Pennsylvania. Photographs by Nicholas Hartmann/Masca.; *Fig. 7.3,* Adapted from D. R. Brothwell and Eric Higgs, *Science in Archaeology,* London: Thames and Hudson, Ltd.; *Fig. 7.4,* After Joseph W. Michels, *Dating Methods in Archaeology,* New

York: Seminar Press, 1973, Fig. 40; *Fig. 7.5,* Courtesy of the University Museum, University of Pennsylvania; *Fig. 7.6,* Redrawn from Ivor Noël Hume, *The Artifacts of Colonial America,* New York: Alfred A. Knopf, Inc., 1969, Fig. 9. Copyright © 1969 by Ivor Noël Hume.

Chapter 8: *Fig. 8.1,* Courtesy of the Danish National Museum; *Fig. 8.2,* Ruth Kirk with Richard D. Dougherty, *Hunters of the Whale,* New York: Wm. Morrow & Co., 1974.

Chapter 10: *Fig. 10.1,* Courtesy of Lesley Newhart; *Fig. 10.2,* Courtesy of University of Colorado Museum, Joe Ben Wheat photo; *Fig. 10.3,* Courtesy of the Peabody Museum, Harvard University; *Fig. 10.4,* Michael Moseley/Anthro-Photo File; *Fig. 10.5,* Cambridge University Collection: Copyright reserved; *Fig. 10.6,* Courtesy of Fondazione Lerici Prospezioni Archeologiche, Rome; *Fig. 10.7,* From John Coles, *Field Archaeology in Britain,* London: Methuen & Co., Copyright © 1972, Fig. 7; *Fig. 10.9,* Courtesy of Norman Hammond; *Fig. 10.10,* Courtesy of Arizona State Museum.

Chapter 11: *Fig. 11.1,* Photograph by Barny Cuniliffe. Courtesy of Oxford University, England; *Fig. 11.2,* Redrawn from Stuart Streuver and James A. Brown, "The Organization of Archaeological Research: An Illinois Example," Fig. 1, in Charles L. Redman, *Research and Theory in Current Archaeology.* New York: John Wiley and Sons, 1973. Also courtesy of the Center for American Archaeology, 1911 Ridge Avenue, P.O. Box 1499, Chicago, IL 60204. *Fig. 11.3,* Courtesy of The University Museum, University of Pennsylvania; *Fig. 11.4,* Courtesy of Sir Mortimer Wheeler and the Society of Antiquaries of London; *Fig. 11.5,* Courtesy of J. A. Tuck Memorial University of Newfoundland; *Fig. 11.6,* Redrawn from Ivor Noël Hume, *Historical Archaeology,* New York: Alfred A. Knopf, Inc., 1968, Fig. 10. By permission of the publisher and Curtis Brown, Ltd., Copyright © 1968 by Ivor Noël Hume; *Fig. 11.7,* Courtesy of the Museum of London; *Fig. 11.9,* Courtesy of Peabody Museum, Harvard University; *Fig. 11.10,* Courtesy of Peabody Museum, Harvard University. Photograph by A. L. Smith; *Fig. 11.11,* Carl W. Blegan and Marion Rawson, *The Palace of Nestor at Pylos in Western Messenia,* Vol. I, Part 2, plates copyright © by Princeton University Press, 1966, Fig. 9. Reprinted by permission of Princeton University Press and the University of Cincinnati; *Fig. 11.12,* Redrawn from Ivor Noël Hume, *Historical Archaeology,* New York: Alfred A. Knopf, Inc., 1968, Fig. 15. Copyright © 1968 by Ivor Noël Hume; *Fig. 11.14,* Courtesy of the Society of Antiquaries of London; *Fig. 11.15,* Copyright H. T. Bunn, University of California at Berkeley.

Reprinted by permission; *Fig. 11.16,* Courtesy of R. S. Peabody Foundation for Archaeology, Andover, Mass.; *Fig. 11.17,* Courtesy of Wilfred Shawcross; *Fig. 11.19,* Courtesy of the Society of Antiquaries of London; *Fig. 11.21,* Courtesy of Patricia M. Christie; *Fig. 11.22,* Courtesy of Winchester Excavations Committee, Winchester, England.

Chapter 12: *Fig. 21.1,* Courtesy of the Society of Antiquaries of London; *Fig. 12.3,* Courtesy of Lowei Museum of Anthropology, University of California, Berkeley; *Fig. 12.4,* From James Deetz, *Invitation to Archaeology,* illustrated by Eric G. Engstrom, Copyright © 1967 by James Deetz. Reproduced by permission of Doubleday & Company, Inc.; *Fig. 12.5,* After J. G. D. Clark, *Star Carr,* New York: Cambridge University Press, 1954, Fig. 35. Used by permission; *Fig. 12.6,* By permission of the Trustees of The British Museum (Natural History); *Fig. 12.7,* Courtesy of Pitt-Rivers Museum.

Chapter 13: *Fig. 13.1,* Redrawn from M. D. Leakey, *Olduvai Gorge,* Vol. III, New York: Cambridge University Press, 1971. Used by permission. *Fig. 13.2a,* Reprinted by permission of Time-Life Books. *Fig. 13.2b,* From Kenneth Oakley, *Frameworks for Dating Fossil Man,* 1968. *Fig. 13.4,* *Life Nature Library/Early Man* © Time, Inc., 1965, 1973. Reprinted by permission; *Fig. 13.5,* Courtesy of Pitt-Rivers Museum, Oxford, England; *Fig. 13.6,* From J. M. Coles and E. S. Higgs, *The Archaeology of Early Man,* London: Faber and Faber, Ltd. Reprinted by permission of Faber and Faber, Ltd.; *Fig. 13.7,* Adapted from F. Bordes, *The Old Stone Age,* London: Weidenfeld & Nicholson, 1968, Fig. 34; *Fig. 13.8a* & *13.8b,* Adapted from F. Bordes, *The Old Stone Age,* London: Weidenfeld & Nicholson, 1968, Fig. 54 and 55; *Fig. 13.8d,* After G. H. Bushnell, *The First Americans,* London: Thames & Hudson, Ltd. and McGraw-Hill, 1967, Fig. 12. Copyright © 1968, Thames & Hudson, London and McGraw-Hill, New York; Courtesy of Robert Edwards, Aboriginal Arts Board; *Fig. 13.10,* Photo by Wyatt Davis. Courtesy Museum of New Mexico (Negative No. 44191); *Fig. 13.11,* Courtesy of the Museum of the American Indian, Heye Foundation, New York. Photograph by Carmelo Guadagno; *Fig. 13.12,* Courtesy of The Art Institute of Chicago; *Fig. 13.14,* Courtesy of The Ohio Historical Society, Columbus, Ohio; *Fig. 13.15,* From G. H. S. Bushnell, *The First Americans: The Pre-Columbian Civilizations,* 1968. Reprinted by permission. *Fig. 13.16,* Courtesy of Michael S. Bisson; *Fig. 13.18,* From K. C. Chang, *The Archaeology of Ancient China,* New Haven: Yale University Press, Copyright © 1971. Also courtesy of the Smithsonian Institution; *Fig. 13.19,* Photograph by Jean Vertut

taken at The British Museum; *Fig. 13.20,* Courtesy of the University of Alaska Museum; *Fig. 13.21,* Ruth Kirk with Richard D. Daugherty, *Hunters of the Whale,* New York: Wm. Morrow & Co., 1974. Photograph by Harvey Rice. *Fig. 13.22,* Courtesy of the Trustees of the British Museum (Natural History).

Chapter 14: *Fig. 14.1,* From Grahame Clark, *Star Carr,* New York: Cambridge University Press, 1954. Used by permission; *Fig. 14.3,* Reproduced by permission of Blackwell Scientific Publications; *Fig. 14.4,* Copyright reserved: University Museum of Archaeology and Ethnology, Cambridge, England; *Fig. 14.5,* From Richard G. Klein, *The Analysis of Animal Bones from Archaeological Sites,* Chicago: The University of Chicago Press, 1984, Fig. 5.4; *Fig. 14.7,* Copyright © 1970 by the regents of the University of California; reprinted by permission of the University of California Press; *Fig. 14.8,* By permission of the Trustees of the British Museum (Natural History); *Fig. 14.9,* Courtesy of the Cave Research Foundation Archaeological Project; photograph by Roger W. Brucker; *Fig. 14.10,* Copyright reserved: University Museum of Archaeology and Ethnology, Cambridge, England; *Fig. 14.11,* Redrawn from J. G. D. Clark, *Prehistoric Europe: The Economic Basis,* Fig. 44, with permission of the publishers, Stanford University Press. Copyright © 1952 by J. G. D. Clark, London: Methuen and Company, Ltd.; *Fig. 14.12,* Redrawn from J. G. D. Clark, *Prehistoric Europe: The Economic Basis,* Fig. 17, with permission of the publisher, Stanford University Press. Copyright © 1952 J. G. D. Clark, London: Methuen and Company, Ltd.; *Fig. 14.14,* Patricia Vinnecombe, "A Fishing Scene from the Tsoelike River, South-Eastern Basutoland," *South African Archaeological Bulletin,* Vol. 15, no. 57, March 1960, p. 15, Fig. 1.

Chapter 15: *Fig. 15.1,* Courtesy of the Smithsonian Institution/Photo No. T13301; *Fig. 15.2,* Courtesy of the Society of Antiquaries of London; *Fig. 15.3,* Redrawn from Richard Lee and Irven DeVore, *Kalahari Hunter Gatherers,* Cambridge, Mass.: Harvard University Press, 1976. Used by permission; *Fig. 15.4,* Richard A. Gould, "The Archaeologist as Ethnographer," *World Archaeology,* 1971, pp. 143–177, Fig. 18. *Fig. 15.5,* From Gordon Willey and Jeremy Sabloff, *A History of American Archaeology,* New York: W. H. Freeman, 1980. Reprinted by courtesy of the authors. Photographs by Lewis Binford. *Fig. 15.6,* Reconstruction by Nelson Reed; courtesy of Illinois State Museum.

Chapter 16: *Fig. 16.2,* Carl Frank/Photo Researchers, Inc.; *Fig. 16.4,* Redrawn from Marcus C. Winter, "Analyzing Household Activities," Fig. 2.17, in Kent V. Flannery, Ed., *The Early Mesoamer-*

ican Village, New York: Academic Press, 1976; *Fig. 16.5*, From Marcus C. Winter, "The Archaeological Household Cluster in the Valley of Oaxaca," *Fig. 2.1*, in Kent V. Flannery, Ed., *The Early Mesoamerican Village*, New York: Academic Press, 1976; *Fig. 16.6*, Redrawn from E. Z. Vogt, *Zinacantan*, Cambridge, Mass.: The Belknap Press of Harvard University Press, 1969. Used by permission; *Fig. 16.7a*, Melvin Konner/Anthro-Photo File; *Fig. 16.7b*, Reproduced by courtesy of the Trustees of the British Museum; *Fig. 16.8*, Lee Boltin; *Fig. 16.9*, After Karl Butzer, *Archaeology as Human Biology*, New York: Cambridge University Press, 1982, p. 16. Used by permission; *Fig. 16.10*, After Karl Butzer, *Archaeology as Human Biology*, New York: Cambridge University Press, 1982, p. 31. Used by permission; *Fig. 16.11*, After Karl Butzer, *Archaeology as Human Biology*, New York: Cambridge University Press, 1982, p. 83. Used by permission; *Fig. 16.13*, Redrawn from Kent V. Flannery, "Empirical Determination of Site Catchments in Oaxaca and Tehuacan," *The Early Mesoamerican Village*, Kent V. Flannery, Ed., New York: Academic Press, 1976, Fig. 4.6; *Fig. 16.15*, Redrawn from Hodder & Orton, *Spatial Analysis in Archaeology*, New York: Cambridge University Press and the Royal Anthropological Institute of Great Britain and Ireland, 1976, p. 461; *Fig. 16.16*, After Karl Butzer, *Archaeology as Human Biology*, New York: Cambridge University Press, 1982, p. 296. Used by permission; *Fig. 16.17*, After Karl Butzer, *Archaeology as Human Biology*, New York: Cambridge University Press, 1982, p. 238. Used by permission.

Chapter 17: *Fig. 17.1*, Courtesy of the American Museum of Natural History; *Fig. 17.3*, Courtesy of the Museum of the American Indian/Heye Foundation, New York; *Fig. 17.4*, Courtesy of the Peabody Museum, Harvard University; *Fig. 17.5*, After Renfrew, in J. S. Sabloff and C. C. Lamberg-Karlovsky, Eds., *Ancient Civilization and Trade*, University of New Mexico Press, 1976; *Fig. 17.6*, *Ramesses II and Queen in Audience*. Stela from 18th Dynasty 09.287, gift of Mrs. Frank E. Peabody. Courtesy of the Museum of Fine Arts; *Fig. 17.7*, Courtesy of the University Museum, University of Pennsylvania; *Fig. 17.8*, Courtesy of the Musée de l'Homme; *Fig. 17.9*, Redrawn from Robert D. Drennan, "Religion and Social Evolution in Formative Mesoamerica," Fig. 11.8, in Kent V. Flannery, Ed., *The Early Mesoamerican Village*, New York: Academic Press, 1976; *Fig. 17.10*, Kent V. Flannery, "Contextual Analysis of Ritual Paraphernalia from Formative Oaxaca," Fig. 11.9, in Kent V. Flannery, Ed., *The Early Mesoamerican Village*, New York: Academic Press, 1976; Fig. 17.

Chapter 18: *Fig. 18.1*, From Gordon R. Wioley, *An Introduction to American Archaeology, Volume One: North and Middle America*, © 1966. Reprinted by permission of Prentice-Hall, Inc. Englewood Cliffs, New Jersey; *Fig. 18.3*, Courtesy of the Metropolitan Museum of Art; Photography by Egyptian Expedition; *Fig. 18.4*, From James Deetz, *Invitation to Archaeology*, illustrated by Eric G. Engstrom. Copyright © 1967 by James Deetz. Reproduced by permission of Doubleday & Company, Inc.; *Fig. 18.5*, Courtesy of the Ohio Historical Society.

Chapter 19: *Fig. 19.1*, From Charles L. Redman, *The Rise of Civilization: From Early Farmers to Urban in the Ancient Near East*, New York: W. H. Freeman and Company, Copyright © 1978.

Chapter 20: *Fig. 20.1*, Printed by courtesy of *Rescue: The Trust for British Archaeology*, Bull Plain, Hertford, SC14, IDX; *Fig. 20.2*, Courtesy of Museum of the American Indian, Heye Foundation, New York; *Fig. 20.3*, Hester A. Davis, "Is There a Future for the Past?" *Archaeology* Vol. 24, no. 4. Copyright 1971, Archaeological Institute of America.

INDEX 🦢

'Ubaid, 426
Uhle, Max, 199, 377
Underwater archaeology, 30, 206, 258, 261, 548
UNESCO, 529, 530
Uniformitarianism, 47–49
Unilinear evolution, 58, 59–62, 391, 514
Urban Revolution, 63, 469
Ur-of-the-Chaldees, 179, 235, 260, 262, 459, 472–473
Use-wear analysis, 316–317, 318, 404
Ussher, Archbishop James, 40, 44, 46, 47, 106

Van der Merwe, N.J., 385
Varves, 133, 147
Vasa (warship), 261
Vegetal remains, 163, 182, 348, 349, 359, 366–375, 385–387
Vegetation, and site identification, 193
Venus figurines, 477, 478
Vertical excavation. *See* Excavation
Vesuvius, 41, 94
Vikings, 22, 62, 170
Village and town sites, 253, 273–276, 418–419. *See also* Communities; Household clusters; Settlement patterns; Structures and specific sites
Vinnecombe, Patricia, 383
Virú Valley, 32, 204–205, 385
Vogel, J.C., 385
Vogt, Evon, 425
Volcanic activity, 41, 94
and dating, 136, 138, 143, 144

Wallace, Alfred, 50
Walpi, 12
Warfare, 173
Warren, Claude N., 380
Waterlogged conditions, 159, 163–167, 166, 256, 261, 283, 339
Waterman, Thomas, 410–411

Webster, David, 517
Weeks, Ken, 210
Wenner Gren Foundation for Anthropological Research, 186
West, 227, 339
Whallon, Michael, 430
Wheat, 370, 373
Wheeler, Sir Mortimer, 35, 94, 109, 178, 234, 246, 272, 394, 395, 504
White, John, 41
White, Leslie, 58, 59, 67, 70, 72, 459, 469
White, Theodore, 365
Willey, Gordon, 32, 65, 67, 204–205, 492, 494
Williamsburg, Colonial, 29, 248, 265
Wiltshire, 274, 414
Winchester, 28, 274–275
Winter, Marcus, 422
Wolvercote, 312
Wooden artifacts and technology, 163, 165, 264, 305, 339–341, 340
preservation of, 163, 165, 339–341
Woolley, Sir Leonard, 179, 235, 237, 260, 472–474, 473
Works Progress Administration (WPA), 532
Worsaae, J.J.A., 91, 107
Wright, Thomas, 5
Writing, 28, 30, 328, 394
Wyoming, 374

Yahi, 411
Yellen, John, 401–403
Yellow Blade Phase, 493, 494

Zagros Mountains, 32, 33, 186
Zambezi Valley, 192, 420
Zambia, 12, 353, 409, 431
Ziggurat, 100, 173, 479
Zimbabwe, 12, 383, 479
Zinacantan, 425, 426
Zooarchaeology, 347, 350–365
Zuñi, 321

8629